KT-215-713

ESSENTIALS OF MANAGEMENT

WITHDRAWN

EDINBURGH NAPIER UNIVERSITY LIBRARY   'ERSITY I

3 8042 00821 4858   00245 1837

McGRAW-HILL SERIES IN MANAGEMENT

Fred Luthans and Keith Davis, Consulting Editors

Also Available from McGraw-Hill

SCHAUM'S OUTLINE SERIES IN ACCOUNTING, BUSINESS AND ECONOMICS

Each outline includes basic theory, definitions, and hundreds of solved problems and supplementary problems with answers.

Current list includes:

Accounting I, 3d edition
Accounting II, 3d edition
Advanced Accounting
Advanced Business Law
Advertising
Bookkeeping and Accounting, 2d edition
Introduction to Business
Business Law
Business Mathematics
Introduction to Business Organization and Management
Business Statistics, 2d edition
College Business Law
Contemporary Mathematics of Finance
Cost Accounting I, 2d edition
Cost Accounting II
Development Economics
Financial Accounting
Intermediate Accounting I, 2d edition
International Economics, 2d edition
Macroeconomic Theory
Managerial Accounting
Managerial Finance
Marketing
Mathematics for Economists
Mathematics of Finance
Microeconomic Theory, 2d edition
Money and Banking
Operations Management
Personal Finance and Consumer Economics
Principles of Economics
Quantitative Methods in Management
Statistics and Econometrics
Tax Accounting

AVAILABLE AT YOUR COLLEGE BOOKSTORE

ESSENTIALS OF MANAGEMENT

FIFTH EDITION

Harold Koontz
Late Professor of Management
University of California, Los Angeles

Heinz Weihrich
Professor of Management and International Business
McLaren College of Business Administration
University of San Francisco

McGraw-Hill, Inc.
New York St. Louis San Francisco Auckland Bogotá
Caracas Lisbon London Madrid Mexico City Milan
Montreal New Delhi San Juan Singapore
Sydney Tokyo Toronto

Library of Congress Cataloging-in-Publication Data

Koontz, Harold, (date).
    Essentials of management / Harold Koontz, Heinz Weihrich. — 5th ed.
    p.   cm. — (McGraw-Hill series in management)
    Includes index.
    ISBN 0-07-035605-X
    1. Management.   I. Weihrich, Heinz.   II. Title.   III. Series.
HD31.K62   1990
658.4—dc20   89-12444

NAPIER UNIVERSITY LIBRARY		
AC / /		ON 0022
LOC SHMK S 658 KOO		SUP PHILKU
CON		PR 27.95

This book is printed on acid-free paper.

ESSENTIALS OF MANAGEMENT

Copyright © 1990, 1986, 1982, 1978, 1974 by McGraw-Hill, Inc. All rights reserved. Printed in the United States of America. Except as permitted under the United States Copyright Act of 1976, no part of this publication may be reproduced or distributed in any form or by any means, or stored in a data base or retrieval system, without the prior written permission of the publisher.

4567890 DOCDOC   94

ISBN   0-07-035605-X

This book was set in Palatino by Black Dot, Inc.
The editors were Kathleen L. Loy, Laura D. Warner, and Eileen Gualberto;
the designer was Chuck Carson;
the production supervisor was Louise Karam.
New drawings were done by Fine Line Illustrations, Inc.
R. R. Donnelley & Sons Company was printer and binder.

Cover photo: Transamerica building in San Francisco./Michele Burgess © 1986; The Stock Market.

About
the Authors

HEINZ WEIHRICH is Professor of Management and International Business at the University of San Francisco. He received his doctorate from the University of California at Los Angeles (UCLA) and was a visiting scholar at the University of California in Berkeley. His fields of work are in management, international management, and behavioral science. He has taught at Arizona State University, at the University of California at Los Angeles, and in Europe.

Dr. Weihrich has published over forty books, including various editions and translations, and is now the sole author of the classic *Management,* ninth edition, by the late Harold Koontz and the late Cyril O'Donnell. Another of his books, *Management Excellence: Productivity through MBO,* discusses a goal-driven management system; it has been translated into Spanish, Italian, German, Greek, Korean, and Japanese. Over eighty of his articles have been published in the United States and abroad.

In addition to pursuing his academic interests, Weihrich is active in management consulting as well as executive and organizational development in the United States, Europe, Africa, and Asia. His consulting and business experiences include work with companies such as Eastman Kodak, Volkswagen, and Hughes Aircraft. He is also an active member of Toastmasters International. Recently he was elected as a Fellow of the International Academy of Management, the highest honor conferred by the international management movement. He is listed in *International Businessmen's Who's Who, Men of Achievement, Dictionary of International Biography, Who's Who in the West,* and *Who's Who in the World.*

The late HAROLD KOONTZ was active as a business and government executive, university professor, company board chairman and director, management consultant, worldwide lecturer to top management groups, and author of many books and articles. From 1950 he was Professor of Management and from

1962 Mead Johnson Professor of Management at the University of California, Los Angeles; from 1978 to 1982 he was World Chancellor of The International Academy of Management. He was author or coauthor of nineteen books and ninety journal articles, and his *Principles of Management* (now in its ninth edition as *Management*) has been translated into sixteen languages. His *Board of Directors and Effective Management* was given the Academy of Management Book Award in 1968. After taking his doctorate at Yale, Professor Koontz served as Assistant to the Trustees of the New Haven Railroad, Chief of the Traffic Branch of the War Production Board, Assistant to the Vice President of the Association of American Railroads, Assistant to the President of Trans World Airlines, and Director of Sales for Convair. He acted as management consultant for, among others, Hughes Tool Company, Hughes Aircraft Company, Purex Corporation, KLM Royal Dutch Airlines, Metropolitan Life Insurance Company, Occidental Petroleum Corporation, and General Telephone Company. Professor Koontz's honors included election as a Fellow of the American and the International Academies of Management, and a term of service as President of the American Academy of Management. He received the Mead Johnson Award in 1962 and the Society for Advancement of Management Taylor Key Award in 1974 and is listed in *Who's Who in America, Who's Who in Finance and Industry,* and *Who's Who in the World.* Harold Koontz passed away in 1984.

To Mary and Ursula

Contents
in Brief

Contents

Part 2   Planning

Part 3   Organizing

Part 5   Leading

Part 6   Controlling

Preface

This book prepares men and women for the exciting, challenging, and rewarding career of managing in the 1990s. The reader is invited to apply its principles, concepts, and theories to become more effective as a person and as a managerial leader.

The fifth edition of *Essentials of Management* is an up-to-date introduction to managing. Prior editions have been translated into many languages and have been well accepted around the world by readers and educators.

Who Will Benefit from This Book?

All persons who work in organizations will benefit from learning about managing. They include students in colleges and universities, aspiring managers, those who already have managerial skills and want to become more effective, and other professionals who want an improved understanding of the organization in which they work. This book is for people in all kinds of organizations, not just business firms; it is relevant to nonbusiness organizations as well, such as government, health care and educational institutions, and other not-for-profit enterprises.

The managerial functions are essentially the same for first-line supervisors, middle managers, and top executives. To be sure, there are considerable variations in environment, scope of authority, and types of problems in the various positions. Yet all managers undertake the same basic functions to obtain results by establishing an environment for effective and efficient performance of individuals working together in groups.

Organization of the Book

Information about managing is classified according to the functions of planning, organizing, staffing, leading, and controlling. A systems model, shown on the inside cover and used throughout the book, integrates these functions into a system; it also links the enterprise with its environment.

Part 1 covers the basis of management science, its theory and practice, and also introduces the systems model which serves as the framework of this book. Parts 2 through 6 discuss the managerial functions of planning, organizing, staffing, leading, and controlling. Part 7 focuses on the challenges in the international environment. In addition, international aspects of managing are mentioned throughout the book. The authors also challenge scholars, researchers, and practicing managers to work toward a unified, global theory of management.

Revision Work in This Edition

This is one of the most comprehensive revisions since the book was first published. While we have retained material that was well received over the years, much new information has been added. For example, we have built on the strong characteristics of the fourth edition, while at the same time adding modern features, ideas, and techniques. Some structural changes have also been made.

In revising this book, we have responded to two major influences. One is the valuable feedback from teachers, scholars, and students who have used past editions at various levels of academic and practical management education in a wide variety of universities and operating enterprises. Another major influence to which we have responded is the great volume of research, new ideas, and advanced techniques, especially those being applied to management from the behavioral, social, and physical sciences. The emphasis is on managerial practice based on sound theory.

Although not all changes can be mentioned here, certain revision work should be pointed out. All chapters have been updated. The number of chapters has been reduced from twenty-five in the previous edition to twenty-two in this book. For example, the chapters "Line and Staff Authority Relationships" and "Decentralization of Authority" have been shortened and combined in this edition. Similarly, the chapters "The Nature and Purpose of Staffing" and "Selection: Matching the Person with the Job" have been combined in the new chapter "Human Resource Management and Selection." While some material has been condensed, other topics have been expanded. Because of the importance of the impact of the external environment, a separate chapter (Chapter 2) is now devoted to the topic of management and society, emphasizing social responsibility and ethics. Similarly, the new chapter on international management discusses managerial practices not only in Asian countries but also in Europe.

New topics   These are some of the new topics in this edition:

- Identification of characteristics of excellent companies (Chapter 1)

- The importance of the role of women in managing (Chapters 1, 11, and 22, for example)

- A model for ethical decision making (Chapter 2)

- Code of ethics for government service (Chapter 2)

- A new tool (TOWS Matrix) for strategy formulation (Chapter 5)

- Porter's generic competitive strategies (Chapter 5)

- Decision support systems (Chapter 6)

- Entrepreneuring and intrapreneuring (Chapter 7)

- Organization culture (Chapter 10)

- Strategic career management (Chapter 12)

- Self-motivation (Chapter 15)

- Equity theory (Chapter 15)

- New challenges created by information technology such as speech recognition devices, telecommuting, and computer networks (Chapter 19 especially)

- Productivity of knowledge workers for gaining a competitive advantage (Chapter 20)

- Computer-aided design (CAD), computer-aided manufacturing (CAM), and manufacturing automation protocol (MAP) (Chapter 20)

- Managing in various countries (Chapter 22)

New or expanded features   Here are some other new or expanded features in this edition:

- Each chapter has a case, either from a domestic environment or from the international environment. Many of these cases are based on our consulting experience. To protect confidentiality, some company names are disguised. But other cases name names: People Express, Honda, McDonald's, Ford, the University of California, South Africa, and so on.

- Throughout the book, many real-life situations illustrate managerial concepts and theories.

- Boxed inserts called "Perspectives" or "International Perspectives" provide additional insights into managing companies such as General Motors, Compaq, 3 M Company, Volvo, Bell Telephone, ITALTEL, Volkswagen, Apple Computers, and Kodak.

- Each chapter has two recommendations for "Exercises/Action Steps" that get students involved.

- Many new figures and tables have been added. See, for example, Figure 2-2 on ethical decision making, Figure 6-5 showing a flowchart for investment decisions in a hospital, and Figure 15-6 depicting the equity theory.

- Frequent references to nonbusiness organizations are made.
- A company index has been added to the comprehensive name and subject indexes.

Learning Assistance

The integrative systems model on the inside of the book cover gives an overview of the book content. Parts 2 through 7 are introduced with this model, with highlighting for the chapters discussed in the individual part.

Each chapter begins with learning objectives and concludes with a summary, key ideas and concepts for review, and discussion questions. The purpose of the new section "Exercises/Action Steps" is to elicit readers' involvement. There are twenty-two cases, many describing domestic and international situations.

The last chapters of Parts 2 through 6, those dealing with the five managerial functions, are followed by summaries of major principles, or guides, related to planning, organizing, staffing, leading, and controlling.

Supplemental Material

Supplemental packages may, at times, be overwhelming to the instructor. We have restricted the supplemental material to the essentials necessary for effective teaching:

- The *Instructor's Resource Manual* has been prepared by John Halff, who is thoroughly familiar with the textbook.
- A set of professionally prepared color and black-and-white *transparencies* of important figures from the book and other sources is available to adopters from the publisher.
- *Transparency masters* of figures and tables are also supplied.
- The *Test Bank*, prepared by Heinz Weihrich, has been thoroughly revised and can be obtained by the instructor from the publisher as a booklet and as a computer disk.

Acknowledgments

The late Dr. Harold Koontz is sorely missed by those who knew him. At a memorial session at the Academy of Management meeting, Professor Ronald Greenwood stated that Howdy Koontz was many years ahead of his time. Indeed, his inspiration and guidance popularized the classification of management knowledge according to the managerial functions, a framework now used around the world. He will be long remembered for his contributions to management and for his many books, especially the first edition of *Principles of Management* (with Cyril O'Donnell), originally published in 1955 and continuously updated ever since.

Professor Koontz and I are indebted to so many persons that a complete acknowledgment would be encyclopedic. Many scholars, writers, and managers are acknowledged through references in the text. Many managers with whom we have served in business, government, education, and other enterprises have contributed by word and example. Thousands of managers in all kinds of enterprises in various countries have honored us over the years by allowing us to test our ideas in executive training classes and lectures. Especially helpful were the many Eastman Kodak managers located around the world who have generously shared their international experiences. To the executives of these and many other companies with whom we have been privileged to work as directors or consultants, we are grateful for the opportunity to gain the clinical practice of managing.

Many colleagues, scholars, managers, and students have contributed their ideas and suggestions to this book. My good friend Professor Keith Davis, at Arizona State University, was particularly helpful with his advice. One of my mentors at UCLA, Professor George S. Steiner, has done much to stimulate my interest in the development of the TOWS Matrix for strategic planning. Professors Peter F. Drucker, George S. Odiorne, and Gene Seyna, to whom my book *Management Excellence: Productivity through MBO* has been dedicated, have sharpened my thinking about goal-driven management systems and managerial productivity.

In previous editions, special appreciation was expressed to those who contributed in many important ways. While they are not named here, their contributions have been important for this edition as well.

We are very indebted to those who reviewed this edition and who made many valuable suggestions. They include Professors Richard D. Babcock, University of San Francisco; Charles F. Chanter, Grand Rapids Junior College; Merlyn Gulker, Dordt College; Charles N. Kaufman, University of South Dakota; James E. Keenan, St. Mary's College; Gary R. Oddou, San Jose State University; Andrew J. Papageorge, California State College; John A. Ritchey, Purdue University; and Stuart A. Rosenkrantz, Eastern Illinois University.

We wish to thank the many people at McGraw-Hill who contributed to this edition, especially Kathleen L. Loy, Laura D. Warner, Susan Gottfried, Eileen Gualberto, and Chuck Carson.

Finally, my wife Ursula has helped greatly with her patient critique. To her and Mary Koontz this book is dedicated.

Heinz Weihrich

ESSENTIALS OF MANAGEMENT

CHAPTER 1

Management: Science, Theory, and Practice

CHAPTER OBJECTIVES

After reading this chapter, you should understand:

1. The nature and purpose of management
2. That management applies to all kinds of organizations and to managers at all organizational levels
3. That the managerial skills required differ in the organizational hierarchy
4. The important role of women in the organization
5. That the goal of all managers is to be productive, that is, to carry out their activities effectively and efficiently and to create a "surplus"
6. That managing as practice is an art in which practitioners apply the underlying theory and science in light of situations
7. That there are various approaches to management
8. The systems approach to management
9. The managerial functions of planning, organizing, staffing, leading, and controlling

One of the most important human activities is managing. Ever since people began forming groups to accomplish aims they could not achieve as individuals, managing has been essential to ensure the coordination of individual efforts. As society has come to rely increasingly on group effort, and as many organized groups have become large, the task of managers has been rising

3

in importance. The purpose of this book is to promote excellence among all persons in organizations, especially among managers, aspiring managers, and other professionals.*

DEFINITION OF MANAGEMENT: ITS NATURE AND PURPOSE

Management is *the process of designing and maintaining an environment in which individuals, working together in groups, efficiently accomplish selected aims*. This basic definition needs to be expanded:

1. As managers, people carry out the managerial functions of planning, organizing, staffing, leading, and controlling.

2. Management applies to any kind of organization.

3. It applies to managers at all organizational levels.

4. The aim of all managers is the same: to create a surplus.

5. Managing is concerned with productivity; this implies effectiveness and efficiency.

The Functions of Management

Many scholars and managers have found that the analysis of management is facilitated by a useful and clear organization of knowledge. In studying management, therefore, it is helpful to break it down into five managerial functions — planning, organizing, staffing, leading, and controlling — around which can be organized the knowledge that underlies those functions. Thus, the concepts, principles, theory, and techniques of management are grouped into these five functions.

This framework has been used and tested for many years. Although there are different ways of organizing managerial knowledge, most textbook authors today have adopted this or a similar framework even after experimenting at times with alternative ways of structuring knowledge.

Some scholars have organized managerial knowledge around the roles of managers, as shown in the Perspective. Indeed, this approach has made some valuable contributions to the study of management, since it also focuses on what managers do and provides evidence of planning, organizing, staffing, leading, and controlling.

Although the emphasis in this book is on managers' tasks that pertain to designing an internal environment for performance within an organization, it must never be overlooked that managers must operate in the external environment of an enterprise as well.[1] Clearly, managers cannot perform their tasks

---

*At times the term "nonmanagers" is used in reference to persons who have no subordinates. Thus, nonmanagers include professionals who may have a high status in organizations.

PERSPECTIVE:
THE TEN MANAGERIAL ROLES IDENTIFIED BY MINTZBERG

Interpersonal roles

1. The figurehead role (performing ceremonial and social duties as the organization's representative)

2. The leader role

3. The liaison role (communicating particularly with outsiders)

Informational roles

1. The recipient role (receiving information about the operation of an enterprise)

2. The disseminator role (passing information to subordinates)

3. The spokesperson role (transmitting information to those outside the organization)

Decision roles

1. The entrepreneurial role

2. The disturbance-handler role

3. The resource allocator role

4. The negotiator role (dealing with various persons and groups of persons)

well unless they have an understanding of, and are responsive to, the many elements of the external environment — economic, technological, social, political, and ethical factors that affect their areas of operations.

Management as an Essential for Any Organization

Managers are charged with the responsibility of taking actions that will make it possible for individuals to make their best contributions to group objectives. Management thus applies to small and large organizations, to profit and not-for-profit enterprises, to manufacturing as well as service industries. The term "enterprise" refers to businesses, government agencies, hospitals, universities, and other organizations, since almost everything said in this book refers to business as well as nonbusiness organizations. Effective managing is the concern of the corporation president, the hospital administrator, the government first-line supervisor, the Boy Scout leader, the bishop in the church, the baseball manager, and the university president.

Managerial Functions at Different Organizational Levels

In this book, no basic distinction is made between managers, executives, administrators, and supervisors. To be sure, a given situation may differ consi-

Figure 1-1

TIME SPENT IN CARRYING OUT MANAGERIAL FUNCTIONS.

Partly based on and adapted from Thomas A. Mahoney, Thomas H. Jerdee, and Stephen J. Carroll, "The Job(s) of Management," *Industrial Relations* (February 1965), pp. 97–110.

derably among various levels in an organization or various types of enterprises. Similarly, the scope of authority held may vary and the types of problems dealt with may be considerably different. Furthermore, the person in a managerial role may be directing people in the sales, engineering, or finance department. But the fact remains that, as managers, all obtain results by establishing an environment for effective group endeavor.

All managers carry out managerial functions. However, the time spent for each function may differ. Figure 1-1 shows an approximation of the relative time spent for each function. Thus, top-level managers spend more time on planning and organizing than do lower-level managers. Leading, on the other hand, takes a great deal of time for first-line supervisors. The difference in the amount of time spent on controlling varies only slightly for managers at various levels.

Managerial skills and the organizational hierarchy   Robert L. Katz identified three kinds of skills for administrators.[2] To these may be added a fourth — the ability to design solutions.

1. **Technical skill** is knowledge of and proficiency in activities involving methods, processes, and procedures. Thus, it involves working with tools and specific techniques. For example, mechanics work with tools, and their supervisors should have the ability to teach them how to use these tools. Similarly, accountants apply specific techniques in doing their job.

2. **Human skill** is the ability to work with people; it is cooperative effort; it is teamwork; it is the creation of an environment in which people feel secure and free to express their opinions.

3. **Conceptual skill** is the ability to see the "big picture," to recognize significant elements in a situation, and to understand the relationships among the elements.

4. **Design skill** is the ability to solve problems in ways that will benefit the enterprise. To be effective, particularly at upper organizational levels, managers must be able to do more than see a problem. They must have, in addition, the skill of a good design engineer in working out a practical solution to a problem. If managers merely see the problem and become "problem watchers," they will fail. Managers must also have that valuable skill of being able to design a workable solution to the problem in the light of the realities they face.

The relative importance of these skills may differ at various levels in the organization hierarchy. As shown in Figure 1-2, technical skills are of greatest importance at the supervisory level. Human skills are also helpful in the frequent interactions with subordinates. Conceptual skills, on the other hand, are usually not critical for lower-level supervisors. At the middle-management level, the need for technical skills decreases; human skills are still essential; the conceptual skills gain in importance. At the top management level, conceptual and design abilities and human skills are especially valuable, but there is relatively little need for technical abilities. It is assumed, especially in large companies, that chief executives can utilize the technical abilities of their subordinates. In smaller firms, however, technical experience may still be quite important.

Women in the organizational hierarchy In the last decade or so, women have made significant progress in obtaining responsible positions in organizations. Among the reasons for this development are laws governing fair employment practices, changing societal attitudes toward women in the workplace, and the desire of companies to project a favorable image by placing qualified women in managerial positions.

Figure 1-2

Skills vary in importance at different management levels.

SKILLS AND MANAGEMENT LEVELS.

In 1965, readers of the *Harvard Business Review* were surveyed to determine their attitudes toward women in business organizations.[3] About half of the men and women (and there was not much difference between them) responding felt that women seldom expected to achieve or even desired positions of authority.

Twenty years later, in 1985, the results showed that the attitudes toward women in business had changed significantly. Only 9 percent of the men and 4 percent of the women in the survey thought that women do not aspire to top positions. Moreover, it was found that men increasingly saw women as competent, equal colleagues. However, over 50 percent of those answering in the survey thought that women would never be completely accepted in business. This may indeed be discouraging to those women who aspire to top management positions. Yet, 20 years ago, few people would have expected the progress toward equality that has been made since 1965.

Some evidence suggests that women do have difficulties making it to the top. For example, there are no women on the way to the chief executive officer's job in the *Fortune* 500 corporations. Discrimination has been given as one reason according to a *Fortune* article.[4] On the other hand, Marisa Bellisario, who will be discussed in greater detail in Chapter 22, is one of the most successful executives in Italy, with the press calling her "Lady Computer" and the "manager in jeans" (she occasionally wears jeans at work). In fact, companies such as IBM, AT&T, and GTE Corporation have unsuccessfully tried to recruit her.

The Goal of All Managers

Nonbusiness executives sometimes say that the aim of business managers is simple — to make a profit. But profit is really only a measure of a surplus of sales dollars (or any other currency) over expense dollars. In a very real sense, in all kinds of organizations, whether business or nonbusiness, the logical and publicly desirable aim of all managers should be a surplus. Thus, managers must establish an environment in which people can accomplish group goals with the least amount of time, money, materials, and personal dissatisfaction or in which they can achieve as much as possible of a desired goal with available resources. In a nonbusiness enterprise such as a police department, as well as in units of a business (such as an accounting department) that are not responsible for total business profits, managers still have goals and should strive to accomplish them with the minimum of resources or to accomplish as much as possible with available resources.

Productivity, Effectiveness, and Efficiency

Another way to view the aim of all managers is to say that they must be productive. After World War II the United States was the world leader in productivity. But in the late 1960s the deceleration of productivity growth began. Today the urgent need for productivity improvement is recognized by gov-

PERSPECTIVE:
WHICH ARE THE EXCELLENT COMPANIES?

In a society such as that in the United States, profitability is an important measure of company excellence. At times, however, other criteria are also used that frequently coincide with financial performance. In their book *In Search of Excellence*, Thomas Peters and Robert Waterman identified 43 companies that they regarded as excellent.[5] In choosing some of the firms, they considered measures such as growth of assets and equity, average return on total capital, and similar factors. They also asked industry experts about the innovativeness of the companies.

The authors identified eight characteristics of excellent enterprises. Specifically, these firms:

- Were oriented toward action

- Learned about the needs of their customers

- Promoted managerial autonomy and entrepreneurship

- Achieved productivity by paying close attention to the needs of their people

- Were driven by a company philosophy often based on the values of their leaders

- Focused on the business they knew best

- Had a simple organization structure with a lean staff

- Were centralized as well as decentralized, depending on appropriateness

Two years after *In Search of Excellence* was published, *Business Week* took a second look at the companies that Peters and Waterman had considered excellent.[6] The magazine's survey revealed that at least 14 of the 43 companies did not measure up very well to several of the eight characteristics of excellence. Nine companies showed a great decline in earnings. While Peters and Waterman have been criticized in several respects (their methods of collecting and interpreting the data, for example, such as extensive use of anecdotes and quotations from leaders in the field rather than more scientific research sources),[7] the performance review of the firms indicated that success may be only transitory and that it demands continuing hard work to adapt to the changes in the environment.

A more recent survey by *Fortune* magazine of 31 industrial groups showed the following ranking of the ten most admired companies:[8] (1) International Business Machines (IBM), (2) 3M, (3) Dow Jones (printing and publishing), (4) Coca-Cola (5) Merck (pharmaceuticals), (6) Boeing, (7) Rubbermaid, (8) Procter & Gamble, (9) Exxon, and (10) J. P. Morgan (banking).

In addition, companies were rated on eight attributes of reputation. IBM ranked first in the following five categories: quality of management; long-term investment value; financial soundness; the ability to attract, develop, and retain talented people; and the use of the assets of the corporation.

In the other three categories these companies ranked first: Dow Jones in quality of products and services, Citicorp in innovativeness, and Eastman Kodak in community and environmental responsibility.

ernment, private industry, and universities. Often we look to Japan to find answers to our productivity problem (a subject to be considered later, in Chapter 22), but we tend to overlook the importance of effectively performing the basic managerial and nonmanagerial activities.

Definition of productivity   Successful companies create a surplus through productive operations. Although there is not complete agreement on the true meaning of **productivity**, let us define it as the *output-input ratio within a time period with due consideration for quality*. It can be expressed as follows:

$$\text{Productivity} = \frac{\text{outputs}}{\text{inputs}} \quad \text{(within a time period, quality considered)}$$

The formula indicates that productivity can be improved (1) by increasing outputs with the same inputs, (2) by decreasing inputs but maintaining the same outputs, or (3) by increasing outputs and decreasing inputs to change the ratio favorably. Companies use several kinds of inputs, such as labor, materials, and capital. Total-factor productivity combines various inputs to arrive at a composite input.[9] In the past, productivity improvement programs were mostly aimed at the worker level.[10] Yet, as Peter F. Drucker, one of the most prolific writers in management, observed, "The greatest opportunity for increasing productivity is surely to be found in knowledge work itself, and especially in management."[11]

Definitions of effectiveness and efficiency   Productivity implies effectiveness and efficiency in individual and organizational performance. **Effectiveness** is the achievement of objectives. **Efficiency** is the achievement of the ends with the least amount of resources. Managers cannot know whether they are productive unless they first know their goals and those of the organization, a topic that will be discussed in Chapter 4.

MANAGING: SCIENCE OR ART?

Managing, like all other practices — whether medicine, music composition, engineering, accountancy, or even baseball — is an art. It is know-how. It is doing things in the light of the realities of a situation. Yet managers can work better by using the organized knowledge about management. It is this knowledge that constitutes a science. Thus, managing as practice is an *art*; the organized knowledge underlying the practice may be referred to as a *science*. In this context science and art are not mutually exclusive; they are complementary.

As science improves, so should art, as has happened in the physical and biological sciences. To be sure, the science underlying managing is fairly crude and inexact. This is true because the many variables with which managers deal are extremely complex. Nevertheless, such management knowledge can certainly improve managerial practice. Physicians without the advantage of science would be little more than witch doctors. Executives who attempt to manage without management science must trust to luck, intuition, or what they did in the past.

In managing, as in any other field, unless practitioners are to learn by trial and error (and it has been said that managers' errors are their subordinates' trials), there is no place they can turn for meaningful guidance other than the accumulated knowledge underlying their practice.

THE ELEMENTS OF SCIENCE

Science is organized knowledge. The essential feature of any science is the application of the scientific method to the development of knowledge. Thus, a science comprises clear concepts, theory, and other accumulated knowledge developed from hypotheses (assumptions that something is true), experimentation, and analysis.

The Scientific Approach

The scientific approach first requires clear **concepts** — mental images of anything formed by generalization from particulars. These words and terms should be exact, relevant to the things being analyzed, and informative to the scientist and practitioner alike. From this base, the **scientific method** involves the determination of facts through observation. After classifying and analyzing these facts, scientists look for causal relationships. When these generalizations or hypotheses are tested for accuracy and appear to be true, that is, to reflect or explain reality, they are called **principles.** They have value in predicting what will happen in similar circumstances. Principles are not always unquestionably or invariably true, but they are considered valid enough to be used for prediction.

Theory is a systematic grouping of interdependent concepts and principles which give a framework to, or tie together, a significant area of knowledge. Scattered data, such as the notations left on a blackboard after a group of engineers has been discussing a problem, are not information unless the observer has knowledge of the theory which will explain relationships. Theory is, as Homans has said, "in its lowest form a classification, a set of pigeon holes, a filing cabinet in which fact can accumulate. Nothing is more lost than a loose fact."[12]

The Role of Management Theory

In the field of management, then, the role of theory is to provide a means of classifying significant and pertinent management knowledge. In the area of designing an effective organization structure, for example, there are a number of principles that are interrelated and that have a predictive value for managers.

Some principles give guidelines for delegating authority; these include the principle of delegating by results expected, the principle of equality of authority and responsibility, and the principle of unity of command.

Principles in management are fundamental truths (or what are thought to be truths at a given time), explaining relationships between two or more sets of variables, usually an independent variable and a dependent variable. Principles may be *descriptive* or *predictive*, and not prescriptive. That is, they describe how one variable relates to another — what will happen when these variables interact. They do not prescribe what people should do. For example, in physics, if gravity is the only force acting on a falling body, the body will fall at an increasing speed; this principle does not say whether anyone should jump off the roof of a high building. Or take the example of **Parkinson's Law:** *Work tends to expand to fill the time available.* Even if Parkinson's somewhat frivolous principle is correct (as it probably is), it does not mean that a manager should lengthen the time available for people to do a job. As another example, in management the **principle of unity of command** states that *the more often an individual reports to a single superior, the more likely it is that the individual will feel a sense of loyalty and obligation and the less likely it is that there will be confusion about instruction.* The principle merely predicts. It in no sense implies that individuals should never report to more than one person. Rather, it implies that if they do so, their managers must be aware of the possible dangers and should take these risks into account in balancing the advantages and disadvantages of multiple command.

Like engineers who apply physical principles to the design of an instrument, managers who apply theory to managing must usually blend principles with realities. An engineer is often faced with the necessity of combining considerations of weight, size, conductivity, and other factors in designing an instrument. Likewise, a manager may find that the advantages of giving a controller authority to prescribe accounting procedures throughout an organizaion outweigh the possible costs of multiple authority. But if they know theory, these managers will know that such costs as conflicting instructions and confusion may exist, and they will take steps (such as making the controller's special authority clear to everyone involved) to minimize disadvantages.

Management Techniques

Techniques are essentially ways of doing things, methods of accomplishing a given result. In all fields of practice they are important. They certainly are in managing, even though few really important managerial techniques have been invented. Among them are budgeting, cost accounting, network planning and control techniques like the Program Evaluation and Review Technique (PERT) or the Critical Path Method (CPM), rate-of-return-on-investment control, various devices of organizational development, all of which will be discussed in later chapters. Techniques normally reflect theory and are a means of helping managers undertake activities most effectively.

PERSPECTIVE:
MANAGEMENT TECHNIQUES OR FADS?

A **management fad** can be defined as a managerial interest or practice followed for a period of time with exaggerated zeal or craze. But fads come and go — some slowly, others quickly; some survive and others fall by the wayside. These managerial fads can be found in all managerial functions. *Business Week* identified some that are out and some that are currently in vogue.[13] Let us look at some of those that are "in" in the various managerial functions.

Fads in planning?   One of the fashionable buzzwords is **strategic alliance**, which essentially means that companies cooperate, as in forming a joint venture. These alliances even cut across national boundaries: American Telephone and Telegraph joins forces with Olivetti in Italy; General Motors builds cars with the Japanese car manufacturer Toyota.[14]

Fads in organizing?   **Corporate culture** is also "in." It pertains to the values and beliefs shared by employees and the general patterns of their behavior.

Fads in staffing?   Organizations have to be staffed by people who are not only competent but also healthy. This requires **wellness** or **fitness** programs and the management of **stress**. Over 90 percent of the 500 largest companies in the United States have a wellness program or are assisting employees in managing stress or improving their health.[15] **Paying for performance** is also currently fashionable.[16] This simply means measuring the contributions of individuals and rewarding them accordingly. Another term you may hear at times is **demassing**, which is a euphemism for laying off employees or demoting managers.

Fads in leading?   Then there is the **intrapreneur**, a person who acts like an entrepreneur but does so within the organizational environment. Gifford Pinchot, who coined the term, describes intrapreneurs as "those who take hands-on responsibility for creating innovation of any kind within an organization. The intrapreneur may be the creator or inventor but he or she is always the dreamer who figures out how to turn an idea into a profitable reality."[17]

Fads in controlling?   People admire success. Managers, rightly or wrongly, look to Japan to solve their productivity or quality problems. Thus, **quality circles**, widely used in Japan, are seen as a way of improving quality and making U.S. products more competitive.

Fads can be become techniques, and they may contribute to the functioning of the organization. (Indeed, some of them will be discussed later in this book.) However, if they are considered short-term solutions to deep-seated problems, or if they are considered quick fixes, then their value may be questioned. On the other hand, if they are integrated into a comprehensive system of management with a real commitment to managerial excellence, then they will be useful techniques.

Figure 1-3   APPROACHES TO MANAGEMENT

CHARACTERISTICS/ CONTRIBUTIONS	LIMITATIONS	ILLUSTRATION
EMPIRICAL, OR CASE, APPROACH		
Studies experience through cases. Identifies successes and failures.	Situations are all different. No attempt to identify principles. Limited value for developing management theory.	
INTERPERSONAL BEHAVIOR APPROACH		
Focus on interpersonal behavior, human relations, leadership, and motivation. Based on individual psychology.	Ignores planning, organizing, and controlling. Psychological training is not enough to become an effective manager.	
GROUP BEHAVIOR APPROACH		
Emphasis on behavior of people in groups. Based on sociology and social psychology. Primarily study of group behavior patterns. The study of large groups is often called "organization behavior."	Often not integrated with management concepts, principles, theory, and techniques. Need for closer integration with organization structure design, staffing, planning, and controlling.	
COOPERATIVE SOCIAL SYSTEMS APPROACH		
Concerned with both interpersonal and group behavioral aspects leading to a system of cooperation. Expanded concept includes any cooperative group with a clear purpose.	Too broad a field for the study of management. At the same time, it overlooks many managerial concepts, principles, and techniques.	
SOCIOTECHNICAL SYSTEMS APPROACH		
Technical system has great effect on social system (personal attitudes, group behavior). Focus on production, office operations, and other areas with close relationships between the technical system and people.	Emphasis only on blue-collar and lower-level office work. Ignores much of other managerial knowledge.	
DECISION THEORY APPROACH		
Focus on the making of decisions, persons or groups making decisions, and the decision-making process. Some theorists use decision making as a springboard to study all enterprise activities. The boundaries of study are no longer clearly defined.	There is more to managing than making decisions. The focus is at the same time too narrow and too wide.	

14

CHARACTERISTICS/ CONTRIBUTIONS	LIMITATIONS	ILLUSTRATION

SYSTEMS APPROACH

Systems concepts have broad applicability. Systems have boundaries, but they also interact with the external environment; i.e., organizations are open systems. Recognizes importance of studying interrelatedness of planning, organizing, and controlling in an organization as well as the many subsystems.	Analyses of the interrelatedness of systems and subsystems as well as the interactions of organizations with their external environment. Can hardly be considered a new approach to management.	Open to external environment

MATHEMATICAL OR "MANAGEMENT SCIENCE" APPROACH

Managing is seen as mathematical processes, concepts, symbols, and models. Looks at management as a purely logical process, expressed in mathematical symbols and relationships.	Preoccupation with mathematical models. Many aspects in managing cannot be modeled. Mathematics is a useful tool, but hardly a school or an approach to management.	

CONTINGENCY OR SITUATIONAL APPROACH

Managerial practice depends on circumstances (i.e., a contingency or a situation). Contingency theory recognizes the influence of given solutions on organizational behavior patterns.	Managers have long realized that there is *no* one best way to do things. Difficulty in determining all relevant contingency factors and showing their relationships. Can be very complex.	

MANAGERIAL ROLES APPROACH

Original study consisted of observations of five chief executives. On the basis of this study, ten managerial roles were identified and grouped into (1) interpersonal, (2) informational, and (3) decision roles.	Original sample was very small. Some activities are not managerial. Activities are evidence of planning, organizing, staffing, leading, and controlling. But some important managerial activities were left out (e.g., appraising managers).	

MCKINSEY'S 7-S FRAMEWORK

The seven S's are (1) strategy, (2) structure, (3) systems, (4) style, (5) staff, (6) shared values, (7) skills.	Although this experienced consulting firm now uses a framework similar to the one found useful by Koontz et al. since 1955 and confirms its practicality, the terms used are not precise and topics are not discussed in depth.	

OPERATIONAL APPROACH

Draws together concepts, principles, techniques, and knowledge from other fields and managerial approaches. The attempt is to develop science and theory with practical application. Distinguishes between managerial and non-managerial knowledge. Develops classification system built around the managerial functions of planning, organizing, staffing, leading, and controlling.	Does not, as some authors do, identify "representing" or "coordination" as a separate function. Coordination, for example, is the essence of managership and is the purpose of managing.	

PATTERNS OF MANAGEMENT ANALYSIS: A MANAGEMENT THEORY JUNGLE?

Although academic writers and theorists contributed notably little to the study of management until the early 1950s (previous writings came largely from practitioners), the past three to four decades have seen a veritable deluge of writing from the academic halls. The variety of approaches to management analysis, the welter of research, and the number of differing views have resulted in much confusion as to what management is, what management theory and science is, and how managerial events should be analyzed. As a matter of fact, the senior author some years ago called this situation "the management theory jungle."[18] Since that time, the vegetation in this jungle has changed somewhat, new approaches have developed, and older approaches have taken on some new meanings with some new words attached to them, but the developments of management science and theory still have the characteristics of a jungle.

Different Approaches to the Analysis of Management

The various approaches to management analysis — summarized in Figure 1-3 — are the following: (1) the empirical, or case, approach, (2) the interpersonal behavior approach, (3) the group behavior approach, (4) the cooperative social systems approach, (5) the sociotechnical systems approach, (6) the decision theory approach, (7) the systems approach, (8) the mathematical, or "management science," approach, (9) the contingency, or situational, approach, (10) Mintzberg's managerial roles approach, shown earlier in the Perspective, (11) McKinsey's 7-S approach, and (12) the operational approach. Understanding the various approaches makes it possible to identify the point of view from which any book or article on management has probably been written.

The Operational, or Management Process, Approach

As Figure 1-3 shows, the operational approach draws on all the other approaches and integrates them in a systematic manner. This approach to management theory and science attempts to bring together the pertinent knowledge of management by relating it to the managerial job — what managers do. Like other operational sciences, it tries to integrate the concepts, principles, and techniques that underlie the task of managing.

The operational approach recognizes that there is a central core of knowledge about managing pertinent only to the field of management. Such matters as line and staff, departmentation, managerial appraisal, and various managerial control techniques involve concepts and theory found only in situations involving managers. In addition, this approach draws on and absorbs knowledge from other fields, including systems theory, decision theory, theories of motivation and leadership, individual and group behavior, social systems, and cooperation and communications, and from the application of mathematical analyses and concepts.

The nature of the operational approach can be seen in Figure 1-4. As this diagram shows, the operational management school recognizes the existence of a central core of science and theory peculiar to managing and also draws important contributions from various other schools and approaches. As the circle shows, the operational theorist is not interested in all the important knowledge in these various fields but only in that which is deemed most useful and relevant to managing.

Figure 1-4

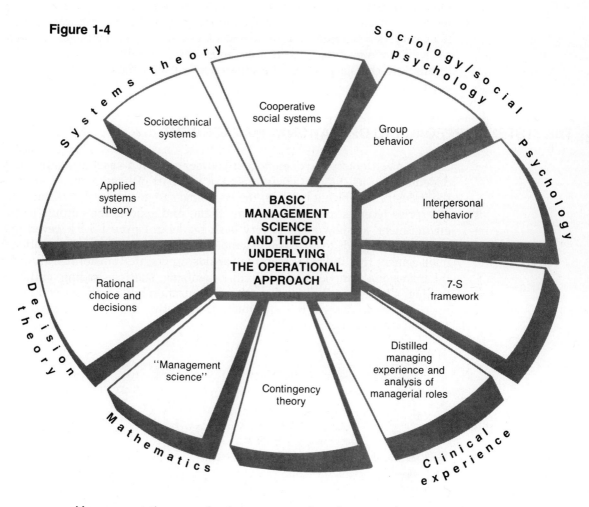

Management theory and science as a system draw on other areas of organized knowledge. The figure shows how operational-management theory and science, here enclosed in the circle, have a core of basic science and theory and draw from other fields of knowledge pertinent to understanding management. Basic management is thus, in part, an eclectic science and theory.

Because the functions of managers are emphasized in the operational approach, it is often called the "management process" school. The great French industrialist and management pioneer Henri Fayol first attempted to organize management knowledge around managerial functions. This approach has been found useful to, and understandable by, practicing managers. It also furnishes a means of distinguishing between managerial knowledge and the special knowledge and expertise of such nonmanagerial fields as marketing and production. In addition, it is a way of integrating into management useful and pertinent knowledge from all schools and approaches.

Although the operationalists generally believe that the fundamentals of management are universal, theorists of this school would readily admit that the problems managers face and the situations in which they operate vary among managerial levels in an enterprise and among different enterprises and that the application of concepts, theories, and techniques will naturally vary. This diversity is characteristic of the difference between theory and practice in any field.

THE SYSTEMS APPROACH TO OPERATIONAL MANAGEMENT

An organized enterprise does not, of course, exist in a vacuum. Rather, it is dependent on its external environment; it is a part of larger systems such as the industry to which it belongs, the economic system, and society. Thus, the enterprise receives inputs, transforms them, and exports the outputs to the environment, as shown by the very basic model in Figure 1-5. However, this simple model needs to be expanded and developed into a model of operational management that indicates how the various inputs are transformed through the managerial functions of planning, organizing, staffing, leading, and controlling. Clearly, any business or other organization must be described by an open-system model that includes interactions between the enterprise and its external environment.

Figure 1-5

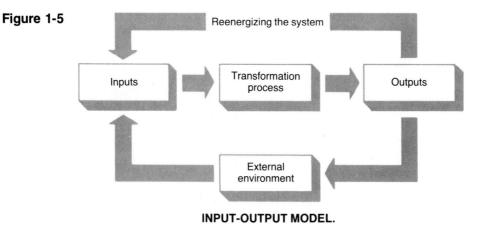

INPUT-OUTPUT MODEL.

Inputs and Claimants

The inputs from the external environment (see Figure 1-6) may include people, capital, and managerial skills, as well as technical knowledge and skills. In addition, various groups of people will make demands on the enterprise. For example, employees want higher pay, more benefits, and job security. On the other hand, consumers demand safe and reliable products at reasonable prices. Suppliers want assurance that their products will be bought. Stockholders want not only a high return on their investment but also security for their money. Federal, state, and local governments depend on taxes paid by the enterprise, but they also expect the enterprise to comply with their laws. Similarly, the community demands that enterprises be "good citizens," providing the maximum number of jobs with a minimum of pollution. Other claimants to the enterprise may include financial institutions and labor unions; even competitors have a legitimate claim for fair play. It is clear that many of these claims are incongruent, and it is the manager's job to integrate the legitimate objectives of the claimants.

The Managerial Transformation Process

It is the task of managers to transform the inputs, in an effective and efficient manner, into outputs. Of course, the transformation process can be viewed from different perspectives. Thus, one can focus on such diverse enterprise functions as finance, production, personnel, and marketing. Writers on management look on the transformation process in terms of their particular approaches to management. Specifically, writers belonging to the human behavior school focus on interpersonal relationships, social systems theorists analyze the transformation by concentrating on social interactions, and those advocating decision theory see the transformation as sets of decisions. Perhaps, however, the most comprehensive and useful approach for discussing the job of managers is to use the managerial functions of planning, organizing, staffing, leading, and controlling as a framework for organizing managerial knowledge (see Figure 1-6).

The Communication System

Communication is essential to all phases of the managerial process for two reasons. First, it integrates the managerial functions. For example, the objectives set in planning are communicated so that the appropriate organization structure can be devised. Communication is essential in the selection, appraisal, and training of managers to fill the roles in this structure. Similarly, effective leadership and the creation of an environment conducive to motivation depend on communication. Moreover, it is through communication that one determines whether events and performance conform to plans. Thus, it is communication which makes managing possible.

The second purpose of the communication system is to link the enterprise with its external environment, where many of the claimants are. For example,

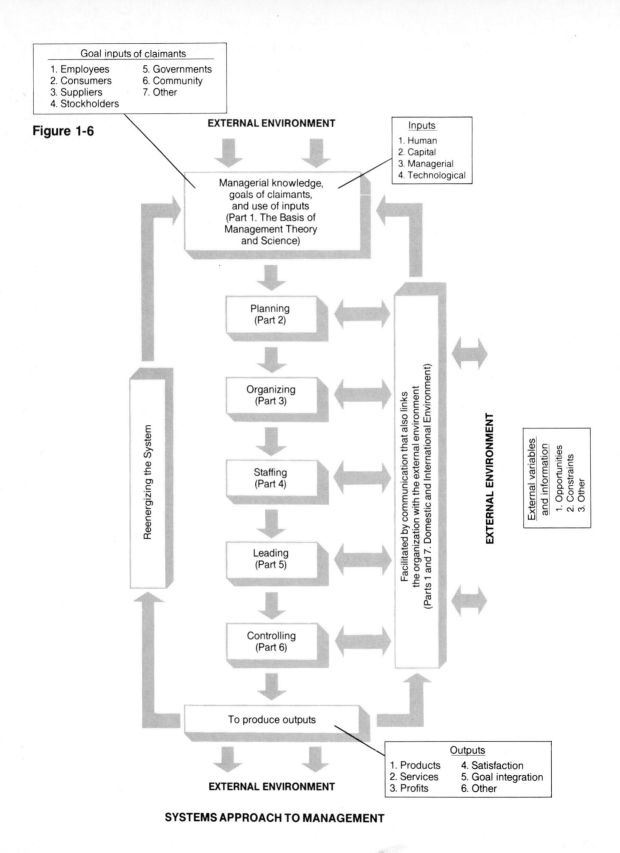

Figure 1-6

Goal inputs of claimants
1. Employees 5. Governments
2. Consumers 6. Community
3. Suppliers 7. Other
4. Stockholders

EXTERNAL ENVIRONMENT

Inputs
1. Human
2. Capital
3. Managerial
4. Technological

Managerial knowledge,
goals of claimants,
and use of inputs
(Part 1. The Basis of
Management Theory
and Science)

Planning
(Part 2)

Organizing
(Part 3)

Staffing
(Part 4)

Leading
(Part 5)

Controlling
(Part 6)

Reenergizing the System

Facilitated by communication that also links
the organization with the external environment
(Parts 1 and 7. Domestic and International Environment)

EXTERNAL ENVIRONMENT

External variables
and information
1. Opportunities
2. Constraints
3. Other

To produce outputs

EXTERNAL ENVIRONMENT

Outputs
1. Products   4. Satisfaction
2. Services   5. Goal integration
3. Profits   6. Other

SYSTEMS APPROACH TO MANAGEMENT

one should never forget that the customer, who is the reason for the existence of virtually all businesses, is outside a company. It is through the communication system that the needs of customers are identified; this knowledge enables the firm to provide products and services at a profit. Similarly, it is through an effective communication system that the organization becomes aware of competition and other potential threats and constraining factors.

External Variables

Effective managers will regularly scan the external environment. While it is true that managers may have little or no power to change the external environment, they have no alternative but to respond to it. The forces acting in the external environment are discussed in various chapters, but especially in Chapters 2, 5, and 22.

Outputs

It is the task of managers to secure and utilize inputs to the enterprise, to transform them through the managerial functions — with due consideration for external variables — to outputs.

Although the kinds of outputs will vary with the enterprise, they usually include many of the following: products, services, profits, satisfaction, and integration of the goals of various claimants to the enterprise. Most of these outputs require no elaboration, and only the last two will be discussed.

The organization must indeed provide many "satisfactions" if it hopes to retain and elicit contributions from its members. It must contribute to the satisfaction not only of basic material needs (for example, employees' needs to earn money for food and shelter or to have job security) but also of needs for affiliation, acceptance, esteem, and perhaps even self-actualization so that one can use his or her potential at the workplace.

Another output is goal integration. As noted above, the different claimants to the enterprise have very divergent — and often directly opposing — objectives. It is the task of managers to resolve conflicts and integrate these aims.

Reenergizing the System

Finally, it is important to notice that in the systems model of operational management some of the outputs become inputs again. Thus, the satisfaction of employees becomes an important human input. Similarly, profits, the surplus of income over costs, are reinvested in cash and capital goods, such as machinery, equipment, buildings, and inventory. You will see shortly that the model shown in Figure 1-6 will serve as a framework in this book for organizing managerial knowledge. But let us first look closer at the managerial functions.

THE FUNCTIONS OF MANAGERS

The functions of managers provide a useful framework for organizing management knowledge. There have been no new ideas, research findings, or techniques that cannot readily be placed in the classifications of planning, organizing, staffing, leading, and controlling.

Planning

Planning involves selecting missions and objectives and the actions to achieve them; it requires decision making, that is, choosing future courses of action from among alternatives. As Chapter 3 will show, there are various types of plans, ranging from overall purposes and objectives to the most detailed actions to be taken, such as ordering a special stainless steel bolt for an instrument or hiring and training workers for an assembly line. No real plan exists until a decision — a commitment of human or material resources or reputation — has been made. Before a decision is made, all that exists is a planning study, an analysis, or a proposal; there is no real plan. The various aspects of planning are discussed in Part 2 of this book.

Organizing

People working together in groups to achieve some goal must have roles to play, much like the parts actors fill in a drama, whether these roles are ones they develop themselves, are accidental or haphazard, or are defined and structured by someone who wants to make sure that people contribute in a specific way to group effort. The concept of a "role" implies that what people do has a definite purpose or objective; they know how their job objective fits into group effort, and they have the necessary authority, tools, and information to accomplish the task.

This can be seen in as simple a group effort as setting up camp on a fishing expedition. Everyone could do anything he or she wanted to do, but activity would almost certainly be more effective and certain tasks would be less likely to be left undone if one or two persons were given the job of gathering firewood, others the assignment of getting water, others the task of starting a fire, others the job of cooking, and so on.

Organizing, then, is that part of managing that involves establishing an intentional structure of roles for people to fill in an organization. It is intentional in the sense of making sure that all the tasks necessary to accomplish goals are assigned and, it is hoped, assigned to people who can do them best. Imagine what would have happened if such assignments had not been made in the program of flying the special aircraft *Voyager* around the globe without stopping or refueling.

The purpose of an organization structure is to help in creating an environment for human performance. It is, then, a management tool and not an end in and of itself. Although the structure must define the tasks to be done, the roles so established must also be designed in the light of the abilities and motivations of the people available.

Designing an effective organization structure is not an easy managerial task. Many problems are encountered in making structures fit situations, including both defining the kind of jobs that must be done and finding the people to do them. These problems and the essential theory, principles, and techniques of handling them are the subjects of Part 3 of this book.

Staffing

Staffing involves filling, and keeping filled, the positions in the organization structure. This is done by identifying work-force requirements; inventorying the people available; and recruiting, selecting, placing, promoting, appraising, planning the careers of, compensating, and training or otherwise developing both candidates and current jobholders to accomplish their tasks effectively and efficiently. This subject is dealt with in Part 4 of this book.

Leading

Leading is the influencing of people so that they will contribute to organization and group goals; it has to do predominantly with the interpersonal aspect of managing. All managers would agree that their most important problems arise from people — their desires and attitudes, their behavior as individuals and in groups — and that effective managers also need to be effective leaders. Since leadership implies followership and people tend to follow those who offer a means of satisfying their own needs, wishes, and desires, it is understandable that leading involves motivation, leadership styles and approaches, and communication. The essentials of these subjects are dealt with in Part 5 of this book.

Controlling

Controlling is the measuring and correcting of activities of subordinates to ensure that events conform to plans. It measures performance against goals and plans, shows where negative deviations exist, and, by putting in motion actions to correct deviations, helps ensure accomplishment of plans. Although planning must precede controlling, plans are not self-achieving. Plans guide managers in the use of resources to accomplish specific goals; then activities are checked to determine whether they conform to the plans.

Control activities generally relate to the measurement of achievement. Some means of controlling, like the budget for expense, inspection records, and the record of labor-hours lost, are generally familiar. Each measures and each shows whether plans are working out. If deviations persist, correction is indicated. But what is corrected? Activities, through persons. Nothing can be done about reducing scrap, for example, or buying according to specifications, or handling sales returns unless one knows who is responsible for these functions. Compelling events to conform to plans means locating the persons who are responsible for results that differ from planned action and then taking the necessary steps to improve performance. Thus, outcomes are controlled by controlling what people do. This subject is treated in Part 6.

Coordination, the Essence of Managership

Some authorities consider coordination to be a separate function of the manager. It seems more accurate, however, to regard it as the essence of managership, for achieving harmony among individual efforts toward the accomplishment of group goals. Each of the managerial functions is an exercise contributing to coordination.

Even in the case of a church or a fraternal organization, individuals often interpret similar interests in different ways, and their efforts toward mutual goals do not automatically mesh with the efforts of others. It thus becomes the central task of the manager to reconcile differences in approach, timing, effort, or interest and to harmonize individual goals to contribute to organization goals.

THE SYSTEMS MODEL OF MANAGEMENT AND THE ORGANIZATION OF THIS BOOK

The model of the Systems Approach to Management is also the foundation for organizing managerial knowledge. Note that in Figure 1-6 the numbers shown in the model correspond to the parts of this book. Part 1 covers the basis of management and the interactions between the organization and its environment. It deals also with social responsibility and ethics. This part cuts across all managerial functions.

As the model in the figure shows, Part 2 deals with the various aspects of **planning** (Chapters 3 to 6). Part 3 is concerned with **organizing** (Chapters 7 to 10), while Part 4 deals with **staffing** (Chapters 11 to 13), Part 5 with **leading** (Chapters 14 to 17), and Part 6 with **controlling** (Chapters 18 to 21).

International topics and future challenges are discussed in Part 7 (Chapter 22). These aspects relate to the inputs, the claimants of the organization, the external variables and information, and the outputs in the model. However, some of the factors external to the organization, such as strategic planning, are also discussed in other chapters. This is as it should be, because the organization is viewed in this book as an open system that interacts with the external environment.

The model shown in Figure 1-6 is repeated at the beginning of Parts 2 to 7; each time, the chapters discussed in that particular part are highlighted. This procedure provides an integrative model that shows the relationships of the topics in this book.

SUMMARY

Management is the process of designing and maintaining an environment for the purpose of efficiently accomplishing selected aims. Managers carry out the functions of planning, organizing, staffing, leading, and controlling. Managing is an essential activity at all organizational levels; however, the managerial skills required vary with organizational levels. Although women have made progress in obtaining responsible positions, they still have a long way to go. The goal of all managers is to create a surplus and to be productive, that is, to achieve a favorable output-input ratio within a specific time period with due consideration for quality. Productivity implies effectiveness (achieving of objectives) and efficiency (using the least amount of resources).

Managing as practice is art; organized knowledge about management is science. The development of management theory involves the development of concepts, principles, and techniques.

There are many theories about management, and each contributes something to our knowledge of what managers do. Each approach has its own characteristics and advantages as well as limitations. The operational, or management process, approach draws on each "school" and systematically integrates them.

The organization is an open system that operates within and interacts with the environment. The systems approach to management includes inputs from the external environment and from claimants, the transformation process, the communication system, external factors, outputs, and a way to reenergize the system. The transformation process consists of the managerial functions which also provide the framework for organizing knowledge in this book.

KEY IDEAS AND CONCEPTS FOR REVIEW

Management
Managerial functions
Managerial skills in the
    organizational hierarchy
Women in the organizational
    hierarchy
The goal of all managers
Characteristics of excellent
    companies
Productivity
Effectiveness
Efficiency
Concepts
Scientific method
Theory

Principles
Parkinson's Law
Techniques
Management theory jungle
Twelve approaches
    to management
Systems approach to
    operational management
Planning
Organizing
Staffing
Leading
Controlling
Coordination

FOR DISCUSSION

1. Is managing a science or an art? Could the same explanation apply to engineering or accounting?

2. In what fundamental way are the basic goals of all managers at all levels and in all kinds of enterprises the same?

3. Look up the terms "science," "theory," and "principle" in a dictionary and determine how they are used. Compare these definitions with the usage of these terms as applied to management in this book. What advantages are there in attempting to identify science, theory, and principles in a book on management?

4. What is meant by the management theory jungle?

5. Identify the various approaches to management. Discuss their characteristics and contributions as well as their limitations.

6. Why do management analysis and practice require a systems approach? Do managers operate in an open or a closed system? Explain.

EXERCISES/ACTION STEPS

1. Interview two local business managers and ask them how they learned about managing. Ask what kind of books they might have read on management (e.g., textbooks or popular books such as *In Search of Excellence* by Thomas J. Peters and Robert H. Waterman, Jr., *The One Minute Manager* by Kenneth H. Blanchard, *Theory Z* by William Ouchi, *The Art of Japanese Management* by Richard Tanner Pascale and Anthony G. Athos, and *Reinventing the Corporation: Transforming Your Job and Your Company for the New Information Society* by John Naisbitt and Patricia Aburdene). Probe to what extent these books have helped them to manage. You may also find it interesting to buy one of the best-selling books on management (most are available in paperback) and mention them in the class discussion.

2. Interview two public administrators and ask them how their job differs from that of business managers. How do they know how well their department, agency, or organization is performing, since profit is probably not one of the criteria for measuring effectiveness and efficiency?

CASE:
PEOPLE EXPRESS[19]

Donald Burr, the founder and chairperson of People Express, has been hailed in his attempt to build a more humane organization. But his leadership style was changing as the organization grew. Managers at People Express had a distinct managerial style: hard-driving, but giving employees a great deal of freedom. All employees are expected to carry out a great variety of tasks. Thus, pilots help out in handling the baggage. Even top executives rotate from job to job to learn the major aspects of the business. Full-time employees must buy stock in the company, although they receive a large discount.

After the company expanded and experienced its first losses, its emphasis on participative management changed. With the acquisition of Frontier Airlines, Inc., People Express became the fifth largest airline in the country — only 5 years after its formation in 1980. With its growth, however, the firm changed its character from a family-style organization to a more traditional one. Critics maintain that within the company it is even risky to ask unpopular questions. One of the original managing directors, Lori Dubose, who was one of the architects of lifetime employment at People Express, was unexpectedly fired. She thinks now that asking Burr challenging questions was risky and probably was a mistake. Another director, Harold Parety, who did not like being told that he had to be at work from 6:00 a.m. to 9:00 p.m. regardless of the work load, quit and formed his own airline (Presidential Airways, Inc.), applying many of People Express's managerial practices.

1. What do you think of Burr's way of firing an officer, although the company has an implied policy of great job security?

2. Should a company be managed the same way regardless of its size or its profitability?

REFERENCES

1. William H. Peace, "I Thought I Knew What Good Management Was," *Harvard Business Review* (March–April 1986), pp. 59–65.

2. Robert L. Katz, "Skills of an Effective Administrator," *Harvard Business Review* (January–February 1955), pp. 33–42; and Robert L. Katz, "Retrospective Commentary," *Harvard Business Review* (September–October 1974), pp. 101–102.

3. Charlotte Decker Sutton and Kris K. Moore, "Executive Women—20 Years Later," *Harvard Business Review* (September–October 1985), pp. 42–66.

4. Susan Fraker, "Why Women Aren't Getting to the Top," *Fortune* (Apr. 16, 1984), pp. 40–45. In certain firms, such as Federal Express and Hewlett-Packard, and in some industries, such as banking and retailing, chances for promotion to upper-level management are better for women. See Irene Pave, "A Woman's Place Is at GE, Federal Express, P&G . . . ," *Business Week* (June 23, 1986), pp. 75–76. But some women are also leaving the work force, as discussed by Alex Taylor III, "Why Women Managers Are Bailing Out," *Fortune* (Aug. 18, 1986), pp. 16–23.

5. Thomas J. Peters and Robert H. Waterman, Jr., *In Search of Excellence* (New York: Harper & Row, 1982).

6. "Who's Excellent Now?" *Business Week* (Nov. 5, 1984), pp. 76–88.

7. Daniel T. Carroll, "A Disappointing Search for Excellence," *Harvard Business Review* (November–December 1983), pp. 78–88. See also Terence R. Mitchell, "In Search of Excellence versus the 100 Best Companies to Work for in America: A Question of Perspectives and Values," *Academy of Management Review* (April 1985), pp. 350–355.

8. Cynthia Hutton, "America's Most Admired Corporations," *Fortune* (Jan. 6, 1986), pp. 16–27. But a year later, IBM slipped to number 7, indicating that success is transitory. See Edward C. Baig, "America's Most Admired Corporations," *Fortune* (Jan. 19, 1987), pp. 18–31.

9. Frank R. Lichtenberg, "What Makes Plant Productivity Grow?" *The Wall Street Journal* (Dec. 24, 1987).

10. Heinz Weihrich, *Management Excellence — Productivity through MBO* (New York: McGraw-Hill Book Company, 1985).

11. Peter F. Drucker, *Management: Tasks, Responsibilities, Practices* (New York: Harper & Row, 1973), p. 69.

12. G. C. Homans, *The Human Group* (New York: Harcourt, Brace & World, 1958), p. 5.

13. John A. Byrne, "Business Fads: What's In — and Out," *Business Week* (Jan. 18, 1986), pp. 52–61. Peter F. Drucker, probably the most prolific writer on management, notes that the fads change about every 2½ years. The next fad may be in accounting to measure productivity. See "Advice from the Dr. Spock of Business," *Business Week* (Sept. 28, 1987), pp. 61–65.

14. Howard V. Perlmutter and David A. Heenan, "Cooperate to Compete Globally," *Harvard Business Review* (March–April 1986), pp. 136–152.

15. Emily T. Smith, Jody Brott, Alice Cuneo, and Jo Ellen Davis, "Stress: The Test Americans Are Failing," *Business Week* (Apr. 18, 1988), pp. 74–76.

16. Jacob M. Schlesinger, "GM's New Compensation Plan Reflects General Trend Tying Pay to Performance," *The Wall Street Journal* (Jan. 26, 1988).

17. Gifford Pinchot III, *Intrapreneuring* (New York: Harper & Row, 1985), p. ix. For a review of books on entrepreneurship, see David E. Gumpert, "Stalking the Entrepreneur," *Harvard Business Review* (May–June 1986), pp. 32–36.

18. See Harold Koontz, "The Management Theory Jungle," *Journal of the Academy of Management* (December 1961), pp. 174–188. See also Harold Koontz, "Making Sense of Management Theory," *Harvard Business Review* (July–August 1962), pp. 24ff, and "The Management Theory Jungle Revisited," *Academy of Management Review* (April 1980), pp. 175–187. Much of this material has been drawn from these articles.

19. The case is based on a variety of sources, including "Up, Up and Away? — Expansion Is Threatening the 'Humane' Culture at People Express," *Business Week* (Nov. 25, 1985), pp. 80–94; James R. Norman, "People Is Plunging, but Burr Is Staying Cool," *Business Week* (July 7, 1986), pp. 31–32. Note that in 1986, Texas Air Corporation acquired People Express. See James R. Norman, "Nice Going, Frank, but Will It Fly?" *Business Week* (Sept. 29, 1986), pp. 34–35.

CHAPTER 2

Management and Society: Social Responsibility and Ethics

CHAPTER OBJECTIVES

After reading this chapter, you should understand:

1. The nature of the pluralistic society
2. The social responsibility of managers and the arguments for and against the social involvement of business
3. The nature and importance of ethics in managing and ways to institutionalize and raise ethical standards
4. Differing ethical standards in various societies

Much of this book deals with the interaction of managers and their subordinates with the environment inside the enterprise, but in most instances the effective manager must also deal with the outside environment. Every time managers plan, they take into account the wants and desires of members of society outside the organization, as well as the needs for material and human resources, technology, and other requirements in the external environment. They do likewise to some degree with almost every other kind of managerial activity.

Figure 2-1

An organization must operate in, and be responsive to, a number of different external environments.

All managers, whether they operate in a business, a government agency, a church, a charitable foundation, or a university, must, in varying degrees, consider the elements and forces of their external environment. While they may be able to do little or nothing to change these constraints, they have no alternative but to respond to them. They must identify, evaluate, and react to the forces outside the enterprise that may affect its operations. The impact of the external environment on the organization is illustrated in Figure 2-1. The constraining influences of external factors on the enterprise are even more crucial in international management (a fact to be discussed later, particularly in Chapter 22).

This chapter deals with the impact of the external environment on the organization and the relationships between business and the society in which it operates. First, the focus is on the nature of the pluralistic environment. Then the discussion expands to the topics of social responsibility and ethical behavior.

OPERATING IN A PLURALISTIC SOCIETY

Managers in the United States operate in a **pluralistic society,** in which many organized groups represent various interests. Each group has an impact on other groups, but no one group exerts inordinate power. Many groups exert some power over business. As explained in Chapter 1, there are many claimants on the organization and they have divergent goals. It is the task of the manager to integrate their aims.

Working within a pluralistic society has several implications for business.[1] First, business power is kept in balance by various groups, such as environmental groups. Second, business interests can be expressed by joining groups such as the Chamber of Commerce. Third, business participates in projects with other responsible groups for the purpose of bettering society; an example is working toward the renewal of inner cities. Fourth, in a pluralistic society there can be conflict or agreement among groups. Finally, in such a society one group is quite aware of what other groups are doing.

THE SOCIAL RESPONSIBILITY OF MANAGERS

In the early 1900s the mission of business firms was exclusively economic. Today, partly due to the interdependencies of the many groups in our society, the social involvement of business has increased. There is indeed a question as to what the social responsibility of business really is. Moreover, the question of social responsibility, originally associated with businesses, is now being posed with increasing frequency in regard to governments, universities, nonprofit foundations, charitable organizations, and even churches. Thus, we talk about the social responsibility and social responsiveness of all organizations, although the focus of this discussion is on business. Society, awakened and vocal by the urgency of social problems, is asking managers, particularly those at the top, what they are doing to discharge their social responsibilities.

Social Responsibility and Social Responsiveness

The concept of social responsibility is not new. Although the idea was already considered in the early part of the twentieth century, the modern discussion of social responsibility got a major impetus with the book *Social Responsibilities of the Businessman* by Howard R. Bowen. He suggested that businesses should consider the social implications of their decisions.[2] As you may expect, there is no complete agreement on the definition. In a survey of 439 executives, 68 percent of the responding managers agreed with the following definition: "**Corporate social responsibility** is seriously considering the impact of the company's actions on society."[3]

A newer concept, but still very similar to social responsibility, is **social responsiveness,** which in simple terms means "the ability of a corporation to relate its operations and policies to the social environment in ways that are mutually beneficial to the company and to society."[4] Both definitions focus on corporations, but these concepts should be expanded (1) to include enterprises other than businesses and (2) to encompass relationships within the enterprise. The main difference between social responsibility and social responsiveness is that the latter implies actions and the "how" of enterprise responses. In this discussion, the terms will be used interchangeably.[5]

Arguments for and against Business Involvement in Social Actions

Although there are arguments for business involvement in social activities, there are also arguments against it, as shown in Table 2-1.

Table 2-1   Arguments for and against Social Involvement of Business

Arguments for social involvement of business

1. Public needs have changed, leading to changed expectations. Business, it is suggested, received its charter from society and consequently has to respond to the needs of society.

2. Improvement of the social environment benefits both society and business. Society gains through better neighborhoods and employment opportunities; business benefits from a better community, since the community is the source of its work force and the consumer of its products and services.

3. Social involvement discourages additional government regulation and intervention. The result is greater freedom and more flexibility in decision making for business.

4. Business has a great deal of power which, it is reasoned, should be accompanied by an equal amount of responsibility.

5. Modern society is an interdependent system, and the internal activities of the enterprise have an impact on the external environment.

6. Social involvement may be in the interest of stockholders.

7. Problems can become profits. Items that may once have been considered waste (for example, empty soft drink cans) can be profitably used again.

8. Social involvement creates a favorable public image. Thus, a firm may attract customers, employees, and investors.

9. Business should try to solve the problems which other institutions have not been able to solve. After all, business has a history of coming up with novel ideas.

10. Business has the resources. Specifically, business should use its talented managers and specialists, as well as its capital resources, to solve some of society's problems.

11. It is better to prevent social problems through business involvement than to cure them. It may be easier to help the hard-core unemployed than to cope with social unrest.

Arguments against social involvement of business

1. The primary task of business is to maximize profit by focusing strictly on economic activities. Social involvement could reduce economic efficiency.

2. In the final analysis, society must pay for the social involvement of business through higher prices. Social involvement would create excessive costs for business, which cannot commit its resources to social action.

3. Social involvement can weaken the international balance of payments. The cost of social programs, the reasoning goes, would have to be added to the price of the product. Thus, American companies selling in international markets would be at a disadvantage when competing with companies in other countries which do not have these social costs to bear.

4. Business has enough power, and additional social involvement would further increase its power and influence.

5. Businesspeople lack the social skills to deal with the problems of society. Their training and experience is with economic matters and their skills may not be pertinent to social problems.

6. There is a lack of accountability of business to society. Unless accountability can be established, business should not get involved.

7. There is not complete support for involvement in social actions. Consequently, disagreements among groups with different viewpoints will cause friction.

Source: Based on Keith Davis and William C. Frederick, *Business and Society,* 5th ed. (New York: McGraw -Hill Book Company, 1984), chap. 2.

Today many businesses are involved in social action. A decision as to whether companies should extend their social involvement requires a careful examination of the arguments for and against such actions. Certainly society's expectations are changing and the trend seems to be toward greater social responsiveness. In fact, most respondents in a study of *Harvard Business Review* readers consider social responsibility a legitimate and achievable aim for business.[6] Still, the mission of the organization must be taken into account.

Reaction or Proaction?

To live within an environment and be responsive to it does not mean that managers should merely react in the face of stress. Since no enterprise can be expected to react very quickly to unforeseen developments, an enterprise must practice ways of anticipating developments through forecasts. An alert company, for example, does not wait until its product is obsolete and sales have fallen off before coming out with a new or improved product. A government agency should not wait until its regulations are obsolete and discredited before looking for another way to achieve its objectives. No enterprise should wait for problems to develop before preparing to face them. *Proaction* is an essential part of the planning process.

The Role of the Government

There are many instances in which social changes can be implemented only by the enactment of legislation. However, many managers in business and elsewhere have found it to their advantage to do something about pressing social problems. For example, many businesses have profited by filtering smoke-stack pollutants and selling or using these recovered wastes. Some companies have made a profit by building low-cost apartment buildings in ghetto areas. The Internal Revenue Service has increased tax collection efficiency and effectiveness by simplifying or eliminating certain burdensome reports and forms. In other words, contributing to the solution of social problems does not always involve net expense. But society may need the bludgeoning force of legislation to get improvements under way.

The Influence of Values and Performance Criteria on Behavior

Even if individual managers have full freedom to act in accordance with the currently conceived social responsibilities, they may not do so because of standards applied in evaluating their performance. Managers, like everyone else, want their performance positively appraised — they seek approval. Therefore, if their success is measured by profit, living within a budget, tax collection as a percentage of income, or the volume of blood contributed to a blood bank, managers will tend to strive for excellence in these regards. If success is measured in terms of pollution control, the number of convicts returned successfully to society, the dollar support for employees seeking university degrees, the ratio of "disadvantaged" to total number of employees, achievements in raising the productivity of subordinates, or combinations of these and similar goals, then managers will strive to achieve them.

In other words, managers will respond to socially approved values and will give priority to those held in highest esteem. If we want to make sure that organizations respond to social forces, we must clarify social values and then reward managers for their success in responding to them, recognizing, of course, that different organizations have a variety of missions.

The Social Audit

The discussion of social responsibility raises the question of how social performance should be evaluated. This led to the concept of the "social audit," first proposed in the 1950s by Howard R. Bowen.[7] But it is only more recently that corporations have seriously concerned themselves with this idea.[8] The **social audit** has been defined as "a commitment to systematic assessment of and reporting on some meaningful, definable domain of the company's activities that have social impact."[9]

One may distinguish between two types of audits. One is *required* by the government and involves, for example, pollution control, product performance requirements, and equal employment standards. The other kind of social audit concerns a great variety of *voluntary* social programs.[10]

One survey of the *Fortune* 500 firms showed that 456 companies (91.2 percent) have made social responsibility disclosures in their annual reports.[11] Although these disclosures may not be equated with a social audit, the large number of firms making such disclosures shows there is a general concern among major corporations about their social responsibility.

It is rather difficult to determine what areas the social audit should encompass. Often the items include pollution and the hiring, training, and promotion of minorities, but there are many other areas. For example, General Electric developed a matrix which facilitates the analysis of the expectations of customers, investors, employees, communities, and other claimants in the following areas: product and technical performance, economic performance, employment performance, environment and natural resources, community welfare and development, government-business relations, as well as international trade and development.[12]

Another difficulty is determining the amount of money an enterprise spends in selected areas. But cost alone is an inadequate measure. It does not necessarily show the results of social involvement. Other problems are the collection of the data and their presentation in a way that accurately reflects the social involvement of an enterprise. There is no doubt that many difficulties are associated with a social audit, but there is evidence that many companies and other organizations in the United States honestly attempt to address themselves to this challenge.

ETHICS IN MANAGING

All persons, whether in business, government, a university, or any other enterprise, are concerned with ethics. In *Webster's Ninth New Collegiate Dictionary*, **ethics** is defined as "the discipline dealing with what is good and bad and with moral duty and obligation." Thus, **personal ethics** has been referred to as "the rules by which an individual lives his or her personal life," and **accounting ethics** pertains to "the code that guides the professional conduct of accountants."[13] **Business ethics** is concerned with truth and justice and has a variety of aspects such as expectations of society, fair competition, advertising, public relations, social responsibilities, consumer autonomy, and corporate behavior in the home country as well as abroad.[14]

Ethical Theories and a Model for Political Behavior Decisions

In organizations, managers compete for information, influence, and resources. The potential for conflicts in selecting the ends as well as the means to the ends is easy to understand, and the question of what criteria should guide ethical behavior becomes acute.

There are three basic types of moral theories in normative ethics. First, the **utilitarian theory** suggests that plans and actions should be evaluated by their consequences. The underlying idea is that plans or actions should produce the greatest good for the greatest number of people. Second, the **theory based on rights** holds that all people have basic rights. Examples are the rights to freedom of conscience, free speech, and due process. A number of those rights can be found in the Constitutional Bill of Rights of the United States. Third, the **theory of justice** demands that decision makers be guided by fairness and equity, as well as impartiality.

Gerald Cavanagh, Dennis Moberg, and Manuel Velasquez point out the strengths and weaknesses of each theory and integrate them into a decision tree, shown in Figure 2-2, which can guide managers in making ethical decisions.[15] The theory is best illustrated by the following example:

Sam and Bob are highly motivated research scientists who work in the new-product development lab at General Rubber. Sam is by far the most technically competent scientist in the lab, and he has been responsible for several patents that have netted the company nearly $6 million in the past decade. He is quiet, serious, and socially reserved. In contrast, Bob is outgoing and demonstrative. While Bob lacks the technical track record Sam has, his work has been solid though unimaginative. Rumor has it that Bob will be moved into an administrative position in the lab in the next few years.

According to the lab policy, a $300,000 fund is available every year for the best new-product development idea proposed by a lab scientist in the form of a competitive bid. Accordingly, Sam and Bob both prepare pro-

Figure 2-2

**A DECISION TREE FOR INCORPORATING ETHICS
INTO POLITICAL BEHAVIOR DECISIONS.**

posals. Each proposal is carefully constructed to detail the benefits to the company and to society if the proposal is accepted, and it is the consensus of other scientists from blind reviews that both proposals are equally meritorious. Both proposals require the entire $300,000 to realize any significant results. Moreover, the proposed line of research in each requires significant mastery of the technical issues involved and minimal need to supervise the work of others.

After submitting his proposal, Sam takes no further action aside from periodically inquiring about the outcome of the bidding process. In contrast, Bob begins to wage what might be termed an open campaign in support of his proposal. After freely admitting his intentions to Sam and others, Bob seizes every opportunity he can to point out the relative advantages of his proposal to individuals who might have some influence over the decision. So effective is this open campaign that considerable informal pressure is placed on those authorized to make the decision on behalf of Bob's proposal. Bob's proposal is funded and Sam's is not.

An ethical analysis of Bob's action in this case could begin by using the decision tree shown in Figure 2-2. The first question in the sequence requires a utilitarian analysis. Clearly, Bob's interests are better served than Sam's. However, the nature of the two proposals seems to require one of the two to be disappointed. Moreover, the outcome in terms of broader interests (i.e., company, society) appears not to be suboptimal, since both proposals were judged equivalent in the blind reviews. Consequently, it is appropriate to answer the first question affirmatively. The second question inquires into the rights respected by Bob's behavior. Here again, the evidence seems persuasive that no one's rights were violated. Sam did not have (did not create) the same opportunity to point out the advantages of his proposal to those at whom Bob directed his lobbying campaign, but Bob's open campaign involved no deceit, and Sam's inaction may be taken as implied consent.

It is in light of the third question that Bob's actions are most suspect. Justice would have best been served in this case if there had been a clear situation-relevant difference between the two proposals. The blind reviews found them equivalent, so some other basis for differentiating between the proposals presumably had to be found. Bob's efforts served to create irrelevant differences between them. If anything, Sam's superior technical track record would have been a more relevant factor than Bob's initiative and social skills in determining who should be favored to perform a technical task. Bob's actions in this regard were therefore unjust. Interestingly, had the proposals required supervision of others or the ability to persuade others, Bob's approach would have been justified.[16]

Managers are facing many situations that require ethical judgments, and often there are no easy answers. The model shown in Figure 2-2 provides a conceptual framework that helps managers analyze and evaluate their decisions, as illustrated by the case.

Institutionalizing Ethics

Managers, and especially top managers, do have a responsibility to create an organizational environment that fosters ethical decision making by institutionalizing ethics. This means applying and integrating ethical concepts into daily action. Theodore Purcell and James Weber suggest that this can be accomplished in three ways: (1) by establishing appropriate company policy or a code of ethics, (2) by using a formally appointed ethics committee, and (3) by teaching ethics in management development programs.[17] The most common way to institutionalize ethics is to establish a code of ethics; much less common is the use of ethics board committees. Management development programs dealing with ethical issues are very seldom used, although companies such as Allied Chemical, International Business Machines, and General Electric have instituted such programs.

Code of Ethics and Its Implementation through Formal Committees

A **code** is a statement of policies, principles, or rules that guide behavior. Certainly codes of ethics do not apply only to business enterprises; they should guide the behavior of persons in all organizations and in everyday life.

Simply stating a code of ethics is not enough, and the appointment of an ethics committee, consisting of internal and external directors, is essential for institutionalizing ethical behavior.[19] The functions of such a committee may include (1) holding regular meetings to discuss ethical issues, (2) dealing with "gray areas," (3) communicating the code to all members of the organization, (4) checking for possible violations of the code, (5) enforcing the code, (6) rewarding compliance and punishing violations, (7) reviewing and updating the code, and (8) reporting activities of the committee to the board of directors.

PERSPECTIVE:
CODE OF ETHICS FOR GOVERNMENT SERVICE

The federal government has established the following code.[18] Any person in government service should:

1. Put loyalty to the highest moral principles and to country above loyalty to persons, party, or Government department.

2. Uphold the Constitution, laws, and regulations of the United States and of all governments therein and never be a party to their evasion.

3. Give a full day's labor for a full day's pay; giving earnest effort and best thought to the performance of duties.

4. Seek to find and employ more efficient and economical ways of getting tasks accomplished.

5. Never discriminate unfairly by the dispensing of special favors or privileges to anyone, whether for remuneration or not; and never accept, for himself or herself or for family members, favors or benefits under circumstances which might be construed by reasonable persons as influencing the performance of governmental duties.

6. Make no private promises of any kind binding upon the duties of office, since a Government employee has no private word which can be binding on public duty.

7. Engage in no business with the Government, either directly or indirectly, which is inconsistent with the conscientious performance of governmental duties.

8. Never use any information gained confidentially in the performance of governmental duties as a means of making private profit.

9. Expose corruption wherever discovered.

10. Uphold these principles, ever conscious that public office is a public trust.

Factors That Raise Ethical Standards

In the study cited earlier, the two factors that raise ethical standards the most, according to the respondents, are (1) public disclosure and publicity and (2) the increased concern of a well-informed public. These factors are followed by government regulations and by education to increase the professionalism of business managers.[20]

For ethical codes to be effective, provisions must be made for their enforcement. Unethical managers should be held responsible for their actions. This means that privileges and benefits should be withdrawn and sanctions should be applied. Although the enforcement of ethical codes may not be easy, the mere existence of such codes can increase ethical behavior by clarifying expectations. On the other hand, one should not expect ethical codes to solve all problems. In fact, they can create a false sense of security. Effective code enforcement requires consistent ethical behavior and support from top management.

Another factor that could raise ethical standards is the teaching of ethics and values in business and other schools and universities. The Harvard Business School has come under severe criticism by its own president, Derek Bok, for the lack of teaching of human values.[21] With the help of business executives, the school hired Dean John McArthur and faculty members trained to teach ethics to give a new direction to the school. While financial aspects received less attention in the revised curriculum, more emphasis was given to people skills and ethical behavior. Since Harvard has one of the largest numbers of business-school graduates holding top managerial positions, a somewhat greater awareness of the ethical dimension in managing may be expected.

The need for improvement of ethical behavior has become clear by way of some widely publicized cases. Saul Gellerman examined three in greater detail: the Manville Corporation, which apparently hid the real danger of asbestos; Continental Illinois Bank, in which some managers misinterpreted the overall interest of the enterprise; and E. F. Hutton and Company, which pleaded guilty to mail and wire fraud.[22]

In light of his analysis, Gellerman made several suggestions, such as:

1. Provide clear guidelines for ethical behavior.
2. Teach ethical guidelines and their importance.
3. In gray areas where there are questions about the ethics of an action, refrain from it.
4. Set up controls (e.g., establish an auditing agency reporting to outside directors) that check on illegal or unethical deeds.
5. Conduct frequent and unpredictable audits.
6. Punish trespassers in a meaningful way, and make it public so that it may deter others.
7. Emphasize regularly that loyalty to the company does not excuse improper behavior or actions.

SUMMARY

Managers operate in a complex environment. They are affected by — and to some extent influence — the environment. In the United States managers operate in a pluralistic society in which many organized groups represent various interests. Corporate social responsibility requires that organizations consider seriously the impact of their actions on society. Similarly, social responsiveness is relating corporate operations and policies to the social environment in ways that are beneficial to the company and society. Determining appropriate relationships between various organizations and society is not an easy task, and one can make arguments for and against business involvement. Still, many corporations and organizations are making serious efforts to establish an environment beneficial to individuals, business, and society.

Ethics deals with what is good and bad and with moral duty and obligation. There are three moral theories in normative ethics: the utilitarian theory, the theory based on rights, and the theory of justice. Some authors have suggested that businesses institutionalize ethics and develop a code of ethics. There are also other factors that raise ethical standards.

KEY IDEAS AND CONCEPTS FOR REVIEW

Pluralistic society
Corporate social responsibility
Social responsiveness
Arguments for and against social
  involvement of business
Role of the government
Values, performance criteria, and behavior
Social audit

Ethics
Utilitarian theory of ethics
Ethical theory based on rights
Ethical theory of justice
Institutionalizing ethics
Code of ethics for government service
Factors raising ethical standards

FOR DISCUSSION

1. What are the major social responsibilities of business or government managers? Have these responsibilities changed over the years? How?

2. Briefly explain the major moral theories in the field of normative ethics. How do they relate to the decision tree for incorporating ethics into political behavior decisions?

3. If you were the chief executive officer of a large corporation, how would you "institutionalize" ethics in the organization?

4. List and discuss the benefits and limitations of some codes of ethics.

5. What ethical codes would you recommend for your university, your class, your family? How should these codes be enforced?

EXERCISES/ACTION STEPS

1. The class should select and read an article published in a recent issue of *The Wall Street Journal, Business Week,* or *Fortune* that involves some ethical issues. Divide the class into groups and analyze the situation using the decision tree shown in this chapter. Each group, through its spokesperson, should present its analysis.

2. Interview one business manager and one administrator in the local government and ask how they perceive their social responsibilities. Do these responsibilities relate primarily to the environment external to the organization, or do they also include internal aspects?

CASE:
BISHOPS' PASTORAL[23]

In 1984 the Catholic bishops issued statements about Catholic social teaching and the U.S. economy. The first draft was debated and criticized as being too negative about the free-market economy in the United States. A second draft was then issued which softened the tone, but the message was the same. Some of the key points are the following:

- Economic decisions must be made with due consideration as to whether they help all people.

- Government, corporations, and individuals must help to reduce the inequities created by the free-market system.

- More resources should be allocated for helping the poor and the jobless instead of for military uses.

The purpose of the document is to influence governmental and individual decisions in a way that would bring about a more humane society. The poor, the letter suggests, have not adequately shared the economic resources, and the government has a role to play to bring this about.

These are some of the recommendations in the draft:

- Pursue fiscal and monetary policies that result in full employment.

- Support job-creating programs.

- Remove employment barriers for women and minorities through affirmative action and job training.

- Reform the welfare system to provide minimum levels of benefit for the poor.

- Support international agencies to reduce poverty in Third World countries.

1. What are the implications for managers?

2. How does the letter relate to the various managerial functions?

REFERENCES

1. George A. Steiner, *Business and Society* (New York: Random House, 1975), chap. 5.

2. Howard R. Bowen, *Social Responsibilities of the Businessman* (New York: Harper & Brothers, 1953).

3. John L. Paluszek, *Business and Society: 1976–2000* (New York: AMACOM, 1976), in George A. Steiner, John B. Miner, and Edmund R. Gray, *Management Policy and Strategy,* 3d ed. (New York: The Macmillan Company, 1986), pp. 38–39.

4. Keith Davis and William C. Frederick, *Business and Society,* 5th ed. (New York: McGraw-Hill Book Company, 1984), p. 564.

5. Edwin Epstein, realizing not only the differences but also a great deal of overlap among business ethics, corporate social responsibility, and corporate social responsiveness, combines the three in his new concept "Corporate Social Policy Process." For a detailed discussion, see Edwin M. Epstein, *Beyond Business Ethics, Corporate Social Responsibility, and Corporate Social Responsivenss: An Introduction to the Corporate Social Policy Process,* Business and Public Policy Working Paper No. BPP-17 (University of California, Berkeley Business School, July 1986).

6. Steven N. Brenner and Earl A. Molander, "Is the Ethics of Business Changing?" *Harvard Business Review* (January–February 1977), pp. 57–71.

7. Bowen, *Social Responsibilities of the Businessman* (1953), pp. 155–156.

8. See also Meinolf Dierkes and Ariane Berthoin Antal, "Whither Corporate Social Reporting: Is It Time to Legislate?" *California Management Review* (Spring 1986), pp. 106–121.

9. Raymond A. Bauer and Dan H. Fenn, Jr., "What is a Corporate Social Audit?" *Harvard Business Review* (January–February 1973), p. 38.

10. Steiner et al, *Management Policy and Strategy* (1986), p. 47.

11. Social Responsibility Disclosure — 1977 Survey of *Fortune* 500 Annual Reports (Cleveland, Ohio: Ernst & Ernst, 1977).

12. Steiner, *Business and Society* (1975), pp. 202–203.

13. Manuel G. Velasquez, *Business Ethics* (Englewood Cliffs, N.J.: Prentice-Hall, 1982), p. 7.

14. Clarence D. Walton (ed.), *The Ethics of Corporate Conduct* (Englewood Cliffs, N.J.: Prentice-Hall, 1977), p. 6. See also La Rue Tone Hosmer, *The Ethics of Management* (Homewood, Ill.: Richard D. Irwin, 1987).

15. The discussion in this section is based on Gerald F. Cavanagh, Dennis J. Moberg, and Manuel Velasquez, "The Ethics of Organizational Politics," *Academy of Management Review* (July 1981), pp. 363–374, and has been used with their permission. See also Manuel Velasquez, Dennis J. Moberg, and Gerald F. Cavanagh, "Organizational Statesmanship and Dirty Politics: Ethical Guidelines for the Organizational Politician," *Organizational Dynamics* (Autumn 1983), pp. 65–80.

16. Cavanagh, Moberg, and Velasquez, "The Ethics" (1981), p. 369.

17. Much of this discussion is based on James Weber, "Institutionalizing Ethics into the Corporation," *MSU Business Topics* (Spring 1981), pp. 47–52; and Theodore V. Purcell, S.J., and James Weber, *Institutionalizing Corporate Ethics: A Case History* (New York: The Presidents Association, The Chief Executive Officers' Division of American Management Association, 1979), Special Study No. 71.

18. Source: Public Law 96–303, July 3, 1980.

19. Weber, "Institutionalizing Ethics" (1981).

20. Brenner and Molander, "Is the Ethics" (1977), p. 63.

21. Gerald F. Cavanagh, *American Business Values,* 2d ed. (Englewood Cliffs, N.J.: Prentice-Hall, 1984), chap. 5; Bruce Nussbaum and Alex Beam, "Remaking the Harvard B-School," *Business Week* (Mar 24, 1986), pp. 54–58.

22. Saul W. Gellerman, "Why 'Good' Managers Make Bad Ethical Choices," *Harvard Business Review* (July–August 1986), pp. 85–90.

23. The case is based on a variety of sources, including Laurie McGinley, "Roman Catholic Bishops Soften Tone of Letter Calling for Action on Poverty," *The Wall Street Journal* (Oct. 7, 1985); "Catholic Social Teaching and the U.S. Economy: First Draft — Bishops' Pastoral," *Origins* (Nov. 15, 1984), pp. 337–383. See also *Second Draft—Pastoral Letter on Catholic Social Teaching and the U.S. Economy* (Oct. 7, 1985). After lengthy discussions, the 115-page letter *Economic Justice for All: Catholic Social Teaching and the U.S. Economy* was approved in November 1986.

Planning

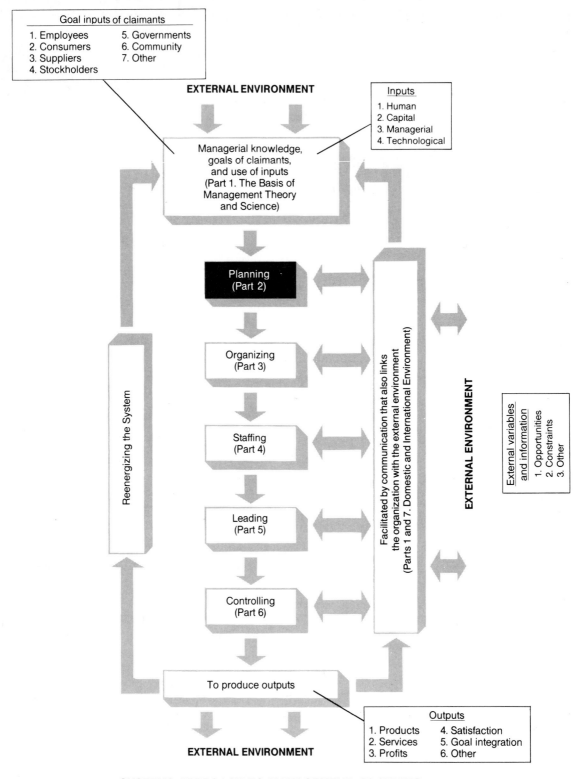

Goal inputs of claimants
1. Employees   5. Governments
2. Consumers   6. Community
3. Suppliers   7. Other
4. Stockholders

EXTERNAL ENVIRONMENT

Inputs
1. Human
2. Capital
3. Managerial
4. Technological

Managerial knowledge,
goals of claimants,
and use of inputs
(Part 1. The Basis of
Management Theory
and Science)

Planning
(Part 2)

Organizing
(Part 3)

Staffing
(Part 4)

Leading
(Part 5)

Controlling
(Part 6)

Reenergizing the System

Facilitated by communication that also links
the organization with the external environment
(Parts 1 and 7. Domestic and International Environment)

EXTERNAL ENVIRONMENT

External variables
and information
1. Opportunities
2. Constraints
3. Other

To produce outputs

Outputs
1. Products   4. Satisfaction
2. Services   5. Goal integration
3. Profits   6. Other

EXTERNAL ENVIRONMENT

SYSTEMS APPROACH TO MANAGEMENT: PLANNING

CHAPTER 3

The Nature and Purpose of Planning

CHAPTER OBJECTIVES

After reading this chapter, you should understand:

1. What managerial planning is and why it is important
2. The various types of plans and how they relate to one another
3. The logical steps in planning and how these steps are essentially a rational approach to setting objectives and selecting the means of reaching them
4. The meaning of the commitment principle
5. The importance of reviewing plans periodically

You are now familiar with basic management theory and have been introduced to the five essential managerial functions: planning, organizing, staffing, leading, and controlling. Chapters 3 to 6 focus on planning and form Part 2 of the book.

In designing an environment for the effective performance of individuals working together in groups, a manager's most essential task is to see that everyone understands the group's purposes and objectives and its methods of attaining them. If group effort is to be effective, people must know what they are expected to accomplish. This is the function of planning. It is the most basic of all the managerial functions. **Planning** involves selecting missions and objectives and the actions to achieve them; it requires decision making, that is,

Figure 3-1

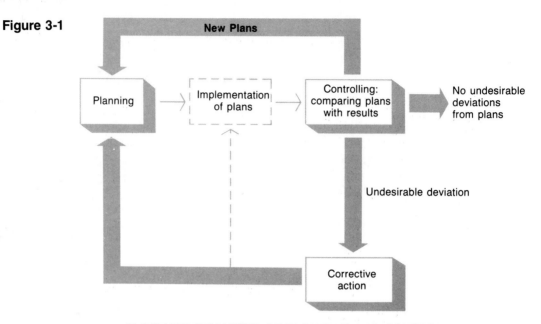

CLOSE RELATIONSHIP OF PLANNING AND CONTROLLING.

choosing from among alternative future courses of action. Plans thus provide a rational approach to preselected objectives. Planning also strongly implies managerial innovation, as will be discussed in Chapter 14.

Planning bridges the gap from where we are to where we want to go. It makes it possible for things to occur which would not otherwise happen. Although we can seldom predict the exact future and although factors beyond our control may interfere with the best-laid plans, unless we plan, we are leaving events to chance. Planning is an intellectually demanding process; it requires that we consciously determine courses of action and base our decisions on purpose, knowledge, and considered estimates.

Planning and *control* are inseparable — the Siamese twins of management (see Figure 3-1). Any attempt to control without plans is meaningless, since there is no way for people to tell whether they are going where they want to go (the result of the task of control) unless they first know where they want to go (part of the task of planning). Plans thus furnish the standards of control.

TYPES OF PLANS

The failure of some managers to recognize that there are a number of different types of plans has often caused difficulty in making planning effective. It is easy to see that a major program, such as one to build and equip a new factory, is a plan. But a number of other courses of future action are also plans. In fact, a plan can encompass any course of future action, which clearly shows that plans are varied. They are classified here as (1) purposes or missions, (2) objectives,

Figure 3-2

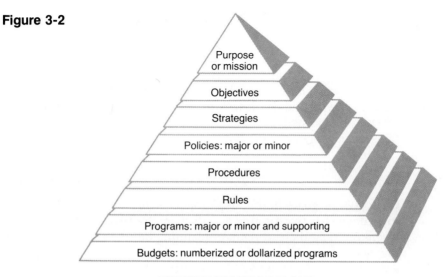

Purpose or mission

Objectives

Strategies

Policies: major or minor

Procedures

Rules

Programs: major or minor and supporting

Budgets: numberized or dollarized programs

THE HIERARCHY OF PLANS.

(3) strategies, (4) policies, (5) procedures, (6) rules, (7) programs, and (8) budgets. To some extent, they are a hierarchy, as illustrated in Figure 3-2.

Purposes or Missions

The **mission** or **purpose** (terms used interchangeably in this book) identifies the basic function or task of an enterprise or agency or of any part of it. Every kind of organized operation has, or at least should have if it is to be meaningful, purposes or missions. In every social system, enterprises have a basic function or task which is assigned to them by society. The purpose of a business generally is the production and distribution of goods and services. The purpose of a state highway department is the design, building, and operation of a system of state highways. The purpose of the courts is the interpretation of law and their application. The purpose of a university is teaching and research. And so on.

Some writers distinguish between purposes and missions. While a business, for example, may have a social purpose of producing and distributing goods and services, it can accomplish this by fulfilling a mission of producing certain lines of products. The missions of an oil company, such as Exxon, are to search for oil and to produce, refine, and market petroleum and a wide variety of petroleum products, from diesel fuel to chemicals. The mission of the Du Pont Company has been expressed as "better things through chemistry," and Kimberly-Clark (noted for its Kleenex trademark) regards its business mission as the production and sale of paper and paper products. In the 1960s, the mission of NASA was to get a person to the moon before the Russians. Hallmark, which has expanded its business beyond greeting cards, defines its mission as "the social expression business."[1] It is true that in some businesses and other enterprises, the purpose or mission often becomes fuzzy. For example, many of the conglomerates have regarded their mission as **synergy,*** which is accomplished through the combination of a variety of companies.

People sometimes think that the mission of a business, as well as its objective, is to make a profit. It is true, as Chapter 1 pointed out, that every kind of enterprise must have a "surplus" — in business, a "profit" — goal or objective if it is to survive and do the task society has entrusted to it. But this basic objective is accomplished by undertaking activities, going in clearly defined directions, achieving goals, and accomplishing a mission.

Objectives

Objectives or **goals** (terms used interchangeably in this book) are the ends toward which activity is aimed — they are the results to be achieved. They represent not only the end point of planning but the end toward which organizing, staffing, leading, and controlling are aimed. While enterprise objectives are the basic plan of the firm, a department may also have its own objectives. Its goals naturally contribute to the attainment of enterprise objectives, but the two sets of goals may be entirely different. For example, the objective of a business might be to make a certain profit by producing a given line of home entertainment equipment, while the goal of the manufacturing department might be to produce the required number of television sets of given design and quality at a given cost. These objectives are consistent, but they differ in that the manufacturing department alone cannot ensure accomplishment of the company's objective.

Strategies

For years the military used the word "strategies" to mean grand plans made in the light of what it is believed an adversary might or might not do. While the term "strategies" still usually has a competitive implication, managers increasingly use it to reflect broad areas of an enterprise operation.

Three definitions are indicative of the most common usages of the term **strategies:** (1) general programs of action and deployment of resources to attain comprehensive objectives; (2) the program of objectives of an organization and their changes, resources used to attain these objectives, and policies governing the acquisition, use, and disposition of these resources; and (3) the determination of the basic long-term objectives of an enterprise and the adoption of courses of action and allocation of resources necessary to achieve these goals.

Thus, a company has to decide what kind of business it is going to be in. Is it a transportation or a railroad company? Is it a container or a paper box manufacturer? The firm also has to decide on its growth goal and its desired

---

*The concept of synergy can be expressed simply as a situation in which 2 plus 2 becomes equal to 5, or in which the whole is greater than the sum of the parts.

> INTERNATIONAL PERSPECTIVE:
> GM'S STRATEGY
>
> Strategies have become increasingly complex and internationally oriented.[2] Take General Motors, which has been threatened by foreign competitors, especially the Japanese. For decades, GM had a "do-it-yourself" strategy. But now some GM cars are made by rival Asian companies such as Suzuki Motors Company and Isuzu Motors Ltd. of Japan. In addition, GM engaged in a joint venture with Toyota Motor Corporation to produce subcompacts in California. Equally surprising is GM's strategic move into nonautomotive businesses such as information processing and robotics. To implement this strategy, GM bought Electronic Data Systems Corporation and engaged in a joint venture with the Japanese robot maker Fanuc Ltd.[3] But a change in strategy usually requires a reorganization, and GM is currently in the process of changing the organization structure that served the company well for over 60 years.

profitability. A strategy might include such major policies as marketing directly rather than through distributors, or concentrating on proprietary products, or having a full line of autos, as General Motors decided to have many years ago.

The purpose of strategies, then, is to determine and communicate, through a system of major objectives and policies, a picture of the kind of enterprise that is envisioned. Strategies do not attempt to outline exactly how the enterprise is to accomplish its objectives, since this is the task of countless major and minor supporting programs. But they furnish a framework for guiding thinking and action. Their usefulness in practice and their importance in guiding planning do, however, justify the separation of strategies as a type of plan for the purpose of analysis.

Policies

Policies also are plans in that they are general statements or understandings which guide or channel thinking in decision making. Not all policies are "statements"; they are often merely implied from the actions of managers. The president of a company, for example, may strictly follow — perhaps for convenience rather than as policy — the practice of promoting from within; the practice may then be interpreted as policy and carefully followed by subordinates. In fact, one of the problems of managers is to make sure that subordinates do not interpret as policy minor managerial decisions that are not intended to serve as patterns.

Policies define an area within which a decision is to be made and ensure that the decision will be consistent with, and contribute to, an objective. Policies help decide issues before they become problems, make it unnecessary to analyze the same situation every time it comes up, and unify other plans, thus permitting managers to delegate authority and still maintain control over what their subordinates do. For example, a certain railroad has the policy of acquiring industrial land to replace all company acreage sold along its right of way.

This policy permits the manager of the land department to develop acquisition plans without continually referring to top management; at the same time, it furnishes a standard of control.

Policies ordinarily exist on all levels of the organization, ranging from major company policies through major department policies to minor policies applicable to the smallest segment of the organization. They may be related to functions such as sales and finance or merely to a project such as the design of a new product to meet a specified competition.

There are many types of policies. Examples include policies of hiring only university-trained engineers or of encouraging employee suggestions for improved cooperation, promoting from within, conforming strictly to a high standard of business ethics, setting competitive prices, or insisting on fixed, rather than cost-plus, pricing.

Since policies are guides to decision making, it follows that they must allow for some discretion. Otherwise, they would be rules. Too often, policies are interpreted as a kind of "ten commandments" that leave no room for discretion. Although discretion, in some instances, is quite broad, it can be exceedingly narrow. For example, a policy of buying from the lowest of three qualified bidders leaves to discretion only the question of which bidders are qualified; a requirement that goods be bought from a certain supplier, regardless of price or service, would, however, be a rule.

Policy is a means of encouraging discretion and initiative, but within limits. The amount of freedom will naturally depend upon the policy and in turn will reflect position and authority in the organization. The president of a company with a policy of aggressive price competition has a broad area of discretion and initiative in which to interpret and apply this policy. The district sales manager (who reports to the regional sales manager) abides by the same basic policy, but the interpretations made by the president, the vice-president for sales, and the regional sales manager become derivative policies that might narrow the district manager's scope to the point of being, for example, only wide enough to approve a special sale price not exceeding a 10 percent reduction to meet competition (see Figure 3-3).

Making policies consistent and integrated enough to realize enterprise objectives is difficult for many reasons. First, policies are too seldom defined in writing and their exact interpretations are too little known. Second, the very delegation of authority that policies are intended to implement leads, through its decentralizing influence, to widespread participation in policymaking and interpretation, with almost certain variations among individuals. Third, it is not always easy to control policy because actual policy may be difficult to ascertain and intended policy may not always be clear.

Procedures

Procedures are plans that establish a required method of handling future activities. They are guides to action, rather than to thinking, and they detail the exact manner in which certain activities must be accomplished. They are chronological sequences of required actions.

Figure 3-3

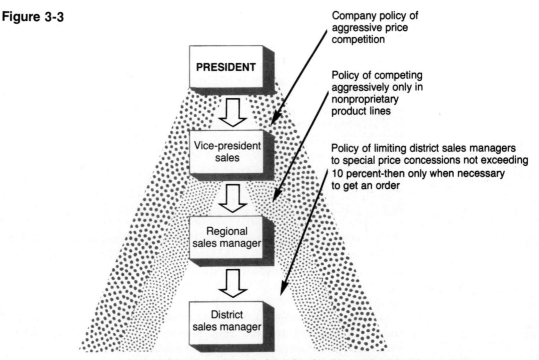

SUCCESSIVE LIMITING OF POLICY BY HIERARCHICAL LEVEL.

Procedures often cut across department lines. For example, in a manufacturing company, the procedure for handling orders will almost certainly involve the sales department (for the original order), the finance department (for acknowledgment of receipt of funds and for customer credit approval), the accounting department (for recording the transaction), the production department (for the order to produce goods or authority to release them from stock), and the traffic department (for determination of shipping means and route).

Let us look at a few examples of the relationship between procedures and policies. Company policy may grant employees vacations; procedures established to implement this policy will provide for scheduling vacations to avoid disruption of work, setting methods and rates of vacation pay, maintaining records to assure each employee of a vacation, and spelling out the means for applying for a vacation. A company may have a policy of shipping orders quickly; particularly in a large company, careful procedures will be necessary to ensure that orders are handled in a specific way. Company policy may require that the public relations department clear its employees' public utterances; to implement this policy, managers must establish procedures for obtaining clearance with minimum inconvenience and delay.

Rules

Rules spell out specific required actions or nonactions, allowing no discretion.[4] They are usually the simplest type of plan.

PERSPECTIVE:
PROCEDURES AND RULES IMPOSED BY THE OUTSIDE

At times, rules and procedures are implemented because of unfavorable publicity. General Dynamics, one of the largest defense contractors, has been accused of some improprieties.[5] In order not to be suspended from bidding on defense contracts, the company had to agree to a list of rules and procedures imposed by the Defense Department.

These new requirements are designed to prevent the shifting of costs from one contract to another. For example, workers have to prepare and sign their own time cards. The supervisor has to check each card; if one is incorrectly filled out, the worker involved has to make the correction, which then has to be initialed by the worker and the boss. The original entry must be left on the card so that it can be checked later. Also, General Dynamics was required to establish tight rules for charging overhead expenses. Employees are not allowed to accept gifts — not even a pen or a calendar.

Thus, rules and procedures can be imposed by an important customer and are examples not only of planning but also of controlling, showing the close relationship between the two functions.

People frequently confuse rules with policies or procedures. Rules are unlike procedures in that they guide action without specifying a time sequence. In fact, a procedure might be looked upon as a sequence of rules. A rule, however, may or may not be part of a procedure. For example, "No smoking" is a rule quite unrelated to any procedure; but a procedure governing the handling of orders may incorporate the rule that all orders must be confirmed the day they are received. This rule allows no deviation from a stated course of action and in no way interferes with the rest of the procedure for handling orders. It is comparable to a rule stating that all fractions of weight of over half an ounce are to be counted as a full ounce or that receiving inspection must count or weigh all materials against the purchase order. The essence of a rule is that it reflects a managerial decision that some certain action must — or must not — be taken.

Be sure you can distinguish rules from policies. The purpose of policies is to guide decision making by marking off areas in which managers can use their discretion. Although rules also serve as guides, they allow no discretion in their application. Many companies and other organizations think they have policies when they really have spelled-out rules. The result is confusion as to when people may use their own judgment, if at all. This can be dangerous. Rules and procedures, by their very nature, are designed to repress thinking; we should use them only when we do not want people in an organization to use their discretion.

Programs

Programs are a complex of goals, policies, procedures, rules, task assignments, steps to be taken, resources to be employed, and other elements necessary to carry out a given course of action; they are ordinarily supported by budgets.

They may be as major as an airline's program for acquiring a $400 million fleet of jets or the 5-year program embarked upon by the Ford Motor Company several years ago to improve the status and quality of its thousands of foremen. Or they may be as minor as a program formulated by a single supervisor to improve the morale of workers in a parts-manufacturing department of a farm machinery company.

A primary program may call for many supporting programs. In the case of the airline mentioned above, the program for investing in new jets, involving many millions of dollars for the purchase of the aircraft and the necessary spare parts, requires many supporting programs if the investment is to be properly used. A program for providing the maintenance and operating bases with spare parts and components must be developed in detail. Special maintenance facilities must be prepared and maintenance personnel trained. Pilots and flight engineers must also be trained; if the new jets mean a net addition to flying hours, flight personnel must be recruited. Flight schedules must be revised and ground station personnel trained to handle the new airplanes and their schedules as service is expanded to new cities in the airline's system. Advertising programs must give adequate publicity to the new service. Plans to finance the aircraft and provide for insurance coverage must be developed.

These and other programs must be devised and implemented before any new aircraft are received and placed in service. Furthermore, all these programs call for coordination and timing, since the failure of any part of this network of supporting plans means delay for the major program as well as unnecessary costs and loss of profits. Some programs, particularly those involving hiring and training of personnel, can be accomplished too soon as well as too late; needless expense results when employees are available and trained before their services are required.

Budgets

A **budget** is a statement of expected results expressed in numerical terms. It may be referred to as a "numberized" program. In fact, the financial operating budget is often called a "profit plan." A budget may be expressed either in financial terms or in terms of labor-hours, units of product, machine-hours, or any other numerically measurable term. It may deal with operations, as the expense budget does; it may reflect capital outlays, as the capital expenditures budget does; or it may show cash flow, as the cash budget does.

Since budgets are also control devices, the principal discussion of budgets appears in Chapter 19, which is on control techniques. However, making a budget is clearly planning. The budget is the fundamental planning instrument in many companies. A budget forces a company to make in advance — whether for a week or 5 years — a numerical compilation of expected cash flow, expenses and revenues, capital outlays, or labor- or machine-hour utilization. The budget is necessary for control, but it cannot serve as a sensible standard of control unless it reflects plans.

Although a budget usually implements a program, it may in itself be a program. One company in difficult financial straits installed an elaborate budgetary control program designed not only to control expenditures but also to instill cost consciousness in management. In fact, one of the major advantages of budgeting is that it makes people plan; because a budget is in the form of numbers, it forces precision in planning.

Budgets vary considerably in accuracy, detail, and purpose. Some budgets vary according to the organization's level of output; these are called **variable** or **flexible** budgets. Government agencies often develop **program budgets** in which the agency (and each department within the agency) identifies goals, develops detailed programs to meet the goals, and estimates the cost of each program. To plan an effective program budget, a manager must do some fairly detailed and thorough planning.

Still another type, which is really a combination of the variable and the program budget, is the **zero-base budget.** A manager using this approach thinks of the goals and the programs needed to achieve them as a "work package," as though the programs were started from scratch, or "base zero."

STEPS IN PLANNING

Although the steps in planning are presented here in connection with major programs, such as the acquisition of a plant or a fleet of jets or the development of a product, managers would follow essentially the same steps in any thorough planning. Since minor plans are usually simpler, some of the steps would be more easily accomplished, but the practical steps listed below, and diagrammed in Figure 3-4, are of general application. In practice, however, managers must study the feasibility of possible courses of action at each stage. For example, in establishing objectives, it is necessary to have some idea about the premises underlying the plans. An ambitious objective of increasing sales by 200 percent may be unrealistic in an environment with a projected economic recession. Similarly, feedback is also essential. In formulating supportive plans, there may be a need to reevaluate and change the overall objectives set earlier. Also, a discriminating manager obviously would not use $100 worth of time to make a decision worth 50 cents, but it is shocking to see 50 cents' worth of time used to make a planning decision involving millions of dollars.

1   Being Aware of Opportunities

Although it precedes actual planning and is therefore not strictly a part of the planning process, an awareness of opportunities* in the external environment

---

*The word "problems" might be used instead of "opportunities." However, a state of disorder or confusion and a need for a solution to achieve a given goal can more constructively be regarded as an opportunity. In fact, one very successful and astute company president does not permit his colleagues to speak of problems, but only of opportunities.

Figure 3-4

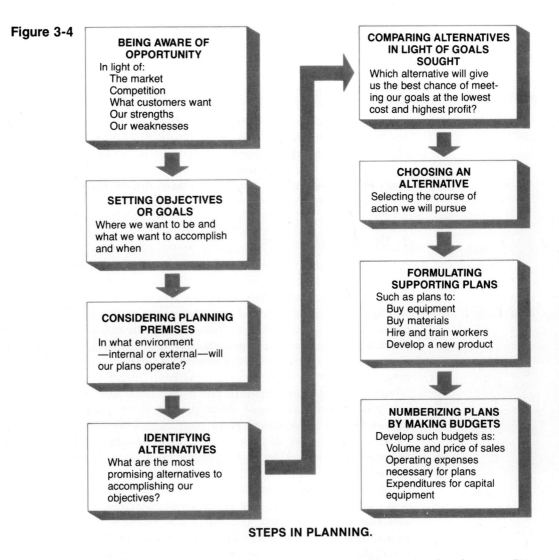

STEPS IN PLANNING.

as well as within the organization is the real starting point for planning. It is important to take a preliminary look at possible future opportunities and see them clearly and completely. All managers should know where they stand in the light of their strengths and weaknesses, understand what problems they wish to solve and why, and know what they expect to gain. Setting realistic objectives depends on this awareness. Planning requires realistic diagnosis of the opportunity situation.

2 Establishing Objectives

The second step is to establish objectives for the entire enterprise and then for each subordinate work unit. This is to be done for the long term as well as for the short range. Objectives specify the expected results and indicate the end points of what is to be done, where the primary emphasis is to be placed, and what is to be accomplished by the network of strategies, policies, procedures, rules, budgets, and programs.

Enterprise objectives give direction to the major plans which, by reflecting these objectives, define the objective of every major department. Major department objectives, in turn, control the objectives of subordinate departments, and so on down the line. In other words, objectives form a hierarchy. The objectives of lesser departments will be more accurate if subdivision managers understand the overall enterprise objectives and the derivative goals. Managers should also have the opportunity to contribute their ideas to setting their own goals and those of the enterprise.

3 Developing Premises

A third logical step in planning is to establish, circulate, and obtain agreement to utilize critical planning premises such as forecasts, applicable basic policies, and existing company plans. They are *assumptions* about the environment in which the plan is to be carried out. It is important for all the managers involved in planning to agree on the premises. In fact, the major **principle of planning premises** is this: *The more thoroughly individuals charged with planning understand and agree to utilize consistent planning premises, the more coordinated enterprise planning will be.*

Forecasting is important in premising: What kinds of markets will there be? What volume of sales? What prices? What products? What technical developments? What costs? What wage rates? What tax rates and policies? What new plants? What policies with respect to dividends? What political or social environment? How will expansion be financed? What are the long-term trends?

Managers have a number of sources to draw from when preparing a forecast for their enterprise. The government publishes a wealth of information that can be useful. Here are just a few examples: Business Cycle Developments, Survey of Current Business, and Economic Indicators. Most large banks publish newsletters on current economic conditions, often on a monthly basis. *Business Week* magazine prepares outlooks for specific industries, such as basic manufacturing (autos, chemicals, machinery, steel), natural resources (agriculture, energy, forest products, communications), and services and consumer products (entertainment, food processing, health care, personal care). Many universities, such as UCLA, make national and regional economic forecasts. Managers interested in long-term trends will find John Naisbitt's book *Megatrends* useful[6].

Because the future is so complex, it would not be profitable or realistic to make assumptions about every detail of the future environment of a plan. Therefore, premises are, as a practical matter, limited to assumptions that are critical, or strategic, to a plan, that is, those which most influence its operation.

4 Determining Alternative Courses

The fourth step in planning is to search for and examine alternative courses of action, especially those not immediately apparent. There is seldom a plan for which reasonable alternatives do not exist, and quite often an alternative that is not obvious proves to be the best.

The more common problem is not finding alternatives but reducing the number of alternatives so that the most promising may be analyzed. Even with mathematical techniques and the computer, there is a limit to the number of alternatives that can be thoroughly examined. The planner must usually make a preliminary examination to discover the most fruitful possibilities.

5 Evaluating Alternative Courses

After seeking out alternative courses and examining their strong and weak points, the next step is evaluating the alternatives by weighing them in the light of premises and goals. One course may appear to be the most profitable, but it may require a large cash outlay and have a slow payback; another may look less profitable but may involve less risk; still another may better suit the company's long-range objectives.

If the only objective were to maximize immediate profits in a certain business, if the future were not uncertain, if cash position and capital availability were not worrisome, and if most factors could be reduced to definite data, this evaluation would be relatively easy. But since planners typically encounter many uncertainties, problems of capital shortage, and various intangible factors, evaluation is usually very difficult, even with relatively simple problems. A company may wish to enter a new product line primarily for purposes of prestige, but the forecast may show a financial loss; even so, the question is still open as to whether the loss is worth the gain in prestige.

There are so many alternative courses in most situations and so many variables and limitations to be considered that evaluation can be exceedingly difficult. Because of these complexities, the newer methodologies and applications of operations research and analysis discussed in Chapter 20 are helpful. Indeed, it is at this step in the planning process that operations research and mathematical as well as computing techniques have their primary application to the field of management.

6 Selecting a Course

This is the point at which the plan is adopted — the real point of decision making. Occasionally, an analysis and evaluation of alternative courses will disclose that two or more are advisable, and the manager may decide to follow several courses rather than the one best course.

7   Formulating Derivative Plans

When a decision is made, planning is seldom complete, and a seventh step is indicated. Derivative plans are almost invariably required to support the basic plan.

8   Numberizing Plans by Budgeting

After decisions are made and plans are set, the final step in giving them meaning, as was indicated in the discussion of types of plans, is to numberize them by converting them to budgets. The overall budgets of an enterprise represent the sum total of income and expenses, with resultant profit or surplus, and budgets of major balance sheet items such as cash and capital expenditures. Each department or program of a business or other enterprise can have its own budgets, usually of expenses and capital expenditures, which tie into the overall budget.

If done well, budgets become a means of adding together the various plans and also set important standards against which planning progress can be measured. Budgets will be discussed in connection with managerial control in Chapter 19.

THE PLANNING PROCESS: A RATIONAL APPROACH TO GOAL ACHIEVEMENT

As indicated by the planning steps above, planning is a rational approach to accomplishing objectives. The process can be illustrated as shown in Figure 3-5. In this diagram, progress (toward more sales, more profits, lower costs, and so forth) is on the vertical axis, and time is on the horizontal axis. Here x indicates where we are (at t_0, or "time zero") and y where we want to be at a future time (at t_n). In short, we are at x and want to go to y. Often we do not have all the data, but we start planning anyway. We may even have to start our planning study at x_1 (at t_{-n}). The line xy is the decision path.

If the future were completely certain, the line xy would be relatively easy to draw. However, in actuality, a myriad of factors may push us away from or toward the desired goal. These are the planning premises. Again, because we cannot forecast or consider everything, we try to develop our path from x to y in the light of the most critical premises.

The essential logic of planning applies regardless of the time interval between t_0 and t_n, whether it is 5 minutes or 20 years. However, the clarity of premises, the attainability of goals, and the simplification of planning are almost certain to be inversely related to the time span. That is, if the time span is long, premises may be unclear, goals may be more difficult to set, and other planning complexities may be great.

Decision making may be the easiest part of planning, although it involves techniques of evaluation and considerable skill in applying them. The real difficulties arise primarily in sharpening and giving meaning to objectives and

Figure 3-5

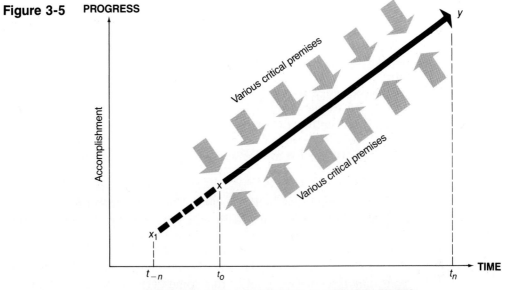

PROGRESS, TIME, AND CRITICAL PLANNING PREMISES.

critical premises, seeing the nature and relationships of the strengths and weaknesses of alternatives, and communicating goals and premises to those throughout the enterprise who must plan.

The Planning Period

Shall plans be for a short period or a long one? How shall short-range plans be coordinated with long-range plans? These questions suggest multiple horizons of planning — in some cases, planning a week in advance may be ample, while in others, the desirable period may be a number of years. Even within the same firm at the same time, various planning periods may exist for various matters.

The Commitment Principle

Some criteria must be used in selecting the time range for company planning. The key to choosing the right planning period seems to lie in the **commitment principle:** *Logical planning encompasses a future period of time necessary to fulfill, through a series of actions, the commitments involved in decisions made today.*

We can readily grasp the logic of planning far enough in the future to foresee, as well as possible, the recovery of capital sunk in a building or a machine. Since capital is the lifeblood of an enterprise and is normally limited in relation to the firm's needs, its expenditure must be accompanied by a reasonable possibility of recovering it, plus a return on investment, through operations. For example, when Lever Brothers sank $35 million into a new factory on the West

Coast, it decided, in effect, that the detergent business would permit the recovery of this investment over a period of time. If this period was 20 years, then logically the plans should have been based on a 20-year projection of business. Of course, the company might have introduced some flexibility and reduced its risk (as it did) by spending extra funds to make the plant modifiable for other purposes.

But a company may make noncost commitments that have various time frames. For example, it may commit itself to a personnel policy of promoting people from within the organization, rather than hiring them from the outside. A company, therefore, may commit itself for varying lengths of time to things that are not always immediately measurable in dollars or any other currency.

What the commitment principle implies   The commitment principle implies that long-range planning is not really planning for future decisions but, rather, planning for the future impact of today's decisions. In other words, a decision is a commitment, normally of funds, direction of action, or reputation. And decisions lie at the core of planning. While studies and analyses preceded decisions, any type of plan implies that some decision has been made. Indeed, a plan does not really exist as such until a decision has been made. Knowing this, the astute manager will recognize the validity of gearing longer-term considerations to present decisions. To do otherwise is to overlook the basic nature of both planning and decision making.

Application of the commitment principle   There is no uniform or arbitrary length of time for which a company should plan or for which a given program or any of its parts should be planned. An airplane company embarking on a new commercial jet aircraft project should probably plan this program for at least 12 years ahead, with 5 or 6 years for engineering and development and at least as many more years for production and sales, in order to recoup total costs and make a reasonable profit. An instrument manufacturer with a product already developed might need to plan revenues and expenses only 6 months ahead, since this period may represent the cycle of raw-materials purchasing, production, inventorying, and sales. But the same company might wish to see much further into the future before assuming a lease for specialized manufacturing facilities, undertaking a program of management training, or developing and promoting a new product. Other examples, showing that different planning areas require different time periods, are illustrated in Figure 3-6.

Coordination of Short- and Long-Range Plans

Often short-range plans are made without reference to long-range plans. This is plainly a serious error. The importance of integrating the two types can hardly be overemphasized, and no short-run plan should be made unless it contributes to the achievement of the relevant long-range plan. Much waste arises from decisions about immediate situations that fail to consider their effect on more remote objectives.

Figure 3-6

EXAMPLE OF KINDS OF COMMITMENTS FOR A MANUFACTURING FIRM

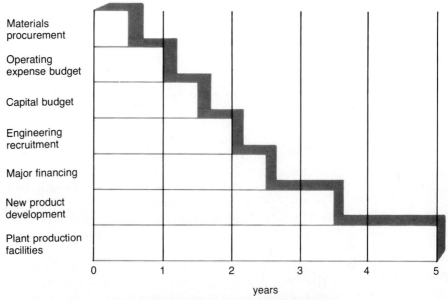

PLANNING AREAS AND TIME PERIODS.
Various management decision areas typically involve planning ahead for differing periods of time. These periods also vary according to the kind of business. For example, a large public utility may plan new power-production plants twenty-five or thirty years into the future, whereas a small garment manufacturer may plan new production facilities only one year ahead.

Sometimes short-range decisions not only fail to contribute to a long-range plan but actually impede, or require changes in, the long-range plan. For example, if a small company accepts a large order without reckoning the effect of the order on its capacity to produce or its supply of cash, this decision may so hamper the company's future ability to finance a systematic expansion that changes may be required in its long-range program. Or, in another company, small additions to the plant (which may be urgently needed) may utilize vacant property so haphazardly as to thwart the land's longer-range use as the site for a large new plant. In other instances, the decision of a plant superintendent to discharge workers without adequate cause may interfere with the company's long-range objective of developing a fair and successful personnel program. The short-range decision of Sewell Avery, chairman of Montgomery Ward, to curtail expansion of the business after World War II because he believed that a serious recession was at hand interfered with the long-range program of enhancing the profitability of the company.

Responsible managers should continually review and revise immediate decisions to determine whether they contribute to long-range programs, and subordinate managers should be regularly briefed on long-range plans so that they will make decisions consistent with the company's long-range goals.

It is far easier to do this than to correct inconsistencies, especially since short-term commitments tend to lead to further commitments along the same line.

SUMMARY

Planning involves selecting missions and objectives and the actions to achieve them. Planning requires decision making, that is, choosing from among alternative future courses of action. Planning and controlling are closely interrelated, although they are discussed separately in this book.

There are many types of plans, such as purposes and missions, objectives or goals, strategies, policies, procedures, rules, programs, and budgets. Once aware of opportunity, a manager plans rationally by establishing objectives, making assumptions (premises) about the present and future environment, finding and evaluating alternative courses of action, and choosing a course to follow. Next, the manager must make supporting plans and devise a budget. These activities must be carried out with attention to the total environment.

According to the commitment principle, plans should cover a period of time that is long enough to fulfill commitments involved in decisions made today. Short-range plans must, of course, be coordinated with long-range plans.

KEY IDEAS AND CONCEPTS FOR REVIEW

Planning	Program
Purpose or mission	Budget
Objectives or goals	Variable or flexible budget
Strategy	Program budget
Policy	Zero-base budget
Procedure	Planning steps
Rule	Commitment principle

FOR DISCUSSION

1. "Planning is looking ahead, and control is looking back." Comment.
2. If planning involves a rational approach to selected goals, how can goals or objectives be a type of plan?
3. Draw up a statement of policy and devise a brief procedure that might be useful in implementing it. Are you sure your policy is not a rule?
4. If all decisions involve commitments and if the future is always uncertain, how can a manager guard against costly mistakes?
5. Using as an example a planning decision with which you are familiar, show to what extent, and how, the commitment principle applies to it.
6. "Planning theory illustrates the open-system approach to management." Comment.

EXERCISES/ACTION STEPS

1. Taking a planning problem which is now facing you, proceed to deal with it in accordance with the planning steps outlined in this chapter.

2. Interview a manager in your area and ask about the planning process (i.e., the steps in planning).

CASE:
INTERNATIONAL MACHINE CORPORATION

Gilbert Brown, the president of International Machine Corporation (IMC), leaned back in his chair and reflected with well-deserved satisfaction on the success of his company, which produces and distributes a line of farm machinery. That afternoon, at a meeting of distributors from various parts of the world, Mr. Brown had been urged to introduce new models to satisfy the changing demands of customers.

The president, who had an engineering background, recognized the implications of the distributors' suggestion. It would require greater investments in research and development. Furthermore, the changes in the highly automated production line would be very costly indeed. Also, having a greater variety of models would require stocking many more spare parts. Depending on the kinds of changes, mechanics also might need to be retrained.

Reflecting on previous staff meetings, the president realized that sales and marketing people always wanted a greater variety of models but never acknowledged the costs involved in changing models. After all, the company had been extremely successful with just a few models. Consequently, the president decided against the introduction of new models. Instead, he considered improving the current models and reducing the cost and price. He felt that what the customer really wants is value. Nevertheless, to test his judgment, the president asked a consultant for an opinion.

1. How would you state the mission of the enterprise?

2. What do you think are the opportunities and threats in the external environment?

3. How would you go about evaluating the strengths and weaknesses of the firm? What factors are critical for success or failure?

4. It is often said that to be successful, an organization must be an open system. What does this mean, and how does it apply to this case?

REFERENCES

1. William L. Glueck and Lawrence R. Jauch, *Business Policy and Strategic Management* (New York: McGraw-Hill Book Company, 1984), chap. 2.

2. Based on a variety of sources, including U. C. Lehner, "With His Bid for EDS, GM's Smith Continues to Make Bold Changes," *The Wall Street Journal* (July 2, 1984); "GM Moves into a New Era," *Business Week* (July 16, 1984), pp. 48–54; "Roger Smith Takes on GM's Critics," *Fortune* (Aug. 18, 1986), pp. 26–27.

3. See also Gene Bylinsky, "Japan's Robot King Wins Again," *Fortune* (May 25, 1987), pp. 53–58.

4. See also F. Neil Brady, "Rules for Making Exceptions to Rules," *Academy of Management Review* (July 1987), pp. 436–444.

5. Ford S. Worthy, "Mr. Clean Charts a New Course at General Dynamics," *Fortune* (Apr. 28, 1986), pp. 70–76.

6. John Naisbitt, *Megatrends* (New York: Warner Books, 1982).

CHAPTER 4

Objectives

CHAPTER OBJECTIVES

After reading this chapter, you should understand:

1. The nature of objectives
2. The evolving concepts in management by objectives (MBO) and the systems approach to MBO
3. The process of managing and appraising by objectives
4. How verifiable objectives can be set for different situations
5. The benefits of MBO
6. The weaknesses of MBO and ways to overcome them

In Chapter 3 **objectives** were defined as the important ends toward which organizational and individual activities are directed. Since writers and practitioners make no clear distinction between the terms "goals" and "objectives," they are used interchangeably in this book. Within the context of the discussion it will become clear whether they are long-term or short-term, broad or specific. The emphasis in this chapter is on **verifiable** objectives; that is, at the end of the period it should be possible to determine whether or not the objective has been achieved. The goal of every manager is to create a surplus (in business organizations this means profits). Clear and verifiable objectives facilitate measurement of the surplus as well as the effectiveness and efficiency of managerial actions.

THE NATURE OF OBJECTIVES

Objectives state end results, and overall objectives need to be supported by subobjectives. Thus, objectives form a hierarchy as well as a network. Moreover, organizations and managers have multiple goals which are sometimes incompatible and may lead to conflicts within the organization, within the group, and even within individuals. A manager may have to choose between short-term and long-term performance, and personal interests may have to be subordinated to organizational objectives.

A Hierarchy of Objectives

As Figure 4-1 shows, objectives form a hierarchy, ranging from the broad aim to specific individual objectives.[1] The zenith of the hierarchy is the purpose, which has two dimensions. First, there is the purpose of society, such as requiring the organization to contribute to the welfare of the people by providing goods and services at a reasonable cost. Second, there is the purpose of the business, which might be to furnish convenient, low-cost transportation for the average person. The stated mission might be to produce, market, and service automobiles. As you will notice, the distinction between purpose and mission is a fine one, and therefore many writers and practitioners do not differentiate between the two terms. At any rate, these aims are, in turn, translated into general objectives and strategies (which will be discussed in Chapter 5), such as designing, producing, and marketing reliable, low-cost, fuel-efficient automobiles.

The next level of the hierarchy contains more specific objectives, such as those in the **key result areas.** These are the areas in which performance is essential for the success of the enterprise. Some examples of objectives for key result areas are the following: to obtain 10 percent return on investment by the end of calendar year 1990 (profitability); to increase the number of units of product X by 7 percent without an increase in cost or a reduction of current quality level by June 30, 1991 (productivity).

The objectives have to be further translated into division, department, and unit objectives down to the lowest level of the organization.

The Process of Setting Objectives and the Organizational Hierarchy[2]

As Figure 4-1 indicates, managers at different levels in the organizational hierarchy are concerned with different kinds of objectives. The board of directors and top managers are very much involved in determining the purpose, the mission, and the overall objectives of the firm, as well as the more specific overall objectives in the key result areas. Middle-level managers, such as the vice-president or manager of marketing or the production manager, are involved in setting key-result-area objectives, division objectives, and department objectives. The primary concern of lower-level managers is setting objectives of departments and units as well as of their subordinates. Although individual objectives, consisting of performance and development goals, are

Figure 4-1

HIERARCHY OF OBJECTIVES

ORGANIZATION HIERARCHY

RELATIONSHIP OF OBJECTIVES AND THE ORGANIZATIONAL HIERARCHY.

Adapted from H. Weihrich and J. Mendleson, *Management: An MBO Approach* (Dubuque, Iowa: Wm. C. Brown| Co., 1978), p. xi. Used with permission.

> **PERSPECTIVE:**
> **KEY RESULT AREAS ACCORDING TO DRUCKER**
>
> Although there is no complete agreement on what the key result areas of a business should be — and they may differ for various enterprises — Peter F. Drucker suggests the following: market standing, innovation, productivity, physical and financial resources, profitability, manager performance and development, worker performance and attitude, public responsibility.[3]

shown at the bottom of the hierarchy, managers at higher levels also should set objectives for their own performance and development.

There is some controversy about whether an organization should use the top-down or the bottom-up approach in setting objectives, as indicated by the arrows in Figure 4-1. In the top-down approach upper-level managers determine the objectives for subordinates, while in the bottom-up approach subordinates initiate the setting of objectives for their positions and present them to their superior.

Proponents of the top-down approach suggest that the total organization needs direction through corporate objectives provided by the chief executive officer (in conjunction with the board of directors). Proponents of the bottom-up approach, on the other hand, argue that top management needs to have information from lower levels in the form of objectives. In addition, subordinates are likely to be highly motivated by, and committed to, goals which they initiate. Personal experience has shown that the bottom-up approach is underutilized but that either approach alone is insufficient. Both are essential, but the emphasis should depend on the situation, including such factors as the size of the organization, the organizational culture, the preferred leadership style of the executive, and the urgency of the plan.

A Network of Objectives

Both objectives and planning programs normally form a network of desired results and events. If goals are not interconnected and if they do not support one another, people very often pursue paths that may seem good for their own department but may be detrimental to the company as a whole.

Goals and plans are seldom linear; that is, when one objective is accomplished, it is not neatly followed by another, and so on. Goals and programs form an interlocking network. Figure 4-2 depicts the network of contributing programs (each of which has appropriate objectives) that constitute a typical new product program. Each of the programs could itself be broken down into an interlocking network. Thus, the product research program shown in Figure 4-2 as a single event might involve within it a network of such goals and programs as development of preliminary schematic design, development of a breadboard model (such as a design that focuses on the product's function but disregards its appearance), simplification of electronic and mechanical elements, packaging design, and other events.

Figure 4-2

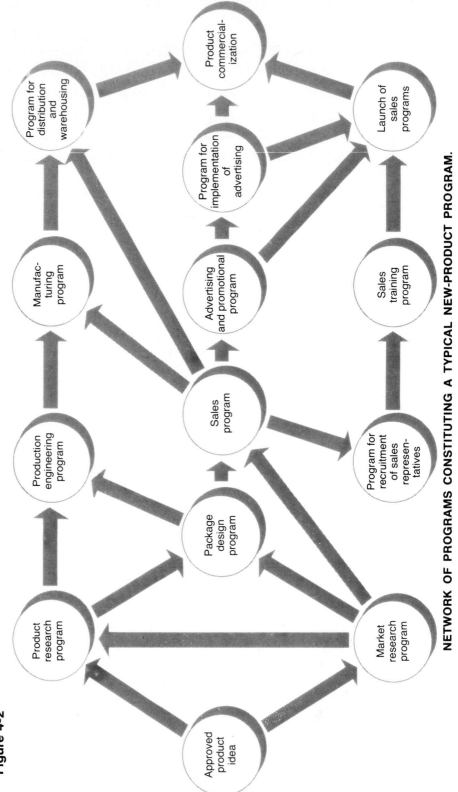

NETWORK OF PROGRAMS CONSTITUTING A TYPICAL NEW-PRODUCT PROGRAM.

Managers must make sure that the components of the network "fit" one another. Fitting is a matter not only of having the various programs carried out but also of timing their completion, since undertaking one program often depends upon first completing another.

It is easy for one department of a company to set goals that may seem entirely appropriate for it, only to find itself operating at cross-purposes with another department. The manufacturing department may see that its goals are best served by long production runs, but this might interfere with the marketing department's desire to have all products in the line readily available or with the finance department's goal of maintaining investment in inventory at a certain low level.

Organizational studies by Gordon Donaldson showed that companies too often set goals that are unrealistic without recognizing the many constraining factors such as the economic condition or the moves by competitors.[4] Moreover, setting the company's financial goals is a continuing process in which conflicting priorities must be balanced. In fact, managers too often see the objectives from their own perspective — based on their self-interest — without understanding the total network of aims.

It is bad enough when goals do not support and interlock with one another. It may be catastrophic when they interfere with one another. What is needed is what one executive described as a matrix of mutually supportive goals.

A Multiplicity of Objectives

Aims are, of course, numerous. Even the mission and broad major enterprise objectives are normally multiple. To say that a university's mission is education and research is not enough. It would be much more accurate (but still not verifiable) to list the overall objectives, as shown in the Perspective.

Likewise, at every level in the hierarchy of objectives, goals are likely to be multiple. Some people think that a manager cannot effectively pursue more than a few objectives, perhaps two to five. The argument is that too many objectives tend to dilute the drive needed for their accomplishment and may unduly highlight minor objectives to the detriment of major ones.

There is something to that position, but two to five objectives seem too arbitrary and too few. It is true that minor goals should not be given the status of important objectives unless a lower-level job is involved. It would hardly be useful for an upper-level manager to occupy his or her time with such lesser objectives as greeting callers, attending meetings, or answering correspondence. There are certain things that any manager is expected to do, and they need not be made into specific and special objectives. Goals are not conceived of as dealing with every facet of a person's job; they should not be confused with activities.

Even if routine matters are excluded, it seems that there is no definite number of objectives. To be sure, if there are so many that none receives adequate attention, planning will be ineffective. At the same time, managers might pursue simultaneously as many as ten or fifteen significant objectives.

> PERSPECTIVE:
> OVERALL OBJECTIVES OF A UNIVERSITY
>
> The overall objectives of a university might be the following:
>
> - Attracting highly qualified students
> - Offering basic training in the liberal arts and sciences as well as in certain professional fields
> - Granting the Ph.D. degree to qualified candidates
> - Attracting a highly regarded faculty
> - Discovering and organizing new knowledge through research
> - Operating as a private school supported principally through tuition and gifts of alumni and friends

However, it would be wise to state the relative importance of each objective. At any rate, the number depends on how much the managers will do themselves and how much they can assign to subordinates, thereby limiting their role to one of assigning, supervising, and controlling.

EVOLVING CONCEPTS IN MANAGEMENT BY OBJECTIVES

Management by objectives (MBO) is now practiced around the world. Yet, despite its wide applications, it is not always clear what is meant by MBO. Some still think of it as an appraisal tool; others see it as a motivational technique; still others consider MBO a planning and control device. In other words, definitions and applications of MBO differ widely, and it is therefore important to highlight the evolving concepts.[5] First, however, MBO should be defined. **Management by objectives** is *a comprehensive managerial system that integrates many key managerial activities in a systematic manner and that is consciously directed toward the effective and efficient achievement of organizational and individual objectives.* This view of MBO as a system of managing is not shared by all. Some still define MBO in a very narrow, limited way.

Early Impetus to MBO

No one person can be called the originator of an approach that emphasizes objectives. Common sense has told people for many centuries that groups and individuals expect to accomplish some end results. However, certain individuals have long placed emphasis on management by objectives and, by doing so, have speeded its development as a systematic process.

One of these is Peter F. Drucker.[6] In 1954 he acted as a catalyst by emphasizing that objectives must be set in all areas where performance affects the health of the enterprise. He laid down a philosophy that emphasizes self-control and self-direction. About the same time, if not earlier, the General Electric Company was using elements of MBO in its reorganization efforts to decentralize managerial decision making. The company implemented this philosophy of appraisal by identifying key result areas and undertaking considerable research on the measurement of performance.

Emphasis on Performance Appraisal

In 1957, in his classic article in the *Harvard Business Review*, Douglas McGregor, a major contributor to the behavioral sciences, criticized traditional appraisal programs that focused on personality trait criteria for evaluating subordinates.[7] In the traditional approach, managers are required to pass judgment on the personal worth of subordinates. Consequently, McGregor suggested a new approach to appraisal based on Drucker's concept of management by objectives. Specifically, subordinates assume the responsibility of setting short-term objectives for themselves, and then they review those objectives with their superior. Of course, the superior has veto power over those objectives, but in the appropriate environment it will hardly need to be used.

Performance is then evaluated against the present objectives, primarily by subordinates themselves. In this new approach, which encourages self-appraisal and self-development, the emphasis is where it ought to be: on performance rather than on personality. The active involvement of subordinates in the appraisal process leads to commitment and creates an environment for motivation.

Emphasis on Short-Term Objectives and Motivation

Researchers, consultants, and practitioners have long recognized the importance of individual goal setting. Early studies at the University of Maryland found that performance was higher when people had specific objectives than when they were simply asked to do their best.[8] Although goal setting is not the only factor in motivating employees, it is an important one (other factors are incentives, participation, and autonomy).[9] Certainly the importance of goal setting as a motivational technique is not restricted to business but is also useful in public organizations.[10] The general vagueness of objectives in many public organizations is a challenge for managers, but there is evidence that this challenge can be met.[11]

Inclusion of Long-Range Planning in the MBO Process

In MBO programs that emphasize performance appraisal and motivation, the focus tends to be on short-term objectives. This orientation, unfortunately, may result in undesirable managerial behavior. For example, a production manager, in an effort to reduce maintenance costs, may neglect the necessary expenses for keeping the machines in good working order. The breakdown of machinery may not be evident at first, but it can result in costly repairs much later. In an effort to show a good return on investment in a given year, the nurturing of good customer relations may be neglected. Similarly, a manager may not invest in new products that would take several years before contributing to profit. Recognizing these shortcomings, many organizations now include long-range and strategic planning in MBO programs.

The Systems Approach to MBO

Management by objectives has undergone many changes; it has been used in performance appraisal, as an instrument for motivating individuals, and, more recently, in strategic planning. But there are still other managerial subsystems that can be integrated into the MBO process; they include design of organizational structures,[12] portfolio management,[13] management development, career development, compensation programs, and budgeting.[14] These various managerial activities need to be integrated into a system. For example, George Odiorne, the most vocal spokesperson for MBO today, considers it to be a system of managerial leadership. Others discuss the systematic relationships of MBO and many other key managerial activities in different environments.[15]

One of the early research studies that investigated MBO as a comprehensive system of managing indicates that most key managerial activities can and should be integrated with the MBO process. The degree of integration, however, differs for individual activities. It was found, for example, that the highest degree of integration of MBO with managerial functions was in controlling, planning, and directing. But several key managerial activities in staffing and organizing also were well integrated into the MBO process. These findings suggest that MBO, to be effective, has to be viewed as a comprehensive system. In short, it must be considered a way of managing, and not an addition to the managerial job.[16]

THE PROCESS OF MANAGING BY OBJECTIVES

The practical importance of objectives in management can best be seen by summarizing how successful managing by objectives works in practice.[17] Figure 4-3 graphically portrays this process. Ideally, the process starts at the top of an organization and has the active support of the chief executive, who gives direction to the organization. It is not essential that objective setting start at the top, however. It can start at the division level, at the marketing-manager level, or even lower. For example, in one company the system was first started in a division where it was carried down to the lowest level of supervision with an interlocking network of goals. Under the personal leadership and tutelage of the division general manager, it succeeded in areas of profitability, cost reduction, and improved operations. Soon, some other division managers and the chief executive became interested in, and attempted to implement, similar programs. In another case, the head of an accounting section developed a system for his group; his success not only earned him recognition (and promotion) but served as the starting point for a companywide program.

Figure 4-3

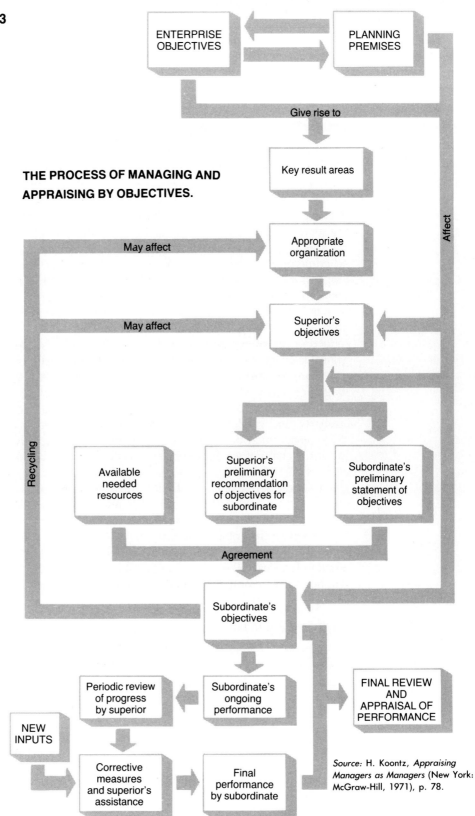

THE PROCESS OF MANAGING AND APPRAISING BY OBJECTIVES.

ENTERPRISE OBJECTIVES

PLANNING PREMISES

Give rise to

Key result areas

Affect

May affect

Appropriate organization

May affect

Superior's objectives

Recycling

Available needed resources

Superior's preliminary recommendation of objectives for subordinate

Subordinate's preliminary statement of objectives

Agreement

Subordinate's objectives

Periodic review of progress by superior

Subordinate's ongoing performance

FINAL REVIEW AND APPRAISAL OF PERFORMANCE

NEW INPUTS

Corrective measures and superior's assistance

Final performance by subordinate

Source: H. Koontz, *Appraising Managers as Managers* (New York: McGraw-Hill, 1971), p. 78.

As in all planning, one of the critical needs in MBO is the development and dissemination of consistent planning premises. No manager can be expected to set goals or establish plans and budgets without guidelines.

Setting Preliminary Objectives at the Top

Given appropriate planning premises, the first step in setting objectives is for the top manager to determine what he or she perceives to be the purpose or mission and the more important goals of the enterprise for a given period ahead. These goals can be set for any period — a quarter, a year, 5 years, or whatever is appropriate in given circumstances. In most instances, objectives are set to coincide with the annual budget or the completion of a major project. But this is not necessary and often is not desirable. Certain goals should be scheduled for accomplishment in a much shorter period and others in a much longer period. Also, typically, as one proceeds down the organizational hierarchy, the length of time set for accomplishing goals tends to get shorter. It is seldom feasible or wise for first-level supervisors, for example, to set many annual goals, since their goal span on most operating matters, such as cost or scrap reduction, rearrangement of facilities, or instituting of special personnel programs, is short (most of these goals may be accomplished in weeks or months).

The goals set by the superior are preliminary, based on an analysis and judgment as to what can and should be accomplished by the organization within a certain period. This requires taking into account the company's strengths and weaknesses in the light of available opportunities and threats. These goals must be regarded as tentative and subject to modification while the entire chain of verifiable objectives is worked out by subordinates. It is usually not advisable to force objectives on subordinates, since force can scarcely give rise to a sense of commitment. Most managers also find that the process of working out goals with subordinates reveals both problems they should deal with and opportunities they were not previously aware of.

When setting objectives, the manager also establishes measures of goal accomplishment. If verifiable objectives are developed, these measures, whether in sales dollars, profits, percentages, cost levels, or program execution, will normally be built into the objectives.

Clarifying Organizational Roles

The relationship between expected results and the responsibility for attaining them is often overlooked. Ideally, each goal and subgoal should be one particular person's clear responsibility. Analyzing an organization's structure, however, often reveals that the responsibility is vague and that clarification or reorganization is needed. Sometimes it is impossible to structure an organization so that a given objective is someone's personal responsibility. In setting goals for launching a new product, for example, the managers of research, marketing, and production must carefully coordinate their activities. Their separate functions can be centralized by putting a product manager in charge. If this is not desirable, at least the specific parts of each coordinating manager's contribution to the program goal can and should be clearly identified.

Setting Subordinates' Objectives

After making sure that subordinate managers have been informed of pertinent general objectives, strategies, and planning premises, the superior can then proceed to work with subordinates in setting their objectives. The superior asks what goals the subordinates believe they can accomplish, in what time period, and with what resources. They will then discuss some preliminary thoughts about what goals seem feasible for the company or department.

The superior's role at this point is extremely important. Questions that she or he should ask include: What can you contribute? How can we improve your operation to help me improve mine? What stands in the way; what obstructions keep you from a higher level of performance? What changes can we make? How can I help? It is amazing how many things can be identified that might obstruct performance and how many constructive ideas can be dredged up from the experience and knowledge of subordinates.

Superiors must also be patient counselors, helping their subordinates develop consistent and supportive objectives and being careful not to set goals that are impossible to achieve. It is human nature to believe that anything can be accomplished a year hence but that much less can be done next week. And one of the things that can weaken a program of managing by objectives is to allow managers to set unrealistic objectives.

At the same time, having subordinates set goals does not mean that people can do whatever they want to do. Superiors must listen to, and work with, their subordinates, but in the end they must take reponsibility for approving subordinates' goals. The superior's judgment and final approval must be based upon what is reasonably attainable with "stretch" and "pull," what is fully supportive of upper-level objectives, what is consistent with goals of other managers in other functions, and what is consistent with the longer-run objectives and interests of the department and the company.

One of the major advantages of carefully setting up a network of verifiable goals and a requirement for doing so effectively is tying in the need of capital, material, and human resources at the same time. All managers at all levels require these resources to accomplish their goals. By relating these resources to the goals themselves, superiors can better see the most effective and most economical way of allocating them.

Recycling Objectives

Objectives can hardly be set by starting at the top and dividing them up among subordinates. Nor should they be started from the bottom. A degree of recycling is required. Recycling is indicated by the arrows in Figures 4-1 and 4-3. Top managers may have some idea of what their subordinates' objectives should be — but they will almost certainly change these preconceived goals as the contributions of the subordinates come into focus. Thus, setting objectives is not only a joint process but also an interactive one. For example, a sales manager may realistically set a goal to achieve product sales that are much higher than what top management has believed possible. In this event, the goals of the manufacturing and finance departments will surely be affected.

HOW TO SET OBJECTIVES

Without clear objectives, managing is haphazard. No individual and no group can expect to perform effectively and efficiently unless there is a clear aim. Table 4-1 illustrates some objectives and how they can be restated in a way that allows measurement.

Quantitative and Qualitative Objectives

To be measurable, objectives must be verifiable. This means one must be able to answer the question: At the end of the period, how do I know if the objective has been accomplished? For example, the objective of making a reasonable profit can at best indicate whether the company made a profit or had a loss (see Table 4-1), but it does not state how much profit is to be made. Also, what is reasonable to the subordinate may not be at all acceptable to the superior. In case of such a disagreement it is, of course, the subordinate who loses the argument. In contrast, a return of investment of 12 percent at the end of the fis-

Table 4-1   Examples of Nonverifiable and Verifiable Objectives

Nonverifiable objectives	Verifiable objectives
1. To make a reasonable profit	1. To achieve a return on investment of 12% at the end of the current fiscal year
2. To improve communication	2. To issue a two-page monthly newsletter beginning July 1, 1991, involving not more than 40 working hours of preparation time (after the first issue)
3. To improve productivity of the production department	3. To increase production output by 5% by December 31, 1991, without additional costs and while maintaining the current quality level
4. To develop better managers	4. To design and conduct a 40-hour in-house program on the "fundamentals of management," to be completed by October 1, 1991, involving not more than 200 working hours of the management development staff and with at least 90% of the 100 managers passing the exam (specified)
5. To install a computer system	5. To install a computerized control system in the production department by December 31, 1991, requiring not more than 500 working hours of systems analysis and operating with not more than 10% downtime during the first 3 months

cal year can be measured; it gives answer to the questions: How much or what? and when?

At times it is more difficult to state results in verifiable terms.[18] This is especially true for staff personnel and also in government. For example, installing a computer system is an important task, but "to install a computer system" is not a verifiable goal. But suppose the objective is "to install a computerized control system (with certain specifications) in the production department by December 31, 1991, with an expenditure of not more than 500 working hours." Then, goal accomplishment can be measured. Moreover, quality can also be specified (in terms of computer downtime).

Setting Objectives in Government

The need of managing by objectives in government has been recognized by Frederic V. Malek, a former special assistant to the President and one of the driving forces in the implementation of MBO in the federal government.[19] He stated: "If the executive branch of government is to be managed effectively, it clearly needs a system for setting priorities, pinpointing responsibility for their achievement, requiring follow-through, and generating enough feedback that programs can be monitored and evaluated from the top." The MBO program initiated in the federal government in the early 1970s indeed had some success. For example, the Department of Health, Education, and Welfare set an objective for training 35,000 welfare recipients and placing them in meaningful jobs, an objective that seemed almost impossible to achieve. The goal was not only achieved but exceeded; 40,000 welfare recipients were trained and placed on payrolls.

To be sure, the management of government has some special problems. Many expenditures are uncontrollable because they are mandated by law. There is also the tendency to perpetuate ineffective programs for political reasons, and congressional members have a political rather than a managerial orientation. Finally, the traditional budgeting process is not conducive to managerial productivity.

Improving the operation of the federal government, and other governments as well, requires:

1. Identifying ineffective programs by comparing performance against pre-established objectives

2. Using zero-base budgeting (a topic to be discussed later, in Chapter 19)

3. Applying MBO concepts for measuring individual performance

4. Preparing short- and long-range objectives and plans

5. Installing effective controls

6. Designing sound organization structures with clear responsibilities and decision-making authority at appropriate levels

7. Developing and preparing government officials for managerial responsibilities

Thus, the setting of objectives, as in MBO programs, not only is essential in making line managers in business organizations more effective but is equally important for improving the performance of staff personnel and public administrators.

Guidelines for Setting Objectives

Setting objectives is indeed a difficult task. It requires intelligent coaching by the superior and extensive practice by the subordinate. The guidelines shown in Table 4-2 will help managers in setting their objectives.

The list of objectives should not be too long, yet it should cover the main features of the job. As this chapter has emphasized, objectives should be verifiable and should state what is to be accomplished and when. If possible, the quality desired and the projected cost of achieving the objectives should be indicated. Furthermore, objectives should present a challenge, indicate priorities, and promote personal and professional growth and development. These and other criteria for good objectives are summarized in Table 4-2. Testing objectives against the criteria shown in the checklist is a good exercise for managers and aspiring managers.

BENEFITS AND WEAKNESSES OF MANAGEMENT BY OBJECTIVES AND SOME RECOMMENDATIONS

Although goal-oriented management is now one of the most widely practiced managerial approaches, its effectiveness is sometimes questioned. Faulty implementation is often blamed, but another reason is that MBO may be applied as a mechanistic technique focusing on selected aspects of the managerial process without integrating them into a system.

A review of 185 studies showed that it is rather difficult to evaluate the true effectiveness of MBO.[20] For one, MBO is defined and practiced differently by various organizations. For some it means simply goal setting, while for others it is a comprehensive system of managing. Also, effectiveness is not easy to define, and an increase or decrease in performance may be due to factors other than MBO. It may take 2 to 5 years to implement an MBO program, and during that time many factors other than the program can influence the operation of the firm. As pointed out several years ago — and it is still true today — if a goal-oriented management approach is to produce results, it has to be adapted to the specific situation.[21]

Nevertheless, one can learn from experience and research by taking a realistic view and analyzing some of the benefits and weaknesses of MBO.

Benefits of Management by Objectives

As pointed out earlier, there is considerable evidence, much of it from laboratory studies, that shows the motivational aspects of clear goals. But there are other benefits.

Table 4-2   Checklist for Manager Objectives

If the objectives meet the criteria, mark " + " in the box at the right of the statement. If they do not, mark " − " in the box.

1. Do the objectives cover the main features of my job?   ☐

2. Is the list of objectives too long? If so, can I combine some objectives?   ☐

3. Are the objectives verifiable; i.e., will I know at the end of the period whether or not they have been achieved?   ☐

4. Do the objectives indicate:
   (a) Quantity (how much)?   ☐
   (b) Quality (how well, or specific characteristics)?   ☐
   (c) Time (when)?   ☐
   (d) Cost (at what cost)?   ☐

5. Are the objectives challenging yet reasonable?   ☐

6. Are priorities assigned to the objectives (ranking, weighing, etc.)?   ☐

7. Does the set of objectives also include:
   (a) Improvement objectives?   ☐
   (b) Personal development objectives?   ☐

8. Are the objectives coordinated with those of other managers and organizational units?   ☐
   Are they consistent with the objectives of my superior, my department, the company?   ☐

9. Have I communicated the objectives to all who need to be informed?   ☐

10. Are the short-term objectives consistent with long-term aims?   ☐

11. Are the assumptions underlying the objectives clearly identified?   ☐

12. Are the objectives expressed clearly and are they in writing?   ☐

13. Do the objectives provide for timely feedback so that I can take any necessary corrective steps?   ☐

14. Are my resources and authority sufficient for achieving the objectives?   ☐

15. Have I given the individuals who are expected to accomplish objectives a chance to suggest their objectives?   ☐

16. Do my subordinates have control over aspects for which they are assigned responsibility?   ☐

Improvement of managing   All the advantages of management by objectives can be summarized by saying that it results in greatly improved management. Objectives cannot be established without planning, and results-oriented planning is the only kind that makes sense. Management by objectives forces managers to think about planning for results, rather than merely planning activities or work. To ensure that objectives are realistic, MBO also requires that managers think of the way they will accomplish results, the organization and personnel they will need to do so, and the resources and assistance they will require. Also, there is no better incentive for control and no better way to know the standards for control than a set of clear goals.

Clarification of organization   Another major benefit of managing by objectives is that it forces managers to clarify organizational roles and structures. To the extent possible, positions should be built around the key results expected of people occupying them.

Companies that have effectively embarked on MBO programs have often discovered deficiencies in their organization. Managers often forget that to get results, they must delegate authority according to the results they expect. As an executive of Honeywell is reported to have said: "There are two things that might also be considered fundamental creed at Honeywell: decentralized management is needed to make Honeywell work and management by objectives is needed to make decentralization work."

Encouragement of personal commitment   One of the great advantages of management by objectives is that it encourages people to commit themselves to their goals. No longer are people just doing work, following instructions, and waiting for guidance and decisions; they are now individuals with clearly defined purposes. They have had a part in actually setting their objectives; they have had an opportunity to put their ideas into planning programs; they understand their area of discretion — their authority — and they have been able to get help from their superiors to ensure that they can accomplish their goals. These are the elements that make for a feeling of commitment. People become enthusiastic when they control their own fate.

Development of effective controls   In the same way that management by objectives sparks more effective planning, it also aids in developing effective controls. Recall that control involves measuring results and taking action to correct deviations from plans in order to ensure that goals are reached. As will be explained in Chapter 18, on the system and process of management control, one of the major problems is knowing what to watch; a clear set of verifiable goals is the best guide.

Weaknesses of Management by Objectives

With all its advantages, a system of management by objectives has a number of weaknesses. Most are due to shortcomings in applying the MBO concepts.

Failure to teach the philosophy of MBO   As simple as management by objectives may seem, managers who would put it into practice must understand and appreciate a good deal about it. They in turn must explain to subordinates what it is, how it works, why it is being done, what part it will play in appraising performance, and, above all, how participants can benefit. The philosophy is built on concepts of self-control and self-direction that are aimed at making managers professionals.

Failure to give guidelines to goal setters   Management by objectives, like any other kind of planning, cannot work if those who are expected to set goals are not given needed guidelines. Managers must know what the corporate goals are and how their own activity fits in with them. If corporation goals are vague, unreal, or inconsistent, it is virtually impossible for managers to tune in with them.

Managers also need planning premises and a knowledge of major company policies. People must have some assumptions as to the future, some understanding of policies affecting their areas of operation, and an awareness of the objectives and programs with which their goals interlock in order to plan effectively. Failure to fill these needs can result in a fatal vacuum in planning.

Difficulty of setting goals   Truly verifiable goals are difficult to set, particularly if they are to have the right degree of stretch or pull, quarter in and quarter out, year in and year out. Goal setting may not be much more difficult than any other kind of effective planning, although it will probably take more study and work to establish verifiable objectives that are formidable but attainable than to develop many plans, which tend only to lay out work to be done. Participants in MBO programs report at times that the excessive concern with economic results puts pressure on individuals that may encourage questionable behavior.[22] To reduce the probability of selecting unethical means for achieving results, top management must agree to reasonable objectives, clearly state behavioral expectations, and give a high priority to ethical behavior, rewarding it as well as punishing unethical activities.

Emphasis on short-run goals   In most MBO programs, managers set goals for the short term, seldom for more than a year and often for a quarter or less. There is clearly a danger of emphasizing the short run, perhaps at the expense of the longer range. This means, of course, that superiors must always assure themselves that current objectives, like any other short-run plan, are designed to serve longer-range goals.

Danger of inflexibility   Managers often hesitate to change objectives. Although goals may cease to be meaningful if they are changed too often and do not represent a well-thought-out and well-planned result, it is nonetheless foolish to expect a manager to strive for a goal that has been made obsolete by revised corporate objectives, changed premises, or modified policies.

Other dangers   There are some other dangers and difficulties in management by objectives. In their desire to make goals verifiable, people may overuse quantitative goals and attempt to use numbers in areas where they are not applicable, or they may downgrade important goals that are difficult to state in terms of end results. A favorable company image may be the key strength of an enterprise, yet it is difficult to state this in quantitative terms. Sometimes managers fail to use objectives as a constructive force even with the full participation and assistance of their superiors. There is also the danger of forgetting that managing involves more than goal setting.

Difficulties may also arise in applying goal-oriented planning in a very dynamic and complex environment. In human services delivery systems it was noted that MBO was rejected because of difficulties in (1) converting broad organizational objectives into more detailed organizational unit objectives, (2) measuring performance and providing feedback, (3) determining what is meritorious performance and rewarding individuals accordingly, (4) stating long-term objectives congruent with short-term goals, and (5) adjusting to the fast-changing environment.[23]

But even with the difficulties and dangers of managing by objectives in certain situations, this system emphasizes in practice the setting of goals long known to be an essential part of planning and managing.

SUMMARY

Objectives are the end points toward which activities are aimed. Objectives are verifiable if it is possible, at the end of the period, to determine whether or not they have been accomplished.

Objectives form both a hierarchy — reaching from corporate purposes and missions down to individual goals — and a network as they are reflected in interlocking programs. Managers can best determine the number of objectives they should realistically set for themselves by analyzing the nature of the job and how much they can do themselves and how much they can delegate. In any case, managers should know the relative importance of each of their goals.

Management by objectives (MBO) has been widely used for performance appraisal and employee motivation, but it is really a system of managing. The MBO process consists of setting goals at the highest level of the organization, clarifying the specific roles of those responsible for achieving the goals, and setting and modifying objectives for subordinates. Goals can be set for line managers as well as for staff personnel. Goals can be qualitative or quantitative.

Among its other benefits, MBO results in better managing, often forces managers to clarify the structure of their organizations, encourages people to commit themselves to their goals, and helps develop effective controls.

Some of its weaknessess are that managers sometimes fail to explain the philosophy of MBO (which emphasizes self-control and self-direction) to subordinates and give them guidelines for their goal setting. In addition, goals themselves are difficult to set, tend to be short-run, and may become inflexible despite changes in the environment of plan operation. People, in their search for verifiability, may overemphasize quantifiable goals.

KEY IDEAS AND CONCEPTS FOR REVIEW

Objectives
Hierarchy of objectives
Network of objectives
Evolving concepts in management
   by objectives (MBO)

Systems approach to managing by
   objectives
MBO process
Quantitative objectives
Qualitative objectives

Verifiability

Objective setting in government

Benefits of MBO

Weaknesses of MBO

Recommendations for
  improving MBO

FOR DISCUSSION

1. To what extent do you believe that managers you have known in business or elsewhere have a clear understanding of their objectives? If, in your opinion, they do not, how would you suggest that they go about setting them?

2. Some people object to defining long-term goals because they think it is impossible to know what will happen over a long period. Do you believe this is an intelligent position to take?

3. Take any program of any kind that you would like to see accomplished and draw up a network of contributing programs and goals that would be necessary for its accomplishment.

4. "The only planning tool we need in this company is the budget. If everyone meets his or her budget, we need nothing else, and management by objectives would be an unnecessary frill." Comment.

5. Why is it that although many business enterprises have talked about and introduced MBO programs, the actual record of performance under these programs has been so poor?

6. Do you believe that managing by objectives could be introduced in a government agency? A university? A college fraternity or sorority?

7. What are your five most important personal objectives? Are they long- or short-range? Are the objectives verifiable?

8. In your organization, what does your superior expect from you in respect to the level of performance? Is it stated in writing? If you wrote your job objective on a sheet of paper and your boss wrote down what he or she expects of you, would the two be consistent?

EXERCISES/ACTION STEPS

1. Make a list of goals you wish to achieve in the next 5 years. Are they verifiable? Are they attainable?

2. Interview two managers in the local community, one in a business enterprise and the other in a government agency. Ask them what the long- and short-term overall objectives of their organizations are. Are the objectives clearly expressed, in writing, and understandable? Also ask the managers about their own objectives. If these organizations have a systematic approach to goal setting, ask about the process and try to diagram it. Present and explain the diagram to the class.

CASE:
THE MUNICIPAL WATER DISTRICT

The district proposed an incentive program for its higher-level managers which would be tried for 1 year. The program, based on MBO concepts, was a response to criticism from citizens in the community. Here is a summary of the proposed program:

The objectives are to be set to represent higher-than-normal performance. Furthermore, the emphasis will be on verifiable objectives against which performance can be measured. One of the objectives, for example, will be to keep the average water bill increase at no more than 75 percent of the inflation rate. The participating managers will receive only half of the cost-of-living increases granted to other employees. To be eligible for the other half, they will have to achieve *some* of the objectives. If, on the other hand, *most* of the above-normal objectives are achieved, their pay increases will be above the inflation rate. No lump-sum bonuses will be granted, but the performance of the managers will be reflected in their wages.

It was calculated that the program would result in savings of $15,000 to $25,000 for the district if none of the objectives were met. On the other hand, if all the objectives were met, the cost to the company would be between $25,000 and $35,000 in salary increases. But the indirect savings were estimated at $1 million or more. This incentive program was submitted to the public through a poll, with arguments presented for and against the plan.

The arguments *for* the incentive program were as follows:

- It would stop the rise in water rates.

- Rewards would be based on performance.

- Turnover of management personnel would be reduced.

- The cost for outstanding performance would be low compared with the potential savings.

The arguments *against* the incentive program were as follows:

- The program would raise current objectives only to what would normally be expected of the managers.

- The company has one of the highest water costs in the state.

- If the general manager were to meet all the objectives, he would get paid more than a U.S. senator. If three other high-level managers were to achieve all their objectives, they would get paid more than the governor of the state.

- Since the budget is prepared by the same person who would be the beneficiary of the incentives, there would be the temptation to "pad" the budget.

- The managers' past performance was considered substandard. No bonus should be offered to managers for improving their substandard performance and doing what they should have been doing in the first place.

- The policy of the company states that it should supply adequate water at the lowest possible cost. If the managers are not capable of performing their job, they should seek employment elsewhere.

1. What do you think about the incentive program?

2. Do you think that the public should be polled on such a program? Why, or why not?

3. As a consultant, what would you recommend?

REFERENCES

1. George A. Steiner, John B. Miner, and Edmund R. Gray, *Management Policy and Strategy,* 3d ed. (New York: The Macmillan Company, 1986), pp. 86–87.

2. Parts of this discussion are based on Heinz Weihrich, "A Hierarchy and Network of Aims," *Management Review* (January 1982), pp. 47–54.

3. Peter F. Drucker, *The Practice of Management* (New York: Harper & Brothers, 1954), p. 63.

4. Gordon Donaldson, "Financial Goals and Strategic Consequences," *Harvard Business Review* (May–June 1985), pp. 57–66.

5. For a detailed discussion of the history of MBO, see George S. Odiorne, "MBO: A Backward Glance," *Business Horizons* (October 1978), pp. 14–24. An excellent discussion of the early history of MBO is by Ronald G. Greenwood, "Management by Objectives: As Developed by Peter Drucker, Assisted by Harold Smiddy," *Academy of Management Review* (April 1981), pp. 225–230.

6. For his original discussion of managing by objectives, see Drucker, *The Practice of Management* (1954), pp. 121–136. In conversation with Harold Koontz, Drucker gave credit for the concept to the late Harold E. Smiddy, then of General Electric. See also Greenwood, "Management by Objectives" (1981), pp. 225–230.

7. Douglas McGregor, "An Uneasy Look at Performance Appraisal," *Harvard Business Review* (May–June 1957), pp. 89–94. In even more recent writings the emphasis in MBO is still on goal setting and appraisal, as shown by Mark L. McConkie, "A Clarification of the Goal Setting and Appraisal Process in MBO," *Academy of Management Review* (January 1979), pp. 29–40. For a discussion of performance appraisal, see also George L. Morrisey, *Performance Appraisal in Business and Industry* (Reading, Mass.: Addison-Wesley Publishing Company, 1983).

8. Edwin A. Locke and Judith F. Bryan, "Performance Goals as Determinants of Level of Performance and Boredom," *Journal of Applied Psychology* (April 1967), pp. 120–130. For other research, see Christina E. Shalley and Greg R. Oldham,

"Effects of Goal Difficulty and Expected External Evaluation on Intrinsic Motivation: A Laboratory Study," *Academy of Management Journal* (September 1985), pp. 628–640. See also Edwin A. Locke and Gary P. Latham, *Goal Setting: A Motivational Technique That Works* (Englewood Cliffs, N.J.: Prentice-Hall, 1984).

9. Edwin A. Locke, "The Ubiquity of the Technique of Goal Setting in Theories of and Approaches to Employee Motivation," *Academy of Management Review* (July 1978), pp. 594–601.

10. James L. Perry and Lyman W. Porter, "Factors Affecting the Context for Motivation in Public Organizations," *Academy of Management Review* (January 1982), pp. 89–98.

11. Heinz Weihrich, "The Application of Management by Objectives in Government," *Faculty Working Paper MG 76–3* (Tempe, Arizona: Arizona State University, 1976).

12. Richard D. Babcock, "Summary of Five Key Elements for Adapting MBO to Different Organizational Designs," *1981 Proceedings, IX Annual Management by Objectives State of the Art Conference* (Washington, D.C., 1981), pp. 14–18.

13. George S. Odiorne, "Portfolio Management and MBO," *1981 Proceedings, IX Annual Management by Objectives State of the Art Conference* (Washington, D.C., 1981), pp. 119–124.

14. M. A. Quereshi and Richard Babcock, "A Proposal for Integrating Budgeting and MBO," in Richard D. Babcock and Peter F. Sorensen, Jr. (eds.), *Strategies and Tactics in Management by Objectives* (Champaign, Ill.: Stripes Publishing Company, 1980), pp. 96–112.

15. Anthony P. Raia, *Management by Objectives* (Glenview, Ill.: Scott, Foresman and Company, 1974); Dale D. McConkey, *MBO for Nonprofit Organizations* (New York: AMACOM, American Management Association, 1975); George L. Morrisey, *Management by Objectives and Results in the Public Sector* (Reading, Mass.: Addison-Wesley Publishing Company, 1976).

16. Heinz Weihrich, "A Study of the Integration of Management by Objectives with Key Managerial Activities and the Relationship to Selected Effectiveness Measures," doctoral dissertation, University of California, Los Angeles, 1973.

17. Some of the material in this section is drawn from Harold Koontz, *Appraising Managers as Managers* (New York: McGraw-Hill Book Company, 1971), chaps. 3 and 4.

18. George S. Odiorne, "Measuring the Unmeasurable: Setting Standards for Management Performance," *Business Horizons* (July–August 1987), pp. 69–75.

19. This discussion is based on Malek's book *Washington's Hidden Tragedy* (New York: The Free Press, 1978), chaps. 7–9. It provides one of the best insights into the operation of MBO in the federal government.

20. Jack N. Kondrasuk, "Studies in MBO Effectiveness," *Academy of Management Review* (July 1981), pp. 419–430.

21. Heinz Weihrich, "An Uneasy Look at the MBO Jungle — Toward a Contingency Approach to MBO," *Management International Review,* vol. 16, no. 4 (1976), pp. 103–109.

22. Charles D. Pringle and Justin G. Longenecker, "The Ethics of MBO," *Academy of Management Review* (April 1982), pp. 305–312.

23. Mark A. Covaleski and Mark W. Dirsmith, "MBO and Goal Directedness in a Hospital Context," *Academy of Management Review* (July 1981), pp. 409–418.

CHAPTER 5

Strategies, Policies, and Planning Premises

CHAPTER OBJECTIVES

After reading this chapter, you should understand:

1. The nature and purpose of strategy and policy
2. The strategic planning process
3. The TOWS Matrix and the Product Portfolio Matrix
4. The major kinds of strategies and policies
5. Porter's generic strategies
6. The requirements for effective implementation of strategies
7. The nature and types of premises and forecasts
8. Effective premising

Today most business enterprises engage in strategic planning, although the degrees of sophistication and formality vary considerably. Conceptually, strategic planning is deceptively simple: Analyze the current and expected future situation, determine the direction of the firm, and develop means for achieving the mission. In reality, this is an extremely complex process which demands a systematic approach for identifying and analyzing factors external to the organization and matching them with the firm's capabilities.

Planning is done in an environment of uncertainty. No one can be sure what the external as well as the internal environment will be even next week, much less several years from now. Therefore, people make assumptions or forecasts about the anticipated environment. Some of the forecasts become assumptions for other plans. For example, the gross national product forecast becomes the assumption for sales planning, which in turn becomes the basis for production planning, and so on.

In this chapter you will learn about (1) the nature and purpose of strategies and policies; (2) the strategic planning process, which identifies the critical aspects of formulating a strategy; (3) the TOWS Matrix, a tool for systematically integrating external and internal factors; (4) the Portfolio Matrix, another tool for allocating resources; (5) the major kinds of strategies; (6) three generic strategies; and (7) the means for effectively implementing strategies. Since plans are made in an environment of uncertainty, you will also learn (8) about premising ànd forecasting and (9) how to make premising effective.

THE NATURE AND PURPOSE OF STRATEGIES AND POLICIES

Strategies and policies are closely related. Both give direction, both are the framework for plans, both are the basis of operational plans, and both affect all areas of managing.

Strategy and Policy

The term "strategy" (which is derived from the Greek word *strategos,* meaning "general") has been used in different ways. Authors differ in at least one major aspect about *strategies.* Some writers focus on both the end points (purpose, mission, goals, objectives) and the means of achieving them (policies and plans). Others emphasize the means to the ends in the strategic process rather than the ends per se. Several meanings of the word "strategies" were discussed in Chapter 3. One of the most comprehensive definitions refers to the determination of basic long-term objectives and of courses of action and allocations of resources to achieve these aims.

Since ends have already been discussed (Chapter 4), let us turn our attention now to the situation analysis. It is assumed that the purpose of the enterprise has already been established yet is subject to change after an evaluation of the situation.

Policies are general statements or understandings which guide managers' thinking in decision making. They ensure that decisions fall within certain boundaries. They usually do not require action but are intended to guide managers in their commitment to the decision they ultimately make.

The essence of policy is discretion. Strategy, on the other hand, concerns the direction in which human and material resources will be applied in order to increase the chance of achieving selected objectives.

The Need for Operational Planning: Tactics

To be effective, strategies and policies must be put into practice by means of plans, increasing in detail until they get down to the nuts and bolts of

---

PERSPECTIVE:
TOP-MANAGEMENT CHOICES

Top managers get paid for making tough decisions, and many of their decisions are strategic for the future of the company. Let us look at some examples of decisions that altered the course of the company.[1]

General Motors.   Roger Smith of General Motors saw the opportunities in the high-tech field and their importance for GM. Consequently, he decided to acquire Electronic Data Systems Corp., a large data processing company. But the resistance to the merger of these two companies (with very different organizational cultures) by GM's staff was substantial. Long-established organizations do not change easily, and Roger Smith learned a great deal about the difficulty of making dramatic changes.

Gould Inc.   William Ylvisaker, the former CEO at Gould Inc., changed the firm from a manufacturer of car batteries and electrical equipment to a high-tech electronics firm. This new direction required a change in personnel; half of Gould's management committee left the company. Making such drastic decisions requires a strong-willed person; Ylvisaker was named one of the ten toughest corporate managers by *Fortune* magazine.

Warner-Lambert.   When Ward Hagan wanted to restructure Warner-Lambert, he had to streamline the drug company. This required selling the eyeglass manufacturer American Optical (a loser) as well as Entenmann, a profitable bakery firm. To give a new direction to the firm, Hagan employed the consulting services of McKinsey & Co. to teach its managers strategic planning. To be sure, nobody can predict the long-term future with great accuracy, but strategic planning forces managers to think critically and analytically about the future. The company sent 500 of its managers to a program that trained them in critical thinking. To demonstrate the importance of strategic thinking, the company rewarded managers who utilized the technique with promotions.

Rolm Corporation.   Rolm Corporation was concerned about its dependence on military customers, which led to a search for related product lines. Despite a thorough search, the results were at first disappointing. Persistence and a continuing search led to the development of digital switching equipment that was more advanced than that of Rolm's competitors. Some risk-taking decisions turned out to be right and made the company a giant in its field before the firm was acquired by IBM.

---

operations. **Tactics,** then, are the action plans through which strategies are executed. Strategies must be supported by effective tactics.

THE STRATEGIC PLANNING PROCESS

Although specific steps in the formulation of the strategy may vary, the process can be built, at least conceptually, around the key elements shown in Figure 5-1.

Figure 5-1

STRATEGIC PLANNING PROCESS.

Adapted from Heinz Weihrich, "The TOWS Matrix: A Tool for Situational Analysis," *Long-Range Planning*, vol. 15, no. 2 (1982), pp. 54–66.

Inputs

The various organizational *inputs,* including the goal inputs of the claimants, were discussed in Chapter 1 and need no elaboration.

Enterprise Profile

The *enterprise profile* is usually the starting point for determining where the company is and where it should go. Thus, top managers determine the basic purpose of the enterprise and clarify the firm's geographic orientation, such as whether it should operate in selected regions, in all states in the United States, or even in different countries. In addition, managers assess the competitive situation of their firm.

Orientation of Top Managers

The enterprise profile is shaped by people, especially *top managers,* and their *orientation* is important for formulating the strategy. They set the organizational climate, and they determine the direction of the firm. Consequently, their values, their preferences, and their attitudes toward risks have to be carefully examined because they have an impact on the strategy.

Purpose and Objectives

The *purpose* and the major *objectives* are the end points toward which the activities of the enterprise are directed. Since the previous chapter dealt with these topics at length, additional discussion here is unnecessary.

External Environment

The present and future *external environment* must be assessed in terms of threats and opportunities. The evaluation focuses on economic, social, political, legal, demographic, and geographic factors. In addition, the environment is scanned for technological developments, for products and services on the market, and for other factors necessary in determining the competitive situation of the enterprise.

Internal Environment

Similarly, the firm's *internal environment* should be audited and evaluated in respect to its resources and its weaknesses and strengths in research and development, production, operations, procurement, marketing, and products and services. Other internal factors important for formulating a strategy include the assessment of human resources, financial resources, and other factors such as the company image, the organization structure and climate, the planning and control system, and relations with customers.

Alternative Strategies

Strategic *alternatives* are developed on the basis of an analysis of the external and internal environment. An organization may pursue many different kinds of strategies. It may *specialize* or *concentrate*, as the Korean Hyundai Company did by producing lower-priced cars (in contrast to General Motors, for example, which has a complete product line ranging from inexpensive to luxurious cars).

Alternatively, a firm may *diversify*, extending the operation into new and profitable markets. Sears not only is in retailing but also provides many financial services.

Still another strategy is to go *international* and expand the operation into other countries. The multinational firms discussed in Chapter 22 provide many examples. The same chapter also examines *joint ventures,* which may be an appropriate strategy for some firms. They are especially suitable for big undertakings in which firms have to pool their resources, as illustrated by the joint venture of General Motors and Toyota to produce small cars in California.

Under certain circumstances, a company may have to adopt a *liquidation* strategy by terminating an unprofitable product line or even dissolving the firm. But in some cases liquidation may not be necessary and a *retrenchment* strategy may be appropriate. In such a situation the company may curtail its operation temporarily.

These are just a few examples of possible strategies. In practice, companies, especially large ones, pursue a combination of strategies.

Evaluation and Choice of Strategies

The various strategies have to be carefully *evaluated* before the *choice* is made. Strategic choices must be considered in light of the risks involved in a particular decision. Some profitable opportunities may not be pursued because a failure in a risky venture could result in bankruptcy of the firm. Another critical element in choosing a strategy is timing. Even the best product may fail if it is introduced to the market at an inappropriate time. Moreover, the reaction of competitors must be taken into consideration. When IBM reduced its price of the PC computer in reaction to the sales success of Apple's Macintosh computer, firms producing IBM-compatible computers had little choice but to reduce their prices as well. This illustrates the interconnection of the strategies of several firms in the same industry.

Medium- and Short-Range Planning, Implementation, and Control

Although not a part of the strategic planning process (and therefore shown by broken lines in Figure 5-1), *medium-* and *short-range planning* as well as the *implementation* of the plans must be considered during all phases of the process. *Control* must also be provided for monitoring performance against plans.[2] The importance of *feedback* is shown by the loops in the model.

Consistency and Contingency

The last key aspect of the strategic planning process is testing for *consistency* and preparing for *contingency plans.* Both topics will be discussed later in this chapter.

THE TOWS MATRIX: A MODERN TOOL FOR ANALYSIS OF THE SITUATION

Today, strategy designers have been aided by a number of matrixes showing the relationships of critical variables. For example, the Boston Consulting Group developed the Business Portfolio Matrix, which will be discussed later. More recently, the TOWS Matrix has been introduced for analyzing the situation.[3]

The TOWS Matrix has a wider scope, and it has different emphases from those of the Business Portfolio Matrix. The former does not replace the latter. The TOWS Matrix is a conceptual framework for a systematic analysis that facilitates matching the external threats and opportunities with the internal weaknesses and strengths of the organization.

It has been common to suggest that companies identify their strengths and weaknesses, as well as the opportunities and threats in the external environment. But what is often overlooked is that combining these factors may require distinct strategic choices. To systematize these choices, the TOWS Matrix has been proposed; "T" stands for threats, "O" for opportunities, "W" for weaknesses, and "S" for strengths. The TOWS model starts with the threats because in many situations a company undertakes strategic planning as a result of a perceived crisis, problem, or threat.

Four Alternative Strategies

Figure 5-2 presents the four alternative strategies of the TOWS Matrix.* The strategies are based on the analysis of the external environment (threats and opportunities) and the internal environment (weaknesses and strengths).

1. The WT strategy (in the lower right-hand corner) aims to minimize both weaknesses and threats. It may require that the company, for example, form a joint venture, retrench, or even liquidate.

2. The WO strategy attempts to minimize the weaknesses and maximize the opportunities. Thus, a firm with certain weaknesses in some areas may either develop those areas within the enterprise or acquire the needed competencies (such as technology or persons with needed skills) from the outside, making it possible to take advantage of opportunities in the external environment.

3. The ST strategy is based on the organization's strengths to deal with threats in the environment. The aim is to maximize the former while minimizing

---

* Although the emphasis is on strategies in this discussion, similar analyses can be made for developing the more detailed tactics and action plans.

Figure 5-2

Internal factors / External factors	Internal strengths (S) e.g., strengths in management, operations, finance, marketing, R&D, engineering	Internal weaknesses (W) e.g., weaknesses in areas shown in the box of "strengths"
External opportunities (O) (Consider risks also) e.g., current and future economic conditions; political and social changes, new products, services, and technology	SO Strategy: Maxi-Maxi Potentially the most successful strategy, utilizing the organization's strengths to take advantage of opportunities	WO Strategy: Mini-Maxi e.g., developmental strategy to overcome weaknesses in order to take advantage of opportunities
External threats (T): e.g., lack of energy, competition, and areas similar to those shown in the "opportunities" box above	ST Strategy: Maxi-Mini e.g., use of strengths to cope with threats or to avoid threats	WT Strategy: Mini-Mini e.g., retrenchment, liquidation or joint venture

THE TOWS MATRIX FOR STRATEGY FORMULATION.

the latter. Thus, a company may use its technological, financial, managerial, or marketing strengths to cope with the threats of a new product introduced by its competitor.

4. The most desirable situation occurs when a company can use its strengths to take advantage of opportunities (the SO strategy). Indeed, it is the aim of enterprises to move from other positions in the matrix to this one. If they have weaknesses, they will strive to overcome them, making them strengths. If they face threats, they will cope with them so that they can focus on opportunities.

Time Dimension and the TOWS Matrix

So far, the factors displayed in the TOWS Matrix pertain to analysis at a particular point in time. However, external and internal environments are dynamic: Some factors change over time, while others change very little. Because of the dynamics in the environment, the strategy designer must prepare several TOWS Matrixes at different points in time, as shown in Figure 5-3. Thus, one may start with a TOWS analysis of the past, continue with an analysis of the present, and, perhaps most important, focus on different time periods (T_1, T_2, etc.) in the future.

THE PORTFOLIO MATRIX: A TOOL FOR ALLOCATING RESOURCES

The Business Portfolio Matrix was developed by the Boston Consulting Group (BCG).[4] Figure 5-4, a simplified version of the matrix, shows the linkages between the growth rate of the business and the relative competitive position

Figure 5-3

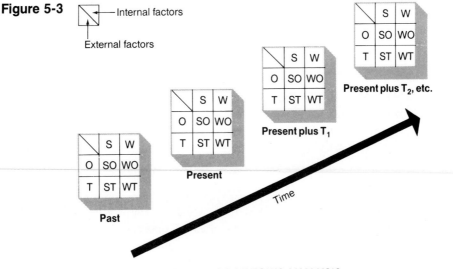

DYNAMICS OF TOWS ANALYSIS.

of the firm, identified by the market share. Businesses in the "question marks" quadrant, with a weak market share and a high growth rate, usually require cash investment so that they can become "stars," the businesses in the high-growth, strongly competitive position. These kinds of businesses have opportunities for growth and profit. The "cash cows," with a strong competitive position and a low growth rate, are usually well established in the market, and such enterprises are in the position of making the products at low cost. Therefore, the products of these enterprises provide the cash needed for their operation. The "dogs" are businesses with a low growth rate and a weak market-share position. These businesses are usually not profitable and generally should be disposed of.

The Portfolio Matrix was developed for large corporations with several divisions that are often organized around strategic business units (a topic to be discussed in Chapter 8). While portfolio analysis was popular in the 1970s, it is not without its critics, who contend that it is too simplistic. Also, the growth-rate criterion has been considered insufficient for the evaluation of an industry's attractiveness. Similarly, the market share as a yardstick for estimating the competitive position may be inadequate.[5]

MAJOR KINDS OF STRATEGIES AND POLICIES

For a business enterprise (and, with some modification, for other kinds of organizations as well), the major strategies and policies that give an overall direction to operations are likely to be in the following areas:*

---

*Although the term "strategies" is used in this section, some may be policies; there is a great deal of overlap between the two, as mentioned earlier in this chapter.

Growth

Growth strategies give answers to such questions as these: How much growth should occur? How fast? Where? How should it occur?

Finance

Every business enterprise and, for that matter, any nonbusiness enterprise must have a clear strategy for financing its operations. There are various ways of doing this and usually many serious limitations.

Organization

Organizational strategy has to do with the type of organizational pattern an enterprise will use. It answers practical questions. For example, how centralized or decentralized should decision-making authority be? What kinds of departmental patterns are most suitable? How should staff positions be designed? Naturally, organization structures furnish the system of roles and role relationships that help people accomplish objectives.

Personnel

There can be many major strategies in the area of human resources and relationships. They deal with such topics as union relations, compensation, selection, hiring, training, and appraisal, as well as with special areas such as job enrichment.

Figure 5-4

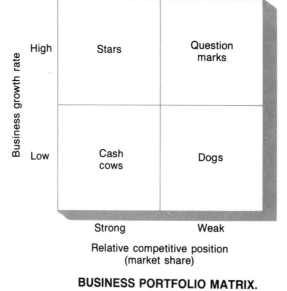

BUSINESS PORTFOLIO MATRIX.

Adapted from *The Product Portfolio Matrix,* copyright © 1970, The Boston Consulting Group, Inc.

Public Relations

Strategies in this area can hardly be independent; they must support other major strategies and efforts. They must also be designed in the light of the company's type of business, its closeness to the public, and its susceptibility to regulation by government agencies. In any area, strategies can be developed only if the right questions are asked. While no set of strategies can be formulated that will fit all organizations and situations, certain key questions will help any company discover what its strategies should be. The right questions will lead to answers. As examples, some key questions are presented below for two major strategic areas: products or services and marketing. With a little thought, you can devise key questions for other major strategic areas.

Products or Services

A business exists to furnish products or services. In a very real sense, profits are merely a measure — although an important one — of how well a company serves its customers. New products or services, more than any other single factor, determine what an enterprise is or will be.

The key questions in this area can be summarized as follows:

What is our business?

Who are our customers?

What do our customers want?

How much will our customers buy and at what price?

Do we wish to be a product leader?

Do we wish to develop our own new products?

What advantages do we have in serving customer needs?

How should we respond to existing and potential competition?

How far can we go in serving customer needs?

What profits can we expect?

What basic form should our strategy take?

Marketing

Marketing strategies are designed to guide managers in getting products or services to customers and in encouraging customers to buy. Marketing strategies are closely related to product strategies; they must be interrelated and mutually supportive. As a matter of fact, Peter Drucker regards the two basic business functions as innovation (e.g., the creation of new goods or services) and marketing. A business can scarcely survive without at least one of these functions and preferably both.

The key questions that serve as guides for establishing a marketing strategy are these:

Where are our customers, and why do they buy?

How do our customers buy?

How is it best for us to sell?

Do we have something to offer that competitors do not?

Do we wish to take legal steps to discourage competition?

Do we need, and can we supply, supporting services?

What are the best pricing strategy and policy for our operation?

THREE GENERIC COMPETITIVE STRATEGIES BY PORTER

Professor Michael Porter at Harvard identified three generic strategies a firm may adopt.[6] These strategies are generic because they may be suitable on a broad level for different kinds of organizations. Any enterprise, however, may use more than one strategy.

Overall Cost Leadership Strategy

This strategic approach aims at reductions in cost, based to a great extent on experience. Thus, the emphasis may be on keeping a close watch on costs in areas such as research and development, sales, and service. The objective is for a company to have a low cost structure compared with that of its competitors. This strategy often requires a large relative market share and cost-efficient facilities, as illustrated by the well-publicized Lincoln Electric Company, which produces arc welding and supplies.

Differentiation Strategy

A company following a differentiation strategy attempts to offer something unique in the industry in respect to products or services. Porsche sports cars are indeed special; so is the Caterpillar Company, which is known for its prompt service and availability of spare parts.

Focused Strategy

A company adopting a focused strategy concentrates on special groups of customers, a particular product line, a specific geographic region, or other aspects that become the focal point of the firm's efforts. Rather than serving the total industry with its products or services, an enterprise may emphasize a specific segment of the market. This may be accomplished by a low-cost strategy, differentiation, or both.

EFFECTIVE IMPLEMENTATION OF STRATEGIES

Strategic planning, to be effective, must go beyond the allocation of resources to achieve organizational objectives. It must be accompanied by strategic thinking that also includes designing an appropriate organization structure, an effective management information system, a budgeting system to facilitate the accomplishments of strategic objectives, and a reward system that supports the strategy.

Strategic Planning Failures and Some Recommendations

Let us look first at some of the reasons why strategic planning may fail and then consider what can be done to improve such planning.

A recent study attributed strategic planning failures to the following factors:[7]

1. Managers are inadequately prepared for strategic planning.

2. The information for preparing the plans is insufficient for planning for action.

3. The goals of the organization are too vague to be of value.

4. The business units (a distinct form of organization that will be discussed in Chapter 8) are not clearly identified.

5. The reviews of the strategic plans of the business units are not done effectively.

6. The link between strategic planning and control is insufficient.

Strategic planning is the job of line managers, who, especially in large companies, may be assisted by staff planners. But in order to do an effective job, line managers must be coached in strategic planning.

The overall strategic plan needs to be supplemented by specific action plans. This, in general, requires the contributions of line managers from different functional departments, such as research and development, engineering, production, marketing, financing, and personnel, to plan for the people required to carry out the plan. But integrating the various functional groups is not easy. Thus, companies have set up a task force, with heavy presentation of middle managers, to cut across the functional barriers.

Goals and objectives, to be meaningful, have to be more than platitudes such as "achieving excellence." The degree of specificity depends on the level in the hierarchy of objectives, as pointed out in Chapter 4.

When organizations become too large, they are frequently broken down into strategic business units (SBUs). These units are expected to operate as if they were relatively independent businesses. But it is important that the boundaries of the different SBUs are correctly drawn. Otherwise, strategic planning may be difficult.

Consider, for example, a large organization with many SBUs, each having its own strategic plan, each competing with the others for scarce resources, each making overly optimistic projections for its own strategic plan. Conflicts are bound to arise at the corporate level. It is indeed an art of the top executive to integrate these strategic plans into a meaningful whole that serves the interest of the total organization. SBUs will be discussed in greater detail in Chapter 8, on departmentation.

Plans are the basis for control. Without plans no control is possible. Too often strategic plans and budgets are in conflict. Too often budgets are based on last year's budgets rather than on the strategic plan. Too often budgets are prepared without a specific action plan to implement the strategy. Strategic plans can also be thwarted by a compensation system that rewards short-term results at the expense of the long-term health of the organization.

From this discussion it is clear that strategic planning needs to be integrated with the total managerial process, such as the organization structure; the appraisal, reward, and motivational system; and the controls used to measure performance against objectives. This is just another illustration that effective management requires a systems approach that recognizes the interdependence of the managerial activities.

Successful Implementation of Strategies

It is one thing to develop clear and meaningful strategies. It is another matter, and one of very great practical importance, to implement strategies effectively.[8] If strategic planning is to be successful, certain steps must be taken to implement it. Following are eight recommendations that should be considered by managers who wish to put their strategies to work.

Communicating strategies to all key decision-making managers   It does little good to formulate meaningful strategies unless they are communicated to all those managers who are in a position to make decisions on programs and plans designed to implement them. Nothing has been communicated unless it is clear to the receiver. Strategies may be clear to the executive committee members and the chief executive who participated in developing them. However, strategies should be communicated in writing, and top executives and their subordinates must make sure that everyone involved in implementing strategies understands them.

Developing and communicating planning premises   The importance of planning premises will be stressed later in this chapter. Managers must develop premises critical to plans and decisions, explain them to all those in the decision-making chain, and give instructions to develop programs and make decisions in line with them. Too few organizations do this. But if premises do not include key assumptions about the environment in which plans will operate, decisions are likely to be based on personal assumptions and predilections. This will almost certainly lead to a collection of uncoordinated plans.

Ensuring that action plans contribute to and reflect major objectives and strategies
Action plans are tactical or operational programs and decisions, major or minor, that take place in various parts of an organization. If they do not reflect desired objectives and strategies, the result will be vague hopes or useless intentions. If care is not taken in this area, strategic planning is not likely to have a bottom-line impact, that is, to have an important effect on company profits.

There are various ways of making sure that action plans contribute to major goals. If every manager understands strategies, all managers can certainly review the recommendations of staff advisers and line subordinates to see that they contribute and are consistent. It might even be a good idea for major decisions to be reviewed by an appropriate small committee, such as one including a manager's superior, the superior's superior, and a staff specialist. Budgets should also be reviewed with objectives and strategies in mind.

Reviewing strategies regularly Even carefully developed strategies may cease to be suitable if conditions change. Therefore, they should be reviewed from time to time, certainly not less than once a year for major strategies and perhaps more often.

Developing contingency strategies and programs If considerable change in competitive factors or other elements in the environment may occur, strategies for such contingencies should be formulated. No one, of course, can wait to make plans until a future environment is certain. Even if there is considerable uncertainty and events may occur that make a given set of objectives, strategies, or programs obsolete, a manager has no choice but to proceed on the most credible set of premises he or she can come up with at a given time. But even then, one need not be totally unprepared if certain possible contingencies do occur. Contingency plans can provide a degree of preparation.

Making the organization structure fit planning needs The organization structure, with its system of delegations, should be designed to help managers accomplish goals and make the decisions necessary to put plans into effect. If possible, one person should be responsible for the accomplishment of each goal and for the implementation of strategies to achieve this goal. In other words, end-result areas and key tasks should be identified and assigned to a single position as far down the organization structure as is feasible. Since such an assignment sometimes cannot be made, there may be no alternative but to utilize a form of matrix organization, a type of organization structure that will be discussed in Chapter 8. If this is done, however, the responsibilities of the various positions in the matrix should be clearly defined.

The role of staff analyst in an organization structure should be so defined as to make it clear that the job of people in a staff position is to advise. Staff studies and recommendations then enter the decision system at the various points where decisions are actually made. Unless they do so, the end result will be independent staff work of no value for planning.

Continuing to emphasize planning and implementing strategy Even if an organization has a workable system of objectives and strategies and their implementation, the system can easily fail unless responsible managers continue to stress the nature and importance of these elements. This process may seem tedious and unnecessarily repetitious, but it is the best way to make sure that members of an organization learn about them. Teaching does not necessarily mean conducting seminars; rather, much of the teaching can take place in the day-to-day interaction between superiors and subordinates.

Creating a company climate that forces planning People tend to allow problems and crises of today to interfere with effective planning for tomorrow. The only way to ensure that planning will be done is to develop strategies carefully and to take pains to implement them.

PREMISING AND FORECASTING

One of the essential and often overlooked steps in effective and coordinate planning is premising, which is the establishment of, and the agreement by managers and planners to utilize, consistent assumptions critical to plans under consideration. **Planning premises** are defined as *the anticipated environment in which plans are expected to operate. They include assumptions or forecasts of the future and known conditions that will affect the operation of plans.* Examples are prevailing policies and existing company plans that control the basic nature of supporting plans.

Planning Premises versus Future Expectancies

A distinction should be drawn between forecasts that are planning premises and forecasts that are translated into future expectancies, usually in financial terms, from actual plans developed. For example, a forecast to determine future business conditions, sales volume, or political environment furnishes premises on which to develop plans. However, a forecast of the costs or revenues from a new capital investment translates a planning program into future expectations. In the first case, the forecast is a prerequisite of planning; in the second case, the forecast is a result of planning.

At the same time, plans themselves and forecasts of their future effects often become premises for other plans. The decision by an electric utility company to construct a nuclear generating plant, for example, creates conditions that give rise to premises for transmission line plans and other plans necessarily dependent upon the generating plant being built.

Effective Premising

Since so many failures occur in planning and planning coordination through poor premising, special attention should be given to this step in planning. It is difficult to identify the factors in a future environment that will affect a manager's plans. But it is also difficult, once these factors have been identified, to achieve practical implementation of consistent and meaningful planning premises. Effective premising is a four-part process.

Selection of the premises which bear materially on the programs   There are many premises that are of strategic importance to one enterprise but not to another. Thus, top managers of every enterprise, and to a certain extent every manager within it, should select their own premises. This basic question should be asked and answered: What factors in the environment, whether external or internal, will influence most the course of plans for which I am responsible?

Development of alternative premises for contingency planning   Since the future cannot be predicted with great certainty, managers should develop plans given different assumptions.

Verification of the consistency of premises   One way of ensuring that premises are consistent is to have each planning staff at headquarters and divisional levels recommend its crucial planning premises, applicable to an enterprise or a division, to the appropriate top executive. Having the top executive approve these premises, usually after consultation with his or her staff, will ensure that the assumptions selected and formulated will be the ones on which the enterprise or division is willing to stake its future.

Communication of the premises   One of the first requirements of effective premise communication is to analyze all managers' "need to know," interpreting this broadly rather than narrowly, and to make sure that premises important for their planning are made available to them. Some companies have found it wise to develop and disseminate to those who need it a manual of planning premises, incorporating assumptions with wide application to planning. These will, of course, be kept current as premises change. In addition, whenever a budget proposal or program recommendation is requested and whenever a major program assignment is made, superiors should develop and distribute supplementary planning premises for the managers reporting to them.

Strategies and policies, then, give direction to the enterprise and provide a framework for developing tactics and other action plans. Meaningful premises facilitate consistency and coordination of plans.

SUMMARY

There are different definitions of strategy. A comprehensive one refers to the determination of basic long-term objectives and of courses of action and allocations of resources to achieve these aims. Policies are general statements or understandings which guide managers' thinking in decision making. Both strategies and policies give direction to plans. They provide the framework for plans and serve as a basis for the development of tactics and other managerial activities.

The strategic planning model shows how the process works. It identifies the critical elements of this process and indicates how they relate to each other. The TOWS Matrix is a modern tool for analyzing the threats and opportunities in the external environment and the relationships to the organization's (internal) weaknesses and strengths. The Portfolio Matrix is a tool for allocating resources, linking the business growth rate with the relative competitive position (measured by market share) of the firm.

Major kinds of strategies and policies need to be developed in areas such as growth, finance, organization, personnel, public relations, products or services, and marketing. Professor Porter identified three generic competitive strategies related to overall cost leadership, differentiation, and focus.

To implement strategies effectively, managers must communicate the strategies and planning premises to all who should know them and must make sure that the plans contribute to and reflect the strategies and goals they serve. Managers also must review strategies regularly, develop contingency strategies, and be sure that the organization structure of the enterprise fits its planning program. Managers need to make learning about planning and implementing strategy an ongoing process.

Planning premises are the anticipated environment. They include assumptions or forecasts of future and known conditions. Effective premising requires proper selection of premises, development of alternative premises for contingency planning, provision for consistency, and communication of the planning premises.

KEY IDEAS AND CONCEPTS FOR REVIEW

Strategies

Policies

Key elements in the strategic planning process

TOWS Matrix by Weihrich

Portfolio Matrix by the Boston Consulting Group

Major kinds of strategies

Three generic strategies by Porter

Requirements for successful implementation of strategies

Planning premises

Requirements for effective premising

FOR DISCUSSION

1. How can you distinguish between strategies and policies?

2. Are strategies and policies as important in a nonbusiness enterprise (such as a labor union, the State Department, a hospital, or a city fire department) as they are in a business? Why and how?

3. Why are contingency strategies important?

4. Choose an organization you know and identify its strengths and weaknesses. What are its special opportunities and threats in the external environment?

5. How would you make an organizational appraisal of your college or university? What kind of "business" is the school in?

6. How can strategies be implemented effectively?

7. Identify major premises which, in your judgment, the Ford Motor Company would need in order to forecast its sales of automobiles for the next 2 years.

8. How would you make premising effective?

EXERCISES/ACTION STEPS

1. Take the concepts of strategic planning and relate them to your life. What are your personal strengths and weaknesses? On the basis of this analysis, what would be a suitable "mission" for you in this world?

2. Take a major decision problem facing you and outline the more critical planning premises surrounding it. How many of these are matters of knowledge, and how many are matters of forecast? How many are qualitative, and how many are quantitative? How many are within your control?

INTERNATIONAL CASE:
McDONALD'S: SERVING FAST FOOD AROUND THE WORLD[9]

Ray Kroc opened the first McDonald's restaurant in 1955. He offered a limited menu of high-quality, moderately priced food served fast in spotless surroundings. McDonald's "QSC&V" (quality, service, cleanliness, and value) was a hit. The chain expanded into every state in the nation. By 1983 it had over 6000 restaurants in the United States.

In 1967 McDonald's opened its first restaurant outside the United States, in Canada. By 1985 international sales represented about one fifth of McDonald's total revenues. Yet fast food has barely touched many cultures. While 90 percent of the Japanese in Tokyo have eaten a McDonald's hamburger, few outside the cities know what a hamburger is. In Europe, McDonald's maintains a very small percentage of restaurant sales but commands a large market share of the fast-food market.

The taste for fast food, American style, is growing more rapidly abroad than at home. McDonald's international sales have been increasing by a large percentage every year. Every day more than 18 million people in over 40 countries eat at McDonald's.

Its traditional menu has been surprisingly successful. People with diverse dining habits have adopted burgers and fries wholeheartedly. Before McDonald's introduced the Japanese to french fries, potatoes were used in Japan only to make starch. The Germans thought hamburgers were people from the city of Hamburg.

The fast, family-oriented service, the cleanliness, and the value accounted for much of McDonald's success. McDonald's was one of the first restaurants in Europe to welcome families with children. Not only are children welcomed, but in many restaurants they are entertained with crayons and paper, a playland, or maybe even Ronald McDonald, who can speak twenty languages.

McDonald's golden arches promise the same basic menu and QSC&V in every restaurant. Its products, handling and cooking procedures, and kitchen layouts are standardized and strictly controlled. McDonald's revoked the first French franchises because they failed to meet its standards for fast service and cleanliness, even though they were highly profitable. This may have delayed its expansion in France.

The restaurants are run by local management and crew. Owners and managers must attend the Hamburger University near Chicago to learn how to operate a McDonald's restaurant and maintain QSC&V. The main campus library and modern electronic classrooms (which include simultaneous translation systems) are the envy of many universities.

McDonald's ensures consistent products by controlling every stage of the distribution. Regional distribution centers purchase products and distribute them to individual restaurants. The centers will buy from local suppliers if the suppliers can meet detailed specifications. McDonald's has had to make some concessions to available products. For example, it is difficult to introduce the Idaho potato in Europe.

McDonald's uses essentially the same competitive strategy in every country: Be first in a market and establish your brand as rapidly as possible by advertising very heavily. New restaurants are opened with a bang. So many people attended the opening of one Tokyo restaurant that the police closed the street to

vehicles. The strategy has helped McDonald's develop a strong market share in the fast-food market, even though its U.S. competitors and new local competitors quickly enter the market.

The advertising campaigns are based on local themes and reflect the different environments. In Japan, where burgers are a snack, McDonald's competes against confectioneries and the new "fast sushi" restaurants. Many of the charitable causes McDonald's supports abroad have been recommended by the local restaurants.

McDonald's has been willing to relinquish the most control to its Far Eastern operations, where many restaurants are joint ventures with local entrepreneurs who own 50 percent or more of the restaurant.

European and South American restaurants are generally company operated or franchised (although there are many affiliates — joint ventures — in France). Like the U.S. franchises, restaurants abroad are allowed to experiment with their menus. In Japan, hamburgers are smaller because they are considered a snack. The "Quarter Pounder" didn't make much sense to people on a metric system, so it is called a "Double Burger." Some of the German restaurants serve beer; some French restaurants serve wine. Some Far Eastern McDonald's offer oriental noodles. But these new items must not disrupt existing operations.

1. What opportunities and threats did McDonald's face? How did it overcome them? What alternatives could it have chosen?

2. Before McDonald's entered the European market, few people believed that fast food could be successful in Europe. Why do you think McDonald's succeeded? What strategies did it follow? How did these differ from its strategies in Asia?

3. What is McDonald's basic philosophy? How does it enforce this philosophy and adapt to different environments?

REFERENCES

1. Myron Magnet, "How Top Managers Make a Company's Toughest Decision," *Fortune* (Mar. 18, 1985), pp. 52–57. See also Roger Evered, "The Strategic Decision Process," in Don Hellriegel and John W. Slocum, Jr. (eds.), *Management in the World Today* (Reading, Mass.: Addison-Wesley Publishing Company, 1975).

2. Peter Lorange, Michael F. Scott Morton, and Sumantra Ghoshal, *Strategic Control* (St. Paul: West Publishing Company, 1986).

3. This discussion and the accompanying figures have been adapted from Heinz Weihrich, "The TOWS Matrix — A Tool for Situational Analysis," *Long Range Planning,* vol. 15, no. 2 (1982), pp. 54–66.

4. Bruce D. Henderson, "The Product Portfolio," in *Perspectives* (Boston Consulting Group, 1970); Bruce D. Henderson, "The Experience Curve Revisited" (Boston Consulting Group, undated); Barry Hedly, "Strategy and the 'Business Portfolio,'" *Long Range Planning* (February 1977), pp. 9–15; Bruce D. Henderson, "The Application and Misapplication of the Experience Curve," *Journal of Business Strategy* (Winter 1984).

5. Charles W. Hofer and Dan E. Schendel, *Strategy Formulation: Analytical Concepts* (St. Paul: West Publishing Company, 1978); Walter Kiechel III, "Oh Where, Oh Where Has My Little Dog Gone? or My Cash Cow? or My Star?" *Fortune* (November 1981), pp. 148–154; Richard G. Hamermesh and Roderick

E. White, "Manage beyond Portfolio Analysis," *Harvard Business Review* (January–February 1984), pp. 103–109.

6. Michael E. Porter, *Competitive Strategy* (New York: The Free Press, 1980). See also by the same author *Competitive Advantage* (New York: The Free Press, 1985).

7. Daniel H. Gray, "Uses and Misuses of Strategic Planning," *Harvard Business Review* (January–February 1986), pp. 89–97.

8. Much of this is drawn from Harold Koontz, "Making Strategic Planning Work," *Business Horizons* (April 1976), pp. 37–47.

9. The case is based on a variety of sources, including interviews and a visit to Hamburger University, as well as the following: Richard Gibson, "McDonald's Sees Nothing to Beef About," *The Wall Street Journal* (Apr. 1, 1988); Frederick H. Katayama, "Japan's Big Mac," *Fortune* (Sept. 15, 1986), pp. 114–120; Stephen Kindel, "Where's the Growth?" *Forbes* (Apr. 23, 1984), p. 80; Nancy Kule, "Fast Food Expands in Europe," *Restaurant Hospitality* (December 1983); Kenneth Labich, "America's International Winners," *Fortune* (Apr. 14, 1986), pp. 34–46; Joan Lang, "McDonald's Japan," *Restaurant Business* (Nov. 1, 1983), pp. 168–169; McDonald's Annual Reports, 1983 and 1984, *Standard & Poor's Industry Survey* (1983); "Those Doubts about McDonald's," *Financial World* (June 15, 1983), pp. 38–40.

CHAPTER 6

Decision Making

CHAPTER OBJECTIVES

After reading this chapter, you should understand:

1. What decision making is
2. The principle of the limiting factor
3. The nature and process of evaluation of alternatives
4. Three approaches for selecting from among alternatives
5. The nature of programmed and unprogrammed decisions
6. Modern approaches to decision making in light of uncertainties
7. Factors determining the importance of the decision
8. The utility of decision support systems (DSSs)
9. The systems approach to decision making

Decision making is defined as *selection of a course of action from among alternatives;* it is at the core of planning. A plan cannot be said to exist unless a decision — a commitment of resources, direction, or reputation — has been made. Until that point, there are only planning studies and analyses. Managers sometimes see decision making as their central job because they must constantly choose what is to be done, who is to do it, and when, where, and occasionally even how it will be done. Decision making is, however, only a step in planning, even when it is done quickly and with little thought or when it influences action for only a few minutes. It is also part of everyone's daily living. A course of action can seldom be judged alone, because virtually every decision must be geared to other plans. The stereotype of the finger-snapping, button-pushing managerial mogul fades as the requirements of systematic research and analysis preceding a decision come into focus.

THE IMPORTANCE AND LIMITATIONS OF RATIONAL DECISION MAKING

In the discussion of the steps in planning in Chapter 3, decision making was considered a major part of planning. As a matter of fact, given an awareness of an opportunity and a goal, the decision process is really the core of planning. Thus, in this context, the process leading to making a decision might be thought of as (1) premising, (2) identifying alternatives, (3) evaluating alternatives in terms of the goal sought, and (4) choosing an alternative, that is, making a decision.

Although this chapter emphasizes the logic and techniques of choosing a course of action, the discussion will show that decision making is really one of the steps in planning.[1]

Rationality in Decision Making

It is frequently said that effective decision making must be rational. But what is rationality? When is a person thinking or deciding rationally?

People acting or deciding rationally are attempting to reach some goal that cannot be attained without action. They must have a clear understanding of alternative courses by which a goal can be reached under existing circumstances and limitations. They also must have the information and the ability to analyze and evaluate alternatives in the light of the goal sought. Finally, they must have a desire to come to the best solution by selecting the alternative that most effectively satisfies goal achievement.

People seldom achieve complete rationality, particularly in managing.[2] In the first place, since no one can make decisions affecting the past, decisions must operate for the future, and the future almost invariably involves uncertainties. In the second place, it is difficult to recognize all the alternatives that might be followed to reach a goal; this is particularly true when decision making involves opportunities to do something that has not been done before. Moreover, in most instances, not all alternatives can be analyzed, even with the newest available analytical techniques and computers.

Limited or "Bounded" Rationality

A manager must settle for limited rationality, or "bounded" rationality. In other words, limitations of information, time, and certainty limit rationality even though a manager tries earnestly to be completely rational. Since managers cannot be completely rational in practice, they sometimes allow their dislike of risk — the desire to "play it safe" — to interfere with their desire to reach the best solution under the circumstances. Herbert Simon has called this **satisficing,** that is, picking a course of action that is satisfactory or good enough under the circumstances. Although many managerial decisions are made with a desire to "get by" as safely as possible, most managers do attempt to make the best decisions they can within the limits of rationality and in the light of the size and nature of risks involved.

> PERSPECTIVE:
> COMPAQ VS. IBM
>
> In 1986 Compaq announced a new personal computer model, the Deskpro 386. The new model was based on Intel's 80386 chip, which was considerably faster than the one in the IBM AT model. The decision to market this new computer in 1986 was rather risky and based on incomplete information. It also was a departure from Compaq's past strategy, which had proved to be very successful. Previously, Compaq had followed IBM standards by making a computer that used IBM software.
>
> But with the Deskpro 386, Compaq assumed the lead over the corporate giant IBM, which was expected to market a computer based on the 80386 technology in 1987.
>
> What, then, was Compaq's dilemma? On the one hand, the company had a head start over its major competitor and gained considerable market share. On the other hand, the new IBM could have included some proprietary features that would have made the Deskpro 386 incompatible with IBM's computer. Moreover, the success of a personal computer depends to a large extent on its software (programs). Thus, software writers may not have been willing to invest their efforts until it was clear that the Compaq computer was indeed truly compatible with the one IBM planned to introduce.[3]

The Principle of the Limiting Factor

Assuming that we know what our goals are and agree on clear planning premises, the first step of decision making is to develop alternatives. There are almost always alternatives to any course of action; indeed, if there seems to be only one way of doing a thing, that way is probably wrong. If we can think of only one course of action, clearly we have not thought hard enough.

The ability to develop alternatives is often as important as being able to select correctly from among them. On the other hand, ingenuity, research, and common sense will often unearth so many choices that all of them cannot be adequately evaluated. The manager needs help in this situation, and this help, as well as assistance in choosing the best alternative, is found in the concept of the limiting or strategic factor.

A **limiting factor** is something that stands in the way of accomplishing a desired objective. Recognizing the limiting factors in a given situation makes it possible to narrow the search for alternatives to those that will overcome the limiting factors.

The **principle of the limiting factor** is as follows: *By recognizing and overcoming those factors that stand critically in the way of a goal, the best alternative course of action can be selected.*

EVALUATION OF ALTERNATIVES

Once appropriate alternatives have been found, the next step in planning is to evaluate them and select the one that will best contribute to the goal. This is the point of ultimate decision making, although decisions must also be made in the other steps of planning — in selecting goals, in choosing critical premises, and even in selecting alternatives.

Quantitative and Qualitative Factors

In comparing alternative plans for achieving an objective, people are likely to think exclusively of **quantitative factors.** These are factors that can be measured in numerical terms, such as time or various fixed and operating costs. No one would question the importance of this type of analysis, but the success of the venture would be endangered if intangible, or qualitative, factors were ignored. **Qualitative,** or **intangible, factors** are those that are difficult to measure numerically, such as the quality of labor relations, the risk of technological change, or the international political climate. There are all too many instances in which an excellent quantitative plan was destroyed by an unforeseen war, a fine marketing plan was made inoperable by a long transportation strike, or a rational borrowing plan was hampered by an economic recession. These illustrations point out the importance of giving attention to both quantitative and qualitative factors when comparing alternatives.

To evaluate and compare the intangible factors in a planning problem and make decisions, a manager must first recognize these factors and then determine whether a reasonable quantitative measurement can be given them. If not, he or she should find out as much as possible about the factors, perhaps rate them in terms of their importance, compare their probable influence on the outcome with that of the quantitative factors, and then come to a decision. This decision may give predominant weight to a single intangible.

Such a procedure allows the manager to make decisions on the basis of the weight of the total evidence. It does involve fallible personal judgments; however, few managerial decisions can be so accurately quantified that judgment is unnecessary. Decision making is seldom simple. It is not without justification that the successful executive has been cynically described as a person who guesses right.

Marginal Analysis

Evaluating alternatives may involve utilizing the techniques of **marginal analysis** to compare additional revenues arising from additional costs. Where the objective is to maximize profits, this goal will be reached, as elementary economics teaches, when the additional revenues and additional costs are equal. In other words, if the additional revenues of a larger quantity are greater than its additional costs, more profits can be made by producing more. However, if the additional revenues of the larger quantity are less than its additional costs, a larger profit can be made by producing less.

Marginal analysis can be used in comparing factors other than costs and revenues. For example, to find the best output of a machine, inputs could be varied against outputs until the additional input equals the additional output.

This would then be the point of maximum efficiency of the machine. Or the number of subordinates reporting to a manager might conceivably be increased to the point at which additional savings in costs, better communication and morale, and other factors equal additional losses in effectiveness of control, leadership, and similar factors.

Cost Effectiveness Analysis

An improvement on, or variation of, traditional marginal analysis is cost effectiveness, or cost benefit, analysis. **Cost effectiveness analysis** seeks the best ratio of benefits and costs; this means, for example, finding the least costly way of reaching an objective or getting the greatest value for given expenditures.

In its simplest terms, cost effectiveness analysis is a technique for choosing the best plan when the objectives are less specific than sales, costs, or profits. For example, a defense objective may be deterring or repelling enemy attack, a social objective may be reducing air pollution or retraining the unemployed, and a business objective may be participating in social objectives through a program of training unemployables.

Nonquantifiable objectives can sometimes be given some fairly specific measures of effectiveness. In a program with the general objective of improving employee morale, for example, a company can measure effectiveness by such verifiable factors as employee turnover, absenteeism, or volume of grievances and can supplement these measurements with such subjective inputs as the judgment of qualified experts.

The major features of cost effectiveness analysis are that it focuses on the results of a program, helps weigh the potential benefits of each alternative against its potential cost, and involves a comparison of the alternatives in terms of the overall advantages.

Although the decision on cost effectiveness involves the same steps as any planning decision, its major distinguishing features are the following:

1. Objectives are normally oriented to output or end result and are usually not precise.

2. Alternatives ordinarily represent total systems, programs, or strategies for meeting objectives.

3. The measures of effectiveness must be relevant to objectives and set in terms as precise as possible, although some may not be subject to quantification.

4. Cost estimates may include nonmonetary as well as monetary costs.

5. Decision standards, while definite but not usually as specific as cost or profit, may include achieving a given objective at least cost, achieving it with resources available, or providing for a trade-off of cost for effectiveness, particularly in the light of the claims of other programs.

SELECTING AN ALTERNATIVE: THREE APPROACHES

When selecting from among alternatives, managers can use three basic approaches: (1) experience, (2) experimentation, and (3) research and analysis. (See Figure 6-1.)

Experience

Reliance on past experience probably plays a larger part than it deserves in decision making. Experienced managers usually believe, often without realizing it, that the things they have successfully accomplished and the mistakes they have made furnish almost infallible guides to the future. This attitude is likely to be more pronounced the more experience a manager has had and the higher in an organization he or she has risen.

To some extent, experience is the best teacher. The very fact that managers have reached their position appears to justify their past decisions. Moreover, the process of thinking problems through, making decisions, and seeing programs succeed or fail does make for a degree of good judgment (at times bordering on intuition). Many people, however, do not profit by their errors, and there are managers who seem never to gain the seasoned judgment required by modern enterprise.

Relying on past experience as a guide for future action can be dangerous, however. In the first place, most people do not recognize the underlying reasons for their mistakes or failures. In the second place, the lessons of experience may be entirely inapplicable to new problems. Good decisions must be evaluated against future events, while experience belongs to the past.

Figure 6-1

**BASES FOR SELECTING FROM AMONG
ALTERNATIVE COURSES OF ACTION.**

On the other hand, if a person carefully analyzes experience, rather than blindly following it, and if he or she distills from experience the fundamental reasons for success or failure, then experience can be useful as a basis for decision analysis. A successful program, a well-managed company, a profitable product promotion, or any other decision that turns out well may furnish useful data for such distillation. Just as scientists do not hesitate to build upon the research of others and would be foolish indeed merely to duplicate it, managers can learn much from others.

Experimentation

An obvious way to decide among alternatives is to try one of them and see what happens. Experimentation is often used in scientific inquiry. People often argue that it should be employed more often in managing and that the only way a manager can make sure some plans are right — especially in view of the intangible factors — is to try the various alternatives and see which is best.

The experimental technique is likely to be the most expensive of all techniques, especially if a program requires heavy expenditures in capital and personnel and if the firm cannot afford to vigorously attempt several alternatives. Besides, after an experiment has been tried, there may still be doubt about what it proved, since the future may not duplicate the present. This technique, therefore, should be used only after considering other alternatives.

On the other hand, there are many decisions that cannot be made until the best course of action can be ascertained by experiment. Even reflections on experience or the most careful research may not assure managers of correct decisions. This is nowhere better illustrated than in the planning of a new airplane.

Experimentation is used in other ways. A firm may test a new product in a certain market before expanding its sale nationwide. Organizational techniques are often tried in a branch office or plant before being applied over an entire company. A candidate for a management job may be tested in the job during the incumbent's vacation.

PERSPECTIVE:
EXPERIMENTATION IN BUILDING AN AIRPLANE

The airplane manufacturer may draw from personal experience and that of other plane manufacturers and new plane users. Engineers and economists may make extensive studies of stress, vibration, fuel consumption, speed, space allocation, and other factors. But all these studies do not answer every question about the flight characteristics and economics of a successful plane; therefore, some experimentation is almost always involved in the process of selecting the right course to follow. Ordinarily, a first-production, or prototype, airplane is constructed and tested, and, on the basis of these tests, production airplanes are made according to a somewhat revised design.

Research and Analysis

One of the most effective techniques for selecting from alternatives when major decisions are involved is research and analysis. This approach means solving a problem by first comprehending it. It thus involves a search for relationships among the more critical of the variables, constraints, and premises that bear upon the goal sought. It is the pencil-and-paper (or, better, the computer-and-printout) approach to decision making.

Solving a planning problem requires breaking it into its component parts and studying the various quantitative and qualitative factors. Study and analysis are likely to be far cheaper than experimentation. Hours of time and reams of paper used for analyses usually cost much less than trying the various alternatives. In manufacturing airplanes, for example, if careful research has not preceded the building and testing of the prototype airplane and its parts, the resulting costs would be enormous.

A major step in the research-and-analysis approach is to develop a model simulating the problem. Thus, architects often make models of buildings in the form of extensive blueprints or three-dimensional renditions. Engineers test models of airplane wings and missiles in a wind tunnel. But the most useful simulation is likely to be a representation of the variables in a problem situation by mathematical terms and relationships. Conceptualizing a problem is a major step toward its solution. The physical sciences have long relied on mathematical models to do this, and it is encouraging to see this method being applied to managerial decision making.

One of the most comprehensive research-and-analysis approaches to decision making is operations research. Since this is an important tool for production and operations management, it will be discussed more fully in Chapter 20.

PROGRAMMED AND NONPROGRAMMED DECISIONS

A distinction can be made between programmed and nonprogrammed decisions.[4] A **programmed decision,** as shown in Figure 6-2, is applied to structured or routine problems. Lathe operators have specifications and rules that tell them whether the part they made is acceptable, has to be discarded, or should be reworked. Another example of a programmed decision is the reordering of standard inventory items. (In fact, there is a formula for doing this, which will be discussed in Chapter 20.) This kind of decision is used for routine and repetitive work; it relies primarily on previously established criteria. It is, in effect, decision making by precedent.

Nonprogrammed decisions are used for unstructured, novel, and ill-defined situations of a nonrecurring nature. Examples are the introduction of the Macintosh computer by Apple Computer, Inc., the development of the four-wheel-drive passenger car by Audi, and the marketing of a small video camera by Kodak. In fact, strategic decisions, in general, are nonprogrammed decisions, since they require subjective judgments.

Figure 6-2

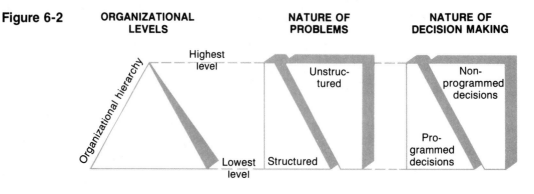

NATURE OF PROBLEMS AND DECISION MAKING IN THE ORGANIZATION.

Most decisions are neither completely programmed nor completely non-programmed; they are a combination of both. As Figure 6-2 indicates, most nonprogrammed decisions are made by upper-level managers; this is because upper-level managers have to deal with unstructured problems.[5] Problems at lower levels of the organization are often routine and well structured, requiring less decision discretion by managers and nonmanagers.

DECISION MAKING UNDER CERTAINTY, UNCERTAINTY, AND RISK

Virtually all decisions are made in an environment of at least some uncertainty.[6] However, the degree will vary from relative certainty to great uncertainty. There are certain risks involved in making decisions.

In a situation involving certainty, people are reasonably sure about what will happen when they make a decision. The information is available and is considered to be reliable, and the cause and effect relationships are known.

In a situation of uncertainty, on the other hand, people have only a meager data base, they do not know whether or not the data are reliable, and they are very unsure about whether or not the situation may change.[7] Moreover, they cannot evaluate the interactions of the different variables. For example, a corporation that decides to expand its operation in a strange country may know little about the country's culture, laws, economic environment, and politics. The political situation may be so volatile that even the experts cannot predict a possible change in government.

In a risk situation, factual information may exist, but it may be incomplete. To improve decision making, one may estimate the objective probabilities of an outcome by using, for example, mathematical models.[8] On the other hand, subjective probability, based on judgment and experience, may be used. Fortunately, there are a number of tools available that help managers make more effective decisions.

MODERN APPROACHES TO DECISION MAKING UNDER UNCERTAINTY

A number of modern techniques improve the quality of decision making under the normal conditions of uncertainty. Among the most important of these are (1) risk analysis, (2) decision trees, and (3) preference theory.

Risk Analysis

All intelligent decision makers dealing with uncertainty like to know the size and nature of the risk they are taking in choosing a course of action. One of the deficiencies in using the traditional approaches of operations research for problem solving is that many of the data used in a model are merely estimates and others are based upon probabilities. The ordinary practice is to have staff specialists come up with "best estimates." However, new techniques have been developed that give a more precise view of risk.

Virtually every decision is based on the interaction of important variables, many of which have an element of uncertainty but, perhaps, a fairly high degree of probability. Thus, the wisdom of launching a new product might depend on a number of critical variables: the cost of introducing the product, the cost of producing it, the capital investment needed, the price that can be set, the size of the potential market, and its share of the total market.

Decision Trees

One of the best ways to analyze a decision is to use so-called decision trees. **Decision trees** depict, in the form of a "tree," the decision points, chance events, and probabilities involved in various courses that might be undertaken. A common problem occurs in business when a new product is introduced. Managers must decide whether to install expensive permanent equipment to ensure production at the lowest possible cost or to undertake cheaper, temporary tooling that will involve a higher manufacturing cost but lower capital investments and will result in lower losses if the product does not sell as well as estimated. In its simplest form, a tree showing the decisions a manager faces in this situation might be similar to that in Figure 6-3.

The decision tree approach makes it possible to see at least the major alternatives and the fact that subsequent decisions may depend upon events in the future. By incorporating the probabilities of various events into the tree, managers can also comprehend the true probability of a decision's leading to the desired results. The "best estimate" may really turn out to be quite risky. One thing is certain: Decision trees and similar decision techniques replace broad judgments with a focus on the important elements in a decision, bring out into the open premises that are often hidden, and disclose the reasoning process by which decisions are made under uncertainty.

Preference Theory

Preference, or **utility, theory** is based on the notion that individual attitudes toward risk will vary: Some individuals are willing to take only smaller risks

Figure 6-3

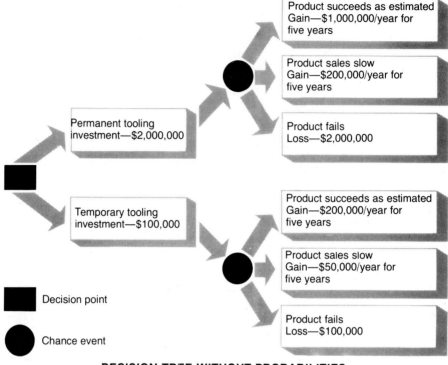

Permanent tooling investment—$2,000,000

Product succeeds as estimated
Gain—$1,000,000/year for five years

Product sales slow
Gain—$200,000/year for five years

Product fails
Loss—$2,000,000

Temporary tooling investment—$100,000

Product succeeds as estimated
Gain—$200,000/year for five years

Product sales slow
Gain—$50,000/year for five years

Product fails
Loss—$100,000

Decision point

Chance event

DECISION TREE WITHOUT PROBABILITIES.

than those indicated by probabilities ("risk averters") and others are willing to take greater risks ("gamblers"). While referred to here as "preference theory," this technique is more classically called "utility theory." Purely statistical probabilities, as applied to decision making, rest upon the assumption that decision makers will follow them. In other words, it might seem reasonable that if there were a 60 percent chance of a decision's being the right one, a person would take it. This is not necessarily true, however; since the risk of being wrong is 40 percent, the individual might not wish to take this risk. Managers avoid risk, particularly if the penalty for being wrong is severe, whether it be in terms of monetary loss, reputation, or job security. If this seems doubtful, consider the likelihood, on a personal basis, of risking, say, $40,000, on the 60 percent chance of making $100,000, realizing that there is still a 40 percent chance of losing $40,000. People might readily risk $4 on a chance of making $10, and gamblers have been known to risk much more on a smaller chance of success.

Attitudes toward risk   In order to give probabilities practical meaning in decision making, it is necessary to understand the individual decision maker's aversion to, or acceptance of, risk. This varies not only with the individual but also with the size of the risk, the level of the manager in an organization, and the source of the funds involved (are they personal, or do they belong to the company?).

Higher-level managers are accustomed to taking larger risks than are lower-level managers, and their decision areas tend to involve larger elements of risk. A company president may have to take great risks in launching a new product, selecting an advertising program, or choosing a vice-president, while a first-level supervisor's risk taking may be limited to hiring or promoting semiskilled workers or approving vacation schedules for subordinates.

Also, the same top managers who may make a decision involving risks of millions of dollars for a company in a given program with a chance of success of, say, 75 percent would not be likely to do that with their own personal fortunes, at least not unless their fortunes were very large. Moreover, the same manager willing to take a 75 percent risk in one case might not be willing to do so in another. Furthermore, a top executive might "go for" a large advertising program for which the chances of success are 70 percent but might decide against an investment in plant and equipment unless the probability of success were higher. In other words, attitudes toward risk vary with events, as well as with people and positions.

Personal risk or preference curves   While not much is known about personal attitudes toward risk, two things are certain: Some people are risk averters in some situations and gamblers in others, and some people have by nature a high aversion to risk and others have a low one. Typical personal risk or preference curves may be drawn as in Figure 6-4. This graph shows both risk averter's and gambler's curves, as well as what is referred to as a "personal" curve. The latter, of course, implies that most of us are gamblers when small stakes are involved but that we soon become risk averters when the stakes rise.

Figure 6-4

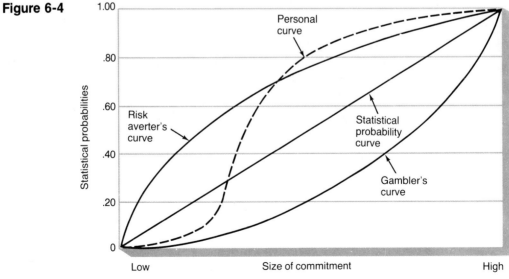

SAMPLE PREFERENCE CURVES.

Most managers (understandably influenced by the dangers of failure) tend to be risk averters to some extent and do not in fact play the averages. Therefore, statistical probabilities are not good enough for practical decision making.

Although perhaps too many managers are risk averters and thereby miss opportunities, few are players of pure statistical averages, at least in important decisions. Therefore, individual preference curves could be substituted for statistical probabilities in decision trees. This can be done, at least roughly, by assessing a person's willingness to take risks in a variety of real or imaginary situations and by developing an individual preference curve for that person. Even if this is not done systematically, those of us who receive recommendations on courses of action from subordinates gain an important advantage if we are aware of the effect of our subordinates' attitude toward risk in making decisions or decision recommendations.

EVALUATING THE IMPORTANCE OF A DECISION

Since managers not only must make correct decisions but also must make them as needed and as economically as possible, and since they must do this often, guidelines to the relative importance of decisions are useful. Decisions of lesser importance do not require thorough analysis and research, and they may even be safely delegated without endangering an individual manager's basic responsibility. The importance of a decision also depends upon the extent of responsibility, so what may be of practically no importance to a corporation president may be of great importance to a section head.

If a decision commits the enterprise to heavy expenditure of funds or to an important personnel program, such as a program for management appraisal and training, or if the commitment can be fulfilled only over a long period, such as by the construction of a new chemical plant, it should be subjected to suitable attention at an upper level of management.

Some plans can be easily changed, some have built into them the possibility of a future change of direction, and others involve action difficult to reverse. Clearly, decisions that involve inflexible courses of action must be more carefully evaluated than decisions that can be easily changed.

If goals and premises are fairly certain, a decision resting on them tends to be less difficult and to require less judgment and analysis than it would if the goals and premises are highly uncertain.

If the goals, inputs, restrictions, and variables can be accurately measured, as with definite inputs in a production machine shop, the importance of the decision, other things remaining the same, tends to be less than if the inputs are difficult to quantify, as in pricing a new consumer product or deciding on its style.

In situations where the impact of a decision on people is great, its importance is high. A doctor's mistake in a hospital can be fatal to a patient. No one making a decision that affects other people can afford to overlook the needs of those people who accept the decision.

OTHER FACTORS IN DECISION MAKING

There are other factors that influence decisionmaking. They will be discussed in more detail in later chapters.

Personal values and organization culture. The strategic planning model shown in the previous chapter indicated that an important variable influencing the direction of the enterprise is personal values, primarily those of top managers. However, values influence decision making at all organizational levels, managers and nonmanagers alike. What is true for individuals is also pertinent to the organization as a whole. Thus, the pattern of behavior, shared beliefs, and values of members of an organization do influence decision making and will be discussed in Chapter 10.

Group decision making. In modern organizations, decisions are often made by groups of individuals, such as committees or teams.[9] Chapter 17 will discuss these organizational forms of managing.

Creativity and innovation. Effective decision making requires creativity and innovation.[10] Both aspects will be discussed in Chapter 14.

DECISION SUPPORT SYSTEMS

Decision support systems (DSSs) use computers to facilitate the decision-making process of semistructured tasks. These systems are designed not to replace managerial judgment but to support it and to make the decision process more effective.[11] Decision support systems also help managers react quickly to changing needs.[12] It is clear, then, that the design of an effective system requires a thorough knowledge of how managers make decisions.

The availability of minicomputers and microcomputers, as well as of communication networks, makes it possible to access and utilize a great deal of information at low cost. Thus, DSS gives managers an important tool for decision making under their own control.

Although there are similarities between management information systems (MISs) and DSSs, there are also differences. Traditionally, the designers of MIS were technical experts, and managers (who had to make the decisions) had only minor inputs. In contrast, DSS focuses on the decision-making process and on managers who, in cooperation with the technical professionals, design the system suitable for a particular position. Managers, having access to data bases in DSS, can manipulate data and explore the effectiveness of alternative courses of action. These and other differences between MIS and DSS are shown in Table 6-1.

Now many software programs are available for microcomputers, such as VisiCalc, Lotus 1–2–3, and Supercalc. The same is true for database software. For example, *InfoWorld,* the newspaper for the microcomputer industry,

Table 6-1 **Comparisons between MIS and DSS**

MIS	DSS
Focus on structured tasks and routine decisions (e.g., use of procedures, use of decision rules)	Focus on semistructured tasks, requiring managerial judgment
Emphasis on data storage	Emphasis on data manipulation
Often only indirect access to data by managers	Direct data access by managers
Reliance on computer expert	Reliance on manager's own judgment
Access to data possibly requiring a wait for manager's turn	Direct access to computer and data
MIS manager not completely understanding the nature of the decision	Manager knowing decision environment
Emphasis on efficiency	Emphasis on effectiveness

Sources: Peter G. W. Keen and Michael S. Scott Morton, *Decision Support System—An Organizational Perspective* (Reading, Mass.: Addison-Wesley Publishing Company, 1978); Ronald R. Wood, "The Personal Computer: How It Can Increase Management Productivity," *Financial Executive* (February 1984); Ernest A. Kallman and Leon Reinharth, *Information System for Planning and Decision Making* (New York: Van Nostrand Reinhold, 1984).

evaluated twenty-four such data bases for the IBM PCs and compatible computers (some of these programs may be familiar to you: Cornerstone, Reflex, and Q&A) and ten such programs for the Macintosh computer (e.g., Filemaker, Overvue, and Reflex).[13] Then there are the many integrated packages, which combine programs for word processors, spreadsheets, data bases, graphics, and communications, with names such as Symphony, Framework, or Jazz. Thus, managers can be overwhelmed by the many choices of programs that aid the decision-making process.

THE SYSTEMS APPROACH AND DECISION MAKING

Decisions cannot usually be made, of course, in a closed-system environment. As already emphasized, many elements of the environment of planning lie outside the enterprise. In addition, every department or section of an enterprise is a subsystem of the entire enterprise; managers of these organizational units must be responsive to the policies and programs of other organizational units and of the total enterprise. Moreover, people within the enterprise are a part of the social system, and their thinking and attitudes must be taken into account whenever a manager makes a decision.

Furthermore, even when managers construct a closed-system model, as they may do with operations research decision models, they do so simply to have a workable program to solve. But in so doing, they make certain assumptions as to environmental forces that heavily influence their decision, they enter inputs into their calculations as they are or appear to be at any given time, and they change the construction of their model when forces and developments beyond its boundaries so require.

> PERSPECTIVE:
> INVESTMENT DECISIONS IN A HOSPITAL
>
> A decision system can become very complex. The flow diagram of information for proposed investments is shown in Figure 6-5.[14]
> Now imagine the many other decisions that have to be made in a hospital pertaining to the well-being of patients, providing the basis for fiscal soundness, and balancing the interests of trustees, administrators, and physicians. More recently, some hospitals began thinking strategically by making decisions that related the hospital's strengths and weaknesses to opportunities and threats in the external environment within the framework of its mission. While it might be difficult to diagram all the various decision processes, and one could be overwhelmed by its complexity, the systems nature of decision making must be recognized. The hospital, it should be kept in mind, cannot be a closed system but must serve the needs of the community of which it is a part.

Saying that managers take into account the various elements in the system environment of their problem does not mean, however, that they abdicate their role as decision makers. Someone must select a course of action from among alternatives, taking into account events and forces in the environment of a decision. It is often not feasible, or advisable, to democratize the decision process to the extent that for all decisions a vote is taken from subordinates or the many other persons who may have some immediate or remote interest in the decision. At some point a decision has to be made.

SUMMARY

Decision making is the process of selecting a course of action from among alternatives; it is the core of planning. Managers must make choices on the basis of limited or bounded rationality. That is, they must make decisions in light of everything they can learn about a situation, which may not be everything they should know. "Satisficing" is a term sometimes used to describe picking a course of action that is satisfactory under the circumstances.

Because there are almost always alternatives — usually many — to a course of action, managers need to narrow them down to those few that deal with the limiting factors. These are the ones that stand in the way of achieving a desired objective. Alternatives are then evaluated in terms of quantitative and qualitative factors. The decision-making techniques include marginal analysis and cost effectiveness analysis. Experience, experimentation, and research and analysis also come into play in making decisions.

Programmed and nonprogrammed decisions are different. The former are suited for structured problems and routine decisions. These kinds of decisions are made especially by lower-level managers and nonmanagers. Nonprogrammed decisions, on the other hand, are used for unstructured problems and nonroutine decisions and are made especially by upper-level managers.

Figure 6-5

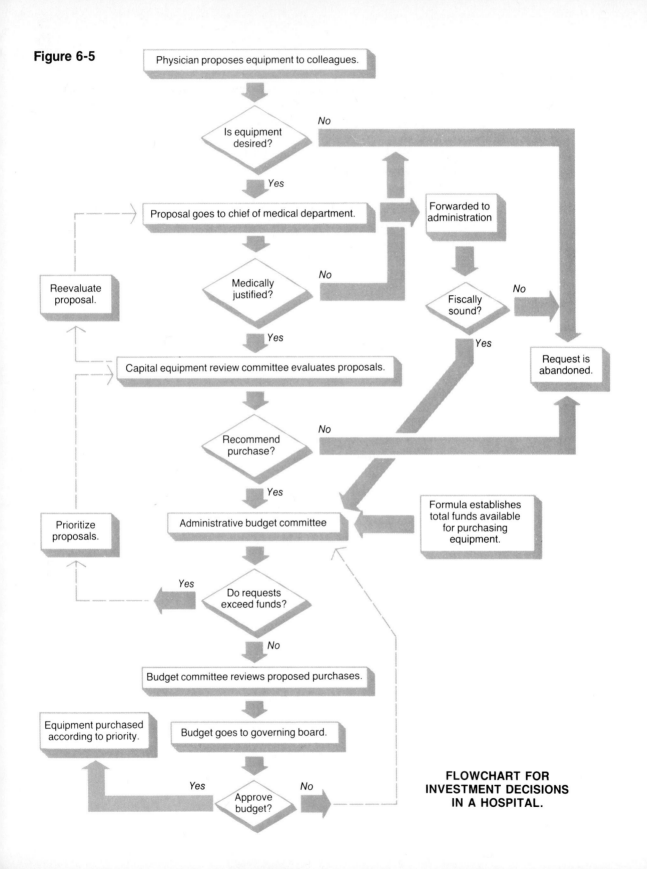

FLOWCHART FOR
INVESTMENT DECISIONS
IN A HOSPITAL.

Some modern approaches to decision making are risk analysis (which assigns mathematical probabilities to the outcomes of decisions), decision trees (which illustrate the decision points, chance events, and probabilities of each possible course of action), and preference theory (which takes into account managers' willingness to take certain risks).

The factors that determine the importance of a decision are the size of the commitment, the flexibility or inflexibility of plans, the certainty or uncertainty of goals and premises, the degree to which variables can be measured, and the impact on people.

Decision support systems (DSSs) use computers to help the decision-making process of semistructured tasks. These systems help managers to make better decisions; they are not a substitute for managerial judgment. Finally, decisions must be made with the recognition that organizations are open systems, interacting with the environment.

KEY IDEAS AND CONCEPTS FOR REVIEW

Decision making
Limited or bounded rationality
Satisficing
Principle of the limiting factor
Marginal analysis
Cost effectiveness analysis
Cost benefit analysis
Three approaches to selecting
   alternatives

Programmed decisions
Nonprogrammed decisions
Risk analysis
Decision trees
Preference, or utility, theory
Factors for evaluating a decision
Decision support systems (DSSs)
Systems approach to decision
   making

FOR DISCUSSION

1. Why is experience often referred to not only as an expensive basis for decision making but also as a dangerous one? How can a manager make best use of experience?

2. In a decision problem you now know of, how and where would you apply the principle of the limiting factor?

3. Identify five decision problems and recommend programmed or nonprogrammed decisions. If the examples are from an organizational setting, did they occur on upper or lower levels?

4. Draw a decision tree for a decision problem you face.

5. "Decision making is the primary task of the manager." Comment.

6. How does risk aversion affect your own life? Given a situation, draw your preference curve.

EXERCISES/ACTION STEPS

1. Your boss offers you a promotion to a position in a location your family does not like. Make the necessary assumptions, and then state how and what you would decide.

2. Interview a manager of a local company and obtain information about the decision-making process in the organization. Discuss with him or her the concept of bounded rationality, and see if it applies to the manager.

CASE:
OLYMPIC TOY COMPANY

"I expect all the managers in my department to act completely rationally in every decision they make," declared Eleanor Johnson, vice-president of marketing for the Olympic Toy Company. "Every one of us, no matter what his or her position, is hired to be a professional rationalist, and I expect all of us not only to know what they are doing and why but to be right in their decisions. I know that someone has said that a good manager needs only to be right in more than half of his or her decisions. But that is not good enough for me. I would agree that you may be excused for occasionally making a mistake, especially if it is a matter beyond your control, but I can never excuse you for not acting rationally."

"I agree with your idea, Eleanor," said Jill Goldberg, her advertising manager, "and I always try to be rational and logical in my decisions. But would you mind helping me be sure of this by explaining just what 'acting rationally' is?"

1. Explain how the vice-president of marketing might describe what is involved in making rational decisions.

2. If Jill Goldberg then declares that there is no way she can be completely rational, what would you suggest as a reply?

REFERENCES

1. The attempts by a number of management specialists to bring logical order to the decision process are outlined and explained in E. R. Archer, "How to Make a Business Decision: An Analysis of Theory and Practice," *Management Review* (February 1980), pp. 30–37.

2. See James G. March and Herbert A. Simon, *Organizations* (New York: John Wiley & Sons, 1958, 1966).

3. Bro Uttal, "Compaq Bids for PC Leadership," *Fortune* (Sept. 29, 1986), pp. 30–32; Jo E. Davis and Geoff Lewis, "Compaq Is Trying to Steal a March on IBM," *Business Week* (Sept. 22, 1986), p. 30; Edward Warner, "Compaq Introduces 386 PC, Challenges

IBM to Match It," *InfoWorld* (Sept. 15, 1986), pp. 1, 8; Jo Ellen Davis and Geoff Lewis, "Who's Afraid of IBM?" *Business Week* (June 29, 1987), pp. 68–74.

4. See, for example, Herbert A. Simon, *The New Science of Management Decisions* (Englewood Cliffs, N.J.: Prentice-Hall, 1977).

5. Weston H. Agor, "How Top Executives Use Their Intuition to Make Important Decisions," *Business Horizons* (January–February 1986), pp. 49–53.

6. Strategic decision making often involves a great deal of uncertainty. See Charles R. Schwenk,

"Cognitive Simplification Processes in Strategic Decision-Making," *Strategic Management Journal* (April–June 1984), pp. 111–128; Agor, "How Top Executives Use Their Intuition" (1986), pp. 49–53.

7. Schwenk, "Cognitive Simplification Processes" (1984), pp. 111–128.

8. See also Jitendra V. Singh, "Performance, Slack, and Risk Taking in Organizational Decision Making," *Academy of Management Journal* (September 1986), pp. 562–585.

9. See also Edwin A. Locke, Gary P. Latham, and David M. Schweiger, "Participation in Decision Making: When Should It Be Used?" *Organizational Dynamics* (Winter 1986), pp. 65ff.

10. For interesting discussions of the topic, see Andre L. Delbecq and Peter K. Mills, "Managerial Practices That Enhance Innovation," *Organizational Dynamics* (Summer 1985), pp. 24–34; M. J. Kirton, "Adaptors and Innovators — Why New Initiatives Get Blocked," *Long Range Planning*, vol. 17, no. 2 (1984), pp. 137–143.

11. Peter G. W. Keen and Michael S. Scott Morton, *Decision Support Systems — An Organizational Perspective* (Reading, Mass.: Addison-Wesley Publishing Company, 1978).

12. Steven Alter, *Decision Support Systems: Current Practice and Continuing Challenges* (Reading, Mass.: Addison-Wesley Publishing Company, 1980), p. xi.

13. *Infoworld* (Sept. 8, 1986), pp. 30–40.

14. Alan D. Meyer, "Mingling Decision Making Metaphors," *Academy of Management Review* (January 1984), pp. 6–17.

SUMMARY OF MAJOR PRINCIPLES, OR GUIDES, OF PLANNING

Perhaps the best way to summarize Part 2, on planning, is to list some of the major principles, or guidelines, that may be used in planning. While others might be added, the most essential guiding principles are those listed below.

The Purpose and Nature of Planning

The purpose and nature of planning may be summarized by reference to the following principles.

Principle of contribution to objectives   The purpose of every plan and all supporting plans is to promote the accomplishment of enterprise objectives.

Principle of objectives   If objectives are to be meaningful to people, they must be clear, attainable, and verifiable.

Principle of primacy of planning   Planning logically precedes all other managerial functions.

Principle of efficiency of plans   The efficiency of a plan is measured by the amount it contributes to purpose and objectives as offset by the costs required to formulate and operate it and by unsought consequences.

The Structure of Plans

Two major principles dealing with the structure of plans can go far in tying plans together, making supporting plans contribute to major plans, and ensuring that plans in one department harmonize with those in another.

Principle of planning premises   The more thoroughly the individuals who are charged with planning understand and agree to utilize consistent planning premises, the more coordinated enterprise planning will be.

Principle of the strategy and policy framework   The more strategies and policies are clearly understood and implemented in practice, the more consistent and effective will be the framework of enterprise plans.

The Process of Planning

Within the process of planning, there are four principles that help in the development of a practical science of planning.

Principle of the limiting factor   In choosing among alternatives, the more accurately individuals can recognize and solve for those factors which are limiting or critical to the attainment of the desired goal, the more easily and accurately they can select the most favorable alternative.

The commitment principle   Logical planning should cover a period of time in the future necessary to foresee as well as possible, through a series of actions, the fulfillment of commitments involved in a decision made today.

Principle of flexibility   Building flexibility into plans will lessen the danger of losses incurred through unexpected events, but the cost of flexibility should be weighed against its advantages.

Principle of navigational change   The more that planning decisions commit individuals to a future path, the more important it is to check on events and expectations periodically and redraw plans as necessary to maintain a course toward a desired goal.

The commitment principle and the principles of flexibility and navigational change are aimed at a contingency approach to planning. Although it makes sense to forecast and draw plans far enough into the future to make reasonably sure of meeting commitments, often it is impossible to do so or the future is so uncertain that it is too risky to fulfill those commitments.

The principle of flexibility deals with that ability to change which is built into plans. The principle of navigational change, on the other hand, implies reviewing plans from time to time and redrawing them if this is required by changed events and expectations. Unless plans have built-in flexibility, navigational change may be difficult or costly.

PART **3**

Organizing

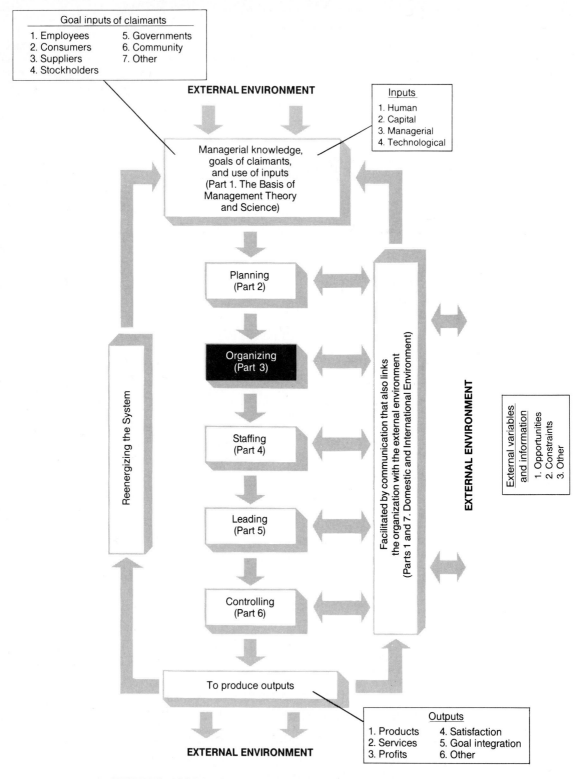

Goal inputs of claimants

1. Employees   5. Governments
2. Consumers   6. Community
3. Suppliers   7. Other
4. Stockholders

EXTERNAL ENVIRONMENT

Inputs

1. Human
2. Capital
3. Managerial
4. Technological

Managerial knowledge,
goals of claimants,
and use of inputs
(Part 1. The Basis of
Management Theory
and Science)

Planning
(Part 2)

Organizing
(Part 3)

Staffing
(Part 4)

Leading
(Part 5)

Controlling
(Part 6)

Reenergizing the System

Facilitated by communication that also links
the organization with the external environment
(Parts 1 and 7. Domestic and International Environment)

EXTERNAL ENVIRONMENT

External variables
and information

1. Opportunities
2. Constraints
3. Other

To produce outputs

Outputs

1. Products   4. Satisfaction
2. Services   5. Goal integration
3. Profits   6. Other

EXTERNAL ENVIRONMENT

SYSTEMS APPROACH TO MANAGEMENT: ORGANIZING

CHAPTER 7

The Nature and Purpose of Organizing

CHAPTER OBJECTIVES

After reading this chapter, you should understand:

1. The purpose of an organization structure
2. The meaning of "organizing" and "organization"
3. The distinction between formal and informal organization
4. That organization structures and their levels are due to the limitations of the span of management
5. That the exact number of people a manager can effectively supervise depends on a number of underlying variables and situations
6. The nature of entrepreneuring and intrapreneuring
7. The logic of organizing and its relationship to other managerial functions
8. That organizing requires taking situations into account

It is often said that good people can make any organization pattern work. Some even assert that vagueness in organization is a good thing in that it forces teamwork, since people know that they must cooperate to get anything done. However, there can be no doubt that good people and those who want to cooperate will work together most effectively if they know the parts they are to play in any team operation and the way their roles relate to one another. This is as true in business or government as it is in football or in a symphony orchestra. Designing and maintaining these systems of roles is basically the managerial function of organizing.

For an **organizational role** to exist and be meaningful to people, it must incorporate (1) verifiable objectives, which, as indicated in Part 2, are a major part of planning; (2) a clear idea of the major duties or activities involved; and (3) an understood area of discretion or authority so that the person filling the role knows what he or she can do to accomplish goals. In addition, to make a role work out effectively, provision should be made for supplying needed information and other tools necessary for performance in that role.

It is in this sense that we think of **organizing** as (1) the identification and classification of required activities, (2) the grouping of activities necessary to attain objectives, (3) the assignment of each grouping to a manager with the authority (delegation) necessary to supervise it, and (4) the provision for coordination horizontally (on the same or similar organizational level) and vertically (e.g., corporate headquarters, division, and department) in the organization structure.

An organization structure should be designed to clarify who is to do what tasks and who is responsible for what results, to remove obstacles to performance caused by confusion and uncertainty of assignment, and to furnish decision-making and communications networks reflecting and supporting enterprise objectives.

"Organization" is a word many people use loosely. Some would say it includes all the behavior of all participants. Others would equate it with the total system of social and cultural relationships. Still others refer to an enterprise, such as the United States Steel Corporation or the Department of Defense, as an "organization." But for most practicing managers, the term **organization** implies a *formalized intentional structure of roles or positions*. In this book, the term is generally used in reference to a formalized structure of roles, although it is sometimes used to denote an enterprise.

What does "intentional structure of roles" mean? In the first place, as already implied in defining the nature and content of organizational roles, people working together must fill certain roles. In the second place, the roles people are asked to fill should be intentionally designed to ensure that required activities are done and that activities fit together so that people can work smoothly, effectively, and efficiently in groups. Certainly most managers believe they are organizing when they establish such an intentional structure.

FORMAL AND INFORMAL ORGANIZATION

Many writers on management distinguish between formal and informal organization. Both types are found in organizations, as shown in Figure 7-1. Let us look at them in more detail.

Formal Organization

In this book, generally, **formal organization** means the intentional structure of roles in a formally organized enterprise. Describing an organization as "formal," however, does not mean there is anything inherently inflexible or unduly confining about it. If a manager is to organize well, the structure must furnish an environment in which individual performance, both present and future, contributes most effectively to group goals.

Formal organization must be flexible. There should be room for discretion, for advantageous utilization of creative talents, and for recognition of individual likes and capacities in the most formal of organizations. Yet individual effort in a group situation must be channeled toward group and organization goals.

Although the attainment of goals must be the reason for any cooperative activity, we must look further for principles to guide the establishment of effective formal organization. These principles—summarized at the end of Part 3 — pertain to the unity of objectives and organizational efficiency.

Informal Organization

Chester Barnard, author of the management classic *The Functions of the Executive*, described informal organization as any joint personal activity without conscious joint purpose, even though contributing to joint results.[1] Thus, the informal relationships established in the group of people playing chess during lunchtime may aid in the achievement of organizational goals. It is much easier to ask for help on an organization problem from someone you know personally, even if he or she may be in a different department, than from someone you know only as a name on an organization chart. More recently, Keith Davis

Figure 7-1

THE FORMAL AND INFORMAL ORGANIZATION.

of Arizona State University, who has written extensively on the topic and whose definition will be used in this book, described the **informal organization** as "a network of personal and social relations not established or required by the formal organization but arising spontaneously as people associate with one another."[2] Thus, informal organizations — relationships not appearing on an organization chart — might include the machine-shop group, the sixth-floor crowd, the Friday evening bowling gang, and the morning coffee "regulars."

ORGANIZATIONAL DIVISION: THE DEPARTMENT

One aspect of organizing is the establishment of departments. The word **department** designates *a distinct area, division, or branch of an organization over which a manager has authority for the performance of specified activities.* A department, as the term is generally used, may be the production division, the sales department, the West Coast branch, the market research section, or the accounts receivable unit. In some enterprises, departmental terminology is loosely applied; in others, especially large ones, a stricter terminology indicates hierarchical relationships. Thus, a vice-president may head a division; a director, a department; a manager, a branch; and a chief, a section. In some organizations, the bureaucratic structure is replaced by an emphasis on teamwork, as shown by the Perspective on Ford Motor Company.

ORGANIZATION LEVELS AND THE SPAN OF MANAGEMENT*

While the purpose of organizing is to make human cooperation effective, the reason for levels of organization is the limitations of the span of management. In other words, organization levels exist because there is a limit to the number of persons a manager can supervise effectively, even though this limit varies depending on situations. The relationships between the span of management and the organizational levels are shown in Figure 7-2. A wide span of management is associated with few organizational levels; a narrow span, with many levels.

Choosing the Span

In every organization, it must be decided how many subordinates a superior can manage. Students of management have found that this number is usually four to eight subordinates at the upper levels of organization and eight to fifteen or more at the lower levels. For example, the prominent British consultant

*In much of the literature of management, this is referred to as the "span of control." Despite the widespread use of this term, in this book "span of management" will be used, since the span is one of management and not merely of control, which is only one function of managing.

PERSPECTIVE:
MANAGEMENT BY TEAMWORK AT FORD

In the early 1980s Ford Motor Company was in trouble. It was even said that "FORD" stood for "fix or repair daily." Indeed, the Ford story shows how a company can be turned around.[3] The Taurus and Mercury's Sable were the turning points for the company; they illustrate that models produced by U.S. carmakers can compete with the very successful Japanese imports.

Problems can become opportunities, and during the 1980 recession there were many difficulties to overcome. It became clear that Ford had to compete not only against U.S. carmakers but against auto manufacturers throughout the world. Drastic steps were necessary: Ford invested $3 billion in its new models, made quality its number-one concern, and learned from other carmakers, especially the Japanese.

One of the first undertakings was to replace the old bureaucratic structure with the team approach, or program management. Previously, it took 5 years to produce a new model. The old approach was as follows: The product planners developed the general concept of the new model, which was then given to the designers. After that, engineers got involved, developing specifications for manufacturing and for the various suppliers. This process was sequential, with little communication among the various groups. When manufacturing, for example, got the specifications, little flexibility was possible, even if changing the design would facilitate assembly. If a problem was discovered at the manufacturing stage, designers and engineers had to be involved again in correcting the problem. However, if parts were already purchased or dies already made, such changes were costly; some were simply not made because of the delay involved. In this approach, the overall responsibility was not clearly defined.

Ford recognized the need for dramatic changes, which were incorporated in the project "Team Taurus." Rather than having each unit do the various tasks sequentially, the company established a team consisting of planners, designers, engineers, manufacturing people, and even suppliers. Thus, representatives from all units were involved in the task right from the beginning. This way, difficulties could be resolved before they became major problems. Ford also involved assembly line workers in the development of the model. They were asked to comment on difficulties they had with assembling the parts and to make recommendations for improvements.

Rather than adopting an attitude of "we know best," Ford people carefully studied cars made by other manufacturers and learned about their best features. For example, Ford noted the accuracy of the Toyota fuel gauge and the good tire storage of the BMW. Ford also tested different seats on young and old, male and female, drivers. Through extensive market studies, Ford learned about other customer preferences.

The chairman, Donald Petersen, gives credit for Ford's turnaround to his team. But *he* took the $3 billion risk in developing the new line of cars. He delegated authority down the organizational hierarchy to the ranks of the workers. Decision making is no longer the prerogative of top management but of the team that takes action. Petersen practiced "management by wandering around," or MBWA, visiting the factories and listening to workers.

Lyndall Urwick found "the ideal number of subordinates for all superior authorities . . . to be four," while "at the lowest level of organization, where what is delegated is responsibility for the performance of specific tasks and not for the supervision of others, the number may be eight or twelve."[4] Others find that a manager may be able to manage as many as twenty to thirty subordinates.

In a survey of 100 large companies made by the American Management Association, the number of executives reporting to the presidents varied from one to twenty-four, and only twenty-six presidents had six or fewer subordinates; the median number was nine.[5] In forty-one smaller companies surveyed, twenty-five of the presidents supervised seven or more subordinates,

Figure 7-2 **Organization with Narrow Spans**

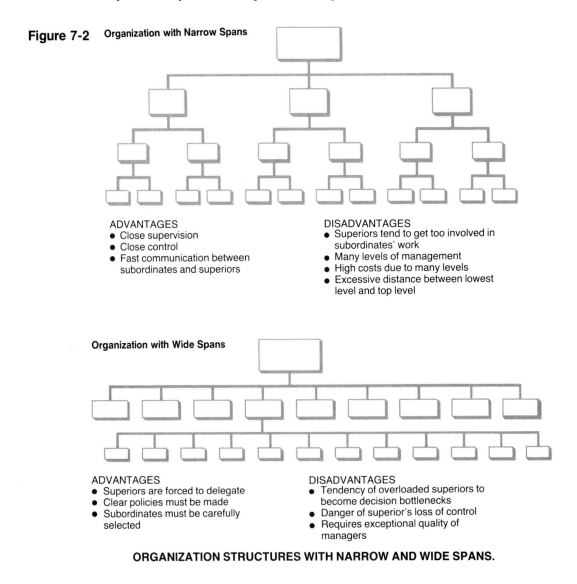

ADVANTAGES
- Close supervision
- Close control
- Fast communication between subordinates and superiors

DISADVANTAGES
- Superiors tend to get too involved in subordinates' work
- Many levels of management
- High costs due to many levels
- Excessive distance between lowest level and top level

Organization with Wide Spans

ADVANTAGES
- Superiors are forced to delegate
- Clear policies must be made
- Subordinates must be carefully selected

DISADVANTAGES
- Tendency of overloaded superiors to become decision bottlenecks
- Danger of superior's loss of control
- Requires exceptional quality of managers

ORGANIZATION STRUCTURES WITH NARROW AND WIDE SPANS.

and the most common number was eight. Comparable results were found in other studies.

In a very real sense, none of these studies is truly indicative of the actual span of management. For one thing, they measure the span only at or near the top of an enterprise. This is hardly typical of what the span may be throughout the enterprise, particularly since every organizer has experienced tremendous pressure for having a large number of the functions report to the top executives. It is probable that spans below the top executive are much narrower. Indeed, a study of more than 100 companies of all sizes revealed a much narrower span in the middle levels of management than at the top.

In addition, the fact that apparently well-managed companies have, among them and certainly within them, widely varying spans indicates that merely counting the numbers in existing spans is not enough to establish what a span *ought* to be. This is true even if it could be assumed that, through trial and error, each company has reached the best number. That might prove only that underlying conditions vary (this will be discussed later in the chapter).

Problems with Organization Levels

There is a tendency to regard organization and departmentation as ends in themselves and to gauge the effectiveness of organization structures in terms of clarity and completeness of departments and department levels. Division of activities into departments, and hierarchical organization and the creation of multiple levels, are not completely desirable in themselves.

In the first place, levels are *expensive*. As they increase, more and more effort and money are devoted to managing, because of the additional managers, the staffs to assist them, and the necessity of coordinating departmental activities, plus the costs of facilities for the personnel. Accountants refer to such costs as "overhead," or "burden," or "general and administrative," in contrast to so-called direct costs. Real production is accomplished by factory, engineering, or sales employees who are, or could logically be accounted for as, "direct labor." Levels above the "firing line" are predominantly staffed with managers whose cost it would be desirable to eliminate, if that were possible.

In the second place, departmental levels *complicate communication*. An enterprise with many levels has greater difficulty communicating objectives, plans, and policies downward through the organization structure than does a firm in which the top manager communicates directly with employees. Omissions and misinterpretations occur as information passes down the line. Levels also complicate communication from the "firing line" to the commanding superiors, which is every bit as important as downward communication. It has been well said that levels are "filters" of information.

Finally, numerous departments and levels *complicate planning and control*. A plan that may be definite and complete at the top level loses coordination and clarity as it is subdivided at lower levels. Control becomes more difficult as levels and managers are added; at the same time the complexities of planning and difficulties of communication make this control more important.

Operational-Management Position: A Situational Approach

The classical school approach to the span of management deals with specifying numbers of subordinates for an effective span. Actual experience does support the classical school opinion that at upper and top levels the span is from three to seven or eight subordinates. However, more recent operational-management theorists have taken the position that there are too many underlying variables in a management situation for us to specify any particular number of subordinates that a manager can effectively supervise. Thus the **principle of the span of management** states that *there is a limit to the number of subordinates a manager can effectively supervise, but the exact number will depend on the impact of underlying factors.*

In other words, the dominant current guideline is to look for the causes of limited span in individual situations, rather than to assume that there is a widely applicable numerical limit. Examining what consumes the time of managers in their handling of superior-subordinate relationships, and ascertaining the devices that can be used to reduce these time pressures, will be not only a helpful approach for determining the best span in individual cases but also a powerful tool for finding out what can be done to extend the span without destroying effective supervision. There can be no argument that the costs of levels of supervision make it highly desirable for every individual manager to have as many subordinates as can be effectively supervised.

FACTORS DETERMINING AN EFFECTIVE SPAN

The number of subordinates a manager can effectively manage depends on the impact of underlying factors. Aside from such personal capacities as comprehending quickly, getting along with people, and commanding loyalty and respect, the most important determinant is a manager's ability to reduce the time he or she spends with subordinates. This ability naturally varies with managers and their jobs, but several factors materially influence the number and frequency of such contacts and therefore the span of management (see Table 7-1).

Subordinate Training

The better the training of subordinates, the fewer the number of necessary superior-subordinate relationships. Well-trained subordinates require not only less of their managers' time but also less contact with their managers.

Training problems increase in new and more complex industries. Managers in the railroad industry, for example, would — because the technology does not change much — tend to be more completely trained than those in the

Table 7-1   Factors Influencing the Span of Management

Narrow span (a great deal of time spent with subordinates) related to:	Wide spans (very little time spent with subordinates) related to:
Little or no training	Thorough subordinate training
Inadequate or unclear authority delegation	Clear delegation to undertake well-defined tasks
Unclear plans for nonrepetitive operations	Well-defined plans for repetitive operations
Nonverifiable objectives and standards	Verifiable objectives used as standards
Fast changes in external and internal environments	Slow changes in external and internal environments
Use of poor or inappropriate communication techniques, including vague instructions	Use of appropriate techniques such as proper organization structure, written and oral communication
Ineffective interaction of superior and subordinate	Effective interaction between superior and subordinate
Ineffective meetings	Effective meetings
Greater number of specialties at lower and middle levels	Number of specialties at upper levels (top managers concerned with external environment)
Incompetent and untrained manager	Competent and trained manager
Complex task	Simple task
Subordinates' unwillingness to assume responsibility and reasonable risks	Subordinates' willingness to assume responsibility and reasonable risks
Immature subordinates	Mature subordinates

aerospace industry. The rapid changes in policy and procedures in the complex electronics and missile industries would increase training problems.

Clarity of Delegation of Authority

Although training enables managers to reduce the frequency and extensiveness of time-consuming contacts, the principal cause of the heavy time burdens of superior-subordinate relationships is to be found in poorly conceived and confused organization. The most serious symptom of poor organization affecting the span of management is inadequate or unclear authority delegation. If a manager clearly delegates authority to undertake a well-defined task, a well-trained subordinate can get it done with a minimum of the manager's time and attention. But if the subordinate's task is not one that can be done, if it is not clearly defined, or if the subordinate does not have the authority to undertake it effectively, either the task will not be performed or the manager will have to spend a disproportionate amount of time supervising and guiding the subordinate's efforts.

Clarity of Plans

Much of the character of a subordinate's job is defined by the plans to be put into effect. If these plans are well defined, if they are workable, if the authority to undertake them has been delegated, and if the subordinate understands what is expected, little of a supervisor's time will be required. Such is often the case with a production supervisor responsible for largely repetitive operations. Thus, in one large-volume work-clothing manufacturer's plant, production supervisors operated satisfactorily with as many as thirty subordinates.

On the other hand, if plans cannot be drawn accurately and subordinates must do much of their own planning, they may require considerable guidance. However, if the superior has set up clear policies to guide decisions and has made sure they are consistent with the operations and goals of a department, and if the subordinate understands them, there will certainly be fewer demands on the superior's time than there would be if these policies were indefinite, incomplete, or not understood.

Use of Objective Standards

A manager must find out, either by personal observation or through use of objective standards, whether subordinates are following plans. Obviously, good objective standards, revealing with ease any deviations from plans, enable managers to avoid many time-consuming contacts and to direct attention to exceptions at points critical to the successful execution of plans.

Rate of Change

Certain enterprises change much more rapidly than others. The rate of change is an important determinant of the degree to which policies can be formulated and the stability of policies maintained. It may explain the organization structure of companies — railroad, banking, and public utility companies, for example — operating with wide spans of management or, on the other hand, the very narrow span of management used by General Eisenhower during World War II.

The effect of slow change on policy formulation and on subordinate training is dramatically shown in the organization of the Roman Catholic Church. This organization, in terms of durability and stability, can probably be regarded as the most successful in the history of Western civilization. Yet the organization levels are few: In most cases bishops report directly to the Pope, and parish pastors to bishops, although in some instances bishops report to archbishops. Thus, there are generally very few levels in this worldwide organization and a consequent wide span of management at each level. Even though it is probably too broad, this extraordinarily wide span is apparently tolerable, partly because the bishops possess a high degree of training and, even more, because the rate of change in the Church has been slow. Changes in procedures or policies are developments of decades, and major objectives have remained the same for almost 2000 years.

Communication Techniques

The effectiveness with which communication techniques are used also influences the span of management. Objective standards of control are a kind of communications device, but many other techniques reduce the time spent with subordinates.

If every plan, instruction, order, or direction has to be communicated by personal contact and every organization change or staffing problem has to be handled orally, a manager's time will obviously be heavily burdened. Many executives use "assistant-to" positions or administrative staff personnel as a communications device to help them solve their problems with key subordinates. Written recommendations by subordinates, summarizing important considerations, frequently speed decision making. Some busy top executives widen their span of management by insisting upon summary presentation of written recommendations, even when these involved enormously important decisions. A carefully reasoned and presented recommendation helps an executive reach a considered decision in minutes when even the most efficient conference would require an hour.

An ability to communicate plans and instructions clearly and concisely also tends to increase a manager's span. The subordinate who, after leaving a superior's office or receiving instructions, is still in doubt about what is wanted or what has been said is sure to request further meetings sooner or later. The subordinate's job is greatly facilitated by superiors who can express themselves well. A manager's casual, easy style may please subordinates, but when this easiness degenerates into confusion and wasted time, it sharply reduces the effective span of management and often lowers morale as well.

Amount of Personal Contact Needed

In many instances, face-to-face meetings are necessary. Many situations cannot be completely handled with written reports, memorandums, policy statements, planning documents, or other communications that do not involve personal contact. An executive may find it valuable and stimulating to subordinates to meet and discuss problems in the give-and-take of a conference. Some problems are of such political delicacy that they can be handled only in face-to-face meetings. This is also true when it comes to appraising people's performance and discussing it with them. And there are other situations in which the best way of communicating a problem, instructing a subordinate, or "getting a feel" for how people really think on some matter is to spend time in personal contact.

One wonders, however, whether the high percentage of executive time spent in meetings and committees might be reduced somewhat by better training, better policymaking and planning, clearer delegation, more thorough staff work, better control systems and objectives standards, and, in general, better application of sound principles of management. One wonders, also, whether much of the time spent in personal contact might not be much better spent in thought and study.

At the other extreme, many companies seem somewhat unaware of how newer personnel techniques affect first-line supervisors, many of whom appear to have spans of management far beyond their abilities to handle them. Merit ratings, insurance programs, grievance procedures, and other personnel matters now requiring supervisors' time in face-to-face relationships have reduced their traditionally wide spans. This is not to say that these innovations are not worth their cost, but span-of-management limitations must be evaluated in the light of these factors. Perhaps the point has been reached at which first-level supervisors, with a traditionally large number of people reporting to them, are the most overworked of all managers.

Variation by Organization Level

Several research projects have found that the size of the most effective span differs by organization level. In one major study, the researchers developed and tested a model to take this variable into account and found that the degree of specialization by individuals ("person specialization") was the most important variable affecting span, although technology and size were also tested, since previous research had concentrated on these.[6] The study revealed that (1) when a greater number of specialties was supervised, effective spans were narrower at lower and middle levels of organization but were increased at upper levels, primarily because top-level managers were most concerned with the interface of the enterprise with its external environment, strategic planning, and major policy matters; (2) routineness (lack of variety of work) of an operation appeared to have little effect at any level; and (3) size (in terms of personnel) had little effect at lower levels but a positive effect at middle levels.

Actually, this study is consistent with the impact of variables outlined above. It found what many practitioners have long known: Neither size nor technology has much to do with an effective span at upper levels of an organization, although the variables outlined in this section do have a significant influence.

Other Factors

Besides the factors discussed above, there are others that affect the span of management. For example, a manager who is competent and well trained can effectively supervise more people than one who is not. Furthermore, simple tasks may allow for a wider span than tasks that are complex and include a great variety of activities. There are still other factors that favor a wider span of management, such as the positive attitudes of subordinates toward assumption of responsibility, as well as their willingness to take reasonable risks. Similarly, with more mature subordinates, the superior may delegate more authority, thus widening the span.

The Need for Balance

There can be no doubt that, despite the desirability of a flat organization structure, the span of management is limited by real and important restrictions.

Managers may have more subordinates than they can manage effectively, even though they delegate authority, carry on training, formulate plans and policies clearly, and adopt efficient control and communication techniques. It is equally true that as an enterprise grows, the span-of-management limitations force an increase in the number of levels simply because there are more people to supervise.

What is required is more precise balancing, in a given situation, of all pertinent factors. Widening spans and reducing the number of levels may be the answer in some cases; the reverse may be true in others. One must balance all the costs of adopting one course or the other, not only the financial costs but costs in morale, personal development, and attainment of enterprise objectives. In a military organization, perhaps the attainment of objectives quickly and without error would be most important. On the other hand, in a department store operation, the long-run objective of profit may be best served by forcing initiative and personal development at the lower levels of the organization.

ORGANIZATIONAL ENVIRONMENT FOR ENTREPRENEURING AND INTRAPRENEURING

At times, special organizational arrangements need to be made for fostering and utilizing entrepreneurship. Frequently, **entrepreneurship** is thought to apply to managing small businesses,[7] but some authors expand the concept to apply also to large organizations and to managers carrying out entrepreneurial roles through which they initiate changes to take advantage of opportunities.[8] Although it is common to search for the "entrepreneurial personality," Peter Drucker suggested that this search may not be successful.[9] Instead, one should look for a commitment to systematic innovation, which is a specific activity of entrepreneurs. The essence of entrepreneurship is innovation, that is, goal-oriented change to utilize the enterprise's potential. As entrepreneurs, managers try to improve the situation.

Gifford Pinchot makes a distinction between the intrapreneur and the entrepreneur. Specifically, an **intrapreneur** is a person who focuses on innovation and creativity and who transforms a dream or an idea into a profitable venture by operating *within* the organizational environment. In contrast, the entrepreneur is a person who does the same, but *outside* the organizational setting.[10] Other authors, however, do not make this distinction; therefore, in this book the term "entrepreneur" designates an enterprising person working either within or outside the organization.

Since it is a managerial responsibility to create an environment for effective and efficient achievement of group goals, managers must promote opportunities for entrepreneurs to utilize their potential for innovation. Entrepreneurs take personal risks in initiating change, and they expect to be rewarded for it. The taking of reasonable risk will, at times, result in failure, but this must be tolerated. Finally, entrepreneurs need some degree of freedom to pursue their ideas; this, in turn, requires that sufficient authority be delegated.

PERSPECTIVE:
POST-IT NOTE PADS

Even in companies with a policy of promoting entrepreneurship and innovation, the development of new products requires perseverance to transform an idea into reality.[11]

Art Fry, the inventor of Post-it note pads, was singing in a church choir. The bookmarks placed in his hymnal fell out after the first church service, making it difficult to find the relevant pages for the second service. The need was clear: An adhesive paper slip that could be easily removed without damaging the page. However, developing an adhesive with appropriate stickiness was not an easy task. In the past, the 3M Company, where Art Fry worked, was known for providing products with great adhesion. For Art's purpose, however, a material was needed that not only had sufficient adhesion but also could be removed. The 3M laboratory did not provide much help in the research and development of such a product. Nor did the marketing department think a great deal of the idea. But being an inventor as well as an innovator, Art Fry pursued his goal with great perseverance. The result was Post-it note pads, which turned out to be a very profitable product for 3M.

Innovative persons often have ideas that are contrary to "conventional wisdom." It is quite common that these individuals are not well liked by their colleagues and that their contributions are often not sufficiently appreciated. It is, therefore, not surprising that entrepreneurs leave large companies and start their own businesses. When Steve Wozniak could not get his dream of building a small computer fulfilled at Hewlett-Packard, he left that prestigious firm to form — together with another entrepreneur, Steve Jobs — Apple Computers. Progressive companies, such as IBM or 3M, consciously try to develop an organizational environment that promotes entrepreneurship within the company.

THE STRUCTURE AND PROCESS OF ORGANIZING

Looking at organizing as a process requires that several fundamentals be considered. In the first place, the structure must reflect objectives and plans, because activities derive from them. In the second place, it must reflect the authority available to an enterprise's management. Authority in a given organization is a socially determined right to exercise discretion; as such, it is subject to change.

In the third place, organization structure, like any plan, must reflect its environment. Just as the premises of a plan may be economic, technological, political, social, or ethical, so may be those of an organization structure. It must be designed to work, to permit contributions by members of a group, and to help people gain objectives efficiently in a changing future. In this sense, a workable organization structure can never be static. There is no single organization structure that works best in all kinds of situations. An effective organization structure depends on the situation.

In the fourth place, since the organization is staffed with people, the groupings of activities and the authority relationships of an organization structure must take into account people's limitations and customs. This is not to say that the structure must be designed around individuals instead of around goals and accompanying activities. But an important consideration is the kind of people who are to staff it.

The Logic of Organizing

There is a fundamental logic to organizing, as shown in Figure 7-3. Although steps 1 and 2 are actually part of planning, the organizing process consists of the following six steps:

1. Establishing enterprise objectives
2. Formulating supporting objectives, policies, and plans
3. Identifying and classifying the activities necessary to accomplish these
4. Grouping these activities in the light of the human and material resources available and the best way, under the circumstances, of using them
5. Delegating to the head of each group the authority necessary to perform the activities
6. Tying the groups together horizontally and vertically, through authority relationships and information flows

Some Misconceptions

Organizing does not imply any extreme occupational specialization, which in many instances makes labor uninteresting, tedious, and unduly restrictive. There is nothing in organization itself that dictates this. To say that tasks should be specific is not to say they must be limited and mechanical. Whether they should be broken down into minute parts — as on a typical assembly line — or be defined broadly enough to encompass the design, production, and sale of a machine is for the organizer to consider in light of the results desired. In any organization, jobs can be defined to allow little or no personal leeway or the widest possible discretion. One must not forget that there is no best way to organize and that the application of structural organization theory must take into account the situation.

BASIC QUESTIONS FOR EFFECTIVE ORGANIZING

It is useful to analyze the managerial function of organizing by raising and answering the following questions:

1. What determines the span of management and hence the levels of organization? (answered in this chapter)

Figure 7-3

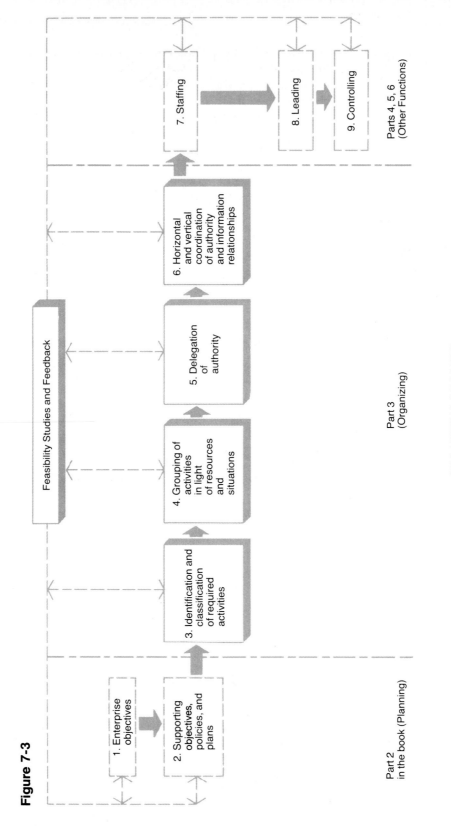

ORGANIZING PROCESS.

2. What determines the basic framework of departmentation, and what are the strengths and weaknesses of the basic forms? (answered in Chapter 8)

3. What kinds of authority relationships exist in organizations? (answered in Chapter 9)

4. How should authority be dispersed throughout the organization structure, and what determines the extent of this dispersion? (answered in Chapter 9)

5. How should the manager make organization theory work in practice? (answered in Chapter 10)

The answers to these questions form a basis for a theory of organizing. When considered along with similar analyses of planning, staffing, leading, and controlling, they constitute an operational approach to management.

SUMMARY

The term "organization" is often used loosely. Formal organization is the intentional structure of roles. Informal organization is a network of personal and social relations neither established nor required by formal authority but arising spontaneously. The term "span of management" refers to the number of people a manager can effectively supervise. A wide span of management results in few organizational levels, and a narrow span results in many levels. There is no definite number of people a manager can always effectively supervise; the number depends on several underlying factors. These include the degree of subordinate training required and possessed, the clarity of authority delegated, the clarity of plans, the rate of change, the use of objective standards, the effectiveness of communication techniques, the amount of personal contact needed, and the level in the organization. The steps in organizing include formulating objectives, subobjectives, policies, and plans to achieve the ends (strictly speaking, this is carried out in planning); identifying and classifying activities; grouping these activities; delegating authority; and coordinating authority as well as information relationships.

KEY IDEAS AND CONCEPTS FOR REVIEW

Organizational role
Organizing
Formal organization
Informal organization
Department
Principle of the span of
    management

Factors determining the span of
    management
Entrepreneuring
Intrapreneuring
Logical steps of organizing
Basic questions for effective
    organizing

FOR DISCUSSION

1. Since people must occupy organization positions, and since an effective organization depends on people, it is often said that the best organization arises when a manager hires good people and lets them do a job in their own way. Comment.

2. A formal organization is often conceived of as a communications system. Is it? How?

3. Construct a diagram depicting the formal organization of an enterprise or activity with which you are familiar. How does this organization chart help or hinder the establishment of an environment for performance?

4. Using the same enterprise or activity as in question 3, chart the informal organization. Does it help or hinder the formal organization? Why?

5. Urwick and other writers seem to say that at top levels the number of persons in the span of management should not exceed six. However, approximately 750 bishops and 1200 other persons have reported directly to the Pope. At one time in the Bank of America organization, over 600 bank managers reported to the chief executive officer. How do you square these facts with the idea that there is a limit to the number of subordinates a manager can supervise?

6. When you become a manager, what criteria will you favor to determine your span?

EXERCISES/ACTION STEPS

1. Organize a family picnic using the steps suggested in this chapter.

2. Interview a manager in your community and ask him or her how many subordinates he or she has. Are different numbers of subordinates supervised at the top, the middle, and the bottom of the organizational hierarchy? What really determines the span of management in this organization? Do you think the span is appropriate for the enterprise?

INTERNATIONAL CASE:
COMPETITIVE CHALLENGES FOR CARMAKERS[12]

The interdependencies of countries can best be illustrated by the global automobile war. About 175 companies produce over 45 million cars, buses, and trucks, which are sold around the world. The competition is so fierce that no country has a clear competitive advantage in all areas. In executive leadership, the American Lee Iacocca of Chrysler is often mentioned. In prestige, the European Mercedes-Benz is frequently cited. The Japanese are considered tough competitors, known for high productivity and adaptability. More recently, inexpensive Korean cars have entered the U.S. market. The beneficiaries of this competition are the car buyers, who can choose from a great variety of features such as Japanese reliability, European handling, and the comfort of the traditional American family car.

The car companies, however, face many problems besides competition: overcapacity in the United States and Europe; traffic congestion in metropolitan areas, which may limit the demand for cars; increasing concern about protectionism in Europe as well as in Japan; and other difficulties. Even so, there are opportunities, such as the demand for large and sporty cars in the United States. Although it has not yet materialized, there is an enormous expected demand for automobiles in less developed countries.

How, then, do the world's carmakers respond to or prepare for such challenges? Each company tries to use its own strength to compete in the world market. Fiat, an Italian car company, seems to have worked out its labor problems and can now focus on beating Volkswagen, the European leader. The strength of VW, on the other hand, is its automated assembly line. Moreover, VW has cooperative ventures with over ten automakers, including the German Daimler-Benz and Porsche, Japanese Nissan, Swedish Volvo, and Spanish SEAT.

Germany has become the second-largest market for Japanese cars (the largest is the United States). The strategy of Japanese automakers in Germany is similar to that in the United States: Get into the market, learn from mistakes and correct them quickly, listen to the customers, and have a flexible production line to adapt to customers' tastes. Carl Hahn, the chairman of VW, admitted that the Japanese cannot be beaten on productivity. The motto underlying a joint project with the Japanese seems to be "If you can't beat them, join them." Thus, Volkswagen and Toyota will produce pickup trucks designed by the Japanese.

Listening to the customers was one of the keys to success of Japanese car companies in Germany. They changed their styling to accommodate European preferences, and they equipped their cars with better suspension and steering to make them suitable for the German freeways, which have no speed limit. Similarly, they identified the need for minivans and four-wheel-drive vehicles and offered models to fill those needs.

One reason many Japanese carmakers can respond quickly to changes in the market is the fact that they deal with many suppliers. It has been estimated that Toyota, for example, buys about 80 percent of its parts from suppliers. The company also strengthened its market position in the United States by a joint venture with General Motors, producing cars in Fremont, California. Indeed, many Japanese carmakers have cooperative arrangements with foreign companies. The exception is Honda, which is quite independent. With its Japanese facilities used to its limits, Honda was one of the first foreign manufacturers (besides VW, which has closed its U.S. plant) to establish itself in the United States. The company's success led to the introduction of a new luxury car marketed under the Acura label.

In the past, General Motor's full model line and its enormous size were considered strengths. But it is now realized that these characteristics can also be weaknesses, hindering quick adaptation to changes in the environment. GM's vertical integration, in which the company produces some 70 percent of its own parts, may also contribute to its inflexibility. Although GM operates worldwide, there has been little cooperation between the U.S. Company and its foreign subsidiaries in the past. In contrast, Ford Motor Company has become truly international, with close coordination among its design centers in the United States, England, and Germany. Chrysler has enlarged its capacity through the purchase of American Motors. The company tries to stay competitive by adapting to changes in consumer demands through the use of flexible manufacturing techniques.

It is quite clear now that executives of major car companies have to take a global view of their business. While opportunities have been increased by internationalization, threats are always present. A shift in the direction of the interdependent economies or a dramatic change in oil prices can make or break the auto-mobile market. The challenges for the car-makers' executives are great indeed.

1. Why have Japanese car companies been so successful in the United States and in Germany?

2. What kind of organization structure is best for competing in the international car war? Why?

REFERENCES

1. Chester I. Barnard, *The Functions of the Executive* (Cambridge, Mass.: Harvard University Press, 1938, 1964).

2. Keith Davis and John Newstrom, *Human Behavior at Work* (New York: McGraw-Hill Book Company, 1985) p. 308.

3. Information has been gathered from a variety of sources, including Brian Dumaine, "A Humble Hero Drives Ford to the Top," *Fortune* (Jan. 4, 1988), pp. 23–24; Alex Taylor III, "Who's Ahead in the World Auto War," *Fortune* (Nov. 9, 1987), pp. 74–88; and James B. Treece, Mark Maremont, and Larry Armstrong, "Will the Auto Glut Choke Detroit?" *Business Week* (Mar. 7, 1987), pp. 54–62.

4. Lyndall Urwick, "Axioms of Organization," *Public Administration Magazine* (London), (October 1955), pp. 348–349. However, in other writings, Urwick modified this position by saying, "No person should supervise more than five, or at the most, six, direct subordinates *whose work interlocks.*" See *Notes on the Theory of Organization* (New York: American Management Association, 1952), p. 53.

5. As summarized in *Business Week* (Aug. 18, 1951), pp. 102–103. Healey found similar variations in his study of 409 manufacturing companies in Ohio, although the median was six subordinates. See J. H. Healey, *Executive Coordination and Control* (Columbus: Ohio State University Press, 1956), p. 66.

6. Robert D. Dewar and Donald P. Simet, "A Level Specific Prediction of Spans of Control Examining the Effects of Size, Technology, and Specialization," *Journal of the Academy of Management* (March 1981), pp. 5–24.

7. Ricky W. Griffin, *Management* (Boston: Houghton Mifflin Company, 1984), chap. 22.

8. Henry Mintzberg, *The Nature of Managerial Work* (New York: Harper & Row, 1973), chap. 4; James Brian Quinn, "Managing Innovation: Controlled Chaos," *Harvard Business Review* (May–June 1985), pp. 73–84. Entrepreneurship has also been extended to public organizations. See Ravi Ramamurti, "Public Entrepreneurs: Who They Are and How They Operate," *California Management Review* (Spring 1986), pp. 142–158.

9. Peter F. Drucker, "The Discipline of Innovation," *Harvard Business Review* (May–June 1985), pp. 67–72. See also Peter F. Drucker, "A Prescription for Entrepreneurial Management," *Industry Week* (Apr. 29, 1985), pp. 33–40.

10. Gifford Pinchot III, *Intrapreneuring* (New York: Harper & Row, 1985).

11. The Post-it story has been reported in various sources, including the videotape "In Search of Excellence"; Pinchot, *Intrapreneuring* (1985); and Lester C. Krogh, "Can the Entrepreneurial Spirit Exist within a Large Company?" *3M: An Executive Message,* delivered at the Conference Board, Conference on Research and Development, New York, Apr. 25, 1984.

12. The case is based on a variety of sources, including Taylor, "Who's Ahead in the World Auto War" (1987); Thomas F. O'Boyle, "German Pride in Cars Doesn't Stop Japan," *The Wall Street Journal* (Oct. 21, 1987); Dale D. Buss, "GM Slows Big Drive for Saturn to Produce Small Car in Five Years," *The Wall Street Journal* (Oct. 30, 1986); Thomas F. O'Boyle, "GM Tries to Reverse Its Losses in Europe," *The Wall Street Journal* (Feb. 12, 1987); James B. Treece, "Detroit Is Bracing for a One-Two Punch," *Business Week* (Nov. 16, 1987), pp. 136–144; John Templeman, "What Ended VW's American Dream," *Business Week* (Dec. 7, 1987), p. 63; Treece, Maremont, and Armstrong, "Will the Auto Glut Choke Detroit?" (1988).

CHAPTER 8

Basic Departmentation

CHAPTER OBJECTIVES

After reading this chapter, you should understand:

1. The basic patterns of traditional departmentation and the advantages and disadvantages of each
2. Matrix organizations and the steps that can be taken to avoid the dangers of disunity of command
3. The modern departmentation according to strategic business units (SBUs)
4. That there is no single best pattern of departmentation and that one must select patterns that will assist in accomplishing objectives in the light of the particular situation.

The limitation on the number of subordinates that can be directly managed would restrict the size of enterprises if it were not for the device of **departmentation.** Grouping activities and people into departments makes it possible to expand organizations — at least in theory — to an indefinite degree. Departments, however, differ with respect to the basic patterns used to group the activities. The nature of these patterns, developed out of logic and practice, and their relative merits will be dealt with in the following sections.

At the outset, it must be emphasized that there is no single best way of departmentizing that is applicable to all organizations or to all situations. The pattern used will depend on given situations and on what managers believe will yield the best results for them in the situation they face.

DEPARTMENTATION BY SIMPLE NUMBERS

Departmentation by simple numbers was once an important method in the organization of tribes, clans, and armies. Although it is rapidly falling into disuse, it still may have certain applications in modern society.

The simple-numbers method of departmentizing is achieved by tolling off persons who are to perform the same duties and putting them under the supervision of a manager. The essential fact is not what these people do, where they work, or what they work with; it is that the success of the undertaking depends only upon the number of people involved in it.

Even though a quick examination may impress an investigator with the number of people departmentized on a human resource basis, the usefulness of this organizational device has declined with each passing century. For one thing, technology has advanced, demanding more specialized and different skills. In the United States, the last stronghold of common labor was agriculture, and even here it is restricted more and more to the harvesting of fewer and fewer crops as farming operations become larger and more specialized.

A second reason for the decline of departmentizing purely by number is that groups composed of specialized personnel are frequently more efficient than those based merely on numbers. The reorganization of the defense forces of the United States on this basis is a case in point. People skilled in the use of different types of weapons have been combined into single units. For example, the addition of artillery and tactical air support to the traditional infantry division makes it a much more formidable fighting unit than it would be if each were organized separately.

A third and long-standing reason for the decline of departmentation by numbers is that it is useful only at the lowest level of the organization structure. As soon as any factor other than pure human power becomes important, the simple-numbers basis of departmentation fails to produce good results.

DEPARTMENTATION BY TIME

One of the oldest forms of departmentation, generally used at lower levels of the organization, is grouping activities on the basis of time. The use of shifts is common in many enterprises where for economic, technological, or other reasons the normal workday will not suffice. Examples of this kind of departmentation can be found in hospitals, where around-the-clock patient care is essential. Similarly, the fire department has to be ready to respond to emergencies at any time. But there are also technological reasons for the use of shifts. A steel furnace, for example, cannot be turned on and off at will; the process of making steel is continuous and requires workers to work in three shifts.

Advantages

These few examples indicate a number of advantages of departmentation by time. First, services can be rendered that go beyond the typical 8-hour day, often extending to 24 hours a day. Second, it is possible to use processes that cannot be interrupted, those that require a continuing cycle. Third, expensive capital equipment can be used more than 8 hours a day when workers in several shifts use the same machines. Fourth, some people — students attending classes during the day, for instance — find it convenient to work at night.

Disadvantages

Departmentation by time also has disadvantages. First, supervision may be lacking during the night shift. Second, there is the fatigue factor; it is difficult for most people to switch, for instance, from a day shift to a night shift and vice versa. Third, having several shifts may cause problems in coordination and communication. In a hospital, for example, nurses from different shifts attending the same patient may not be familiar with the patient's particular problems. In a factory, the night shift may not clean up the machines to be used by the day shift people. Fourth, the payment of overtime rates can increase the cost of the product or service.

DEPARTMENTATION BY ENTERPRISE FUNCTION

Grouping activities in accordance with the functions of an enterprise — **functional departmentation** — embodies what enterprises typically do. Since all enterprises undertake the creation of something useful and desired by others, the basic enterprise functions are production (creating utility or adding utility to a good or service), selling (finding customers, patients, clients, students, or members who will agree to accept the good or service at a price or for a cost), and financing (raising and collecting, safeguarding, and expending the funds of the enterprise). It has been logical to group these activities into such departments as engineering, production, sales or marketing, and finance. Figure 8-1 shows a typical functional grouping for a manufacturing company.

Often, these particular functional designations do not appear in the organization chart. First, there is no generally accepted terminology: A manufacturing enterprise employs the terms "production," "sales," and "finance"; a wholesaler is concerned with such activities as "buying," "selling," and "finance"; and a railroad is involved with "operations," "traffic," and "finance."

A second reason for the variance of terms is that basic activities often differ in importance: Hospitals have no selling departments; churches, no production departments. This does not mean that these activities are not undertaken, but merely that they are unspecialized or of such minor importance that they are combined with other activities.

A third reason for the absence of sales, production, or finance departments on many organization charts is that other methods of departmentation may have been deliberately selected. Those responsible for the enterprise may decide to organize on the basis of product, customer, territory, or marketing channel (the way goods or services reach the user).

Figure 8-1

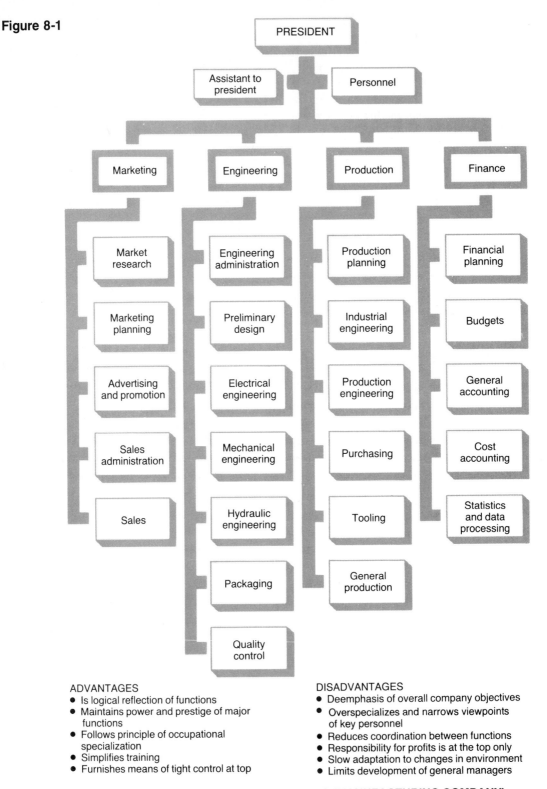

ADVANTAGES
- Is logical reflection of functions
- Maintains power and prestige of major functions
- Follows principle of occupational specialization
- Simplifies training
- Furnishes means of tight control at top

DISADVANTAGES
- Deemphasis of overall company objectives
- Overspecializes and narrows viewpoints of key personnel
- Reduces coordination between functions
- Responsibility for profits is at the top only
- Slow adaptation to changes in environment
- Limits development of general managers

A FUNCTIONAL ORGANIZATION GROUPING (MANUFACTURING COMPANY).

Functional departmentation is the most widely employed basis for organizing activities and is present in almost every enterprise at some level in the organization structure. The characteristics of the selling, production, and finance functions of enterprises are so widely recognized and thoroughly understood that they are the basis not only of departmental organization but also, most often, of departmentation at the top level.

Coordination of activities may be achieved through rules and procedures, various aspects of planning (e.g., goals and budgets), the organizational hierarchy, personal contacts, and sometimes liaison departments. Such a department may be used between engineering and manufacturing to handle design or change problems.[1]

Advantages

The most important advantage of functional departmentation is that it is a logical and time-proven method. It is also the best way of making certain that the power and prestige of the basic activities of the enterprise will be defended by the top managers. This is an important consideration among functional managers, for they see on every side the encroachments of staff and service groups, which sometimes threaten the security of the principal line executives. Another advantage is that functional departmentation follows the principle of occupational specialization and thereby facilitates efficiency in the utilization of people. Still other advantages are that it simplifies training and, because the top managers are responsible for the end results, furnishes a means of tight control at the top.

Disadvantages

In spite of the advantages of functional departmentation, there are times when the claims of other methods seem even stronger. The size of the geographic area over which an enterprise operates may call for territorial grouping of activities; the production or purchase of numerous product lines, or of products designed for certain buyer classifications, may call for grouping along product or customer lines. In addition, functional departmentation may tend to de-emphasize overall enterprise objectives. Accountants, production experts, and salespeople, working in specialized departments, often have problems seeing the business as a whole, and coordination among them is frequently difficult to achieve. They develop attitudes and other behavior patterns involving loyalty to a functional department and not to the enterprise as a whole. Such "walls" between functional departments are common, and considerable effort is required to break them down.

Another disadvantage is that only the chief executive officer can be held responsible for profits. In small firms, this is all right, but in large firms the burden becomes too heavy for one person to bear. Also, this kind of departmentation makes it difficult to adapt quickly to environmental changes.[2] What is perhaps most important is that since the lowest general managerial position is that of the president or the executive vice-president, the functionally organized company is not the best training ground for promotable top-management people.

DEPARTMENTATION BY TERRITORY OR GEOGRAPHY

Departmentation based on territory is rather common in enterprises that operate over wide geographic areas. In this case, it may be important that activities in a given area or territory be grouped and assigned to a manager, for example, as shown in Figure 8-2.

Figure 8-2

ADVANTAGES

- Places responsibility at a lower level
- Places emphasis on local markets and problems
- Improves coordination in a region
- Takes advantage of economies of local operations
- Better face-to-face communication with local interests
- Furnishes measurable training ground for general managers

DISADVANTAGES

- Requires more persons with general manager abilities
- Tends to make maintenance of economical central services difficult and may require services such as personnel or purchasing at the regional level
- Increases problem of top management control

**A TERRITORIAL, OR GEOGRAPHIC, ORGANIZATION GROUPING
(MANUFACTURING COMPANY).**

Extent of Use

Territorial departmentation is especially attractive to large-scale firms or other enterprises whose activities are physically or geographically dispersed. However, a plant may be local in its activities and still assign the personnel in its security department on a territorial basis, placing two guards, for example, at each of the south and west gates. Department stores assign floorwalkers on this basis, and it is a common way to assign janitors, window washers, and the like. Business firms resort to this method when similar operations are undertaken in different geographic areas, as in automobile assembling, chain retailing and wholesaling, and oil refining. Many government agencies — the Internal Revenue Service, the Federal Reserve Board, the federal courts, and the Postal Service, among others — adopt this basis of organization in their efforts to provide like services simultaneously across the nation. Territorial departmentation is most often used in sales and in production; it is not used in finance, which is usually concentrated at the headquarters.

Advantages

Departmentation by territory, or geography, offers a number of advantages. It places responsibility at a lower level, encourages local participation in decision making, and improves coordination of activities in a region. Managers can give special attention to the needs and problems of local markets. Thus, they may recruit local salespeople who are familiar with the special situation in the area. Moreover, these salespeople can spend more time selling and less time traveling.

Production may also be organized on a territorial basis by establishing plants in a particular region. This can reduce transportation costs and delivery time. Moreover, labor rates may be lower in certain regions, and producing things locally may create jobs and goodwill in the local community.

Geographic departmentation improves face-to-face communication with local people. Also, since the manager in a territory has to carry out many different functional and managerial activities, this type of organization provides a good training ground for general managers.

Disadvantages

There are also disadvantages in organizing territorially. This kind of departmentation requires more persons with general managerial abilities, and a shortage of them is often a factor limiting the growth of an enterprise. Moreover, geographic departmentation tends to lead to duplication of services. Thus, managers of a territory want to have their own purchasing, personnel, accounting, and other services — services that are also carried out in the home office. This duplication, naturally, can be costly. Finally, geographic departmentation may increase the problem of control by top managers at the headquarters, who may find it difficult to monitor the activities of the departments located in various territories.

CUSTOMER DEPARTMENTATION

Grouping activities so that they reflect a primary interest in customers is common in a variety of enterprises. Customers are the key to the way activities are grouped when each of the different things an enterprise does for them is managed by one department head. The industrial sales department of a wholesaler that also sells to retailers is a case in point. Business owners and managers frequently arrange activities on this basis to cater to the requirements of clearly defined customer groups, and educational institutions offer regular and extension courses to serve different groups of students.

There are difficult decisions to be made in separating some types of customer departments from product departments. For example, in the great central cash markets for agricultural products, the loan officers of commercial banks frequently specialize in fruit, vegetables, or grain, even to the point where an individual officer will make loans only on wheat or oranges. This is a case of customer departmentation, since loan service is provided by type of customer. Figure 8-3 illustrates a typical customer departmentation in a large bank.

Figure 8-3

ADVANTAGES

- Encourages concentration on customer needs
- Gives customers feeling that they have an understanding supplier (banker)
- Develops expertness in customer area

DISADVANTAGES

- May be difficult to coordinate operations between competing customer demands
- Requires managers and staff expert in customers' problems
- Customer groups may not always be clearly defined (for example, large corporate firms vs. other corporate businesses)

CUSTOMER DEPARTMENTATION IN A LARGE BANK.

Advantages

Customer departmentation can address the special and widely varied needs of customers for clearly defined services. The manufacturer that sells to both wholesalers and industrial buyers frequently can meet their special needs by setting up separate departments.

Nonbusiness groups follow similar practices. The extension services of universities, such as night-school divisions, are arranged, with respect to time, subject matter, and sometimes instructors, to appeal to an entirely different group of students than those who attend the university on a full-time day basis. The operations of a United Way drive are arranged on the basis of different "customer" classifications. And departments of the federal government are set up to care for farmers, businesspeople, industrial workers, the elderly, and other specific groups.

Disadvantages

Customer departmentation is not without certain drawbacks. There is, for instance, the difficulty of coordination between this type of department and those organized on other bases, with constant pressure from the managers of customer departments for special treatment.

Another disadvantage is the possibility of underemployment of facilities and labor-specialized workers in customer groups. In periods of recession, some customer groups may all but disappear, for example, machine-tool buyers; in periods of expansion, the unequal development of customer groups and demands is characteristic.

PROCESS OR EQUIPMENT DEPARTMENTATION

Manufacturing firms often group activities around a process or a type of equipment. Such a basis of departmentation can be found in paint or electroplating process grouping or in the arrangement in one plant area of punch presses or automatic screw machines. In this kind of departmentation, people and materials are brought together in order to carry out a particular operation. Figure 8-4 illustrates such an organizational arrangement.

One common example of equipment departmentation is the electronic data processing department. As installations for data processing have become expensive and complex, with ever-increasing capacities, they have tended to be organized in a separate department. Most large and even medium-size companies have such departments. In some cases, computer stations connected to an enterprise's central computer (or to an outside one on a time-sharing or leasing basis), minicomputers, and electronic desktop computers have tended to slow the growth of centralized computer departments. However, major data processing departments will unquestionably continue to exist and to be placed fairly high in the organization structure.

Figure 8-4

ADVANTAGES
- Achieves economic advantage
- Uses specialized technology
- Utilizes special skills

DISADVANTAGES
- Coordination of departments is difficult
- Responsibility for profit is at the top
- Is unsuitable for developing general managers

PROCESS OF EQUIPMENT DEPARTMENTATION.

DEPARTMENTATION BY PRODUCT

Grouping activities on the basis of product or product lines has long been growing in importance in multiline, large-scale enterprises. It can be seen as an evolutionary process. Typically, companies and other enterprises adopting this form of departmentation were organized by enterprise functions. With the growth of the firm, production managers, sales and service managers, and engineering executives encountered problems of size. The managerial job became complex, and the span of management limited their ability to increase the number of immediate subordinate managers. At this point, reorganization on a product division basis became necessary. This structure permits top management to delegate to a division executive extensive authority over the manufacturing, sales, service, and engineering functions that relate to a given product or product line and to exact a considerable degree of profit responsibility from each of these managers. Figure 8-5 shows an example of a typical product organization grouping for a manufacturing company.[3]

Advantages

Product or product line is an important basis for departmentation because it facilitates the use of specialized capital (e.g., a press for molding car bodies), promotes a certain type of coordination, and permits the maximum use of personal skills and specialized knowledge. For example, the sales effort of a particular person may be most effective when confined to lubricants, or conveyors, or power plants, each of which is best sold by an expert thoroughly familiar with the product. For companies whose potential volume of business is high enough to justify fully employing such salespeople, the advantages of product departmentation are significant. If production of an item, or closely related items, is on a scale sufficient to warrant fully specialized facilities, strong pressure may be felt for product departmentation in order to realize economic advantages in manufacturing, assembly, or handling. Note also that this kind of departmentation permits growth and diversity of products and services offered by the firm.

If it is important for activities relating to a particular product to be coordinated, then product departmentation may be preferred. Better timing and customer service can thus sometimes be provided. If sales and engineering efforts are also located in the plant, cooperation with production can be exceptionally good. However, other factors, which will be considered later, may reduce this advantage.

Finally, profit responsibility can be exacted from product department managers. When such executives supervise the sales, production, engineering,

Figure 8-5

ADVANTAGES
- Places attention and effort on product line
- Facilitates use of specialized capital, facilities, skills, and knowledge
- Permits growth and diversity of products and services
- Improves coordination of functional activities
- Places responsibility for profits at the division level
- Furnishes measurable training ground for general managers

DISADVANTAGES
- Requires more persons with general manager abilities
- Tends to make maintenance of economical central services difficult
- Presents increased problem of top management control

A PRODUCT ORGANIZATION GROUPING (MANUFACTURING COMPANY).

service, and cost functions, they may be held responsible for certain profit goals. Along with other similarly organized groups, they have the responsibility of producing a profit, and this enables top managers to evaluate more intelligently the contribution of each product line to total profit. Moreover, this kind of departmentation provides a measurable training ground for general managers.

Some Notes of Caution

In considering these advantages, however, it is essential to avoid oversimplification. Product-line managers may be saddled with heavy overhead costs, allocated from the expense of operating the headquarters office, perhaps a central research division, and, frequently, many central service divisions. Product managers understandably resent being charged with costs over which they have no control.

Disadvantages

The disadvantages of product departmentation are similar to those of territorial departmentation. They include the necessity of having available more persons with general managerial abilities, the dangers of increased costs through duplication of central service and staff activities, and the problem of maintaining top-management control. The latter is especially important because a product division manager is, to a very great extent, in the same position as the chief executive of a single-product-line company. Enterprises that operate with product divisions must have enough decision making and control at the headquarters level to ensure that the entire enterprise does not disintegrate.

MATRIX ORGANIZATION

Another kind of departmentation is matrix or grid organization, or project or product management. As will be explained later, however, pure project management need not imply a grid or matrix. The essence of **matrix organization** normally is the combining of functional and product patterns of departmentation in the same organization structure. As shown in Figure 8-6, which depicts matrix organization in an engineering department, there are functional managers in charge of engineering functions and an overlay of project managers responsible for the end product. While this form has been common in engineering and in research and development, it has also been widely used, although seldom drawn as a matrix, in product marketing organization.

This kind of organization occurs frequently in construction (e.g., building a bridge), in aerospace (e.g., designing and launching a weather satellite), in marketing (e.g., an advertising campaign for a major new product), in the installation of an electronic data processing system, or in management consulting firms in which professional experts work together on a project.[4]

Figure 8-6

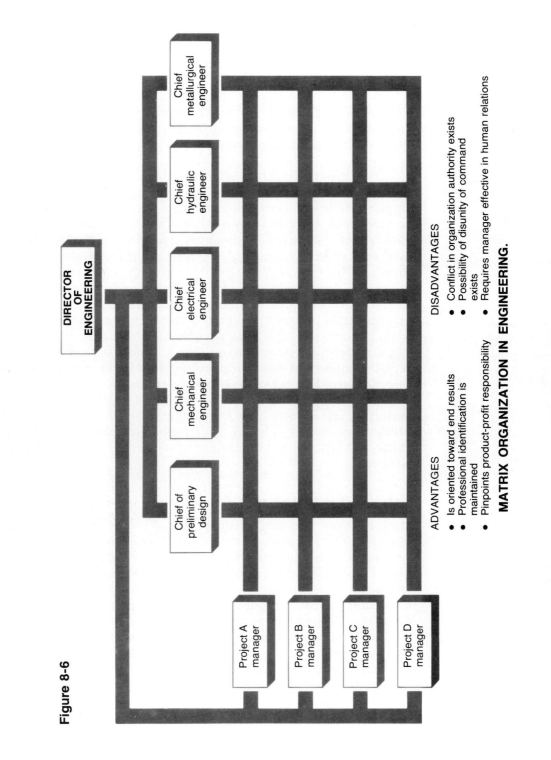

DIRECTOR OF ENGINEERING

Chief of preliminary design

Chief mechanical engineer

Chief electrical engineer

Chief hydraulic engineer

Chief metallurgical engineer

Project A manager

Project B manager

Project C manager

Project D manager

ADVANTAGES
- Is oriented toward end results
- Professional identification is maintained
- Pinpoints product-profit responsibility

DISADVANTAGES
- Conflict in organization authority exists
- Possibility of disunity of command exists
- Requires manager effective in human relations

MATRIX ORGANIZATION IN ENGINEERING.

Why Matrix Management Is Used

As companies and customers have become increasingly interested in end results, that is, in the final product or completed project, there has been pressure to establish responsibility for ensuring such end results. Of course, this could be accomplished by organizing along traditional product department lines. This is often done, even in engineering, where a project manager is put in charge of all the engineering and support personnel necessary to accomplish an entire project. This kind of organization is depicted in Figure 8-7.

But pure project organization may not be feasible for a number of reasons. For example, the project may not be able to utilize certain specialized engineering personnel or equipment full time: a solid-state physicist may be needed only occasionally or the project may need only part-time use of an expensive environmental test laboratory or a prototype shop. Also, the project may be of relatively short duration. Although there is no logical reason why an organization structure should not be changed daily or monthly, there is the practical reason that people, particularly highly trained professionals, simply may not tolerate the insecurity of frequent organization change. Another reason why pure project organization may not be feasible is that highly trained professionals (and some that are not so highly trained) generally prefer to be allied organizationally with their professional group. They feel more at home in the functional department; they feel that their professional reputation and advancement will be better served by belonging to such a group than by being allied with a project; and they believe that their superiors, if they are professionals in the same field, will be more likely to appreciate their expertise at times of salary advances, promotions, or layoffs. These feelings ordinarily exist not only among engineers and scientists but also among lawyers, accountants, and university professors.

Variations in Practice

There are many variations of the project or product manager role. In some cases, the project or product managers have no authority to tell any functional department to do anything; they may be only information gatherers, keeping tabs on how their project or product is proceeding and reporting to a top executive when significant deviations from plans occur. In other cases, they might be persuaders, using knowledge and personal persuasiveness to get results. Obviously, these roles have some very serious drawbacks, particularly if the manager without any organization power whatsoever is actually held responsible for end results. No wonder that turnover among those who hold such positions has been high!

Another variation in practice is simply to draw a grid or matrix, like that in Figure 8-6, showing certain managers in charge of functional departments and others in charge of projects or products. This grid is usually intended to represent a pure case of dual command. The results are predictable. If something goes wrong with a project or product, it is often difficult for a top superior to know who is at fault and where the difficulties really lie. Also, in

Figure 8-7

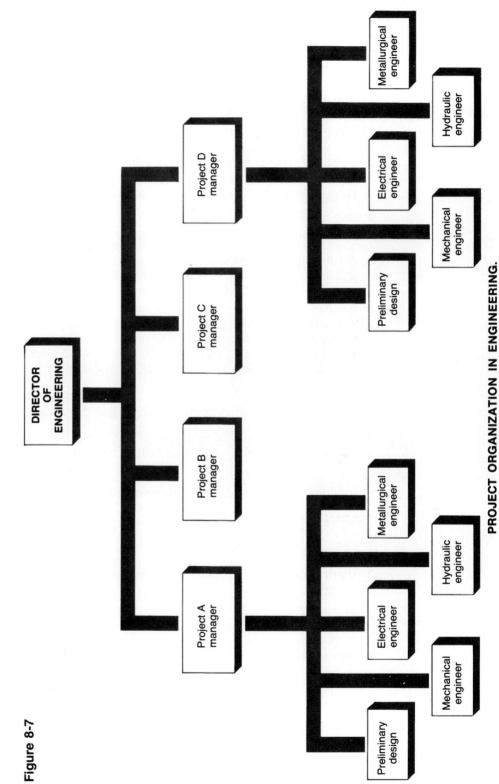

PROJECT ORGANIZATION IN ENGINEERING.

such cases, there tend to arise the usual friction, buck-passing, and confusion one would expect to result from disunity of command.

Problems with Matrix Management

Let us summarize some typical problems found in matrix management.[5]

1. A state of conflict exists between functional and project managers, as both compete for limited resources (e.g., financial and human). Moreover, members on the project team may encounter role ambiguity.

2. Role conflict, role ambiguity, and role overload may result in stress for the functional and project managers as well as for the team members.

3. An imbalance of authority and power, as well as horizontal and vertical influence of the project and functional managers, can also lead to problems in matrix organizations.[6] If, for example, the functional manager has too much power, work on a particular project may receive a low priority, thereby delaying its completion. An imbalance of authority in favor of the project manager, on the other hand, may result in inefficiencies. The functional manager, for example, may frequently be required to change the machine setup to accommodate work on various projects.

4. Because of the potential conflicts, managers may want to protect themselves against blame by putting everything in writing, which increases administration costs.

5. Matrix organization requires many time-consuming meetings.[7]

Guidelines for Making Matrix Management Effective[8]

Matrix management can be made more effective by following these guidelines:

1. Define the objectives of the project or task.

2. Clarify the roles, authorities, and responsibilities of managers and team members.

3. Ensure that influence is based on knowledge and information, rather than on rank.

4. Balance the power of functional and project managers.

5. Select an experienced manager for the project who can provide leadership.

6. Undertake organization and team development.

7. Install appropriate cost, time, and quality controls that report deviations from standards in a timely manner.

8. Reward project managers and team members fairly.

STRATEGIC BUSINESS UNITS

More recently, companies have been using an organizational device generally referred to as a **strategic business unit** (SBU). SBUs are distinct little businesses set up as units in a larger company to ensure that a certain product or product line is promoted and handled as though it were an independent business. One of the earlier users of this organizational device was the General Electric Company. This special organization unit was introduced to ensure that each product or product line of the hundreds offered by the company would receive the same attention as it would if it were developed, produced, and marketed by an independent company. In some cases companies have also used the device for a major product line. Occidental Chemical Company, for example, used it for such products as phosphates, alkalis, and resins.[9]

To be called an SBU, a business unit must meet specific criteria. An SBU, for example, must (1) have its own mission, distinct from the missions of other SBUs, (2) have definable groups of competitors, (3) prepare its own integrative plans, fairly distinct from those of other SBUs, (4) manage its resources in key areas, and (5) have a proper size — neither too large nor too small.[10] Obviously, in practice it might be difficult to define SBUs that meet all of these criteria.

For each SBU a manager (usually a "business manager") is appointed with responsibility for guiding and promoting the product from the research laboratory through product engineering, market research, production, packaging, and marketing and with bottom-line responsibility for its profitability.[11] Thus, an SBU is given its own missions and goals, as well as a manager who, with the assistance of a full-time or part-time staff (people from other departments assigned to the SBU on a part-time basis), will develop and implement strategic and operating plans for the product. The organization of a typical SBU, that for phosphates in the Occidental Chemical Company, is shown in Figure 8-8. Note that reporting to the business manager for phosphates are all the functions that would be found necessary in a separate company.

Obviously, the major benefit of utilizing an SBU organization is to provide assurance that a product will not get "lost" among other products (usually those with larger sales and profits) in a large company. It preserves the attention and energies of a manager and staff whose job it is to guide and promote a product or product line. It is thus an organizational technique for preserving the entrepreneurial attention and drive so characteristic of the small company. In fact, it is an excellent means of promoting entrepreneurship, which is likely to be so lacking in the large company.

CHOOSING THE PATTERN OF DEPARTMENTATION

There is no one best way of departmentizing applicable to all organizations and all situations.[12] Managers must determine what is best by looking at the situation they face — the jobs to be done and the way they should be done, the people involved and their personalities, the technology employed in the

Figure 8-8

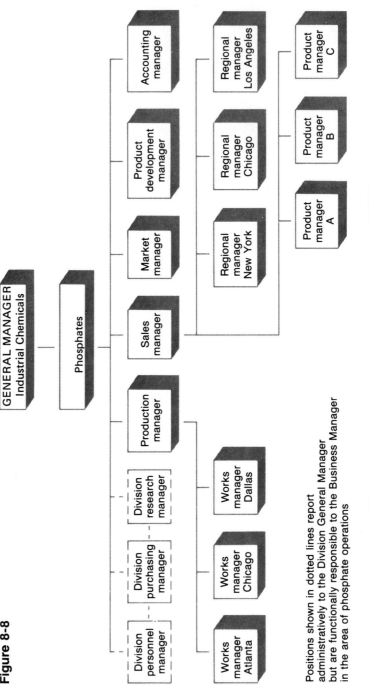

Positions shown in dotted lines report
administratively to the Division General Manager
but are functionally responsible to the Business Manager
in the area of phosphate operations

**TYPICAL STRATEGIC BUSINESS UNIT ORGANIZATION
IN A LARGE INDUSTRIAL CHEMICAL COMPANY.**

department, the users being served, and other internal and external environmental factors in the situation. However, if they know the various departmentation patterns, and the advantages, disadvantages, and dangers of each, practicing managers should be able to design the organization structure most suitable for their particular operations.[13]

The Aim: Achieving Objectives

Departmentation is not an end in itself but is simply a method of arranging activities to facilitate the accomplishment of objectives. Each method has its advantages and disadvantages. Consequently, the process of selection involves a consideration of the relative advantages of each pattern at each level in the organization structure. In all cases, the central question concerns the type of organizational environment that the manager wishes to design and the situation being faced. The preceding discussion of the alternative methods of departmentation showed that each method yields certain gains and involves certain costs.

Mixing Types of Departmentation

Another point to be highlighted concerns the mixing of types of departmentation within a functional area. For example, a wholesale drug firm has grouped the buying and selling activities relating to beverages in one product department, but it has grouped, on the same level, all other selling activities on a territorial basis. A manufacturer of plastic goods has territorialized both the production and the sale of all its products except dinnerware, which is itself a product department. A functional department manager may, in other words, employ two or more bases for grouping activities on the same organizational levels. Such practices may be justified on logical grounds: The objective of departmentation is not to build a rigid structure, balanced in terms of levels and characterized by consistency and identical bases, but to group activities in the manner which will best contribute to achieving enterprise objectives. If a variety of bases does this, there is no reason why managers should not take advantage of the alternatives before them.

The logic of this view is frequently ignored by those who design organization structures. For some reason, possibly to make an organization chart look pretty or to maintain control, specialists often insist that all departmentized activities below the primary level of organization be grouped in exactly the same manner. For instance, the organization structure of the Internal Revenue Service at the regional and district levels is essentially the same, despite tremendous variation in district sizes. Firms with multiplants often organize them in the same way; thus, the same departments will be found in virtually all Sears, Roebuck and Company stores.

Creating an identical organization structure in similar enterprise groupings merely to make an organizational chart look nice is really not good practice

The organization planner may think it "looks better," but this is a poor reason for organizing in a particular way. The matter of control, however, is quite different. There may be very important reasons for comparing the operation of similarly organized plants, stores, and agencies. They all may be comparable profit centers; consequently, their managers can be more readily compared within this organization structure. Even though these, and others, are important arguments for similarity of organization structure, it must be remembered that no one organizes to control; people organize to produce efficiently and effectively. If the latter purpose is sacrificed for the former, the cost of control is too great.

SUMMARY

The grouping of activities and people into departments makes organizational expansion possible. Departmentation can be done by simple numbers, by time, by enterprise function, by territory or geography, by the kinds of customer served, and by the process of equipment required. Relatively new kinds of departmentation are the product, matrix or grid, or project organization and the strategic business unit.

There is no single best way to organize; the most appropriate pattern depends on various factors in a given situation. These factors include the kind of job to be done, the way the task must be done, the kinds of people involved, the technology, the people served, and other internal and external considerations. At any rate, the selection of a specific departmentation pattern should be done so that organizational and individual objectives can be achieved effectively and efficiently. Accomplishing this goal often requires mixing forms of departmentation.

KEY IDEAS AND CONCEPTS FOR REVIEW

Departmentation by simple numbers
Departmentation by time
Departmentation by enterprise function
Departmentation by territory or geography
Customer departmentation

Process or equipment departmentation
Departmentation by product
Matrix organization (or grid, or project, or product)
Strategic business units (SBUs)

FOR DISCUSSION

1. Some sociologists tell us that organization structuring is a social invention. What do you think they mean? Do they imply that there is a "right" or "wrong" way to organize? What test of whether an organization structure is "right" would you suggest?

2. If you were the president of a company that was organized along functional lines and a consultant suggested that you organize along territorial or product lines, what might concern you in following this recommendation?

3. Why do you think that many large companies have organized along product lines (e.g., General Motors and DuPont), while other large companies have territorial departments (e.g., Prudential Life Insurance Company)?

4. Why do most large department store and supermarket chains organize their stores on a territorial basis and then organize the internal store units by products? Give examples from your own experience.

5. Why do most small companies use functionally organized departments?

6. Why are so many federal government agencies organized primarily on a territorial basis?

7. Do you see any reasons why managing by objectives may result in increased use of matrix organizational structures?

8. How does this chapter illustrate a situational approach to management?

EXERCISES/ACTION STEPS

1. Divide the class into groups of four or five students (depending on class size). Assign one pattern of departmentation to each group (assign two to each if the class is small). The groups should discuss (*a*) the nature of the assigned departmentation, (*b*) companies that use this departmental arrangement, (*c*) the advantages of the departmentation, and (*d*) the disadvantages of the departmentation.

2. Select a company and identify the departmentation pattern (or patterns) used by the enterprise. Draw an organization chart for the firm. Why do you think the company selected the type of departmentation it did? Would you recommend a different departmentation arrangement? State your reasons for your recommendation.

CASE:
AGRICULTURAL FERTILIZER DIVISION OF THE NORTHERN CHEMICAL CORPORATION

At the end of a busy day, a group of middle-level managers of the Agricultural Fertilizer Division of the Northern Chemical Corporation gathered to reflect on their problems. The headquarters of Northern Chemical had recently set up a central data processing department in Houston, where all the corporation's data processing would be done for its various divisions located throughout the United States. At that time, the data processing equipment of every division had been taken away; each division headquarters office was given a terminal connected to Houston, and each division was required to get any report processing it needed from the Houston facility.

The headquarters of the Agricultural Fertilizer Division was located in Sacramento, California. This division had long concentrated on developing and selling fertilizers to the large agricultural growers in the West and on distributing its garden and house plant fertilizers to stores throughout the country. It had been very successful, with sales growing rapidly and profits even faster. But the line managers of the division were quite unhappy about not being able to have their own computer facilities to give them the analyses and reports they needed.

Bill Jacobs, production planning and control supervisor, was particularly disturbed about the change to centralized data processing. "There is no way," said Jacobs, "that I can plan our products, especially with our many products and customers and the demands of our large growers for good service, if Houston runs our programs. The people there do not always have the data needed in their data bank, and, by the time I get it worked out with them, I have lost much valuable time."

Barry Hill, district sales manager for Northern California, was even unhappier. He pointed out that he often needed to run productivity and profitability studies for large growers and he could not do so unless the division had a computer operation in its own offices in Sacramento. "The growers will never understand why I cannot make these analyses for them quickly, nor will they understand why they must be made in Houston; they will soon tell me that there are other companies that can serve their needs," moaned Hill.

"You do have a problem," said Mona Fredericks, head of statistical analyses and reports in the division controller's office. "But yours is a small one compared with mine. I have to get many special and regular reports to headquarters, to the division managers, and to all you people in sales, market research, product development, and production. You always want them right away and in the form you can use most easily. How can I do that for you now?"

The frustration reached its peak when Joe Morey, cost control supervisor, startled the group by saying: "Did you know that all the departments in our division are being charged fees each month for Houston's services and that these are higher than the costs when we each had our own little computer system?"

1. Do you agree that these people have a serious problem?

2. If you were one of them, what would you do about it?

3. If you were to look at this purely as an organization problem, what conclusions would you draw?

REFERENCES

1. Jay R. Galbraith, "Matrix Organization Designs: How to Combine Functional and Project Forms," in Harold Koontz, Cyril O'Donnell, and Heinz Weihrich (eds.), *Management: A Book of Readings,* 5th ed. (New York: McGraw-Hill Book Company, 1980), pp. 292–300.

2. Thomas J. Peters and Robert H. Waterman, Jr., *In Search of Excellence* (New York: Harper & Row, 1982).

3. Product management is also used in nonmanufacturing companies. See, for example, Robert B. Fetter and Jean L. Freeman, "Diagnosis Related Groups: Product Line Management within Hospitals," *Academy of Management Review* (January 1986), pp. 41–54.

4. John M. Stewart, "Making Project Management Work" in Harold Koontz and Cyril O'Donnell (eds.), *Management: A Book of Readings,* 2d ed. (New York: McGraw-Hill Book Company, 1968), pp. 202–213; Kenneth Knight, in Koontz, O'Donnell, and Weihrich, *Management* (1980), pp. 301–312.

5. Based primarily on Knight, in *Management* (1980).

6. Although not directly related to matrix organization, an interesting discussion of power relationships is by Fernando Bartolome and Andre Laurent, "The Manager: Master and Servant of Power," *Harvard Business Review* (November–December 1986), pp. 77–81.

7. For additional information on limitations of matrix management, see Robert A. Pitts and John D. Daniels, "Aftermath of the Matrix Mania," *Columbia Journal of World Business* (Summer 1984), pp. 48–54.

8. Stewart, in *Management* (1968); Knight, in *Management* (1980); Jay Galbraith, *Designing Complex Organizations* (Reading, Mass.: Addison-Wesley Publishing Company, 1973), chap. 5. See also William H. Hoffmann, "Strategy Matrix," *Managerial Planning* (May–June 1985), pp. 4–9, 75.

9. For a discussion of SBUs, see W. K. Hall, "SBUs: Hot, New Topic in the Management of Diversification," *Business Horizons* (February 1978), pp. 13–23.

10. Frederick W. Gluck, "A Fresh Look at Strategic Management," *Journal of Business Strategy* (Fall 1985), pp. 4–19.

11. For a discussion of the effective use of business units, see Boris Yavitz and William H. Newman. "What the Corporation Should Provide Its Business Units," *Journal of Business Strategy* (Summer 1982), pp. 14–19.

12. An argument for using relatively simple organizational forms, even for multinational companies, has been made after a study of four Swedish firms by Gunnar Hedlund, "Organization In-Between: The Evolution of the Mother-Daughter Structure of Managing Foreign Subsidiaries in Swedish MNCs," *Journal of International Business Studies* (Fall 1984), pp. 109–122.

13. For an interesting review of books on organizing, see P. H. Ginyer, "Designing Effective Organizations — Book Review Articles," *Long Range Planning* (April 1984), pp. 151–156.

CHAPTER 9

Line/Staff Authority and Decentralization

CHAPTER OBJECTIVES

After reading this chapter, you should understand:

1. The nature of authority and power
2. The difference between line and staff, realizing their nature as relationships rather than positions or people
3. The nature and use of functional authority as a mixture of line and staff
4. Centralization, decentralization, and delegation of authority
5. The importance of obtaining balance in the centralization and decentralization of authority

Now that the patterns of departmentation have been discussed, it is time to consider another essential question: What kind of authority is found in an organizational structure? The question has to do with the nature of authority relationships — the problem of line and staff. This chapter will also deal with the question: How much authority should be delegated? The answer concerns decentralization of authority. Without authority — the power to exercise discretion in making decisions — properly placed in managers, various departments cannot become smoothly working units harmonized for the accomplishment of enterprise objectives. Authority relationships, whether vertical or horizontal, are the factors that make organization possible, facilitate departmental activities, and bring coordination to an enterprise.

AUTHORITY AND POWER

Before concentrating on the authority in organization, it will be useful to distinguish between authority and power. **Power,** a much broader concept than authority, is the ability of individuals or groups to induce or influence the beliefs or actions of other persons or groups.[1] **Authority** in organization is the right in a position (and, through it, the right of the person occupying the position) to exercise discretion in making decisions affecting others. It is, of course, one type of power, but power in an organization setting.

Although there are many different **bases of power,** the power of primary concern in this book is *legitimate* power.[2] It normally arises from position and derives from our cultural system of rights, obligations, and duties whereby a "position" is accepted by people as being "legitimate." In a privately owned business, authority of position arises primarily from the social institution (a "bundle of rights") of private property. In government, this authority arises basically from the institution of representative government. A traffic officer who gives you a traffic ticket gets the power to do so because we have a system of representative government in which we have elected legislators to make laws and provide for their enforcement.

Power may also come from the *expertness* of a person or a group. This is the power of knowledge. Physicians, lawyers, and university professors may have considerable influence on others because they are respected for their special knowledge. Power may further exist as *referent* power, that is, influence which people or groups may exercise because people believe in them and their ideas. Thus, Martin Luther King had very little legitimate power, but, by the force of his personality, his ideas, and his ability to preach, he strongly influenced the behavior of many people. Likewise, a movie star or a military hero might possess considerable referent power.

In addition, power arises from the ability of some people to grant rewards. Purchasing agents, with little position power, might be able to exercise considerable influence by their ability to expedite or delay a much-needed spare part. Likewise, university professors have considerable *reward* power; they can grant or withhold high grades.

Coercive power is still another type. Although closely related to reward power and normally arising from legitimate power, it is the power to punish, whether by firing a subordinate or withholding a merit increase.

While organization authority is the power to exercise discretion in decision making, it almost invariably arises from the power of position, or legitimate power.[3] When people speak of authority in managerial settings, they are usually referring to the power of positions. At the same time, other factors, such as personality and style of dealing with people, are involved in leadership.[4]

LINE AND STAFF CONCEPTS

Much confusion has arisen both in literature and among managers as to what "line" and "staff" are; as a result, there is probably no area of management that causes more difficulties, more friction, and more loss of time and effectiveness. Yet line and staff relationships are important as an organizational way of life, and the authority relationships of members of an organization must necessarily affect the operation of the enterprise.

One widely held view of line and staff is that line functions are those that have direct impact on the accomplishment of the objectives of the enterprise. On the other hand, staff functions are those that help the line persons work most effectively in accomplishing the objectives. The people who hold to this view almost invariably classify production and sales (and sometimes finance) as line functions, and purchasing, accounting, personnel, plant maintenance, and quality control as staff functions.

The confusion arising from such a concept is immediately apparent. It is argued that purchasing, for example, merely helps in achieving the main goals of business because, unlike the production departments, such as painting or parts assembly, it is not directly essential. But is purchasing really any less essential than production departments to the achievement of company objectives? Is it not possible for the company to store up painted or assembled parts and get along without these departments for a while, just as it could get along for a while without purchasing? And could not the same question be asked about other so-called staff and service departments, such as accounting, personnel, and plant maintenance? There is probably nothing that could stop the satisfactory production and sale of most manufactured goods more completely than the failure of quality control.

The Nature of Line and Staff Relationships[5]

A more precise and logically valid concept of line and staff is that they are simply a matter of relationships. Line authority gives a superior a line of authority over a subordinate. It exists in all organizations as an uninterrupted scale or series of steps. Hence, the **scalar principle** in organization: *The clearer the line of authority from the ultimate management position in an enterprise to every subordinate position, the clearer will be the responsibility for decision making and the more effective will be organization communication.* In many large enterprises, the steps are long and complicated, but even in the smallest, the very fact of organization introduces the scalar principle.

It therefore becomes apparent from the scalar principle that **line** authority is that relationship in which a superior exercises direct supervision over a subordinate — an authority relationship in direct line or steps.

The nature of the **staff** relationship is advisory. The function of people in a pure staff capacity is to investigate, research, and give advice to line managers.

PERSPECTIVE:
LINE OR STAFF? WHAT IS YOUR CAREER GOAL?

The goal of many MBA graduates is to work in staff positions, using their analytical skills to advise line managers. It has been reported that in 1985 over a third of Harvard's MBA graduates chose such a career.[6] In earlier years, this percentage was even higher.

In the 1980s, partly due to the economy and the competitive pressure, the situation was changing as many large companies reduced their staff. For example, the task of strategy formulation was carried out more frequently by the line managers, who also had to implement the strategy, rather than by the strategic planners in headquarters. Consequently, people who had been used to plan, advise, and analyze business situations moved into line positions in which they were required to set priorities, make decisions, and motivate people to contribute to the aims of the enterprise.

While some staff personnel made an effective transition into line positions, others failed. One of the problems these "newcomers" encountered was the resentment of the "old-time" managers, who saw the positions they had aspired to taken by former staff. Clearly, line work is different from staff tasks. Having real authority for executing decisions can be exciting, but not everyone can make the transition. Thus, aspiring managers should carefully analyze their strengths, weaknesses, and motivations before choosing their career paths.

Line and Staff Relationships or Departmentation?[7]

Some managers and writers regard line and staff as types of departments. Although a department may stand in a predominantly line or staff position with respect to other departments, line and staff are distinguished by *authority relationships* and not by what people do.

For example, one may think of the public relations department, to the extent that it is primarily advisory to the top executives, as a staff department. But within the department are line relationships; the director will stand in a line authority position with respect to his or her immediate subordinates. On the other hand, the vice-president in charge of production may head what is clearly and generally known as a line department. His or her job is not primarily advisory to the chief executive officer. If, however, the vice-president counsels the chief executive on overall company production policy, the relationship becomes one of staff.

When one looks at an organization structure as a whole, the general character of line and staff relationships for the total organization emerges. Certain departments are predominantly staff in their relationship to the entire organization; other departments are primarily line.

Figure 9-1 portrays a simplified organization chart of a manufacturing company. The activities of the director of research and the director of public relations are apt to be mainly advisory to the mainstream of corporate operations and are consequently often considered staff activities. The finance,

Figure 9-1

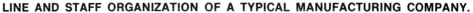

LINE AND STAFF ORGANIZATION OF A TYPICAL MANUFACTURING COMPANY.

production, and sales departments, with activities generally related to the main corporate functions, are ordinarily considered line departments.

Although it is often convenient and even correct to refer to one department as a line department and to another as a staff department, their activities do not so characterize the departments. Line and staff are characterized by relationships and not by departmental activities.

FUNCTIONAL AUTHORITY

Functional authority *is the right which is delegated to an individual or a department to control specified processes, practices, policies, or other matters relating to activities undertaken by persons in other departments.* If the principle of unity of command were followed without exception, authority over these activities would be exercised only by their line superiors. But numerous reasons — including a lack of special knowledge, a lack of ability to supervise processes, and the danger of diverse interpretations of policies — explain why these managers are occasionally not allowed to exercise this authority. In such cases, the line managers are deprived of some authority. It is delegated by their common superior to a staff specialist or to a manager in another department. For example, a company controller is ordinarily given functional authority to prescribe the system of accounting throughout the company, but this specialized authority is really a delegation from the chief executive.

Functional authority is not restricted to managers of a particular type of department. It may be exercised by line, service, or staff department heads, although more often by the latter two because service and staff departments are usually composed of specialists whose knowledge becomes the basis for functional controls.

Delegation of Functional Authority

One can better understand functional authority by thinking of it as a *small slice of the authority of a line superior.* A corporation president, for example, has complete authority to manage a corporation, subject only to limitations placed by such superior authority as the board of directors, the corporate charter and bylaws, and government regulations. In the pure staff situation, the advisers on personnel, accounting, purchasing, or public relations have no part of this line authority, their duty being merely to offer counsel. But when the president delegates to these advisers the right to issue instructions directly to the line organizations, as shown in Figure 9-2, that right is called "functional authority."

The four staff and service executives have functional authority over the line organizations with respect to procedures in the fields of accounting, personnel, purchasing, and public relations. What has happened is that the president, feeling it is unnecessary to clear such specialized matters personally, has delegated line authority to staff assistants (or managers) to issue their own instructions to the operating department. Of course, subordinate managers can use the same device, as in the case of a factory superintendent who dele-

Figure 9-2

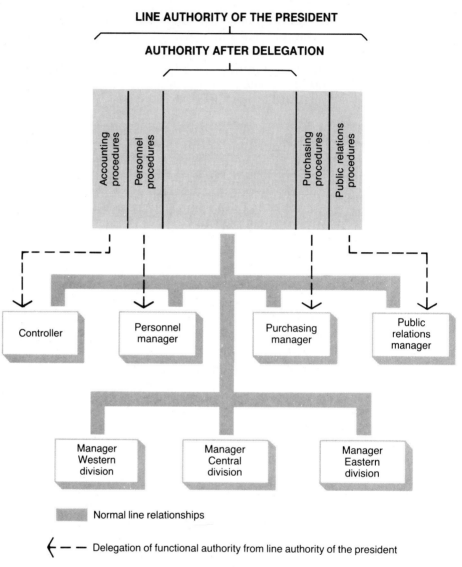

LINE AUTHORITY OF THE PRESIDENT

AUTHORITY AFTER DELEGATION

Accounting procedures

Personnel procedures

Purchasing procedures

Public relations procedures

Controller

Personnel manager

Purchasing manager

Public relations manager

Manager Western division

Manager Central division

Manager Eastern division

Normal line relationships

Delegation of functional authority from line authority of the president

FUNCTIONAL AUTHORITY DELEGATION.

gates to cost, production control, and quality control supervisors the functional authority to prescribe procedures for the operating supervisors.

Restricting the Area of Functional Authority

Functional authority should be carefully restricted. A purchasing manager's functional authority, for example, is generally limited to setting the procedures for divisional or departmental purchasing and does not include telling departments what they can purchase or when. When these managers conduct certain purchasing activities that relate to the whole company, they are acting as heads of service departments. The functional authority of the personnel manager over the general line organization is likewise ordinarily limited to prescribing procedures for handling grievances, for sharing in the administration of wage and salary programs, and for handling vacation procedures and similar matters.

BENEFITS OF STAFF

There are, of course, many important benefits in using staff. The necessity of having the advice of well-qualified specialists in various areas of an organization's operations can scarcely be overestimated, especially as operations become more complex. The U.S. Army learned this the hard way in 1898: In the Spanish-American War, troops were sent into Cuba in woolen uniforms despite the tropical heat and were expected to take territory although they lacked accurate road and topographic maps.

Today, staff advice is far more critical for business, government, and other enterprises than it was in the past. Operating managers are now faced with making decisions that require expert knowledge in economic, technical, political, legal, and social areas. Moreover, it may be necessary, in many instances where highly specialized knowledge is required, to give specialists some functional authority to make decisions for their bosses.

Another major advantage of staff is that these specialists may be allowed the time to think, to gather data, and to analyze, whereas their superiors, busy managing operations, cannot do so. It is a rare operating manager, especially at top levels, who has the time, or will take the time, to do those things that a staff assistant can do so well.

Therefore, not only can a staff help line managers to be effective, but, as problems grow more complex, staff analysis and advice are becoming an urgent necessity. Moreover, despite the dangers of multiple command, even functional authority delegated to staff specialists is often imperative.

LIMITATIONS OF STAFF

Although staff relationships are usually necessary to an enterprise and can do much to make it successful, the nature of staff authority and the difficulty of understanding it lead to certain problems in practice.

Danger of Undermining Line Authority

Operating managers often view staff personnel with skepticism. Too frequently, a president brings in staff executives, clothes them with authority (frequently very vague), and commands all other managers to cooperate. The proposals of staff specialists are received by the president with enthusiasm, and pressure is brought to bear upon the managers involved to put them into effect. What is actually taking place here is that the authority of department managers is being undermined; yet, grudgingly and resentfully, the proposals will be accepted because all will recognize the high tide of the staff specialists' prestige. A continuation of this situation might harm or even destroy operating departments. Capable managers, not willing to submit to indignity or wait until the tide ebbs, might resign; or they might put the matter bluntly to their boss — fire the staff specialists or get along without the line managers!

Operating departments represent the main line of the enterprise, and their managers gain a degree of indispensability. If staff advisers forget that they are there to counsel and not to order, if they overlook the fact that their value lies in the extent to which they strengthen line managers, and if — worse yet — they undermine line authority, they risk becoming expendable. If there is an expendable person in an organization, it is likely to be the staff assistant.

Lack of Staff Responsibility

Advisory departments only propose a plan; others must make the decision to adopt the plan and put it into operation. This creates an ideal situation for shifting blame for mistakes. The staff will claim that it was a good plan and that it failed because the operating manager was unqualified, uninterested, or intent on sabotage. The manager who must make the plan work will claim that it was a poor plan hatched by inexperienced and impractical theorists.

Thinking in a Vacuum

The argument that a staff position gives planners time to think is appealing, but it overlooks an important point: Because staff people do not implement what they recommend, it is possible that staff may think in a vacuum. The alleged impracticality of staff recommendations often results in friction, loss of morale, and even sabotage.

Another weakness in the suggestion that planners must be set off from line departments in order to think is the implication that operating managers are without creative ability. They may, indeed, be without specialized knowledge, but this can be furnished by able staff assistants. Good operating managers can analyze plans, see long-range implications, and spot fatal weaknesses far better than most staff assistants.

Managerial Problems

Few would deny the importance of maintaining unity of command. It is not easy for a department head to be responsible to two or more people; at the worker level, it may be disastrous to attempt multiple responsibility. Some disunity in command may be unavoidable, since functional authority relationships are often unavoidable. But managers should remain aware of the difficulties of multiple authority and should either limit it—even with the loss of some uniformity or of the fruits of specialization—or else carefully clarify it.

Furthermore, too much staff activity may complicate a line executive's job of leadership and control. A corporation president may be so busy dealing with the recommendations of a large number of staff assistants and straightening twisted lines of authority that time and attention may not be available for operating departments. Similarly, a business may become so intent on making policies and setting procedures that there is little time left to make instruments or provide transportation service.

DECENTRALIZATION OF AUTHORITY

The previous section focused on the kinds of authority relationships, such as line, staff, and functional authority. This section emphasizes the dispersion of authority in the organization.

The Nature of Decentralization

Organization authority is merely the discretion conferred on people to use their judgment to make decisions and issue instructions. **Decentralization** is the tendency to disperse decision-making authority in an organized structure. It is a fundamental aspect of delegation; to the extent the authority is not delegated, it is centralized. How much should authority be concentrated in or dispersed throughout the organization? There could be absolute centralization of authority in one person, but that implies no subordinate managers and therefore no structured organization. Some decentralization exists in all organizations. On the other hand, there cannot be absolute decentralization, for if managers delegated all their authority, their status as managers would cease, their position would be eliminated, and there would, again, be no organization. Centralization and decentralization are tendencies, as indicated in Figure 9-3.

Figure 9-3

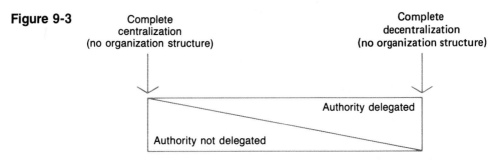

Complete
centralization
(no organization structure)

Complete
decentralization
(no organization structure)

Authority delegated

Authority not delegated

CENTRALIZATION AND DECENTRALIZATION AS TENDENCIES.

Different Kinds of Centralization

The term "centralization" has several meanings:

1. **Centralization of performance** (further discussed later in this chapter) pertains to geographic concentration; it characterizes, for example, a company operating in a single location.

2. **Departmental centralization** refers to concentration of specialized activities, generally in one department. For example, maintenance for a whole plant may be carried out by a single department.

3. **Centralization as an aspect of management** is the tendency to restrict delegation of decision making. A high degree of authority is held at or near the top by managers in the organizational hierarchy.

Decentralization as a Philosophy and Policy

Decentralization implies more than delegation: It reflects a philosophy of organization and management. It requires careful selection of which decisions to push down into the organization structure and which to hold near the top, specific policymaking to guide the decision making, proper selection and training of people, and adequate controls. A policy of decentralization affects all areas of management and can be looked upon as an essential element of a managerial system. In fact, without it, managers could not use their discretion to handle the ever-changing situations they face.

DELEGATION OF AUTHORITY

As simple as delegation of authority appears to be, studies have shown that many managers fail because of poor delegation. Delegation is necessary for an organization to exist. Just as no one person in an enterprise can do all the tasks necessary for accomplishing a group purpose, so is it impossible, as an enterprise grows, for one person to exercise all the authority for making decisions. As explained in Chapter 7, there is a limit to the number of persons managers can effectively supervise and make decisions for. Once this limit has been passed, authority must be delegated to subordinates, who will make decisions within the area of their assigned duties.

How Authority Is Delegated

Authority is delegated when a superior gives a subordinate discretion to make decisions. Clearly, superiors cannot delegate authority they do not have, whether they are board members, presidents, vice-presidents, or supervisors.

PERSPECTIVE:
SPLINTERED AUTHORITY AT THE RAILROAD

One of the authors observed the solution of a problem involving a Western railroad whose headquarters were in Chicago. The problem was relatively minor, but a decision on it in Los Angeles required the consolidated authority of the traffic department, the operating department, and the public relations department. It could have been referred up the line by each of the managers to the president's office, where sufficient authority for making the decision was concentrated. But if such decisions were always handled by upward reference, the president's office would be swamped. In this case, the managers of the three departments in the Los Angeles office met briefly, pooled their delegated authority, and quickly made the decision.

The **process of delegation** involves (1) determining the results expected from a position, (2) assigning tasks to a position, (3) delegating authority for accomplishing these tasks, and (4) holding the person in that position responsible for the accomplishment of the tasks. In practice, it is impossible to split this process, since expecting a person to accomplish goals without giving him or her the authority to achieve them is unfair, as is delegating authority without knowing the end results for which it will be used. Moreover, since the superior's responsibility cannot be delegated, a boss has no practical alternative but to hold subordinates responsible for completing their assignments.

Splintered Authority

Splintered authority exists wherever a problem cannot be solved or a decision made without pooling the authority delegations of two or more managers. For example, the superintendent of plant A may see an opportunity to reduce costs through a minor modification in her procedures and those in plant B, but her authority cannot encompass the change. But if the superintendents of the two plants can agree upon the change (and if it affects no other managers), all they need to do is pool their authority and make the decision. Individually, their authority is said to be "splintered." In day-to-day operations of any company, there are many cases of splintered authority. Many managerial conferences are held because of the necessity of pooling authority to make a decision.

Such problems could be handled by merely referring the decision upward until it reaches a person with the authority to make it unilaterally. In the case of the two plant superintendents, it might lie within the authority of the vice-president in charge of manufacturing. In many cases, the splinters of authority, although far down in the organization, exist in departments that have a common superior only in the office of the president.

Splintered authority cannot be wholly avoided in making decisions. However, recurring decisions on the same matters may be evidence that authority delegations have not been properly made and that some reorganization is required.

THE ART OF DELEGATION

Most failures in effective delegation occur not because managers do not understand the nature and principles of delegation but because they are unable or unwilling to apply them. Delegation is, in a way, an elementary act of managing. Yet studies of managerial failures almost invariably find that poor or inept delegation is at or near the top of the list of causes. Much of the reason lies in personal attitudes toward delegation.

Personal Attitudes toward Delegation

Although charting an organization and outlining managerial goals and duties will help in making delegations, and knowledge of the principles of delegation will furnish a basis for it, certain personal attitudes underlie real delegation.

Receptiveness   An underlying attribute of managers who will delegate authority is a willingness to give other people's ideas a chance. Decision making always involves some discretion, and a subordinate's decision is not likely to be exactly the one a superior would have made. The manager who knows how to delegate must be able not only to welcome the ideas of others but also to help others and to compliment them on their ingenuity.

Willingness to let go   A manager who will effectively delegate authority must be willing to release the right to make decisions to subordinates. A major fault of some managers who move up the executive ladder — or of the pioneer who has built a large business from the small beginning of, say, a garage machine shop — is that they want to continue to make decisions for the positions they have left. Corporate presidents and vice-presidents who insist upon confirming every purchase or approving the appointment of every laborer or secretary waste time and attention needed for far more important decisions.

If the size or complexity of the organization forces delegation of authority, managers should realize that there is a "law of comparative managerial advantage," somewhat like the law of comparative economic advantage that applies to nations. Well known to economists and logically sound, the latter states that a country's wealth will be enhanced if it exports what it produces most efficiently and imports what it produces least efficiently, even though it could produce the imported goods more cheaply than any other nation. Likewise, managers enhance their contributions to the firm if they concentrate on tasks that contribute most to the firm's objectives and assign to subordinates other tasks, even though they could accomplish them better themselves.

Willingness to let others make mistakes   Although no responsible manager would sit idly by and let a subordinate make a mistake that might endanger the company or the subordinate's position in the company, continual checking to ensure that no mistakes are ever made will make true delegation impossible. Since everyone makes mistakes, a subordinate must be allowed to make some, and their cost must be considered an investment in personal development.

Serious or repeated mistakes can be largely avoided without nullifying delegation or hindering development of a subordinate. Patient counseling, asking leading or discerning questions, and carefully explaining the objectives and policies are some of the methods available to the manager who would delegate well. None of these techniques involves discouraging subordinates with intimidating criticism or harping on their shortcomings.

Willingness to trust subordinates Superiors have no alternative to trusting their subordinates, for delegation implies a trustful attitude between them. This trust is sometimes hard to come by. A superior may put off delegation with the thought that subordinates are not yet experienced enough, that they cannot handle people, that they have not yet developed judgment, or that they do not appreciate all the facts bearing on a situation. Sometimes these considerations are true, but then a superior should either train subordinates or else select others who are prepared to assume the responsibility. Too often, however, bosses distrust their subordinates because they do not wish to let go, are threatened by subordinates' successes, do not delegate wisely, or do not know how to set up controls to ensure proper use of the authority.

Willingness to establish and use broad controls   Since superiors cannot delegate responsibility for performance, they should not delegate authority unless they are willing to find means of getting feedback, that is, of assuring themselves that the authority is being used to support enterprise or department goals and plans. Obviously, controls cannot be established and exercised unless goals, policies, and plans are used as basic standards for judging the activities of subordinates. More often than not, reluctance to delegate and to trust subordinates comes from the superior's inadequate planning and understandable fear of loss of control.

Guides for Overcoming Weak Delegation

The following practical guides will facilitate successful delegation:

1. **Define assignments and delegate authority in the light of results expected.** Or, to put it another way, grant sufficient authority to make possible the accomplishment of goal assignments.

2. **Select the person in the light of the job to be done.** Although the good organizer will approach delegation primarily from the standpoint of the task to be accomplished, in the final analysis staffing as a part of the total system of delegation cannot be ignored.

3. **Maintain open lines of communication.** Since the superior does not delegate all authority or abdicate responsibility and since managerial independence therefore does not exist, decentralization should not lead to insulation. There should be a free flow of information between superior and subordinate, furnishing the subordinate with the information needed to make decisions and to interpret properly the authority delegated. Delegations, then, do depend on situations.

4. **Establish proper controls.** Because no manager can relinquish responsibility, delegations should be accompanied by techniques for ensuring that the authority is properly used. But if controls are to enhance delegation, they must be relatively broad and be designed to show deviations from plans, rather than interfering with routine actions of subordinates.

5. **Reward effective delegation and successful assumption of authority.** Managers should be ever-watchful for means of rewarding both effective delegation and effective assumption of authority. Although many of these rewards will be monetary, the granting of greater discretion and prestige — both in a given position and by promotion to a higher position — is often even more of an incentive.

BALANCE: THE KEY TO DECENTRALIZATION[8]

To avoid pitfalls, any program for decentralization of authority must take into consideration the advantages and limitations summarized in Table 9-1.

Table 9-1 **Advantages and Limitations of Decentralization**

Advantages of decentralization

1. Relieves top management of some burden of decision making and forces upper-level managers to let go.
2. Encourages decision making and assumption of authority and responsibility.
3. Gives managers more freedom and independence in decision making.
4. Promotes establishment and use of broad controls which may increase motivation.
5. Makes comparison of performance of different organizational units possible.
6. Facilitates setting up of profit centers.
7. Facilitates product diversification.
8. Promotes development of general managers.
9. Aids in adaptation to fast-changing environment.

Limitations of decentralization

1. Makes it more difficult to have a uniform policy.
2. Increases complexity of coordination of decentralized organizational units.
3. May result in loss of some control by upper-level managers.
4. May be limited by inadequate control techniques.
5. May be constrained by inadequate planning and control systems.
6. Can be limited by the availability of qualified managers.
7. Involves considerable expenses for training managers.
8. May be limited by external forces (national labor unions, governmental controls, tax policies).
9. May not be favored by economies of scale of some operations.

As noted earlier, strong forces favor the practice of decentralization. At the same time, extensive decentralization is not to be blindly undertaken. Perhaps the principal problem of decentralization is loss of control. No enterprise can decentralize to the extent that its existence is threatened and the achievement of its goals is frustrated. If organizational disintegration is to be avoided, decentralization must be tempered by selective centralization in certain major policy areas. The company with well-balanced decentralization will probably centralize decisions at the top on such things as financing, overall profit goals and budgeting, major facilities and other capital expenditures, important new product programs, major marketing strategies, basic personnel policies, and the development and compensation of managerial personnel.

The achievement of balance is perhaps one of the greatest accomplishments of Alfred Sloan in his management of General Motors over the years. Although practicing and preaching decentralization, he and his top management team realized that no department or division could be given complete freedom. As a result, within GM, despite its large size, authority has been retained at the very top for major policy and program decisions on matters affecting the soundness and success of the entire company. Through decentralization, however, once major program and strategy decisions have been made at the top, the countless decisions involving their execution are made by operating divisions.

SUMMARY

There are a number of different bases of power. Power can be legitimate, expert, referent, reward, or coercive. There are also various ways to conceptualize line and staff. Generally, line and staff are characterized by relationships and not by people or departments. Line authority is that relationship in which a superior exercises direct supervision over subordinates. The staff relationship, on the other hand, consists of giving advice and counsel. Functional authority is the right to control *selected* processes, practices, policies, or other matters in departments other than a person's own. Functional authority is a small slice of a line manager's authority and should be used sparingly.

Using staff has benefits as well as limitations such as the danger of undermining line and the lack of responsibility of staff. There are also the possibilities of making impractical recommendations and of undermining the unity of command.

Another important concept is decentralization, which is the tendency to disperse decision-making authority. Centralization, on the other hand, is the concentration of authority. It may refer to geographic concentration, departmental centralization, or the tendency to restrict delegation of decision making. The process of delegation of authority includes determining the results to be achieved, assigning tasks, delegating authority, and holding people responsible for results.

Delegation, which is an art, is influenced by personal attitudes. In addition, practical guides exist that can help managers overcome weak delegation. Balance is the key to proper decentralization.

KEY IDEAS AND CONCEPTS FOR REVIEW

Power	Decentralization
Authority	Centralization
Bases of power	Process of delegation
Line	Splintered authority
Staff	Attitudes toward delegation
Functional authority	Guides for overcoming weak delegation
Limitations of staff	Advantages and limitations of decentralization

FOR DISCUSSION

1. Why has there been a conflict between line and staff for so long and in so many companies? Can this conflict be removed?

2. Take as examples a number of positions in any kind of enterprise (business, church, government, etc.). Classify each as line or staff.

3. If the task of a person in a purely staff position is to offer advice, how can an individual receiving this advice make sure that it is independent, well researched, and realistic?

4. How many cases of functional authority in organization have you seen? Analyzing a few, do you agree that they could have been avoided? If avoidance had been possible, would you have eliminated them? If they could not have been avoided or if you had not wanted to eliminate them, how would you remove most of the difficulties which might arise?

5. If you were asked to advise a young college graduate who has accepted a staff position as assistant to a factory manager, what suggestions would you make?

6. Why is poor delegation of authority often found to be the most important cause of managerial failure?

7. In many foreign countries where companies have grown from within and are often family-owned, very little authority is decentralized. What do you think would explain this? What effect does it have?

8. If you were a manager, would you decentralize authority? State several reasons for your answer. How would you make sure that you did not decentralize too much?

9. Should authority be pushed down in an organization as far as it will go?

EXERCISES/ACTION STEPS

1. Interview a line manager and a staff person at a local company. Ask them what they like and dislike about their jobs. Reflect upon the interviews and ask yourself whether a line position or a staff one is the major aim of your career plan.

2. Interview two line managers about their views on delegation. Do they think that their superior delegates sufficient authority to them? Also inquire how they feel about delegating authority to their subordinates?

INTERNATIONAL CASE:
FORD'S GLOBAL STRATEGY: CENTERS OF EXCELLENCE[9]

In 1986 Ford passed its bigger competitor, General Motors, with earnings of $3.3 billion. Ford's market share is about 20 percent. But success, in many instances, may be only temporary, and Ford's chairman, Donald E. Petersen, is concerned about complacency. Indeed, the company has to work hard to maintain its reputation for stylish, aerodynamic cars and high quality.

Under the former leadership of Henry Ford II, the company was very centralized. But Petersen's plan is to make Ford an integrated global enterprise. Thus, a great deal of authority for the development of specific models or components is now centralized in the company's various technical centers around the world rather than in Detroit. Under this plan, the car or its components are developed in the technical center with the best expertise in a particular field, anywhere in the world. This could save the company a lot of money by avoiding duplication in development and reducing tooling costs. For example, Ford of Europe, located in England, is the center for developing the platform for the new model that will replace the European Sierra and the American Tempo and Topaz. Ford will sell the new cars in Europe and in the United States. Similarly, in Japan Mazda (Ford owns 25 percent of the company), which has much experience in building small cars, will be the center for developing the platform for the replacement car for the Escort. The North American center of excellence will focus on midsize cars. Similar centers are planned for major components such as transmissions and engines. While these centers of excellence develop platforms and key components, exterior and interior styling will be the responsibility of companies in the various regions.

The concept of the centers of excellence may seem promising, yet a previous attempt in the early 1980s to build a "world car" in Europe failed. It is said that the American car, the Escort, shared only one part with its European counterpart, namely, a seal in the water pump.

1. What do you think of Ford's overall decentralization with centralized authority for development of specific cars and components at the technical centers?

2. Why does Ford think that the concept of having centers of excellence located in various parts of the world will be the correct organization structure for the twenty-first century?

REFERENCES

1. The concept of power has been widely discussed in the literature. See, for example, the thorough discussion by Gerald R. Salancik and Jeffrey Pfeffer, "Who Gets Power—and How They Hold On to It: A Strategic-Contingency Model of Power," in David A. Nadler, Michael L. Tushman, and Nina G. Hatvany (eds.), *Managing Organizations—Readings and Cases* (Boston: Little, Brown and Company, 1982), pp 385–399.

2. John R. P. French, Jr., and Bertram Raven, "The Bases of Social Power," in Walter E. Natemeyer (ed.), *Classics of Organizational Behavior* (Oak Park, Ill.: Moore Publishing Company, 1978), pp. 198–210.

3. But authority patterns may vary with culture. See Trudy Heller, "Changing Authority Patterns: A Cultural Perspective," *Academy of Management Review* (July 1985), pp. 488–495.

4. For a research study on the topic of power, see Anthony T. Cobb, "An Episodic Model of Power: Toward an Integration of Theory and Research," *Academy of Management Review* (July 1984), pp. 482–493.

5. For an interesting discussion of line and staff relationships in large organizations, see Jerome Wilkenfield, "Managing Staff Functions in a Large Corporation," *Management Review* (June 1986), pp. 41–44.

6. Jeff Bailey, "Where the Action Is: Executives in Staff Jobs Seek Line Positions," *The Wall Street Journal* (Aug. 12, 1986); see also David Wessel, "Do as I Do: More Consultants Quit Profession to Start New Businesses," *The Wall Street Journal* (Oct. 15, 1986).

7. Hall L. Logan, "Line and Staff: An Obsolete Concept?" in Harold Koontz, Cyril O'Donnell, and Heinz Weihrich (eds.), *Management: A Book of Readings,* 5th ed. (New York: McGraw-Hill Book Company, 1980), pp. 322–325.

8. See also John G. Staiger, "What Cannot Be Decentralized," in Koontz, O'Donnell, and Weihrich, *Management* (1980), pp. 319–321.

9. The case is based on a variety of sources, including James B. Treece et al., "Can Ford Stay on Top?" *Business Week* (Sept. 28, 1987), pp. 78–86.

CHAPTER 10

Effective Organizing and Organizational Culture

CHAPTER OBJECTIVES

After reading this chapter, you should understand:

1. How to avoid mistakes in organizing by planning
2. How organizing can be improved by maintaining flexibility and by making staff more effective
3. How to avoid conflict by clarifying the organization structure and ensuring an understanding of organizing
4. The importance of the organization culture
5. Major principles, or guidelines, to be kept in mind in developing organization structure

Organizing involves developing an intentional structure of roles for effective performance. Organizing requires a network of decision and communication centers for coordinating efforts toward group and enterprise goals. To work, an organization structure must be understood, and principles must be put into practice. As emphasized at the outset, in organizing, as elsewhere in managing, there is no one best way. What works will always depend on the specific situation.

AVOIDING MISTAKES IN ORGANIZING BY PLANNING

As with the other functions of managing, establishment of objectives and orderly planning are necessary for good organization. As Urwick said in his classic book, "Lack of design (in organization) is illogical, cruel, wasteful, and inefficient."[1] It is illogical because good design, or planning, must come first, whether one speaks of engineering or social practice. It is cruel because "the main sufferers from a lack of design in organization are those individuals who work in an undertaking." It is wasteful because "unless jobs are clearly put together along lines of functional specialization, it is impossible to train new men (or women) to succeed to positions as the incumbents are promoted, resign or retire." And it is inefficient because if management is not based on principles, it will be based on personalities, with the resultant rise of company politics, for "a machine will not run smoothly when fundamental engineering principles have been ignored in construction."

Planning for the Ideal

The search for an ideal organization to reflect enterprise goals under given circumstances is the impetus to planning. The search entails charting the main lines of organization, considering the organizational philosophy of the enterprise managers (e.g., whether authority should be centralized as much as possible or whether the company should divide its operations into semi-independent product or territorial divisions), and sketching out consequent authority relationships. The ultimate form established, like all plans, seldom remains unchanged, and continuous remolding of the ideal plan is normally necessary. Nevertheless, an ideal organization plan constitutes a standard, and by comparing present structure with it, enterprise leaders know what changes should be made when possible.

An organizer must always be careful not to be blinded by popular notions in organizing, because what may work in one company may not work in another. Principles of organizing have general application, but the background of each company's operations and needs must be considered in applying these principles. Organization structure needs to be tailor-made.

Modification for the Human Factor

If available personnel do not fit into the ideal structure and cannot or should not be pushed aside, the only choice is to modify the structure to fit individual capabilities, attitudes, or limitations. Although this modification may seem like organizing around people, in this case one is first organizing around the goals to be met and activities to be undertaken and only then making modifications for the human factor. Thus, planning will reduce compromising the necessity for principle whenever changes occur in personnel.

Advantages of Organization Planning

Planning the organization structure helps determine future personnel needs and required training programs. Unless it knows what managerial personnel will be needed and what experience should be demanded, an enterprise cannot intelligently recruit people and train them.

Furthermore, organization planning can disclose weaknesses. Duplication of effort, unclear lines of authority, overlong lines of communication, excessive red tape, and obsolete practices show up best when desirable and actual organization structures are compared.

AVOIDING ORGANIZATIONAL INFLEXIBILITY

One basic advantage of organization planning is the avoidance of organizational inflexibility. Many enterprises, especially those which have been in operation for many years, become too rigid to meet the first test of effective organization structure: the ability to adapt to a changing environment and meet new contingencies. This resistance to change can cause considerable loss of efficiency in organizations.

Signs of Inflexibility

Some older companies provide ample evidence of inflexibility: an organization pattern that is no longer suited to the times, a district or regional organization that could be either abolished or enlarged because of improved communications, or a structure that is too highly centralized for an enlarged enterprise requiring decentralization.

Avoiding Inflexibility through Reorganization

Although reorganization is intended to respond to changes in the enterprise environment, there may be other compelling reasons for reorganization. Those related to the business environment include changes in operations caused by acquisition or sale of major properties, changes in product line or marketing methods, business cycles, competitive influences, new production techniques, labor union policy, government regulatory and fiscal policy, or the current state of knowledge about organizing. New techniques and principles may become applicable, such as developing managers by allowing them to manage decentralized semi-independent units of a company. Or new methods may come into use, such as gaining adequate financial control with a high degree of decentralization.

Moreover, a new chief executive officer and new vice-presidents and department heads are likely to have some definite organizational ideas of their own. Shifts may be due merely to the desire of new managers to make changes based on ideas formulated through their previous experience or to the fact that their methods of managing and their personalities require a changed organization structure.

Furthermore, reorganization may be caused by demonstrated deficiencies in an existing structure. Some of these arise from organizational weaknesses: excessive spans of management, an excessive number of committees, lack of uniform policy, slow decision making, failure to accomplish objectives, inability to meet schedules, excessive costs, or breakdown of financial control. Other deficiencies may stem from inadequacies of managers. Lack of knowledge or skill on the part of a manager who for some reason cannot be replaced may be avoided by organizing in a way that moves much of the authority for decision making to another position.

Personality clashes between managers also may be solved by reorganization. Staff-line conflicts may develop to such an extent that they can be resolved only by reorganization.

The Need for Readjustment and Change

In addition to pressing reasons for reorganization, there is a certain need for moderate and continuing readjustment merely to keep the structure from becoming stagnant. "Empire building" (i.e., building up a large organization so that the manager appears to be more important) is not so attractive when all those involved know that their positions are subject to change. As a company president told his subordinates: "Don't bother to build any empires, because I can assure you that you won't be in the same position three years from now." Some managers, realizing that an organization structure must be a living thing, make structural changes merely to accustom subordinates to change.

Much can be said for developing a tradition of change. People who are used to change tend to accept it without the frustration and demoralization that result when need for reorganization is allowed to reach the stage at which change must be revolutionary. On the other hand, a company continually undertaking major reorganization may damage morale, and people may spend much of their time wondering what will happen to them because of organizational changes.

MAKING STAFF WORK EFFECTIVE

The line-staff problem is not only one of the most difficult that organizations face but also the source of an extraordinarily large amount of inefficiency. Solving this problem requires great managerial skill, careful attention to principles, and patient teaching of personnel.

Understanding Authority Relationships

Managers must understand the nature of authority relationships if they want to solve the problems of line and staff. As long as managers regard line and staff as groups of people or groupings of activities (e.g., service departments), confusion will result. Line and staff are authority relationships and many jobs have elements of both. The line relationship involves making decisions and acting on them. The staff relationship, on the other hand, implies the right to assist and counsel. In short, the line may "tell," but the staff must "sell" (its recommendations).

Making Line Listen to Staff

If staff counsel and advice are justifiable at all, it is because of the need for assistance either from experts or from those freed from more pressing duties to give such assistance. Obviously, if staff help is not used, it would make sense to abolish it. Line managers should realize that competent staff assistants offer suggestions to aid and not to undermine or criticize. Although line-staff friction may stem from ineptness or overzealousness on the part of staff people, trouble also arises when line executives too carefully guard their authority and resent the very assistance they need.

Line managers should be encouraged or required to consult with staff. Enterprises would do well to adopt the practice of compulsory staff assistance, wherein the line must listen to staff. At General Motors, for example, product division managers consult with the headquarters staff divisions before proposing a major program or policy to the top executive or the finance committee. They may not be required to do so, but they are likely to find that this practice results in smoother sailing for their proposals; and if they can present a united front with the staff division concerned, there will unquestionably be a better chance for the adoption of their proposals.

Keeping Staff Informed

Common criticisms of staff are that specialists operate in a vacuum, fail to appreciate the complexity of the line manager's job, or overlook important facts in making recommendations. To some extent, these criticisms are warranted, because specialists cannot be expected to know all the fine points of a manager's job. Specialists should take care that their recommendations deal only with matters within their competence, and operating managers should not lean too heavily on a recommendation if it deals only with part of a problem.

Many criticisms arise because staff assistants are not kept informed on matters within their field. Even the best assistant cannot advise properly in such cases. If line managers fail to inform their staff of decisions affecting its work or if they do not pave the way — through announcements and requests for cooperation — for staff to obtain the requisite information on specific problems, the staff cannot function as intended. In relieving their superiors of the necessity for gathering and analyzing such information, staff assistants largely justify their existence.

Requiring Completed Staff Work

Many staff persons overlook the fact that in order to be most helpful, their recommendations should be complete enough to make possible a simple positive or negative answer by a line manager. Staff assistants should be problem solvers and not problem creators. They create problems for managers when their advice is indecisive or vague, when their conclusions are wrong, when they have not taken into account all the facts or have not consulted the persons seriously affected by a proposed solution, or when they do not point out to superiors the pitfalls as well as the advantages of a recommended course of action.

Completed staff work implies presentation of a clear recommendation based upon full consideration of a problem, clearance with persons importantly affected, suggestions about avoiding any difficulties involved, and, often, preparation of the paperwork — letters, directives, job descriptions, and specifications — so that a manager can accept or reject the proposal without further study, long conferences, or unnecessary work. Should a recommendation be accepted, thorough staff work provides line managers with the machinery to put it into effect. People in staff positions who learn to do these things can find themselves highly valued and appreciated.

Making Staff Work as a Way of Organizational Life

An understanding of staff authority lays the foundation for an organizational way of life. Wherever staff is used, its responsibility is to develop and maintain a climate of favorable personal relations. Essentially, the task of staff assistants is to make responsible line managers "look good" and to help them do a better job. A staff assistant should not attempt to assume credit for an idea. Not only is this a sure way of alienating line teammates who do not like being shown up by a staff assistant, but operating managers who accept ideas actually bear responsibility for implementation of the proposals.

Even under the best of circumstances, it is difficult to coordinate line and staff authority, for people must be persuaded to cooperate. Staff persons must gain and hold the confidence of their fellow workers. They must keep in close touch with operating departments, know their managers and staffs, and understand their problems. They must, through precept and example, convince their line teammates that their prime interest is the welfare of operating managers, and they must downgrade their own contributions while embellishing those of the persons they assist. People in a staff capacity have succeeded in their role when line executives seek their advice and ask them to study their problems.

AVOIDING CONFLICT BY CLARIFICATION

A major reason for conflict in organizations is that people do not understand their assignments and those of their coworkers. No matter how well conceived an organization structure may be, people must understand it to make it work. Understanding is aided materially by the proper use of organization charts, accurate job descriptions, the spelling out of authority and informational relationships, and the introduction of specific goals for specific positions.

Organization Charts

Every organization structure, even a poor one, can be charted, for a chart merely indicates how departments are tied together along the principal lines of authority. It is therefore somewhat surprising to find top managers occasionally taking pride in the fact that they do not have an organization chart or, if they do have one, feeling that the chart should be kept a secret.

Advantages A prominent manufacturer once said that although he could see some use for an organization chart for his factory, he had refused to chart the organization above the level of factory superintendent. His argument was that charts tend to make people overly conscious of being superiors or inferiors, tend to destroy team feeling, and give persons occupying a box on the chart too great a feeling of "ownership." Another top executive once said that if an organization is left uncharted, it can be changed more easily and that the absence of a chart also encourages a competitive drive for higher executive positions on the part of the uncharted middle-management group.

These reasons for not charting organization structures are clearly unsound. Subordinate-superior relationships exist not because of charting but, rather, because of essential reporting relationships. As for a chart's creating a too-comfortable feeling and causing a lack of drive on the part of those who have "arrived," these are matters of top leadership — of reorganizing whenever the enterprise environment demands, of developing a tradition of change, and of making subordinate managers continue to meet adequate and well-understood standards of performance. Managers who believe that team spirit can be produced without clearly spelling out relationships are fooling themselves and preparing the way for politics, intrigue, frustration, buck-passing, lack of coordination, duplicated effort, vague policy, uncertain decision making, and other evidences of organizational inefficiency.

Since a chart maps lines of decision-making authority, sometimes merely charting an organization can show inconsistencies and complexities and lead to their correction. A chart also reveals to managers and new personnel how they tie into the entire structure.

Limitations Organization charts are subject to important limitations. In the first place, a chart shows only formal authority relationships and omits the many significant informal and informational relationships. Figure 10-1 shows many, but not nearly all, of the informal relationships found in a typical organized enterprise. It shows also the major line, or formal, relationships. It does not show how much authority exists at any point in the structure. While it would be interesting to chart an organization with lines of different widths to denote formal authority of varying degrees, authority is not subject to such measurement. And if the multiple lines of informal relationships and of communication were drawn, they would so complicate a chart that it could not be understood.

Many charts show structures as they are supposed to be or used to be, rather than as they really are. Managers hesitate or neglect to redraft charts, forgetting that organization structures are dynamic and that charts should not be allowed to become obsolete.

Another difficulty with organization charts is that individuals may confuse authority relationships with status. The staff officer reporting to the corporation president may be shown at the top of the organization chart, while a regional line officer may be shown one or two levels lower. Although good

Figure 10-1

━━━━━ Formal relationships
━ ━ ━ ━ Informal or informational relationships

THE FORMAL AND INFORMAL OR INFORMATIONAL ORGANIZATION.

charting attempts to make levels on the chart conform to levels of enterprise importance, it cannot always do so. This problem can be handled by clearly spelling out authority relationships and by using that best indicator of status — salary and bonus levels. No one is likely, for example, to hear that the general manager of Chevrolet in General Motors feels a sense of inferiority because his position on the chart is below that of the company secretary.

Position Descriptions

Every managerial position should be defined. A good position description informs everyone of the incumbent's reponsibilities. A modern position description is not a detailed list of all the activities an individual is expected to undertake, and it certainly does not specify how to undertake them. Rather, it states the basic function of the position, the major end-result areas for which the manager is responsible, and the reporting relationships. The description also clarifies the authority in a position and states the verifiable objectives for the end-result areas.

Position descriptions have many benefits. As jobs are analyzed, duties and responsibilities are brought into focus and areas of overlapping or neglected duties come to light. Forcing people to consider what should be done and who should do it is more than worth the effort. Further benefits of job descriptions include the guidance they provide in training new managers, in drawing up candidate requirements, and in setting salary levels. Finally, as a means of control over organization, the position description furnishes a standard against which to judge whether a position is necessary and, if so, what its organization level and exact location in the structure should be.

ENSURING UNDERSTANDING OF ORGANIZING

All the members of an enterprise must understand the structure of their organization in order for that structure to work. This requires teaching. Also, since formal organization is supplemented by informal organization, members of an enterprise must understand the general working of informal as well as formal organization.

Teaching the Nature of Organizing

Many soundly conceived organization plans fail because organization members do not understand them. A well-written organization manual — containing a statement of organization philosophy, programs, charts, and an outline of job descriptions — goes far toward making organizing understandable. If an organization structure is put into written words and charts, it has a better chance of being clear than if it is not. However, because even the best-written words and charts do not always clearly convey the same meaning to every reader, effective managers cannot stop with written clarification. They must teach those in their operation the meaning of the organization structure, their position in it, and the relationships involved.

Managers may do this by individual coaching, by holding staff or special meetings, or by simply watching how the structure works. If subordinates pass decisions up the line that they should be making themselves, managers can take this opportunity to clarify authority. Likewise, if communication among members of a group seems to be inadequate, managers can look for causes in either a poorly conceived or a poorly understood organization structure. Too many group meetings or too much committee work is a signal for managers to do some investigating. Thus, managers are obligated continually to teach the fundamentals of organizing, for if they do not, their enterprise or department is likely to fail.

Recognizing the Importance of Informal Organization and the Grapevine

Another way of making the formal organization work effectively is to recognize and take full advantage of informal organization. The nature of informal organizations and their distinction from formal organizations were discussed in Chapter 7. Many informal organizations arise from the formal organization in which they operate. They include interrelationships that are not usually charted, such as the unwritten rules of organizational conduct, the way to "learn the ropes," the people in an enterprise who have power not implied by or coming from an organization position, and gossip. One of the best-known examples of an important informal organization, one which seems to exist in every department and organization, is the "grapevine."

The grapevine   Informal organization tends to exist when members of a formal organization (perhaps a company department) know one another well enough to pass on information — sometimes only gossip — that is in some way connected with the enterprise. In the typical enterprise — whose members spend many hours a day deriving material security and status, as well as social satisfaction, from the grapevine — the desire for information concerning the organization and its people is strong enough that such information is rapidly transmitted between persons who know and trust one another.

The grapevine, of course, thrives on information not openly available to the entire group, whether because that information is regarded as confidential, or because formal lines of communication are inadequate to spread it, or because it is of the kind, like much gossip, that would never be formally disclosed. Even managers who conscientiously inform employees through company bulletins or newspapers never so completely or quickly disclose all information of interest as to make the grapevine purposeless.

Since all forms of informal organization serve essential human communication needs, the grapevine is inevitable and valuable. Indeed, an intelligent top manager would probably be wise to feed it accurate information, since it is very effective for quick communication. There is much to be said for a manager's getting a place — personally or through a trusted staff member or secretary — on the company grapevine.

Benefits Informal organization brings a kind of cohesiveness to formal organization. It imparts to members of a formal organization a sense of belonging, status, self-respect, and satisfaction. Many managers, understanding this fact, consciously use informal organizations as channels of communication and molders of employee morale.

PROMOTING AN APPROPRIATE ORGANIZATION CULTURE

The effectiveness of an organization is also influenced by the organization culture, which affects the way the managerial functions of planning, organizing, staffing, leading, and controlling are carried out. Illustrations of organization culture are listed in Table 10-1. Given the choice, most people would probably prefer to work in an organization such as environment B, in which one can participate in the decision-making process, one is evaluated on performance criteria rather than on the basis of friendship, one has open communi-

Table 10-1   Illustrations of Organization Culture and Management Practice

Environment A	Environment B
Planning	
Goals are set in autocratic manner. Decision making is centralized.	Goals are set with a great deal of participation. Decision making is decentralized.
Organizing	
Authority is centralized. Authority is narrowly defined.	Authority is decentralized. Authority is widely defined.
Staffing	
People are selected on the basis of friendship.	People are selected on the basis of performance criteria.
Training is in a narrowly defined specialty.	Training is in many functional areas.
Leading	
Managers exercise directive leadership. Communication flow is primarily top-down.	Managers practice participative leadership. Communication flow is top-down, bottom-up, horizontal, and diagonal.
Controlling	
Superiors exercise strict control. Focus is on financial criteria.	Individuals exercise a great deal of self-control. Focus is on multiple criteria.

cation channels in all directions, and one has the opportunity to exercise a great deal of self-control. In their search for excellent companies, Thomas Peters and Robert Waterman, the authors of a best-selling book on management, found that the dominance of a coherent culture characterized these organizations.[2]

But the recognition of the importance of corporate culture is not new at all (although some management gurus want you to believe it is).[3] Over 2000 years ago, in 431 B.C., Pericles in ancient Greece eloquently urged the Athenians, who were at war with the Spartans, to adhere to values such as those inherent in democracy: informality in communication, the importance of individual dignity, and promotion based on performance. Pericles realized that the underlying values might mean victory or defeat. These values are not so different from those espoused by many U.S. companies.

Defining Organization Culture

As it relates to organizations, **culture** is the general pattern of behavior, shared beliefs, and values that members have in common.[4] Culture can be inferred from what people say, do, and think within an organizational setting. It involves the learning and transmitting of knowledge, beliefs, and patterns of behavior over a period of time, which means that an organization culture is fairly stable and does not change fast.[5] It often sets the tone for the company and establishes implied rules for the way people should behave. Many give a general idea of what a particular company stands for.[6] Here are some examples:

> For General Electric, it is "Progress is our most important product."
>
> American Telephone & Telegraph Company is proud of its "universal service."
>
> DuPont makes "better things for better living though chemistry."
>
> Delta Airlines describes its internal climate with the slogan "the Delta family feeling."

Similarly, IBM wants to be known for its service, Sears for quality and price, Caterpillar for its 24-hour parts service, Polaroid for its innovation, Maytag for its reliability, and so on. Indeed, the orientation of these companies, often expressed in slogans, contributed to the successful conduct of their businesses.

The Influence of the Leader on Organization Culture

Managers, and especially top managers, create the climate for the enterprise. Their values influence the direction of the firm. Although the term "value" is used differently, a **value** can be defined as a fairly permanent belief about what is appropriate and what is not that guides the actions and behavior of

> ### PERSPECTIVE:
> ### MERGING CORPORATE CULTURES AT GENERAL MOTORS
>
> General Motors' chairman, Roger B. Smith, is attempting to change the company's culture.[7] One of the major tasks is to merge GM's culture with the very different ones of its newly acquired firms, such as the high-tech aerospace Hughes Aircraft Company and the computer services company Electronic Data Systems (EDS), headed by the colorful, action-oriented entrepreneur Ross Perot. While GM emphasized bureaucratic processes and procedures, EDS focused on achieving results in a militarylike fashion. While decision making was slow at GM and risk taking usually not rewarded, Hughes, being at the forefront of technology, continuously had to scan the environment for new developments and opportunities, making decisions that, at times, involved a great deal of risk.
>
> To give direction to the divergent cultures, Smith distributes "culture cards" that state the company's mission: "The fundamental purpose of General Motors is to provide products and services of such quality that our customers will receive superior value, our employees and business partners will share our success, and our stockholders will receive a sustained, superior return on their investment."[8]

employees in fulfilling the organization's aims. Values can be thought of as forming an ideology that permeates everyday decisions.

In many successful companies, value-driven corporate leaders serve as role models, set the standards for performance, motivate employees, make the company special, and are a symbol to the external environment. It was Edwin Land, the founder of Polaroid, who created a favorable organizational environment for research and innovation. It was Jim Treybig of Tandom, in the Silicon Valley near San Francisco, who made it a point to emphasize that every person is a human being and deserves to be treated accordingly. It was William Cooper Procter of Procter & Gamble who ran the company with the slogan "Do what is right." It was Theodore Vail of AT&T who addressed the needs of customers by emphasizing service. The organization culture created by corporate leaders can result in managerial functions being carried out in quite different ways.

A clear vision of a common purpose elicits commitment. Moreover, when people participate in the decision-making process and exercise self-direction and self-control, they feel committed to their own plans. But espoused values need to be reinforced through rewards and incentives, ceremonies, stories, and symbolic actions.[9]

SUMMARY

Organizing involves developing an intentional structure of roles for effective performance. Many mistakes in organizing can be avoided by first planning the ideal organization for goal achievement and then making modifications for the human or other situational factors. Organization planning identifies staffing needs and helps overcome staffing deficiencies. It also discloses duplication of effort, unclear authority and communication lines, and obsolete ways of doing things. An effective organization remains flexible and adjusts for changes in the environment.

To make staff work effectively, it is important to teach the authority relationships, to make line listen to staff people, and to keep staff informed. Furthermore, effectiveness demands that staff prepares complete recommendations and that the utilization of staff becomes a way of organizational life.

Organizational conflict can be reduced by the use of organization charts and position descriptions. Organizing is improved by teaching its nature and by recognizing the informal organization and the grapevine. Moreover, effective enterprises develop and nurture an appropriate organization culture.

KEY IDEAS AND CONCEPTS FOR REVIEW

Avoiding mistakes in organizing by planning   Understanding of organizing
Avoiding organizational inflexibility   Informal organization
Effective staff work   The grapevine
Avoiding conflict by clarification   Organization culture
Organization charts   Values
Position description

FOR DISCUSSION

1. Many psychologists have pointed to the advantages of "job enlargement," that is, assigning tasks that are not so specialized that an individual loses a sense of doing things which are meaningful. Assuming that managers wish to limit specialization of tasks and "enlarge" jobs, can they do so and still apply the basic principles of organizing?

2. Taking an organized enterprise with which you have some familiarity, can you find any of the deficiencies that commonly occur in organization structures?

3. It is sometimes stated that the typical organization chart is undemocratic in that it emphasizes the superiority and inferiority of people and positions. Comment.

4. What, in your judgment, makes an organization structure "good"? How do "good" organization structures support leadership?

5. What would you need to know to plan an organization structure? How far ahead should you plan it? How would you go about making such a plan?

6. Take an organization you know and discuss its culture. Is the culture helping or hindering the organization in achieving its goals?

EXERCISES/ACTION STEPS

1. Visit a company in your area which is considered a model of effective management. Get any information on this company that gives you some insight into the operation. What makes this organization excellent? Would you like to work for this enterprise? Why, or why not?

2. Gather information on a company that is considered poorly managed. If it is a local company, talk to people and read the newspaper. If the firm is not in your area, gather the information from magazines (e.g., *Fortune, Forbes, Business Week*) and newspapers (e.g., *The Wall Street Journal*). What are some of the problems? What would you recommend to make this firm more effective? Present your findings and your recommendations to the class.

CASE:
ORGANIZATION CULTURE AT IBM[10]

Everyone at IBM is expected to follow three fundamental principles: Respect individuals, strive for excellence, and provide the best service. Thomas Watson founded a patriarchy to instill these principles. His successors have maintained them in the face of rapid growth and changing technology by moving toward a more entrepreneurial system.

One way top management shows its respect for individuals is by treating all employees as equals. IBM hires employees for life. No one will lose his or her job unless he or she consistently fails to meet clear standards or violates the ethics code. There is no distinction between white-, blue-, and pink-collar workers. Many employees will move through line and staff positions over the course of their career. All employees are encouraged to continue their education and prepare themselves for promotions. Almost all middle- and upper-level positions are filled by existing IBM employees.

New employees undergo up to 9 months of training to prepare them for their job and to indoctrinate them in the IBM philosophy. Those who stay rapidly adapt to the corporate culture by dressing conservatively, engaging in competition and team sports, attending various company events, and embracing other aspects of corporate life. Another mark of respect for the individual is the attention top management pays to employee suggestions. The firm has a tradition of open doors at the highest levels. At least once a year, employees discuss matters important to them with their managers. In turn, managers publicly respond to all comments received in suggestion boxes. A suggestion program rewards ideas that reduce costs or improve products or quality control. Between 1975 and 1984, IBM paid workers almost $60 million for suggestions which saved the company $300 million.

Top management monitors employee morale through questionnaires and roundtable discussions at all levels. It holds branch and division managers accountable for any problems and actively helps them improve morale. Most employees are happy being a part of the IBM family and stay with the company for their entire professional life.

IBM is well known for dependable service. Top management emphasizes its commitment to service by focusing on the people who provide that service: the marketing representatives. Most of the top executives, including

Thomas Watson, began their career as salesmen.

Representatives are given full responsibility for pleasing customers. If representatives lose an account, the original sales commission for that account is deducted from their salary. Not surprisingly, the representatives spend much of their time helping customers to maintain their system.

Distinction at IBM is based on merit. The system is designed to foster achievers. Managers establish realistic goals and exuberantly reward employees when they reach them. Almost 25 percent of the employees get bonuses, many receive gifts or a dinner for two, and they receive frequent praise.

The merit system is most obvious in the sales force. Annual sales quotas are set so that approximately 80 percent of the sales representatives will meet them. The representatives' monthly sales are posted on bulletin boards. Managers are expected to help subordinates to meet their goals. Those who achieve their quota join the "100% Club." They attend a lavish three-day annual celebration. The 10 percent of the sales representatives who have the highest sales join the "Golden Circle" and celebrate their success at a posh resort. Those who consistently fail to meet quotas are dismissed.

The competition is tempered by a rigorously enforced code of ethics and team spirit. No matter what their levels, managers' successes depend on their teams' efforts. Because the teams are small, managers can give extensive personal attention to their subordinates. In addition, the sales branches hold monthly rallies to review progress and reward top performers.

As IBM grew, the organization became a vast bureaucracy. Growth has spawned many rules and controls. The hierarchy in such a large organization may slow down communication between departments. Thus, despite their immediate superior's attention to their professional needs, some employees feel insignificant and do not know the direction of the company.

IBM's customer orientation helped the firm to respond rapidly to changes in the market despite the bureaucracy. When personal computers became popular, top management realized it had ignored a product its customers wanted. To get a personal computer on the market fast, top management bypassed its bureaucracy by forming an independent business unit (IBU). The vice-president and his team were freed from other duties so that they could devote their full attention to developing, manufacturing, and marketing the IBM personal computer (PC) without interference from the rest of the organization.

The PC team made several revolutionary decisions, including buying components from other companies, using "open architecture" so other companies could provide software and compatible equipment, and distributing the PC through computer stores. Previously, IBM had insisted on providing all computer services and equipment itself, and its technical specifications had been jealously guarded secrets.

IBM is now exploiting opportunities in telecommunications, robotics, electronics, scientific instrumentation, and computer software by buying into existing companies or forming IBUs. The company has also moved toward decentralization, giving individuals more autonomy without relinquishing its founder's basic philosophy.

1. What is IBM's culture? How does it affect employees? What symbols, traditions, and norms typify IBM?

2. How has the culture changed? How did it help or hinder IBM's adaptation to the external environment?

3. What problems could acquisitions and IBUs create? How should IBM integrate them?

REFERENCES

1. Lyndall Urwick, *The Elements of Administration* (New York: Harper & Row, 1944), p. 38.

2. Thomas J. Peters and Robert H. Waterman, Jr., *In Search of Excellence* (New York: Harper & Row, 1982).

3. John K. Clemens, "A Lesson from 431 B.C.," *Fortune* (Oct. 13, 1986), pp. 161–164.

4. Vijay Sathe, "Some Action Implications of Corporate Culture: A Manager's Guide to Action," *Organizational Dynamics* (Autumn 1983), pp. 4–23; S. R. Luce, "Managing Corporate Culture," *Canadian Business Review* (Spring 1984), pp. 40–43; Stanley M. Davis, "Corporate Culture and Human Resource Management: Two Keys to Implementing Strategy," *Human Resource Planning*, vol. 6, no. 3 (1983), pp. 159–167; Edgar H. Schein, "What You Need to Know about Organizational Culture," *Training and Development Journal* (January 1986), pp. 30–33.

5. B. Littal, "The Corporate Culture Vultures," *Fortune* (Oct. 17, 1983), pp. 66–72.

6. Terrence E. Deal and Allan A. Kennedy, *Corporate Cultures* (Reading, Mass.: Addison-Wesley Publishing Company, 1982), chap. 2.

7. David E. Whiteside, "Roger Smith's Campaign to Change the GM Culture," *Business Week* (Apr. 7, 1986), pp. 84–85; Russell Mitchell, "How General Motors Is Bringing Up Ross Perot's Baby," *Business Week* (Apr. 14, 1986), pp. 96–100; Melinda Grenier Guiles, "GM's Smith Presses for Sweeping Changes, but Questions Arise," *The Wall Street Journal* (Mar. 14, 1985). Partly due to cultural differences, Ross Perot parted with General Motors.

8. Clemens, "A Lesson from 431 B.C." (1986), p. 164.

9. James M. Kouzes, David F. Caldwell, and Barry Z. Posner, "Organizational Culture: How It Is Created, Maintained, and Changed," presentation by the authors, 1983.

10. The case is based on a variety of sources, including the following: P. H. Dorn, "The Song Remains the Same," Datamation (February 1984), pp. 105–110; L. W. Foster, "From Darwin to Now: The Evolution of Organizational Strategies," *Journal of Business Strategy* (Spring 1985), pp. 94–98; B. Jeffery, "With a Little Help from Some Friends," Datamation (February 1984), pp. 147–150; D. Kneal, J. Marcom, Jr., and Randall Smith, "IBM: Behind the Monolith – A Special Report," *The Wall Street Journal* (Apr. 7, 1986), pp. 19–22; L. Luciano, "Seeing the Future Work at IBM," *Money* (November 1985); Peter D. Petre, "Meet the Lean, Mean New IBM," *Fortune* (June 13, 1983), p. 69; T. Sweeny, "Corporate Culture," *San Francisco Business* (February 1986), p. 6; Jo Ellen Davis and Geoff Lewis, "Who's Afraid of IBM?" *Business Week* (June 29, 1987), pp. 68–74; "The Greatest Capitalist in History," *Fortune* (Aug. 31, 1987), pp. 24–35.

SUMMARY OF MAJOR PRINCIPLES, OR GUIDES, OF ORGANIZING

Although the science of organizing has not yet developed to the point at which its principles are infallible laws, there is considerable agreement among management scholars and practitioners about a number of them. These principles are truths (or are believed to be truths) of general applicability, although their application is not precise enough to give them the exactness of the laws of pure science. They are more in the nature of essential criteria for effective organizing. The most essential guiding principles of organizing are summarized in this section.

The Purpose of Organizing

The purpose of organizing is to aid in making objectives meaningful and to contribute to organizational efficiency.

Principle of unity of objectives   An organization structure is effective if it enables individuals to contribute to enterprise objectives.

Principle of organizational efficiency   An organization is efficient if it is structured to aid the accomplishment of enterprise objectives with a minimum of unsought consequences or costs.

The Cause of Organizing

The basic cause of organization structure is the limitation of the span of management. If there were no such limitation, an unorganized enterprise might have only one manager.

Span-of-management principle   In each managerial position, there is a limit to the number of persons an individual can effectively manage, but the exact number will depend on the impact of underlying variables.

The Structure of Organization: Authority

Authority is the cement of organization structure, the thread that makes it possible, the means by which groups of activities can be placed under a manager and coordination of organizational units can be promoted. It is the tool by which a manager is able to exercise discretion and to create an environment for individual performance. Some of the most useful principles of organizing are related to authority.

Scalar principle   The clearer the line of authority from the ultimate management position in an enterprise to every subordinate position, the clearer will be the responsibility for decision making and the more effective will be organization communication.

Principle of delegation by results expected   Authority delegated to all individual managers should be adequate enough to ensure their ability to accomplish the results expected.

Principle of absoluteness of responsibility   The responsibility of subordinates to their superiors for performance is absolute, and superiors cannot escape responsibility for the organization activities of their subordinates.

Principle of parity of authority and responsibility   The responsibility for actions cannot be greater than that implied by the authority delegated, nor should it be less.

Principle of unity of command   The more complete an individual's reporting relationships to a single superior, the smaller the problem of conflicting instructions and the greater the feeling of personal responsibility for results.

Authority-level principle   Maintenance of intended delegation requires that decisions within the authority of individual managers should be made by them and not be referred upward in the organization structure.

The Structure of Organization: Departmentized Activities

Organization involves the design of a departmental framework. Although there are several principles in this area, one is of major importance.

Principle of functional definition   The more a position or a department has a clear definition of the results expected, activities to be undertaken, and organization authority delegated and has an understanding of authority and informational relationships with other positions, the more adequately the responsible individual can contribute toward accomplishing enterprise objectives.

The Process of Organizing

The various principles of authority delegation and of departmentation are fundamental truths about the process of organizing. They deal with phases of the two primary aspects of organizing — authority and activity groupings. There are other principles that deal with the process of organizing. It is through their application that managers gain a sense of proportion or a measure of the total organizing process.

Principle of balance   In every structure there is need for balance. The application of principles or techniques must be balanced to ensure the overall effectiveness of the structure in meeting enterprise objectives.

The principle of balance is common to all areas of science and to all functions of the manager. The inefficiencies of broad spans of management must be balanced against the inefficiencies of long lines of communication. The losses from multiple command must be balanced against the gains from expertness and uniformity in delegating functional authority to staff and service departments. The savings of functional specialization in departmentalizing must be balanced against the advantages of establishing profit-responsible, semi-independent product or territorial departments. It is apparent, once again, that the application of management theory depends on the specific situation.

Principle of flexibility   The more that provisions are made for building flexibility into an organization structure, the more adequately an organization structure can fulfill its purpose.

Devices and techniques for anticipating and reacting to change must be built into every structure. Every enterprise moves toward its goal in a changing environment, both external and internal. The enterprise that develops inflexibilities, whether these are resistance to change, too-complicated procedures, or too-firm departmental lines, is risking the inability to meet the challenges of economic, technical, biological, political, and social change.

Principle of leadership facilitation   The more an organization structure and its delegations of authority enable managers to design and maintain an environment for performance, the more they will help the leadership abilities of those managers.

Since managership depends to a great extent upon the quality of leadership of those in managerial positions, it is important for the organization structure to do its part in creating a situation in which a manager can most effectively lead. In this sense, organizing is a technique of promoting leadership. If the authority allocation and the structural arrangements create a situation in which heads of departments tend to be looked upon as leaders and in which their task of leadership is aided, organization structure has accomplished an essential task.

PART 4

Staffing

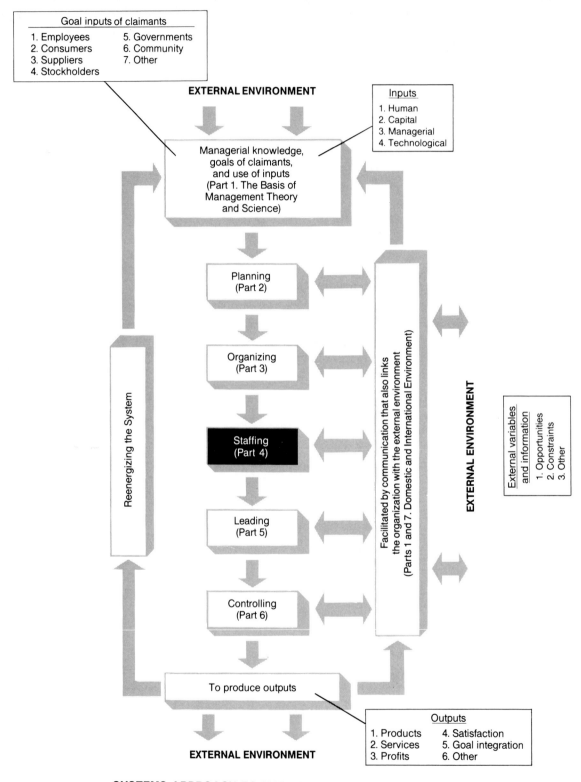

Goal inputs of claimants
1. Employees   5. Governments
2. Consumers   6. Community
3. Suppliers   7. Other
4. Stockholders

EXTERNAL ENVIRONMENT

Inputs
1. Human
2. Capital
3. Managerial
4. Technological

Managerial knowledge,
goals of claimants,
and use of inputs
(Part 1. The Basis of
Management Theory
and Science)

Planning
(Part 2)

Organizing
(Part 3)

Staffing
(Part 4)

Leading
(Part 5)

Controlling
(Part 6)

Reenergizing the System

Facilitated by communication that also links
the organization with the external environment
(Parts 1 and 7. Domestic and International Environment)

EXTERNAL ENVIRONMENT

External variables
and information
1. Opportunities
2. Constraints
3. Other

To produce outputs

Outputs
1. Products   4. Satisfaction
2. Services   5. Goal integration
3. Profits   6. Other

EXTERNAL ENVIRONMENT

SYSTEMS APPROACH TO MANAGEMENT: STAFFING

CHAPTER 11

Human Resource Management and Selection

CHAPTER OBJECTIVES

After reading this chapter, you should understand:

1. The managerial function of staffing and what it means to be a manager
2. The systems approach to human resource management
3. The manager inventory and factors in the external and internal environment
4. The policy of open competition and ways to make staffing more effective
5. The important aspects of the systems approach to manager selection
6. Position requirements, important characteristics of job design, and characteristics needed by managers
7. The matching of manager qualifications with position requirements
8. The orientation and socialization process of new employees

Few executives would argue with the fact that people are vital for the effective operation of a company. Managers often say that people are their most important asset. Yet the "human assets" are virtually never shown on the balance sheet as a distinct category, although a great deal of money is invested in the recruitment, selection, and training of people. It is for this reason that the late Rensis Likert and his colleagues suggested maintaining accounts of the valuable human assets. They refer to this process as "human resource accounting."[1] This approach is not without its problems,[2] and there is even conflict among management experts, between the proponents of human resource accounting and the financial people who have to develop the system for measuring the human assets.[3] What is important here is the recognition that staffing is a crucial function of managers and one that may well determine the success or failure of an enterprise.

This chapter begins with a definition of the managerial function of staffing and an explanation of what it means to be a manager, then introduces an overview of the systems approach to human resource management, and concludes with a discussion of the various aspects of selecting the right person.

DEFINITION OF STAFFING

The managerial function of **staffing** is defined as *filling, and keeping filled, positions in the organization structure.* This includes identifying work-force requirements, inventorying the people available, and recruiting, selecting, placing, promoting, appraising, planning the careers of, compensating, and training or otherwise developing both candidates and current jobholders to accomplish their tasks effectively and efficiently.* It is clear that staffing must be closely linked to organizing, that is, to the setting up of intentional structures of roles and positions.

Many writers on management theory discuss staffing as a phase of organizing. In this book, however, staffing is identified as a separate managerial function for several reasons. First, the staffing of organizational roles includes knowledge and approaches not usually recognized by practicing managers, who often think of organizing as just setting up a structure of roles and give little attention to filling these roles. Second, making staffing a separate function facilitates placing an even greater emphasis on the human element in selection, appraisal, career planning, and manager development. Third, an important body of knowledge and experience has been developed in the area of staffing. Fourth, managers often overlook the fact that staffing is their responsibility — not that of the personnel department. To be sure, this department provides valuable assistance, but it is the job of managers to fill the positions in their organization and keep them filled with qualified people.

DEFINING THE MANAGERIAL JOB

Complete agreement does not exist as to what exactly constitutes the job of a manager. In fact, the nature of managerial tasks has been studied from several different perspectives.[4] One group of writers, known as the *great man school,*

---

*Another term now frequently used for the managerial function of staffing is "human resource management."

studied successful managers and described their behaviors and habits. Although the stories about these people are interesting, the authors usually do not provide an underlying theory to explain the success of their subjects. Other writers — primarily economists — focus on the *entrepreneurial* aspects of managing. Their main concern is profit maximization, innovation, risk taking, and similar activities. Yet another group of writers emphasizes *decision making,* especially the kinds of decisions that cannot be easily programmed. An additional view of the managerial job draws attention to *leadership,* with an emphasis on particular traits and managerial styles. Closely related to this approach is the discussion about *power* and *influence,* that is, the leader's control of the environment and subordinates. Other writers focus their attention on the *behavior of leaders* by examining the content of the manager's job. Finally, the approach favored by Henry Mintzberg is based on observing the *work activities* of managers.[5] He found through observations of five executives that their work was characterized by brevity, variety, discontinuity, and action orientation. He also found that executives favor oral communication and that they engage in many activities that link the enterprise with its environment.

It is useful, as already emphasized, to organize the key tasks of managers into the five functions of planning, organizing, staffing, leading, and controlling, which constitute the framework of this book.

THE SYSTEMS APPROACH TO HUMAN RESOURCE MANAGEMENT: AN OVERVIEW OF THE STAFFING FUNCTION

Figure 11-1 shows how the managerial function of staffing relates to the total management system.* Specifically, enterprise plans (discussed in Part 2 of this book) become the basis for organization plans (Part 3), which are necessary to achieve enterprise objectives. The present and projected organization structure determines the number and kinds of managers required. These demands for managers are compared with available talent through the management inventory. On the basis of this analysis, external and internal sources are utilized in the processes of recruitment, selection, placement, promotion, and separation. Other essential aspects of staffing are appraisal, career strategy, and training and development of managers.

Staffing, as seen in the model, affects leading and controlling. For instance, well-trained managers create an environment in which people, working together in groups, can achieve enterprise objectives and at the same time accomplish personal goals. In other words, proper staffing facilitates leading (Part 5). Similarly, selecting quality managers affects controlling, for example, by preventing many undesirable deviations from becoming major problems (Part 6).

---

*Figure 11-1 is an overview of the staffing function. The variables not discussed in this chapter, but which also focus on staffing, are enclosed with broken lines.

Figure 11-1

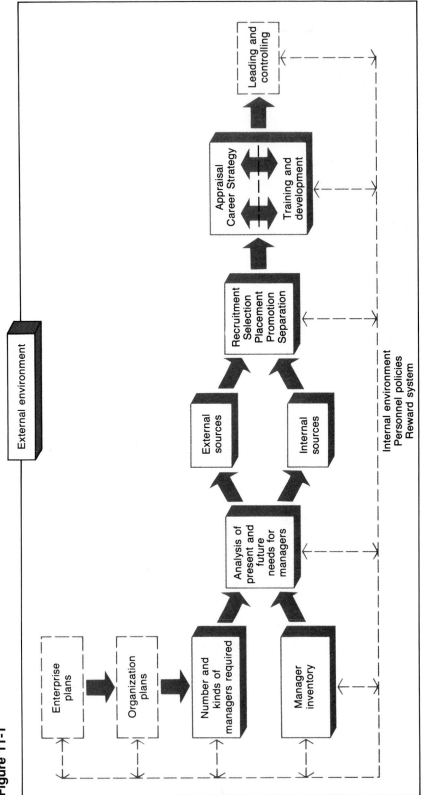

SYSTEMS APPROACH TO STAFFING.

Staffing requires an open-system approach. It is carried out within the enterprise, which, in turn, is linked to the external environment. Therefore, internal factors of the firm — such as personnel policies, the organizational climate, and the reward system — must be taken into account. Clearly, without adequate rewards it is impossible to attract and keep quality managers. The external environment cannot be ignored either; high technology demands well-trained, well-educated, and highly skilled managers. Inability to meet the demand for such managers may well prevent an enterprise from growing at a desired rate.

Factors Affecting the Number and Kinds of Managers Required

The number of managers needed in an enterprise depends not only upon its size but also upon the complexity of the organization structure, the plans for expansion, and the rate of turnover of managerial personnel. The ratio between the number of managers and the number of employees does not follow any law. It is possible, by enlarging or contracting the delegation of authority, to modify a structure so that the number of managers in a given instance will increase or decrease regardless of the size of an operation.

Although the need for determining the number of managers required has been stressed here, it is clear that numbers are only part of the picture. Specifically, the qualifications for individual positions must be identified so that the best-suited managers can be chosen. This kind of detailed analysis of position requirements will be discussed later in this chapter.

Determination of Available Managerial Resources: The Management Inventory

It is common for any business, as well as for most nonbusiness enterprises, to keep an inventory of raw materials and goods on hand to enable it to carry on its operations. It is far less common for enterprises to keep an inventory of available human resources, particularly managers, despite the fact that the required number of competent managers is a vital requirement for success. Keeping abreast of the management potential within a firm can be done by the use of an inventory chart,* which is simply an organization chart of a unit with managerial positions indicated and keyed as to the promotability of each incumbent.

Figure 11-2 depicts a typical inventory chart. At a glance the controller can see where he or she stands with respect to the staffing function. The controller's successor is probably the manager of general accounting, and this person in turn has a successor ready for promotion. Supporting that person in turn is a subordinate who will be ready for promotion in 1 year, but below that

---

*Another term for "inventory chart" is "management replacement chart."

Figure 11-2

MANAGER INVENTORY CHART.

Note: The age shown on the inventory chart must not be used to discriminate against employees on the basis of their age. (That is illegal.)

position are one person who does not have potential and two newly hired employees.

The cost accounting manager represents the all-too-frequent case of a person who is acceptable but not promotable. This individual stands in the way of one subordinate who is promotable now. The remaining people in this department represent extremes of nonpromotability and good potential. Overall, the staffing pattern in this department is not satisfactory.

The manager of budget and analysis has considerable development to accomplish before being ready for promotion. There is no immediately promotable successor. To complicate matters, no further potential exists among the remaining two subordinates.

Contract pricing portends some problems. Its manager is not promotable, but there is good potential in the subordinates.

Advantages and Limitations of the Manager Inventory Chart

The manager inventory chart, as seen from the preceding discussion, has certain general advantages:

1. The chart gives an overview of the staffing situation of an organization.

2. Managers who are ready for promotion can now be easily identified. Prompt action in finding a suitable position within the organization may reduce the propensity of managers to seek employment outside the company.

3. The chart also shows the future internal supply of managers by indicating who is promotable in a year or more.

4. Managers who do not perform satisfactorily are identified, and the need for training or replacement is indicated.

5. If the organization has insufficient "depth," recruitment and training plans can be initiated immediately to ensure the future supply of managers.

6. Managers who are close to retirement can be identified, and preparations can be made for their replacement.

7. The chart facilitates the transfer of managers not only to strengthen weak departments but also to broaden the managers' experience.

8. One can identify and prevent the hoarding of promotable people by their immediate superiors, a practice quite common, especially in large enterprises. Naturally, superiors dislike depriving themselves of able subordinates by letting them transfer to other organizational units. But the overall interest of the enterprise is more important than the self-interest of an individual manager.

9. Managers can counsel subordinates about their career paths and relate them to employment opportunities within the company.

Despite its many advantages, the manager inventory chart also has limitations:

1. The chart does not show to what position the manager may be promotable. If an opening occurs in another organizational unit, the person who is "promotable now" will not necessarily be able to fit this position, since knowledge or skills may be required in specialized areas. A promotable manager in a production department can hardly fill the job of vice-president of sales.

2. The data shown on the chart are not sufficient for making a fair assessment of all the capabilities of individuals. It is still necessary to keep records of each individual's skills, performance, and other biographical information.

3. Although the chart is useful for counseling subordinates, it is often not practical to share the information with all employees. Instead, only the top manager of a division or a department may have this information available.

4. It takes time and effort to keep the chart up to date.

5. Upper-level managers may be reluctant to make their charts available to other upper-level managers because they may be afraid they will lose competent subordinates to other organizational units.

Analysis of the Need for Managers: External and Internal Information Sources

As shown in Figure 11-1, the need for managers is determined by enterprise and organizational plans and, more specifically, by an analysis of the number of managers required and the number available as identified through the management inventory. But there are other factors, internal and external, that influence the demand for and supply of managers. The external forces include economic, technological, social, political, and legal factors. For example, economic growth may result in increased demand for the product, which requires an expansion of the work force, thus increasing the demand for managers. At the same time, competing companies may also expand and recruit from a common labor pool, thus reducing the supply of managers. One must also consider the trends in the labor market, the demographics, and the composition of the community with respect to knowledge and skills of the labor pool and the attitude toward the company. Information about the long-term trends in the labor market may be obtained from several sources. The U.S. government, for example, publishes the *Monthly Labor Review* and the annual *Manpower Report of the President*, which makes long-term projections. Some trade associations and unions also project the demand for labor.

The data about the need and the availability of personnel give rise to four demand-and-supply situations, each requiring a different emphasis in personnel actions. This is illustrated in the matrix shown in Figure 11-3.

With a high supply of managers and a high demand, the focus will be on selection, placement, and promotion. Consequently, particular efforts are made to match the available managers with enterprise needs most effectively.

Figure 11-3

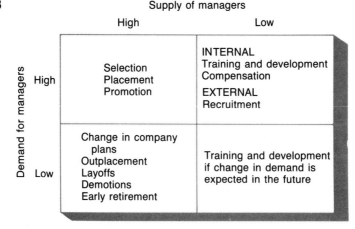

PERSONNEL ACTIONS BASED ON MANAGER SUPPLY AND DEMAND WITHIN THE ENTERPRISE.

A low supply of managers and a high demand requires a different emphasis. If the company favors internal promotions — and many firms do — special emphasis would be placed on training and development to enlarge and improve the pool of managers. But this takes time, and planning far in advance of actual needs is essential. Staffing may be based on open competition for available jobs, and managers from outside the firm should also be considered. Thus, recruitment would be another option. In a situation with a high demand for managers within the enterprise, chances are that there is also a general demand for managers in the external environment. It is therefore crucial that compensation be competitive. This is important for retaining managers already employed by the enterprise, and it is also essential for recruiting managers.

A company with a high supply of managers and a low demand has several alternatives available. The firm can change plans to provide for growth, which would increase the demand for managers and thus take advantage of the managerial assets. The company may also resort to replacement or "outplacement" (a conscious attempt to help managers find and select other suitable employment),[6] layoffs, demotions, or early retirements.

An enterprise with a low supply of managers and a low demand should give special attention to enterprise plans, because this situation indicates a degree of stagnation in the firm. Since developing managers takes a long time, the company should start the process early if there are prospects of growth and of changes in demand for managers in the future.

Other Important Aspects in the Systems Approach to Staffing

After the need for managerial personnel has been determined, a number of candidates may have to be *recruited*. (See Figure 11-1.) This involves attracting qualified candidates to fill organizational roles. From these, managers or potential managers are *selected*; this is the process of choosing from among the candidates the most suitable ones. The aim is to *place* people in positions that allow them to utilize their personal strengths and, perhaps, overcome their weaknesses by getting experience or training in those skills in which they need improvement. Finally, placing a manager in a new position within the enterprise often results in a *promotion*, which normally involves more responsibility. Since recruitment, selection, placement, and promotion are complex processes, they will be discussed in greater detail later in this chapter. Similarly, appraisal, career strategy, training, and development will be discussed in the following staffing chapters. The reference to leading and controlling in Figure 11-1 indicates that effective staffing influences these functions.

SITUATIONAL FACTORS AFFECTING STAFFING

The actual process of staffing shown in Figure 11-1 is affected by many environmental factors. Specifically, external factors include the level of education, the prevailing attitudes in society (such as the attitude toward work), the many laws and regulations that directly affect staffing, the economic conditions, and the supply of and demand for managers outside the enterprise.

There are also many internal factors that affect staffing. They include, for example, organizational goals, tasks, technology, organization structure, the kinds of people employed by the enterprise, the demand for and the supply of managers within the enterprise, the reward system, and various kinds of policies. Some organizations are highly structured; others are not. For some positions — such as the position of a sales manager — skill in human relations may be of vital importance, while the same skill may be less critical for a research scientist working fairly independently in a laboratory. Effective staffing, then, requires recognition of many external and internal situational factors, but the focus here is on those that have a particular relevance to staffing.

The External Environment

Factors in the external environment do affect staffing to various degrees. These influences can be grouped into educational, sociocultural, legal-political, and economic constraints or opportunities. For example, the high technology used in many industries requires extensive and intensive education. Similarly, managers in the sociocultural environment in the United States generally do not accept orders blindly; they want to become active participants in the decision-making process. Furthermore, now and in the future, managers will have to be more oriented toward the public than they have been in the past, responding to the public's legitimate needs and adhering to high ethical standards.

The economic environment — including the competitive situation — determines the external supply of, and the demand for, managers. Legal and political constraints require that firms follow laws and guidelines issued by various levels of government. Table 11-1 summarizes some major federal legislation and orders relating to fair employment that influence the staffing function. The following discussion focuses on equal employment opportunity and the role of women in management, as well as on the staffing of international business.

Equal employment opportunity   Several laws have been passed that provide for equal employment opportunity (EEO). The laws prohibit employment practices that discriminate on the basis of race, color, religion, national origin, sex, or age (in specified age ranges).[7] EEO is based on federal, state, and local laws, and these laws impact on staffing. Recruitment and selection for promotion must be in compliance with these laws. This means that managers making decisions in these areas must be knowledgeable about the laws and the way they apply to the staffing function.

Women in management   In the last decade or so, women have made significant progress in obtaining responsible positions in organizations. Reasons for this development include laws governing fair employment practices, changing societal attitudes toward women in the workplace, and the desire of companies to project a favorable image by placing qualified women in management.

Table 11-1   Major Federal Laws Governing EEO

Major equal employment opportunity laws	Objectives	Jurisdiction
Equal Pay Act (1963)	Equal pay for equal work regardless of sex	Employers engaged in interstate commerce and most employees of federal, state, and local governments
Title VII of the Civil Rights Act (1964) (as amended in 1972)	Equal Employment Opportunity (EEO) for different races, colors, religions, sexes, and national origins	Employers with fifteen or more employees; unions with fifteen or more members; employment agencies; union hiring halls; institutions of higher education; federal, state, and local governments
Age Discrimination in Employment Act (1967) (as amended from age 65 to 70 in 1978)	EEO for ages 40 to 70	Employers with twenty or more employees; unions with twenty-five or more members; employment agencies; federal, state, and local governments
Vocational Rehabilitation Act (1973)	EEO and reasonable affirmative action for handicapped people	Federal government agencies and government contractors with contracts of $2500 or more
Pregnancy Discrimination Act (1978)	EEO during pregnancy	Same as Civil Rights Act

Source: Keith Davis and John W. Newstrom, *Human Behavior at Work: Organizational Behavior* (New York: McGraw-Hill Book Company, 1985), p. 402. Used with permission.

Evidence indicates that women also have some difficulty making it to the top. For example, no women are major candidates for the position of chief executive officer in the *Fortune* 500 corporations. Discrimination has been given as one reason, according to a *Fortune* article.[8] On the other hand, women's representation on boards of directors is increasing.[9] Nevertheless, the total number of women serving on boards is still rather small.

Staffing in the international environment   One must look beyond the immediate external environment and recognize the worldwide changes brought about primarily by advanced communication technology and by the existence of multinational corporations.[10] It is not unusual for large international firms to have top-management teams composed of managers of many different nationalities. The geocentric attitude is the basis for viewing the organization as a worldwide entity engaged in global decision making, including staffing decisions.

The Internal Environment

The internal factors selected for this discussion concern staffing managerial positions with personnel from within the firm as well as from the outside, determining the responsibility for staffing, and recognizing the need for top-management support in overcoming resistance to change.

Promotion from within   Originally, promotion from within implied that workers proceeded into front-line supervisory positions and then upward through the organizational structure. Thus, a firm was pictured as receiving a flow of non-managerial employees from which future managers emerged. As used to be said in the railroad industry, "When a president retires or dies, we hire a new office worker."

As long as the matter is considered in general terms, there is little doubt that employees overwhelmingly favor a policy of promotion from within. The banning of outsiders places limits on competition for positions and gives employees an established monopoly on managerial openings. Employees come to doubt the wisdom of the policy, however, when they are confronted with a specific case of selection of one of their own for promotion. This feeling is present at all levels of the organization, largely because of jealousy or because of rivalry for promotion. The difficulty becomes most evident when a general manager is being selected from among the sales, production, finance, or engineering managers. Top managers are often inclined to choose the easy way and avoid problems by selecting an outsider.

Promoting from within the enterprise not only has positive values relating to morale, employees' long-run commitment to the company, and the firm's reputation but also permits taking advantage of the presence of potentially fine managers among the firm's employees. However, even though these positive but unmeasurable values are important, executives should not be blind to the dangers of either overemphasizing this source or relying upon it exclusively.

A danger presented by an exclusive policy of promoting from within is that it may lead to the selection of persons for promotion who have, perhaps, only imitated their superiors. This is not necessarily a fault, especially if only the best methods, routines, and viewpoints are cultivated, but this is likely to be an unapproachable ideal. The fact is that enterprises often need people from the outside to introduce new ideas and practices. Consequently, there is good reason to avoid a policy of exclusive promotion from within.

Promotion from within in large companies   On the other hand, a policy of promotion from within may be quite suitable for a very large company such as Sears, DuPont, or General Motors. Nevertheless, large business and nonbusiness organizations usually have so many qualified people that promotion from within actually approaches a condition similar to an open-competition policy. Even in these large companies, however, it may be necessary to go outside, as General Motors did when it hired a university professor as vice-president to head its environmental control staff.

The policy of open competition   Managers must decide whether the benefits of a policy of promotion from within outweigh the policy's shortcomings. There are clear-cut reasons for implementing the principle of open competition by opening vacant positions to the best-qualified persons available, whether inside or outside the enterprise. It gives the firm, in the final analysis, the opportunity to secure the services of the best-suited candidates. It counters the shortcomings of an exclusive policy of promotion from within, permits a firm to adopt the best techniques in recruiting managers, and motivates the complacent "heir apparent." To exchange these advantages for the morale advantages attributed to internal promotion would appear questionable.

A policy of open competition is a better and more honest means of ensuring managerial competence than is obligatory promotion from within. However, it does put the managers who use it under a special obligation. If morale is to be protected in applying an open-competition policy, the enterprise must have fair and objective methods of appraising and selecting its people. It should also do everything possible to help people develop so that they can qualify for promotions.

When these requirements are met, it would be expected that every manager making an appointment to a vacancy or a new position would have available a roster of qualified candidates within the entire enterprise. If people know that their qualifications are being considered, if they have been fairly appraised and have been given opportunities for development, they are far less likely to feel a sense of injustice if an opening goes to an outsider. Other things being equal, present employees should be able to compete with outsiders. If a person has the ability for a position, he or she has the considerable advantage of knowing the enterprise and its personnel, history, problems, policies, and objectives. For the superior candidate, the policy of open competition should be a challenge and not a hindrance to advancement.

Responsibility for staffing   While responsibility for staffing should rest with every manager at every level, the ultimate responsibility is with the chief executive officer and the policymaking group of top executives. They have the duty of developing policy, assigning its execution to subordinates, and ensuring its proper application. Policy considerations, for example, include decisions about the development of a staffing program, the desirability of promoting from within or securing managers from the outside, the sources for candidates, the selection procedure to follow, the kind of appraisal program to use, the nature of manager and organization development, and the promotion and retirement policies to follow.

Line managers should certainly make use of the services of staff members — usually from the personnel department — to assist in recruiting, selecting, placing, promoting, appraising, and training people. In the final analysis, however, it is the manager's responsibility to fill positions with the best-qualified persons.

Need for top-management support in overcoming resistance to effective staffing
The prestige and power of top management must be brought to bear if staffing is to be effective. Some managers within the organization will resent losing promising subordinates, even though they can make a greater contribution to the enterprise in a different department. Others will resist changes required

by managerial and organizational development efforts. There are also those who may be threatened by imaginative and achievement-oriented subordinates. Still others may not see staffing as a pressing matter and may neglect it altogether. To overcome these human tendencies, top-management involvement in staffing is necessary.

SELECTION: MATCHING THE PERSON WITH THE JOB

Plant, equipment, materials, and people do not make a business any more than airplanes, tanks, ships, and people make an effective military force. One other element is indispensable: effective managers. The quality of managers is one of the most important factors determining the continuing success of any organization. It necessarily follows, therefore, that the selection of managers is one of the most critical steps in the entire process of managing. **Selection** is the process of choosing from among candidates, from within the organization or from the outside, the most suitable person for the current position or for future positions.

SYSTEMS APPROACH TO SELECTION: AN OVERVIEW

Since qualified managers are critical to the success of an enterprise, a systematic approach is essential to manager selection and to the assessment of present and future needs for managerial personnel.

An overview of the systems approach to selection is illustrated in Figure 11-4. The variables that are closely related to selection, but are not discussed in this section, are marked with broken lines in the model. The position requirements plan is based on the firm's objectives, forecasts, plans, and strategies. This plan is translated into position and job design requirements which are matched with such individual characteristics as intelligence, knowledge, skills, attitudes, and experience. To meet organizational requirements, managers recruit, select, place, and promote people. This, of course, must be done with due consideration for the internal environment (for example, company policies, supply and demand of managers, and the organizational climate) and the external environment (laws, regulations, availability of managers). After people have been selected and placed in positions, they must be introduced to the new job. This orientation involves learning about the company, its operation, and its social aspects.

The newly placed managers then carry out their managerial and nonmanagerial functions (such as marketing), resulting in managerial performance, which eventually determines enterprise performance. Subsequently, managerial performance is appraised, and managers are rewarded. (See Chapter 12.) On the basis of this evaluation, manager and organization development is initiated (Chapter 13). Finally, appraisal may also become the basis for promotion, demotion, replacement, and retirement decisions.

That is the selection model in brief; now each major variable in the model will receive closer attention.

Figure 11-4

SYSTEMS APPROACH TO SELECTION.

Variables marked with broken lines are staffing and other activities that are discussed in other chapters.

POSITION REQUIREMENTS AND JOB DESIGN

Selecting a manager effectively requires a clear understanding of the nature and purpose of the position which is to be filled. An objective analysis of position requirements must be made, and, as far as possible, the job must be designed to meet organizational and individual needs. In addition, positions must be evaluated and compared so that the incumbents can be treated equitably. Among other factors to consider are the skills required — technical, human, conceptual, and design — since these vary with the level in the organizational hierarchy and the personal characteristics needed by managers. (See Chapter 1.)

Identifying Job Requirements

In identifying job requirements, firms must answer questions such as these: What has to be done in this job? How is it done? What background knowledge, attitudes, and skills are required? Since positions are not static, additional questions may have to be considered: Can the job be done differently? If so, what are the new requirements? Finding answers to these and similar questions requires that the job be analyzed. This can be done through observation, interviews, questionnaires, or even a systems analysis. Thus, a job description, based on job analysis, usually lists important duties, authority-responsibility, and the relationship to other positions. More recently, some firms have also included objectives and expected results in job descriptions.

There is, of course, no foolproof rule for designing managerial jobs. Nevertheless, firms can avoid mistakes by following some guidelines.

Appropriate scope of the job   A job too narrowly defined provides no challenge, no opportunity for growth, and no sense of accomplishment. Consequently, good managers will be bored and dissatisfied. On the other hand, a job must not be so broad that it cannot be effectively handled. The result will be stress, frustration, and loss of control.

Full-time challenge of the job   Sometimes managers are given a job that does not require their full time and effort. They are not challenged by their task and they feel underutilized. Consequently, they often meddle in the work of their subordinates, who then also feel that they do not have sufficient authority and discretion to do their jobs. Some time ago, when a utility company asked for help in solving organizational conflicts, it was found that people did not have full-time jobs; they were quarreling about jobs, duties, and tasks; they were in each other's way. Thus, they channeled their energy against one another instead of toward the aims of the company. The need to design jobs with challenging objectives, duties, and responsibilities should be obvious.

Managerial skills required by job design   Generally, the design of the job should start with the tasks to be accomplished. The design is usually broad enough to accommodate people's needs and desires. But some writers on management suggest that it may be necessary to design the job to fit the leadership style of a particular person.[11] It may be especially appropriate to design jobs for exceptional persons, in order to utilize their potential. The problem, of course, is that such a position would probably have to be restructured every time a new manager occupied it. The job description, then, must provide a clear idea of the performance requirements for a person in a particular position but must also allow some flexibility so that the employer can take advantage of individual characteristics and abilities.

Any position description is contingent on the particular job and the organization. For example, in a bureaucratic and fairly stable organization environment, the position may be described in relatively specific terms. In contrast, in a dynamic organization with an unstable, fast-changing environment, a job description may have to be more general and most likely will have to be reviewed more frequently. A situational approach to job descriptions and job designs is called for.

Job Design

People spend a great deal of time on the job, and it is therefore important to design jobs so that individuals feel good about their work. This requires an appropriate job structure in terms of content, function, and relationships.

Design of jobs for individuals and work teams The focus of job design can be on the individual position or on work groups.[12] First, individual jobs can be enriched by grouping tasks into natural work units. This means putting tasks that are related into one category and assigning an individual to carry out the tasks. A second related approach is to combine several tasks into one job. For example, rather than having the tasks of assembling a water pump carried out by several persons on the assembly line, workstations can be established with individuals doing the whole task of putting the unit together and even testing it. A third way of enriching the job is to establish direct relationships with the customer or client. A systems analyst may present findings and recommendations directly to the managers involved in the systems change rather than reporting to his or her superior, who would then make the recommendations to top management. Fourth, prompt and specific feedback should be built into the system whenever appropriate. In one retail store, for example, salespersons received the sales figures for each day and summary figures for each month. Fifth, jobs can be enriched through vertical job loading, which is increasing individuals' responsibility for planning, doing, and controlling their job.

Similar arguments can be made for improving the design of jobs for work teams.[13] Jobs should be designed so that groups have a complete task to perform. Moreover, teams may be given authority and freedom to decide how well the jobs shall be performed, giving the groups a great deal of autonomy. Within the team, individuals can often be trained so that they can rotate to different jobs within the group. Finally, rewards may be administered on the basis of group performance, which tends to induce cooperation rather than competition among team members.

> ### INTERNATIONAL PERSPECTIVE:
> ### JOB DESIGN AT VOLVO IN SWEDEN
>
> Job design receives considerable attention abroad as well as in the United States. At the Volvo truck assembly plant in Sweden, work teams have a great deal of autonomy. For example, these teams choose their own supervisor, assign the work among themselves, set their own outputs within specified limits, and assume responsibility for quality control. In Kalmar, Sweden, Volvo designed an auto plant for teams of fifteen to twenty-five employees; each team handles a specific major task. Employees also receive immediate feedback on hourly production rates, which are displayed on screens.

Factors influencing job design   In designing jobs, the requirements of the enterprise have to be taken into account. But other factors must be considered in order to realize maximum benefits; they include individual differences, the technology involved, the costs associated with restructuring the jobs, the organization structure, and the internal climate.

People have different needs. Those with unused capabilities and a need for growth and development usually want to have their job enriched and to assume greater responsibility. While some people prefer to work by themselves, others with social needs usually work well in groups. The nature of the task and the technology related to the job must also be considered. While it may be possible for work teams to assemble automobiles, as is done at a Volvo plant in Sweden, it may not be efficient to use the same work design for the high production runs at General Motors in the United States. The costs of changing to new job designs must also be considered. It makes a great deal of difference whether a plant is newly designed or an old plant has to be redesigned and changed to accommodate new job design concepts.

The organization structure must also be taken into account. Individual jobs must fit the overall structure. Autonomous work groups, for example, may work well in a decentralized organization, but they may be inappropriate in a centralized structure. Similarly, the organizational climate influences job design. Groups may function well in an atmosphere that encourages participation, job enrichment, and autonomous work, while they may not fit into an enterprise with an autocratic top-down approach to managerial leadership.

SKILLS AND PERSONAL CHARACTERISTICS NEEDED BY MANAGERS

To be effective, managers need various skills ranging from technical to design. The relative importance of these skills varies according to the level in the organization, as discussed in Chapter 1. In addition, analytical and problem-solving abilities and certain personal characteristics are sought in managers.

Analytical and Problem-Solving Abilities

One of the frequently mentioned skills desired of managers is analytical and problem-solving ability. But as Alan Stoneman, former president of the Purex

Corporation, used to say, "We have no problems here; all are opportunities; all a problem should be is an opportunity." In other words, managers must be able to identify problems, analyze complex situations, and by solving the problems encountered, exploit the opportunities presented. They must scan the environment and identify, through a rational process, those factors that stand in the way of opportunities. Thus, analytical skills should be used to find needs of present customers — or potential ones — and then to satisfy those needs with a product or service. It has been amply demonstrated that this opportunity-seeking approach can mean corporate success. For example, Edwin H. Land of Polaroid filled the needs of people who wanted instant photographs. But problem identification and analysis are not enough. Managers also need the will to implement the solutions; they must recognize the emotions, needs, and motivations of the people involved in initiating the required change as well as of those who resist change.

Personal Characteristics Needed by Managers

In addition to the various skills that effective managers need, several personal characteristics are also important. They are (1) a desire to manage, (2) the ability to communicate with empathy, (3) integrity and honesty, and (4) the person's experience — his or her past performance as a manager — which is a very significant characteristic.

Desire to manage The successful manager has a strong desire to manage, to influence others, and to get results through team efforts of subordinates. To be sure, many people want the privileges of managerial positions, which include high status and salary, but they lack the basic motivation to achieve results by creating an environment in which people work together toward common aims. The desire to manage requires effort, time, energy, and, usually, long hours of work.

Communication skills and empathy Another important characteristic of managers is the ability to communicate through written reports, letters, speeches, and discussions. Communication demands clarity, but even more, it demands *empathy*. This is the ability to understand the feelings of another person and to deal with the emotional aspects of communication. Communication skills are important for effective *intragroup communication,* that is, communication with people in the same organizational unit. As one moves up in the organization, however, *intergroup communication* becomes increasingly important. This is communication not only with other departments but also with groups outside the enterprise: customers, suppliers, governments, the community, and, of course, the stockholders in business enterprises.

Integrity and honesty Managers must be morally sound and worthy of trust. Integrity in managers includes honesty in money matters and in dealing with others, effort to keep superiors informed, adherence to the full truth, strength of character, and behavior in accordance with ethical standards.

Many of these qualities, and others, have been cited by top executives of major companies. Henry Ford II, former chairperson of Ford Motor Company, mentioned as appealing qualities honesty, candor, and openness. Similarly, Donald M. Kendall, chairperson of Pepsico, Inc., listed work ethics and integrity as essential characteristics of executives. Noah Dietrich, who ran the Howard Hughes empire for 32 years, identified honesty and candor as the top qualities of his subordinates. His attitude was "I cannot do my job if the executives who report to me do not tell me the truth about their operations."

Past performance as a manager   Another very important characteristic for selection is past performance as a manager. It is probably the most reliable forecast of a manager's future performance. Of course, an assessment of managerial experience is not possible in selecting first-line supervisors from the ranks, since they have not had such experience. But past accomplishments are important considerations in the selection of middle- and upper-level managers. In a survey of Fortune 500 companies, most CEOs said that experience within the company was the key to their successful careers.[14]

MATCHING QUALIFICATIONS WITH POSITION REQUIREMENTS

After the organizational positions are identified, managers are obtained through recruitment, selection, placement, and promotion. (See variable in Figure 11-4.) There are basically two sources of managerial personnel: People from within the enterprise may be promoted or transferred, and managers may be hired from the outside. For *internal* promotions, a computerized information system may help to identify qualified candidates. It can be used in conjunction with a comprehensive human resource plan. Specifically, it can be utilized to anticipate staff requirements, new openings, attritions, development needs, and career planning.

There are also several *external* sources available, and the enterprise may use different methods in finding qualified managers. Many employment agencies — public and private — and executive recruiters (sometimes called "headhunters") locate suitable candidates for positions. Other sources for managers are professional associations, educational institutions, referrals from people within the enterprise, and, of course, unsolicited applications from persons interested in the firm.

Recruitment of Managers

Recruiting involves attracting candidates to fill the positions in the organization structure. Before recruiting begins, the position's requirements — which should relate directly to the task — must be clearly identified. This makes it easier to recruit suitable candidates from the outside. Enterprises with a favorable public image find it easier to attract qualified candidates. A company such as IBM (International Business Machines) has a well-recognized image, while small firms — which frequently offer excellent growth and development opportunities — may have to make great efforts to communicate to the applicant the kinds of products, services, and opportunities the firm offers.

Recruitment in the public sector has many similarities to recruitment in the private sector. However, government regulations or policies may demand that managers adhere to special hiring guidelines. For example, legislation may require that potential employees live within a municipality's boundaries. Another difference is that applicants for public sector positions often have to take competitive tests such as civil service examinations, although an increasing number of privately owned enterprises are using written and oral tests as well.

Unfortunately, the selection process in government is not always as objective and rational as it should be, and the practice of making decisions on criteria other than competence is probably not unusual. Frederic V. Malek, a former special assistant to the President and now a business executive himself, reports that it is unthinkable for a major corporation to put a person without considerable managerial experience in charge of 5000 people, yet in government this is not uncommon.[15] Thus, in order to improve the effectiveness and efficiency of government, a better selection process is required.

Information Exchange Contributing to Successful Selection

The exchange of information works two ways in recruitment and selection: An enterprise provides applicants with an objective description of the company and the position, while the applicants provide information about their capabilities. (See Figure 11-5.)

Business and other organizations attempt to project a favorable image, stress opportunities for personal growth and development, highlight potential challenges, and indicate promotion possibilities. They also convey information about pay, fringe benefits, and, perhaps, job security. This can, of course, be overdone, raising unrealistic expectations in the applicant. In the long run, there may be undesirable side effects resulting in low job satisfaction, high turnover, and unfulfilled dreams. Certainly the enterprise should present itself in an attractive light, yet the opportunities should be discussed in a factual and realistic manner, covering limitations and even unfavorable aspects of the job.

On the other hand, management should elicit from all the applicants an objective demonstration of their knowledge, skills, abilities, aptitudes,

Figure 11-5

EXCHANGE OF INFORMATION IN SELECTION OF MANAGERS.

motivation, and past performance. A number of techniques and instruments can reveal this information (they will be discussed later in the chapter). To be sure, the collection of data about an applicant can go too far and can become an invasion of privacy. The managerial candidate will tolerate only a reasonable amount of interviewing, testing, and disclosure of personal information. Clearly, managers must exercise restraint and request information that is essential and relevant to the job.

Selection, Placement, and Promotion

Selecting a manager is choosing from among the candidates the one that best meets the position requirements. Since the selection may be for a specific job opening or for future managerial requirements, there are two approaches to filling organizational positions. In the *selection approach*, applicants are sought to fill a position with rather specific requirements; in the *placement approach*, the strengths and weaknesses of the individual are evaluated and a suitable position is found or even designed.

Promotion is a change within the organization to a higher position that has greater responsibilities and requires more advanced skills. It usually involves higher status and an increase in pay. The various facets of selection generally apply also to promotion, which may be a reward for outstanding performance or a result of the firm's desire to better utilize an individual's skills and abilities. Promotions may be a reward for past performance, but only if there is evidence of potential competency. Otherwise, persons may be promoted to a level at which they are incompetent.

PERSPECTIVE:
MEET THE YOUNG WORK FORCE

While some observers paint a gloomy picture for the baby-boomers, others look more optimistically into the future.[16] About half of the U.S. labor force is now under 35, and these men and women will be determining the success of enterprises and, on a broader scale, the well-being of the country.

Demographics suggest that there may be an oversupply of managers. Yet the salaries of the young managers have not been eroded. Some factors, such as decentralization of organizations, have increased the demand for general managers. On the other hand, the extensive use of computers may have a particular impact on middle managers, as the discussion on management information systems (Chapter 19) will show. It seems likely that the competition for managerial jobs is going to increase.

What kind of work force will these managers lead? *Fortune* magazine interviewed about 100 workers across the country and found that they are very much aware of the economic — including the Japanese — challenges. At the same time, they are willing to adapt. In fact, they are eager to learn new skills, are willing to relocate, and are open to changing jobs if necessary. The vitalization of industry will depend to a great extent on the young work force: managers and nonmanagers alike.

The Peter Principle

Errors in selection are possible, perhaps even common. According to Laurence J. Peter and Raymond Hall, authors of *The Peter Principle*, managers tend to be promoted to the level of their incompetence.[17] Specifically, if a manager succeeds in a position, this very success may lead to promotion to a higher position, often one requiring skills that the person does not possess. Such a promotion may involve work that is over the manager's head. While the possibility of individual growth must not be overlooked, the Peter Principle can serve as a warning not to take the selection and promotion process lightly.

Responsibility for Selection

The final decision in the selection of a person for a new position should rest with the candidate's prospective superior; only then can the selector be held accountable for the performance of the chosen candidate. It is also advisable to get the opinions of others, especially those with whom the candidate will have working relationships. In addition, the superior of the selector should be involved, approving, rather than actually making, the selection decision. This gives additional assurance that the selecting manager is choosing people on the basis of adequate qualifications and potential for growth rather than on the basis of friendships.

SELECTION PROCESS, TECHNIQUES, AND INSTRUMENTS

This section presents an overview of the selection process, followed by a discussion of a number of instruments and techniques, including interviews, tests, and the assessment center. For good selection, the information about the applicant should be both *valid* and *reliable*. When people ask if data are **valid,** they raise the question: Are the data measuring what they are supposed to be measuring? In selection, validity is the degree to which the data predict the candidate's success as a manager. The information should also have a high degree of **reliability,** a term which refers to the accuracy and consistency of the measurement. For example, a reliable test, if repeated under the same conditions, would give essentially the same results.

The Selection Process

There are some variations of the specific steps in the selection process. For example, the interview of a candidate for a first-level supervisory position may be relatively simple when compared with the rigorous interviews for a top-level executive. Nevertheless, the following broad outline is indicative of the typical process.

First, the selection criteria are established, usually on the basis of current — and sometimes future — job requirements. These criteria include such items as education, knowledge, skills, and experience. Second, the candidate is requested to complete an application form (this step may be omitted if the candidate for the position is from within the organization). Third, a screening interview is conducted to identify the more promising candidates. Fourth, additional information may be obtained by testing the candidate's qualifications for the position. Fifth, formal interviews are conducted by the manager, his or her superior, and other persons within the organization. Sixth, the information provided by the candidate is checked and verified. Seventh, a physical examination may be required. Eighth, on the basis of the results of previous steps, the candidate is either offered the job or informed that he or she has not been selected for the position. Let us examine some parts of the selection process in greater detail.

Interviews

Virtually every manager hired or promoted by a company is interviewed by one or more people. Despite its general use, the interview is considerably distrusted as a reliable and valid means for selecting managers. Various interviewers may weigh or interpret the obtained information differently. Interviewers often do not ask the right questions. They may be influenced by the interviewee's general appearance, which may have little bearing on job performance. They also frequently make up their minds early in the interview, before they have all the information necessary to make a fair judgment.

Several techniques can be used to improve the interviewing process and overcome some of these weaknesses. First, interviewers should be trained so that they know what to look for. For example, in interviewing people from within the enterprise, they should analyze and discuss past records. They should study the results achieved as well as the way key managerial activities were performed. Chapter 12, on appraisal, shows in greater detail how this can be done. When selecting managers from outside the firm, interviewers find that these data are more difficult to obtain, and they usually get them by checking with the listed references.

Second, interviewers should be prepared to ask the right questions. There are structured, semistructured, and unstructured interviews. In an *unstructured* interview, an interviewer may say something like "Tell me about your last job." In the *semistructured* interview, the manager follows an interview guide but may also ask other questions. In a *structured* interview, the interviewer asks a set of prepared questions, such as the following:

What were your specific duties and responsibilities in your last job?

What did you achieve in this job, and how does this compare with the normal output for this job?

Who could be asked to verify these achievements?

To what extent were these achievements due to your efforts?

What were the contributions of other people?

Who are they?

What did you like and dislike about your job?

What innovations did you make in your job?

Why do you want to change your job?

A third way to improve selection is to conduct multiple interviews utilizing different interviewers. Thus, several people can compare their evaluations and perceptions. However, not all interviewers should vote in selecting the candidate; rather, they should provide additional information to the manager who will be responsible for the final decision.

Fourth, the interview is just one aspect of the selection process. It should be supplemented by data from the application form, the results of various tests, and the information obtained from persons listed as references. Reference checks and letters of recommendation may be necessary to verify the information given by the applicant. For a reference to be useful, the person giving the reference must know the applicant well and give a truthful and complete assessment of the applicant. Many people are reluctant to provide complete information, so an applicant's strong points are often overemphasized while his or her shortcomings may be glossed over. The Privacy Act of 1974 and related legislation and judicial rulings have made it even more difficult to obtain objective references. Under this act, the applicant has a legal right to inspect letters of reference unless this right is waived. This is one of the reasons that teachers are sometimes reluctant to make objective and accurate job referrals for their students.

Tests

The primary aim of testing is to obtain data about the applicants that help predict their probable success as managers. Some of the benefits from testing include finding the best person for the job, obtaining a high degree of job satisfaction for the applicant, and reducing turnover. The most commonly used tests can be classified as follows:

1. **Intelligence tests** are designed to measure mental capacity and to test memory, speed of thought, and ability to see relationships in complex problem situations.
2. **Proficiency and aptitude tests** are constructed to discover interests, existing skills, and potential for acquiring skills.
3. **Vocational tests** are designed to show a candidate's most suitable occupation or the areas in which the candidate's interests match the interests of people working in that occupation.
4. **Personality tests** are designed to reveal candidates' personal characteristics and the way candidates may interact with others, thereby giving a measure of leadership potential.

Tests have a number of limitations, however. First, competent industrial psychologists agree that tests are not accurate enough to be used as the sole measure of candidates' characteristics but must be interpreted in the light of each individual's entire history. Second, the test user must know what tests do and what their limitations are. One of the major limitations is uncertainty about whether tests are really applicable; even psychologists are not highly confident that present-day tests are effective in measuring managerial abilities and potentials. Third, before any test is widely used, it should be tried out, if possible on personnel currently employed in an enterprise, to see whether it is valid for employees whose managerial abilities are already known. Fourth, it is also important that tests be administered and interpreted by experts in the field. Finally, tests should not discriminate unfairly and should be consistent with laws and government guidelines.

Assessment Centers

The assessment center is not a location but a technique for selecting and promoting managers. This approach may be used in combination with training. Assessment centers were first used for selecting and promoting lower-level supervisors, but now they are applied to middle-level managers as well. They seem, however, to be inappropriate for top executives. The assessment center technique is not new. It was used by the German and British military in World War II and the American Office of Strategic Services. But its first corporate use in the United States is generally attributed to the American Telephone and Telegraph Company in the 1950s.

Intended to measure how a potential manager will act in typical managerial situations, the usual center approach is to have candidates take part in a series of exercises. During this period they are observed and assessed by psychologists or experienced managers. A typical assessment center will have the candidates do the following:

Take various psychological tests.

Engage in management games in small groups.

Engage in "in-basket" exercises, in which they are asked to handle a variety of matters that they might face in a managerial job.

Give a brief oral presentation on a particular topic or theme, usually recommending a course of desirable action to a mythical superior.

Engage in various other exercises, such as preparing a written report.

During these exercises, the candidates are observed by their evaluators, who also interview them from time to time. At the end of the assessment center period, the assessors summarize their appraisals of each candidate's performance, compare their evaluations with those of other assessors, come to conclusions with them concerning each candidate's managerial potential, and write a summary report on each candidate. These reports are made available to appointing managers for their guidance. They are also often used as guides for management development. In many cases candidates are given feedback on their evaluation; in other cases feedback is given only when candidates request it. Sometimes the summary evaluation as to promotability remains confidential, even though candidates may be informed by assessors about their performance in the various exercises.

Evidence of the usefulness of the assessment center approach — although not conclusive — is encouraging. Specifically, its reliability seems high enough to suggest that further use is warranted.

Assessment centers do present some problems, however. First, they are costly in terms of time, especially since many effective programs extend over a 5-day period. Second, training assessors is a problem, particularly in those companies which believe, with some justification, that the best assessors are likely to be experienced line managers rather than trained psychologists. Third, although a number of different exercises are used to cover the kinds of things a manager does, questions have been raised as to whether these exercises are the best criteria for evaluation. An even greater problem exists in determining which evaluation measures should be applied to each exercise. Most assessment centers, being highly oriented to individual and interpersonal behavior under various circumstances, may be overlooking the most important element in selecting managers, especially those about to enter the managerial ranks for the first time. That element is motivation — whether or not a person truly wants to be a manager. To be so motivated, candidates must know what managing is, what it involves, and what is required to be a successful manager. Obviously, motivation is a difficult quality to evaluate. However, by making clear to a candidate what managing involves and requires and then asking the candidate to think this over, the interviewer can give the candidate a good basis on which to determine whether he or she really wants to be a manager.

Limitations of the Selection Process

The diversity of selection approaches and tests indicates that there is no one perfect way to select managers. Experience has shown that even carefully chosen selection criteria are still imperfect in predicting performance. Furthermore, there is a distinction between what persons *can do,* that is, their ability to perform, and what they *will do,* which relates to motivation. The latter is a function of the individual and the environment. For example, a person's needs may be different at various times. The organizational environment also changes. The climate of an enterprise may change from one that encourages initiative to one that restricts it because a new top management introduces a different managerial philosophy. Therefore, selection techniques and instruments are not a sure way to predict what people will do, even though they may have the ability to do it.

Testing itself, especially psychological testing, has limitations. Specifically, the seeking of certain information may be considered an invasion of privacy. In addition, it has been charged that some tests unfairly discriminate against women or members of minority groups. These complex issues are not easily resolved, yet they cannot be ignored when an enterprise is selecting managers.

Still other concerns in selection and hiring are the time and cost involved in making personnel decisions. It is important to identify such factors as advertising expenses, agency fees, costs of test materials, time spent interviewing candidates, costs for reference checks, medical exams, start-up time required for the new manager to get acquainted with the job, relocation, and orientation of the new employee. When recruiting costs are recognized, it becomes evident that turnover can be very expensive to an enterprise.

ORIENTING AND SOCIALIZING NEW EMPLOYEES

The selection of the best person for the job is only the first step in building an effective management team. Even companies that make great efforts in the recruitment and selection process often ignore the needs of new managers after they have been hired. Yet the first few days and weeks can be crucial for integrating the new person into the organization.

Orientation involves the introduction of new employees to the enterprise, its functions, tasks, and people. Large firms usually have a *formal orientation program* which explains these features of the company: history, products and services, general policies and practices, organization (divisions, departments, and geographic locations), benefits (insurance, retirement, vacations), requirements for confidentiality and secrecy (especially in defense contracts), safety and other regulations. These may be further described in detail in a company booklet, but the orientation meeting provides new employees with an opportunity to ask questions. Although these formal programs are usually conducted by persons from the personnel department, the primary responsibility for orienting the new manager still rests with the superior.

There is another and perhaps even more important aspect of orientation: the socialization of new managers. **Organizational socialization** is defined in several different ways. A global view includes three aspects: acquisition of work skills and abilities, adoption of appropriate role behaviors, and adjustment to the norms and values of the work group.[18] So, in addition to meeting the specific requirements of the job, new managers will usually encounter new values, new personal relationships, and new modes of behavior. They do not know people they can ask for advice, they do not know how the organization works, and they have a fear of being unsuccessful in the new job. All this uncertainty can cause a great deal of anxiety for a new employee, especially management trainees. Because the initial experience in an enterprise can be very important for future management behavior, the first contact of trainees should be with the best superiors in the enterprise, people who can serve as models for future behavior.

SUMMARY

Staffing means filling positions in the organization structure. It involves identifying work-force requirements, inventorying the people available, and recruiting, selecting, placing, promoting, appraising, planning the careers of, compensating, and training people.

In the systems approach to staffing, enterprise and organization plans become important inputs for staffing tasks. The number and quality of managers required to carry out crucial tasks depend on many different factors. One major step in staffing is to determine the people available by making a management inventory. This can be done by using an inventory chart.

Staffing does not take place in a vacuum; one must consider many situational factors — both internal and external. Staffing requires adherence to equal employment opportunity (EEO) laws so that practices do not discriminate, for example, against minorities or women. Also, one must evaluate the pros and cons of promoting people from within the organization or selecting people from the outside.

In the systems model for selection, the comprehensive managerial requirements plan is the basis for position requirements. In designing jobs, the manager must see that the scope of the job is appropriate, that the position involves a full-time, challenging job, and that it reflects required skills. The job structure must be appropriate in terms of content, function, and relationships. Jobs can be designed for individuals or work teams. The importance of technical, human, conceptual, and design skills varies with the level in the organizational hierarchy. The position requirements are matched with the various skills and characteristics of individuals. The matching is important in recruitment, selection, placement, and promotion.

Errors in selection can lead to actualization of the Peter Principle, which states that managers tend to be promoted to the level of their incompetence. Although the advice of several people should be sought, the selection decision should generally rest with the immediate superior of the candidate for the position.

The selection process may include interviews, various tests, and the use of assessment centers. To avoid dissatisfaction and employee turnover, new employees must be introduced to, and integrated with, other persons in the organization.

KEY IDEAS AND CONCEPTS FOR REVIEW

Staffing	Recruitment
Systems approach to human resource management	Selection
Management inventory	Placement
Situational factors affecting staffing	Promotion
Equal employment opportunity (EEO)	Peter Principle
Women in management	Validity
Promotion from within	Reliability
Policy of open competition	Selection process
Systems approach to selection	Kinds of tests
Position and job requirements	Assessment centers
Job design	Orientation and socialization

FOR DISCUSSION

1. Why is the function of staffing seldom approached logically? Briefly describe the systems approach to staffing. How is staffing related to other managerial functions and activities?

2. List and evaluate external factors affecting staffing. Which ones are most critical today? Explain.

3. What are the key characteristics of a manager inventory chart? Discuss the advantages and disadvantages of such a chart.

4. What are the dangers and difficulties in applying a policy of promotion from within? What is meant by a policy of open competition? Do you favor such a policy? Why, or why not?

5. What is the systems approach to selection of managers? Why is it called a systems approach? How does it differ from other approaches?

6. What are some of the factors that are important in designing individual jobs and jobs for work teams? Which ones seem most important to you? Why?

7. The Peter Principle has been widely quoted in management circles. What do you think of it? Do you think that it could ever apply to you? Does it mean that all chief executives are incompetent? Explain.

8. What is an assessment center? How does it work? Would you like to participate in such a center? Why, or why not?

EXERCISES/ACTION STEPS

1. Select an organization you know and evaluate the effectiveness of the enterprise's recruitment, selection, and appraisal of people. How systematically are these and other staffing activities carried out?

2. Go to the library and research the background of successful CEOs. You may begin by looking at *Fortune* magazine or reading the biography of Lee Iacocca, the CEO at Chrysler.

CASE:
BELDEN ELECTRONICS COMPANY

Belden Electronics Company (BEC) has an excellent national and international reputation, and its employees are proud to work for the firm. But the company demands total loyalty from its employees and even tries to influence their behavior and appearance after work.

Christine Sharp, a bright young woman working for BEC for over 10 years, was highly respected by her colleagues and did a fine job as a divisional sales manager. It was generally agreed that she had excellent potential for advancement. For 2 months, Ms. Sharp had been dating Frank Simmons, who worked in the electronics division of a competing company. One day, Ralph Schmidt, Christine's boss, approached her about this matter, stating that there might be a possible conflict of interest in her association with an employee of the competitor. He made it clear that BEC has an unwritten policy that demands (and rewards) complete loyalty from all its employees.

Shortly after this emotional confrontation with her boss, Ms. Sharp was transferred to a nonmanagerial position without any loss in pay.

She also noted that even her friends at BEC tried to avoid her. But Ms. Sharp felt very strongly that the company had no business suggesting whom she could and could not see after working hours; as a result, she quit her job.

1. Can a company demand loyalty to the extent indicated in the case? Would your answer be different if Ms. Sharp had access to important company trade secrets?

2. What would you do in Ms. Sharp's position?

3. What would you do in the supervisor's position?

REFERENCES

1. Rensis Likert, *The Human Organization: Its Management and Value* (New York: McGraw-Hill Book Company, 1967), chap. 9.

2. For a detailed discussion of problems, see Phil H. Mirvis and Barry A. Macy, "Human Resource Accounting: A Measurement Perspective," *Academy of Management Review* (April 1976), pp. 74–83.

3. J. D. Powell, H. A. Sciullo, and G. Mattson, "Human Resource Accounting: Why the Delay?" *Journal of Management* (Fall 1976), pp. 25–31.

4. For a comprehensive review, see Henry Mintzberg, *The Nature of Managerial Work* (New York: Harper & Row, 1973), chap. 2.

5. Henry Mintzberg, "The Manager's Job: Folklore and Fact," *Harvard Business Review* (July–August 1975), pp. 49–61.

6. Since job security cannot always be guaranteed, outplacement may be a way of helping employees. See the discussion with Peter F. Drucker in "Advice from the Dr. Spock of Business," *Business Week* (Sept. 28, 1987), pp. 61–65.

7. See, for example, David G. Scalise and Daniel J. Smith, "Legal Update: When Are Job Requirements Discriminatory?" *Personnel* (March 1986), pp. 41–48.

8. Susan Fraker, "Why Women Aren't Getting to the Top," *Fortune* (Apr. 16, 1984), pp. 40–45.

9. Clare Ansberry, "Board Games," *The Wall Street Journal*, special report (Mar. 24, 1986).

10. See also Simcha Ronen, *Comparative and Multinational Management* (New York: John Wiley & Sons, 1986), chap. 12.

11. See, for example, Fred E. Fiedler, "Engineering the Job to Fit the Manager," *Harvard Business Review* (September–October 1965), pp. 115–122. His theory is discussed in Chapter 18.

12. This discussion of job design is based in part on David A. Nadler, J. Richard Hackman, and Edward E. Lawler III, *Managing Organizational Behavior* (Boston: Little, Brown and Company, 1979), chap. 5.

13. Nadler et al., *Managing Organizational Behavior* (1979). See also the discussion of sociotechnical systems in Chapter 2 of this book.

14. Maggie McComas, "Atop the Fortune 500: A Survey of the C.E.O.s," *Fortune* (Apr. 28, 1986), pp. 26–31.

15. Frederic V. Malek, *Washington's Hidden Tragedy* (New York: The Free Press, 1978), p. 68.

16. Myron Magnet, "Baby-Boom Executives Are Making It," *Fortune* (Sept. 2, 1985), pp. 22–28; and Michael Brody, "Meet Today's Young American Worker," *Fortune* (Nov. 11, 1985), pp. 90–98.

17. Laurence J. Peter and Raymond Hall, *The Peter Principle* (New York: Bantam Books, 1969). See also Laurence J. Peter, *The Peter Pyramid: Or Will We Ever Get the Point?* reviewed by Peter Shaw, "A Management Guru Peters Out," *The Wall Street Journal* (Jan. 24, 1986).

18. Daniel C. Feldman, "The Multiple Socialization of Organization Members," *Academy of Management Review* (April 1981), pp. 309–318.

CHAPTER 12

Performance Appraisal and Career Strategy

CHAPTER OBJECTIVES

After reading this chapter, you should understand:

1. The importance of effectively appraising managers
2. The qualities that should be measured in appraising managers
3. That traditional trait appraisals have not been effective
4. The system of managerial appraisal based on evaluating performance against verifiable objectives and performance as a manager
5. The rewards and stress of managing
6. The important aspects of career planning

Managerial appraisal has sometimes been referred to as the Achilles' heel of managerial staffing, but it is probably a major key to managing itself. It is the basis for determining who is promotable to a higher position. It is also important to management development, because if a manager's strengths and weaknesses are not known, it is difficult to determine whether development efforts are aimed in the right direction. Appraisal is, or should be, an integral part of a system of managing. Knowing how well a manager plans, organizes, staffs, leads, and controls is really the only way to ensure that those occupying managerial positions are actually managing effectively. If a business, a government agency, a charitable organization, or even a university is to reach its goals effectively and efficiently, ways of accurately measuring management performance must be found and implemented.

There are other reasons why effective managerial appraisal is important. One of the most compelling arises from the provisions of Title VII of the Civil Rights Act of 1964 (as amended) and the regulations of the Equal Employment Opportunity Commission and the Office of Federal Contract Compliance. These agencies have been highly critical of many appraisal programs, finding that they often result in discrimination, particularly in areas of race, age, and sex. Courts have supported the federal agencies in their insistence that, to be acceptable, an appraisal program must be reliable and valid.[1] That these are rigorous standards is apparent.

Effective performance appraisal should also recognize the legitimate desire of employees for progress in their professions. One way to integrate organizational demands and individual needs is through career management, which can be a part of performance appraisal, as this chapter will explain.

THE PURPOSES AND USES OF APPRAISAL

Appraisals serve different organizational and individual needs. Some important studies are discussed below.

The Conference Board Study[2]

An extensive study by The Conference Board showed that the *objectives* of appraisals, on the basis of the frequency mentioned, were the following: (1) management development, (2) performance appraisal, (3) performance improvement, (4) compensation, (5) potential identification, (6) feedback, (7) work-force planning, and (8) communication.

However, when respondents were asked how the companies *used* appraisals, the ranking differed and showed the following results: (1) performance feedback, (2) compensation administration, (3) promotion decisions, (4) identification of management development needs, (5) work-force planning, and (6) validation of selection procedures.

The differences between the stated objectives of appraisals and the way they were used may be an important reason for the dissatisfaction with appraisals that was indicated by some of the personnel managers participating in this study. Note also that the objectives and uses of appraisals have a different orientation. In determining compensation, or often even in evaluating performance, superiors assume the role of judges. In contrast, when the aim is to develop subordinates, managers need to be counselors, helpers, and teachers.

The General Electric Studies

Some of the best-known studies on performance appraisals were done at the General Electric Company.[3] The findings of the initial study showed that

(1) criticism had a negative impact on goal accomplishment, (2) praise had little effect, (3) specific goals improved performance, (4) critical appraisal resulted in defensiveness and inferior performance, (5) coaching should be done on a day-to-day basis rather than once a year, (6) joint objective setting, not criticism, improved performance, (7) meetings with the primary purpose of improving performance should not be conducted at the same time that salary or promotion is being considered, and (8) subordinates' participation in setting objectives improved performance.

In light of the findings, General Electric developed a new appraisal program called "Work Planning and Review" (WP&R). This new approach emphasized frequent discussions of performance without summary ratings. Moreover, salary actions were discussed at separate meetings. Finally, problem solving and joint objective setting were emphasized. The experience at General Electric suggests that the two purposes of performance appraisal should be separated because if the appraisal is used as the basis for salary action, the superior assumes the role of a judge, while in the attempt to motivate employees, the manager takes the role of a coach. It is through recognizing the split roles in performance appraisal and by setting specific goals mutually agreed upon by the superior and the subordinates that productivity can be improved.

THE PROBLEM OF MANAGEMENT APPRAISAL

Managers have long been reluctant to appraise subordinates. However, in an activity as important as managing, there should be no reluctance to measure performance as accurately as possible. In almost all kinds of group enterprises, whether in work or in play, performance has usually been rated in some way. Moreover, most people, and particularly people of ability, want to know how well they are doing.

It is difficult to believe that the controversy, the misgivings, and even the disillusionment that are still so widespread with respect to managerial performance appraisal have come from the practices of measuring and evaluating. Rather, it appears that they have arisen from the things measured, the standards used, and the way measurement is done.

Managers can understandably take exception, feel unhappy, or resist when they believe that they are evaluating, or being evaluated, inaccurately or against standards that are inapplicable, inadequate, or subjective. However, some light and hope have emerged in the past 30 years and offer promise of making evaluation effective. The interest in evaluating managers by comparing actual performance against present verifiable objectives or goals is a development of considerable potential.

Even appraisal against verifiable objectives is not enough. It needs to be supplemented by an appraisal of managers as managers. Moreover, neither system is without difficulties and pitfalls, and neither can be operated by simply adopting the technique and doing the paperwork. More must be done. In the first place, it is essential that managing by verifiable objectives, as explained in Chapter 4, be a way of life in an enterprise. In the second place, managers need not only a clear understanding of the managerial job and the fundamentals underlying it but also an ability to apply these fundamentals in practice.

CHOOSING THE APPRAISAL CRITERIA

The appraisal should measure performance in accomplishing goals and plans as well as performance as a manager. No one wants a person in a managerial role who appears to do everything right as a manager but who cannot turn in a good record of profit making, marketing, controllership, or whatever the area of responsibility may be. Nor should we be satisfied to have a "performer" in a managerial position who cannot operate effectively as a manager. Some star performers may have succeeded through no fault of their own.

Performance in Accomplishing Goals

In assessing performance, systems of appraising against verifiable preselected goals have extraordinary value. Given consistent, integrated, and understood planning designed to reach specific objectives, probably the best criteria of managerial performance relate to the ability to set goals intelligently, to plan programs that will accomplish those goals, and to succeed in achieving them. Those who have operated under some variation of this system often claim that these criteria are inadequate and that elements of luck or other factors beyond the manager's control are taken into account when arriving at any appraisal. But, in too many cases, managers who achieve results owing to sheer luck are promoted, and others, who do not achieve expected results because of factors beyond their control, are blamed for failures. Thus, appraisal against verifiable objectives is, by itself, insufficient.

Performance as Managers

The system of measuring performance against preestablished objectives should be supplemented by an appraisal of a manager *as a manager.* Managers at any level also undertake nonmanagerial duties, and these cannot be overlooked. The primary purpose for which managers are hired and against which they should be measured, however, is their performance as managers — that is, they should be appraised on the basis of how well they understand and undertake the managerial functions of planning, organizing, staffing, leading, and controlling. The standards to use in this area are the fundamentals of management, but first some traditional appraisal programs should be examined.

TRADITIONAL TRAIT APPRAISALS

For many years, managers have been evaluated against standards of personal traits and work characteristics. Typical trait-rating evaluation systems may list ten to fifteen personal characteristics, such as ability to get along with people, leadership, analytical competence, industry, judgment, and initiative. The list may also include such work-related characteristics as job knowledge, ability to carry through on assignments, production or cost results, or success in seeing that plans and instructions are carried out. However, at least until recent years, personal traits have far outnumbered work-related characteristics. On the basis of these standards, the rater appraises subordinates, rating them from unacceptable to outstanding.

Weaknesses of Trait Appraisal

Managers resist doing this type of evaluation or tend to go through the paperwork without knowing exactly how to rate. Even in firms that have made earnest attempts to "sell" such programs, to indoctrinate managers, and to train them in the meaning of traits so that they can improve their appraisal ability, few managers can or will evaluate properly.

One practical problem of the trait approach to appraisal is that because trait evaluation cannot be objective, serious and fair-minded managers do not wish to utilize their obviously subjective judgment on a matter as important as performance. And employees who receive less than the top rating almost invariably feel that they have been dealt with unfairly.

Another problem is that the basic assumption of trait appraisals is open to question. The connection between performance and possession of specific traits is doubtful. What is evaluated tends to be outside of — separated from — a manager's actual operations. Trait appraisal substitutes someone's opinion of an individual for what that individual really does.

Many managers look upon trait rating as only a paperwork exercise that must be done because someone has ordered it. When people have this attitude, they go through the paperwork and tend to make ratings as painless (for the subordinate and themselves) as possible. Consequently, they tend not to be very discriminating. It is interesting, but hardly surprising, that a study of ratings of U.S. Navy officers several years ago came up with an arithmetical paradox: Of all the officers rated over a period of time, some 98.5 percent were outstanding or excellent, and only 1 percent were average!

Trait criteria are at best nebulous. Raters are dealing with a blunt tool, and subordinates are likely to be vague about what qualities they are being rated on. In the hands of most practitioners, it is a crude device, and since raters are painfully aware of this, they are reluctant to use it in a manner that would damage the careers of their subordinates. One of the principal purposes of appraisal is to provide a basis upon which to discuss performance and to plan for improvement. But trait evaluations provide few tangible things to discuss, little on which participants can agree as fact, and therefore little mutual understanding of what is required to obtain improvement.

Attempts to Strengthen Trait Rating

As the deficiencies of trait rating have come to be recognized, a number of changes and additions have been introduced. Some are aimed at making the traits more comprehensible to raters. In a rating form used by a well-known business corporation, a person's "judgment" is defined as his or her capability to recognize the significant from the less significant in arriving at sound conclusions. Likewise, attempts are made to give meanings to various grades under each category.

Often, too, trait and work-quality forms are supplemented by open-ended evaluations in which, without specific guidance, appraisers are asked to supply whatever evidence on performance they feel is pertinent. Sometimes, also, this approach is used for the entire appraisal. Appraisers may be given a broad outline to guide them; for example, they may be asked for comments under such categories as operations, organization, personnel, and finance, and they may be asked specifically to consider such things as quality, quantity, time required to complete work, customer relations, and subordinate employee morale. Although these categories are helpful, experience has shown that they do not greatly improve the quality of ratings.

Attempts have also been made to improve the effectiveness of the rating process. In some systems, subordinates are required to rate themselves, and superiors must compare their own ratings with those made by subordinates. In other instances, the superior's superior is asked to rate the former's subordinate or at least to carefully review the evaluation made by the immediate superior. Sometimes, a rater is forced by an appraisal system to rank subordinates from the best to the least able. In still other cases, rating has been done through the use of critical incidents that are assumed to give meaning to the grades given. These incidents are important events or decisions critical for effective performance in a particular job. Such incidents may represent outstanding or unsatisfactory performance.

These and other devices have been used to offset the disadvantages of trait rating. They have helped, but they cannot overcome the fact that traits and work qualities are subjective and are not correlated with what a manager's job really is.

APPRAISING MANAGERS AGAINST VERIFIABLE OBJECTIVES

One widely used approach to managerial appraisal is the system of evaluating managerial performance against the setting and accomplishing of verifiable objectives. As was noted in Chapter 4, a network of meaningful and attainable objectives is basic to effective managing. This is simple logic, since people cannot be expected to accomplish a task with effectiveness or efficiency unless they know what the end points of their efforts should be. Nor can any organized enterprise in business or elsewhere be expected to do so.

The Appraisal Process

Once a program of managing by verifiable objectives is operating, appraisal is a fairly easy step. Supervisors determine how well managers set objectives and how well they have performed against them. In cases where appraisal by results has failed or been disillusioning, the principal reason is that managing by objectives was seen only as an appraisal technique. The system is not likely to work if used only for this purpose. Management by objectives must be a way of managing, a way of planning, as well as the key to organizing, staffing, leading, and controlling. When this is the case, appraisal boils down to whether or not managers have established adequate but reasonably attainable objectives and how they have performed against them in a certain period.

Look at the system of managing and appraising by objectives in Figure 4-3. As the figure shows, appraising is merely a last step in the entire process.

There are other questions too. Were the goals adequate? Did they call for "stretched" (high but reasonable) performance?* These questions can be answered only through the judgment and experience of a person's superior, although this judgment can become sharper with time and experience, and it may be even more objective if the superior can use the goals of other managers in similar positions for comparison.

In assessing the accomplishment of goals, the evaluator must take into account such considerations as whether the goals were reasonably attainable in the first place, whether factors beyond a person's control unduly helped or hindered in accomplishing goals, and what the reasons for the results were. The reviewer should also note whether an individual continued to operate against obsolete goals when situations changed and revised goals were called for.

Three Kinds of Reviews

The simplified model of performance appraisal shown in Figure 12-1 indicates three kinds of appraisals: (1) a comprehensive review, (2) progress or periodic reviews, and (3) continuous monitoring.

There is general agreement that a *formal comprehensive appraisal* should be conducted at least once a year, but some people suggest that such discussions should take place more frequently. Some enterprises do all the reviews within a short period of time each year, while others schedule the appraisals throughout the year, often at the employment anniversary. A case could be made against any rigid schedule of annual performance reviews. Instead, it may be argued, with good reason, that performance should be reviewed, for example, after the completion of a major project. Obviously, no universally applicable suggestion can be made about the time frame for the formal comprehensive review. It depends on the nature of the task, past company practices, and other situational factors. Once, twice, or even three times may be appropriate for a particular organization or a person who is new in a job.

What is important is that the formal comprehensive reviews be supplemented by frequent *progress* or *periodic reviews.* These reviews can be short and relatively informal, but they help identify problems or barriers that hinder effective performance. They also keep communication open between the

---

*For additional questions, see the checklist in Table 4-2.

Figure 12-1

THE APPRAISAL PROCESS.

Redrawn from Heinz Weihrich, *Management Excellence: Productivity through MBO* (New York: McGraw-Hill Book Company, 1985), p. 125.

superior and subordinates. Furthermore, priorities can be rearranged and objectives can be renegotiated if warranted by changed situations. It certainly is inappropriate to pursue obsolete or even unsuitable objectives that were agreed upon in an environment of uncertainties.

Finally, there is *continuous monitoring* of performance. With this system, when performance deviates from plans, one does not have to wait for the next periodic review to correct it. The superior and the subordinate discuss the situation immediately so that corrective actions can be taken at once in order to prevent a small deviation from developing into a major problem.

Strengths of Appraisal against Verifiable Objectives

The strengths of appraising against accomplishment of objectives are almost the same as those of managing by objectives. Both are part of the same process, both are basic to effective managing, and both are means of improving the quality of managing.

In the area of appraising, there are special and important strengths. Appraising on the basis of performance against verifiable objectives has the great advantage of being operational. Appraisals are not apart from the job that managers do but are a review of what they actually did as managers.

There are always questions of how well a person did; of whether goals were missed or accomplished, and for what reasons; and of how much in the way of goal attainment should be expected. But information about what a person has done, measured against what that individual agreed was a reasonable target, is available. This information furnishes strong presumptions of objectivity and reduces the element of pure judgment in appraisal. Moreover, the appraisal can be carried on in an atmosphere in which superiors cooperatively work with subordinates rather than sitting in judgment of them.

Weaknesses of Appraisal against Verifiable Objectives

As noted in Chapter 4, there are certain weaknesses in the implementation of managing by objectives. These, of course, apply with equal force to appraisal. One of them is that it is entirely possible for persons to meet or miss goals through no fault of their own. Luck often plays a part in performance. For example, a new product's acceptance may be far beyond expectations, and its success will make a marketing manager look exceptionally good, even though the quality of the marketing program and its implementation might actually be poor. Or an unpredictable cancellation of a major military contract might make the record of a division manager look unsatisfactory.

Most evaluators will say that they always take uncontrollable or unexpected factors into account in assessing goal performance, and to a very great extent they do. But it is extremely difficult to do so. In an outstanding sales record, for example, how much can anyone be sure how much was due to luck and how much to competence? Outstanding performers are rated highly, at least as long as they perform. Nonperformers can hardly escape having a cloud cast over them.

With its emphasis on accomplishing operating objectives, the system of appraising against these may overlook needs for individual development. Goal attainment tends to be short-run in practice. Even if longer-range goals are included, seldom are they so long-range as to allow for adequate long-term development of managers. Managers concerned primarily with results might be driven by the system to take too little time to plan, implement, and follow through with programs required for their development and that of their subordinates.

On the other hand, since managing by objectives gives better visibility to managerial needs, development programs can be better pinpointed. If individual development is to be ensured, however, goals in this area should be specifically set.

From an appraisal as well as an operating management point of view, perhaps the greatest deficiency of management by objectives is that it appraises operating performance only. Not only is there the question of luck, mentioned previously, but also there are other factors to appraise, notably an individual's *managerial* abilities. This is why an adequate appraisal system must appraise performance as a manager as well as performance in setting and meeting goals.

A SUGGESTED PROGRAM: APPRAISING MANAGERS AS MANAGERS

The most appropriate standards to use for appraising managers as managers are the fundamentals of management. It is not enough to appraise a manager broadly, evaluating only performance of the basic functions of the manager; appraisal should go further.

The best approach is to utilize the basic techniques and principles of management as standards. If they are basic, as they have been found to be in a wide variety of managerial positions and environments, they should serve as reasonably good standards. As crude as they may be, and even though some judgment may be necessary in applying them to practice, they give the evaluator some benchmarks for measuring how well subordinates understand and are following the functions of managing. They are definitely more specific and more applicable than evaluations based on such broad standards as work and dress habits, cooperation, intelligence, judgment, or loyalty. They at least focus attention on what may be expected of a manager *as a manager.* And, when used in conjunction with appraisal of the performance of plans and goals, they can help remove much of the weakness in many management appraisal systems.

In brief, the program involves classifying the functions of the manager as done in this book and then dealing with each function by a series of questions. The questions are designed to reflect the most important fundamentals of managing in each area. Although the total list of key questions, the form used, the system of ratings, and the instructions for operating the program are too extensive to be treated in this book,[4] some sample "checkpoints" are presented below.

Sample Questions for Appraising Managers as Managers

In the area of *planning,* a manager's rating would be determined through questions such as the following. Does the manager:

- Set for the departmental unit both short-term and long-term goals in verifiable terms that are related in a positive way to those of superiors and of the company?

- Check plans periodically to see whether they are consistent with current expectations?

- In choosing from among alternatives, recognize and give primary attention to those factors which are limiting or critical to the solution of a problem?

In the area of *organizing,* questions such as the following are asked. Does the manager:

- Delegate authority to subordinates on the basis of results expected of them?

- Refrain from making decisions in that area once authority has been delegated to subordinates?

- Regularly teach subordinates, or otherwise make sure that they understand, the nature of line and staff relationships?

In the three other areas of managing — staffing, leading, and controlling — evaluators ask similar questions. In all, there are seventy-three checkpoints.

Semantics has always been a problem in management. Therefore, it is wise to use a standard book on management (such as this one) and refer to the pages that correspond to the questions.[5] This approach leads to a fair degree of managerial development.

Managers are rated on how well they perform the activities. The scale used is from 0 for "inadequate" to 5 for "superior." To give the numerical ratings more rigor, each rating is defined. For example, "superior" means "a standard of performance which could not be improved under any circumstances or conditions known to the rater."

To further reduce subjectivity and to increase the discrimination among performance levels, the program requires that (1) in the comprehensive annual appraisal, incident examples be given to support certain ratings, (2) the ratings be reviewed by the superior's superior, and (3) the raters be informed that their own evaluation will depend in part on how well they discriminate on the ratings of performance levels when evaluating their subordinates. Obviously, objectivity is enhanced by the number (seventy-three) and the specificity of the checkpoint questions.

Advantages of the New Program

Experience with this program in a multinational company showed certain advantages. By focusing on the essentials of management, this method of evaluation gives operational meaning to what management really is. Also, the use of a standard reference text for interpretation of concepts and terms removes many of the semantic and communication difficulties so commonly encountered. Such things as variable budgets, verifiable objectives, staff, functional authority, and delegation take on consistent meaning. Likewise, many management techniques become uniformly understood.

The system, furthermore, has proved to be a tool for management development; in many cases, it has brought to managers' attention certain basics that they may have long disregarded or not understood. In addition, it has been found useful in pinpointing areas in which weaknesses exist and to which development should be directed. Finally, as intended, the program acts as a supplement to, and a check on, appraisal of managers' effectiveness in setting and achieving goals. If a manager has an outstanding performance in goal accomplishment but is found to be a less-than-average manager, those in charge would look for the reason. Normally, one would expect a truly effective manager to be effective also in meeting goals.

Weaknesses of the New Program

There are, however, a number of weaknesses or shortcomings in the approach. It applies only to managerial aspects of a given position and not to such technical qualifications as marketing or engineering abilities that might also be important. These, however, can be weighed on the basis of goals selected and achieved. There is also the apparent complexity of the seventy-three checkpoints; rating on all of them does take time, but the time is well spent.

Perhaps the major shortcoming in appraising managers as managers is the subjectivity involved. As mentioned earlier, some subjectivity in rating each checkpoint was found to be unavoidable. However, the program still has a high degree of objectivity and is far more objective than appraisal of managers only on the broader areas of the managerial functions. At least the checkpoints are specific and pertain to the essentials of managing.

REWARDS AND STRESS OF MANAGING

Managers are different; they have different needs, desires, and motives. The essentials of motivation will be discussed in Chapter 15. The concern here is with some of the general rewards, as well as the stressful aspects, of managing.

Rewards of Managing

Since managerial candidates differ widely in age, economic position, and level of maturity, they want many things, but these usually include opportunity, power, and income. Most managerial candidates desire the opportunity for a progressive career that provides depth and breadth of managerial experience. Related to this is the challenge found in meaningful work. Most people, but perhaps managers in particular, want to feel that they have the power to make a significant contribution to the aims of an enterprise and even to society.

In addition, managers want to be, and should be, rewarded for their contributions, although the size of the financial rewards has been criticized. The

---

PERSPECTIVE:
FINANCIAL REWARDS OF CEOs

The thirty-sixth annual compensation survey by *Business Week* and Sibson & Company identified the twenty-five highest-paid executives.[6] In 1985 the total pay was $12,739,000 for Victor Posner of DWG, $11,426,000 for Lee A. Iacocca of Chrysler, and $8,431,000 for T. Boone Pickens, Jr., the chairman of Mesa Petroleum. Even the twenty-fifth-ranked executive, Peter T. Buchanan, president of First Boston, received a total pay of $2,533,000. By far the biggest "golden parachute" (severance pay) was given to Revlon's Michel C. Bergerac, who received a total package worth $35 million. A survey of CEOs in the *Fortune* 500 largest industrial and the 500 largest service companies showed the median compensation for those surveyed to be $543,400. This figure was considerably higher than in 1976, when it was $209,000.[7]

Perspective specifies the compensation of some of the highest-paid executives in 1985.

There is, however, some concern about whether the shareholders get their money's worth and whether the compensation is fair. The *Fortune* survey, mentioned in the Perspective, found that compensation of CEOs in the industrial companies increased by 25.3 percent when adjusted for inflation. But the return on the equity of shareholders declined from 13.3 percent in 1976 to 11.5 percent in 1986. At times, then, there is little correlation between executive pay and performance. In another survey, 76 percent of the public thought that top executives are not worth the compensation they receive.[8] One study found that their salaries and bonuses increased by 12.2 percent annually over a 10-year period ending in 1987.[9] During the same time, wages of hourly workers rose only 6.1 percent per year and profits only 0.75 percent.

One can also compare the compensation of top managers in other countries. Even with the weak dollar, CEOs in the United States earned about 40 percent more than those in Japan, more than twice as much as those in Great Britain, and about 3.5 times as much as top managers in Australia. Moreover, in U.S. firms, the compensation of CEOs, on average, was about 14 times that of college graduates entering their companies; in Japan, it was 10 times as much; and in Australia, 4 times as much.[10]

Peter F. Drucker, one of the most perceptive writers on management, suggests that if executive pay is not reformed Congress will do it.[11] In Japan, known for its high productivity, executives receive about 8 times the pay of blue-collar workers. In the United States, the multiplier is much higher. American workers, professionals, and managers are outraged by what they perceive as exorbitant pay for top executives. Unions, for example, were requested to make concessions, only to find out later that executives received high bonuses and stock options.[12]

More recently, efforts have been made to link pay to performance and to induce managers to make decisions that are in the long-term intersts of the enterprise.[13] At Ford, for example, more emphasis is given to stock grants that reward the achievement of 5-year objectives. These criteria include not only return on equity but also measures such as customer satisfaction, involvement of employees, and product quality. Moreover, performance is compared with that of competitors. For instance, even though quality may have improved at Ford, if more quality improvements have been made by a competitor, this will be held against Ford's managers — if their quality has not improved sufficently.

Stress in Managing

Stress is a very complex phenomenon. It is, therefore, no surprise that there is no commonly accepted definition. A widely used working definition is *an adaptive response, mediated by individual differences and/or psychological processes, that is, a consequence of any external (environmental) action, situation, or event that places excessive psychological and/or physical demands on a person.*[14]

Hans Selye, probably the leading authority on the concept of stress, described stress as "the rate of all wear and tear caused by life."[15] Alvin Toffler, the author of *Future Shock*, said "Dr. Hans Selye knows more about stress than any other scientist alive."[16]

There are many *physical sources* of stress, such as work overload, irregular work hours, loss of sleep, loud noises, bright light, and insufficient light. *Psychological sources* of stress may be due to a particular situation, such as a boring job, inability to socialize, lack of autonomy, resonsibility for results without sufficient authority, unrealistic objectives, role ambiguity or role conflict, and dual-career marriages. But what might be stressful to one person may be less so to another; people react differently to situations.

Stress can have various *effects* on the individual as well as on the organization. There are the physiological effects that may be linked to a variety of illnesses. Then there are psychological effects such as burnout or boredom. Various kinds of behavior, such as drug and alcohol abuse, inordinate food consumption, accidents, or withdrawal from the stressful situation (absenteeism, excessive labor turnover), may be a reaction to stress. Clearly, not only does the individual suffer, but the organization may also be affected by the turnover or impaired decision making of its managers and nonmanagers alike.

Individuals and organizations have attempted to deal with stress in various ways.[17] Individuals, for example, may try to reduce stress through better management of their time, healthful nutrition, exercises, career planning, change in jobs, promotion of psychological health, relaxation,[18] meditation, and prayer. Organizations may provide counseling or recreation facilities or may improve the job design by matching the person with the job.

Fitting the Needs of the Individual to the Demands of the Job

Managing, then, offers rewards but also involves stress. An individual aspiring to a managerial position should evaluate both the advantages and the disadvantages of managing before pursuing this career. A proper fit between individual needs and the demands of the task will benefit both the individual and the enterprise. Career management will help to achieve this fit.

FORMULATING THE CAREER STRATEGY[19]

The appraisal of performance should identify the strengths and weaknesses of an individual; this identification can be the starting point for a career plan. The personal strategy should be designed to utilize strengths and overcome weaknesses in order to take advantage of career opportunities. Although there are different approaches to career development, it is considered here as a process of developing a personal strategy that is conceptually similar to an organization strategy. This process is shown in Figure 12-2.

1 Preparation of a Personal Profile

One of the most difficult tasks is gaining insight into oneself, yet this is an essential first step in developing a career strategy. Managers should ask themselves: Am I an introvert or an extrovert? What are my attitudes toward time,

Figure 12-2

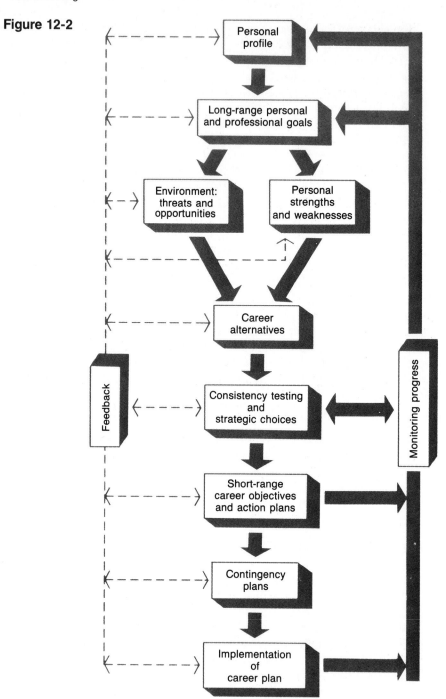

FORMULATION OF CAREER STRATEGY.

achievement, work, material things, and change? The answers to these and similar questions and a clarification of values will help in determining the direction of the professional career.

2   Development of Long-Range Personal and Professional Goals

No airplane would take off without a flight plan including a destination. Yet how clear are managers about the direction of their lives? People often resist career planning because it involves making decisions. By choosing one goal, a person gives up opportunities to pursue others; if an individual studies to become a lawyer, she or he usually cannot become a doctor at the same time. Managers also resist goal setting because uncertainties in the environment cause concern about making commitments. Furthermore, there is the fear of failing to achieve goals, because the nonachievement of objectives is a blow to one's ego.

But by understanding the factors that inhibit goal setting, one can take steps to increase commitment. First, when the setting of performance goals becomes a part of the appraisal process, identifying career goals is easier. Moreover, one does not set career goals all at once. Rather, goal setting is a continuing process that allows flexibility; professional goals can be revised in the light of changing circumstances. Another factor that reduces resistance to goal setting is the integration of long-term aims with the more immediate requirement for action. For example, the aim of becoming a doctor makes it easier to study boring subjects that are necessary for the medical degree.

How far in advance should one plan? The answer may be found in the commitment principle discussed in the planning section. It states that planning should cover a period of time necessary for the fulfillment of commitments involved in the decision made today. Therefore, the time frame for career planning will differ with the circumstances. For example, if a person wants to become a professor, it is necessary to plan for university studies of 7 to 9 years. On the other hand, if the career goal is to become a taxi driver, the time span is much shorter. At any rate, the long-term aim has to be translated into short-term objectives. Before this is done, however, it is necessary to make a careful assessment of the external environment, including its threats and opportunities.

3   Analysis of the Environment: Threats and Opportunities

In the analysis of the environment inside and outside the organization, many diverse factors need to be taken into account. They include economic, social, political, technological, and demographic factors; they also include the labor market, competition, and other factors relevant to a particular situation. For example, joining an expanding company usually provides more career opportunities than working for a mature company that is not expected to grow. Similarly, working for a mobile manager means an increased probability that the position of the superior will become vacant; or one might "ride the coattails" of a competent mobile superior by following him or her through a series of promotions up the organizational hierarchy. At any rate, successful career planning requires a systematic scanning of the environment for opportunities and threats.

One has to be concerned not only about the present but also about the future environment. This requires forecasting. Since there are a great many factors that need to be analyzed, planning one's career necessitates being selective and concentrating on those factors critical to personal success.

4   Analysis of Personal Strengths and Weaknesses

For successful career planning, the environmental opportunities and threats must be matched with the strengths and weaknesses of individuals. Capabilities may be categorized as technical, human, conceptual, or design. As Figure 1-2 illustrated, the relative importance of these skills differs for the various positions in the organizational hierarchy, with technical skills being very important on the supervisory level, conceptual skills being crucial for top managers, and human skills being important at all levels.

5   Development of Strategic Career Alternatives

In developing a career strategy, one usually has several alternatives. The most successful strategy would be to build on one's strengths to take advantages of opportunities. For example, if a person has an excellent knowledge of computers and many companies are looking for computer programmers, he or she should find many opportunities for a satisfying career. On the other hand, if there is a demand for programmers, and if an individual is interested in programming but lacks the necessary skills, the proper approach would be a developmental strategy to overcome the weakness and develop the skills in order to take advantage of the opportunities.

It may also be important to recognize the threats in the environment and to develop a strategy to cope with them. A person with excellent managerial and technical skills may work in a declining company or industry. The appropriate strategy might be to find employment in an expanding firm or in a growing industry.

6   Consistency Testing and Strategic Choices

In developing a personal strategy, one must realize that the rational choice based on strengths and opportunities is not always the most fulfilling alternative. Although one may have certain skills demanded in the job market, a career in that field may not be congruent with personal values or interests. For example, a person may prefer dealing with people to programming computers. Some may find great satisfaction in specialization, while others prefer to broaden their knowledge and skills.

Strategic choices require trade-offs. Some alternatives involve high risks, others low risks. Some choices demand action now; other choices can wait. Careers that were glamorous in the past may have an uncertain future.

Rational and systematic analysis is just one step in the career-planning process, for a choice also involves personal preferences, personal ambitions, and personal values.

7   Development of Short-Range Career Objectives and Action Plans

So far, concern has centered on career direction. But the strategy has to be supported by short-term objectives and action plans, which can be a part of the performance appraisal process. Thus, if the aim is to achieve a certain management position that requires a master of business degree, the short-term objective may be to complete a number of courses. Here is an example of a short-term verifiable objective: to complete the course Fundamentals of Management by May 30 with a grade of A. This objective is measurable, as it states the task to be done, the deadline, and the quality of performance (the grade).

Objectives often must be supported by action plans. Continuing with the example, the completion of the management course may require a schedule for attending classes, doing the homework, and obtaining the support of the spouse, who may suffer because attending classes takes time that might otherwise be spent with the family. It is obvious that the long-term strategic career plan needs to be supported by short-term objectives and action plans.

8   Development of Contingency Plans

Career plans are developed in an environment of uncertainty, and the future cannot be predicted with great accuracy. Therefore, contingency plans based on alternative assumptions should be prepared. While one may enjoy working for a small, fast-growing venture company, it may be wise to prepare an alternative career plan based on the assumption that the venture may not succeed.

9   Implementation of the Career Plan

Career planning may start during the performance appraisal. At that time, the person's growth and development should be discussed. Career goals and personal ambitions can be considered in selecting and promoting and in designing training and development programs.

10   Monitoring Progress

Monitoring is the process of evaluating progress toward career goals and making necessary corrections in the aims or plans. An opportune time for assessing career programs is during the performance appraisal. This is the time not only to review performance against objectives in the operating areas but also to review the achievement of milestones in the career plan. In addition, progress should be monitored at other times, such as at the completion of an important task or project.

Dual-Career Couples

An effective career strategy requires that consideration be given to the career of the spouse. Dual-career couples, with both partners working, sometimes have to make very stressful choices. For example, if both partners have successful careers, the opportunity for a promotion that requires relocation is a particularly painful decision. Merrill Lynch Relocation Management, Inc., conducted a survey of 600 major companies and found that 60 percent of relocations involved dual-career couples. It has been estimated that by 1990, the figure will be 75 percent.[20]

Some companies are accommodating the special needs of dual-career couples by having a flexible approach to transfers that involve relocation, considering the needs of both partners in career planning, helping to find employment for the spouse either within the company or outside, and providing maternity leave and day-care services for children. With the large number of married women in the work force, an increasing number of companies have recognized the stressful situation of dual-career couples and implemented more flexible policies, career planning, personnel selection, placement, and promotion.

SUMMARY

Appraisal is essential for effective managing. The Conference Board study showed differences between the stated objectives of appraisals and the way they were actually used. These differences may have caused dissatisfaction. In the Work Planning and Review approach to appraisal, General Electric emphasized frequent performance discussions. Moreover, performance ratings and salary actions were discussed at separate meetings.

Appraisal should measure performance in achieving goals and plans and performance as a manager, that is, how well a person carries out key managerial activities. Traditional appraisal methods that attempt to measure personality traits have serious limitations.

An effective method is to appraise managers against verifiable objectives, as exemplified by the discussion of management by objectives (MBO) in Chapter 4. This approach is operational, related to the manager's job, and relatively objective. Still, a person may perform well (or badly) because of luck of factors beyond his or her control. Therefore, the management-by-objectives approach should be supplemented by appraisal of managers as managers, that is, appraisal of how well they perform their key managerial activities.

There are three kinds of reviews: (1) the formal comprehensive appraisal, (2) progress or periodic reviews, and (3) continuous monitoring. In a suggested appraisal program, key managerial activities are presented as checklist questions and grouped under the categories of planning, organizing, staffing, leading, and controlling.

Since managers differ greatly, they look for different rewards, such as opportunity and income. But the job of a manager is also stressful, and this can affect the individual as well as the organization. Therefore, various ways of coping with stress have evolved.

Career planning can be effectively integrated with performance appraisal. Although the specific steps in developing a career strategy may vary, the process is similar to developing an organization strategy. Since dual-career couples are quite common, an effective career strategy must include consideration of the spouse's career.

KEY IDEAS AND CONCEPTS FOR REVIEW

Purposes and uses of appraisal
Work Planning and Review at General Electric
Weaknesses of trait appraisal
Steps in the appraisal process (against verifiable objectives)

Three kinds of reviews
Strengths and weaknesses of appraisal against verifiable objectives
Suggested performance appraisal of managers
Ten steps in formulating a career strategy

FOR DISCUSSION

1. Do you think managers should be appraised regularly? If so, how?

2. What problems may arise from the fact that different managers on the same level appraise differently, some generally rating higher than others?

3. Many firms evaluate managers on such personality factors as aggressiveness, cooperation, leadership, and attitude. Do you think this kind of rating makes sense?

4. An argument has been made in this book for appraising managers on their ability to manage. Should anything more be expected of them?

5. How do you feel about an appraisal system based upon results expected and realized? Would you prefer to be appraised on this basis? If not, why not?

6. What is your assessment of the degree of objectivity or subjectivity of the appraisal approaches suggested in this chapter? Can you suggest any further means of making appraisals more objective?

7. On what basis should your performance in college be appraised?

8. What would you say to a student who tells you that he studied at least 4 hours every day in preparation for the midterm exam and still got only a "C"?

9. Describe the most rewarding and most stressful aspects of your job or your college experience.

10. What is your career goal? Have you developed a plan to achieve your goal? If not, why not?

EXERCISES/ACTION STEPS

1. Interview two managers. Ask them what criteria are used for their performance appraisal. Are the criteria verifiable? Do these managers think that the performance evaluation measures their performance in a fair manner?

2. Develop a career plan for yourself. Identify a personal profile for yourself and state your long-range personal and professional goals. What are your strengths and weaknesses? Follow the steps explained in this chapter to develop a comprehensive strategic career plan for yourself.

CASE: FORESITE INCORPORATED

Carl Fisher was the president of Foresite, Inc., a multidivisional company in the high-technology field. The large company was well known for its technical innovations and the high caliber of its scientists and engineers. But competition was on the increase, and the president realized that the success of the firm depended on effective management. It was felt that planning was one of the very weak areas where improvement was needed. Therefore, the president invited John Weigand, a management consultant, to "look at his company" and to explore alternative ways of improving the organization. At the first meeting considerable trust developed between Fisher and Weigand, and in the course of the discussion it was agreed that any major organization intervention should be based on facts (that is, on data collected from the organization itself). Weigand began by interviewing three major department heads — Ms. Albani, Mr. Johnson, and Mr. Baker — to get an overview of the firm and the quality of its managers. The president agreed, tentatively, to a long-range systematic organizational development effort. However, the immediate problem was making some selections for key managerial positions.

Managers have to be well versed in all managerial functions, but at this point it was felt that aspects of planning were particularly important. With the guidance of the consultant, Carl Fisher assessed the planning activities of three managers considered for the positions of (1) head of the corporate planning group and (2) division manager. He found useful the appraisal approach developed by Harold Koontz and described in the text.

The instructions for rating the candidates for the positions were as follows: In rating each question, give the following marks for each (for each level of rating use only one of two numbers, such as 4.0 or 4.5 for *Excellent;* use no other decimals). The possible marks were:

X = Not applicable to position

N = Do not know accurately enough for rating

5.0 = *Superior:* A standard of performance which could not be improved upon under any circumstances or conditions known to the rater

4.0 or 4.5 = *Excellent:* A standard of performance which leaves little or any consequence to be desired

3.0 or 3.5 = *Good:* A standard of performance above the average and meeting all normal requirements of the position

2.0 or 2.5 = *Average:* A standard of performance regarded as average for the position involved and the people available

1.0 or 1.5 = *Fair:* A standard of performance which is below the normal requirements of the position, but one that may be regarded as marginally or temporarily acceptable

0.0 = *Inadequate:* A standard of performance regarded as unacceptable for the position involved

The results of the evaluations are shown in the table below.

To gain greater confidence in his judgment, Carl Fisher asked two of his vice-presidents to rate the three candidates. Their evaluations were consistent with the president's appraisal.

Assume that all three candidates have similar technical and managerial skills besides those shown in the table and that their performance results are similar.

1. Whom would you select as a head of the corporate planning staff? Why?

2. Whom would you choose as manager of the division?

3. What other factors would you consider in making the selection?

4. What training and development would you recommend for each of the managers?

Performance as a Manager

Planning	Florence Albani	Ted Johnson	George Baker
1. Does the manager set for the departmental unit both short-term and long-term goals in verifiable terms (either qualitative or quantitative) that are related in a positive way to those of the superior and the company?	N	3.5	4.5
2. To what extent does the manager make sure that the goals of the department are understood by those who report to him or her?	3.0	3.0	4.0
3. How well does the manager assist those who report to him or her in establishing verifiable and consistent goals for their operations?	3.5	3.0	4.5
4. To what extent does the manager utilize consistent and approved planning premises in planning and see that subordinates do likewise?	4.5	3.5	4.0
5. Does the manager understand the role of company policies in decision making and ensure that subordinates do likewise?	4.5	4.0	4.0
6. Does the manager attempt to solve problems of subordinates by policy guidance, coaching, and encouragement of innovation, rather than by rules and procedures?	4.0	3.0	4.5
7. Does the manager help subordinates get the information they need to assist them in their planning?	4.5	3.5	4.0
8. To what extent does the manager seek out applicable alternatives before making a decision?	4.0	4.0	3.5
9. In choosing from among alternatives, does the manager recognize and give primary attention to those factors which are limiting, or critical, to the solution of a problem?	4.0	N	3.5
10. In making decisions, how well does the manager bear in mind the size and length of commitment involved in each decision?	4.5	4.0	3.5
11. Does the manager check plans periodically to see if they are still consistent with current expectations?	3.0	4.5	4.0
12. To what extent does the manager consider the need for, as well as the cost of, flexibility in arriving at a planning decision?	4.0	4.5	4.5

Performance as a Manager *(Continued)*

Planning	Florence Albani	Ted Johnson	George Baker
13. In developing and implementing plans, does the manager regularly consider long-range implications of the decisions along with the short-range results expected?	4.0	4.5	4.0
14. When the manager submits problems to the superior, or when a superior seeks help in solving problems, does he or she submit considered analyses of alternatives (with advantages and disadvantages) and recommended suggestions for solution?	4.0	4.0	3.5
Total number of questions in which ratings are made:	13	13	14
Total score on questions given ratings:	51.5	49.0	56
Average of ratings in Planning:	4.0	3.8	4.0

REFERENCES

1. For research on the possible rater's bias, see Eileen A. Hogan, "Effects of Prior Expectations on Performance Ratings: A Longitudinal Study," *Academy of Management Journal* (June 1987), pp. 354–368.

2. Robert I. Lazer and Walter S. Wikstrom, *Appraising Managerial Performance: Current Practices and Future Directions* (New York: The Conference Board, 1977).

3. Herbert H. Meyer, Emanuel Kay, and John R. P. French, Jr., "Split Roles in Performance Appraisal," *Harvard Business Review* (January–February 1965), pp. 123–129.

4. All the key questions are given in Harold Koontz, *Appraising Managers as Managers* (New York: McGraw-Hill Book Company, 1971), chaps. 5 and 6 and apps. 2–5.

5. This has been done, for example, in the text booklet accompanying the cassette recording program *Measuring Managers: A Double-Barreled Approach,* by Harold Koontz and Heinz Weihrich (New York: American Management Association, 1981).

6. John A. Byrne, "Executive Pay: How the Boss Did in '85," *Business Week* (May 5, 1986), pp. 48–58.

7. Maggie McComas, "Atop the Fortune 500: A Survey of the C.E.O.s," *Fortune* (Apr. 28, 1986), pp. 26–31.

8. "Top Executive Pay Peeves the Public," *Business Week* (June 25, 1984), p. 15; see also "Chrysler Officials' Raises Are Called Lavish by UAW," *The Wall Street Journal* (Apr. 8, 1986); Doron P. Levin, "Chrysler's Iacocca Got a 35% Raise While '85 Net Fell," *The Wall Street Journal* (Apr. 7, 1986).

9. Amanda Bennett, "Corporate Chief's Pay Far Outpaces Inflation and the Gains of Staffs," *The Wall Street Journal* (Mar. 28, 1988).

10. Bennett, "Corporate Chief's Pay" (1988).

11. Peter F. Drucker, "Reform Executive Pay or Congress Will," *The Wall Street Journal* (Apr. 24, 1984).

12. The process of determining executive pay has been described by Monci Jo Williams, "Why Chief Executives' Pay Keeps Rising," *Fortune* (Apr. 1, 1985), pp. 66–76.

13. Amanda Bennett, "More Managers Find Salary, Bonus Are Tied Directly to Performance," *The Wall Street Journal* (Feb. 28, 1986); Byrne, "Executive Pay" (1986); "Rewarding Executives for Taking the Long View," *Business Week* (Apr. 2, 1984), pp. 99–100, 108.

14. James L. Gibson, John M. Ivancevich, and James H. Donnelly, Jr., *Organizations,* 5th ed. (Plano, Texas: Business Publications, 1985), p. 220.

15. Hans Selye, *The Stress of Life,* rev. ed. (New York: McGraw-Hill Book Company, 1976), p. viii.

16. Hans Selye, *The Stress without Distress* (New York: New American Library, 1975), book cover.

17. Emily T. Smith, Jody Brott, Alice Cuneo, and Jo Ellen Davis, "Stress: The Test Americans Are Failing," *Business Week* (Apr. 18, 1988), pp. 74–76.

18. See, for example, Herbert Benson, *The Relaxation Response* (New York: Avon Books, 1975).

19. Adapted from Heinz Weihrich, *Management Excellence — Productivity through MBO* (New York: McGraw-Hill Book Company, 1985).

20. Irene Pave, "Move Me, Move My Spouse: Relocating the Corporate Couple," *Business Week* (Dec. 16, 1985), pp. 57–60.

CHAPTER 13

Manager and Organization Development

CHAPTER OBJECTIVES

After reading this chapter, you should understand:

1. Managerial development, managerial training, and organization development
2. The manager development process and training
3. How to manage change and conflicts
4. The nature and processes of organization development

This chapter deals with change. First, the focus is on the change of individuals, specifically, manager development and training. But people do not operate in isolation. Consequently, in the second part of this chapter the emphasis shifts to groups of individuals and organizations.

Excellent executives look to the future and prepare for it. One important way to do this is to develop and train managers so that they are able to cope with new demands, new problems, and new challenges. Indeed, executives have a responsibility to provide training and development opportunities for their employees so that the employees can reach their full potential.

The costs of training represent major investments, so executives are justifiably concerned about the effectiveness of training. Companies spend billions of dollars every year to educate their work forces, and most of this money is

PERSPECTIVE:
MAKING MANAGEMENT EDUCATION RELEVANT

In order to make business courses more meaningful, many schools invite guest speakers to share their experiences.[1] This creates close ties between business schools and enterprises. Executives become aware of the quality of the school's curriculum and students may find it advantageous to know about the companies when they are looking for a job. Moreover, executives often serve on advisory boards, which makes the schools aware of the needs of the business community. This does not mean, however, that market-driven schools should adopt any management fad.[2] Instead, management education must be broad enough to encompass the teaching of all key managerial activities in planning, organizing, staffing, leading, and controlling.

spent on in-house training and development. It is important that management education be effective and efficient, and therefore this chapter emphasizes the need for a systematic approach to manager and organization development.

The term **manager development** refers to the progress a person makes in learning how to manage. **Managerial training,** on the other hand, pertains to the programs that facilitate the learning process. However, it is quite common to refer to management or manager development when one is talking about programs or approaches. There is even less agreement on the definition of organization development (OD). In this book, **organization development** is a systematic, integrated, and planned approach to improving the effectiveness of groups of people and of the whole organization or a major organizational unit. Organization development uses various techniques for identifying and solving problems.

Essentially, then, OD focuses on the total organization (or a major segment of it), while manager development concentrates on individuals. These approaches support each other and should be integrated to improve the effectiveness of both the managers and the enterprise.

MANAGER DEVELOPMENT PROCESS AND TRAINING

Before specific training and development programs are chosen, three kinds of needs must be considered. The needs of the organization include such items as the objectives of the enterprise, the availability of managers, and turnover rates. Needs related to the operations and the job itself can be determined from job descriptions and performance standards. Data about individual training needs can be gathered from performance appraisals, interviews with the jobholder, tests, surveys, and career plans for individuals. Let us look more closely at the steps in the manager development process, focusing first on the present job, then on the next job in the career ladder, and finally on the long-term future needs of the organization. The steps in manager development are depicted in Figure 13-1.

Figure 13-1

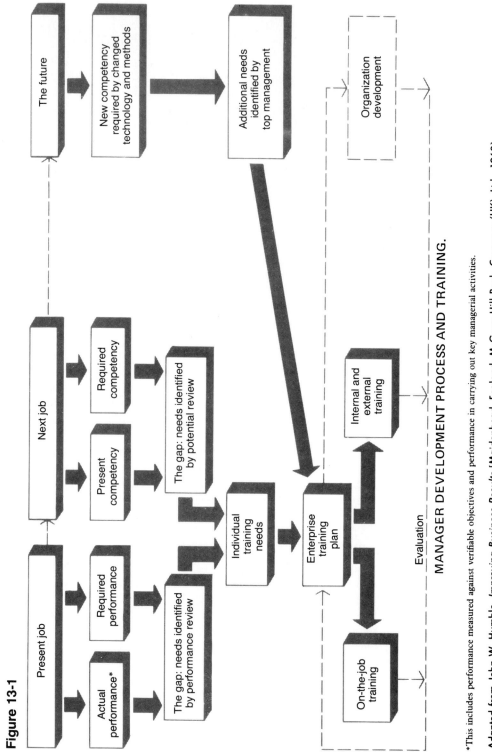

MANAGER DEVELOPMENT PROCESS AND TRAINING.

*This includes performance measured against verifiable objectives and performance in carrying out key managerial activities.

Adapted from John W. Humble, *Improving Business Results* [Maidenhead, England: McGraw-Hill Book Company (UK), Ltd., 1968].

Present Job

Manager development and training must be based on a needs analysis derived from a comparison of actual performance and behavior with required performance and behavior. Such an analysis is shown in Figure 13-2. A district sales manager has decided that the selling of 1000 units is a reasonable expectation, but the actual sales are only 800, 200 units short of the sales target. Analysis of the deviation from the standard might indicate that the manager lacks the knowledge and skills for making a forecast and that conflicts among subordinate managers hinder effective teamwork. On the basis of this analysis, training needs and methods for overcoming the deficiencies are identified. Consequently, the district sales manager enrolls in courses in forecasting and conflict resolution. Furthermore, organization development efforts are undertaken to facilitate cooperation among organization units.

Next Job

As shown in Figure 13-1, a similar process is applied in the identification of the training needs for the next job. Specifically, present competency is compared with the competency demanded by the next job. For instance, a person who has worked mainly in production may be under consideration for a job as a project manager. This position requires training in functional areas such as engineering, marketing, and even finance. This systematic preparation for a new assignment certainly is a more professional approach than simply thrusting a person into a new work situation without training.

Future Needs

Progressive organizations go one step further in their training and development approach; they prepare for the more distant future. This requires that they forecast what new competencies will be demanded by changing technol-

Figure 13-2

TRAINING NEEDS ANALYSIS.

ogy and methods. For example, energy shortages may again occur, and this requires that managers be trained not only in the technical aspects of energy conservation but also in energy-related long-range planning and creative problem solving. These new demands — created by the external environment — have to be integrated into enterprise training plans which focus on the present and the future. These plans are contingent not only on the training needs but also on the various approaches to manager development that are available.

APPROACHES TO MANAGER DEVELOPMENT: ON-THE-JOB TRAINING

Many opportunities for development can be found on the job. Trainees can learn as they contribute to the aims of the enterprise. However, because this approach requires competent higher-level managers who can teach and coach trainees, there are limitations to on-the-job training.

Planned Progression

Planned progression is a technique that gives managers a clear idea of their path of development. Managers know where they stand and where they are going. For example, a lower-level manager may have available an outline of the path from superintendent to works manager and eventually to production manager. The manager then knows the requirements for advancement and the means of achieving it. Unfortunately, there may be an overemphasis on the next job instead of on good performance of present tasks. Planned progression may be perceived by trainees as a smooth path to the top, but it really is a step-by-step approach which requires that tasks be done well at each level.

Job Rotation

The purpose of job rotation is to broaden the knowledge of managers or potential managers. Trainees learn about the different enterprise functions by rotating into different positions. They may rotate through (1) nonsupervisory work, (2) observation assignments (observing what managers do, rather than managing themselves), (3) various managerial training positions, and (4) middle-level "assistant" positions, and there is even (5) unspecified rotation to various managerial positions in different departments such as production, sales, and finance.

The idea of job rotation is good, but there are difficulties. As the term indicates, in some job rotation programs participants do not actually have managerial authority. Instead, they observe or assist line managers, but they do not have the responsibility they would have if they were actually managing. Even in rotations to managerial positions, the participants in the training program may not remain long enough in the position to prove their future effectiveness as managers. Furthermore, when the rotation program is completed, there may be no suitable positions available for the newly trained managers. Despite these drawbacks, if the inherent difficulties are understood by both managers and trainees, job rotation has positive aspects and should benefit trainees.

Creation of "Assistant-to" Positions

"Assistant-to" positions are frequently created to broaden the viewpoints of trainees by allowing them to work closely with experienced managers who can give special attention to the developmental needs of trainees. Managers can, among other things, give selected assignments to test the judgment of trainees. As in job rotation, this approach can be very effective when superiors are also qualified teachers who can guide and develop trainees until they are ready to assume full responsibilities as managers.

Temporary Promotions

Individuals are frequently appointed as "acting" managers when, for example, the permanent manager is on vacation, is ill, or is making an extended business trip or even when a position is vacant. Thus, temporary promotions are a developmental device as well as a convenience to the enterprise.

When the acting manager makes decisions and assumes full responsibility, the experience can be valuable. On the other hand, if such a manager is merely a figurehead, makes no decisions, and really does not manage, the developmental benefit may be minimal.

Committees and Junior Boards

Committees and "junior boards," also known as "multiple management," are sometimes used as developmental techniques. These give trainees the opportunity to interact with experienced managers. Furthermore, trainees, usually from the middle, but sometimes from the lower level, become acquainted with a variety of issues that concern the whole organization. They learn about the relationships among different departments and the problems created by the interaction of these organizational units. Trainees may be given the opportunity to submit reports and proposals to the committee or the board and to demonstrate their analytical and conceptual abilities. On the other hand, trainees may be treated in a paternalistic way by senior executives; although trainees are appointed to committees or junior boards, they may not be given opportunities to participate, an omission that might frustrate and discourage them. The program would then be detrimental to their development.

Coaching

On-the-job training is a never-ending process. A good example of on-the-job-training is athletic coaching. To be effective, coaching, which is the responsibility of every line manager, must be done in a climate of confidence and trust between superior and trainees. Patience and wisdom are required of superiors, who must be able to delegate authority and give recognition and praise for jobs well done. Effective coaches will develop the strengths and potentials of subordinates and help them overcome their weaknesses. Coaching requires time, but, if done well, it will save time and money and will prevent costly mistakes by subordinates; thus, in the long run, it will benefit all — the superior, the subordinates, and the enterprise.

APPROACHES TO MANAGER DEVELOPMENT: INTERNAL AND EXTERNAL TRAINING

Besides on-the-job training, there are many other approaches to manager development. These programs may be conducted within the company or they may be offered externally by educational institutions and management associations, as indicated in Figure 13-1.

Sensitivity Training, T-Groups, and Encounter Groups

Sensitivity training, also called *T-group* ("T" stands for training), *encounter group,* or *leadership training,* is a controversial approach to manager development. Although popular in the 1960s and early 1970s, T-groups have lost favor as a managerial training technique in many companies. Still, certain aspects of sensitivity training may be used in team-building efforts. The objectives of sensitivity training generally include (1) better insight into one's own behavior and the way one "appears" to others, (2) better understanding of group processes, and (3) development of skills in diagnosing and intervening in group processes.

Although the sensitivity-training process has many variations, one general characteristic is that people interact and then receive feedback on their behavior from the trainer and other group members, who express their opinions freely and openly. The feedback may be candid and direct: "Jim, I do not get a good feeling when you approach the topic the way you just did. Could we talk about it?"

Jim may accept this comment and resolve to change his behavior. But he may also feel hurt and withdraw from the group. The T-group process may lead to personal anxieties and frustrations, but, if properly administered, it can result in collaborative and supportive behavior.

The benefits of sensitivity training must be balanced against the criticisms of it.[3] For example, some people may be psychologically harmed because they simply cannot cope with the concurrent invasions of privacy. Owing to the group pressure and group dynamics, participants may reveal more about themselves than they actually intended to. There also is concern that some trainers may not be qualified to conduct sessions that become highly emotional.

Finally, the relevancy of the outcomes of sensitivity training to the work situation has been questioned.

Despite the concerns of researchers and observers, certain enterprises do use T-groups in their development efforts. The following guidelines can help to reduce potential harm and increase effectiveness:

1. Participation in T-groups should be voluntary.

2. Participants should be screened, and those who could be harmed, for example, highly defensive people, should be excluded from this experience.

3. Trainers should be carefully evaluated and their competence clearly established.

4. Potential participants should be informed about the goals and process before they commit themselves to sensitivity training.

5. Before using sensitivity training, organizations should clearly identify development and training needs and objectives. Given these needs and objectives, other methods should also be considered.

Conference Programs

Conference programs may be used in internal or external training. During conference programs, managers or potential managers are exposed to the ideas of speakers who are experts in their field. Within the company, people

---

PERSPECTIVE:
THE VARIETY OF CONFERENCE PROGRAMS

There is a great variety of conference programs available. The American Management Association offers programs such as these:

- **Time management.** To help managers make better use of their time and the time of their subordinates

- **Managing stress.** To help people in stressful environments, such as those with rapidly changing technologies

- **Interpersonal skills.** To be more effective in dealing with people

- **Computer graphics.** To communicate information effectively through the application of graphics

Or consider the sessions offered by the Association for Management Excellence (AME), with topics such as these:

- Increasing productivity through people

- Designing a simple, lean organization

- Developing your entrepreneurial skills

may be instructed in the history of the firm and its purposes, policies, and relationships with customers, consumers, and other groups. External conferences may vary greatly, ranging from programs on specific managerial techniques to programs on broad topics, such as the relationship between business and society.

These programs can be valuable if they satisfy a training need and are thoughtfully planned. A careful selection of topics and speakers will increase the effectiveness of this training device. Furthermore, conferences can be made more successful by including discussions; two-way communication allows participants to ask for clarification of specific topics that are particularly relevant to them.

University Management Programs

Besides offering undergraduate and graduate degrees in business administration, many universities now conduct courses, workshops, conferences, institutes, and formal programs for training managers. These offerings may include evening courses, short seminars, live-in programs, a full graduate curriculum, or even programs custom-designed for the needs of individual companies. Some executive development centers even provide career development assistance with programs designed to fit typical training and development needs of first-line supervisors, middle managers, and top executives.

These university programs expose managers to theories, principles, and new developments in management. In addition, there is usually a valuable interchange of experience among managers who, in similar positions, face similar challenges.

PERSPECTIVE:
UNIVERSITY EXECUTIVE PROGRAMS

Many major business schools offer a variety of management development programs. The 1987 Stanford Executive Program, which lasts for 8 weeks, includes topics such as these:

- The functional business areas of accounting, finance, and marketing

- The managerial process and organizational behavior

- Modern methods for quantitative and qualitative decision making

- Assessment of personal values and goals

Besides offering programs for top executives, the Harvard Business School also has an intensive 12-week program for functional managers. The MIT Sloan School of Management, located just a short distance from Harvard, offers a 9-week program for senior executives and a 12-month program for middle and upper managers that leads to a master's degree in management.

Readings

Another approach to development is planned reading of relevant and current management literature. This is essentially self-development. A manager may be aided by the training department, which often develops a reading list of valuable books. This learning experience can be enhanced through discussion of articles and books with other managers and the superior.

Business Simulation, Experiential Exercises, and Expert Systems

Business games and experiential exercise have been used for some time, but the introduction of microcomputers has made these approaches to training and development even more popular. The computer, however, is only one of several tools; many of the exercises do not require any hardware at all.

The great variety of business simulations is best illustrated by the topics discussed at meetings of the Association for Business Simulation and Experiential Learning (ABSEL).* The approaches range from behavioral exercises dealing, for example, with attitudes and values to simulations in courses such as marketing, accounting, decision support systems, and business policy and strategic management.

Recently, **expert systems** have received a great deal of attention. They are a subset of artificial intelligence (AI), which involves the use of computers to duplicate the functioning of the brain.[4] AI was initially used for problem solving in games such as checkers and chess. Later it was applied in medicine. Researchers at Stanford developed a knowledge-based system to serve as an "intelligent consultant" to help in the diagnosis and treatment of specific diseases. Similar systems are now being developed to assist managers in making decisions. For example, expert systems are used for checking sales orders, for oil drilling, for monitoring steam turbines at Westinghouse, for credit authorization at American Express, for tax accounting decisions at Coopers & Lybrand, for pricing systems bids at IBM, and for capital investments at Texas Instruments.[5]

Expert systems are an exciting new frontier for training and development, but a great deal of research will have to be done to validate the systems, especially those for unstructured decisions such as in strategic management.

Special Training Programs

Management development must take an open-system approach that responds to the needs and demands of the external environment. Recently, government and industry have become aware of the need for training programs specifically designed for members of minority groups and for individuals who are physically handicapped. Many firms have made special efforts to train these people so that they may utilize their full potential while contributing to the aims of the enterprise.

*Such as the fifteenth annual meeting held in March 1988 in San Diego.

Evaluation and Transfer

Determining the effectiveness of training programs is difficult. It requires measurements against standards and a systematic identification of training needs and objectives.

In general, developmental objectives include (1) an increase in knowledge, (2) development of attitudes conducive to good managing, (3) acquisition of skills, (4) improvement of management performance, and (5) achievement of enterprise objectives.

If training is to be effective, it is extremely important that the criteria used in the classroom situation resemble as closely as possible the criteria relevant in the working environment. One of the authors observed a T-group which had as its goals openness and frank feedback on each person's conduct in the group. The behavioral change of one of the participants would have had to be rated "excellent" when measured against the T-group criteria. However, when this person attempted to transfer his new values and behavior to the job, he met resistance and outright hostility. Arguments occurred, and as a result, this person had to leave the company. Although the person changed, his boss did not; nor did his coworkers or the total work environment. This illustration shows that manager development requires a situational approach in which training objectives, techniques, and methods should be sufficiently congruent with the values, norms, and characteristics of the environment.

MANAGING CHANGE

The forces for change may come from the environment external to the firm, from within the organization, or from the individuals themselves.

Changes That Affect Manager and Organization Development

Several trends, some of them already occurring, will have implications for developing human resources. Here are some illustrations:[6]

1. The increasing use of computers, especially microcomputers, requires that teachers as well as students become computer-literate.

2. Education extends into the adult life. Lifelong learning becomes a necessity, and educational institutions and enterprises must recognize the special educational needs of adults.

3. The proportion of knowledge workers will increase and the need for skill workers will decrease, which may require more training in knowledge, conceptual, and design skills.

4. The shift from manufacturing to service industries requires retraining in preparation for new positions.

5. The choice of educational opportunities will increase. For example, many companies already are conducting their own training programs.[7]

6. There may be greater cooperation and interdependence between the private and the public sectors — at least in some countries, such as Canada.

7. Internationalization will continue, and managers in different countries must learn to communicate and to adapt to each other. Companies need to train with a global perspective.

There are various ways to respond to these forces. One approach is simply to react to a crisis. Unfortunately, this is usually not the most effective response. Another approach is to deliberately plan the change. This may require new objectives or policies, organizational rearrangements, or a change in leadership style and organization culture.

Techniques for Initiating Change

Organizations may be in a state of equilibrium, with forces pushing for change on one hand and forces resisting change by attempting to maintain the status quo on the other. Kurt Lewin expressed this phenomenon in his **field force theory,** which suggests that an equilibrium is maintained by *driving* forces and *restraining* forces, as shown in Figure 13-3.[8] In initiating change, the tendency is to increase the driving forces. This may indeed produce some movement, but it usually also increases resistance by strengthening the restraining forces. Another approach, and one that is usually more effective, is to reduce or eliminate the restraining forces and then move to a new level of equilibrium. In organizations, therefore, a change in policy is less resisted when those affected by it participate in the change.

The change process involves three steps:[9] (1) unfreezing, (2) moving or changing, and (3) refreezing. The first stage, unfreezing, creates motivation for change. If people feel uncomfortable with the present situation, they may see the need for change. However, in some cases an ethical question may arise regarding the legitimacy of deliberately creating discomfort that may initiate change.

The second stage is the change itself. This change may occur through assimilation of new information, exposure to new concepts, or development of a different perspective.

The third stage, refreezing, stabilizes the change. Change, to be effective, has to be congruent with a person's self-concept and values. If the change is incongruent with the attitudes and behaviors of others in the organization, chances are that the person will revert back to the old behavior. Thus, reinforcement of the new behavior is essential.

Figure 13-3

MOVING AN ORGANIZATIONAL EQUILIBRIUM.

Resistance to Change

There are many reasons why people resist change. Here are some examples:

1. What is not known causes fear and induces resistance. An organizational restructuring can leave a person uncertain about its effect on his or her job. People want to feel secure and have some control over the change.

2. Not knowing the reason for the change also causes resistance. In fact, it is often unclear to those affected why the change is necessary at all.

3. Change may also result in reduction of benefits or a loss of power.

Reduction of resistance can be achieved in many ways. Involvement of organizational members in planning the change can reduce uncertainty. Communication about proposed changes also helps clarify reasons or effects of the changes. Some approaches focus on the people involved in the change; others involve changes in organization structure or technology. The sociotechnical systems approach (see Chapter 1) suggests that effective organization requires consideration of both social and technical dimensions in an enterprise. There are many other approaches to improving organizational effectiveness; some are discussed later in this chapter.

ORGANIZATIONAL CONFLICT

Conflict is a part of organizational life and may occur within the individual, between individuals, between the individual and the group, and between groups. While conflict is generally perceived as dysfunctional, it can also be beneficial because it may cause an issue to be presented in different perspectives. One top executive of a major company maintained that if there was no conflict on an issue, it could not have been sufficiently analyzed, and the final decision on the issue was usually postponed until all aspects were critically evaluated.

Sources of Conflict

There are many potential sources of conflict. Today's organizations are characterized by complex relationships and a high degree of task interdependence that can cause frictions. Moreover, the goals of the parties are often incompatible, especially when the parties compete for limited resources. People also have different values and different perceptions of issues. A production manager, for example, may take the position that streamlining the product line and concentrating on a few products can make the organization more productive, while a sales manager may desire a broad product line that will satisfy diverse customer demands. An engineer may want to design the best product regardless of cost or market demand considerations.

Conflict can arise from other sources as well. There may be conflicts between people in line and staff positions. A superior's autocratic leadership style may cause conflicts. Differing educational backgrounds are potential sources of conflict. Perhaps most often mentioned is lack of communication. Many of these topics are discussed in various chapters of this book.

Managing Conflict

Conflict can be managed in different ways, some focusing on interpersonal relationships and others on structural changes. *Avoidance* of the situation that causes the conflict is an example of an interpersonal approach.[10] Another way of coping with conflict is through *smoothing*, emphasizing the areas of agreement and common goals and de-emphasizing disagreements. A third way is *forcing*, pushing one's own view on others; this, of course, will cause overt or covert resistance. A traditional way of coping with conflict is to *compromise*, agreeing in part with the other person's view or demand.

Attempts can also be made to *change the behavior* of individuals, a very difficult task indeed. At times, it may also be possible to *reassign* an individual to another organizational unit. In many situations, conflicts are resolved by a *person higher up in the organization* who has sufficient authority to decide an issue. The problem is that the loser may attempt to get even with the winner at a later time, thus perpetuating the conflict. In the *problem-solving* approach to organizational conflicts, differences are openly confronted and the issues are analyzed as objectively as possible.

Another way of coping with conflict is to make structural changes. This means modifying and integrating the *objectives* of groups with different viewpoints. Moreover, the *organization structure* may have to be changed and authority-responsibility relationships clarified. New ways of *coordinating* activities may have to be found. *Tasks* and *work locations* can also be rearranged. In one workroom, for example, machines were placed in a way that prevented conflicting parties from interacting with one another. Often one must not only decide on the necessary changes but also select the appropriate process. For this reason, the next section focuses on organization development.

ORGANIZATION DEVELOPMENT

Organization development, typically shortened to OD, is a systematic, integrated, and planned approach to improving enterprise effectiveness. It is designed to solve problems that decrease operating efficiency at all levels. Such problems may include lack of cooperation, excessive decentralization, and poor communication.

The techniques of OD may involve laboratory training (for example, people communicating in a group situation), managerial-grid training, and survey feedback.[11] Some OD practitioners also use team building, process consultation, job enrichment, organizational behavior modification, job design, stress management, career and life planning, and management by objectives as part of their approach.[12]

The Organization Development Process

Organization development is a situational or contingency approach to improving enterprise effectiveness. Although various techniques are utilized, the process often involves the steps shown in Figure 13-4. An example can illustrate the application of the model.

Figure 13-4

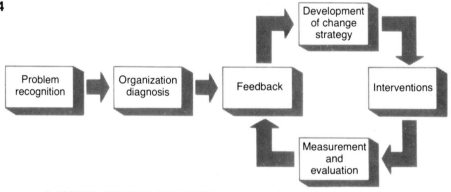

A MODEL OF THE ORGANIZATION DEVELOPMENT PROCESS.

Adapted from H. M. F. Rush, *Organization Development: A Reconnaissance* (New York: National Industrial Conference Board, Inc., 1973), p. 6. Used by permission.

Consider a firm that experiences certain problems: conflict among organizational units, low morale, customer complaints, and increasing costs (*problem recognition* in the model). The chief executive contacts an OD expert to discuss the situation. The two agree on the necessity of an *organizational diagnosis.* The consultant then collects information from several organizational units, using questionnaires, interviews, and observations. The data are analyzed and prepared for feedback.

The executive confers with other managers and sets up a meeting with them. At the meeting, after some introductory comments, the consultant presents the findings under the headings "relations between departments," "enterprise goals," and "customer relations" *(feedback).* The group then ranks the problems in order of their importance. With the guidance of the consultant, the group discusses the difficulties, identifies the underlying causes, and explores possible solutions.

The role of the consultant is that of a coach facilitating the process. Short lectures and exercises on decision making, team building, and problem solving are integrated into the process. At times, subgroups are established to deal with specific issues. The emphasis is on openness and objectivity. The meeting ends with an agreement on a *change strategy.*

The specific *interventions* may include a change in the organization structure, a more effective procedure for handling customer complaints, and the establishment of a team charged with the responsibility of implementing a cost reduction program. Furthermore, the group agrees to meet again in 3 months to *measure and evaluate* the effectiveness of the OD efforts.

Although three phases complete the OD cycle, the effort does not end. Instead, OD becomes a *continuous process* — planned, systematic, and focused on change — that aims at making the enterprise more effective.

Grid Organization Development and Other Methods

One systematic program in organization development is the grid approach.[13] Because the grid itself is discussed in Chapter 16, the emphasis here is on the six phases of grid organization development.

Phase 1 is an introduction to the basic concept of the grid. Robert Blake and Jane Mouton state that the concern for people and the concern for production are not mutually exclusive; they are complementary. The aim of the grid exercise is to develop a high concern for both.

Phase 2 is a continuation of Phase 1, but the focus is on the *team* instead of the individual. In this phase, group members set standards, develop ways of achieving objectives, and identify barriers to achievement of the full potential of the enterprise.

Phase 3 concerns *intergroup development.* It is in this phase that OD really begins. The focus is now on the organization, rather than on individuals. The aim is to reduce conflicts among groups that work together.

Phase 4 involves *organizational goal setting.* In this phase, top managers identify the aims of the enterprise and *design an ideal strategic corporate model.*

Managers from different enterprise functions, including production, engineering, sales, finance, and personnel, are usually members of this policy-setting team.

Phase 5 is the *implementation of the strategic model*. This phase may extend over several years. Managers from all levels of the organization hierarchy have responsibilities in carrying out the activities necessary to achieve the goals set in the previous phase.

Phase 6 is a *systematic critique*. During this phase managers evaluate achievements as well as mistakes made in the previous phases. They also discuss new challenges.

The managerial grid is but one of several approaches to OD. Another one is the *survey feedback method*; it emphasizes the collection, organization, analysis, and feedback of data to participants. Still another technique of OD is *process consultation*, which is concerned with the role of the consultant in facilitating processes within and between groups. In *team building*, people who work together meet to identify barriers to effective functioning of the group. Then the team members develop change objectives and action plans to make the group more effective in achieving enterprise goals.

As these approaches indicate, the parameters of OD are not clearly defined. Instead, OD is eclectic in the sense that it chooses from a variety of tools, methods, and techniques that facilitate the solving of particular enterprise problems.

OD in Action

General Motors (GM) used OD to improve the effectiveness of its management system. OD as a long-range, situational effort is based on action research and problem-solving techniques.[14] Scientific analysis was used to identify factors that bore on a particular problem. In light of the findings, improvements were made through interventions such as changes in the job content, the organization structure, and the enterprise environment.

At GM's Oldsmobile division, the OD program reduced absenteeism and turnover; the Chevrolet group improved employee job satisfaction; and the Buick division, using a job enrichment program, increased productivity, reduced petty grievances, improved departmental morale, and facilitated better interpersonal relationships.[15]

Organization development is not restricted to business but is widely practiced in the military, which may be a surprise to those who perceive the military as an autocratic, mechanistic organization with values apparently incompatible with OD technologies.[16] The U.S. Army tried a number of new managerial approaches, including OD, which the army named "organizational effectiveness" (OE). Among the techniques employed were team building, goal setting, and developmental efforts based on surveys. These decentralized and flexible OE efforts had the strong support of top management, which may have been an important factor in the effectiveness of the program as perceived by respondents in a study.

The OD efforts in the U.S. Navy emphasized survey feedback. The pilot program, called "command development," was not a spectacular success. Nevertheless, the OD efforts were continued under the name "human resource management" (HRM). This program (summarized in Table 13-1) is quite standardized. Although a high percentage of participants felt positive about the program, others did not like the survey or felt that the process was too time-consuming.

Table 13-1 The Navy's Human Resource Management Cycle

Time phasing	Time to conduct	Step activity
Weeks 1–2	1½ days	1. Initial meetings between commanding officer (CO) and consultants
Week 2	½ day	2. Data-gathering planning meetings: Will interview be conducted? What questions? Are additional survey questions desired? Schedule the survey administration
Week 3	1 hour per person	3. Survey administration (mandatory): To all hands
Week 4	As required	4. Conduct interviews (optional)
Week 5	1 day	5. Return survey results to CO: Brief printout format, terms Study and analysis
Weeks 6–7	½ day per working group	6. Survey feedback to work groups (optional): Familiarization with data Source of perceptions? Supervisory self-knowledge Possible solutions/recommendations for action
Weeks 8–9	½ day	7. Action-planning meeting (optional): Develop plans for human resource availability week: OD, equal opportunity, alcohol, drug abuse, and overseas diplomacy
Week 10	1–3 days per group	8. Human resource workshops (optional): Vertical slice of ship or intact work group Modular training packages (standardized series of lectures, films, and exercises on such topics as motivation, communication, MBO, leadership, and race relations)
	2 days	9. Command action-planning workshop (optional): Selected members of crew normally (CO participates part-time) CO approves plan (a command action plan is mandatory)
Week 11	Indefinite	10. Action phase: Implement action plans
Weeks 25–30	½ day	11. Follow-up by consultant: Determine effect of human resource activities through interviews and discussions Meet with CO
Weeks 11–104	As negotiated	12. Follow-on activities (optional): Survey readministered Conduct additional workshops or training activities

Source: D. D. Umstot, "Organization Development Technology and the Military: A Surprising Merger?" *Academy of Management Review* (April 1980), p. 194. Used with permission.

The U.S. Air Force does not have a centralized program but relies on a variety of approaches such as laboratory training, team building, survey feedback, and job enrichment. The results were also mixed. Here, as elsewhere, most claims for the effectiveness of OD are based on testimonials and anecdotes. There is little solid empirical evidence that OD efforts changed the organizations or improved performance.

Although the results of the various kinds of OD efforts in different organizations are mixed, some are encouraging. Still, more research needs to be done in a variety of companies under different conditions to make a definitive evaluation of OD. Today, there is still a major gap in research on the cost and effectiveness of OD efforts. No doubt such research is a complex task, because it is not easy to isolate cause and effect relationships. For instance, improved enterprise performance may be attributable to favorable market conditions and not to OD efforts. However, the great interest in measuring productivity — indicated by several writings[17] — may eventually result in development of more sophisticated tools for assessing the effects of OD and other managerial approaches.

SUMMARY

Manager development refers to the progress a manager makes in learning how to manage effectively. Frequently, it also pertains to developmental programs. Organization development (OD), on the other hand, is a systematic, integrated, and planned approach to making the whole organization or an organization unit effective.

Good results can be achieved through a systematic approach to manager development and training. On-the-job training includes planned progression, job rotation, creation of "assistant-to" positions, temporary promotions, use of committees and junior boards, and coaching. Manager development may include a variety of internal and external training programs.

There are many sources of conflicts. Ways of managing conflict include avoiding the situation, smoothing, forcing, compromising, changing behavior, reassigning individuals, resolving the conflict at higher levels, and problem solving. Another approach is to make structural changes: modifying objectives, developing new methods of coordination, and rearranging authority-responsibility relationships, tasks, and work locations.

The typical organization development process includes the recognition of problems, the diagnosis of an organization, feedback of information on the organization, the development of a change strategy, interventions, and measurement and evaluation of the change efforts. A number of different OD programs are used to improve organizational effectiveness and efficiency.

KEY IDEAS AND CONCEPTS FOR REVIEW

Manager development	T-groups
Managerial training	Business simulation
Organization development (OD)	Experiential exercises
Manager development process	Expert systems
On-the-job training	Sources of organizational conflict
Internal and external training and development	Ways of managing organizational conflict
	Organization development process
Sensitivity training	Grid organization development

FOR DISCUSSION

1. It has been argued that firms have an obligation to train and develop all employees with managerial potential. Do you agree?

2. What are some typical failures in manager development and training? Can you explain these failures? What would you recommend to overcome the shortcomings?

3. Evaluate the advantages and limitations of different approaches to on-the-job training.

4. Evaluate sensitivity training as a technique for training managers. Do you think sensitivity training would make you a better manager? Explain.

5. In the job you now have or the one you expect to have in the future, what kind of coaching and management development would be most beneficial to you?

6. What is an expert system, and how can it help managers make decisions?

7. What are the main characteristics of organization development? How does OD differ from manager development? Do you think OD might work in your organization? Explain why or why not.

EXERCISES/ACTION STEPS

1. Select an organization you know and analyze its management development efforts.

2. What kinds of conflicts have you experienced in an organization with which you are familiar? What were the causes of the conflicts? What was done, if anything, about resolving these conflicts?

CASE:
MANAGEMENT EDUCATION AT
THE HARVARD BUSINESS SCHOOL[18]

Harvard is one of the leading business schools. Yet there is growing concern about whether the school is moving in the right direction. Harvard's mission has been to educate "general managers and business leaders," but recently, over 50 percent of its graduates took jobs in investment banking and management consulting. Moreover, less than one-fourth of the 1987 MBAs went into manufacturing companies, and of those, most moved into staff, rather than line, positions.

Investment houses and consulting firms are eager to recruit at Harvard, offering attractive starting salaries. While some critics accuse the students of being greedy, many professors supplement their salaries by teaching in corporations, consulting, appearing as expert witnesses, or serving on corporate boards. While consulting can enhance teaching, there is a maximum time officially allowed for outside activities.

The approach to teaching has also changed. The case approach, for which Harvard is famous, used to stress the role of the general manager. While cases are still used, more analytical tools have become increasingly important. For example, the course Business Policy has changed to Competitive Strategy under the leadership of Professor Michael Porter, who, with a background in economics, uses concepts and theories in making competitive analyses.

Harvard, once known for developing business leaders, now increasingly educates specialists. Most of the students have shown little interest in joining manufacturing firms. Yet manufacturing may be critical for making the United States competitive.

1. Do you think Harvard is moving in the right direction?

2. How does Harvard's approach compare with the one used in your school?

REFERENCES

1. Ed Bean, "By Practicing What It Preaches, Fuqua Wins a Place among Top Business Schools," *The Wall Street Journal* (May 13, 1986).

2. John A. Byrne, "Business Fads: What's In — And Out," *Business Week* (Jan. 20, 1986), pp. 52–61; and Kenneth Dreyfack and John A. Byrne, "When Companies Tell B-Schools What to Teach," *Business Week* (Feb. 10, 1986), pp. 60–61.

3. For an evaluation of sensitivity training, see Alan C. Filley, Robert J. House, and Steven Kerr, *Managerial Process and Organizational Behavior*, 2d ed. (Glenview, Ill.: Scott, Foresman and Company, 1976), pp. 498–503.

4. Norman E. Sondak and Robert O. Briggs, "Expert Systems — The New Business Simulation Tool"; Theodore F. Gautschi and Mohad Prasad, "An Initial Step towards Developing and Using an Expert System with a Business Simulation"; and Marian Sackson and Andrew Varanelli, Jr., "The Use of an Expert System to Develop Strategic Scenarios"; all three articles appeared in Patricia Sanders and Tom Pray (eds.), *Developments in Business Simulation & Experiential Exercises*, Proceedings of the Fifteenth Annual Conference of ABSEL, San Diego, March 16–18, 1988.

5. Dorothy Leonard-Barton and John J. Sviokla, "Putting Expert Systems to Work," *Harvard Business Review* (March–April 1988), pp. 91–98.

6. Based, in part, on Norman B. Wright, "The Revolution around Us: Human Resource Development in the 80's," *Business Quarterly* (Fall 1984), pp. 6–8.

7. Lucia Solorzano, "Why Business Spends Billions Educating Workers," *U.S. News & World Report* (Feb. 10, 1986), pp. 50–51.

8. Kurt Lewin, *Field Theory in Social Science: Selected Theoretical Papers* (New York: Harper & Brothers, 1951).

9. Edgar H. Schein, *Organizational Psychology*, 3d ed. (Englewood Cliffs, N.J.: Prentice-Hall, 1980), chap. 13; D. D. Warrick, *Managing Organization Change and Development* (Chicago: Science Research Associates, 1984).

10. See Robert R. Blake and Jane S. Mouton, *Building a Dynamic Corporation through Grid Organization Development* (Reading, Mass.: Addison-Wesley Publishing Company, 1969), chap. 6.

11. A survey feedback approach was used by Xerox and is discussed by Norman Deets and Richard Morano, "Xerox's Strategy for Changing Management Styles," *Management Review* (March 1986), pp. 31–35.

12. For a discussion of the history of OD and the contributions to the field, see Wendell L. French, "The Emergence and Early History of Organization Development: With Reference to Influences upon and Interactions among Some of the Key Actors," *Group and Organization Studies* (September 1983).

13. Blake and Mouton, *Building a Dynamic Corporation* (1969); Robert R. Blake and Jane S. Mouton, *The Versatile Manager — A Grid Profile* (Homewood, Ill.: Richard D. Irwin, 1981), pp. 157–178.

14. This is the purpose of the concept of double-loop learning as discussed by Chris Argyris, "The Executive Mind and Double-Loop Learning," *Organizational Dynamics* (Autumn 1982), pp. 4–22; Chris Argyris, "Double Loop Learning in Organizations," in David A. Kolb, Irwin M. Rubin, and James M. McIntyre (eds.), *Organizational Psychology*, 4th ed. (Englewood Cliffs, N.J.: Prentice-Hall, 1984), pp. 45–58.

15. Stephen P. Robbins, *The Administrative Process* (Englewood Cliffs, N.J.: Prentice-Hall, 1976), pp. 340–345, 347–349.

16. This discussion is drawn from Denis D. Umstot, "Organizational Development Technology and the Military: A Surprising Merger?" *Academy of Management Review* (April 1980), pp. 189–201.

17. For more information on improving managerial productivity, see, for example, Paul Mali, *Improving Total Productivity* (New York: John Wiley & Sons, 1978), Heinz Weihrich, *Management Excellence — Productivity through MBO* (New York: McGraw-Hill Book Company, 1985).

18. Walter Kiechel III, "New Debate about Harvard Business School," *Fortune* (Nov. 9. 1987), pp. 34–48.

SUMMARY OF MAJOR PRINCIPLES, OR GUIDES, OF STAFFING

There are no universally accepted staffing principles. Nevertheless, those listed below are useful as guidelines for understanding the staffing function. These principles are grouped under the purpose and process of staffing.

The Purpose of Staffing

The purpose of staffing is summarized by the following principles.

Principle of the objective of staffing   The objective of managerial staffing is to ensure that organization roles are filled by those qualified employees who are able and willing to occupy them.

Principle of staffing   The clearer the definition of organization roles and their human requirements, and the better the techniques of manager appraisal and training employed, the higher the managerial quality.

The first principle stresses the importance of the desire and ability to undertake the responsibilities of management. There is considerable evidence of failure to achieve results when these qualities are lacking. The second principle rests upon an important body of knowledge concerning management practices. Those organizations that have no established job definitions, no effective appraisals, and no system for training and development will have to rely on coincidence or outside sources to fill positions with able managers. On the other hand, enterprises applying the systems approach to staffing and human resource management will utilize the potentials of individuals in the enterprise more effectively and efficiently.

The Process of Staffing

The following principles indicate the means for effective staffing.

Principle of job definition   The more precisely the results expected of managers are identified, the more the dimensions of their positions can be defined.

This principle is similar to the principle of functional definition discussed in Part 3 on organizing. Since organizational roles are occupied by people with different needs, these roles must have many dimensions — such as pay, status, power, discretion, and possibility of accomplishment — that induce managers to perform.

Principle of managerial appraisal The more clearly verifiable objectives and required managerial activities are identified, the more precise can be the appraisal of managers against these criteria.

The principle suggests that performance should be measured both against verifiable objectives — as in an appraisal approach based on management by objectives — and against standards of performance as managers. The appraisal of managers as managers considers how well the key managerial activities within the functions of planning, organizing, staffing, leading, and controlling are carried out.

Principle of open competition The more an enterprise is committed to the assurance of quality management, the more it will encourage open competition among all candidates for management positions.

Violation of this principle has led many firms to appoint managers with inadequate abilities. Although social pressures strongly favor promotion from within the firm, these forces should be resisted whenever better candidates can be brought in from the outside. At the same time, the application of this principle obligates an organization to appraise its people accurately and to provide them with opportunities for development.

Principle of management training and development The more management training and development are integrated with the management process and enterprise objectives, the more effective the development programs and activities will be.

This principle suggests that, in the systems approach, training and development efforts are related to the managerial functions, the aims of the enterprise, and the professional needs of managers.

Principle of training objectives The more precisely the training objectives are stated, the more likely are the chances of achieving them.

The analysis of training needs is the basis for training objectives that give direction to development and facilitate the measurement of the effectiveness of training efforts. This principle brings into focus the contribution that training makes to the purpose of the enterprise and the development of individuals.

Principle of continuing development The more an enterprise is committed to managerial excellence, the more it requires that managers practice continuing self-development.

This principle suggests that in a fast-changing and competitive environment, managers cannot stop learning. Instead, they have to update their managerial knowledge continuously, reevaluate their approaches to managing, and improve their managerial skills and performance to achieve enterprise results.

PART 5

Leading

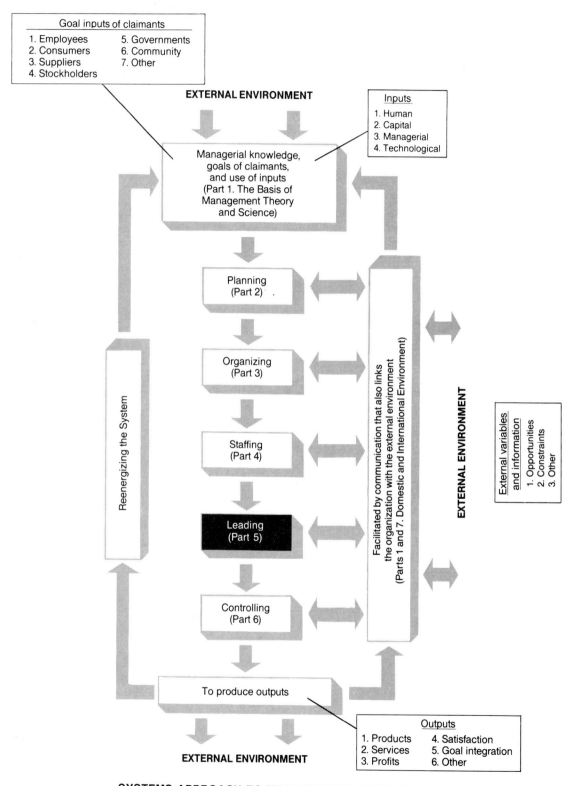

Goal inputs of claimants

1. Employees   5. Governments
2. Consumers   6. Community
3. Suppliers   7. Other
4. Stockholders

EXTERNAL ENVIRONMENT

Inputs

1. Human
2. Capital
3. Managerial
4. Technological

Managerial knowledge,
goals of claimants,
and use of inputs
(Part 1. The Basis of
Management Theory
and Science)

Planning
(Part 2)

Organizing
(Part 3)

Staffing
(Part 4)

Leading
(Part 5)

Controlling
(Part 6)

Reenergizing the System

Facilitated by communication that also links
the organization with the external environment
(Parts 1 and 7. Domestic and International Environment)

EXTERNAL ENVIRONMENT

External variables
and information

1. Opportunities
2. Constraints
3. Other

To produce outputs

Outputs

1. Products   4. Satisfaction
2. Services   5. Goal integration
3. Profits   6. Other

EXTERNAL ENVIRONMENT

SYSTEMS APPROACH TO MANAGEMENT: LEADING

CHAPTER 14

Managing and the Human Factor

CHAPTER OBJECTIVES

After reading this chapter, you should understand:

1. The nature of leading and leadership
2. The basic human factors affecting managing
3. Various models of the nature of people and their implications for managing
4. The need for an eclectic view of behavioral models
5. The importance of creativity and innovation in managing
6. The importance of harmonizing objectives

Management and leadership are often thought of as the same thing. Although it is true that the most effective manager will almost certainly be an effective leader and that leading is an essential function of managers, there is more to managing than just leading. As indicated in previous chapters, managing involves doing careful planning, setting up an organization structure that will aid people in achieving plans, and staffing the organization structure with people who are as competent as possible. The measurement and correction of people's activities through controlling is also an important function of management, as Part 6 will show. However, all these managerial functions accomplish little if managers do not know how to lead people and to understand the human factor in their operations in such a way as to produce desired results.

The managerial function of **leading** is defined as the process of influencing people so that they will contribute to organization and group goals. As the discussion of this function will show, it is in this area that the behavioral sciences make their major contribution to managing. In its analysis of the pertinent knowledge in leading, Part 5 of this book will focus on the human factor, motivation, leadership, and communication.

In this chapter, discussion centers on a variety of human factors important for managing. The concept of what people are like influences managerial behavior. Therefore, several models of people will be introduced. Creativity also plays an important role in managing people. Effective managers draw from various theories and experiences in their efforts to harmonize individual and organizational objectives, which is the key to leading.

HUMAN FACTORS IN MANAGING

It is obvious that while enterprise objectives may differ somewhat in various organizations, the individuals involved also have needs and objectives that are especially important to them. Through the function of leading, managers help people see that they can satisfy their own needs and utilize their potential and at the same time contribute to the aims of an enterprise. Managers thus require an understanding of the roles assumed by people, the individuality of people, and the personalities of people.

Multiplicity of Roles

Individuals are much more than merely a productive factor in management's plans. They are members of social systems of many organizations; they are consumers of goods and services, and thus they vitally influence demand; they are members of families, schools, churches, trade associations, and political parties. In these different roles, they establish laws that govern managers, ethics that guide behavior, and a tradition of human dignity that is a major characteristic of our society. In short, managers and the people they lead are interacting members of a broad social system.

No Average Person

People act in different roles, but they are also different themselves. There is no average person. Yet, in organized enterprises, the assumption is often made that there is. Firms develop rules, procedures, work schedules, safety standards, and position descriptions — all with the implicit assumption that people are essentially alike. Of course, this assumption is necessary to a great extent in organized efforts, but it is equally important to acknowledge that individuals are unique — they have different needs, different ambitions, different attitudes, different desires for responsibility, different levels of knowledge and skills, and different potentials.

Unless managers understand the complexity and individuality of people, they may misapply the generalizations about motivation, leadership, and communication. Principles and concepts, although generally true, have to be adjusted to fit specific situations. In an enterprise, not all the needs of individuals can be completely satisfied, but managers do have considerable latitude in making individual arrangements. Although position requirements are usually derived from enterprise and organization plans, this fact does not necessarily exclude the possibility of arranging the job to fit the person in a specific situation.

The Importance of Personal Dignity

Managing involves achieving enterprise objectives. Achieving results is important, but the means must never violate the dignity of people. The concept of individual dignity means that people must be treated with respect, no matter what their position in the organization. The president, vice-president, manager, first-line supervisor, and worker all contribute to the aims of the enterprise. Each is unique, with different abilities and aspirations, but all are human beings and all deserve to be treated as such.[1]

Considering the Whole Person

We cannot talk about the nature of people unless we consider the whole person, not just separate and distinct characteristics, such as knowledge, attitudes, skills, or personality traits. A person has them all to different degrees. Moreover, these characteristics interact with one another, and their predominance in specific situations changes quickly and unpredictably. The human being is a total person influenced by external factors. People cannot divest themselves of the impact of these forces when they come to work. Managers must recognize these facts and be prepared to deal with them.

BEHAVIORAL MODELS

In order to understand the complexity of people, writers on management have developed several models. Managers, whether they consciously know it or not, have in mind a model of individual and organizational behavior that is based on assumptions about people. These assumptions and their related theories influence managerial behavior.

Over the years, various views about the basic nature of people have been suggested. Dealing with all of them would not be practical here, but consideration is given to models by Schein and by Porter and his colleagues and to McGregor's classic assumptions about people. Also included is an examination of organization behavior models by Miles on the macro level.

From the Rational-Economic View to the Complex Person

Edgar H. Schein developed four conceptions about people. The first concept, *rational-economic assumptions,* is based on the idea that people are primarily motivated by economic incentives.[2] Since these incentives are controlled by the enterprise, people are generally passive and are manipulated, motivated, and controlled by the organization. These assumptions are similar to those listed as Theory X by McGregor, which will be discussed shortly.

The second concept, concerning *social assumptions,* is based on Elton Mayo's idea that, basically, people are motivated by social needs. Thus, social forces of the peer group are more important than controls by managers.

The third concept, concerning *self-actualizing assumptions,* suggests that motives fall into five classes in a hierarchy ranging from the simple needs for survival to the highest needs of self-actualization with maximum use of a person's potential. According to this conception, people are self-motivated — they want to be, and can be, mature.

The fourth concept, based on *complex assumptions,* presents Schein's own view of people. His underlying assumptions are that people are complex and variable and have many motives which combine into a complex motive pattern. In addition, people are able to learn new motives and to respond to different managerial strategies.

Contrasting Views and Models of People

Because the understanding of the behavior of people is so dependent on their nature, it is no surprise that many attempts have been made to categorize the basic views about the underlying nature of people. Lyman Porter and his colleagues have identified six models of people, which are discussed below.[3] This will be followed by an examination of Douglas McGregor's Theory X and Theory Y assumptions about the nature of people.

Rational or emotional?   According to the *rational view,* people behave rationally: They collect and evaluate information systematically and make decisions on the basis of an objective analysis of the different alternatives available. A manager with this view probably would try to interact with people on a rational basis but would tend to ignore their feelings, their emotions, and the human side of their personalities. The *emotional view* holds that people are ruled primarily by their emotions, some of which are uncontrollable. A manager with this view might, for example, play the role of amateur psychiatrist by trying to unearth the underlying psychological causes of employees' behavior.

Behavioristic or phenomenological?   The *behavioristic view* is that people's behavior is controlled by their environment. Managerial strategies based on this theory would suggest changing the environment to get the desired behavior from subordinates. Directly opposed is the *phenomenological view,* which holds that people are unpredictable, unique, subjective, and relative (rather than absolute) but have potential. A manager adopting this model would probably have to understand the complex functioning of the brains of subordinates, because it is there that behavior originates. Since this is not possible, people cannot be understood through scientific and behavioral observation.

Economic or self-actualizing?   According to the *economic view,* people are motivated by economic factors. Thus, it is assumed that people act rationally to get satisfaction from material rewards. Managers with this view probably would see money as the prime (if not the only) way to elicit contributions from subordinates. Furthermore, these managers would create a competitive environment in which people's primary concern is self-interest. In contrast, the *self-actualizing view* holds that people want to increase their competence, want to develop, and strive to use their potential. A manager adhering to this model would establish an environment in which people could exercise self-direction and reach their full capabilities.

McGregor's Theory X and Theory Y

Another view about the nature of people has been expressed in two sets of assumptions developed by Douglas McGregor and commonly known as "Theory X" and "Theory Y."[4] Managing, McGregor suggested, must start with the basic question of how managers see themselves in relation to others. This viewpoint requires some thought on the perception of human nature. Theory X and Theory Y are two sets of assumptions about the nature of people. McGregor chose these terms because he wanted neutral terminology without any connotation of being "good" or "bad."

Theory X assumptions   The "traditional" assumptions about the nature of people, according to McGregor, are included in Theory X as follows:

1. Average human beings have an inherent dislike of work and will avoid it if they can.

2. Because of this human characteristic of disliking work, most people must be coerced, controlled, directed, and threatened with punishment to get them to put forth adequate effort toward the achievement of organizational objectives.

3. Average human beings prefer to be directed, wish to avoid responsibility, have relatively little ambition, and want security above all.

Theory Y assumptions   The assumptions under Theory Y are seen by McGregor as follows:

1. The expenditure of physical effort and mental effort in work is as natural as play or rest.

2. External control and the threat of punishment are not the only means for producing effort toward organizational objectives. People will exercise self-direction and self-control in the service of objectives to which they are committed.

3. The degree of commitment to objectives is in proportion to the size of the rewards associated with their achievement.

4. Average human beings learn, under proper conditions, not only to accept responsibility but also to seek it.

5. The capacity to exercise a relatively high degree of imagination, ingenuity, and creativity in the solution of organizational problems is widely, not narrowly, distributed in the population.

6. Under the conditions of modern industrial life, the intellectual potentialities of the average human being are only partially utilized.

These two sets of assumptions obviously are fundamentally different. Theory X is pessimistic, static, and rigid. Control is primarily external, that is, imposed on the subordinate by the superior. In contrast, Theory Y is optimistic, dynamic, and flexible, with an emphasis on self-direction and the integration of individual needs with organizational demands. There is little doubt that each set of assumptions will affect the way managers carry out their managerial functions and activities.

Clarification of the theories   McGregor was apparently concerned that Theory X and Theory Y might be misinterpreted.[5] The following points will clarify some of the areas of misunderstanding and keep the assumptions in proper perspective. First, Theory X and Theory Y assumptions are just that: They are assumptions only. They are not prescriptions or suggestions for managerial strategies. Rather, these assumptions must be tested against reality. Furthermore, these assumptions are intuitive deductions and are not based on research. Second, Theories X and Y do not imply "hard" or "soft" management. The "hard" approach may produce resistance and antagonism. The "soft" approach may result in laissez-faire management and is not congruent with Theory Y. The effective manager recognizes the dignity and capabilities, as well as the limitations, of people and adjusts behavior as demanded by the situation. Third, Theories X and Y are not to be viewed as being on a continuous scale, with X and Y on opposite extremes. They are not a matter of degree; rather, they are completely different views of people.

Fourth, the discussion of Theory Y is not a case for consensus management, nor is it an argument against the use of authority. Under Theory Y, authority is seen as only one of the many ways a manager exerts leadership. Fifth, different tasks and situations require a variety of approaches to management. At times, authority and structure may be effective for certain tasks, as found in the research by John J. Morse and Jay W. Lorsch.[6] They suggest that different approaches are effective in different situations. Thus, the productive enterprise is one that fits the task requirements to the people and the particular situation.

A Dual-Model Theory

According to Raymond E. Miles, the managerial task is to integrate organizational variables (goals, technology, and structure) with human variables (capabilities, attitudes, values, needs, and demographic characteristics) into an effective and efficient sociotechnical system.[7] This integration, shown in Table 14-1, is achieved through activities such as directing, selecting, training, appraising, communicating, and controlling. It also includes designing the organization and jobs, developing people, and rewarding individuals for their contributions. The framework, as you will readily recognize, is similar to the managerial activities discussed in this book.

Miles suggests that the manager's own concepts about managing partially determine the way the key managerial activities are carried out. Consequently, he identifies three "theories" of management known as the traditional, the human relations, and the human resources models.[8] In developing these models, Miles draws extensively from McGregor.[9] The traditional model is similar to Theory X, while the human resources model is closely related to Theory Y. The human relations model may be seen as Theory X with pseudo-participation.

The models shown in Table 14-1 begin with assumptions about people; then policies related to these assumptions are described; finally, the expected results are stated. The important point is that managers apparently subscribe not only to one model but to two. One concerns the way they manage subordinates, and the other concerns the way they believe they should be managed by their superiors.

Three managerial models In the *traditional model*, emphasis is on control and directing. The underlying assumption is that members of the enterprise will comply if tasks and procedures are specified and members are properly selected, trained, and paid. The *human relations model* gives attention to social and egoistic needs. Thus, it is recognized that fair treatment and pay are not enough. Nevertheless, the emphasis by managers is still on controlling, although preventive steps are also taken to obtain the desired contributions of enterprise members. The *human resources model* is different. The manager is seen as a developer and facilitator who helps subordinates achieve performance aims. There is a great deal of participation in goal setting. Furthermore, if problems occur, several factors — rather than a single cause — are evaluated as potential reasons for the difficulties. Although self-direction and self-control are important to this model, the need for other controls is also recognized.

Table 14-1 **Alternative Theories of Management**

Traditional model	Human relations model	Human resources model
Assumptions		
1. Work is inherently distasteful to most people. 2. What workers do is less important than what they earn for doing it. 3. Few want or can handle work which requires creativity, self-direction, or self-control.	1. People want to feel useful and important. 2. People desire to belong and to be recognized as individuals. 3. These needs are more important than money in motivating people to work.	1. Work is not inherently distasteful. People want to contribute to meaningful goals which they have helped establish. 2. Most people can exercise far more creative, responsible self-direction and self-control than their present jobs demand.
Policies		
1. The manager's basic task is to closely supervise and control his subordinates. 2. He must break tasks down into simple, repetitive, easily learned operations. 3. He must establish detailed work routines and procedures and enforce these firmly but fairly.	1. The manager's basic task is to make each worker feel useful and important. 2. He should keep his subordinates informed and listen to their objections to his plans. 3. The manager should allow his subordinates to exercise some self-direction and self-control on routine matters.	1. The manager's basic task is to make use of his "untapped" human resources. 2. He must create an environment in which all members may contribute to the limits of their ability. 3. He must encourage full participation on important matters, continually broadening subordinate self-direction and control.
Expectations		
1. People can tolerate work if the pay is decent and the boss is fair. 2. If tasks are simple enough and people are closely controlled, they will produce up to standard.	1. Sharing information with subordinates and involving them in routine decisions will satisfy their basic needs to belong and to feel important. 2. Satisfying these needs will improve morale and reduce resistance to formal authority—subordinates will "willingly cooperate."	1. Expanding subordinate influence, self-direction, and self-control will lead to direct improvements in operating efficiency. 2. Work satisfaction may improve as a "by-product" of subordinates' making full use of their resources.

Source: Raymond E. Miles, *Theories of Management: Implications for Organizational Behavior and Development* (New York: McGraw-Hill Book Company, 1975), p. 35. Used with permission.

> **PERSPECTIVE:**
> **SOME EXPERIENCES SUPPORTING THE DUAL-MODEL THEORY**
>
> The findings by Miles have repeatedly been noted in a variety of consulting and management development experiences. For example, in seminars on MBO there is little disagreement among participants about the desirability of participation in goal setting; they favor placing responsibility for planning at the level where actions are carried out and providing an environment in which people can use their potential, self-control, self-direction, and accountability for results. Frequently heard from seminar participants are phrases such as "Great idea, but my boss should really attend this session," and "If only top management would practice this participative philosophy." However, if the same people are observed interacting with their subordinates in the organizational setting, it is not unusual to find that they do not practice what they supposedly believe to be effective. In other words, their position is that the human resources model is effective at their own level but not in their relationships with subordinates.

Separate theories for subordinates and for managers themselves   On the basis of extensive research evidence, Miles concluded that managers actually believe in two models: one for subordinates and the other for themselves. Studies conducted at Stanford University and at the University of California at Berkeley showed a basic agreement about the desirability of the concept concerning participation in decision making by subordinates, sharing of information, and increasing self-control. However, managers did not indicate strong belief in the capabilities of their subordinates and, in fact, exhibited a lack of confidence in them. Nor did these managers think that the capacity for leadership was widely distributed among subordinates. Thus, these managers seem to have rejected the human resources model when it came to their own relationships with their subordinates.

The picture was quite different, however, for managers viewing their relationships with their own superiors. There was a tendency for these managers to rate themselves as equal to, or higher than, their superiors on factors such as creativity, ingenuity, flexibility, and willingness to change. In addition, these managers felt that their superiors should use participation, which, in turn, would result in better enterprise performance at their level. In summary, then, these managers appear to have suggested that their superiors should follow practices which would allow them to operate consistently with the human resources model. On the other hand, these same managers, in their relationships with subordinates, seem to have subscribed to the human relations model.

TOWARD AN ECLECTIC VIEW OF BEHAVIORAL MODELS

Which of these many views of individuals is valid? Earlier in this chapter, it was noted that Schein suggested four conceptions of people, ranging from the rational-economic view to a view that stresses complex motivations. Porter and his colleagues presented six different views about the nature of individuals, and McGregor grouped assumptions into Theory X and Theory Y. Finally, Miles suggested three different models. Which model, then, is valid?

Many similarities can be found among the various models, but it appears that no single model is sufficient to explain the full range of individual and organizational behavior. People behave differently in diverse situations, and, to complicate matters, they even behave differently in similar situations at different times. In some situations people act rationally; in other situations they are guided by emotions. It is the manager's responsibility to create an environment in which people are induced to contribute to the aims of the enterprise. Yet assuming that people can be manipulated ignores their individuality and underestimates their intelligence. Economic rewards certainly are important in an enterprise, but people often want more than money from a job. They usually want to develop their capabilities, their competence, and their potential as well.

The effective manager will take an eclectic approach by drawing from different models that describe the nature of people. At the very least, one must recognize that people are different and do not fit neatly into a single conceptual model. They must be treated with respect and dignity; they must be considered as whole persons; and they must be seen in the context of their total environment, in which they assume different roles. It is important to realize that different situations require a variety of managerial approaches for utilizing most effectively and efficiently the most valuable resource of the enterprise, namely, people.

CREATIVITY AND INNOVATION

An important factor in managing people is creativity. A distinction can be made between creativity and innovation. The term **creativity** usually refers to the ability and power to develop new ideas. **Innovation,** on the other hand, usually means the use of these ideas. In an organization, this can mean a new product, a new service, or a new way of doing things. Although this discussion centers on the creative process, it is implied that organizations not only generate new ideas but also translate them into practical applications.

The Creative Process

The creative process is seldom simple and linear. Instead, it generally consists of four overlapping and interacting phases: (1) unconscious scanning, (2) intuition, (3) insight, and (4) logical formulation.[10]

The first phase, *unconscious scanning*, is difficult to explain because it is beyond consciousness. This scanning usually requires an absorption in the problem which may be vague in the mind. Yet managers working under time constraints often make decisions prematurely rather than dealing thoroughly with ambiguous, ill-defined problems.

The second phase, *intuition*, connects the unconscious with the conscious. This stage may involve a combination of factors that may seem contradictory at first. For example, in the 1920s Donaldson Brown and Alfred Sloan of General Motors conceived the idea of a decentralized division structure with centralized control — concepts which seem to contradict each other. Yet the idea makes sense when one recognizes the underlying principles of (1) giving responsibility for the operations to the general manager of each division, and (2) maintaining centralized control in headquarters over certain functions. It took the intuition of two great corporate leaders to see that these two principles could interact in the managerial process.

Intuition needs time to work. It requires that people find new combinations and integrate diverse concepts and ideas. Thus, one must think through the problem. Intuitive thinking is promoted by several techniques such as brainstorming and synectics, which will be discussed shortly.

Insight, the third phase of the creative process, is mostly the result of hard work. For example, many ideas are needed in the development of a usable product, a new service, or a new process. Interestingly, insight may come at times when the thoughts are not directly focused on the problem at hand. Moreover, new insights may last for only a few minutes, and effective managers may benefit from having paper and pencil ready to make notes of their creative ideas.

The last phase in the creative process is *logical formulation* or *verification*. Insight needs to be tested through logic or experiment. This may be accomplished by continuing to work on an idea or by inviting critiques from others. Brown and Sloan's idea of decentralization, for example, needed to be tested against organizational reality.

Techniques to Enhance Creativity

Creativity can be taught.[11] Creative thoughts are often the fruits of extensive efforts, and several techniques are available to nurture those kinds of thoughts, especially in the decision-making process. Some techniques focus on group interactions; others focus on individual actions. As illustrative of the various techniques, two popular ones are brainstorming and synectics.

Brainstorming   One of the best-known techniques for facilitating creativity has been developed by Alex F. Osborn, who has been called "the father of brainstorming."[12] The purpose of this approach is to improve problem solving by finding new and unusual solutions. In the brainstorming session, a multiplication of ideas is sought. The rules are as follows:

1. No ideas are ever criticized.

2. The more radical the ideas are, the better.

3. The quantity of idea production is stressed.

4. The improvement of ideas by others is encouraged.

Brainstorming, which emphasizes group thinking, was widely accepted after its introduction. However, the enthusiasm was dampened by research which showed that individuals could develop better ideas working by themselves than they could working in groups. Additional research, however, showed that in some situations the group approach may work well. This may be the case when the information is distributed among various people or when a poorer group decision is more acceptable than a better individual decision which, for example, may be opposed by those who have to implement it. Also, the acceptance of new ideas is usually greater when the decision is made by the group charged with its implementation.[13]

Synectics   Originally known as the Gordon technique (named after its creator, William J. Gordon), this system was further modified and became known as synectics.[14] In this approach, the members of the synectics team are carefully selected for their suitability to deal with the problem, a problem which may involve the entire organization.

The leader of the group plays a vital role in this approach. In fact, only the leader knows the specific nature of the problem. This person narrows and carefully leads the discussion without revealing the actual problem itself. The main reason for this approach is to prevent the group from reaching a premature solution to the problem. The system involves a complex set of interactions from which a solution emerges — frequently the invention of a new product.

Limitations of Traditional Group Discussion

Although the techniques of brainstorming and synectics may result in creative ideas, it would be incorrect to assume that creativity flourishes only in groups. Indeed, the usual group discussion can inhibit creativity.[15] For example, group members may pursue an idea to the exclusion of other alternatives. Experts on a topic may not be willing to express their ideas in a group for fear of being ridiculed. Also, lower-level managers may be inhibited in expressing their views in a group with higher-level managers. Pressures to conform can discourage the expression of deviant opinions. The need for getting along with others can be stronger than the need for exploring creative but unpopular alternatives to the solution of a problem. Finally, because they need to arrive at a decision, groups may not make the effort of searching for data relevant to a decision.

The Creative Manager

All too often it is assumed that most people are noncreative and have little ability to develop new ideas. This assumption, unfortunately, can be detrimental to the organization, for in the appropriate environment virtually all people are capable of being creative, even though the degree of creativity varies considerably among individuals.

Generally speaking, creative people are inquisitive and come up with many new and unusual ideas; they are seldom satisfied with the status quo.

Although intelligent, they not only rely on the rational process but also involve the emotional aspects of their personality in problem solving. They appear to be excited about solving a problem, even to the point of tenacity. Creative individuals are aware of themselves and capable of independent judgment. They object to conformity and see themselves as being different.

Unquestionably, creative people can make great contributions to an enterprise. At the same time, however, they may also cause difficulties in organizations. Change — as any manager knows — is not always popular. Moreover, change frequently has undesirable and unexpected side effects. Similarly, unusual ideas, pursued stubbornly, may frustrate others and inhibit the smooth functioning of an organization. Finally, creative individuals may be disruptive by ignoring established policies, rules, and regulations.

As a result, the creativity of most individuals is probably underutilized in many cases, despite the fact that unusual innovations can be of great benefit to the firm. However, individual and group techniques can be effectively used to nurture creativity, especially in the area of planning. But creativity is not a substitute for managerial judgment. It is the manager who must determine and weigh the risks involved in pursuing unusual ideas and translating them into innovative practices.

Innovation and Entrepreneurship

Recently, innovation and entrepreneurship have received considerable attention. When hearing these terms, one thinks immediately of the success stories of people such as Steven Jobs of Apple Computers and Ross Perot of Electronic Data Processing (acquired by General Motors). It may be an appealing thought to get rich and get rich quick, often by establishing new companies.[16] While some authors examine the individual entrepreneur, others focus on entrepreneurship in companies.*

Peter Drucker suggests that innovation applies not only to high-tech companies but equally to low-tech, established businesses. Worthwhile innovation is not a matter of sheer luck; it requires systematic and rational work, well organized and managed for results.[17]

What does entrepreneurship imply? It suggests dissatisfaction with how things are and awareness of a need to do things differently. Innovation comes about because of some of the following situations:

1. The unexpected event, failure, or success

2. The incongruous — what is assumed and what really is

3. The process or task that needed improvement

4. Changes in the market or industry structure

5. Changes in demographics

*See also the discussion of "intrapreneurship" mentioned in Chapter 7.

> **PERSPECTIVE:**
> **CREATIVE THINKING AT BELL TELEPHONE LABORATORY**
>
> The Bell Telephone Laboratory has been referred to as "probably the greatest invention factory." The organizational climate in this firm, which allows for great freedom, was probably set many years ago by Theodore Vail, AT&T's president, who himself had an innovative vision in formulating the strategy for the telephone company. In the early 1900s, when the Bell System was almost a monopoly, Vail formalized the purpose of the organization as *providing service.* A simple insight? Perhaps, but it was a significant one because it charted the successful course of the company for many years to come.

6. Changes in meaning or in the way things are perceived

7. Innovation based on knowledge

Innovations based solely on bright ideas may be very risky and are, at times, not successful. General Electric's ambitious plans for the "factory of the future" may have been a costly mistake.[18] These plans may have been based on unrealistic forecasts and GE's unrealistic expectations to automate industry. The concept of the new factory expressed the wish of the chairperson, who wanted to promote entrepreneurship in an organization that was known to be highly structured.

The most successful innovations are often the mundane ones. Take the Japanese, who make minor innovations (providing, for example, little conveniences that customers like) in their cars or in their electronic equipment.[19] James Brian Quinn found in his research that successful large companies are listening carefully to the needs of their customers. They establish teams that search for creative alternatives to serve their customers — but within a limiting framework and with clear goals in mind.[20]

Innovation is not only relevant to high-tech firms but also crucial for old-line, traditional companies which may not survive without the infusion of innovation. Managers in those companies must create an environment that fosters entrepreneurial spirit and actions.

HARMONIZING OBJECTIVES: THE KEY TO LEADING

Understanding the human factor in enterprises is important for the managerial function of leading. How a manager views human nature influences the selection of motivational and leadership approaches. A number of models presenting various conceptions of the nature of people have been proposed; however, no single view is sufficient to understand the whole person. Therefore, an *eclectic view* of the nature of people is suggested.

People do not work in isolation; rather, they work to a great extent in groups toward the achievement of personal and enterprise objectives. Unfortunately, these objectives are not always harmonious. Likewise, the goals of subordinates are not always the same as those of the superior. Therefore, one of the most important activities of managers is to harmonize the needs of individuals with the demands of the enterprise.

Leading bridges the gap between, on the one hand, logical and well-considered plans, carefully designed organization structures, good programs of staffing, and efficient control techniques, and, on the other hand, the need for people to understand, to be motivated, and to contribute all they are capable of to enterprise and department goals. There is no way that a manager can utilize the desires and goals of individuals to achieve enterprise objectives without knowing what these individuals want. Even then, managers must be able to design an environment that will take advantage of these individual drives. Managers must know how to communicate with and guide their subordinates so that they will see how they serve their own interests by working creatively for an organization.

SUMMARY

Leading is the process of influencing people so that they will contribute to organization and group goals. People assume different roles, and there is no average person. While working toward goals, the manager must take into account the dignity of the whole person.

There are different views and assumptions about human nature. Schein proposed four sets of assumptions: the rational-economic, social, self-actualization, and complex assumptions. McGregor called his sets of assumptions about people Theory X and Theory Y. Miles identified three models: the traditional, the human relations, and the human resources models. In addition, he concluded that managers subscribe to two models: one for subordinates and the other for themselves (dual-model theory). But no single model is sufficient to explain the complexities of people. Consequently, it is preferable to take an eclectic view, drawing from different models to describe human nature.

Creativity, the ability and power to develop new ideas, is important for effective managing. Innovation is the use of these ideas. The creative process consists of four overlapping phases: (1) unconscious scanning, (2) intuition, (3) insight, and (4) logical formulation. Two popular techniques for enhancing creativity are brainstorming and synectics. Innovation is important for entrepreneurship.

Managers need to understand the various behavioral patterns of themselves and their subordinates that help in harmonizing objectives.

KEY IDEAS AND CONCEPTS FOR REVIEW

Leading	Eclectic view of people
Human factors in managing	Creative process
Individual dignity	Brainstorming
Schein's assumptions about people	Synectics
McGregor's Theory X and Y assumptions	Innovation and entrepreneurship
Dual-model theory	Harmonizing objectives

FOR DISCUSSION

1. What are Theory X and Theory Y assumptions? State your agreements or disagreements with these assumptions. What are some misunderstandings of Theories X and Y?

2. What are some possible implications of Theories X and Y for carrying out the managerial functions of planning, organizing, staffing, leading, and controlling?

3. According to Miles, managers may subscribe to *two* managerial models. What does this actually mean? What has been your experience?

4. Think of a problem that was creatively solved. Did the solution come about through group discussion, or was it an individual effort? Reconstruct the steps of the creative process.

5. Do you — as a student, as an employee, or as a manager — work at your capacity? Why, or why not?

6. Why is harmonizing of personal and enterprise objectives seen as a key to leading?

EXERCISES/ACTION STEPS

1. Interview two managers and ask them what they think about the basic nature of people. For example, do they think that people are basically lazy and need to be controlled? Or do they think that employees want to work and contribute to the company's goals. In preparation for presenting your findings to the class, analyze the managers' responses in light of the theories you learned in this chapter.

2. Read some books and articles on creativity and innovation, and try to apply some of the principles, concepts, or theories to your life. You may start by looking at the references for this chapter.

CASE:
CUSTOMER'S ELECTRIC APPLIANCE COMPANY

John Caldwell, the president of the Customer's Electric Appliance Company, had just received the latest report of the state of the firm. He did not like what he read: sales down, costs increased, profits decreased, customer complaints up, and labor turnover extremely high. He immediately asked his secretary to order all the vice-presidents from the functional areas, the controller, and the other key staff personnel to come to his office. At the meeting, Mr. Caldwell stated: "I have just received the report on key indicators, and I think the poor performance of the firm is directly attributable to your lack of leadership. This company has become a country club. When I walk through the corridors, I see people standing around as if they were at a cocktail party. Their concern is to do less for more money and more fringe benefits. They have completely forgotten that we are in business to make a profit. You must remember that people want to do as little as possible and to squeeze the last dime out of the company. What is needed is closer supervision and more control. When people are not performing, you warn them once — if they do not shape up, fire them. Recently, several customers complained that they would not get any service if their requests would not result in sales and commissions for the salesperson. I want you to check the salespeople very closely on their dealings with the customers. Do not hesitate to listen in on their telephone conversations. Perhaps you might even make recordings of these conversations and bring them to my attention."

The executives at the meeting nodded approvingly to the president's remarks. Only Carolyn Jung, a 28-year-old staff assistant, raised some questions. She wondered whether the company should go that far in installing controls. In fact, she suggested that people basically want to work, want to contribute, and want to do a good job, provided opportunities are given. She even suggested that the company perhaps did not really utilize the people's poten-

tials, because employees today are better educated than ever before and they want to participate in the decision-making process. She recommended that the president should explain to the employees the company's poor performance and then solicit their help in improving productivity.

The president, stunned by Ms. Jung's comments, said that she must have been misled by some of the newfangled ideas she might have heard when she recently took courses to complete her M.B.A. degree. Mr. Caldwell then abruptly closed the meeting with the order that all officers come to a meeting scheduled for the following Monday and report on the specific steps each one would undertake to bring the company under control.

1. If you were employed by the firm and attended the meeting (let's say you had been employed for 6 months), what would you have said, if anything?

2. What is the president's view of the nature of people?

3. What are the underlying assumptions about people expressed in Ms. Jung's comments?

4. If you were an outside consultant attending this meeting, what recommendations would you make to the president to improve the human organization?

REFERENCES

1. This is also one of the important messages in the *Second Draft — Pastoral Letter on Catholic Social Teaching and the U.S. Economy* (Oct. 7, 1985). The letter *Economic Justice for All: Catholic Social Teaching and the U.S. Economy* was approved in November 1986.

2. Edgar H. Schein, *Organizational Psychology,* 3rd ed. (Englewood Cliffs, N.J.: Prentice-Hall, 1980), pp. 52–101.

3. Lyman W. Porter, Edward E. Lawler III, and J. Richard Hackman, *Behavior in Organizations* (New York: McGraw-Hill Book Company, 1975), chap. 2.

4. Douglas McGregor, *The Human Side of Enterprise* (New York: McGraw-Hill Book Company, 1960).

5. Harold M. F. Rush, *Behavioral Science — Concepts and Management Application* (New York: National Industrial Conference Board, 1969), pp. 13–16; Douglas McGregor, *The Professional Manager* (New York: McGraw-Hill Book Company, 1969), chap. 5.

6. John J. Morse and Jay W. Lorsch, "Beyond Theory Y," *Harvard Business Review* (May–June 1970), pp. 61–68.

7. Raymond E. Miles, *Theories of Management: Implications for Organizational Behavior and Development* (New York: McGraw-Hill Book Company, 1975), especially chap. 2.

8. A theory is defined by Miles in this context as "simply a more or less complete explanation of how and why someone or something behaves, occurs, or responds as he or it does under a given set of circumstances." In Miles, *Theories of Management* (1975), p. 32.

9. See John B. Miner, *Theories of Organizational Behavior* (Hinsdale, Ill.: The Dryden Press, 1980), chap. 10.

10. Much of the discussion of the creative process is based on Michael B. McCaskey, *The Executive Challenge — Managing Change and Ambiguity* (Marshfield, Mass.: Pitman Publishing, 1982), chap. 8.

11. Emily T. Smith, "Are You Creative? Research Shows Creativity Can Be Taught — and Companies Are Listening," *Business Week* (Sept. 30, 1985), pp. 80–84.

12. Alex F. Osborn, *Applied Imagination,* 3d rev. ed. (New York: Charles Scribner's Sons, 1963).

13. Irvin Summers and David E. White, "Creativity Techniques: Toward Improvement of the Decision Process," *Academy of Management Review* (April 1976), pp. 99–107.

14. William J. Gordon, "Operational Approach to Creativity," *Harvard Business Review* (November–December 1956), pp. 41–51; William J. Gordon, *Synectics* (New York: Harper & Brothers, 1961).

15. George S. Steiner, John B. Miner, and Edmund R. Gray, *Management Policy and Strategy,* 3d ed. (New York: The Macmillan Company, 1986), pp. 174–177; Andre L. Delbecq, Andrew H. Van de Ven, and David H. Gustafson, *Group Techniques for Program Planning* (Glenview, Ill.: Scott, Foresman and Company, 1975).

16. For a critical review of some books on entrepreneurship, see David E. Gumpert, "Stalking the Entrepreneur," *Harvard Business Review* (May–June 1986), pp. 32–36.

17. Peter F. Drucker, *Innovation and Entrepreneurship — Practices and Principles* (New York: Harper & Row, 1985); Peter F. Drucker, "The Discipline of Innovation," *Harvard Business Review* (May–June 1985), pp. 67–72; John W. Wilson, "The New Economy According to Drucker," *Business Week* (June 10, 1985), p. 10–12; and Everett Groseclose, "A Management Sage's Shibboleths for Success," *The Wall Street Journal* (Oct. 7, 1985).

18. Peter Petre, "How GE Bobbled the Factory of the Future," *Fortune* (Nov. 11, 1985), pp. 52–63.

19. More recently, Japan has been breaking with tradition and now begins funding of basic research. See Stephen K. Yoder, "Going Crazy in Japan," *The Wall Street Journal,* A Special Report on Technology in the Workplace (Nov. 10, 1986).

20. James B. Quinn, "Managing Innovation: Controlled Chaos," *Harvard Business Review* (May–June 1985), pp. 73–84.

CHAPTER 15

Motivation

CHAPTER OBJECTIVES

After reading this chapter, you should understand:

1. The meaning of motivation, motivators, and satisfaction
2. The reasons why motives are often complex and even conflicting
3. Various theories of motivation and their strengths and weaknesses
4. Special motivational techniques and job enrichment
5. The systems and contingency approach to motivation, with special emphasis on developing an organizational climate to ensure motivation

Managing requires the creation and maintenance of an environment in which individuals work together in groups toward the accomplishment of common objectives. A manager cannot do this job without knowing what motivates people. The building of motivating factors into organizational roles, the staffing of these roles, and the entire process of leading people must be built on a knowledge of motivation. This chapter emphasizes the importance of knowing and taking advantage of motivating factors, but that does not mean managers should become amateur psychiatrists. The manager's job is not to manipulate people but, rather, to recognize what motivates people.

The basic element of all human behavior is some kind of activity, whether physical or mental. Thus, human behavior can be seen as a series of activities. The question arises as to which activities human beings will undertake at any given time, and why. Activities are goal-oriented; that is, people do things that lead them to accomplish something. But individual goals can be baffling.

Sometimes people know exactly why they do things; often, however, individual drives lie buried in the subconscious. For example, do you know why you did what you did today and what all your various activities were designed to achieve?

The primary task of managers is to get people to contribute activities that help achieve the mission and goals of an enterprise or of any department or other organized unit within it. Clearly, guiding people's activities in desired directions requires knowing, to the best of any manager's ability, what leads people to do things, what motivates them.

MOTIVATION AND MOTIVATORS

Human motives are based on needs, whether consciously or subconsciously felt. Some are primary needs, such as the physiological requirements for water, air, food, sleep, and shelter. Other needs may be regarded as secondary, such as self-esteem, status, affiliation with others, affection, giving, accomplishment, and self-assertion. Naturally, these needs vary in intensity and over time among different individuals.

PERSPECTIVE:
SELF-MOTIVATION

Managers are responsible for providing an environment conducive to performance. But individuals themselves are responsible for self-motivation. One approach is through strategic career management (which was discussed in Chapter 12). George Odiorne, management professor, scholar, and experienced consultant, made specific recommendations.[1] Here are some:

1. Set a goal for yourself and do not lose sight of it. Lee Iacocca (currently president at Chrysler) set the goal of becoming vice-president at the Ford Motor Company by age 35, and for 15 years this aim motivated him and guided his behavior.

2. Supplement your long-term objectives with short-term goals and specific actions. It has been said that to get something done is to begin.

3. Learn a challenging new task each year. Learning to become a manager does not stop with a bachelor's or master's degree in business. A degree is the real beginning, not the end, of learning. Learning and applying the new microcomputer technology might be such a challenging task.

4. Make your job a different one. Set improvement objectives for your position. With some imagination, you probably can considerably increase your productivity.

5. Develop an area of expertise. Build on your strengths or develop one of your weaknesses into a strength. You might want to be known as the best accountant or the best engineer in your specific area of competence.

6. Give yourself feedback and reward yourself. Setting verifiable goals provides you with a standard against which you can measure your performance. Why not have a special dinner to celebrate your accomplishments?

Motivation

Motivation is a general term applying to the entire class of drives, desires, needs, wishes, and similar forces. To say that managers motivate their subordinates is to say that they do those things which they hope will satisfy these drives and desires and induce the subordinates to act in a desired manner.

The Need-Want-Satisfaction Chain

It is possible, then, to look at motivation as involving a chain reaction: Felt needs give rise to wants or goals sought, which cause tensions (that is, unfulfilled desires), which give rise to actions toward achieving goals, which finally result in satisfying actions. This chain is shown in Figure 15-1.

The chain explanation is complex. In the first place, except for physiological needs, such as hunger, needs are not independent of a person's environment. Many physiological needs, however, are stimulated by environmental factors: The smell of food may cause hunger, a low thermometer reading may cause chills, or the sight of a cold drink may cause an overwhelming thirst.

Environment has a major influence on our perception of secondary needs. The promotion of a colleague may kindle one's desire for a higher position. A challenging problem may whet one's desire to accomplish something by solving it. A congenial social group may increase one's need for affiliation; and, of course, being alone more than one wants to be can give a strong motivation for wanting to be with people.

In the second place, the need-want-satisfaction chain does not always operate as simply as portrayed. Needs do cause behavior, but needs also may result from behavior. Satisfying one need may lead to a desire to satisfy more needs. For example, a person's need for accomplishment may be made keener by the satisfaction gained from achieving a desired goal or it may be dulled by failure. The one-way nature of the chain has also been challenged by the work of some biological scientists who have found that needs are not always the cause of human behavior but may be a result of it. In other words, behavior is often what people do and not why they do it.

Figure 15-1

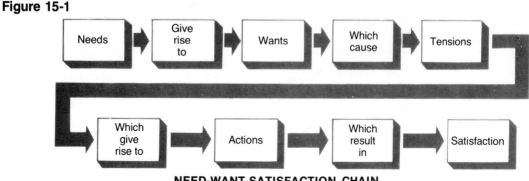

NEED-WANT-SATISFACTION CHAIN.

Complexity of Motivation

It takes only a moment's thought to realize that at any given time, an individual's motives may be quite complex and often conflicting. A person may be motivated by a desire for economic goods and services (groceries, a better house, a new car, or a trip), and even these desires may be complex and conflicting (should one buy a new house or a new car?). At the same time an individual may want self-esteem, status, a feeling of accomplishment, or relaxation (who has not felt a conflict between the time demands of a job and the desire to play golf or go to a movie?).

Motivators Motivators are things which induce an individual to perform. While motivations reflect wants, motivators are the identified rewards, or incentives, that sharpen the drive to satisfy these wants. They are also the means by which conflicting needs may be reconciled or one need heightened so that it will be given priority over another.

A manager can do much to sharpen motives by establishing an environment favorable to certain drives. For example, people in a business which has developed a reputation for excellence and high quality tend to be motivated to contribute to this reputation. Similarly, the environment of a business in which managerial performance is effective and efficient tends to breed a desire for high-quality management among most, or all, managers and personnel.

A motivator, then, is something that influences an individual's behavior. It makes a difference in what a person will do. Obviously, in any organized enterprise, managers must be concerned about motivators and also inventive in their use. People can often satisfy their wants in a variety of ways. A person can, for example, satisfy a desire for affiliation by being active in a social club rather than in a business, meet economic needs by performing a job just well enough to get by, or satisfy status needs by spending time working for a political party. What a manager must do, of course, is use those motivators which will lead people to perform effectively for the enterprise that employs them. No manager can expect to hire the whole person, since people always have desires and drives outside the enterprise. But if a company or any other kind of enterprise is to be efficient and successful, enough of every person's drives must be stimulated and satisfied to ensure effective performance.

Difference between motivation and satisfaction Motivation refers to the drive and effort to satisfy a want or goal. **Satisfaction** refers to the contentment experienced when a want is satisfied. In other words, motivation implies a drive toward an outcome, and satisfaction is the outcome already experienced, as shown in Figure 15-2.

From a management point of view, then, a person might have high job satisfaction but a low level of motivation for the job, or the reverse might be true. Understandably, the probability exists that highly motivated persons with low job satisfaction will look for other positions. Likewise, people who find their positions rewarding but are being paid considerably less than they desire or think they deserve will probably search for other jobs.

Figure 15-2

DIFFERENCES BETWEEN MOTIVATION AND SATISFACTION.
Motivation is the drive to satisfy a want (achieve an outcome); satisfaction is experienced when the outcome has been achieved.

MOTIVATION: THE CARROT AND THE STICK

The various leading theories of motivation and motivators seldom make reference to the carrot and the stick. This metaphor relates, of course, to the use of rewards and penalties in order to induce desired behavior. It comes from the old story that to make a donkey move, one must put a carrot in front of him or jab him with a stick from behind.

Despite all the research on and theories of motivation that have come to the fore in recent years, reward and punishment are still considered strong motivators. For centuries, however, they were too often thought of as the only forces that could motivate people. As the succeeding sections will explain, there are many other motivators.

At the same time, in all theories of motivation, the inducements of some kind of "carrot" are recognized. Often this is money in the form of pay or bonuses. Even though money is not the only motivating force, it has been and will continue to be an important one. The trouble with the money "carrot" approach is that too often everyone gets a carrot, regardless of performance, through such practices as salary increases and promotion by seniority, automatic "merit" increases, and executive bonuses not based on individual manager performance. It is as simple as this: If a person put a donkey in a pen full of carrots and then stood outside with a carrot, would the donkey be encouraged to come out of the pen?

The "stick," in the form of fear — fear of loss of job, loss of income, reduction of bonus, demotion, or some other penalty — has been and continues to be a strong motivator. Yet it is admittedly not the best kind. It often gives rise to defensive or retaliatory behavior, such as union organization, poor-quality work, executive indifference, failure of a manager to take any risks in decision making, or even dishonesty. But fear of penalty cannot be overlooked. Whether managers are first-level supervisors or chief executives, the power of their position to give or withhold rewards or impose penalties of various kinds gives them an ability to control, to a very great extent, the economic and social well-being of their subordinates. It is hardly a wonder that many subordinates are "yes-sayers," simply agreeing with their superiors rather than using their considered judgment.

THE HIERARCHY OF NEEDS THEORY

One of the most widely mentioned theories of motivation is the hierarchy of needs theory put forth by psychologist Abraham Maslow.[2] Maslow saw human needs in the form of a hierarchy, ascending from the lowest to the highest, and he concluded that when one set of needs is satisfied, this kind of need ceases to be a motivator.

The Needs Hierarchy[3]

The basic human needs placed by Maslow in an ascending order of importance and shown in Figure 15-3 are these:

1. **Physiological needs** These are the basic needs for sustaining human life itself, such as food, water, warmth, shelter, and sleep. Maslow took the position that until these needs are satisfied to the degree necessary to maintain life, other needs will not motivate people.

2. **Security, or safety, needs** These are the needs to be free of physical danger and of the fear of losing a job, property, food, or shelter.

Figure 15-3

Need for self-actualization

Esteem needs

Affiliation or acceptance needs

Security or safety needs

Physiological needs

MASLOW'S HIERARCHY OF NEEDS.

3. **Affiliation, or acceptance, needs** Since people are social beings, they need to belong, to be accepted by others.

4. **Esteem needs** According to Maslow, once people begin to satisfy their need to belong, they tend to want to be held in esteem both by themselves and by others. This kind of need produces such satisfactions as power, prestige, status, and self-confidence.

5. **Need for self-actualization** Maslow regards this as the highest need in his hierarchy. It is the desire to become what one is capable of becoming — to maximize one's potential and to accomplish something.

Questioning the Needs Hierarchy

Maslow's concept of a hierarchy of needs has been subjected to considerable research. Edward Lawler and J. Lloyd Suttle collected data on 187 managers in two different organizations over a period of 6 to 12 months.[4] They found little evidence to support Maslow's theory that human needs form a hierarchy. They did note, however, that there were two levels of needs — biological and other needs — and that the other needs would emerge only when biological needs were reasonably satisfied. They found, further, that at the higher level, the strength of needs varied with the individual; in some individuals social needs predominated, while in others self-actualization needs were strongest.

In another study of Maslow's needs hierarchy involving a group of managers over a period of 5 years, Douglas T. Hall and Khalil Nougaim did not find strong evidence of a hierarchy.[5] They found that as managers advance in an organization, their physiological and safety needs tend to decrease in importance and their needs for affiliation, esteem, and self-actualization tend to increase. They insisted, however, that the upward movement of need prominence resulted from upward career changes and not from the satisfaction of lower-order needs.

THE MOTIVATION-HYGIENE APPROACH TO MOTIVATION

Maslow's need approach has been considerably modified by Frederick Herzberg and his associates.[6] Their research purports to find a **two-factor theory** of motivation. In one group of needs are such things as company policy and administration, supervision, working conditions, interpersonal relations, salary, status, job security, and personal life. These were found by Herzberg and his associates to be only **dissatisfiers** and not motivators. In other words, if they exist in a work environment in high quantity and quality, they yield no dissatisfaction. Their existence does not motivate in the sense of yielding satisfaction; their lack of existence would, however, result in dissatisfaction. Herzberg called them *maintenance, hygiene,* or *job context factors.*

In the second group, Herzberg listed certain **satisfiers** — and therefore motivators — all related to *job content.* They include achievement, recognition, challenging work, advancement, and growth in the job. Their existence will yield feelings of satisfaction or no satisfaction (not dissatisfaction). As Figure 15-4 indicates, the satisfiers and dissatisfiers identified by Herzberg are similar to the factors suggested by Maslow.

The first group of factors (the dissatisfiers) will not motivate people in an organization; yet they must be present, or dissatisfaction will arise. The second group, or the job content factors, Herzberg found to be the real motivators because they have the potential of yielding a sense of satisfaction. Clearly, if this theory of motivation is sound, managers must give considerable attention to upgrading job content.

The Herzberg research has not gone unchallenged.[7] Some researchers question Herzberg's methods, saying that his investigation methods tended to prejudice his results. For example, the well-known tendency of people to attribute good results to their own efforts and to blame others for poor results is thought to have prejudiced Herzberg's findings. Other researchers, not following his methods, have arrived at conclusions that do not support Herzberg's theory.

Figure 15-4

COMPARISON OF MASLOW'S AND HERZBERG'S THEORIES OF MOTIVATION.

THE EXPECTANCY THEORY OF MOTIVATION

Another approach, one that many believe goes far in explaining how people are motivated, is the **expectancy theory.** One of the leaders in advancing and explaining this theory is the psychologist Victor H. Vroom. He holds that people will be motivated to do things to reach a goal if they believe in the worth of that goal and if they can see that what they do will help them in achieving it.[8] In a sense, this is a modern expression of what Martin Luther observed centuries ago when he said, "Everything that is done in the world is done in hope."

In greater detail, Vroom's theory is that people's motivation toward doing anything will be determined by the value they place on the outcome of their effort (whether positive or negative), multiplied by the confidence they have that their efforts will materially aid in achieving a goal. In other words, Vroom makes the point that motivation is a product of the anticipated worth that an individual places on a goal and the chances he or she sees of achieving that goal. Using his own terms, Vroom's theory may be stated as

Force = valence × expectancy

where **force** is the strength of a person's motivation, **valence** is the strength of an individual's preference for an outcome, and **expectancy** is the probability that a particular action will lead to a desired outcome. When a person is indifferent about achieving a certain goal, a valence of zero occurs; there is a negative valence when the person would rather not achieve the goal. The result of either would be, of course, no motivation. Likewise, a person would have no motivation to achieve a goal if the expectancy were zero or negative. The force exerted to do something will depend on *both* valence and expectancy. Moreover, a motive to accomplish some action might be determined by a desire to accomplish something else. For example, a person might be willing to work hard to get out a product for a valence in the form of pay. Or a manager might be willing to work hard to achieve company goals in marketing or production for a promotion or pay valence.

The Vroom Theory and Practice

One of the great attractions of the Vroom theory is that it recognizes the importance of various individual needs and motivations. It thus avoids some of the simplistic features of the Maslow and Herzberg approaches. It does seem more realistic. It fits the concept of harmony of objectives (explained in Chapter 14): Individuals have personal goals different from organizational goals, but these can be harmonized. Furthermore, Vroom's theory is completely consistent with the system of managing by objectives.

The strength of Vroom's theory is also its weakness. His assumption that senses of value vary among individuals at different times and in various places appears to fit real life more accurately. It is consistent also with the idea that a manager's job is to *design* an environment for performance, necessarily taking into account the differences in various situations. On the other hand, Vroom's theory is difficult to apply in practice. Despite its difficulty in application, the logical accuracy of Vroom's theory indicates that motivation is much more complex than the approaches of Maslow and Herzberg seem to imply.

The Porter and Lawler Model

Lyman W. Porter and Edward E. Lawler III derived a substantially more complete model of motivation, built in large part on expectancy theory. In their study, they have applied this model primarily to managers.[9] It is summarized in Figure 15-5.

As this model indicates, the amount of effort (the strength of motivation and energy exerted) depends on the value of a reward plus the amount of energy a person believes is required and the probability of receiving the reward. The perceived effort and probability of actually getting a reward are, in turn, also influenced by the record of actual performance. Clearly, if people know they can do a job or if they have done it, they have a better appreciation of the effort required and know better the probability of rewards.

Actual performance in a job (the doing of tasks or the meeting of goals) is determined principally by effort expended. But it is also greatly influenced by an individual's ability (knowledge and skills) to do the job and by his or her perception of what the required task is (the extent to which the person understands the goals, required activities, and other elements of a task). Performance, in turn, is seen as leading to intrinsic rewards (such as a sense of accomplishment or self-actualization) and extrinsic rewards (such as working conditions and status). These rewards, tempered by what the individual sees as equitable, lead to satisfaction. But performance also influences sensed equitable rewards. Understandably, what the individual sees as a fair reward for effort will necessarily affect the satisfaction derived. Likewise, the actual value of rewards will be influenced by satisfaction.

Implications for Practice

The Porter and Lawler model of motivation, while more complex than other theories of motivation, is almost certainly a more adequate portrayal of the system of motivation. To the practicing manager, this model means that motivation is not a simple cause and effect matter. It means, too, that managers should carefully assess their reward structures and that through careful planning, managing by objectives, and clearly defining duties and responsibilities through a good organization structure, the effort-performance-reward-satisfaction system can be integrated into an entire system of managing.

Figure 15-5

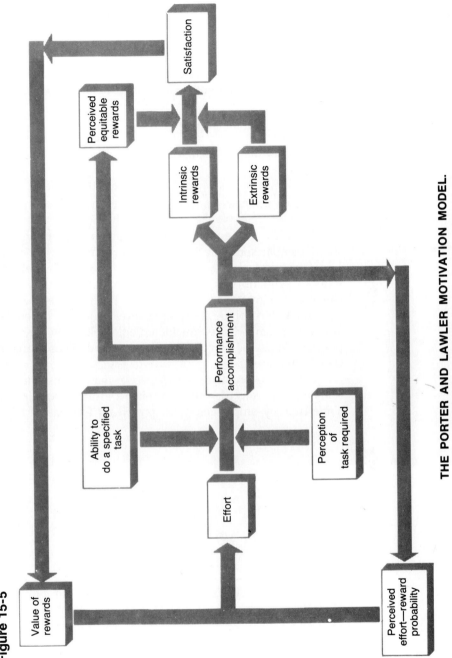

THE PORTER AND LAWLER MOTIVATION MODEL.

Adapted from L. W. Porter and E. E. Lawler, *Managerial Attitudes and Performance* (Homewood, Ill.: Richard D. Irwin, Inc., 1968), p. 165.

EQUITY THEORY

An important factor in motivation is whether individuals perceive the reward structure as being fair. One way of addressing this issue is through **equity theory,** which refers to an individual's subjective judgments about the fairness of the reward she or he got, relative to the inputs (which include many factors such as effort, experience, education, and so on), in comparison with the rewards of others. J. Stacy Adams has received a great deal of credit for the formulation of the equity (or inequity) theory.[10] The essential aspects of the equity theory may be shown as follows:

$$\frac{\text{Outcomes by a person}}{\text{Inputs by a person}} = \frac{\text{outcomes by another person}}{\text{inputs by another person}}$$

There should be a balance of the outcomes-inputs relationship for one person in comparison with that for another person.

If people feel they are inequitably rewarded, they may be dissatisfied, reduce the quantity or quality of output, or leave the organization. They also can ask for a greater reward. If people perceive the rewards as equitable, they probably will continue at the same level of output. If people think the rewards are greater than what is considered equitable, they may work harder. It is also possible that some may discount the reward. These three situations are illustrated in Figure 15-6.

One of the problems is that people may overestimate their own contributions and the rewards others receive. Certain inequities may be tolerated for some time by employees.[11] But prolonged feelings of inequity may result in

Figure 15-6

EQUITY THEORY.

strong reactions to an apparently minor occurrence. For example, an employee-being reprimanded for being a few minutes late may get angry and decide to quit the job, not so much because of the reprimand but because of long-standing feelings that the rewards for his or her contributions are inequitable in comparison with others' rewards. Likewise, a person may be very satisfied with a weekly salary of $500 until he or she finds out that another person doing similar work gets $10 more.

REINFORCEMENT THEORY

Psychologist B. F. Skinner of Harvard developed an interesting — but controversial — technique for motivation. This approach, called **positive reinforcement** or **behavior modification,**[12] holds that individuals can be motivated by proper design of their work environment and praise for their performance and that punishment for poor performance produces negative results.

Skinner and his followers do far more than praise good performance. They analyze the work situation to determine what causes workers to act the way they do, and then they initiate changes to eliminate troublesome areas and obstructions to performance. Specific goals are then set with workers' participation and assistance, prompt and regular feedback of results is made available, and performance improvements are rewarded with recognition and praise. Even when performance does not equal goals, ways are found to help people and praise them for the good things they do. It has also been found highly useful and motivating to give people full information on a company's problems, especially those in which they are involved.

This technique sounds almost too simple to work, and many behavioral scientists and managers are skeptical about its effectiveness. However, a number of prominent companies have found the approach beneficial. Emery Air Freight Corporation, for example, observed that this approach saved the company a substantial amount of money by merely inducing employees to take great pains to ensure that containers were properly filled with small packages before shipment.[13]

Perhaps the strength of the Skinner approach is that it is so closely akin to the requirements of good managing. It emphasizes removal of obstructions to performance, careful planning and organizing, control through feedback, and the expansion of communication.

McCLELLAND'S NEEDS THEORY OF MOTIVATION

David C. McClelland has contributed to the understanding of motivation by identifying three types of basic motivating needs.[14] He classified them as the need for power (n/PWR), need for affiliation (n/AFF), and need for achievement (n/ACH). Considerable research has been done on methods of testing people with respect to these three types of needs, and McClelland and his associates have done substantial research, especially on the need for achievement.[15]

All three drives — power, affiliation, and achievement — are of particular relevance to management, since all must be recognized to make an organized enterprise work well. Because any organized enterprise and every department in it represents groups of individuals working together to achieve goals, the need for achievement is of paramount importance.

Need for Power

McClelland and other researchers have found that people with a high need for power have a great concern for exercising influence and control.[16] Such individuals generally are seeking positions of leadership; they are frequently good conversationalists, though often argumentative; they are forceful, outspoken, hardheaded, and demanding; and they enjoy teaching and public speaking.

Need for Affiliation

People with a high need for affiliation usually derive pleasure from being loved and tend to avoid the pain of being rejected by a social group. As individuals, they are likely to be concerned with maintaining pleasant social relationships, to enjoy a sense of intimacy and understanding, to be ready to console and help others in trouble, and to enjoy friendly interaction with others.

Need for Achievement[17]

People with a high need for achievement have an intense desire for success and an equally intense fear of failure. They want to be challenged, and they set moderately difficult (but not impossible) goals for themselves. They take a realistic approach to risk; they are not likely to be gamblers but, rather, prefer to analyze and assess problems, assume personal responsibility for getting a job done, and like specific and prompt feedback on how they are doing. They tend to be restless, like to work long hours, do not worry unduly about failure if it does occur, and tend to like to run their own shows.

How McClelland's Approach Applies to Managers

In research studies by McClelland and others, entrepreneurs — people who start and develop a business or other enterprise — showed very high need-for-achievement and fairly high need-for-power drives but were quite low in their need for affiliation. Managers generally showed high on achievement and power and low on affiliation, but not as high or low as entrepreneurs.

McClelland found the patterns of achievement motivation clearest in people in small companies, with the president normally having very high achievement motivation. In large companies, interestingly enough, he found chief executives to be only average in achievement motivation and often stronger in drives for power and affiliation. Managers in the upper-middle level of management in such companies rated higher than their presidents in achievement motivation. Perhaps, as McClelland indicated, these scores are understandable. The chief executive has "arrived," and those below are striving to advance.

The question is often raised as to whether all managers should rate high on achievement motivation. People who do rate high tend to advance faster than those who do not. But because so much of managing requires other characteristics besides achievement drive, every company should probably have many managers who, while possessing fairly strong achievement motivation, also have a high need for affiliation. This latter need is important for working with people and for coordinating the efforts of individuals working in groups.

SPECIAL MOTIVATIONAL TECHNIQUES

After looking at the theories of motivation, one may well ask what they mean to managers. What motivational techniques can managers use? While motivation is so complex and individualized that there can be no single best answer, some of the major motivational techniques can be identified.

Money

As mentioned earlier, in the discussion of the carrot and the stick, money can never be overlooked as a motivator. Whether in the form of wages, piecework (getting paid for units produced at a certain quality level) or any other incentive pay, bonuses, stock options, company-paid insurance, or any of the other things that may be given to people for performance, money is important. And, as some writers have pointed out, money is often more than monetary value. It can also mean status or power.

Economists and most managers have tended to place money high on the scale of motivators,[18] while behavioral scientists tend to place it low.[19] Probably neither view is right. But if money is to be the kind of motivator that it can and should be, managers must remember several things.

First, money, as money, is likely to be more important to people who are raising a family, for example, than to people who have "arrived" in the sense that their money needs are not so urgent. Money is an urgent means of achieving a minimum standard of living, although this minimum has a way of getting higher as people become more affluent. For example, an individual who was once satisfied with a small house and low-priced car may now be able to derive the same satisfaction only from a large and comfortable house and a fairly luxurious automobile. And yet it is impossible to generalize in even these terms. For some people money will always be of the utmost importance, while for others it may never be.

Second, it is probably quite true that in most kinds of businesses and other enterprises money is used as a means of keeping an organization adequately

PERSPECTIVE:
THE OTHER SIDE OF THE COIN

The lure of money and power can lead to inappropriate and illegal actions. Ivan F. Boesky has been accused of insider trading that resulted in huge personal profits — and a $100 million fine. The scandal, one of the worst on Wall Street since the 1920s, has shaken public confidence with the fear that stock trading may be rigged.[20] While money is often used for motivating, it also addresses itself to human greed that dulls the conscience and may result in unethical and illegal behavior.

staffed and not primarily as a motivator. Various enterprises make wages and salaries competitive within their industry and their geographic area to attract and hold people.

Third, money as a motivator tends to be dulled somewhat by the practice of making sure that salaries of various managers in a company are reasonably similar. In other words, organizations often take great care to ensure that people on comparable levels are given the same, or nearly the same, compensation. This is understandable, since people usually evaluate their compensation in the light of what their equals are receiving.

Fourth, if money is to be an effective motivator, people in various positions, even though at a similar level, must be given salaries and bonuses that reflect their individual performance. Even if a company is committed to the practice of comparable wages and salaries, a well-managed firm need never be bound to the same practice with respect to bonuses. In fact, it appears that unless bonuses for managers are based to a major extent on individual performance, an enterprise is not buying much motivation with them. The way to ensure that money has meaning, as a reward for accomplishment and as a way of giving people pleasure from accomplishment, is to base compensation as much as possible on performance.

It is almost certainly true that money can motivate only when the prospective payment is large relative to a person's income. The trouble with many wage and salary increases, and even bonus payments, is that they are not large enough to motivate the receiver. They may keep the individual from being dissatisfied and from looking for another job, but unless they are large enough to be felt, they are not likely to be a strong motivator.[21]

Participation

One technique that has been given strong support as the result of motivation theory and research is the increased awareness and use of participation. Only rarely are people not motivated by being consulted on action affecting them — by being "in on the act." In addition, most people in the center of an operation have knowledge both of problems and of solutions to them. As a consequence, the right kind of participation yields both motivation and knowledge valuable for enterprise success.

Participation is also a means of recognition. It appeals to the need for affiliation and acceptance. Above all, it gives people a sense of accomplishment. But encouraging participation should not mean that managers weaken their positions. Although they encourage participation of subordinates on matters with which the latter can help, and although they listen carefully, on matters requiring their decision they must decide themselves. The best subordinates would not have it any other way, and few subordinates ever have respect for a weak superior.

Quality of Working Life (QWL)

One of the most interesting approaches to motivation is the **quality of working life** (QWL) program, which is a systems approach to job design and a promising development in the broad area of job enrichment, combined with a grounding in the sociotechnical systems approach to management. QWL is not only a very broad approach to job enrichment but also an interdisciplinary field of inquiry and action combining industrial and organization psychology and sociology, industrial engineering, organization theory and development, motivation and leadership theory, and industrial relations. Although QWL rose to prominence only in the 1970s, there are now hundreds of case studies and practical programs and a number of QWL centers, primarily in the United States, Great Britain, and Scandinavia.[22]

PERSPECTIVE:
QWL IN ACTION

In the development of a QWL program, certain steps are normally undertaken. Usually, a labor-management steering committee is set up, ordinarily with a QWL specialist or staff, which is charged with finding ways of enhancing the dignity, attractiveness, and productivity of jobs through job enrichment and redesign. The participation of workers and their unions (if an operation is unionized) in the effort is thought to be very important, not only because of the exercise of industrial democracy but also because of the great practical advantage it offers: People on a job are the ones who are best able to identify what would enrich the job for them and make it possible for them to be more productive. This typical QWL technique tends to solve the problem encountered in many job enrichment cases in which workers have mistakenly not been asked what would make the job more interesting for them.

Out of the deliberations of this committee, a number of changes may be suggested in the design of jobs and in the entire working environment. The recommendations of the committee may extend to such matters as reorganization of the organization structure, means of improving communication, problems that may never have surfaced before and their solutions, changes in work arrangements through technical modifications such as the redesign of an assembly line, better quality control, and other things that might improve organization health and productivity.

QWL has received enthusiastic support from a number of sources. Managers have regarded it as a promising means of dealing with stagnating productivity, especially in the United States and Europe. Workers and union representatives have also seen it as a means of improving working conditions and productivity and as a means of justifying higher pay. Government agencies have been attracted to QWL as a means of increasing productivity and reducing inflation and as a way of obtaining industrial democracy and minimizing labor disputes.

It is no wonder that QWL, with such possible important yields, has been spreading fast, especially in larger companies. Nor is it a surprise that leaders in adopting QWL programs should be such well-managed companies as General Motors, Procter & Gamble, American Aluminum (ALCOA), and AT&T.

JOB ENRICHMENT

Research and analysis of motivation point to the importance of making jobs challenging and meaningful. This applies to the jobs of managers as well as to those of nonmanagers. Job enrichment is related to Herzberg's theory of motivation, in which factors such as challenge, achievement recognition, and responsibility are seen as the real motivators. Even though his theory has not gone unchallenged, it has led to a widespread interest, both in the United States and overseas, in developing ways to enrich job content, particularly for nonmanagerial employees.

Job enrichment should be distinguished from job enlargement (but some authors do not make this distinction). **Job enlargement** attempts to make a job more varied by removing the dullness associated with performing repetitive operations. It means enlarging the scope of the job by adding similar tasks without enhancing responsibility. For example, a production line worker may install not only the bumper on a car but also the front hood. Critics would say that this is simply adding one dull job to another, since it does not increase the worker's responsibility. In **job enrichment,** the attempt is to build into jobs a higher sense of challenge and achievement. A job may be enriched by variety. But it also may be enriched by (1) giving workers more freedom in deciding about such things as work methods, sequence, and pace or the acceptance or rejection of materials; (2) encouraging participation of subordinates and interaction between workers; (3) giving workers a feeling of personal responsibility for their tasks; (4) taking steps to make sure that workers can see how their tasks contribute to a finished product and the welfare of an enterprise; (5) giving people feedback on their job performance, preferably before their supervisors get it; and (6) involving workers in the analysis and change of physical aspects of the work environment, such as layout of office or plant, temperature, lighting, and cleanliness.

The Claims of Job Enrichment

A number of companies have introduced programs of job enrichment. The first company to do so on a fairly large scale was Texas Instruments, and other companies, such as AT&T, Procter & Gamble, and General Foods, have had considerable experience with it. In all these companies, claims have been made that productivity was increased, that absenteeism and turnover were reduced, and that morale improved.

Perhaps the most glowing claims for job enrichment are contained in the 1973 report of a study made by the U.S. Department of Health, Education, and Welfare.[23] As the result of an analysis of worker attitudes and the quality of working life, this study concluded that (1) the primary cause of dissatisfaction of workers is the nature of their work — the quality of their working life — and (2) blue-collar workers will work harder if their jobs are enriched and expanded so as to give them greater control over their work and more freedom from their supervisor.

Limitations of Job Enrichment

Even the strongest supporters of job enrichment readily admit that there are limitations in its application.[24] One of these is technology. With specialized machinery and assembly line techniques, it may not be possible to make all jobs very meaningful. Another limitation is cost. General Motors tried six-person and three-person teams in the assembly of motor homes but found that this approach was too difficult, slow, and costly. On the other hand, two Swedish auto manufacturers, Saab and Volvo, have used the team approach and have found costs to be only slightly higher, and they believe that this increase was more than offset by reductions in absenteeism and turnover. Another problem has been the difficulty of enriching any job that requires low levels of skill.

There is also some question as to whether workers really want job enrichment, especially of the kind that changes the basic content of their jobs. Various surveys of worker attitudes, even the attitudes of assembly line workers, have shown that a high percentage of workers are not dissatisfied with their jobs and that few want "more interesting" jobs. What these workers seem to want above all is job security and pay. Moreover, workers are concerned that changing the nature of the task to increase productivity may mean a loss of jobs.

The limitations of job enrichment apply mainly to jobs requiring low skill levels. The jobs of highly skilled workers, professionals, and managers already contain varying degrees of challenge and accomplishment. Perhaps these could be enriched considerably more than they are. But this can probably be done best by modern management techniques such as managing by objectives, utilizing more policy guidance with delegation of authority, introducing more status symbols in the form of titles and office facilities, and tying bonuses and other rewards more closely to performance.

Problems with Job Enrichment

On the surface, job enrichment as a response to motivating factors is an attractive idea, but it apparently has not worked as well as anticipated. There do seem to be a number of problems in the way it has been approached.

One of the major problems appears to be the tendency of top managers and personnel specialists to apply their own scale of values for challenge and accomplishment to other people's personalities. Some people are challenged by jobs that would appear dull to many others. In one company, an employee who had spent his life doing no more than keeping daily records of orders received honestly felt he had one of the most important jobs in the company. In another business, a woman who had a job-enriched position with a variety of tasks told her supervisor that she was greatly relieved to be freed of such responsibility when she was given a repetitive assembly line job. Similarly, a woman who was found to have considerable leadership ability in her outside activities with the Girl Scouts and Parent Teacher Association turned down a supervisory position because her present job allowed her to think about the problems and programs she was interested in outside the company.

Another difficulty is that job enrichment is usually imposed on people; they are told about it, rather than being asked whether they would like it and how their jobs could be made more interesting. This appeared to be, at least in part, the problem General Motors encountered in enlarging the jobs of assembly line workers at the Vega plant in Lordstown, where workers interpreted the attempts to make jobs more varied and meaningful as only a scheme of the company to get them to work harder. One should never overlook the importance of consultation, of getting people involved.

Also, there has been little or no support of job enrichment by union leaders. If job enrichment were so important to workers, it would probably be translated into union demands, a move that apparently has seldom occurred.

Making Job Enrichment Effective

Several approaches can be used to make job enrichment appeal to higher-level motivations. First, organizations need a better understanding of what people want. As a number of motivation researchers have pointed out, wants vary with people and situations. Research has shown that workers with few skills want such factors as job security, pay, benefits, less restrictive plant rules, and more sympathetic and understanding supervisors. As people move up the ladder in an enterprise, they find that other factors become increasingly important. But little job enrichment research has been done on high-level professionals and managers.

Second, if productivity increases are the main goal of enrichment, the program must show how workers will benefit. For example, in one company with fleets of unsupervised two-person service trucks, a program of giving these employees 25 percent of the cost savings from increased productivity, while still making it clear that the company would profit from their efforts, resulted in a startling rise in output and a much greater interest in these jobs.

Third, people like to be involved, to be consulted, and to be given an opportunity to offer suggestions. They like to be considered as people. In one aerospace missile plant, increased morale and productivity, as well as greatly reduced turnover and abseenteeism, resulted from the simple technique of having all employees' names on placards at their workstations and of having each program group — from parts production and assembly to inspection — work in an area in which machines and equipment were painted a different color.

Fourth, people like to feel that their managers are truly concerned with their welfare. Workers like to know what they are doing and why. They like feedback on their performance. They like to be appreciated and recognized for their work.

A SYSTEMS AND CONTINGENCY APPROACH TO MOTIVATION

The foregoing analysis of theory, research, and application demonstrates that motivation must be considered from a systems and contingency point of view. Given the complexity of motivating people with individual personalities and in different situations, risks of failure exist when any single motivator, or group of motivators, is applied without taking into account these variables. Human behavior is not a simple matter but must be looked upon as a system of variables and interactions of which certain motivating factors are an important element.

Dependency of Motivation on Organizational Climate

Motivating factors definitely do not exist in a vacuum. Even individual desires and drives are conditioned by physiological needs or by needs arising from a person's background. But what people are willing to strive for is also affected by the organizational climate in which they operate. At times a climate may curb motivations; at other times it may arouse them.

Motivation, Leadership, and Managership

The interaction of motivation and organizational climate not only underscores the systems aspects of motivation but also emphasizes how motivation both depends on and influences leadership styles and management practice. Leaders and managers (who, if effective, will almost certainly be leaders) must respond to the motivations of individuals if they are to design an environment in which people will perform willingly.[25] Likewise, they can design a climate that will arouse or reduce motivation. Styles of leadership will be discussed in Chapter 16.

As for the ways and means by which managers design an environment for performance, they are really the subject of this entire book. In short, managers do this when they see that verifiable goals are set, strategies are developed and communicated, and plans to achieve objectives are made. They do it also in designing a system of organizational roles in which people can be effective. (It should be pointed out in this connection that "organization structure" is not used here in the restrictive bureaucratic sense.) Managers do it also when they make sure that the structure is well staffed. Their styles of leadership and their ability to solve communication problems are also central to managing. And managers do much to create an effective environment when they make sure that control tools, information, and approaches furnish people with the feedback knowledge they must have for effective motivation.

SUMMARY

Motivation is not a simple concept; instead, motivation pertains to various drives, desires, needs, wishes, and other forces. Managers motivate by providing an environment that induces organization members to contribute. The need-want-satisfaction chain is somewhat oversimplified. Indeed, motives are often conflicting.

Maslow's theory holds that human needs form a hierarchy ranging from the lowest-order needs (physiological needs) to the highest-order need (the need for self-actualization). According to Herzberg's two-factor theory, there are two sets of motivating factors. In one set are the dissatisfiers, which are related to the job context (circumstances, conditions). The absence of these factors results in dissatisfaction. In the other set are the satisfiers, or motivators, which are related to the content of the job.

Vroom's expectancy theory of motivation suggests that people are motivated to reach a goal if they think that the goal is worthwhile and can see that their activities will help them achieve the goal. The Porter and Lawler model has many variables. Essentially, performance is a function of ability, the perception of the task required, and effort. Effort is influenced by the value of rewards and the perceived effort-reward probability. Performance accomplishment, in turn, is related to rewards and satisfaction.

Equity theory refers to an individual's subjective judgment about the fairness of the reward received for inputs in comparison with the rewards of others. Reinforcement theory was developed by Skinner, who suggested that people are motivated by praise of desirable behavior; people should participate in setting their goals and should receive regular feedback with recognition and praise. McClelland's theory is based on the need for power, the need for affiliation, and the need for achievement.

Special motivational techniques include using money, encouraging participation, and improving the quality of working life (QWL). Job enrichment aims at making jobs challenging and meaningful. Although there have been some successes, certain limitations must not be overlooked.

The complexity of motivation requires a contingency approach that takes into account the environmental factors, including the organizational climate.

KEY IDEAS AND CONCEPTS FOR REVIEW

Motivation
Need-want-satisfaction chain
Motivators
Maslow's needs hierarchy
Herzberg's motivation-hygiene approach
Vroom's expectancy theory
Porter and Lawler's motivation model

Equity theory
Positive reinforcement
Behavior modification
McClelland's needs theory
Quality of working life (QWL)
Job enrichment
Organizational climate and motivation

FOR DISCUSSION

1. What is motivation? How does effective managing take advantage of, and contribute to, motivation?

2. Why is the need-want-satisfaction chain too simplified an explanation of motivation?

3. Why has the Maslow theory of needs been criticized? To what extent, if any, is it valid?

4. Compare and contrast the Maslow and Herzberg theories of motivation. On what grounds has the Herzberg theory been criticized? Why would you suspect that Herzberg's approach has been so popular with practicing managers?

5. Explain Vroom's expectancy theory of motivation. How is it different from the Porter and Lawler approach? Which appeals to you as being more accurate? Which is more useful in practice?

6. Explain McClelland's theory of motivation. How does it fit into a systems approach? What does the impact of organizational climate show?

7. "You cannot motivate managers. They are self-propelled. You just get out of their way if you really want performance." Comment.

8. To what extent, and how, is money an effective motivator?

9. What motivates you in striving toward excellence in your work at school? Are these motivating forces shown in any of the models discussed in this chapter?

EXERCISES/ACTION STEPS

1. The instructor may take a survey in the class and ask the students to respond to two questions: (1) "Can you describe in detail when you felt exceptionally good about your job?" and (2) "Can you describe in detail when you felt exceptionally bad about your job?" Students should write

their answers on a sheet of paper. Then each individual should be encouraged to share his or her good and bad work experiences with the class. The instructor can classify these responses according to Herzberg's two-factor theory and point out the weakness in this research design.

2. Collect information on an organization you know, and identify the reasons why people contribute to the goals of the enterprise.

CASE:
CONSOLIDATED MOTORS CORPORATION

One of the problems that had long concerned the top managers of the Consolidated Motors Corporation was the lack of workers' interest in doing their jobs on both the components and the final car assembly lines, with the result that quality had to be ensured by the inspection department. For the problem of cars that could not pass final inspection, the company's only solution was to set up groups of highly skilled mechanics in a special shop where quality problems were fixed at the end of the line. Not only was this costly but it also caused considerable concern, since most of the problems were the result of carelessness in assembling components and of the design of the automobile itself.

At the urging of the company president, the division general manager called a meeting of his key department heads to see what could be done about the problem.

Bill Burroughs, production manager, claimed that some of the problems were a matter of engineering. He held that if only engineering would design components and the automobile carefully enough, many quality problems would disappear. He also blamed the personnel department for not selecting workers more carefully and for not getting the union business agent involved in the problem. He pointed out especially that there was a high turnover, more than 5 percent per month, among assembly workers and that absenteeism on Mondays often reached 20 percent. His position was that no production department could operate effectively with this kind of labor force.

Charles Wilson, chief engineer, held that the components and cars were engineered well enough. He claimed that if engineering tolerances were any stricter, the fitting of parts would be so difficult and time-consuming that the company's automobiles would be too costly to make.

Alice Turner, the personnel manager, accounted for the personnel problems in several ways. First, she pointed out that her department had little or no control over whom the company hired or kept, in view of the strong labor union the company had. Second, she observed that assembly work was dull, deadening drudgery and that the company should not expect people to have much interest in this work beyond their paychecks.

But Ms. Turner did say she was convinced that the company could develop more worker interest, and consequently higher-quality work and less absenteeism and turnover, if assembly jobs were enlarged. When asked for suggestions, Ms. Turner recommended that the company do two things: (1) Have each worker handle several operations on the assembly line, with employees working in teams, instead of doing only one simple task, and (2) rotate workers each week from one location on the line to a completely different one in order to give them new and more challenging work.

These suggestions were adopted and put into effect. To everyone's surprise, the workers expressed great dissatisfaction with the new program. After a week, the assembly lines were closed down by a strike. The workers claimed that the new program was only a management scheme to get them to do more work than they had done before and to train them to replace other workers without any increase in pay.

The division manager and the personnel manager were surprised. When asked by the division manager what had happened, Ms.

Turner could only say: "This is a mystery to me. We make their jobs more interesting, and they strike!"

1. What do you believe went wrong with the program?

2. What would you have done if you had been the personnel manager? Would you have used this program, a different one, or none at all? Why?

REFERENCES

1. Most of the recommendations are based on *The George Odiorne Letter,* (Nov. 8, 1985).

2. Abraham Maslow, *Motivation and Personality* (New York: Harper & Row, 1954).

3. A variation of Maslow's hierarchy of needs theory of motivation has been suggested by Clayton P. Alderfer, which he refers to as the ERG (existence, relatedness, and growth) theory of needs. See his *Existence, Relatedness, and Growth: Human Needs in Organizational Settings* (New York: The Free Press, 1972).

4. Edward Lawler III and J. Lloyd Suttle, "A Causal Correlation Test of the Need-Hierarchy Concept," *Organizational Behavior and Human Performance* (April 1972), pp. 265–287.

5. Douglas T. Hall and Khalil Nougaim, "An Examination of Maslow's Hierarchy in an Organization Setting," *Organizational Behavior and Human Performance* (February 1968), pp. 12–35. For an additional evaluation of the need-hierarchy theory, see John B. Miner, *Theories of Organizational Behavior* (Hinsdale, Ill.: The Dryden Press, 1980), chap. 2.

6. Frederick Herzberg, Bernard Mausner, Robert A. Peterson, and D. Capwell, *Job Attitudes: Review of Research and Opinion* (Pittsburgh: Psychological Services of Pittsburgh, 1957); Frederick Herzberg, Bernard Mausner, and Barbara B. Snyderman, *The Motivation to Work* (New York: John Wiley & Sons, 1959).

7. See, for example, H. Randolph Bobbitt and O. Behling, "Defense Mechanism as an Alternate Explanation of Herzberg's Motivator-Hygiene Results," *Journal of Applied Psychology* (January 1972), pp. 24–27; D. A. Ondrack, "Defense Mechanism and the Herzberg Theory: An Alternate Test," *Academy of Management Journal* (March 1974), pp. 79–89; Edwin

A. Locke and Roman J. Whiting, "Sources of Satisfaction and Dissatisfaction among Solid Waste Management Employees," *Journal of Applied Psychology* (April 1974), pp. 145–156.

8. Victor H. Vroom, *Work and Motivation* (New York: John Wiley & Sons, 1964). See also David A. Nadler and Edward E. Lawler III, "Motivation: A Diagnostic Approach," In J. Richard Hackman, Edward E. Lawler III, and Lyman W. Porter (eds.), *Perspectives on Behavior in Organizations,* 2d ed. (New York: McGraw-Hill Book Company, 1983), pp. 67–87.

9. Lyman W. Porter and Edward E. Lawler III, *Managerial Attitudes and Performance* (Homewood, Ill.: Richard D. Irwin, 1968); Cynthia M. Pavett, "Evaluation of the Impact of Feedback on Performance and Motivation," *Human Relations* (July 1983), pp. 641–654.

10. J. Stacy Adams, "Toward an Understanding of Inequity," *Journal of Abnormal and Social Psychology* vol. 67 (1963), pp. 422–436; J. Stacy Adams, "Inequity in Social Exchange," in L. Berkowitz (ed.), *Advances in Experimental Social Psychology* (New York: Academic Press, 1965), pp. 267–299.

11. Richard A. Cosier and Dan R. Dalton, "Equity Theory and Time: A Reformulation," *Academy of Management Review* (April 1983), pp. 311–319. See also Richard C. Huseman, John D. Hatfield, and Edward W. Miles, "A New Perspective on Equity Theory: The Equity Sensitivity Construct," *Academy of Management Review* (April 1987), pp. 222–234.

12. Fred Luthans and Robert Kreitner, *Organizational Behavior Modification and Beyond: An Operant and Social Learning Approach* (Glenview, Ill.: Scott, Foresman and Company, 1984).

13. For an extensive discussion of the benefits of behavior modification, see W. Clay Hamner and

Ellen P. Hamner, "Behavior Modification on the Bottom Line," in J. Richard Hackman et al., *Perspectives on Behavior* (1983), pp. 310–324.

14. David C. McClelland, *The Achievement Motive* (New York: Appleton-Century-Crofts, 1953), *Studies in Motivation* (New York: Appleton-Century-Crofts, 1955), and *The Achieving Society* (Princeton, N.J.: Van Nostrand Company, 1961). See also his "Achievement Motivation Can be Developed," *Harvard Business Review* (January–February 1965), pp. 6–24, 178, and (with David G. Winter) *Motivating Economic Achievement* (New York: The Free Press, 1969).

15. For a thorough evaluation of the theory, see John B. Miner, *Theories of Organizational Behavior* (1980), chap. 3.

16. See, for example, David C. McClelland and David H. Burnham, "Power Is the Great Motivator," *Harvard Business Review* (March–April 1976), pp. 100–110.

17. David C. McClelland, "That Urge to Achieve," in Max D. Richards (ed.), *Readings in Management,* 7th ed. (Cincinnati: South-Western Publishing Company, 1986), pp. 367–375.

18. See Aaron Bernstein and Michael A. Pollock, "Executive Pay: Who Made the Most," *Business Week* (May 5, 1985), pp. 78–103.

19. George S. Odiorne, "When Money Has Lost Its Motivational Power, What Else Can You Use to Motivate Your People?" *The George Odiorne Letter* (Mar. 21, 1986), pp. 1–3.

20. William B. Glaberson, Jeffrey M. Laderman, Christopher Power, and Vicky Cahan, "Who'll Be the Next to Fall?" *Business Week* (Dec. 1, 1986), pp. 28–30; Chris Welles and Gary Weiss, "A Man Who Made a Career of Tempting Fate," *Business Week* (Dec. 1, 1986), pp. 34–35.

21. For a discussion of a compensation plan, see Jay R. Schuster, "Compensation Plan Design," *Management Review* (May 1985), pp. 21–25. Also, more recently, employee ownership has become more common; see J. C. Louis, "Employee Ownership: The Rising Tide," *Management Review* (March 1985), pp. 40–43.

22. For a pioneering work in this field, see Louis E. Davis and Albert B. Cherns, *Quality of Working Life* (New York: The Free Press, 1975). Among the more prominent QWL centers are the Tavistock Institute in Great Britain, under Eric L. Trist; the center at the University of California, Los Angeles, under Louis E. Davis; and the Institute for Social Research in Industry in Trondheim, Norway, under M. Elder.

23. DHEW, *Work in America* (Washington: Government Printing Office, 1973). See also Antone Alber, "Job Enrichment for Profit," *Human Resource Management* (Spring 1979), pp. 15–25.

24. The appropriateness of job enrichment depends on the situation. The need for balancing internal and external factors has been pointed out by Randall B. Dunham, Jon L. Pierce, and John W. Newstrom, "Job Context and Job Content: A Conceptual Perspective," *Journal of Management* (Fall–Winter 1983), pp. 187–202.

25. Abraham Zaleznik makes a distinction between managers and leaders, but the difference is primarily in the way he describes managers (a rather negative way), which certainly is not our view of an effective manager. See Abraham Zaleznik, "Managers and Leaders: Are They Different?" *Harvard Business Review* (May–June 1986), p. 48.

CHAPTER **16**

Leadership

CHAPTER OBJECTIVES

After reading this chapter, you should understand:

1. The nature and ingredients of leadership
2. The trait approaches to leadership and their limitations
3. The various leadership styles based on the use of authority
4. Likert's four systems of management
5. The two dimensions of Blake and Mouton's managerial grid and the resulting extreme leadership styles
6. Leadership as a continuum, with managerial power and influence ranging from low to high
7. Fiedler's contingency approach to leadership
8. The path-goal approach to leadership effectiveness.

Although some people treat the terms "managership" and "leadership" as synonyms, two should be distinguished. As a matter of fact, there can be leaders of completely unorganized groups, but there can be managers, as conceived here, only where organized structures create roles. Separating leadership from managership has important analytical advantages. It permits leadership to be singled out for study without the encumbrance of qualifications relating to the more general issue of managership.

Leadership is an important aspect of managing. As this chapter will show, the ability to lead effectively is one of the keys to being an effective manager; also, undertaking the other essentials of managing — doing the entire managerial job — has an important bearing on ensuring that a manager will be an effective leader. Managers must exercise all the functions of their role in order to combine human and material resources to achieve objectives. The key to doing this is the existence of a clear role and a degree of discretion or authority to support managers' actions.

The essence of leadership is followership.[1] In other words, it is the willingness of people to follow that makes a person a leader. Moreover, people tend to follow those whom they see as providing a means of achieving their own desires, wants, and needs.

Leadership and motivation are closely interconnected. By understanding motivation, one can appreciate better what people want and why they act as they do. Also, as noted in the previous chapter, leaders may not only respond to subordinates' motivations but also arouse or dampen them by means of the organizational climate they develop. Both these factors are as important to leadership as they are to managership.

DEFINING LEADERSHIP

Leadership has different meanings to various authors.[2] In this book, **leadership** is defined as influence, that is, the art or process of influencing people so that they will strive willingly and enthusiastically toward the achievement of group goals. Ideally, people should be encouraged to develop not only willingness to work but also willingness to work with zeal and confidence. Zeal is ardor, earnestness, and intensity in the execution of work; confidence reflects experience and technical ability. Leaders act to help a group attain objectives through the maximum application of its capabilities. They do not stand behind a group to push and prod; they place themselves before the group as they facilitate progress and inspire the group to accomplish organizational goals. A good example is an orchestra leader, whose function is to produce coordinated sound and correct tempo through the integrated effort of the musicians. Depending upon the quality of the director's leadership, the orchestra will repond.

PERSPECTIVE:
LEADERSHIP AT SOUTHWEST AIRLINES

Let us consider the leadership style of Herbert Kelleher, the chairman of Southwest Airlines.[3] He attempts to create a family feeling among his employees by remembering their names and personally sending out birthday cards. In an attempt to stay competitive in the deregulated airline industry, he asked for, and received, considerable concessions from employees and their union. His hands-on leadership style won him the respect and followership of his employees. The austerity measures apply equally to management and employees. His office, for example, is in a barrack-style building. Leading by example those who follow him, he seems concerned about both the tasks to be done and the people who work for him.

INGREDIENTS OF LEADERSHIP

Leaders envision the future; they inspire organization members and chart the course of the organization. Chrysler's Lee Iacocca and General Electric's Jack Welch have provided a vision for their companies. Leaders must instill values — whether it be concern for quality, honesty, and calculated risk taking or for employees and customers.[4]

Every group of people that performs near its total capacity has some person as its head who is skilled in the art of leadership. This skill seems to be a compound of at least four major ingredients: (1) the ability to use power effectively and in a responsible manner, (2) the ability to comprehend that human beings have different motivation forces at different times and in different situations, (3) the ability to inspire, and (4) the ability to act in a manner that will develop a climate conducive to responding to and arousing motivations.

The first ingredient of leadership is power. The nature of power and the differences between power and authority were discussed in Chapter 9.

The second ingredient of leadership is a fundamental understanding of people. As in all practices, it is one thing to know motivation theory, kinds of motivating forces, and the nature of a system of motivation but another thing to be able to apply this knowledge to people and situations. A manager or any other leader who at least knows the present state of motivation theory and who understands the elements of motivation is more aware of the nature and strength of human needs and is more able to define and design ways of satisfying them and to administer so as to get the desired responses.

The third ingredient of leadership is the rare ability to inspire followers to apply their full capabilities to a project. While the use of motivators seems to center on subordinates and their needs, inspiration also comes from group heads. They may have qualities of charm and appeal that give rise to loyalty, devotion, and a strong desire on the part of followers to promote what leaders want. This is not a matter of need satisfaction; it is, rather, a matter of people giving unselfish support to a chosen champion. The best examples of inspirational leadership come from hopeless and frightening situations: an unprepared nation on the eve of battle, a prison camp with exceptional morale, or a defeated leader undeserted by faithful followers. Some may argue that such devotion is not entirely unselfish, that it is in the interests of those who face catastrophe to follow a person they trust. But few would deny the value of personal appeal in either case.

The fourth ingredient of leadership has to do with the style of the leader and the climate he or she develops. As Chapter 15 has shown, the strength of motivation greatly depends on expectancies, perceived rewards, the amount of effort believed to be required, the task to be done, and other factors which are part of an environment, as well as on organizational climate. Awareness of these factors has led to considerable research on leadership behavior and to the development of various pertinent theories. The views of those who have long approached leadership as a psychological study of interpersonal relationships have tended to converge with the personal viewpoint expressed in this book,

PERSPECTIVE:
CAN LEADERSHIP BE TAUGHT?

A frequently raised question is whether leadership can be taught. Professor Noel Tichy of the University of Michigan estimates that 80 percent of leadership growth derives from experience on the job whereas 20 percent can be acquired through training and study.[5] This, of course, is difficult to prove and depends on the individual, but it points out that on-the-job training and classroom training must go hand in hand. At an early stage in their careers, potential leaders at Johnson & Johnson are given the opportunity to demonstrate their ability to manage one of the company's rather autonomous business units. The idea behind this practice is that a tough assignment can be an opportunity for learning and development.

that is, that the primary tasks of managers are the design and maintenance of an environment for performance.

Almost every role in organized enterprise is made more satisfying for participants and more productive for the enterprise by those who can help others fulfill their desire for such things as money, status, power, or pride of accomplishment. The fundamental **principle of leadership** is this: *Since people tend to follow those who, in their view, offer them a means of satisfying their own personal goals, the more managers understand what motivates their subordinates and how these motivations operate, and the more they reflect this understanding in carrying out their managerial actions, the more effective they are likely to be as leaders.*

Because of the importance of leadership in all kinds of group action, there is a considerable volume of theory and research concerning it.[6] It is difficult to summarize such a large body of research in a form relevant to day-to-day management. However, examined below are several major types of leadership theory and research, together with outlines of some basic kinds of leadership styles.

TRAIT APPROACHES TO LEADERSHIP

Prior to 1949, studies of leadership were based largely on an attempt to identify the traits that leaders possess.[7] Starting with the "great man" theory that leaders are born and not made, a belief dating back to the ancient Greeks and Romans, researchers have tried to identify the physical, mental, and personality traits of various leaders. The "great man" theory lost much of its acceptability with the rise of the behaviorist school of psychology.

Many studies of traits have been made.[8] Ralph M. Stogdill found that various researchers have identified specific traits related to leadership ability: five physical traits (such as energy, appearance, and height), four intelligence and ability traits, sixteen personality traits (such as adaptability, aggressiveness, enthusiasm, and self-confidence), six task-related characteristics (such as achievement drive, persistence, and initiative), and nine social characteristics (such as cooperativeness, interpersonal skills, and administrative ability).[9]

In general, the study of leaders' traits has not been a very fruitful approach to explaining leadership. Not all leaders possess all the traits, and many non-leaders may possess most or all of them. Also, the trait approach gives no guidance as to *how much* of any trait a person should have. Furthermore, the dozens of studies that have been made do not agree as to which traits are leadership traits or what their relationships are to actual instances of leadership. Most of these so-called traits are really patterns of behavior.

LEADERSHIP BEHAVIOR AND STYLES

There are several theories on leadership behavior and styles. This section focuses on (1) leadership based on the use of authority, (2) Likert's four systems of managing, (3) the managerial grid, and (4) leadership involving a variety of styles, ranging from a maximum to a minimum use of power and influence.

Styles Based on Use of Authority

Some earlier explanations of leadership styles classified them on the basis of how leaders use their authority. Leaders were seen as applying three basic styles. The **autocratic leader** commands and expects compliance, is dogmatic and positive, and leads by the ability to withhold or give rewards and punishment. The **democratic,** or **participative,** leader consults with subordinates on proposed actions and decisions and encourages participation from them. This type of leader ranges from the person who does not take action without subordinates' concurrence to the one who makes decisions but consults with subordinates before doing so.

The **free-rein** leader uses his or her power very little, if at all, giving subordinates a high degree of independence in their operations. Such leaders depend largely on subordinates to set their own goals and the means of achieving them, and they see their role as one of aiding the operations of followers by furnishing them with information and acting primarily as a contact with the group's external environment. Figure 16-1 illustrates the flow of influence in the three leadership situations.

There are variations within this simple classification of leadership styles. Some autocratic leaders are seen as "benevolent autocrats." Although they listen considerably to their followers' opinions before making a decision, the decision is their own. They may be willing to hear and consider subordinates' ideas and concerns, but when a decision is to be made, they may be more autocratic than benevolent.

A variation of the participative leader is the person who is supportive. Leaders in this category may look upon their task as not only consulting with followers and carefully considering their opinions but also doing all they can to support subordinates in accomplishing their duties.

The use of any style will depend on the situation. A manager may be highly autocratic in an emergency; one can hardly imagine a fire chief holding a long meeting with the crew to consider the best way of fighting a fire.

Figure 16-1

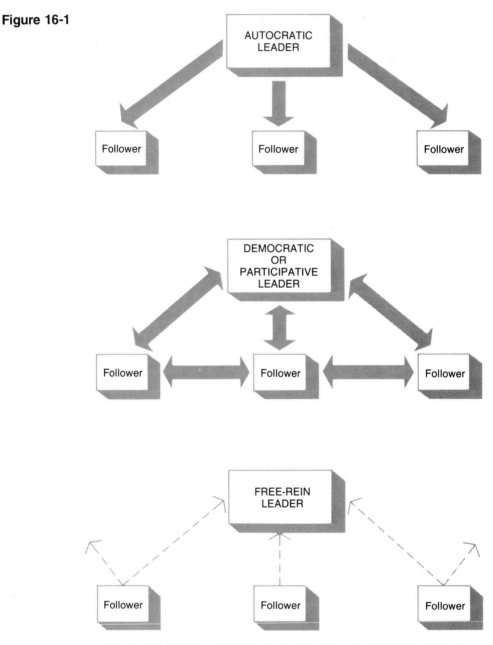

THE FLOW OF INFLUENCE WITH THREE LEADERSHIP STYLES.

Managers may also be autocratic when they alone have the answers to certain questions.

A leader may gain considerable knowledge and a better commitment on the part of persons involved by consulting with subordinates. As already noted, this is true in developing verifiable objectives under systems of managing

PERSPECTIVE:
MANAGEMENT BY WALKING AROUND (MBWA)

Leadership demands information about what is really going on in the organization. Managers who never leave the office, and who rely on formal communication channels, may receive only the information that places subordinates in a favorable light. To overcome their isolation, managers need to supplement the formal communication channels with informal ones.

In their search for excellent companies, Thomas Peters and Robert Waterman noted that managers at United Airlines practice what has been labeled "management by walking around."[10] A similar practice is called "management by wandering around" at Hewlett Packard. The belief is that managers will improve informal communication channels by walking through the plant.

However, a survey of CEOs in *Fortune* 500 enterprises indicated that executives spend little time with lower-level employees.[11] Professor Henry Mintzberg, who previously studied the activities of executives, interpreted the findings as showing that "management by walking around" is not very prevalent in these large companies. Managers spend a lot of time with those who are at similar organizational levels.

by objectives. Furthermore, a manager dealing with a group of research scientists may give them free rein in developing their inquiries and experiments. But the same manager might be quite autocratic in enforcing a rule stipulating that employees wear protective covering when they are handling certain potentially dangerous chemicals.

Likert's Four Systems of Management

Professor Rensis Likert and his associates at the University of Michigan have studied the patterns and styles of leaders and managers for three decades.[12] In the course of this research, Likert has developed certain ideas and approaches important to understanding leadership behavior. He sees an effective manager as strongly oriented to subordinates, relying on communication to keep all parties working as a unit. All members of the group, including the manager or leader, adopt a supportive attitude in which they share in one another's common needs, values, aspirations, goals, and expectations. Since it appeals to human motivations, Likert views this approach as the most effective way to lead a group.

As guidelines for research and for the clarification of his concepts, Likert has suggested four systems of management. **System 1** management is described as "exploitive-authoritative"; its managers are highly autocratic, have little trust in subordinates, motivate people through fear and punishment and only occasional rewards, engage in downward communication, and limit decision making to the top. **System 2** management is called "benevolent-authoritative"; its managers have a patronizing confidence and trust in subordinates, motivate with rewards and some fear and punishment, permit some upward communication, solicit some ideas and opinions from subordinates, and allow some delegation of decision making but with close policy control.

System 3 management is referred to as "consultative." Managers in this system have substantial but not complete confidence and trust in subordinates, usually try to make use of subordinates' ideas and opinions, use rewards for motivation with occasional punishment and some participation, engage in communication flow both down and up, make broad policy and general decisions at the top while allowing specific decisions to be made at lower levels, and act consultatively in other ways.

Likert saw **System 4** management as the most participative of all and referred to it as "participative-group." System 4 managers have complete trust and confidence in subordinates in all matters; they always get ideas and opinions from subordinates and constructively use them. They also give economic rewards on the basis of group participation and involvement in such areas as setting goals and appraising progress toward goals. They engage in much communication down and up and with peers, encourage decision making throughout the organization, and operate among themselves and with their subordinates as a group.

In general, Likert found that those managers who applied the System 4 approach to their operations had greatest success as leaders. Moreover, he noted that departments and companies managed by the System 4 approach were most effective in setting goals and achieving them and were generally more productive. He ascribed this success mainly to the degree of participation and the extent to which the practice of supporting subordinates was maintained.

Figure 16-2 shows the profile of a new manager in a General Motors assembly plant. The organization operated previously in System 3 but moved toward System 4. This manager, aided by the survey feedback improvement approach, used the data of the profile to focus on those areas that needed improvement.

Although there is considerable support for System 4 theory, the approach is not without its critics.[13] The research focus of this theory is on small groups, yet the discussion is frequently extrapolated and applied to the total organization. Furthermore, the research has primarily been conducted at lower organizational levels and may not be supported when data from top-level managers are separated.[14] Likert and his associates realize the need for clarity in role definitions, but at the same time they suggest, for example, matrix departmentation, which usually increases role conflict and uncertainty. Since System 4 is often introduced when companies are profitable, the results attributed to the survey feedback method may actually be due to general prosperity of the firm. It appears, then, that those evaluating System 4 theory should take careful account of the surrounding circumstances. For the practicing manager this means that the benefits attributed to System 4 theory must be viewed with some caution.

The Managerial Grid

A well-known approach to defining leadership styles is the **managerial grid,** developed some years ago by Robert Blake and Jane Mouton.[15] Building on

Figure 16-2

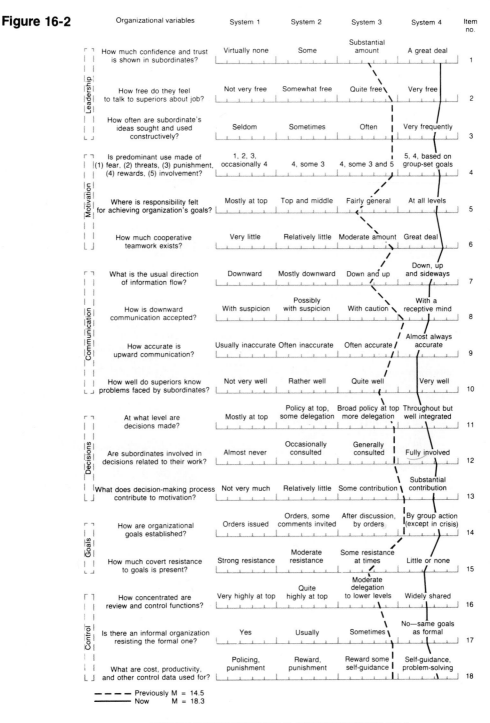

PROFILE OF ORGANIZATIONAL CHARACTERISTICS OF A NEW PLANT MANAGER AT A GENERAL MOTORS PLANT.

R. Likert and J. G. Likert, *New Ways of Managing Conflict* (New York: McGraw-Hill Book Company, 1976), p. 75. Used with permission.

previous research that showed the importance of a manager's having concern both for production and for people, Blake and Mouton devised a clever device to dramatize this concern. This grid, shown in Figure 16-3, has been used throughout the world as a means of training managers and of identifying various combinations of leadership styles.

The grid dimensions   The grid has two dimensions: concern for people and concern for production. As Blake and Mouton have emphasized, the phrase "concern for" is meant to convey "how" managers are concerned about production or "how" they are concerned about people, and not such things as "how much" production they are concerned about getting out of a group.

"Concern for production" includes the attitudes of a supervisor toward a wide variety of things, such as the quality of policy decisions, procedures and

Figure 16-3

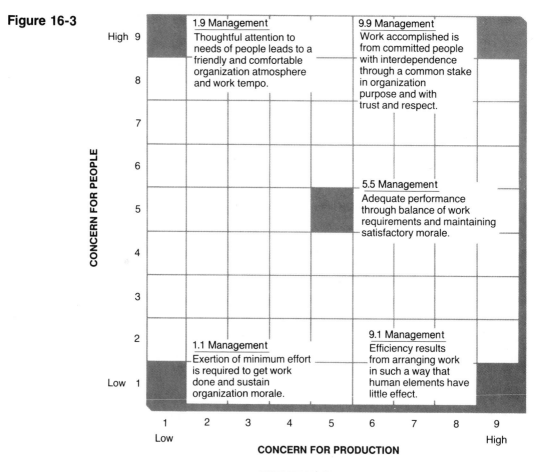

THE MANAGERIAL GRID.

Adapted from R. R. Blake and J. S. Mouton, *The Managerial Grid* (Houston, Texas: Gulf Publishing Company, 1964), p. 10.

processes, creativeness of research, quality of staff services, work efficiency, and volume of output. "Concern for people" is likewise interpreted in a broad way. It includes such elements as degree of personal commitment toward goal achievement, maintenance of the self-esteem of workers, placement of responsibility on the basis of trust rather than obedience, provision of good working conditions, and maintenance of satisfying interpersonal relations.

The four extreme styles Blake and Mouton recognize four extremes of style. Under the **1.1** style (referred to as "impoverished management"), managers concern themselves very little with either people or production and have minimum involvement in their jobs; to all intents and purposes, they have abandoned their jobs and only mark time or act as messengers communicating information from superiors to subordinates. At the other extreme are the **9.9** managers, who display in their actions the highest possible dedication both to people and to production. They are the real "team managers" who are able to mesh the production needs of the enterprise with the needs of individuals.

Another style is **1.9** management (called "country club management" by some), in which managers have little or no concern for production but are concerned only for people. They promote an environment in which everyone is relaxed, friendly, and happy and no one is concerned about putting forth coordinated effort to accomplish enterprise goals. At another extreme are the **9.1** managers (sometimes referred to as "autocratic task managers"), who are concerned only with developing an efficient operation, who have little or no concern for people, and who are quite autocratic in their style of leadership.

By using these four extremes as points of reference, every managerial technique, approach, or style can be placed somewhere on the grid. Clearly, **5.5** managers have medium concern for production and for people. They obtain adequate, but not outstanding, morale and production. They do not set goals too high, and they are likely to have a rather benevolently autocratic attitude toward people.

The managerial grid is a useful device for identifying and classifying managerial styles, but it does not tell us why a manager falls into one part or another of the grid. To determine the reason, one has to look at underlying causes, such as the personality characteristics of the leader or the followers, the ability and training of managers, the enterprise environment, and other situational factors that influence how leaders and followers act.

Leadership as a Continuum

The adaptation of leadership styles to different contingencies has been well characterized by Robert Tannenbaum and Warren H. Schmidt, developers of the **leadership continuum** concept.[16] As Figure 16-4 shows, they see leadership as involving a variety of styles, ranging from one that is highly boss-centered to one that is highly subordinate-centered. The styles vary with the degree of freedom a leader or manager grants to subordinates. Thus, instead of suggesting a choice between the two styles of leadership — authoritarian or

Figure 16-4

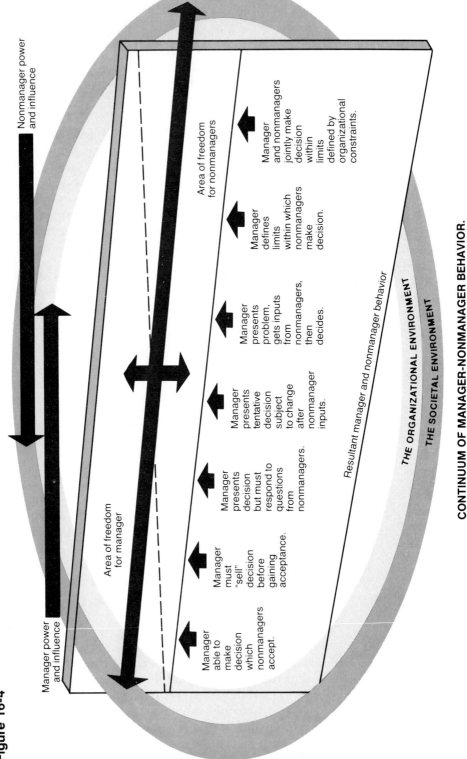

CONTINUUM OF MANAGER-NONMANAGER BEHAVIOR.

Used with permission from Robert Tannenbaum and Warren H. Schmidt, "Retrospective Commentary" on "How to Choose a Leadership Pattern," *Harvard Business Review,* vol. 51, no. 3 (May–June 1973), p. 167.

democratic — this approach offers a range of styles, with no suggestion that one is always right and another is always wrong.

The continuum theory recognizes that which style of leadership is appropriate depends on the leader, the followers, and the situation. To Tannenbaum and Schmidt, the most important elements that may influence a manager's style can be seen along a continuum as (1) the forces operating in the manager's personality, including his or her value system, confidence in subordinates, inclination toward leadership styles, and feelings of security in uncertain situations; (2) the forces in subordinates (such as their willingness to assume responsibility, their knowledge and experience, and their tolerance for ambiguity) that will affect the manager's behavior; and (3) the forces in the situation, such as organization values and traditions, the effectiveness of subordinates working as a unit, the nature of a problem and the feasibility of safely delegating the authority to handle it, and the pressure of time.

In reviewing their continuum model in 1973 (it was first formulated in 1958), Tannenbaum and Schmidt placed circles around the model, as shown in Figure 16-4, to represent the influences on style imposed by both the organizational environment and the societal environment.[17] This was done to emphasize the open-system nature of leadership styles and the various impacts of the organizational environment and of the social environment outside an enterprise. In their 1973 commentary, they put increased stress on the interdependency of leadership style and environmental forces — such as labor unions, greater pressures for social responsibility, the civil rights movement, and the ecology and consumer movements — that challenge the rights of managers to make decisions or handle their subordinates without considering interests outside the organization.

SITUATIONAL, OR CONTINGENCY, APPROACHES TO LEADERSHIP

As disillusionment with the "great man" and trait approaches to understanding leadership increased, attention turned to the study of situations and the belief that leaders are the product of given situations. A large number of studies have been made on the premise that leadership is strongly affected by the situation from which the leader emerges and in which he or she operates. That this is a persuasive approach is indicated by the rise of Hitler in Germany in the 1930s, the earlier rise of Mussolini in Italy, the emergence of Franklin Delano Roosevelt in the Great Depression of the 1930s in the United States, and the rise of Mao Tse-tung in China in the period after World War II. This approach to leadership recognizes that there exists an interaction between the group and the leader. It supports the follower theory that people tend to follow those whom they perceive (accurately or inaccurately) as offering them a means of accomplishing their own personal desires. The leader, then, is the person who recognizes these desires and does those things, or undertakes those programs, designed to meet them.

INTERNATIONAL PERSPECTIVE:
LEADERSHIP AT ITALTEL

In 1981, when Marisa Bellisario became director and CEO of ITALTEL, a state-owned telecommunication equipment manufacturer in Italy, the company was in trouble: high losses, large debts, insufficient research and development, and an overstaffed, unionized organization.[18] Ms. Bellisario took some major steps to turn the company around and to improve productivity. Here are some examples of the new direction:

- Restructuring the organization into business units
- Reducing the number of employees by more than one-third between 1980 and 1985, which was accomplished through open communication and cooperation with the union
- Leading the company into electronics, which required retraining employees
- Developing a program to upgrade low-skilled women in the work force
- Pushing for intra-European cooperation with companies in France, England, and West Germany
- Improving efficiency through innovation in products and manufacturing processes

Leadership such as this has to be analyzed in terms of the characteristics of the leader (technical, human, conceptual, and design skills); good relations with the followers, especially the unionized work force; and the situation, which in the early 1980s demanded a strong leader to deal with the crisis.

Situational, or contingency, approaches obviously have much meaning for managerial theory and practice. They also tie into the system of motivation discussed in Chapter 15, and they are important for practicing managers, who must consider the situation when they design an environment for performance.

Fiedler's Contingency Approach to Leadership

Although their approach to leadership theory is primarily one of analyzing leadership style, Fred E. Fiedler and his associates at the University of Illinois have suggested a **contingency theory of leadership.**[19] The theory holds that people become leaders not only because of the attributes of their personalities but also because of various situational factors and the interactions between leaders and group members.

Critical dimensions of the leadership situation   On the basis of his studies, Fiedler described *three critical dimensions* of the leadership situation that help determine what style of leadership will be most effective:

1. **Position power.** This is the degree to which the power of a position, as distinguished from other sources of power, such as personality or expertise, enables a leader to get group members to comply with directions; in the case of managers, this is the power arising from organizational authority.

As Fiedler points out, a leader with clear and considerable position power can obtain good followership more easily than one without such power.

2. **Task structure.** With this dimension, Fiedler had in mind the extent to which tasks can be clearly spelled out and people held responsible for them. If tasks are clear (rather than vague and unstructured), the quality of performance can be more easily controlled and group members can be held more definitely responsible for performance.

3. **Leader-member relations.** Fiedler regarded this dimension as the most important from a leader's point of view, since position power and task structure may be largely under the control of an enterprise. It has to do with the extent to which group members like and trust a leader and are willing to follow that leader.

Leadership styles   To approach his study, Fiedler set forth two major styles of leadership. One of these is primarily task-oriented, that is, the leader gains satisfaction from seeing tasks performed. The other is oriented primarily toward achieving good interpersonal relations and attaining a position of personal prominence.

Favorableness of situation was defined by Fiedler as the degree to which a given situation enables a leader to exert influence over a group. To measure leadership styles and determine whether a leader is chiefly task-oriented, Fiedler used an unusual testing technique. He based his findings on two sources: (1) scores on the *least preferred coworker* (LPC) scale — these are ratings made by people in a group as to those with whom they would least like to work; and (2) scores on the *assumed similarity between opposites* (ASO) scale — ratings based on the degree to which leaders see group members to be like themselves, on the assumption that people will like best, and work best with, those who are seen as most like themselves. Today the LPC scale is most commonly used in research. In developing this scale, Fiedler asked respondents to identify the traits of a person with whom they could work least well.[20] Respondents described the person by rating sixteen items on a scale of attributes, such as the following:

Pleasant : ___ : ___ : ___ : ___|___ : ___ : ___ : ___ : Unpleasant

Rejecting : ___ : ___ : ___ : ___|___ : ___ : ___ : ___ : Accepting

On the basis of his studies with this method, as well as studies done by others, Fiedler found that people who rated their coworkers high (that is, in favorable terms) were those who derived major satisfaction from successful interpersonal relationships. People who rated their "least preferred coworker" low (that is, in unfavorable terms) were seen as deriving their major satisfaction from task performance.

From his research, Fiedler came to some interesting conclusions. Recognizing that personal perceptions may be unclear and even quite inaccurate, Fiedler nonetheless found the following to be true:

Leadership performance depends as much on the organization as it depends on the leader's own attributes. Except perhaps for the unusual case, it is simply not meaningful to speak of an effective leader or an ineffective leader; we can only speak of a leader who tends to be effective in one situation and ineffective in another. If we wish to increase organizational and group effectiveness we must learn not only how to train leaders more effectively but also how to build an organizational environment in which the leader can perform well.[21]

Fiedler's contingency model of leadership is presented as a graph in Figure 16-5. This figure is really a summary of Fiedler's research, in which he found that in "unfavorable" or "favorable" situations the task-oriented leader would be the most effective. In other words, when leader position power is weak, the task structure is unclear, and leader-member relations are moderately poor, the situation is unfavorable for the leader and the most effective leader will be one who is task-oriented. (Each dot in the graph's lower right-hand corner represents findings from a research study.) At the other extreme, in which position power is strong, the task structure is clear, and leader-member relations are good — a favorable situation for the leader — Fiedler found that the task-oriented leader will also be most effective. However, if the situation is only moderately unfavorable or favorable (the middle of the scale in the figure), the human relations–oriented leader will be most effective.

In a highly structured situation, such as in the military during a war, where the leader has strong position power and good relations with members, there is a favorable situation in which task orientation is most appropriate. The other extreme, an unfavorable situation with moderately poor relations, an unstructured task, and weak position power, also suggests task orientation by the leader, who may reduce anxiety or ambiguity that could be created by the loosely structured situation. Between the two extremes (the middle of the scale in Figure 16-5), the suggested approach emphasizes cooperation and good relations with people.

Fiedler's research and management   In reviewing Fiedler's research, one finds that there is nothing automatic or "good" in either the task-oriented or the people-satisfaction-oriented style. Leadership effectiveness depends upon the various elements in the group environment. This might be expected. Cast in the desired role of leaders, managers who apply knowledge to the realities of the group reporting to them will do well to recognize that they are practicing an art. But in doing so, they will necessarily take into account the motivations to which people will respond and their ability to satisfy them in the interest of attaining enterprise goals.

Several scholars have put Fiedler's theory to the test in various situations. Some have questioned the meaning of the LPC score, and others suggest that the model does not explain the causal effect of the LPC score on performance. Some of the findings are not statistically significant, and situational measures may not be completely independent of the LPC score.

Despite such criticism, it is important to recognize that effective leadership style depends on the situation. Although this idea may not be new, Fiedler and his colleagues drew attention to this fact and stimulated a great deal of research.

Figure 16-5

FIEDLER'S MODEL OF LEADERSHIP.

Adapted from F. E. Fiedler, *A Theory of Leadership Effectiveness* (New York: McGraw-Hill Book Company, 1967), p. 146. Used with permission.

The Path-Goal Approach to Leadership Effectiveness

The **path-goal theory** suggests that the main function of the leader is to clarify and set goals with subordinates, help them find the best path for achieving the goals, and remove obstacles. Proponents of this approach have studied leadership in a variety of situations.[22] As stated by Robert House, the theory builds on various motivational and leadership theories of others.[23]

In addition to the expectancy theory variables, other factors contributing to effective leadership should be considered. These situational factors include (1) characteristics of subordinates, such as their needs, self-confidence, and abilities; and (2) the work environment, including such components as the task, the reward system, and the relationship with coworkers (see Figure 16-6).

Leader behavior is categorized into four groups:

1. *Supportive leadership* behavior gives consideration to the needs of subordinates, shows a concern for their well-being, and creates a pleasant organizational climate. It has the greatest impact on subordinates' performance when they are frustrated and dissatisfied.

2. *Participative leadership* allows subordinates to influence the decisions of their superiors and can result in increased motivation.

3. *Instrumental leadership* gives subordinates rather specific guidance and clarifies what is expected of them; this includes aspects of planning, organizing, coordinating, and controlling by the leader.

4. *Achievement-oriented leadership* involves setting challenging goals, seeking improvement of performance, and having confidence that subordinates will achieve high goals.

Figure 16-6

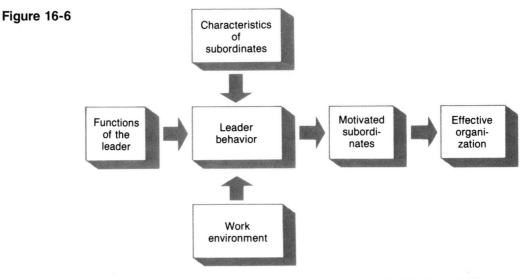

PATH–GOAL APPROACH TO LEADERSHIP EFFECTIVENESS.

Rather than suggesting that there is one best way to lead, this theory suggests that the appropriate style depends on the situation. Ambiguous and uncertain situations can be frustrating for subordinates, and a more task-oriented style may be called for. In other words, when subordinates are confused, then the leadr may tell them what to do and show them a clear path to goals. On the other hand, for routine tasks, such as those found on the assembly line, additional structure (usually provided by a task-oriented leader) may be considered redundant; subordinates may see such efforts as overcontrolling, which, in turn, may be dissatisfying. To put it differently, employees want the leader to stay out of their way because the path is already clear enough.

The theory proposes that the behavior of the leader is acceptable and satisfies subordinates to the extent that they see it as a source for their satisfaction. Another proposition of the theory is that the behavior of the leader increases the effort of subordinates, that is, it is motivating, insofar as (1) this behavior makes satisfaction of the needs of subordinates dependent on effective performance and (2) the behavior enhances the subordinates' environment through coaching, directing, supporting, and rewarding.

The key to the theory is that the leader influences the paths between behavior and goals. The leader can do this by defining positions and task roles, by removing obstacles to performance, by enlisting the assistance of group members in setting goals, by promoting group cohesiveness and team effort, by increasing opportunities for personal satisfaction in work performance, by reducing stresses and external controls, by making expectations clear, and by doing other things that meet people's expectations.

The path-goal theory makes a great deal of sense to the practicing manager. At the same time, one must realize that the model needs further testing before the approach can be used as a definite guide for managerial action.

SUMMARY

Leadership is the art or process of influencing people so that they contribute willingly and enthusiastically toward group goals. Leadership requires followership. There are various approaches to the study of leadership, ranging from the trait to the contingency approach. One such approach focuses on three styles: the autocratic, the democratic or participative, and the free-rein. Likert identified four systems of management, ranging from System 1 (exploitive-authoritative) through System 4 (participative-group), which he considers the most effective system.

The managerial grid identifies two dimensions: concern for production and concern for people. On the basis of these dimensions, four extreme styles and a middle-of-the-road style are identified. Leadership can also be viewed as a continuum. At one extreme of the continuum, the manager has a great deal of freedom while subordinates have very little. At the other extreme, the manager has very little freedom whereas subordinates have a great deal.

Still another approach to leadership, built on the assumption that leaders are the product of given situations, focuses on the study of situations. Fiedler's contingency approach takes into account the position power of the leader, the structure of the task, and the relations between the leader and group members. The conclusion is that there is no one best leadership style and that managers can be successful if placed in appropriate situations. The path-goal approach to leadership suggests that the most effective leaders help subordinates achieve enterprise and personal goals.

KEY IDEAS AND CONCEPTS FOR REVIEW

Leadership	Managerial grid
Ingredients of leadership	Leadership as a continuum
Leadership traits	Situational approach to leadership
Leadership styles based on the use of authority	Fiedler's contingency theory
Likert's four systems of management	Path-goal approach to leadership

FOR DISCUSSION

1. What do you see as the essence of leadership?

2. How are leadership theory and styles related to motivation?

3. Why has the trait approach as a means of explaining leadership been so open to question?

4. Can you see why the managerial grid has been so popular as a training device?

5. Select a business or political leader you admire, and identify his or her style of leading by applying the managerial grid or the continuum-of-behavior model of Tannenbaum and Schmidt.

6. What is Fiedler's theory of leadership? Applying it to cases of leaders you have known, do you perceive it as being accurate?

7. What are the advantages and limitations of the path-goal approach to leadership?

8. If you were selected to be the group leader for a class project (e.g., to make a case study of a particular company), which leadership style or what behavior would you use? Why?

EXERCISES/ACTION STEPS

1. Analyze a situation in which you were the leader. Which leadership approach discussed in this chapter helps explain why you were a leader?

2. Analyze a case in this book by using the group approach. Specifically, the class should be divided into groups of about five students. Each group should select a spokesperson who should present the analysis of the case to

the class. For each group, one observer (this person should not be a participant in the case discussion) should describe the interactions in the group. Was there a leader in the group? If the answer is "yes," why was he or she considered a leader? Was it due to the leader's personality, the other group members (followers), or the nature of the task (situation)? Explain the group processes in light of any leadership theory or concepts discussed in this chapter.

CASE:
PALMER MACHINERY COMPANY

Palmer Machinery Company has encountered hard times, not only because of an economic recession but also because of competition from products imported from Japan. In the past, labor relations have been rather poor. The unions usually asked for big pay increases for the workers and got them. But things have changed during the last few months, and labor and management have realized that they are in for some bad times ahead.

The company, maintaining it is in a precarious condition, has asked labor for concessions and givebacks. The union has called a membership meeting to discuss the situation. While Ann Stewart, an assembler, thinks that she is overpaid and argues for a wage reduction, the majority of those present disagree and do not want to make any concessions. In fact, there is a great mistrust of management's intentions and the workers feel that giving concessions will encourage the company to ask for additional ones. After a long discussion some workers are more agreeable to concessions if management makes similar sacrifices. But management does not make any commitments. During the next few weeks the situation gets worse; faced with a layoff, the union agrees to some cutbacks with the understanding that employees will share in some way in the profits of the company when things get better.

One month later, a national-magazine survey of executives' salaries at major companies shows that the executives at Palmer received a substantial increase in compensation. One worker remarks: "You just can't trust top management. I wish our situation was like the one in Japan, where in hard times the dividends are cut first, then the salary of top management is reduced, and later middle-level managers get a pay cut; the workers' pay is affected last."

1. Do you think the workers should have made concessions and agreed to givebacks?

2. If you were the president of the company, how would you have handled the situation?

3. What do you think of the Japanese approach to dealing with economic problems?

REFERENCES

1. For a review of research on followership, see Trudy Heller and Jon Van Til, "Leadership and Followership: Some Summary Propositions," *Journal of Applied Behavioral Science*, vol. 18, no. 3 (1982), pp. 405–414. For other discussions, see William Litzinger and Thomas Schaefer, "Leadership through Followership," *Business Horizons* (September–October 1982), pp. 78–81.

2. See Bernard M. Bass, *Stogdill's Handbook of Leadership: A Survey of Theory and Research*, rev. ed. (New York: The Free Press, 1981).

3. "Why Herb Kelleher Gets So Much Respect from Labor," *Business Week* (Sept. 24, 1984), pp. 112–114.

4. Jeremy Main, "Wanted: Leaders Who Can Make a Difference," *Fortune*, (Sept. 28, 1987), pp. 92–102.

5. Main, "Wanted: Leaders" (1987).

6. For an evaluation of the extensive research, see John B. Miner, "The Validity and Usefulness of Theories in an Emerging Organizational Science," *Academy of Management Review* (April 1984), pp. 296–306.

7. For a discussion of leadership traits, see Gary A. Yukl, *Leadership in Organizations* (Englewood Cliffs, N.J.: Prentice-Hall, 1981), chap. 4.

8. David A. Kenny and Stephen J. Zaccaro, "An Estimate of Variance Due to Traits in Leadership," *Journal of Applied Psychology* (November 1983), pp. 678–685.

9. Ralph M. Stogdill, *Handbook of Leadership: A Survey of Theory and Research* (New York: The Free Press, 1974). See also his earlier study, "Personal Factors Associated with Leadership: A Survey of the Literature," *Journal of Psychology,* vol. 25 (1948), pp. 35–71.

10. Thomas J. Peters and Robert H. Waterman, Jr. *In Search of Excellence* (New York: Harper & Row, 1982), chap. 5.

11. Maggie McComas, "Atop of the Fortune 500: A Survey of the C.E.O.s," *Fortune* (Apr. 28, 1986), pp. 26–31.

12. See especially his *New Patterns of Management* (New York: McGraw-Hill Book Company, 1961) and *The Human Organization* (New York: McGraw-Hill Book Company, 1967), from which material in this section has been drawn. Also see Rensis Likert and Jane G. Likert, *New Ways of Managing Conflict* (New York: McGraw-Hill Book Company, 1976).

13. John B. Miner, *Theories of Organizational Structure and Process* (Hinsdale, Ill.: The Dryden Press, 1982), chap. 2.

14. David G. Bowers, "Hierarchy, Function and the Generalizability of Leadership Practices," in James G. Hunt and Lars L. Larson (eds.), *Leadership Frontiers* (Kent, Ohio: Kent State University Press, 1975), pp. 167–180.

15. Robert R. Blake and Jane Mouton, *The Managerial Grid* (Houston, Tex.: Gulf Publishing Company, 1954) and *Building a Dynamic Corporation through Grid Organization Development* (Reading, Mass.: Addison-Wesley Publishing Company, 1969). The grid concept has been further refined in Robert R. Blake and Jane S. Mouton, *The Versatile Manager: A Grid Profile* (Homewood, Ill.: Richard D. Irwin, 1981) and *The Managerial Grid III* (Houston, Tex.: Gulf Publishing Company, 1985).

16. Robert Tannenbaum and Warren H. Schmidt, "How to Choose a Leadership Pattern," *Harvard Business Review* (March–April 1958), pp. 95–101. See also Heinz Weihrich, "How to Change a Leadership Pattern," *Management Review* (April 1979), pp. 26–28, 37–40.

17. Tannenbaum and Schmidt, "How to Choose a Leadership Pattern," reprinted with a commentary by the authors in *Harvard Business Review* (May–June 1973), pp. 162–180.

18. The perspective is based on a variety of sources, including Lawrence Ingrassia, "A Revitalized ITALTEL Wants to Test Wings in the Global Market," *The Wall Street Journal* (June 17, 1985); Parker Hodges, "The Continental Challenge," *Datamation* (Nov. 1, 1985); "ITALTEL's New Chief Gets What She Wants," *Business Week* (Apr. 30, 1984); "European Companies Link Up for Strategic Growth," *International Management* (June 1985); and personal correspondence.

19. Fred E. Fiedler, *A Theory of Leadership Effectiveness* (New York: McGraw-Hill Book Company, 1967). See also Fred E. Fiedler and Martin M. Chemers, *Leadership and Effective Management* (Glenview, Ill.: Scott, Foresman and Company, 1974); Fred E. Fiedler and Martin M. Chemers, with Linda Mahar, *Improving Leadership Effectiveness* (New York: John Wiley & Sons, 1977).

20. Fiedler, *A Theory of Leadership Effectiveness* (1967), p. 41.

21. Fiedler, p. 261.

22. For a meta-analysis of the research on the path-goal theory, see Julie Indvik, "Path-Goal Theory of Leadership: A Meta-Analysis," in John A. Pearce II and Richard B. Robinson, Jr. (eds.), *Academy of Management Best Papers — Proceedings 1986*, Forty-Sixth Annual Meeting of the Academy of Management, Chicago, August 13–16, 1986, pp. 189–192.

23. Robert J. House, "A Path-Goal Theory of Leadership Effectiveness," *Administrative Science Quarterly* (September 1971), pp. 321–338; Robert J. House and Terence R. Mitchell, "Path-Goal Theory of Leadership," in Harold Koontz, Cyril O'Donnell, and Heinz Weihrich (eds.), *Management: A Book of Readings,* 5th ed. (New York: McGraw-Hill Book Company, 1980), pp. 533–540; Alan C. Filley, Robert J. House, and Steven Kerr, *Managerial Process and Organizational Behavior* (Glenview, Ill., Scott, Foresman and Company, 1976), chap. 12.

CHAPTER 17

Communication

CHAPTER OBJECTIVES

After reading this chapter, you should understand:

1. The nature of communication and its function in an organization
2. The basic communication process
3. The flow of communication in an organization
4. The characteristics of written, oral, and nonverbal communication
5. Barriers and breakdowns in communication and approaches for improvement
6. Effective communication in committees
7. The role of the electronic media in communication

Although communication applies to all phases of managing, it is particularly important in the function of leading. Communication is the transfer of information from a sender to a receiver with the information being understood by the receiver. This definition, then, becomes the basis for the communication process model discussed in this chapter. The model focuses on the sender of the communication, the transmission of the message, and the receiver of the message. The model also draws attention to noise, which interferes with good communication, and feedback, which facilitates communication. This chapter also examines the impact of the electronic media on communication.

THE COMMUNICATION FUNCTION IN ORGANIZATIONS

It is no exaggeration to say that the communication function is the means by which organized activity is unified. It may be looked upon as the means by which social inputs are fed into social systems. It is also the means by which behavior is modified, change is effected, information is made productive, and goals are achieved. Whether it is within a church, a family, a scout troop, or a business enterprise, the transfer of information from one individual to another is absolutely essential.

The Importance of Communication

Over the years, the importance of communication in organized effort has been recognized by many authors. Chester I. Barnard, for example, viewed communication as the means by which people are linked together in an organization to achieve a common purpose.[1] This is still the fundamental function of communication. Indeed, group activity is impossible without communication, because coordination and change cannot be effected.

Psychologists have also been interested in communication. They emphasize human problems that occur in the communication process of initiating, transmitting, and receiving information. They have focused on the identification of barriers to good communication, especially those that involve the interpersonal relationships of people. Sociologists and information theorists, as well as psychologists, have concentrated on the study of communication networks.

Figure 17-1   **THE MANAGEMENT PROCESS**

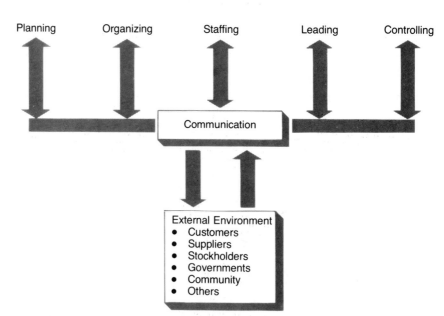

THE PURPOSE AND FUNCTION OF COMMUNICATION.

The Purpose of Communication

In its broadest sense, the purpose of communication in an enterprise is to effect change — to influence action toward the welfare of the enterprise. Communication is essential for the *internal* functioning of enterprises, because it integrates the managerial functions. Especially, communication is needed to (1) establish and disseminate goals of an enterprise, (2) develop plans for their achievement, (3) organize human and other resources in the most effective and efficient way, (4) select, develop, and appraise members of the organization, (5) lead, direct, motivate, and create a climate in which people want to contribute, and (6) control performance.

Figure 17-1 graphically shows not only that communication facilitates the managerial functions but also that communication relates an enterprise to its *external* environment. It is through information exchange that managers become aware of the needs of customers, the availability of suppliers, the claims of stockholders, the regulations of governments, and the concerns of a community. It is through communication that any organization becomes an open system interacting with its environment, a fact whose importance is emphasized throughout this book.

THE COMMUNICATION PROCESS

Simply stated, the **communication process,** diagrammed in Figure 17-2, involves the sender, the transmission of a message through a selected channel, and the receiver. Let us examine closely the specific steps in the process.

The Sender of the Message

Communication begins with the sender, who has a *thought* or an idea which is then encoded in a way that can be understood by both the sender and the receiver. While it is usual to think of *encoding* a message into the English language, there are many other ways of encoding, such as translating the thought into computer language.

Use of a Channel to Transmit the Message

The information is transmitted over a *channel* that links the sender with the receiver. The message may be oral or written, and it may be transmitted through a memorandum, a computer, the telephone, a telegram, or television. Television, of course, also facilitates the transmission of gestures and visual clues. At times, two or more channels are used. In a telephone conversation, for instance, two people may reach a basic agreement that they later confirm by a letter. Since many choices are available, each with advantages and disadvantages, the proper selection of the channel is vital for effective communication.

Figure 17-2

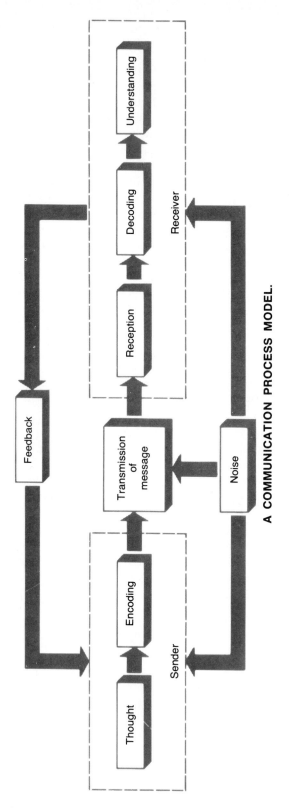

A COMMUNICATION PROCESS MODEL.

The Receiver of the Message

The receiver has to be *ready* for the message so that it can be decoded into thought. A person thinking about an exciting football game may pay insufficient attention to what is being said about an inventory report, for example, thus increasing the probability of a communication breakdown. The next step in the process is *decoding,* in which the receiver converts the message into thoughts. Accurate communication can occur only when both the sender and the receiver attach the same or at least similar meanings to the symbols that compose the message. Thus, it is obvious that a message encoded into French requires a receiver who understands French. Less obvious, and frequently overlooked, is the fact that a message in technical or professional jargon requires a recipient who understands such language. So communication is not complete unless it is understood. *Understanding* is in the mind of both the sender and the receiver. Persons with closed minds will normally not completely understand messages, especially if the information is contrary to their value system.

Noise and Feedback in Communication

Unfortunately, communication is affected by "noise," which is anything — whether in the sender, the transmission, or the receiver — that hinders communication. For example:

- A noise or a confined environment may hinder the development of a clear thought.

- Encoding may be faulty because of the use of ambiguous symbols.

- Transmission may be interrupted by static in the channel, such as may be experienced in a poor telephone connection.

- Inaccurate reception may be caused by inattention.

- Decoding may be faulty because the wrong meaning may be attached to words and other symbols.

- Understanding can be obstructed by prejudices.

- Desired change may not occur because of the fear of possible consequences of the change.

To check the effectiveness of communication, a person must have *feedback.* One can never be sure whether or not a message has been effectively encoded, transmitted, decoded, and understood until it is confirmed by feedback. Similarly, feedback indicates whether individual or organizational change has taken place as a result of communication.

Situational and Organizational Factors in Communication

Many situational and organizational factors affect the communication process. Such factors in the external environment may be educational, sociological, legal-political, and economic. For example, a repressive political environment will inhibit the free flow of communication. Another situational factor is geographic distance. A direct face-to-face communication is different from a telephone conversation with another person on the other side of the globe and different from an exchange of cables or letters. Time must also be considered in communication. The busy executive may not have sufficient time to receive and send information accurately. Other situational factors that affect communication within the enterprise include the organization structure, managerial and nonmanagerial processes, and technology. An example of the latter is the pervasive impact of computer technology on handling very large amounts of data.

In summary, the communication model provides an overview of the communication process, identifies the critical variables, and shows their relationships. This, in turn, helps managers pinpoint communication problems and take steps to solve them, or even better, to prevent the difficulties from occurring in the first place.

COMMUNICATION IN THE ENTERPRISE

In today's enterprises, information must flow faster than ever before. Even a short stoppage on a fast-moving production line can be very costly in lost output. It is, therefore, essential that production problems be communicated quickly for corrective action. Another important element is the amount of information, which has greatly increased over the years, frequently causing an information overload. What is often needed is not more information but relevant information. It is necessary to determine what kind of information the manager needs to have for effective decision making. Obtaining this information frequently requires getting information from managers' superiors and subordinates and also from departments and people elsewhere in an organization.

The Manager's Need to Know

To be effective, a manager needs information necessary to carry out managerial functions and activities. Yet even a casual glance at communication systems shows that managers often lack vital information for decision making, or they may get too much information, resulting in overload. It is evident that managers must be discriminating in selecting information. A simple way for a manager to start is to ask, "What do I really need to know for my job?" Or, "What would happen if I did not get this information on a regular basis?" It is not maximum information a manager needs but pertinent information. Clearly, there is no universally applicable communication system; rather, it must be tailored to the manager's needs.

The Communication Flow in the Organization

In an effective organization, communication flows in various directions: downward, upward, and crosswise. Traditionally, *downward* communication was emphasized, but there is ample evidence that if communication flows only downward, problems will develop. In fact, one could argue that effective communication has to start with the subordinate, and this means primarily *upward* communication. Communication also flows *horizontally,* that is, between people on the same or similar organizational levels, and *diagonally,* involving persons from different levels who are not in direct reporting relationships with one another. The different kinds of information flows are diagrammed in Figure 17-3.

Downward communication Downward communication flows from people at higher levels to those at lower levels in the organizational hierarchy. This kind of communication exists especially in organizations with an authoritarian atmosphere. The kinds of media used for downward *oral* communication include instructions, speeches, meetings, the telephone, loudspeakers, and even the grapevine. Examples of *written* downward communication are memoranda, letters, handbooks, pamphlets, policy statements, procedures, and electronic news displays.[2]

Unfortunately, information is often lost or distorted as it comes down the chain of command. Top management's issuance of policies and procedures does not ensure communication. In fact, many directives are not understood or even read. Consequently, a feedback system is essential for finding out whether information was perceived as intended by the sender.

Downward flow of information through the different levels of the organization is time-consuming. Indeed, delays may be so frustrating that some top managers insist that information be sent directly to the person or group requiring it.

Figure 17-3

INFORMATION FLOW IN AN ORGANIZATION.

* Since horizontal and diagonal communication flows have some common characteristics, we call them crosswise communication and discuss them together later in this chapter.

Upward communication Upward communication travels from subordinates to superiors and continues up the organizational hierarchy. Unfortunately, this flow is often hindered by managers in the communication chain who filter the messages and do not transmit all the information — especially unfavorable news — to their bosses. Yet objective transmission of information is essential for control purposes. Upper management needs to know specifically about production performance, marketing information, financial data, what lower-level employees are thinking, and so on.

Upward communication is primarily nondirective and is usually found in participative and democratic organizational environments. Typical means for upward communication — besides the chain of command — are suggestion systems, appeal and grievance procedures, complaint systems, counseling sessions, joint setting of objectives, the grapevine, group meetings, the practice of open-door policy, morale questionnaires, exit interviews, and the ombudsperson.

The concept of the **ombudsperson** was used relatively little in the United States until recently. It originated in Sweden, where a civil servant could be approached by a citizen to investigate complaints about the federal bureaucracy. Now some U.S. companies have established a position for a person who investigates employees' concerns. Anheuser-Busch, Control Data, General Electric, McDonnell Douglas, and AT&T are just a few of the companies using the ombudsperson for promoting upward communication. There is now even a Corporate Ombudsman Association. At General Dynamics, over 3000 calls were made to the ombudsperson in 1986, suggesting that workers trust the person in such a position.[3] Companies have found that the position of the

---

PERSPECTIVE:
LACK OF UPWARD COMMUNICATION CAN BE DISASTROUS

The lack of upward communication can be disastrous. In the 1986 space shuttle disaster vital information apparently did not reach the top management at NASA.[4] Other examples of a breakdown of upward communication are these: Bank of America's top officials were surprised about the poor quality of their mortgage portfolio, which resulted in substantial losses for the bank. E. F. Hutton's executives were apparently unaware of the incorrect check-writing scheme of their lower-level managers.

In some organizations, upward communication is hindered by an organization culture and climate that "punishes" managers who communicate bad news or information with which top management does not agree. Indeed, the tendency to report only good news upward is quite common. Yet correct information is absolutely necessary for managing an enterprise.[5]

So what can managers do to facilitate the free flow of information? First, managers must create an informal climate that encourages upward communication. An open-door policy is only useful when it is practiced. Second, the formal structure of information flow must be clear. Third, managers can learn a great deal by just wandering through the corridors. Hewlett Packard is often mentioned as an example of open communication by the practice of "management by wandering around."

ombudsperson can provide a valuable upward communication link and avert front-page scandals and legal costs by bringing improprieties to the attention of the appropriate person before they become major problems.

Effective upward communication requires an environment in which subordinates feel free to communicate. Since the organizational climate is greatly influenced by upper management, the responsibility for creating a free flow of upward communication rests to a great extent — although not exclusively — with superiors.

Crosswise communication   Crosswise communication includes the *horizontal* flow of information, among people on the same or similar organizational levels, and the *diagonal* flow, among persons at different levels who have no direct reporting relationships. This kind of communication is used to speed information flow, to improve understanding, and to coordinate efforts for the achievement of organizational objectives. A great deal of communication does not follow the organizational hierarchy but cuts across the chain of command.

The enterprise environment provides many occasions for *oral* communication. They range from informal meetings of the company bowling team and lunch hours employees spend together to more formal conferences and committee and board meetings. This kind of communication also occurs when individual members of different departments are grouped into task teams or project organizations. Finally, communication cuts across organizational boundaries when, for example, staff with functional or advisory authority interacts with line managers in different departments.

In addition, *written* forms of communication keep people informed about the enterprise. These written forms include the company newspaper or magazine and bulletin boards. Modern enterprises use many kinds of oral and written crosswise communication patterns to supplement the vertical flow of information.

Because information may not follow the chain of command, proper safeguards need to be taken to prevent potential problems. Specifically, crosswise communication should rest on the understanding that (1) crosswise relationships will be encouraged wherever they are appropriate, (2) subordinates will refrain from making commitments beyond their authority, and (3) subordinates will keep superiors informed of important interdepartmental activities. In short, crosswise communication may create difficulties, but it is a necessity in many enterprises in order to respond to the needs of the complex and dynamic organizational environment.

Written, Oral, and Nonverbal Communication

Written and oral communication media have favorable and unfavorable characteristics; consequently, they are often used together so that the favorable qualities of each can complement the other. In addition, visual aids may be used to supplement both oral and written communications. For example, the lecture in the management training session may be made more effective when written handouts, transparencies, videotapes, and films are used. Evidence has shown that when a message is repeated through several media, the people receiving it will more accurately comprehend and recall it.

In selecting the media, one must consider the communicator, the audience, and the situation. An executive who feels uncomfortable in front of a large audience may choose written communication rather than a speech. On the other hand, certain audiences who may not read a memo may be reached and become motivated by direct oral communication. Situations may also demand a specific medium. For example, former President Reagan, an effective communicator, used press conferences in trying to clarify the arm shipments to Iran. Face-to-face interaction was demanded by the news media to deal with the many aspects of the transactions.

Written communication   Written communication has the *advantage* of providing records, references, and legal defenses. The message can be carefully prepared and then directed to a large audience through mass mailings. Written communication can also promote uniformity in policy and procedure and can reduce costs, in some cases.

The *disadvantages* are that written messages may create mountains of paper, may be poorly expressed by ineffective writers, and may provide no immediate feedback. Consequently, it may take a long time to know whether a message has been received and properly understood.

Oral communication   A great deal of information is communicated orally. Oral communication can occur in a face-to-face meeting of two people or in a manager's presentation to a large audience; it can be formal or informal, and it can be planned or accidental.

The principal *advantage* of oral communication are that it makes possible speedy interchange with immediate feedback. People can ask questions and clarify points. In a face-to-face interaction, the effect can be noted. Furthermore, a meeting with the superior may give the subordinate a feeling of importance. Clearly, informal or planned meetings can greatly contribute to the understanding of the issues.

However, oral communication also has *disadvantages*. It does not always save time, as any manager knows who has attended meetings in which no results or agreements were achieved. These meetings can be costly in terms of time and money.

Nonverbal communication   People communicate in many different ways. What a person says can be reinforced (or contradicted) by nonverbal communication, such as facial expressions and body gestures. Nonverbal communication is expected to support the verbal, but it does not always do so. For example, an autocratic manager may pound a fist on the table while announcing that from now on participative management will be practiced; such contradictory communications will certainly create a credibility gap. Similarly, managers may state that they have an open-door policy, but then they may have a secretary carefully screen people who want to see them; this creates an incongruency between what they say and what they do. Clearly, nonverbal communication may support or contradict verbal communication, giving rise to the saying that actions often speak louder than words.

BARRIERS AND BREAKDOWNS IN COMMUNICATION

It is probably no surprise that managers frequently cite communication breakdowns as one of their most important problems. However, communication problems are often symptoms of more deeply rooted problems. For example, poor planning may be the cause of uncertainty about the direction of the firm. Similarly, a poorly designed organization structure may not clearly communicate organizational relationships. Vague performance standards may leave managers uncertain about what is expected of them. Thus, the perceptive manager will look for the causes of communication problems instead of just dealing with the symptoms. Barriers can exist in the sender, in the transmission of the message, in the receiver, or in the feedback. Specific communication barriers are discussed below.

Lack of Planning

Good communication seldom happens by chance. Too often people start talking and writing without first thinking, planning, and stating the purpose of the message. Yet giving the reasons for a directive, selecting the most appropriate channel, and choosing proper timing can greatly improve understanding and reduce resistance to change.

Unclarified Assumptions

Often overlooked, yet very important, are the uncommunicated assumptions that underlie messages. A customer may send a note stating that she will visit a vendor's plant. Then she may assume that the vendor will meet her at the airport, reserve a hotel room, arrange for transportation, and set up a full-scale review of the program at the plant. But the vendor may assume that the customer is coming to town mainly to attend a wedding and will make a routine call at the plant. These unclarified assumptions in both instances may result in confusion and the loss of goodwill.

Semantic Distortion

Another barrier to effective communication is semantic distortion, which can be deliberate or accidental. An advertisement that states "We sell for less" is deliberately ambiguous; it raises the question: Less than what? Words may evoke different responses. To some people, the word "government" may mean interference or deficit spending; to others, the same word may mean help, equalization, and justice.

Poorly Expressed Messages

No matter how clear the idea in the mind of the sender of communication, it may still be marked by poorly chosen words, omissions, lack of coherence, poor organization of ideas, awkward sentence structure, platitudes, unnecessary jargon, and a failure to clarify the implications of the message. This lack of clarity and precision, which can be costly, can be avoided through greater care in encoding the message.

Communication Barriers in the International Environment

Communication in the international environment becomes even more difficult because of different languages, cultures, and etiquette.[6] Translating advertising slogans is very risky. The slogan "Put a Tiger in Your Tank" by Exxon was very effective in the United States, yet it is an insult to the people in Thailand. Colors have different meanings in various cultures. Black is often associated with death in many Western countries, while in the Far East white is the color of mourning. In business dealings it is quite common in the United States to communicate on a first-name basis, yet in most cultures, especially in those with a pronounced hierarchical structure, persons generally address one another by their last names.[7]

To overcome communication barriers in the international environment, large corporations have taken a variety of steps. Volkswagen, for example, provides extensive language training. Furthermore, the company maintains a large staff of translators. Frequently, local nationals, who know the host-country's language and culture, are hired for top positions. In the United States, foreign firms find it advantageous to hire students from their own country who are attending U.S. universities.

Loss by Transmission and Poor Retention

In a series of transmissions from one person to the next, the message becomes less and less accurate. Poor retention of information is another serious problem. Thus, the necessity of repeating the message and using several channels is rather obvious. Consequently, companies often use more than one channel to communicate the same message.

Poor Listening and Premature Evaluation

There are many talkers but few listeners. Everyone probably has observed people entering a discussion with comments that have no relation to the topic. One reason may be that these persons are pondering their own problems — such as preserving their own egos or making a good impression on other group members — instead of listening to the conversation. Listening demands full attention and self-discipline. It also requires that the listener avoid premature evaluation of what another person has to say. A common tendency is to judge — to approve or disapprove what is being said — rather than trying to understand the speaker's frame of reference. Yet listening without making hasty judgments can make the whole enterprise more effective and more efficient. For example, sympathetic listening can result in better labor-management relations and greater understanding among managers. Specifically, sales personnel may better understand the problems of production people, and the credit manager may realize that an overrestrictive credit policy may lead to a disproportionate loss in sales. In short, listening with empathy can reduce some of the daily frustrations in organized life and result in better communication.

Impersonal Communication

Effective communication is more than simply transmitting information to employees. It requires face-to-face communication in an environment of openness and trust. The Perspective illustrates how this simple but effective communication technique may be overlooked. As the events in the Perspective indicate, real improvement of communication often requires not expensive and sophisticated (and impersonal) communication media but the willingness of superiors to engage in face-to-face communication. Such informal gatherings, without status trappings or a formal authority base, may be threatening to a top executive, but the risks involved are outweighed by the benefits that better communication can bring.

Distrust, Threat, and Fear

Distrust, threat, and fear undermine communication. In a climate containing these forces, any message will be viewed with skepticism. Distrust can be the result of inconsistent behavior by the superior, or it can be due to past experiences in which the subordinate was punished for honestly reporting unfavorable, but true, information to the boss. Similarly, in the light of threats — whether real or imagined — people tend to tighten up, become defensive, and distort information. What is needed is a climate of trust, which facilitates open and honest communication.

PERSPECTIVE:
THE CLOSED-CIRCUIT TELEVISION FAILURE[8]

A company was about to install a sophisticated $300,000 closed-circuit television system to improve the transmission of information to employees. When a management consultant recommended instead that the president should join his people during the coffee break, rather than sipping his coffee in a closed group of top executives, the president was skeptical. The suggestion seemed radical, but he agreed to try it. The experiment was a failure because the president found that his employees would not talk to him. After some soul-searching, the president again tried meeting with his employees face-to-face during the coffee break, but this time he talked about *their* concern (the opening of a European plant that could result in the elimination of jobs). To the president's surprise, employees talked openly about what was on their minds. In fact, the communication went so well that the president requested that his executive group mingle with their people for "kaffeeklatsches."

Insufficient Period for Adjustment to Change

The purpose of communication is to effect change that may seriously concern employees: shifts in the time, place, type, and order of work or shifts in group arrangements or skills to be used. Some communications point to the need for further training, career adjustment, or status arrangements. Changes affect people in different ways, and it may take time to think through the full meaning of a message. Consequently, for maximum efficiency, it is important not to force change before people can adjust to its implications.

Information Overload[9]

One might think that more and unrestricted information flow would help people overcome communication problems.[10] But unrestricted flow may result in too much information. People respond to information overload in various ways.[11] First, they may *disregard* certain information. A person getting too much mail may ignore letters that should be answered. Second, if they are overwhelmed with too much information, people *make errors* in processing it. For example, they may leave out the word "not" in a message, which reverses the intended meaning. Third, people may *delay* processing information either permanently or with the intention of catching up in the future. Fourth, people may *filter* information. Filtering may be helpful when the most pressing and most important information is processed first and the less important messages receive lower priority. However, chances are that attention will be given first to matters that are easy to handle, while more difficult but perhaps critical messages are ignored. Finally, people respond to information overload by simply *escaping* from the task of communication. In other words, they ignore information or do not communicate information because of an overload.

Some responses to information overload may be adaptive tactics that can, at times, be functional. For example, delaying the processing of information until the amount is reduced can be effective. On the other hand, withdrawing from the task of communicating is usually not a helpful response. Another way to approach the overload problem is to reduce the demands for information. Within an enterprise, this may be accomplished by insisting that only essential data be processed, such as information showing critical deviations from plans. Reducing external demands for information is usually more difficult because these demands are less controllable by managers. An example may be the government's demand for detailed documentation on governmental contracts. Companies that do business with the government simply have to comply with these requests.

Other Communication Barriers

Besides the mentioned barriers to effective communication, there are many others. In *selective perception* people tend to perceive what they expect to perceive. In communication this means that they hear what they want to hear and ignore other relevant information.

Closely related to perception is the influence of *attitude*, which is the predisposition to act or not to act in a certain way; it is a mental position regarding a fact or state. Clearly, if people have made up their minds, they cannot objectively listen to what is said.

Still other barriers to communication are differences in *status* and *power* between the sender and the receiver of communication. Also, when information has to pass through several *levels* in the organization hierarchy, it tends to be distorted.

TOWARD EFFECTIVE COMMUNICATION

The communication process model introduced at the beginning of this chapter (Figure 17-2) helps identify the critical elements in the communication process. At each stage, breakdowns can occur — in the encoding of the message by the sender, in the transmission of the message, and in the decoding and understanding of the message by the receiver. Certainly, noise can interfere with effective communication at each stage of the process.

Guidelines for Improving Communication

Effective communication is the responsibility of all persons in the organization, managers as well as nonmanagers, who work toward a common aim. Whether communication is effective can be evaluated by the intended results. The following guidelines can help overcome the barriers to communication:

1. Senders of messages must clarify in their minds what they want to communicate. This means that one of the first steps in communicating is clarifying the purpose of the message and making a plan to achieve the intended end.

2. Effective communication requires that encoding and decoding be done with symbols that are familiar to the sender and the receiver of the message. Thus the manager (and especially the staff specialist) should avoid unnecessary technical jargon, which is intelligible only to the experts in their particular field.

3. The planning of the communication should not be done in a vacuum. Instead, other people should be consulted and encouraged to participate: to collect the facts, analyze the message, and select the appropriate media. For example, a manager may ask a colleague to read an important memo before it is distributed throughout the organization. The content of the message should fit the recipients' level of knowledge and the organizational climate.

4. It is important to consider the needs of the receivers of the information. Whenever appropriate, one should communicate something that is of value to them, in the short run as well as in the more distant future. At times, unpopular actions that affect employees in the short run may be more easily

accepted if they are beneficial to them in the long run. For instance, short-ening the workweek may be more acceptable if it is made clear that this action will strengthen the competitive position of the company in the long run and avoid layoffs.

5. There is a saying that the tone makes the music. Similarly, in communica-tion the tone of voice, the choice of language, and the congruency between what is said and how it is said influence the reactions of the receiver of the message. An autocratic manager ordering subordinate supervisors to prac-tice participative management will create a credibility gap that will be diffi-cult to overcome.

6. Too often information is transmitted without communicating, since com-munication is complete only when the message is understood by the receiver. And one never knows whether communication is understood unless the sender gets feedback. This is accomplished by asking questions, requesting a reply to a letter, and encouraging receivers to give their reac-tions to the message.

7. The function of communication is more than transmitting information. It also deals with emotions that are very important in interpersonal relation-ships between superiors, subordinates, and colleagues in an organization. Furthermore, communication is vital for creating an environment in which people are motivated to work toward the goals of the enterprise while they achieve their personal aims. Another function of communication is control. As explained in the discussion of management by objectives (MBO), control does not necessarily mean top-down control. Instead, the MBO philosophy emphasizes self-control, which demands clear communication with an understanding of the criteria against which performance is measured.

8. Effective communicating is the responsibility not only of the sender but also of the receiver of the information. Thus, listening is an aspect that needs additional comment.

Listening: The Key to Understanding

The rushed, never-listening manager will seldom get an objective view of the functioning of the organization. Time, empathy, and concentration on the com-municator's messages are prerequisites to understanding. People want to be heard, want to be taken seriously, want to be understood. Thus, the manager must avoid interrupting subordinates and putting them on the defensive. It is also wise both to give and to ask for feedback, for without it one can never be sure whether the message is understood. To elicit honest feedback a manager should develop an atmosphere of trust and confidence and a supportive leader-ship style, with a de-emphasis on status (such as barricading oneself behind an extrawide executive desk).

Listening is a skill that can be developed. Keith Davis and John W. New-strom proposed ten guides to improve listening: (1) Stop talking, (2) put the talker at ease, (3) show the talker that you want to listen, (4) remove distractions, (5) empathize with the talker, (6) be patient, (7) hold your temper, (8) go easy on arguments and criticism, (9) ask questions, and (10) stop talking! The first and the last guides are the most important; people have to stop talking before they can listen.[12]

Carl R. Rogers and F. J. Roethlisberger suggest a simple experiment.[13] It goes like this. The next time you have an argument try to use the following simple rule: A person may speak only after the ideas and feelings of the previous speaker are repeated accurately to the speaker's satisfaction. This rule sounds simple yet is difficult to practice. It requires listening, understanding, and empathy. But managers who have used this technique have reported a considerable number of cases in which they were not communicating accurately.

Some Tips for Improving Written Communication

Effective writing may be the exception rather than the rule; nor do education and intelligence guarantee good writing. Many people fall into the habit of using technical jargon that can be understood only by experts in the same field. Common problems in written communications are that writers omit the conclusion or bury it in the report, are too wordy, and use poor grammar, ineffective sentence structure, and incorrect spelling. Yet a few guidelines may do much to improve written communication:[14]

Use simple words and phrases.

Use short and familiar words.

Use personal pronouns (such as "you") whenever appropriate.

Give illustrations and examples; use charts.

Use short sentences and paragraphs.

Use active verbs such as "The manager plans . . . "

Avoid unnecessary words.

John Fielden suggests that the writing style should fit the situation and the effect the writer wants to achieve.[15] Specifically, he recommends a *forceful* style when the writer has power; the tone should be polite, but firm. The *passive* style is appropriate when the writer is in a position lower than that of the recipient of the message. The *personal* style is recommended for communicating good news and making persuasive requests for action. The *impersonal* style is generally right for conveying negative information. The *lively* or *colorful* style is suitable for good-news items, advertisements, and sales letters. On the other hand, a *less colorful* style, combining the impersonal with the passive, may be appropriate for common business writing.

Effective Communication in the Group: The Committee

Managers spend a great deal of time in committees. The use of committees is due not only to the democratic tradition in American social life but also to a growing emphasis on group management and group participation in organizations. Some of the disadvantages of committees can be overcome by applying the following guidelines for more effective communication.

Authority   The committee's authority should be spelled out so that members know whether their responsibility is to make decisions, make recommendations, or merely deliberate and give the chairperson some insights into the problem under discussion.

Size   The size of the committee is very important. The complexity of interrelationships greatly increases with the size of the group. If the group is too large, there may not be enough opportunities for adequate communication among its members. On the other hand, if the group consists of only three persons, there is the possibility that two may form a coalition against the third member. No precise conclusions can be drawn here about the appropriate size. As a general rule, a committee should be large enough to promote deliberation and include the breadth of expertise required for the job but not so large as to waste time or foster indecision. The optimum committee size is thought by some to be at least five or six members but not more than fifteen or sixteen. An analysis of small-group research indicates that the ideal committee size may be five when the five members possess adequate skills and knowledge to deal with problems facing the committee.[16] It is obvious that the larger the group, the greater the difficulty in obtaining a "meeting of the minds" and the more time necessary to allow everyone to contribute.

Membership   The members of the committee must be selected carefully. If a committee is to be successful, the members must be representative of the interests they are intended to serve. They must also possess the required authority and be able to perform well in a group. Finally, the members should have the capacity for communicating well and reaching group decisions by integrated group thinking rather than by inappropriate compromise.

Subject matter   The subject matter must be carefully selected. Committee work should be limited to subject matter that can be handled in group discussion. Certain kinds of subjects lend themselves to committee action, while others do not. Jurisdictional disputes and strategy formulation, for example, may be suitable for group deliberation, while certain isolated, technical problems may be better solved by an expert in the specialized field. Committees will be more effective if an agenda and relevant information are circulated well in advance so that the members can study the subject matter before the meeting.

Chairperson   The selection of the chairperson is crucial for an effective committee meeting. Such a person can avoid the wastes and drawbacks of committees by planning the meeting, preparing the agenda, seeing that the results of research are available to the members ahead of time, formulating definite proposals for discussion or action, and conducting the meeting efficiently. The chairperson sets the tone of the meeting, integrates the ideas, and keeps the discussion from wandering.

Minutes   Effective communication in committees usually requires circulating minutes and checking conclusions. At times, individuals leave the meeting with varying interpretations as to what was agreed. This can be avoided by taking careful minutes of the meeting and circulating them in draft form for correction or modification before the final copy is approved by the committee.

Cost effectiveness   The committee must be worth its cost. It may be difficult to count the benefits, especially such intangible factors as morale, enhanced status of committee members, and the committee's value as a training device to enhance teamwork. But the committee can be justified only if the costs are offset by tangible and intangible benefits.

ELECTRONIC MEDIA IN COMMUNICATION

Managers have studied and are gradually adopting various electronic devices, that improve communication. Electronic equipment includes mainframe computers, minicomputers, personal computers, electronic mail systems, and electronic typewriters, as well as cellular telephones for making telephone calls from cars and beepers for keeping in contact with the office. The impact of computers on all phases of the management process will be discussed in Chapter 19 in connection with management information systems and will therefore be mentioned only briefly here. Let us first look at telecommunication in general and at the increasing use of teleconferencing in particular.

Telecommunication

Although telecommunication is just emerging, a number of companies have already effectively utilized the new technology in a variety of ways, as shown by the following examples:[17]

- A large bank supplies hardware and software to its customers so that they can easily transfer funds to their suppliers.

- Several banks now make bank-by-phone services available even to individuals.

- Facsimile mail service ensures delivery of a document across the country within hours.

- The computerized airline reservation system facilitates making travel arrangements.

- One large medical supply company gained a competitive edge by providing hospital purchasing agents with the opportunity to enter supply orders directly at the computer terminal.

- Many firms now have detailed personnel information — including performance appraisals and career development plans — in a data bank.

As you can see, there are many applications of telecommunication. But to make telecommunication systems effective, the technical experts must make every effort to identify the real needs of managers and customers and to design systems that are useful.[18] Let us now turn to a specific application of the new technology: teleconferencing.

Teleconferencing

For some time now companies such as IBM, Bank of America, and Hughes have used teleconferencing.[19] However, due to the wide variety of systems, including audio systems, audio systems with snapshots displayed on the video monitor, and live video systems, the term "teleconferencing" is difficult to define. In general, most people think of a **teleconference** as a group of people interacting with each other by means of audio and video media with moving or still pictures.

Full-motion video is frequently used to hold meetings among managers. Not only do they hear each other, but they can also see each other's expressions or discuss some visual display. This kind of communication is, of course, rather expensive, and audio in combination with still video may be used instead. This method of communicating may be useful for showing charts or illustrations during a technical discussion.

Advantages   Some of the potential advantages of teleconferencing include savings in travel expenses and travel time. Also, conferences can be held whenever necessary, since there is no need to make travel plans long in advance. Because meetings can be held more frequently, communication is improved between, for example, headquarters and geographically scattered divisions.

Disadvantages   There are also drawbacks to teleconferencing. Because of the ease in arranging meetings in this manner, they may be held more often than necessary. Moreover, since this approach uses rather new technology, the equipment is subject to breakdowns. Most important, perhaps, teleconferencing is still a poor substitute for meeting with other persons face-to-face. Despite these limitations, an increased use of teleconferencing is likely in the future.

The Use of Computers for Information Handling

Electronic data processing now makes it possible to handle large amounts of data and to make information available to a large number of people. Thus, one can obtain, analyze, and organize timely data quite inexpensively. But it must never be forgotten that data are not necessarily information; information must inform someone. The new computer graphics can inform visually, displaying important company information. At PepsiCo Inc. managers used to dig through reams of computer printouts for information; now they can quickly display a colored map showing their competitive picture.[20] There will be more about the impact of the computer on the process of managing in Chapter 19.

SUMMARY

Communication is the transfer of information from the sender to the receiver, with the information being understood by both the sender and the receiver. The communication process begins with the sender, who encodes an idea which is sent in oral, written, visual, or some other form to the receiver. The receiver decodes the message and gains an understanding of what the sender wants to communicate. This, in turn, may result in some change or action. But the communication process may be interrupted by "noise," that is by anything that hinders communication. In an organization, managers should have the information necessary for doing a good job. The information may flow not only downward or upward in the organization structure but also horizontally or diagonally. Communication can be in written form, but more information is communicated orally. In addition, people communicate through gestures and facial expressions.

Communication is hindered by barriers and breakdowns in communication. Understanding these barriers and applying the guides for effective communicating and listening facilitate not only understanding but also managing. A great deal of time is spent communicating in committee meetings; applying the guidelines for group communication will make these meetings more productive. The electronic media can improve communication, as illustrated by teleconferencing and the application of computers, two of many approaches to handling the increasing amount of information in organizations.

KEY IDEAS AND CONCEPTS FOR REVIEW

Communication
Communication process model
"Noise" in communication
Downward communication
Crosswise communication
Written communication — advantages and disadvantages
Oral communication — advantages and disadvantages

Nonverbal communication
Barriers and breakdowns in communication
Responses to information overload
Guidelines for improving communication
Recommendations for making committees effective
Teleconferencing

FOR DISCUSSION

1. Briefly describe the communication process model. Select a communication problem and determine the cause (or causes) by applying the model in your analysis.

2. List different channels for transmitting a message. Discuss the advantages and disadvantages of the various channels.

3. What are some kinds of downward communication? Discuss those used most frequently in an enterprise you are familiar with. How effective are the various types?

4. What are some problems in upward communication? What would you suggest for overcoming the difficulties?

5. What are the advantages and disadvantages of written and oral communication? Which do you prefer? Under what circumstances?

6. What is information overload? Do you ever experience it? How do you deal with it?

7. How well do you listen? How could you improve your listening skills?

8. Discuss means for making committees more effective.

9. Discuss the role of electronic media in communications.

EXERCISES/ACTION STEPS

1. Recall a situation that occurred at home or at work and identify the communication problems you observed or experienced. Discuss how the communication model in this chapter can help you locate the problems.

2. Go to the library and do research on a public figure who communicates well. Discuss this person's characteristics as they relate to communication.

CASE:
HAYNES FASHION STORES, INCORPORATED

After graduating from college, Joyce Haynes went to work for her father, Dudley Haynes, who was president of Haynes Fashion Stores, Incorporated, a chain of women's apparel stores. The company had been founded by Ms. Haynes's grandfather over 50 years ago. With her grandfather's and, for the past 20 years, her father's drive and knowledge of women's fashions and of how to buy and sell them, the company had developed from a single store in Hartford, Connecticut, to a fairly large and highly profitable chain of thirty stores in the New England area. Dudley Haynes was much like his father. He knew what he was doing and how to do it, and he prided himself on being able to keep his hands on details in buying, advertising, and store management. Every one of his store managers, as well as his top vice-presidents and headquarters staff people, met with him every 2 weeks in Hartford. Between these meetings, Mr. Haynes spent 2 or 3 days each week visiting the stores and working with store managers.

His major worries were communication and motivation. Although he felt that all his managers and staff people listened carefully at the conferences he held, their subsequent actions made him wonder whether they had heard him at all. He observed that many of his policies were not being strictly followed in the stores; he often had to rewrite advertising copy; and in some of the stores the employees had joined the clerks union. He increasingly heard things he did not like, such as reports that many employees and even some managers felt they did not know the company's goals and believed they could do better if they had a chance to communicate with the executives at headquarters. He also had a strong feeling that many of his managers and most of the store clerks were merely doing their jobs without showing any real imagination or drive. An additional concern was the fact that some of his best people had quit and taken positions with a competitor.

When his daughter walked into his office to begin work as his special assistant, he said:

"Joyce, I'm worried about how things are going. Apparently, my two problems are communication and motivation. Now, I know that you took some courses in management in school. I've heard you talk of the problems, barriers, and techniques of communication, and you've mentioned some fellows — Maslow, Herzberg, Vroom, McClelland, and others — who knew a great deal about motivation. While I doubt that these psychology types knew much about business and I feel that I know what motivates people — primarily money, good bosses, and a good place to work — I wonder if you've learned anything that will help me communicate better. I hope so, for that college education of yours has cost me a lot of money. What do you suggest?"

1. If you were Ms. Haynes, what would you say to your father?

2. How would you go about analyzing the communication problem, and what difficulties do you see already from the case?

3. Suggest ways that the motivation and communication theories you have studied might be applied to Haynes Fashion Stores. Is there anything else you would want to know?

4. How would you apply the Rogers and Roethlisberger experiment discussed in this chapter to the case?

REFERENCES

1. Chester I. Barnard, *The Functions of the Executive* (Cambridge, Mass.: Harvard University Press, 1938).

2. Walter Kiechel III, "No Word from on High," *Fortune* (Jan. 6, 1986), pp. 125–126.

3. Michael Brody, "Listen to Your Whistleblower," *Fortune* (Nov. 24, 1986), pp. 77–78.

4. Michael Brody, "NASA's Challenge: Ending Isolation at the Top," *Fortune* (Mar. 12, 1986), pp. 26–32.

5. Charles E. Beck and Elizabeth A. Beck, "The Manager's Open Door and the Communication Climate," *Business Horizons* (January–February 1986), pp. 15–19.

6. See John D. Daniels, Ernest W. Ogram, Jr., and Lee H. Radebaugh, *International Business*, 3d ed. (Reading, Mass.: Addison-Wesley Publishing Company, 1982), chaps. 4 and 19; Simcha Ronen, *Comparative and Multinational Management* (New York: John Wiley & Sons, 1986), chap. 4.

7. V. H. Kirpalani, *International Marketing* (New York: Random House, 1985), chap. 4.

8. Roger D'Aprix, "The Oldest (and Best) Way to Communicate with Employees," *Harvard Business Review* (September–October 1982), pp. 30–32.

9. See also Rodger W. Griffeth, Kerry D. Carson, and Daniel B. Marin, "Information Overload: A Test

of an Inverted U Hypothesis with Hourly and Salaried Employees," *Academy of Management Best Papers — Proceedings 1988,* Forty-Eighth Annual Meeting of the Academy of Management, Anaheim, California, August 7–10, 1988, pp. 232–235.

10. See also Eric M. Eisenberg and Marsha G. Witten, "Reconsidering Openness in Organizational Communication," *Academy of Management Review* (July 1987), pp. 418–426.

11. For a detailed discussion of this topic, see Miller's analysis of information overload in Daniel Katz and Robert L. Kahn, *The Social Psychology of Organizations* (New York: John Wiley & Sons, 1978), pp. 451–455.

12. Keith Davis and John W. Newstrom, *Human Behavior at Work: Organizational Behavior,* 7th ed. (New York: McGraw-Hill Book Company, 1985), p. 436.

13. Carl R. Rogers and F. J. Roethlisberger, "Barriers and Gateways to Communication," *Business Classics: Fifteen Key Concepts for Managerial Success* (Boston: Resident and Fellows of Harvard College, 1975), pp. 44–50.

14. Davis and Newstrom, *Human Behavior At Work* (1985), p. 438.

15. John S. Fielden, "What Do You Mean You Don't Like My Style?" *Harvard Business Review* (May–June 1982), pp. 128–138.

16. See A. C. Filley, "Committee Management: Guidelines from Social Science Research," *California Management Review* (Fall 1970), pp. 13–21.

17. Eric K. Clemons and F. Warren McFarlan, "Telecom: Hook Up or Lose Out," *Harvard Business Review* (July–August 1986), pp. 91–97; Anne R. Field and Catherine L. Harris, "The Information Business," *Business Week* (Aug. 25, 1986), pp. 82–90.

18. For a series of articles on telecommunications, see *The Wall Street Journal — A Special Report: Telecommunications* (Feb. 24, 1986).

19. Robert Johansen and Christine Bullen, "What to Expect from Teleconferencing," *Harvard Business Review* (March–April 1984), pp. 164–174.

20. "Management Warms Up to Computer Graphics," *Business Week* (Aug. 13, 1984), pp. 96–101.

SUMMARY OF MAJOR PRINCIPLES, OR GUIDES, OF LEADING

For the managerial function of leading, several principles, or guides, can be summarized. They are the following:

Principle of harmony of objectives The more managers can harmonize the personal goals of individuals with the goals of the enterprise, the more effective and efficient the enterprise will be.

Principle of motivation Since motivation is not a simple cause and effect matter, the more managers carefully assess a reward structure, look upon it from a situation and contingency point of view, and integrate it into the entire system of managing, the more effective a motivational program will be.

Principle of leadership Since people tend to follow those who, in their view, offer them a means of satisfying their personal goals, the more managers understand what motivates their subordinates and how these motivators operate, and the more they reflect this understanding in carrying out their managerial actions, the more effective they are likely to be as leaders.

Principle of communication clarity Communication tends to be clear when it is expressed in a language and transmitted in a way that can be understood by the receiver.

The responsibility of the sender is to formulate the message so that it is understandable to the receiver. This responsibility pertains primarily to written and oral communication and points to the necessity for planning the message, stating the underlying assumptions, and applying the generally accepted rules for effective writing and speaking.

Principle of communication integrity The greater the integrity and consistency of written, oral, and nonverbal messages, as well as of the moral behavior of the sender, the greater the acceptance of the message by the receiver.

Principle of supplemental use of informal organization Communication tends to be more effective when managers utilize the informal organization to supplement the communication channels of the formal organization.

Informal organization is a phenomenon managers must accept. Information, true or not, flows quickly through the informal organization. Consequently, managers should take advantage of this device to correct misinformation and to provide information that cannot be effectively sent or appropriately received through the formal communication system.

Controlling

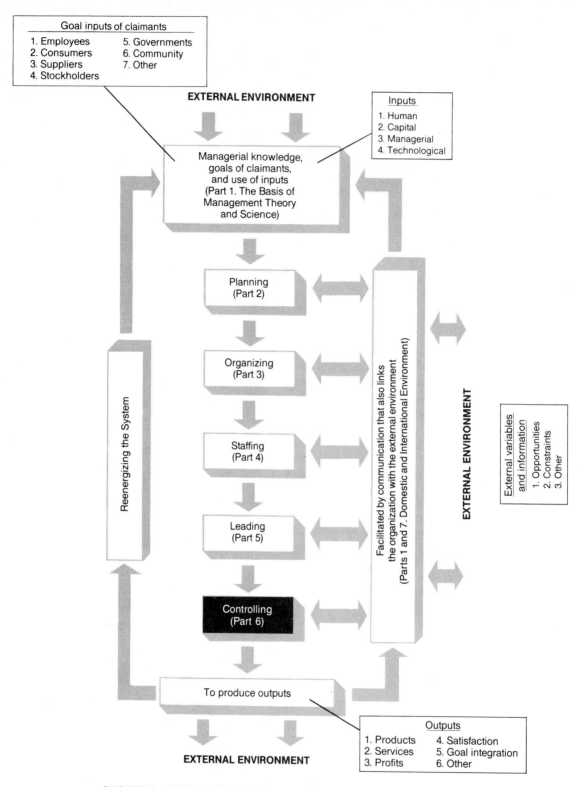

Goal inputs of claimants

1. Employees
2. Consumers
3. Suppliers
4. Stockholders
5. Governments
6. Community
7. Other

EXTERNAL ENVIRONMENT

Inputs

1. Human
2. Capital
3. Managerial
4. Technological

Managerial knowledge,
goals of claimants,
and use of inputs
(Part 1. The Basis of
Management Theory
and Science)

Planning
(Part 2)

Organizing
(Part 3)

Staffing
(Part 4)

Leading
(Part 5)

Controlling
(Part 6)

To produce outputs

Reenergizing the System

Facilitated by communication that also links
the organization with the external environment
(Parts 1 and 7. Domestic and International Environment)

EXTERNAL ENVIRONMENT

External variables
and information

1. Opportunities
2. Constraints
3. Other

Outputs

1. Products
2. Services
3. Profits
4. Satisfaction
5. Goal integration
6. Other

EXTERNAL ENVIRONMENT

SYSTEMS APPROACH TO MANAGEMENT: CONTROLLING

CHAPTER 18

The System and Process of Controlling

CHAPTER OBJECTIVES

After reading this chapter, you should understand:

1. The steps in the basic control process
2. The importance of critical control points and standards
3. Control as a feedback system
4. That real-time information will not solve all the problems of management control
5. That feedforward control systems can make management control more effective
6. The requirements for effective controls

The managerial function of **controlling** is the measurement and correction of performance in order to make sure that enterprise objectives and the plans devised to attain them are accomplished. Planning and controlling are closely related. In fact, some writers on management think that these functions cannot be separated. It is wise to separate them conceptually, however, which is why they are discussed individually in Parts 2 and 6 of this book. Still, planning and controlling may be viewed as the blades of a pair of scissors; the scissors cannot work unless there are two blades. Without objectives and plans, control is not possible, because performance has to be compared against some established criteria.

Controlling is the function of every manager from president to supervisor. Some managers, particularly at lower levels, forget that the primary responsibility for the exercise of control rests in every manager charged with the execution of plans. Occasionally, because of the authority of upper-level managers and their resultant responsibility, top- and upper-level control is so emphasized that people assume that little controlling is needed at lower levels. Although the scope of control varies among managers, those at all levels have responsibility for the execution of plans, and control is therefore an essential managerial function at every level.

Although control is often treated superficially in management literature, Giovanni B. Giglioni and Arthur G. Bedeian found a valuable body of knowledge in the following areas: control concepts, the process of control, characteristics of control systems, the problems encountered in control and the lessons learned from them, the variety of control models and techniques, and some principles for effective and efficient control.[1] Part 6 will cover all these topics, as well as others such as management information systems and tools for production and operation management.

THE BASIC CONTROL PROCESS

Control techniques and systems are essentially the same for cash, office procedures, morale, product quality, or anything else. The **basic control process,** wherever it is found and whatever is being controlled, involves three steps: (1) establishing standards, (2) measuring performance against these standards, and (3) correcting variations from standards and plans.

Establishment of Standards

Because plans are the yardsticks against which managers devise controls, the first step in the control process logically would be to establish plans. However, since plans vary in detail and complexity and since managers cannot usually watch everything, special standards are established. **Standards** are by definition simply criteria of performance. They are the selected points in an entire planning program at which measures of performance are made so that managers can receive signals about how things are going and thus do not have to watch every step in the execution of plans.

There are many kinds of standards. Among the best are verifiable goals or objectives, as suggested in the discussion of managing by objectives (see Chapter 4). You will learn more about standards, especially about those that point out deviations at critical points, in the next section.

Measurement of Performance

Although such measurement is not always practicable, the measurement of performance against standards should ideally be done on a forward-looking basis so that deviations may be detected in advance of their occurrence and avoided by appropriate actions. The alert, forward-looking manager can sometimes predict probable departures from standards. In the absence of such ability, however, deviations should be disclosed as early as possible.[2]

If standards are appropriately drawn and if means are available for determining exactly what subordinates are doing, appraisal of actual or expected performance is fairly easy. But there are many activities for which it is difficult to develop accurate standards, and there are many activities that are hard to measure. It may be quite simple to establish labor-hour standards for the production of a mass-produced item, and it may be equally simple to measure performance against these standards, but if the item is custom-made, the appraisal of performance may be a formidable task because standards are difficult to set.

Moreover, in the less technical kinds of work, not only may standards be hard to develop but also appraisal will be difficult. For example, controlling the work of the finance vice-president or the industrial relations director is not easy because definite standards are not easily developed. The superior of these managers often relies on vague standards, such as the financial health of the business, the attitude of labor unions, the absence of strikes, the enthusiasm and loyalty of subordinates, the expressed admiration of business associates, and the overall success of the department (often measured in a negative way by lack of evidence of failure). The superior's measurements are often equally vague. At the same time, if the department seems to be making the contribution expected of it at a reasonable cost and without too many serious errors, and if the measurable accomplishments give evidence of sound management, a general appraisal may be adequate. The point is that as jobs move away from the assembly line, the shop, or the accounting machine, controlling them becomes more complex and often even more important.

Correction of Deviations

Standards should reflect the various positions in an organization structure. If performance is measured accordingly, it is easier to correct deviations. Managers know exactly where, in the assignment of individual or group duties, the corrective measures must be applied.

Correction of deviations is the point at which control can be seen as a part of the whole system of management and can be related to the other managerial functions. Managers may correct deviations by redrawing their plans or by modifying their goals. (This is an exercise of the principle of navigational change.) Or they may correct deviations by exercising their organizing function through reassignment or clarification of duties. They may correct, also, by additional staffing, by better selection and training of subordinates, or by that ultimate restaffing measure — firing. Or, again, they may correct through better leading — fuller explanation of the job or more effective leadership techniques.

CRITICAL CONTROL POINTS AND STANDARDS

Standards are yardsticks against which actual or expected performance is measured. In a simple operation a manager might control through careful personal observation of the work being done. However, in most operations this is not possible because of the complexity of the operations and the fact that a manager has far more to do than personally observe performance for a whole day. A manager must choose points for special attention and then watch them to be sure that the whole operation is proceeding as planned.

The points selected for control should be *critical*, in the sense either of being limiting factors in the operation or of showing better than other factors whether plans are working out. With such standards, managers can handle a larger group of subordinates and thereby increase their span of management, with resulting cost savings and improvement of communication. The **principle of critical-point control,** one of the more important control principles, states: *Effective control requires attention to those factors critical to evaluating performance against plans.*

Questions for Selecting Critical Points of Control

The ability to select critical points of control is one of the arts of management, since sound control depends on them. In this connection, managers must ask themselves such questions as these: What will best reflect the goals of my department? What will best show me when these goals are not being met? What will best measure critical deviations? What will tell me who is responsible for any failure? What standards will cost the least? For what standards is information economically available?

Types of Critical-Point Standards

Every objective, every goal of the many planning programs, every activity of these programs, every policy, every procedure, and every budget become standards against which actual or expected performance might be measured. In practice, however, standards tend to be of the following types: (1) physical standards, (2) cost standards, (3) capital standards, (4) revenue standards, (5) program standards, (6) intangible standards, (7) goals as standards, and (8) strategic plans as control points for strategic control.

Physical standards   Physical standards are nonmonetary measurements and are common at the operating level, where materials are used, labor is employed, services are rendered, and goods are produced. They may reflect quantities such as labor-hours per unit of output, pounds of fuel per horsepower produced, ton-miles of freight traffic carried, units of production per machine-hour, or feet of wire per ton of copper. Physical standards may also reflect quality, such as hardness of bearings, closeness of tolerances, rate of climb of an airplane, durability of a fabric, or fastness of a color.

Cost standards   Cost standards are monetary measurements and, like physical standards, are common at the operating level. They attach monetary values to the costs of operations. Illustrative of cost standards are such widely used measures as direct and indirect costs per unit produced, labor cost per unit or per hour, material cost per unit, machine-hour costs, costs per plane reservation, selling costs per dollar or unit of sales, and costs per foot of oil well drilled.

Capital standards   There are a variety of capital standards, all arising from the application of monetary measurements to physical items. They have to do with the capital invested in the firm rather than with operating costs and are therefore primarily related to the balance sheet rather than to the income statement. Perhaps the most widely used standard for new investment, as well as for overall control, is return on investment. The typical balance sheet will disclose other capital standards, such as the ratios of current assets to current liabilities, debt to net worth, fixed investment to total investment, cash and receivables to payables, and notes or bonds to stock, as well as the size and turnover of inventories.

Revenue standards   Revenue standards arise from attaching monetary values to sales. They may include such standards as revenue per bus passenger–mile, average sale per customer, or sales per capita in a given market area.

Program standards   A manager may be assigned to install a variable budget program, a program for formally following the development of new products, or a program for improving the quality of a sales force. Although some subjective judgment may have to be applied in appraising program performance, timing and other factors can be used as objective standards.

Intangible standards   More difficult to set are standards not expressed in either physical or monetary measurements. What standard can a manager use for determining the competence of the divisional purchasing agent or personnel director? What can one use for determining whether the advertising program meets both short- and long-term objectives? Or whether the public relations program is successful? Are supervisors loyal to the company's objectives? Is the office staff alert? Such questions show the difficulty of establishing standards or goals for clear quantitative or qualitative measurement.

Many intangible standards exist in business, partially because adequate research into what constitutes desired performance has not been done above the level of the shop, the district sales office, the shipping room, or the accounting department. Perhaps a more important reason is that where human relationships count in performance, as they do above the basic operating levels, it is very hard to measure what is "good," "effective," or "efficient." Tests, surveys, and sampling techniques developed by psychologists and sociometrists have made it possible to probe human attitudes and drives, but many managerial controls over interpersonal relationships must continue to be based upon intangible standards, considered judgment, trial and error, and even, on occasion, sheer hunch.

Goals as standards   With the present tendency for better-managed enterprises to establish an entire network of verifiable qualitative or quantitative goals at every level of management, the use of intangible standards, while still important, is diminishing. In complex program operations, as well as in the performance of managers themselves, modern managers are finding that through research and thinking it is possible to define goals that can be used as performance standards. While the quantitative goals are likely to take the form of the standards outlined above, definition of qualitative goals represents an important development in the area of standards. For example, if the program of a district sales office is spelled out to include such elements as training salespeople in accordance with a plan with specific characteristics, the plan and its characteristics themselves furnish standards which tend to become objective and, therefore, "tangible."

Strategic plans as control points for strategic control   A great deal has been written about strategic planning, but relatively little is known about strategic control. According to a recent book on the topic, **strategic control** comprises systematic monitoring at strategic control points as well as modifying the organization's strategy on the basis of this evaluation.[3] The book's authors agree with the viewpoint expressed in this text, namely, that planning and controlling are closely related. Therefore, strategic plans require strategic control. Moreover, since controls facilitate comparisons of intended goals with actual performance, they also provide opportunities for learning, which, in turn, is the basis for organization change. Finally, through the use of strategic control one gains insights not only about organizational performance but also about the ever-changing environment by monitoring it.

CONTROL AS A FEEDBACK SYSTEM

Managerial control is essentially the same basic control process as that found in physical, biological, and social systems. Many systems control themselves through information feedback, which shows deviations from standards and initiates changes. In other words, systems use some of their energy to feed back information that compares performance with a standard and initiates corrective action. A simple feedback system was shown in Chapter 3 (see Figure 3-2).

Management control is usually perceived as a feedback system similar to that which operates in the usual household thermostat.[4] This can be seen clearly by looking at the feedback process in management control shown in Figure 18-1. This system places control in a more complex and realistic light than would regarding it merely as a matter of establishing standards, measuring performance, and correcting for deviations. Managers do measure actual performance, compare this measurement against standards, and identify and analyze deviations. But then, to make the necessary corrections, they must develop a program for corrective action and implement this program in order to arrive at the performance desired.

PERSPECTIVE:
EXAMPLES OF FEEDBACK SYSTEMS

The steam engine governor is a simple mechanical feedback system; in other words, it is a system of feedback of information for control. In order to control an engine's speed under different load conditions, weights (balls) are whirled. As the speed increases, centrifugal force makes these weights exercise an outward thrust; this force, in turn, transmits a message to cut down the input of steam and thereby reduce the speed. As speed is reduced, the reverse occurs. Likewise, in the human body, a number of feedback systems control temperature, blood pressure, motor reactions, and other conditions. Another example of feedback is the grade a student receives on a midterm test. This is intended, of course, to give students information about how they are doing and, if performance is less than desirable, to send a signal suggesting improvement. In social systems, even excluding the managed formal organizations, one also finds feedback. For example, in the social system of baseball, there are such standards as three strikes and out, and even the seventh-inning stretch, which are accomplished, essentially, by the feedback of information which corrects those who would deviate.

REAL-TIME INFORMATION AND CONTROL

One of the interesting advances arising from the use of the computer and from electronic gathering, transmission, and storage of data is the development of systems of **real-time information.** This is information about what is happening while it is happening. It is technically possible through various means to obtain real-time data on many operations. For years, airlines have obtained information about vacant seats simply by pushing a flight number, trip segment (for example, Los Angeles to New York), and date into a memory system that immediately responds with information on seat availability. Supermarkets and department stores have electronic cash registers in operation that immediately transmit data on every sale to a central data storage facility, where

Figure 18-1

FEEDBACK LOOP OF MANAGEMENT CONTROL.

inventory, sales, gross, profit, and other data can be obtained as they occur. A factory manager can have a system that reports at any time the status of production programs in terms of such things as production point reached and labor-hours accumulated and even whether a project is late or on time in the manufacturing process.

Some people see real-time information as a means of getting real-time control in areas of importance to managers — in other words, control effected at the very time information shows a deviation from plans. But reference to the management control feedback loop in Figure 18-1 shows that real-time information does not, except possibly in the simplest and most unusual cases, make possible real-time control. It is possible in many areas to collect real-time data that measure performance. It may also be possible in many of these cases to compare these data with standards and even to identify deviations. But the analysis of causes of deviations, the development of programs of correction, and the implementation of these programs are likely to be time-consuming tasks.

In the case of quality control, for example, it may take considerable time to discover what is causing factory rejects and more time to put corrective measures into effect. In the more complex case of inventory control, particularly in a manufacturing company, which has many items — raw materials, component parts, goods in process, and finished goods — the correction time may be very long. Once it is learned that an inventory is too high, the steps involved in getting it back to the desired level may take a number of months. And so it goes with most instances of management control problems: Time lags are unavoidable.

This does not mean that prompt measurement of performance is unimportant. The sooner managers know that activities for which they are responsible are not proceeding in accordance with plans, the faster they can take action to make corrections. Even so, there is always the question of whether the cost of gathering real-time data is worth the few days saved. Often it is, as in the case of the airline business, in which ready information on seat availability is likely to be crucial to serving customers and filling airplanes. But in a major defense company producing one of the highest-priority defense equipment items, there was little real-time information in an otherwise highly sophisticated control information system. Even for this program, it was thought that the benefit of gathering real-time data was not worth the expense because the correction process took so long.

FEEDFORWARD CONTROL[5]

The time lag in the management control process shows that control must be directed toward the future if it is to be effective. It illustrates the problem of only using feedback from the output of a system and measuring this output as a means of control. It shows the deficiency of historical data such as those received from accounting reports. One of the difficulties with such historical data is that they tell business managers in November that they lost money in October (or even September) because of something that was done in July. At this late time, such information is only a distressingly interesting historical fact.

What managers need for effective control is a system that will tell them, in time to take corrective action, that problems will occur if they do not do something about them now. Feedback from the output of a system is not good enough for control. It is little more than a postmortem, and no one has found a way to change the past.

Future-directed control is largely disregarded in practice, mainly because managers have been so dependent for purposes of control on accounting and statistical data.[6] To be sure, in the absence of any means of looking forward, reference to history — on the questionable assumption that what is past is prologue — is admittedly better than no reference at all.

Techniques of Future-Directed Control

Neglect of future-directed control does not mean that nothing has been done. One common way many managers have practiced it is through careful and repeated use of forecasts based on the latest available information: By comparing what is desired with the forecasts, managers can introduce program changes that will make the forecasts more promising. For example, if a company makes a sales forecast indicating that sales will be at a lower level than desirable, managers may develop new plans for advertising, sales promotion, or introduction of new products in order to improve the sales forecast.

Likewise, most businesses and other enterprises engage in future-directed control when managers carefully plan the availability of cash to meet requirements. Businesses, for example, would hardly find it wise to wait for a report at the middle or end of May to determine whether they had enough cash in the banks to cover checks issued in April.

One of the better techniques of future-directed control in use today is network planning, exemplified by PERT (Program Evaluation and Review Technique) networks (a topic to be discussed in Chapter 19). This technique of planning and control enables managers to see that they will have problems in such areas as costs or on-time delivery unless they take action now.

Feedforward in Human Systems

There are many examples of feedforward control in human systems. A motorist, for example, who wishes to maintain a constant speed in going up a hill would not usually wait for the speedometer to signal a drop in speed before depressing the accelerator. Instead, knowing that the hill represents a disturbing variable in the system, the driver would probably correct for this by pressing the accelerator before speed falls. Likewise, a hunter will always aim ahead of a duck's flight to correct for the time lag between a shot and a hoped-for hit.

Feedforward versus Feedback Systems

Simple feedback systems measure outputs of a process and feed into the system or the inputs of a system corrective actions to obtain desired outputs. For most management problems, because of time lags in the correction process, this is not good enough. Feedforward systems monitor *inputs* into a process to ascertain whether the inputs are as planned; if they are not, the inputs, or perhaps the process, are changed in order to obtain desired results.

A comparison of feedforward and feedback systems is depicted in Figure 18-2. In a sense, a feedforward control system is really a kind of feedback system. However, the information feedback is at the *input* side of the system so that corrections can be made before the system output is affected. Also, even with a feedforward system, a manager would still want to measure the final system output, since nothing can be expected to work perfectly enough to ensure that the final output will always be exactly as desired.

Feedforward in Management

An idea of what feedforward means in management control can be conveyed through the examples of cash and inventory planning systems. Figures 18-3 and 18-4 illustrate what is involved.

The somewhat simplified schematic figures of input variables shown in the charts for cash and for inventory planning and control indicate that if managers are to exercise effective control over either cash or inventories, they must identify each as an interacting system. As can be seen in each instance, some of the variables interact, and some have either a negative or a positive effect on either cash or inventory.

Also, if the system of variables and their impact on a process are accurately portrayed — and each enterprise should design its own system, appropriate to the realities of its situation — a deviation from any planned input can

Figure 18-2

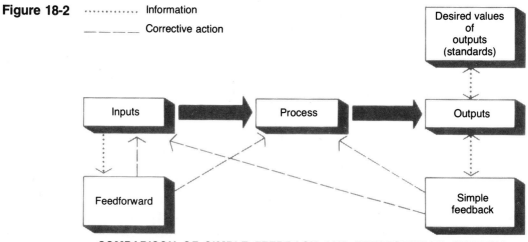

.... Information

— — — — Corrective action

COMPARISON OF SIMPLE FEEDBACK AND FEEDFORWARD SYSTEMS.

Figure 18-3

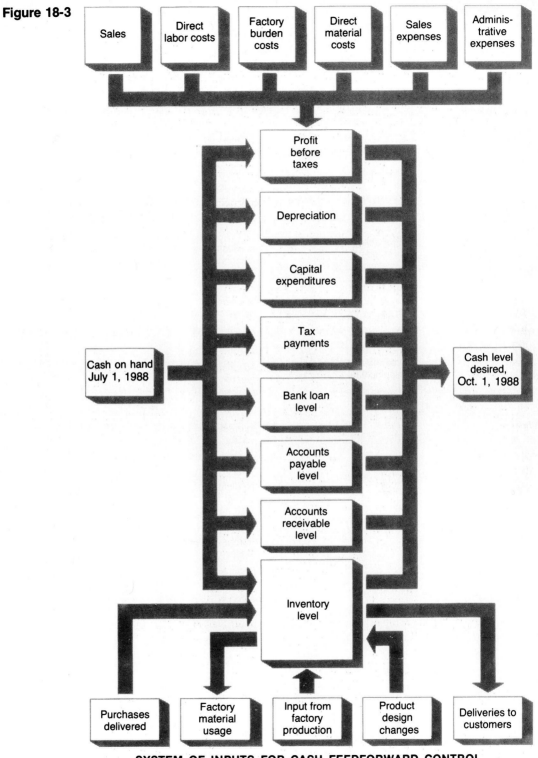

SYSTEM OF INPUTS FOR CASH FEEDFORWARD CONTROL.

Figure 18-4

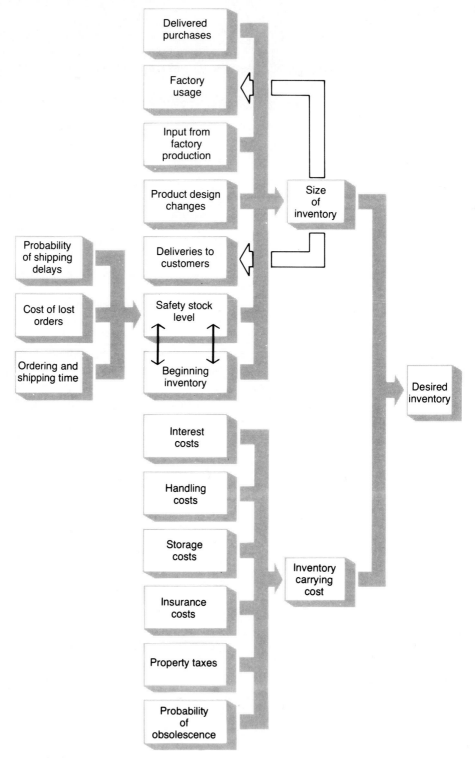

SYSTEM OF INPUTS FOR FEEDFORWARD INVENTORY CONTROL.

result in an unplanned output unless something is done about it in time. For example, in the case of the inventory model, if purchase deliveries are greater than planned or if factory usage turns out to be less than planned, the result will be a higher-than-planned inventory unless corrective action is taken. Of course, to make feedforward work in practice, inputs must be carefully monitored.

In the best kind of feedforward control program, the model of input variables should include inputs in the system model that materially influence the key inputs. For example, purchase deliveries tend to increase inventories; but these deliveries are, of course, dependent on orders placed, and the placing of orders is in turn dependent on other factors.

The system of feedforward may appear to be rather complex. But for major problem areas, at least, it should not be difficult to identify system input variables, to see them as an interacting system, and to computerize the model. From that point it should be an easy matter to gather information on the inputs and to determine on a regular basis their effect on the desired end result. Certainly, in view of its importance to meaningful management control, this would not appear to be too much trouble to take.

One of the problems in all feedforward control systems is the necessity of watching for what engineers call "disturbances." These are factors which have not been taken into account in the input model but which may have an impact on the system and desired end results. Obviously, it would be impracticable to take into account in a model all inputs that might possibly affect the operation of a program. For example, for a company with a long history of adequate flow of bank loans for financing needs, the possibility that the company's bank may suddenly have to restrict credit might not have been a variable put into the input system. Or the bankruptcy of a large customer or supplier might be an unanticipated, and unprogrammed, input variable. Since unprogrammed events do sometimes occur and may upset a desired output, monitoring regular inputs must be supplemented by watching for, and taking into account, unusual or unexpected "disturbances."

Requirements for Feedforward Control

The requirements for a workable feedforward control system may be summarized as follows:

1. Make a thorough and careful analysis of the planning and control system, and identify the more important input variables.

2. Develop a model of the system.

3. Take care to keep the model up to date; in other words, the model should be reviewed regularly to see whether the input variables identified and their interrelationships continue to represent realities.

4. Collect data on input variables regularly and put them into the system.

5. Regularly assess the variations of actual input data from planned-for inputs and evaluate the impact on expected end results.

6. Take action. Like any other technique of planning and control, all that the system can do is indicate problems; people must obviously take action to solve them.

REQUIREMENTS FOR EFFECTIVE CONTROLS

All alert managers want to have an adequate and effective system of controls to assist them in making sure that events conform to plans.[7] It is sometimes not realized that the controls used by managers must be designed for the specific task and person they are intended to serve. While the basic process and the fundamentals of control are universal, the actual system requires special design.

Indeed, if controls are to work, they must be specially tailored. In short, they must be tailored to plans and positions, to the individual managers and their personalities, and to the needs for efficiency and effectiveness.

Tailoring Controls to Plans and Positions

All control techniques and systems should reflect the plans they are designed to follow. Every plan and every kind and phase of an operation has unique characteristics. What managers need is the information that will tell them how the plans for which they are responsible are progressing. Certainly, the information needed for following the progress of a marketing program will be quite different from that needed for checking on a production plan.

In the same way, controls should be tailored to positions. What will be appropriate for a vice-president in charge of manufacturing will certainly not be suitable for a shop supervisor. Controls for the sales department will differ from those for the finance department, and both will differ from controls for the purchasing department. A small business will need some controls that differ from those in a large business. The very nature of control emphasizes the fact that the more controls are designed to deal with and reflect the specific nature and structure of plans, the more effectively they will serve managerial needs.

Certain techniques, such as budgets, standard hours and costs, and various financial ratios, have general application in various situations. However, none of these widely used techniques is completely applicable in any given situation. Managers must always be aware of the critical factors in their plans and operations requiring control, and they must use techniques and information suited to them.

Controls should also reflect the organization structure. Being the principal means of clarifying the roles of people in an enterprise, organization structure shows who is responsible for the execution of plans and for any deviation from them. Controls must therefore reflect the organization structure, and the more carefully controls are designed to reflect the place in the organization where responsibility for action lies, the more they will enable managers to correct deviations from plans.

Tailoring Controls to Individual Managers

Controls must also be tailored to individual managers. Control systems and information are of course intended to help individual managers carry out their function of control. If they are not of a type that a manager can or will understand, they will not be useful. It really does not matter whether people cannot understand a control technique or control information or whether they are just unwilling to understand it. In either case, it is not understood. What individuals cannot understand they will not trust. And what they do not trust they will not use.

Some people — for instance, certain statisticians and accountants — like their information in the form of complex tables of data or voluminous computer printouts; in such cases, they should have it that way. Other people like their information in chart form; if so, it should be furnished that way. And a few people — for instance, scientists and mathematicians — may even like their information in mathematical model form; in this event, it should be given to them that way. It is sometimes said that if people will not understand the information they need in any other way, one should consider giving it to them in comic-book form. The important thing is that people should get the information they need in a form they will understand and use.

What is said about tailoring information for understanding is true also of control techniques. Even quite intelligent people may be "turned off" by some of the sophisticated techniques of the expert. Sophisticated techniques of planning and control, like variable budgeting or network planning, can fail in practice solely because the systems either were not comprehensible to the people who had to use them or appeared to be too complex for them. Experts in these matters must not try to show others how expert they are; rather, they should design a system at the level of ready comprehension so that people will use it. Obtaining 80 percent of the possible benefit from a fairly crude system is far better than obtaining no benefit from a more perfect, but unworkable, system.

Controls Pointing Up Exceptions at Critical Points

One of the most important ways of tailoring controls to the needs for efficiency and effectiveness is to make sure that they are designed to *point up exceptions*. In other words, by concentrating on exceptions from planned performance, managers can use controls based on the time-honored exception principle to detect those areas that require their attention.

But it is not enough merely to look at exceptions. Some deviations from standards have little meaning, and others have a great deal. Small deviations in certain areas may have greater significance than larger exceptions in other areas. A manager, for example, might be concerned if the cost of office labor deviated from budget by 5 percent but might be unworried if the cost of postage stamps deviated from budget by 20 percent.

Consequently, the exception principle should be accompanied in practice by the *principle of critical-point control*. It is not enough just to look for exceptions; one must look for them at critical points. Certainly, the more that managers concentrate their control efforts on exceptions, the more efficient their control will be. But this principle had best be considered in light of the fact that effective control requires that managers pay primary attention to those things which are most important.

Objectivity of Controls

Management necessarily has many subjective elements, but whether a subordinate is doing a good job should ideally not be a matter for subjective determination. If controls are subjective, a manager's or a subordinate's personality may influence judgments of performance and make them less accurate; but people have difficulty in explaining away control of their performance, particularly if the standards and measurements are kept up to date through periodic review. This requirement may be summarized by saying that effective control requires objective, accurate, and suitable standards.

Flexibility of Controls

Controls should remain workable in the face of changed plans, unforeseen circumstances, or outright failures. If controls are to remain effective despite failure or unexpected changes of plans, they must be flexible.

The need for flexible control can readily be illustrated. A budget system may project a certain level of expenses and grant authority to managers to hire labor and purchase materials and services at this level. If, as is usually the case, this budget is based on a forecast of a certain level of sales, it may become meaningless as a system of control if the actual sales volume is considerably above or below the forecast. Budget systems have been brought into ill repute among some companies because of inflexibility in such circumstances. What is needed, of course, is a system that will reflect sales variations as well as other deviations from plans. This requirement is provided by the flexible, or variable, budget, as Chapter 19 will show.

Fitting the Control System to the Organizational Climate

To be most effective, any control system or technique must fit the organizational climate. For example, in an organization where people have been given considerable freedom and participation, a tight control system may go so strongly against the grain that it will be doomed to failure. On the other hand, if subordinates have been managed by a superior who allows little participation in decision making, a generalized and permissive control system would hardly succeed. People who have little desire to participate, or who have not been accustomed to participating, are likely to want clear standards and measurements and specific directions.

Economy of Controls

Controls must be worth their cost. Although this requirement is simple, it is often difficult to accomplish in practice. A manager may have difficulty in ascertaining what a paticular control system is worth or what it costs. Economy is relative, since the benefits vary with the importance of the activity, the size of the operation, the expense that might be incurred in the absence of control, and the contribution the system can make.

A limiting factor of control systems is their cost; this, in turn, will depend a great deal on managers' selecting for control only critical factors in areas important to them. If tailored to the job and to the size of the enterprise, control will probably be economical. One of the economies of large-scale enterprise is being able to afford expensive and elaborate control systems. Often, however, the magnitude of the problems, the wider area of planning, the difficulty of coordinating plans, and poor management communication in a large organization require such expensive controls that their overall efficiency suffers in comparison with lesser controls in a small business. Control techniques and approaches are efficient when they bring to light the causes of actual or potential deviations from plans with the minimum of costs.

Controls Leading to Corrective Action

An adequate system will disclose where failures are occurring and who is responsible for them, and it will ensure that some corrective action is taken. Control is justified only if deviations from plans are corrected through appropriate planning, organizing, staffing, and leading.

SUMMARY

The managerial function of controlling is the measurement and correction of performance in order to ensure that enterprise objectives and the plans devised to attain them are being accomplished. It is a function of every manager from president to supervisor.

Control techniques and systems are basically the same regardless of what is being controlled. Wherever it is found and whatever is being controlled, the basic control process involves three steps: (1) establishing standards, (2) measuring performance against these standards, and (3) correcting variations from standards and plans. There are different kinds of standards, and they should point out deviations at critical points.

Managerial control is usually perceived as a simple feedback system similar to the common household thermostat. However, no matter how quickly information is available on what is occurring (even real-time information, which is information on what is happening as it happens), there are unavoidable delays in analyzing deviations, developing plans for taking corrective action, and implementing these programs. In order to overcome these time lags in control, it is suggested that managers utilize a feedforward control approach and not rely on simple feedback alone. Feedforward control requires designing a model of a process or system and monitoring inputs with a view to detecting future deviations of results from standards and plans, thereby giving managers time to take corrective action.

If controls are to work, they must be specially tailored (1) to plans and positions, (2) to individual managers, and (3) to the needs for efficiency and effectiveness. To be effective, controls also should be designed to point up exceptions at critical points, to be objective, to be flexible, to fit the organizational climate, to be economical, and to lead to corrective action.

KEY IDEAS AND CONCEPTS FOR REVIEW

Controlling	Techniques of future-directed control
Steps in controlling	Feedforward control in management
Critical-point control	Requirements for feedforward control
Types of critical-point standards	Requirements for adequate controls
Feedback systems	Exception principle
Real-time information system	

FOR DISCUSSION

1. Planning and control are often thought of as a system; control is also often referred to as a system. What is meant by these observations? Can both statements be true?

2. Why is real-time information not good enough for effective control?

3. What is feedforward control? Why is it important to managers? Besides the examples of cash and inventory control mentioned in this chapter, can you think of any other areas in which feedforward would be used? Selecting one of these, how would you proceed?

4. If you were asked to institute a system of "tailored" controls in a company, how would you go about it? What would you need to know?

5. Develop a set of standards for any area of interest to you over which you might wish to exercise effective control.

EXERCISES/ACTION STEPS

1. Design a control system for measuring the progress you make in your course work. Apply the feedback and feedforward concepts discussed in this chapter.

2. Interview two managers about the controls used in their companies. Can you identify standards against which performance can be accurately measured? How is performance measured against the standard and how timely is the reporting of deviations? If deviations are detected, how long does it take before corrections are made in specific situations?

CASE:
THE KAPPA CORPORATION

As George House, vice-president of finance, and Helen Robbins, controller, walked into the office of Adrian Barnes, chairperson and chief executive officer of Kappa Corporation, they were met with the following outburst from the company's top officer:

"Why doesn't someone tell me things? Why can't I know what is going on around here? Why am I kept in the dark? No one informs me about how the company is doing, and I never seem to hear of our problems until they become crises. Now, I want you both to work out a system for keeping me informed, and I want to know by next Monday how you will do it. I am tired of

being isolated from the things I must know if I am to take responsibility for this company."

After George House had left Mr. Barnes's office, he turned to his controller and muttered, "That silly jerk! Everything he wants to know or could possibly want to know is in that stack of reports on the table in back of his desk."

1. Who was right — Adrian Barnes or George House? Was Barnes getting information?

2. What would you do to make sure that the chairperson did get the information he needed for control purposes?

REFERENCES

1. For an excellent summary of pioneering writers on control, see Giovanni B. Giglioni and Arthur G. Bedeian, "A Conspectus of Management Control Theory: 1900–1972," *Academy of Management Journal* (June 1974), pp. 292–305.

2. Richard L. Daft and Norman B. Macintosh, "The Nature and Use of Formal Control Systems for Management Control and Strategy Implementation," *Journal of Management* (Fall 1984), pp. 43–66.

3. Peter Lorange, Michael F. Scott Morton, and Sumantra Ghoshal, *Strategic Control* (St. Paul, Minn.: West Publishing Company, 1986), p. xvii. See also Daft and Macintosh, "The Nature and Use of Formal Control Systems" (1984).

4. There are also limitations and problems in relying on feedback. See Geert Hofstede, "The Poverty of Management Control Philosophy," in Richards, *Readings* (1986), pp. 302–315. Some of the limitations of traditional controls will be discussed in Chapter 21 under the topic "preventive controls."

5. For a discussion of feedforward control techniques, see Harold Koontz and Robert W. Bradspies, "Managing through Feedforward Control," in Harold Koontz, Cyril O'Donnell, and Heinz Weihrich, (eds.) *Management: A Book of Readings*, 5th ed. (New York: McGraw-Hill Book Company, 1980), pp. 576–585. Much of the material in this section is drawn from that paper.

6. The idea of future-directed control was emphasized by one of the authors many years ago. See Harold Koontz, "A Preliminary Statement of Principles of Planning and Control," *Academy of Management Journal* (April 1958), pp. 45–61. Now many authors discuss this concept but they give it different names. For example, the term "steering controls" has been used by James A. F. Stoner and Charles Wankel, *Management*, 3d ed. (Englewood Cliffs, N.J.: Prentice-Hall, 1986), p. 579; and John R. Schermerhorn, Jr., *Management for Productivity*, 2d ed. (New York: John Wiley & Sons, 1986), p. 402.

7. See also Robert N. Anthony, John Dearden, and Norton M. Bedford, *Management Control Systems*, 5th ed. (Homewood, Ill., Richard D. Irwin, 1984).

CHAPTER 19

Control Techniques and Information Technology

CHAPTER OBJECTIVES

After reading this chapter, you should understand:

1. The nature of budgeting and types of budgets
2. Modern techniques of budgeting, including variable and zero-base budgets
3. Nonbudgetary control devices
4. Time-event networks as major techniques of planning and control
5. The nature and applications of information technology
6. The importance of computers in handling information
7. The challenges created by the new information technology.

Although the basic nature and purpose of management control do not change, a variety of tools and techniques have been used over the years to help managers control. As this chapter will show, all these techniques are in the first instance tools for planning. They illustrate the fundamental truth that the task of controls is to make plans succeed; naturally, in doing so, controls must reflect plans, and planning must precede control.

Some of these tools may be classed as traditional in the sense that they have long been used by managers, although variable budgeting and zero-base budgeting, for example, are refinements of traditional budgeting. Others, like Program Evaluation and Review Technique (PERT) and program budgeting, represent a newer generation of planning and control tools. While there are many more of these than discussed here, the newer tools generally reflect the systems techniques long used in the physical sciences. Operations research (discussed in Chapter 20) is such a technique. Since information is vital for managing effectively, this chapter also examines the newer information technology and its challenges, as well as the use of computers.

In spite of all the newer techniques of planning and control, the traditional tools are still extremely important.

CONTROL TECHNIQUES: THE BUDGET*

A widely used device for managerial control is the budget. Indeed, it has sometimes been assumed that budgeting is *the* device for accomplishing control. However, many nonbudgetary devices are also essential.

The Concept of Budgeting

Budgeting is the formulation of plans for a given future period in numerical terms. As such, budgets are statements of anticipated results, either in financial terms — as in revenue and expense and capital budgets — or in nonfinancial terms — as in budgets of direct-labor-hours, materials, physical sales volume, or units of production. It has sometimes been said, for example, that financial budgets represent the "dollarizing" of plans.

The Purpose of Budgeting

By stating plans in terms of numbers and breaking them into parts that parallel the parts of an organization, budgets correlate planning and allow authority to be delegated without loss of control. In other words, reducing plans to numbers forces a kind of orderliness that permits the manager to see clearly what capital will be spent by whom and where, and what expense, revenue, or units of physical input or output the plans will involve. Having ascertained this, the manager can more freely delegate authority to effect the plan within the limits of the budget. Moreover, a budget, to be useful to a manager at any level, must reflect the organizational pattern. Only when plans are complete, coordinated, and developed enough to be fitted into departmental operations can a useful departmental budget be prepared as an instrument of control.

Types of Budgets

There are many types of budgets. They may be classified into several basic types, with a budget summary (discussed in Chapter 21) portraying the total

---

*Primarily because of the negative implications of budgeting in the past, the more positive phrase "profit planning" is sometimes used and the budget is then known as the "profit plan."

planning picture of all the budgets: (1) revenue and expense budgets, (2) time, space, material, and product budgets, (3) capital expenditure budgets, and (4) cash budgets.

Revenue and expense budgets   By far the most common budgets spell out plans for revenues and operating expenses in dollar terms. The most basic of these is the sales budget (for a simple example, see Table 19-1), which is a formal and detailed expression of the sales forecast. Just as the sales forecast is the cornerstone of planning, so is the sales budget the foundation of budgetary control. Although a company may budget other revenues, such as expected income from rentals, royalties, or miscellaneous sources, the revenue from sales of products or services furnishes the principal income to pay operating expenses and yield profits.

    Operating expense budgets of the typical enterprise can be as numerous as the expense classifications in its chart of accounts and the units of organization in its structure. These budgets may deal with individual items of expense, such as travel, data processing, entertainment, advertising, telephone, and insurance. Sometimes a department head will budget only major items and lump together other items in one control summary. For example, if the manager of a small department is expected to take one business trip a year at a cost of $720, budgeting this cost each month at $60 would mean little for monthly planning or control.

Time, space, material, and product budgets   Many budgets are better expressed in quantities rather than in monetary terms. Although such budgets are usually translated into monetary terms, they are much more significant at a certain stage in planning and control if they are expressed in terms of quantities. Among the more common of these are the budgets for direct-labor-hours, machine-hours, units of materials, square feet allocated, and units produced.

Table 19-1   **A Typical Sales Budget**
(For the year ending December 31, 1992)

Product and area	Unit sales volume	Unit selling price	Total sales
Product A:			
Area 1	26,000	$10	$260,000
Area 2	15,000	10	150,000
Area 3	20,000	10	200,000
Total			$610,000
Product B:			
Area 1	30,000	$15	$ 450,000
Area 2	20,000	15	300,000
Area 3	22,000	15	330,000
Total			$1,080,000
Total revenue from sales			$1,690,000

Most firms budget product output, and most production departments budget their share of the output of components of the final product. In addition, it is common to budget labor, in either labor-hours or labor-days or by types of labor required. Obviously, such budgets cannot be well expressed in monetary terms, since the dollar cost would not accurately measure the resources used or the results intended.

Capital expenditure budgets   Capital expenditure budgets outline specifically capital expenditures for plant, machinery, equipment, inventories, and other items. Whether for a short term or a long one, these budgets require care because they give definite form to plans for spending the funds of an enterprise. Since capital is generally one of the most limiting factors of any enterprise and since a business takes a long time to recover its investment in plant and equipment through charges as costs, thereby leading to a high degree of inflexibility, capital expenditure budgets should usually be tied in with fairly long-range planning.

Cash budgets   The cash budget is simply a forecast of cash receipts and disbursements against which actual cash "experience" is measured. Whether called a budget or not, this is one of the most important controls in an enterprise. The availability of cash to meet obligations as they fall due is the first requirement of existence, and handsome business profits do little good when tied up in inventory, machinery, or other noncash assets. Cash budgeting also shows the availability of excess cash, thereby making it possible to plan for profit-making investment of surpluses.

Dangers in budgeting

Budgets are used for planning and control. Unfortunately, some budgetary control programs are so complete and detailed that they become cumbersome, meaningless, and unduly expensive.

Overbudgeting   There is a danger in overbudgeting through spelling out minor expenses in detail and depriving managers of needed freedom in managing their departments. For example, a department head in a poorly budgeted company was hindered in an important sales promotion because expenditures for office supplies exceeded budgeted estimates; new expenditures had to be limited, even though his total departmental expenses were well within the budget and he had funds to pay personnel for writing sales promotion letters. In another department, expenses were budgeted in such useless detail that the actual budgeting cost of many items exceeded the expenses controlled.

Overriding enterprise goals   Another danger lies in allowing budgetary goals to become more important than enterprise goals. In their zest to keep within budget limits, managers may forget that they owe primary loyalty to enterprise objectives. In one company with a budgetary control program, the sales department could not obtain needed information from the engineering department on the grounds that the latter's budget would not stand such expense! This conflict between partial and overall control objectives, the excessive departmental independence generated, and the lack of coordination are symptoms of inadequate management, since plans should constitute a supporting and interlocking network and every plan should be reflected in a budget in a way that will aid in achieving enterprise goals.

Hiding inefficiencies Another danger in budgeting is that it may be used to hide inefficiencies. Budgets have a way of growing from precedent; the fact that a certain expenditure was made in the past can become evidence of its reasonableness in the present. Thus, if a department once spent a given amount for supplies, this cost becomes a minimum for future budgets. Also, managers sometimes learn that budget requests are likely to be pared down in the course of final approval, and therefore they ask for much more than they need. Unless budget making is accomplished by constant reexamination of standards and conversion factors by which planned action is translated into numerical terms, the budget may become an umbrella under which slovenly and inefficient management can hide.

Causing inflexibility Perhaps inflexibility is the greatest danger in budgets. Even if budgeting is not used to replace managing, the reduction of plans to numerical terms gives them a kind of misleading definiteness. It is entirely possible that events will prove that a larger amount should be spent for this kind of labor or that kind of material and a smaller amount for another, or that sales will exceed or fall below the amount forecast. Such differences may make a budget obsolete almost as soon as it is formulated; if managers must stay within the straitjacket of their budgets in the face of such events, the usefulness of budgets is reduced or nullified. This is especially true when budgets are made for long periods in advance.

Variable Budgets

Because dangers arise from inflexibility in budgets and because maximum flexibility consistent with efficiency underlies good planning, attention has been increasingly given to **variable, or flexible, budgets.** These are designed to vary usually as the volume of sales or some other measure of output varies and so are limited largely to expense budgets. The variable budget is based upon an analysis of expense items to determine how individual costs *should* vary with volume of output. Some costs do not vary with volume, particularly in so short a period as 1 month, 6 months, or a year. Among these are depreciation, property taxes and insurance, maintenance of plant and equipment, and costs of keeping a minimum staff of supervisory and other key personnel. Some of these standby, or period, costs — such as those of maintaining a minimum number of key or trained personnel for advertising or sales promotion and for research — depend upon managerial policy.

Costs that vary with volume of output range from those that are completely variable to those that are only slightly variable. The task of variable budgeting involves selecting some unit of measure that reflects volume; inspecting the various categories of costs (usually by reference to the chart of accounts); and, by statistical studies, methods of engineering analyses, and other means, determining how these costs should vary with volume of output. At this stage, each category of cost is related to volume, sometimes with recognition of "steps" as volume increases. Each department is given these variable cost items, along with definite dollar amounts for its fixed, or standby, costs. Periodically — usually each month — department heads are then given the volume forecast for the immediate future, from which is calculated the dollar amounts of variable costs that make up the budget. In this way, a basic budget can be established for 6 or 12 months in advance, but it can be made variable with shorter-term changes in sales and output.

The variable budget chart in Figure 19-1 is based on the assumption that period costs will remain the same for a volume output of 0 to 6000 units. In most cases, a variable budget will represent a range of output in which plant,

Figure 19-1

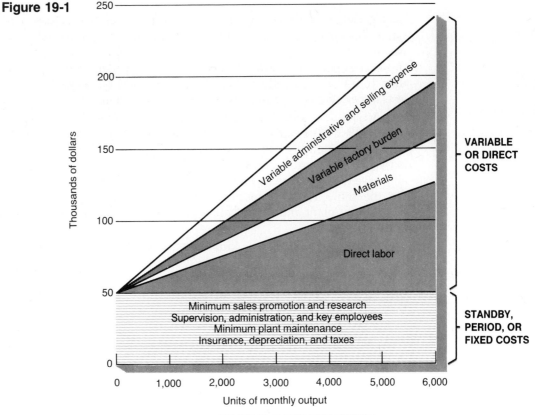

VARIABLE BUDGET CHART.

Table 19-2 A Typical Variable Budget for an Entire Company
(In thousands of dollars)

Item of expense	Monthly sales volume						
	$575	**$625**	**$675**	**$725**	**$775**	**$825**	**$875**
Material	$184	$200	$216	$232	$248	$264	$280
Direct labor	70	76	82	88	94	100	106
Overhead costs	150	155	161	168	170	171	174
Cost of production	$404	$431	$459	$488	$512	$535	$560
Engineering	$ 35	$ 36	$ 38	$ 38	$ 38	$ 38	$ 40
Research and development	10	10	10	10	12	12	12
Sales and advertising	64	66	69	72	73	74	75
Administrative costs	60	62	63	63	64	65	66
Total costs	$573	$605	$639	$671	$699	$724	$753
Profits from operations	$2	$20	$36	$54	$76	$101	$122
Percentage of profit to sale	0.3%	3.2%	5.4%	7.5%	9.8%	12.3%	14%

managerial, organizational, and other elements of period cost will be the same. But, in practice, this may be over a range of 3000 to 10,000 units. If it were less than 3000 units, a different variable budget would be required with the level of period costs more suitable for the smaller volume; if it were more than 10,000 units, another variable budget would be necessary to reflect the level of period costs necessitated by a larger operation.

A typical variable budget resulting from the analysis in the text is shown in Table 19-2. This expense budget, for an entire company, is based on a range of expected monthly sales volume of $575,000 to $875,000. The assumption is that if sales were thought to be below $575,000, the company would probably have to reorganize its operations to sustain this smaller volume profitably. On the other hand, if monthly sales rose above $875,000, an expansion of company plant and organization would require a completely new variable budget.

When using the various kinds of variable budgets, department managers must still make future plans. It may be easy to tell a certain supervisor that during the month of May he can have twelve trained electronic assemblers; then, several weeks later, that he may have fifteen in June; and a month later, that his budget for July will permit him to have only ten. But the problems of hiring and training competent personnel make the process of accomplishing these variations more costly than the savings they are intended to produce. In other words, efficiency may demand that department managers not vary certain of their expenses with short-term variations in volume. In the search for flexibility in budgets, as with other tools of management, an intelligent manager will not lose sight of basic objectives and efficiencies by blindly following any system.

Variable budgets work best when sales or other measures of volume can be reasonably well forecast and when longer-range plans are made, so that the level of expense will not have to be changed so often and on such short notice as to make the job of supervisors intolerable. Under these circumstances, one might well ask: What are the advantages of variable budgeting? Although a fixed budget will work as well with good plans and sales forecasts, a variable budget forces study of, and preoccupation with, factors which translate work load into labor or expense needs. Conversion factors — carefully worked out and applied in advance — are necessary for any good budgeting. This, rather than flexibility itself, appears to be the principal advantage of variable budgeting.

Alternative and Supplementary Budgets

Another method of obtaining variable budgeting is to establish **alternative budgets.** Sometimes a company will establish budgets for a high level of operation, a medium level, and a low level, and the three budgets will be approved for the company as a whole and for each organizational segment for 6 or 12 months in advance. Then, at stated times, managers will be informed as to which budget to use in their planning and control. Alternative budgets are a modification of variable budgets, the latter being virtually infinitely variable instead of being limited to a few alternatives.

Budget flexibility is also obtained with a plan referred to as the **supplemental monthly budget.** Under this plan, a 6-month or 1-year budget is prepared for the primary purpose of outlining the framework of the company's plans, coordinating them among departments, and establishing department objectives. This is a basic or minimum budget. Then a supplementary budget is prepared each month on the basis of the volume of business forecast for that month. This budget gives each manager authority for scheduling output and spending funds above the basic budget if, and to the extent that, the shorter-term plans so justify. It avoids some of the detailed calculations necessary under the typical variable budget. But these budget approaches do not usually have the advantage of forcing complete analysis of all costs and relating them to volume.

Zero-Base Budgeting

Another type of budgeting, the purpose of which has much in common with the purpose of a well-operated system of variable budgeting, is **zero-base budgeting.** The idea behind this technique is to divide enterprise programs into "packages" composed of goals, activities, and needed resources and then to calculate costs for each package from the ground up. By starting the budget of each package from base zero, costs are calculated afresh for each budget period, thus avoiding the common tendency in budgeting of looking only at changes from a previous period.

This technique has generally been applied to so-called support areas, rather than to actual production areas, on the assumption that there is some room for discretion in expenditures for most programs in such areas as marketing, research and development, personnel, planning, and finance. The various programs thought to be desirable are costed and reviewed in terms of their benefits to the enterprise and are then ranked in accordance with those benefits and selected on the basis of which package will yield the benefit desired.

The principal advantage of this technique is, of course, the fact that it forces managers to plan each program package afresh. As managers do so, they review established programs and their costs in their entirety, along with newer programs and their costs.

Effective Budgetary Control

If budgetary controls are to work well, managers must remember that budgets are designed only as tools and not as replacements for managing, that they have limitations, and that they must be tailored to each job. Moreover, they are the tools of all managers and not only of the budget administrator or the controller. The only persons who can administer budgets, since they are plans, are the managers responsible for budgeted programs. No successful budget program can be truly "directed" or "administered" by a budget director. This staff officer can assist in the preparation and use of budgets by the responsible managers, but, unless the entire company management is to be turned over to the budget officer, this person should not be given the job of making budget-commitment or expenditure decisions.

Top-management support   To be most effective, budget making and administration must receive the wholehearted support of top management. Establishing an office of budget administrator by decree and then forgetting about it leads to haphazard budget making and to saddling subordinate managers with another procedure or set of papers to prepare. On the other hand, if top management actively supports budget making and grounds a budget firmly on plans, requires divisions and departments to make and defend their budgets, and participates in this review, then budgets encourage alert management throughout the organization.

Participation   Related to the participation of top management, another means of making budgets work is to make sure that all managers expected to operate and live under budgets have a part in their preparation. Real participation in budget making is necessary to ensure success. Most budget administrators and controllers recognize this fact, but too often in practice participation amounts to managers' being simply pressured to "accept" budgets.

Although budgets do furnish a means of delegating authority without loss of control, there is danger, as noted earlier, that they will be so detailed and inflexible that little real authority is, in fact, delegated. Some executives even believe that the best budget to give managers is one that lumps all their allowable expenditures for a period of time into a single amount and then gives them complete freedom regarding how these funds are to be spent in pursuance of the company's goals. This kind of decentralization has much to recommend it, although better planning and control might be achieved by allowing the department manager to participate actively in budget making. It may be a good idea, however, to give department managers a reasonable degree of latitude in changing their budgets and in shifting funds, as long as they meet their *total* budgets.

Standards   One of the keys to successful budgeting is to develop and make available standards by which programs and work can be translated into needs for labor, operating expenses, capital expenditures, space, and other resources. Many budgets fail for lack of such standards, and some upper-level managers hesitate to allow subordinates to submit budget plans for fear that they may have no logical basis for reviewing budget requests. With conversion factors available, superior managers can review such requests and justify their approval or disapproval of them. Moreover, by concentrating on the resources required to do a planned job, managers can base their request on what they need to have for meeting output goals and improving performance. They no longer must cope with arbitrary across-the-board budget cuts — a very frustrating technique. In fact, across-the-board cuts are the surest evidence of poor planning and loss of control.

Information   Finally, if budgetary control is to work, managers need ready information about actual and forecast performance under budgets by their departments. This information must be designed to show them how well they are doing. Unfortunately, such information is usually not available until it is too late for the manager to avoid budget deviations.

TRADITIONAL NONBUDGETARY CONTROL DEVICES

There are, of course, many traditional control devices not connected with budgets, although some may be related to, and used with, budgetary controls. Among the more important of them are (1) statistical data, (2) special reports and analyses, (3) the operational audit, and (4) personal observation.

Statistical Data

Statistical analyses of the innumerable aspects of an operation and the clear presentation of statistical data, whether of a historical or a forecast nature, are important to control. It is probably safe to say that most managers understand statistical data best when the data are presented in chart or graphic form, since trends and relationships are then easier to see. Moreover, if data are to be meaningful, even when presented on charts, they should be formulated in such a way that comparisons to some standard can be made. What is the significance of a 3 or a 10 percent rise or fall in sales or costs? Who is responsible? Clear presentation of statistical data in graphic, tabular, or chart form is an art that requires imagination.

Moreover, since no manager can do anything about history, it is essential that statistical reports show trends so that the viewer can extrapolate where things are going. This means that most data, when presented on charts, should be made available as averages to rule out variations due to accounting periods, seasonal factors, accounting adjustments, and other periodic variations. In the 12-month moving average, for example, the total for 12 consecutive months, divided by 12, is used. The difference in clarity can be seen in the comparative data presented graphically in Figure 19-2.

Special Reports and Analyses

For control purposes, special reports and analyses help in particular problem areas. Although routine accounting and statistical reports furnish a good share of necessary information, there are often areas in which they are

Figure 19-2

ACTUAL MONTHLY DATA VERSUS 12-MONTH MOVING AVERAGE.
Sales of company X, 1981–1986.

inadequate. One successful manager of a complicated operation hired a small staff of trained analysts and gave them no assignment other than that of investigating and analyzing operations under his control. This group developed a surprising sense for situations in which things did not seem just right. Almost invariably, their investigation disclosed opportunities for cost improvement or better utilization of capital that no statistical chart would have revealed.

It may be that some of the funds spent for elaborate information programs could be more profitably spent for special analyses. Their nonroutine nature can highlight the usual and, in so doing, reveal places for significant improvement in efficiency. In routinely searching for pennies and accounting for them, managers may be overlooking opportunities for saving dollars.

Operational Audit

Another effective tool of managerial control is the internal audit, or, as it is now coming to be called, the operational audit. **Operational auditing,** in its broadest sense, is the regular and independent appraisal, by a staff of internal auditors, of the accounting, financial, and other operations of an enterprise. Although often limited to the auditing of accounts, in its most useful form operational auditing includes appraisal of operations in general, weighing actual results against planned results. Thus, operational auditors, in addition to assuring themselves that accounts properly reflect the facts, appraise policies, procedures, use of authority, quality of management, effectiveness of methods, special problems, and other phases of operations.

Personal Observation

One should never overlook the importance of control through personal observation. Budgets, charts, reports, ratios, auditors' recommendations, and other devices are essential to control. But the manager who relies wholly on these devices and sits, so to speak, in a soundproof control room reading dials and manipulating levers can hardly expect to do a thorough job of control. Managers, after all, have the task of seeing that enterprise objectives are accomplished by *people,* and although many scientific devices aid in ensuring that people are doing that which has been planned, the problem of control is still one of measuring activities of human beings. It is amazing how much information an experienced manager can get from personal observation, even from an occasional walk through a plant or an office. In some companies this is called "management by walking around."

TIME-EVENT NETWORK ANALYSES

Another planning and control technique is a time-event network analysis called the Program Evaluation and Review Technique (PERT). Before the development of PERT, there were other techniques designed to assess how the parts of a program fit together during the passage of time and events.

Gantt Charts

The first of these techniques was the chart system (see Figure 19-3) developed by Henry L. Gantt early in the twentieth century and culminating in the bar chart bearing his name. Although simple in concept, this chart, showing time relationships between "events" of a production program, has been regarded as revolutionary in management. What Gantt recognized was that total program goals should be regarded as a series of interrelated supporting plans (or events) that people can comprehend and follow. The most important developments of control reflect this simple principle as well as basic principles of control such as picking out the more critical elements of a plan to watch carefully.

Milestone Budgeting

As a result of the development of further techniques from the principles of the Gantt chart, and with better appreciation of the network nature of programs, "milepost" or "milestone" budgeting and PERT have been devised, contributing much to better control of many projects and operations. Used by an increasing number of companies in recent years in controlling engineering and development, milepost or milestone budgeting breaks a project down into controllable pieces and then carefully follows them. As noted in the discussion of planning, even relatively simple projects contain a network of supporting plans or projects. In this approach to control, "milestones" are defined as identifiable segments. When accomplishment of a given segment occurs, cost or other results can be determined.

Program Evaluation and Review Techniques

Developed by the Special Projects Office of the U.S. Navy,* the Program Evaluation and Review Technique (PERT) was first formally applied to the planning and control of the Polaris Weapon System in 1958 and worked well in expediting the successful completion of that program. For a number of years, it was so enthusiastically received by the armed services that it became virtually a required tool for major contractors and subcontractors in the armament and space industry. Although PERT is no longer much heard of in defense and space contracts for reasons that will be noted presently, its fundamentals are still essential tools of planning and control. Moreover, in a host of nongovernmental applications, including construction, engineering and tooling projects, and even such simple things as the scheduling of activities to get out monthly financial reports, PERT or its companion network technique, the Critical Path Method (CPM), may be used.

---

*The technique was also separately developed as the Critical Path Method by engineers at the Du Pont Company at virtually the same time. Only PERT is discussed here because the Critical Path Method, although different in some respects, utilizes the same principles.

Figure 19-3

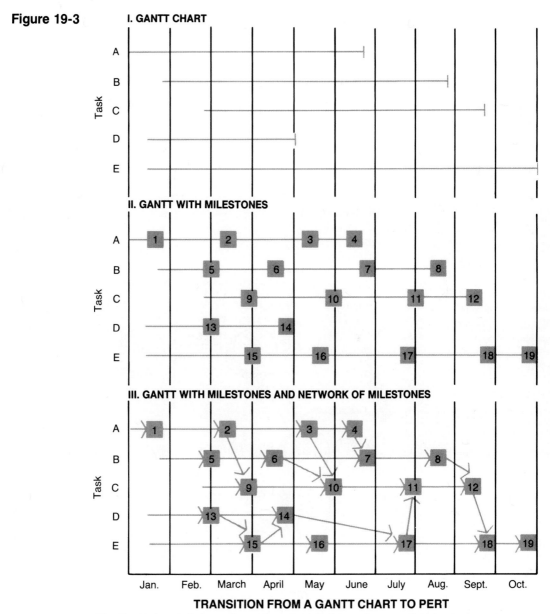

I. GANTT CHART

II. GANTT WITH MILESTONES

III. GANTT WITH MILESTONES AND NETWORK OF MILESTONES

Jan.   Feb.   March   April   May   June   July   Aug.   Sept.   Oct.

TRANSITION FROM A GANTT CHART TO PERT

The Gantt chart in I above shows the scheduled time of accomplishing a task, such as procurement (Task A), and the related schedules of doing other tasks, such as manufacture of parts (Task B). When each of these tasks is broken down into milestones, such as the preparation of purchase specifications (Task A-1), and when network relationships among the milestones of each task to those of other tasks are worked out, the result provides the basic elements of a PERT chart.

Major features PERT is a time-event network analysis system in which the various events in a program or project are identified, with a planned time established for each. These events are placed in a network showing the relationships of each event to the other events. In a sense, PERT is a variation of milestone budgeting (see Figure 19-3).

Figure 19-4 shows a PERT flowchart for the major assembly of an airplane. This very simple example illustrates the basic nature of PERT. Each *circle* represents an event — a supporting plan whose completion can be measured at a given time. The circles are numbered in the order in which the events occur. Each *arrow* represents an activity — the time-consuming element of a program, the effort that must be made between events. *Activity time*, represented by the numbers beside the arrows, is the elapsed time required to accomplish an event.

Figure 19-4

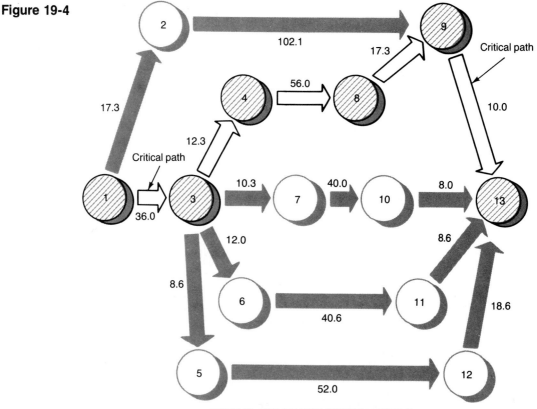

PERT FLOW CHART: TIME IN WEEKS.

Major assembly of an airplane. Events (major milestone of progress) are: (1) order program go-ahead; (2) initiate engine procurement; (3) complete plans and specifications; (4) complete fuselage drawings; (5) submit GFAE* requirements; (6) award tail assembly subcontract; (7) award wings subcontract; (8) complete manufacture of fuselage; (9) complete assembly of fuselage engine; (10) receive wings from subcontractors; (11) receive tail assembly from subcontractors; (12) receive GFAE; (13) complete aircraft.
*Note: GFAE stands for government-furnished airplane equipment.

In this example only a single time is shown, but in the original PERT program there were *three time estimates:* "optimistic" time, an estimate of the time required if everything goes exceptionally well; "most likely" time, an estimate based on the time the project engineer really believes is necessary for the job; and "pessimistic" time, a time estimate based on the assumption that some logically conceivable bad luck — other than a major disaster — will be encountered. These estimates are often included in PERT because it is very difficult, in many engineering and development projects, to estimate time accurately. When several estimates are made, they are usually averaged, with special weight given to the most likely estimate; a single estimate is then used for calculations.

The next step is to compute the *critical path,* that is, the sequence of events which takes the longest time and which has zero (or the least) slack time. In Figure 19-4, the critical path comprises events 1–3–4–8–9–13. Over this path, the activity time for this sequence of events is 131.6 weeks; if promised delivery is in 135 weeks, even this critical path would have been completed 3.4 weeks ahead of time. Some of the other paths are almost as long as the critical path. For example, the path 1–2–9–13 is 129.4 weeks. This is not unusual in PERT charts, and it is customary to identify several crucial paths in order of importance. Although the critical path has a way of changing as key events are delayed in other parts of the program, identifying it at the start makes possible close monitoring of this particular sequence of events to ensure that the total program is on schedule.

Typical PERT analyses involve hundreds or thousands of events. Even though smaller PERT analyses can be done manually, estimates indicate that when more than 200 to 300 events are involved, it is virtually impossible to handle the calculations without a computer.

It is customary to summarize very large and complex time-event networks by subnetworks and to prepare the summarized network for top-management consideration. Thus, the top-management network might include some forty or fifty major events, each a summary of a number of subsidiary events. In fact, it is possible to group, or to break down, events so that there is a PERT network appropriate to every level of management.

Strengths and weaknesses   There are five important advantages of PERT. First, it forces managers to plan, because it is impossible to make a time-event analysis without planning and seeing how the pieces fit together. Second, it forces planning all the way down the line, because each subordinate manager must plan the event for which he or she is responsible. Third, it concentrates attention on critical elements that may need correction. Fourth, it makes possible a kind of forward-looking control; a delay will affect succeeding events and possibly the whole project unless the manager can make up the time by shortening the time allocated to some action in the future. Fifth, the network system with its subsystems enables managers to aim reports and pressure for action at the right spot and level in the organization structure at the right time.

PERT also has certain limitations. Because of the importance of activity time to its operation, the technique is not useful when a program is nebulous and no reasonable "guesstimates" of schedule can be made; even in this case, however, insurance can be "bought" by such practices as putting two or more groups of people to work on an event when costs permit. A major disadvantage of PERT has been its emphasis on time only, not on costs. While this focus is suitable for programs in which time is of the essence or in which, as so often is the case, time and costs have a close direct relationship, the tool is more useful when considerations other than time are introduced into the analysis. (There is, however, another program called PERT/COST which does consider costs.)

PERT is not a cure-all. It will not do the planning, although it forces planning. It will not make control automatic, although it establishes an environment where sound control principles can be appreciated and used. And it apparently involves rather less expense than one might expect. Setting up the network, its analysis, and its interpretation and reporting from it probably require little, if any, more expense than most other planning and control techniques, unless, of course, these are made unduly complicated.

INFORMATION TECHNOLOGY

The systems model of management shows that communication is needed for carrying out the managerial functions and for linking the organization with its external environment. The management information system (MIS) provides the communication link that makes managing possible.

The term **management information system** has been used differently by various authors. It is defined here as a formal system of gathering, integrating, comparing, analyzing, and dispersing information internal and external to the enterprise in a timely, effective, and efficient manner.

The management information system has to be tailored to specific needs and may include routine information, such as monthly reports, information that points out exceptions, especially at critical points, and information necessary to predict the future. The guidelines for designing a management infor-

---

**INTERNATIONAL PERSPECTIVE:
PLANNING AND CONTROL AT VOLKSWAGEN**

Siegfried Hoehn, director of strategy and investment at Volkswagen A.G. (VW), writing from the perspective of a practitioner, points out that the information system affects the whole system of managing, but especially planning and controlling.[1] Figure 19-5 provides an overview of the planning and control model used by the VW Group.

Although the planning and control system at VW is quite comprehensive, Hoehn suggests that new developments in information technology will change planning and control in the future. Some of the trends include the use of integrative systems, multifunction terminals, telecommunication networks, and computer systems. Moreover, greater decentralization allows the system to be tailored to the specific functions of the users. The application of computers facilitates the automation of workplaces, with computers doing more of the routine work.[2]

mation system are similar to those for designing systems and procedures and other control systems. Since they have been discussed elsewhere, they need not be elaborated here.

Electronic equipment permits fast and economical processing of huge amounts of data. The computer can, with proper programming, process data toward logical conclusions, classify them, and make them readily available for a manager's use. In fact, data do not become information until they are processed into a usable form that informs.

Expanding Basic Data

The focus of attention on management information, coupled with its improved processing, has led to the reduction of long-known limitations. Managers have recognized for years that traditional accounting information, aimed at the calculation of profits, has been of limited value for control. Yet in many companies this has been virtually the only regularly collected and analyzed type of

Figure 19-5

**INFORMATION, PLANNING, AND CONTROL
IN THE MANAGEMENT SYSTEM OF THE VOLKSWAGEN GROUP.**

From Siegfried Hoehn, "How Information Technology Is Transforming Corporate Planning," *Long Range Planning* (August 1986), p. 19. Used with permission.

data. Managers need all kinds of nonaccounting information about the external environment, such as social, economic, political, and technical developments. In addition, managers need nonaccounting information on internal operations. The information should be qualitative as well as quantitative.

While not nearly enough progress has been made in meeting these requirements, the computer, plus operations research, has led to an enormous expansion of available managerial information. One sees this especially in relation to data on marketing, competition, production and distribution, product cost, technological change and development, labor productivity, and goal accomplishment.

Information Indigestion

Managers who have experienced the impact of better and faster data processing are justly concerned with the danger of "information indigestion." With their appetite for figures whetted, the data originators and processors are turning out material at an almost frightening rate. Managers are complaining that they are being buried under printouts, reports, projections, and forecasts which they do not have time to read or cannot understand or which do not fill their particular needs.

Intelligence Services

One attempt at solving the information overload is the establishment of intelligence services and the development of a new profession of intelligence experts. The service would be provided by specialists who know (or find out) what information managers need and who know how to digest and interpret such information for managerial use. Some companies have established organizational units under such names as "administrative services" or "management analyses and services" for making information understandable and useful.[3]

THE USE OF COMPUTERS IN HANDLING INFORMATION

The computer can store, retrieve, and process information. Often a distinction is made between kinds of computers. The *mainframe* is a full-scale computer, often costing millions of dollars, that is capable of handling huge amounts of data. Some of these "supercomputers" are used for engineering, simulation, and the manipulation of large data bases. The *minicomputer* has less memory and is smaller than the mainframe. This kind of computer is often connected with peripheral equipment. The *microcomputer* is even smaller and may be a desk computer, home computer, personal computer, portable computer, or small computer for a business system. Increasingly, however, minicomputers are used by large organizations either as stand-alone computers or as parts of a network.

But the distinction between the various classes of computers is disappearing. With the introduction of the new microcomputers based on the 80386 microprocessor, these computers have become very powerful. However, the full utilization of the hardware (the computers) depends to a considerable degree on the lagging development of the software programs.

Among the many business applications of the computer are material requirements planning, manufacturing resource planning, computer-aided control of manufacturing machinery, project costing, inventory control, and purchasing. The computer also aids design and engineering, an application which made the U.S. space program possible. Then there are the many uses in processing financial information such as accounts receivable and accounts payable, payroll, capital budgeting, and financial planning.

The Impact of Computers on Managers at Different Organizational Levels

Information needs differ at various organizational levels. Therefore, the impact of computers will also be different.

At the *supervisory level* activities are usually highly programmable and repetitive. Consequently, the use of computers is widespread at this level. Scheduling, daily planning, and controlling of the operation are just a few examples.

Middle-level managers, such as department heads or plant managers, are usually responsible for administration and coordination. But much of the information important to them is now also available to top management if the company has a comprehensive information system. For this reason, some people think that the need for middle-level managers will be reduced by the computer. Others predict that their roles may be expanded and changed.

Top-level managers are responsible for the strategy and overall policy of the organization.[4] In addition to determining the general direction of the company, they are responsible for the appropriate interaction between the enterprise and its environment. Clearly, the tasks of CEOs are not easily programmable. Yet top managers can use the computer to retrieve information from a data base that facilitates the application of decision models.[5] This enables the company to make timely responses to changes in the external environment. Still, the use of the computer will probably affect the jobs of top managers less severely than it will affect the jobs of those at lower levels.

The Application and Impacts of Microcomputers

The personal computer (PC) is becoming increasingly appealing to managers because it is flexible and relatively inexpensive and can be used more quickly than the mainframe computer. Its applications include the following:

Budget preparation	Simulation models
Graphic presentation	Forecasting
Electronic spreadsheets	Electronic mail
Financial analyses	Tapping into data bases
Word processing	Time-sharing

The implications of the increasing use of the microcomputer are manifold. There is a need for specialized staff support, education for managers and nonmanagers, and a redefinition of jobs. For example, the distinction between line and staff is becoming less clear. The information that was formerly gathered by staff can now be obtained with ease by other managers by accessing a common data base. On the other hand, information that was the prerogative of upper-level managers can also be made available to personnel at lower levels, possibly resulting in the shift of power to lower levels in the organization. But not all information should be accessible to all people in the company. Thus, one of the problems currently faced by many firms is maintaining the security of information.

CHALLENGES CREATED BY INFORMATION TECHNOLOGY

Eliminating the unauthorized use of information is just one of many challenges. Others include reducing resistance to the use of computers, adapting to speech recognition devices and telecommuting, and implementing computer networks.

Resistance to Computer Application

While high school students may feel comfortable using the computer, some managers fear it. One study revealed that the typical executive affected by this phobia is male, is about 50 years old, and has worked most of his life for the same company. This fear might explain why certain managers are reluctant to use the computer. They are afraid of looking unskilled if they are not able to understand the new technology or do not have the typing skills often necessary for inputting data to the computer. In the past, typing was considered the task of the secretary, not the manager.[6]

A survey of CEOs in *Fortune* 500 companies showed that over 50 percent of the respondents never used the computer and over 70 percent of them did not have a computer in their office.[7] On the other hand, a majority of the top executives thought that computers assist managers in doing their jobs, which suggests that computers are considered useful below the level of the CEO. Those not favorably inclined to the use of computers made various comments, such as that their time is too valuable to be spent learning computer skills.

The application of graphics can help overcome the resistance to computers. Instead of being buried in reams of computer printouts, information is displayed as easy-to-understand graphics. PepsiCo, for example, invested $250,000 in decision support graphics over 3 years, generating 80,000 charts and slides.[8] At any rate, as more sophisticated technology makes the use of the computer easier, its acceptance is likely to increase.

Speech Recognition Devices

Another way to encourage the use of computers is through speech recognition devices.[9] The aim is to input data into the computer by speaking in a normal manner, rather than by using the keyboard. Several companies are working on such devices, but it may still take several years before they can be widely applied, although simple speech recognition has been in limited use for some time. Merely expanding the vocabulary through larger memory is not enough. Imagine the program sophistication needed to distinguish between similar sounds such as "then" and "than," "to" and "too" and "two." Despite the complex problems, some people think that the efforts made in this area will result in products that may revolutionize office operation.

Telecommuting

The widespread use of computers and the ease of linking them through telephone lines to a company's mainframe computer has led to **telecommuting.** This means that a person can work at a computer terminal at home instead of commuting to work. Some of the advantages claimed include greater flexibility in scheduling work, the avoidance of traffic congestion, and a reduced need for office space.

The futurist Alvin Toffler envisioned an "electronic cottage" with computer terminals installed at home. But John Naisbitt, in his book *Megatrends,* is skeptical of the idea and suggested that after telecommuting for some time, workers will miss the office gossip and the human interactions with coworkers.[10] Some companies that have contracted work to telecommuters have been criticized for not providing the benefits usually given to office workers. At Pacific Bell, however, participants in the voluntary program are considered full-time employees.[11] Moreover, some employees go to the office at least once a week to check their mail and to mingle with coworkers.

With the increasing traffic congestion, especially in metropolitan areas, one may see a somewhat greater use of telecommuting. But it is doubtful that it will replace the office as we know it today.[12]

Computer Networks

The widespread use of stand-alone computers often results in duplication of efforts. The data base in the mainframe or the minicomputer, for example, may not be accessible from the desktop computer. Therefore, computer networks have been developed that link workstations with each other, with larger computers, and with peripheral equipment.

Persons at several workstations can communicate with each other as well as access other computers.[13] Moreover, workstations can be connected to costly hardware that may be underutilized by a single user. For example, several users can share laser printers or tape backup units that ensure saving of the data files. There are many other applications of computer networks, such as electronic mail and the gathering and disseminating of industry data and future trends. Although computer networking is still in its infancy, new technological developments are rapidly changing the system of information handling.

SUMMARY

A variety of tools and techniques have been used to help managers control. These techniques are generally, in the first instance, tools for planning, and they illustrate the fact that controls must reflect plans. Some of these tools have long been used by managers; others, such as variable budgeting and zero-base budgeting, are more recent refinements of traditional budgeting. The Program Evaluation and Review Technique (PERT) represents a newer generation of planning and control tools.

One of the older control techniques is the budget. Budgeting is the formulation of plans in numerical terms. There are several types of budgets: (1) revenue and expense budgets, (2) time, space, material, and product budgets, (3) capital expenditure budgets, and (4) cash budgets. There are a number of dangers in budgeting, but the major danger, inflexibility, can be largely avoided by using variable budgets. These are budgets designed to vary with the volume of output, with expenses divided among those items that vary usually as the volume of sales or some other measure of output varies. Flexibility may also be obtained by providing alternative or supplementary budgets. Budgeting is made much more precise by zero-base budgeting, in which programs are divided into "packages." Costs for each package are calculated from a base of zero. In order to make budgetary control effective in practice, managers must always realize that budgets are tools and are not intended to replace managing.

Among the traditional nonbudgetary control devices are statistical data and their analyses, special reports and analyses, the operational audit, and personal observation.

One of the newer techniques of planning and control is time-event network analyses. The Program Evaluation and Review Technique (PERT) is a refinement of the original Gantt charts, which were designed to show, in bar-chart form, the various things that must be done, and when, in order to accomplish a program. PERT is also a refinement of "milestone" budgeting, in which the things that have to be done are broken down into identifiable and controllable pieces called milestones. When milestones are connected to form a network and the time required to complete each milestone is identified, the result is a PERT/TIME network. Using the sequence of events and the times required for each, one can determine the critical path, which is the sequence that takes the longest time and has zero (or the least) slack time.

The management information system (MIS) is a formal system of gathering, integrating, comparing, analyzing, and dispersing information internal and external to the enterprise in a timely, effective, and efficient manner.

Computers (mainframe, minicomputers, and microcomputers) are now extensively used. Their impact on managers at various organizational levels differs. Information technology provides many challenges. Some managers still resist using computers, but speech recognition devices encourage computer use. Computers have also contributed to telecommuting, which means that persons may work at home at a computer terminal which is linked to a company's mainframe computer. Increasingly, computer networks link workstations with each other.

KEY IDEAS AND CONCEPTS FOR REVIEW

Budgeting
Types of budgets
Budgeting problems
Variable budgets
Alternative and supplementary budgets
Zero-base budgeting
Nonbudgetary control devices
Operational audit
Gantt charts
Milestone budgeting
Program Evaluation and Review Technique (PERT)

Critical path in PERT
Management information system (MIS)
Mainframe computer
Minicomputer
Microcomputer
Impact of computers on managers
Application of minicomputers
Speech recognition devices
Telecommuting
Computer networks

FOR DISCUSSION

1. The techniques of control appear to be as much techniques of planning as they are of control. In what ways is this true? Why would you expect it to be so?

2. "Variable budgets are flexible budgets." Discuss.

3. It is often claimed that an operating expense budget must be set at a level lower than expected in order to ensure the attainment of cost and profit goals. Do you agree?

4. To what extent, and how, can budgeting be approached on a grass roots basis, that is, from the bottom of the organization upward?

5. If you were going to institute a program of special control reports and analyses for a top manager, how would you go about it?

6. PERT is a management invention that takes basic principles and knowledge and, through design to get a desired result, comes up with a useful technique of planning and control. Analyze PERT with this in mind.

7. Give examples of how information technology has affected you.

8. Why do you think computers have a different impact on managers at various organization levels?

EXERCISES/ACTION STEPS

1. Use PERT to plan your college study program. What are the advantages in using this technique? What are some problems?

2. Select an organization you know and show how it uses computers.

CASE:
THE WHOLESALE DRUG COMPANY

The Wholesale Drug Company grew rapidly to become one of the largest firms of its kind. The success was due primarily to the leadership of the president, Ms. Johnson. Since many similar, but smaller, enterprises used computers for recordkeeping and data processing, Ms. Johnson was under great pressure to install a computerized control system to keep track of twenty distribution centers scattered throughout the nation.

Up to that time, expenses and income were recorded by means of a relatively simple ledger sheet and a journal showing the data for the twenty centers. This kind of recordkeeping, which was done by hand, allowed for easy comparison of the centers. Payrolls were done in a similar manner, and checks were usually processed within 24 hours. At that time five people and two supervisors were employed in the accounting department.

Several computer companies looked at the system, but their analysis showed that cost savings were hardly possible. However, one firm made a rather convincing case for a new data processing system. The consulting firm predicted the following benefits: (1) faster processing of information, (2) more detailed information on the operation, and (3) a reduction in costs.

After 2 years of using the new system, Ms. Johnson, who had reluctantly agreed to the computerization, related the following story: "Before the use of the computer, we had seven people in the accounting department. Now we have nine plus seven people in the data processing center. It is true that it takes only a few minutes to get the output from the computer, but we cannot run the program until the last distribution center provides the data. Unfortunately, this means delays, because we depend on the slowest operational unit for their input. It is true that we can get more detailed information, but I do not know if anybody ever looks at it. It is just too time-consuming to find the relevant information in the stacks of computer printouts and to interpret the data. I just wish we could go back to the old ledger system. But we invested so much money, and have reached a point of no return."

1. Why did the computerized system not live up to its expectations?

2. What should Ms. Johnson do now?

3. How would you design a computerized system? What factors would you consider?

REFERENCES

1. Siegfried Hoehn, "How Information Technology Is Transforming Corporate Planning," *Long Range Planning* (August 1986), pp. 18–30.

2. See also John C. Papageorgiou, "Decision Making in the Year 2000," *Interfaces* (April 1983), pp. 77–86.

3. For organizational issues in establishing an MIS unit, see Mark Klein, "Information Politics," *Datamation* (Aug. 1, 1985), pp. 87–92.

4. Clark Holloway thinks that in the 1990s supercomputers may share many functions of top executives. See his article "Strategic Management and Artificial Intelligence," *Long Range Planning* (October 1983), pp. 89–93. The use of information technology for formulating a strategy is discussed by Sid L. Huff, "Information Technology and Corporate Strategy," *Business Quarterly* (Summer 1985), pp. 18ff.

5. While some argue that senior managers can keep better control of the operation as well as of subordinates, others consider the impact on top management minimal. For discussions of this topic, see John Dearden, "SMR Forum: Will the Computer Change the Job of Top Management?" *Sloan Management Review* (Fall 1983), pp. 195–204; John C. Camillus and Albert L. Lederer, "Corporate Strategy and the Design of Computerized Information Systems," *Sloan Management Review* (Spring 1985), p. 35ff.

6. See also Alice LaPlante, "Baby-Sitting the Boss," *InfoWorld* (Aug. 8, 1988), pp. 1 and 89.

7. Lisa L. Spiegelman, "Top-Level Managers Not Using PCs, Survey Finds," *InfoWorld* (May 26, 1988), p. 24.

8. "Management Warms Up to Computer Graphics," *Business Week* (Aug. 13, 1984), pp. 96–101.

9. Paul Duke, Jr., "Can We Talk?" *The Wall Street Journal*, A Special Report: Technology in the Work Place (Nov. 10, 1986).

10. John Naisbitt, *Megatrends* (New York: Warner Books, 1982), chap. 1.

11. David Needle, "Telecommuting: Off to a Slow Start," *InfoWorld* (May 19, 1986), pp. 43–46.

12. Margrethe H. Olson, "Do You Telecommute?" *Datamation* (Oct. 15, 1985), pp. 129–132.

13. For a discussion of local area networks, see Laurie Flynn, "LANs," *InfoWorld* (Oct. 27, 1986), pp. 45–46.

CHAPTER 20

Productivity and Operations Management[*]

CHAPTER OBJECTIVES

After reading this chapter, you should understand:

1. The nature of productivity issues and ways to improve effectiveness and efficiency
2. The nature of production and operations management as an applied case of managerial planning and control
3. The managerial techniques that are especially useful for operations planning and control as well as other areas of enterprise operation
4. Techniques for improving productivity
5. Probable future developments in operations planning and control

In a real sense, the whole book is about the improvement of productivity. But this important topic will receive special attention in this chapter, with an emphasis on the micro level of production and operations management.[1]

[*]Additional topics in production and operations management are discussed in other parts of the book. See, for example, Chapter 6 for various aspects of decision making, including the topic of decision support systems; Chapter 11 for job design; and Chapter 19 for management information systems and for different kinds of control techniques.

PRODUCTIVITY PROBLEMS AND MEASUREMENT

Undoubtedly, productivity will be one of the major concerns of managers not only for the remaining part of the 1980s but also for the 1990s, and probably beyond. This concern extends beyond the boundaries of the United States into many parts of the world. Even Japan, which is admired for productivity improvements, is now concerned about remaining competitive in the world market.

Productivity Problems

Productivity implies measurement, which, in turn, is an essential step in the control process. Although there is general agreement about the need for improving productivity, there is little consensus about the fundamental causes of the problem and what to do about them.[2] The blame has been attributed to various factors. Some people place it on the greater proportion of less skilled workers in respect to the total labor force, but others disagree. There are those who see the cutback in research and the emphasis on immediate results as the main culprit. Another reason given for the productivity dilemma is the growing affluence of people, which makes them less ambitious. Still others cite the breakdown in family structure, the workers' attitudes, and government policies and regulations. Increasingly, attention shifts to management as the cause of the problem — as well as the solution, which is the focus of this book.

Measuring Productivity of Knowledge Workers

As defined in Chapter 1, **productivity** is *the input-output ratio within a time period with due consideration for quality.* This definition can be applied to the productivity of organizations, managers, staff personnel, and workers. Measurement of skills work is relatively easy, but it becomes more difficult for knowledge work.

PERSPECTIVE:
APPROACHES TO PRODUCTIVITY IMPROVEMENT

There is no one best approach to productivity improvement, but there are many.[3] Here are some examples:

- Kaiser Aluminum and Chemical Corporation emphasized the formulation of improvement objectives, the measurement of performance against these objectives, an effective reporting system, and frequent reinforcement of good performance.
- Hughes Aircraft Company, in which a very large portion of the employees are knowledge workers, provided principles and guidelines for productivity improvement covering areas such as recognition of good performance, use of work modules, design of meaningful work, emphasis on goals, and development of the ability to work with people.

The difference between the two kinds of work is the relative use of knowledge and skills. Thus, a person on the production line would be considered a skill worker, while the assistant to the manager with planning as his or her main function would be a knowledge worker. Managers, engineers, and programmers are knowledge workers because the relative amount of their work does not consist of utilizing skills, as would be the case for bricklayers, mechanics, and butchers. But the job title cannot be the sole guide for making distinctions. The owner of a gas station may schedule the day's tasks, determine priorities, and direct subordinates, but the owner may also change brakes, adjust the carburetor, or realign the front wheels on a car.

It is clear that, in general, the productivity of the knowledge worker is more difficult to measure than that of the skill worker. (Note also that worker productivity measurement is somewhat artificial because it often ignores the cost of capital.) One difficulty in measuring the productivity of knowledge workers is that some outputs are really activities that help achieve end results. Thus, the engineer contributes indirectly to the final product. Another difficulty is that knowledge workers often assist other organizational units. The advertising manager's efforts should improve sales, but it is hard to say for sure what the exact contribution is. Still another difficulty is that the quality of the knowledge workers' outputs is often difficult to measure. The effects of a strategic decision, for example, may not be evident for several years, and even then the success or failure of the new strategic direction may depend on many external forces beyond the control of the manager.

It is evident, then, that productivity improvement is achieved by the good management practices advocated throughout this book. But the discussion will now turn to the specific area of production and operations management, where measurement is relatively easy and consequently has been the focus of productivity improvement programs in the past.

PRODUCTION AND OPERATIONS MANAGEMENT [4]

One of the major areas in any kind of enterprise, whether business, government, or others, is production and operations management. It is also the area where managing as a scientifically based art got its start. The contributions of such management pioneers as Taylor, Gantt, and Gilbreth, to mention only a few, indicate that their interest was largely in improving productivity and manufacturing products most efficiently while still recognizing, as they did, the importance of the human factor as an indispensable input.

In the past, **production management** was the term used to refer to those activities necessary to manufacture products. However, in recent years, the area has been generally expanded to include such activities as purchasing, warehousing, transportation, and other operations from the procurement of raw materials through various activities until a product is available to the buyer. The term **operations management** refers to activities necessary to produce and deliver a service as well as a physical product.

There are, of course, other essential activities undertaken by a typical enterprise. In addition to production, these enterprise functions often include research and development, engineering, marketing and sales, accounting, and financing. This chapter deals only with what has come to be called "operations management" or "production management," and often "production and operations management" (POM). It should be pointed out that this is not, of course, the same thing as "operational"-management theory. As explained earlier, operational-management theory is the study of the practice (managing) which that theory or science is designed to underpin.

OPERATIONS MANAGEMENT SYSTEMS

Operations management has to be seen as a system. Figure 20-1 gives an overview of the operations function. In the operations management model the *inputs* include needs of customers, information, technology, labor and management, fixed assets, and variable assets that are relevant to the transformation process. Managers and workers use the information and physical factors to produce outputs. Some physical elements, such as land, plant sites, buildings, machines, and warehouses, are relatively permanent. Other physical

Figure 20-1

OPERATIONS MANAGEMENT SYSTEM.

Table 20-1   Examples of Operations Systems

Inputs	Transformation	Outputs
1. Plant, factory machines, people, materials	Assembling bicycles	Completed bicycles
2. Students with limited knowledge, skills, and attitudes	Lectures, cases, experiential exercises, term papers	Students with enhanced knowledge, skills, and attitudes
3. Client problem	Consulting: data-collection analysis, evaluation of alternatives, selection of alternative, recommendation	Consulting report recommending course of action

elements, such as materials and supplies, are consumed in the process of producing outputs. The *transformation process* incorporates planning, operating, and controlling the system. There are many tools and techniques available to facilitate the transformation process. The model also reflects a constant concern for improving the system. *Outputs* consist of products and services and may even be information, such as that provided by a consulting organization.

The last part of the model shows that operations are influenced by *external factors,* such as safety regulations or fair labor practices. Since the external environment is discussed elsewhere in this book, especially in planning, it will not be expanded upon here; the important point is that operations management must be an open system interacting with its surroundings.

The operations management model (Figure 20-1) serves as a framework for the discussions that follow. There is a close relationship between this model and the one introduced in Chapter 1, since this operations model may be regarded as a subsystem of a total management system. Examples of operations systems[5] with inputs, transformation (sometimes also called "process"), and outputs are presented in Table 20-1.

Planning Operations

Objectives, premises, and strategies of an enterprise (discussed in Part 2 of this book) determine the search for and the selection of the product or service. In this discussion, the production of physical products is emphasized, but the concepts can also be applied to the provision of services. After an end product has been selected, the specifications are determined and the technological feasibility of producing it is considered. The design of an operations system requires decisions concerning the location of facilities, the process to be used, the quantity to be produced, and the quality of the product.

Special interests in a product decision   One of the basic decisions an enterprise makes is selecting a product or products it intends to produce and market. This requires gathering product ideas that will satisfy the needs of customers and contribute to the goals of an enterprise while being consistent with the strategy of the firm.[6] In a product decision, the various interests of functional managers must be considered. For example, a production manager may want a product that can be produced without difficulty, at a reasonable cost, and with long production runs. Engineers may share many of these aims, but they are often looking for engineering sophistication rather than ways of producing the product at a reasonable cost.

The sales or marketing manager's interest is likely to be the needs of customers, and his or her aim is to increase the sales of products through ready availability and competitive prices. Moreover, sales managers may want to offer a broad product line without considering the engineering, production, transportation, and warehousing costs and the problems involved. The finance manager's concerns are likely to be costs and profits, high return on investment, and low financial risks. The divergent interests of these functionally oriented managers and professionals influence what products will be produced and marketed, but it is the general manager who has to integrate the various interests and balance revenues with costs, profits with risks, and long-term with short-term growth.

Product and production design   The design of a product and its production require a number of activities. The following steps have often been suggested:

1. Create product ideas by searching for consumer needs and screening the various alternatives.

2. Select the product on the basis of various considerations, including data from market and economic analyses, and make a general feasibility study.

3. Prepare a preliminary design by evaluating various alternatives, taking into consideration reliability, quality, and maintenance requirements.

4. Reach a final decision by developing, testing, and simulating the processes to see if they work.

5. Decide whether the enterprise's current facilities are adequate or if new or modified facilities are required.

6. Select the process for producing the product; consider the technology and the methods available.

7. After the product is designed, prepare the layout of the facilities to be used,[7] plan the system of production, and schedule the various things that must be done.

Systems design   In producing a product, companies can consider several basic kinds of production layouts.[8] One alternative is to arrange the layouts in the order in which the product is *produced* or *assembled*. For example, a truck assembly line may be arranged so that the preassembled front and rear axles are attached to the frame, followed by the installation of the steering, the engine, and the transmission. Then the brake lines and electrical cables are connected, and other parts are assembled and painted. Finally, the truck is road tested.

A second alternative is to lay out the production system according to the *process* employed. In a hospital, for example, specific steps are likely to be followed, beginning with the admission of the patient, the treatment of the patient — which usually involves specific subprocesses — billing for service, and dismissal. This may be followed up by posthospitalization treatment.

In a third kind of layout (sometimes called *fixed-position* layout) the product stays in one place for assembly. This layout is used for the assembly of extremely large and bulky items such as printing presses, large strip-mining machines, or ships.

The fourth kind of layout is arranged according to the nature of the *project.* Building a bridge or tunnel is normally a one-time project designed to fit specific geographic requirements.

In the fifth kind of layout the production process is arranged to facilitate the *sale* of products. In a supermarket basic food items, such as dairy products, are normally located away from the checkout counter. This causes customers to walk through the long aisles and, it is hoped, select other items on the way to the dairy section.

A sixth basic approach to production layout is to design the process so that it facilitates *storage or movement* of products. Storage space is costly, and an effective and efficient design can keep the storage costs low. Also, in order to reach an item it should not be necessary to move many other items.

Operating the System

After the products have been selected and the systems for producing them have been designed and built, the next major step is to operate the system. This requires setting up an organization structure, staffing the positions, and training people. Managers are needed who can provide the supervision and leadership to carry out activities necessary to produce desired products or provide services. Other activities, such as purchasing and maintaining the inventory, are also required in operating the system. The aim is to obtain the best productivity ratio within a time period with due consideration to quality.

Controlling Operations with Emphasis on Information Systems

Controlling operations, as in any case of managerial control, requires setting performance criteria, measuring performance against them, and taking actions to correct undesirable deviations. Thus, one can control production, product quality and reliability levels, inventory levels, and work-force performance. A number of tools and techniques have been developed to do this. Because their application extends beyond operations or production, they have been discussed previously. Some, however, are important to operations; examined here is the role of information systems in operations control.

One type of planning and control system, and one which has been available for several years, integrates information on virtually an instantaneous basis, thereby reducing considerably the delays that usually impede effective control. With the development of computer hardware and software, it is now possible for virtually any measurable data to be reported as events occur. Systems are available for quickly and systematically collecting data bearing on total operation, for keeping these data readily available, and for reporting without delay the status of any of a large number of projects at any instant. They are thus primarily information systems designed to provide effective planning and control.[9]

PERSPECTIVE:
HOW AN INFORMATION SYSTEM WORKS

Applied widely now to purchasing, storing, manufacturing, and shipping, information systems may operate through dispatch stations and input centers located throughout a plant. At the dispatch centers, events are recorded as they occur and the information is dispatched immediately to a computer. For example, when a worker finishes an assigned task on the assembly of a product, the work-order time card is put into a transactor, which electrically transmits to a computer the information that item x has passed through a certain process, has accumulated y hours of labor, may or may not be on schedule, and other pertinent data. The input centers are equipped to originate information needed for a production plan automatically from programmed instructions, purchase orders, shop orders, and other authorizations. These data are fed into a computer and compared against plans, which are used as standards against which actual operations can be compared.

In addition to providing fast entry, comparison, and retrieval of information, such an integrated operations control system furnishes needed information for planning programs in such areas as purchasing, production, and inventory control. Moreover, it permits almost instantaneous comparison of results with plans, pinpointing where they differ and providing a regular (daily or more often, if needed) system of reports on deviations from plans, such as items that are behind schedule or costs that are running above budget.

Other planning, control, and information systems have been developed to reflect quickly the interaction between production and distribution operations and such key financial measures as costs, profit, and cash flow. Companies with real-time computer models can give operating managers virtually instant analysis of such "what-if" questions as the effects of reducing or increasing output, the impact of a reduction in demand, and the sensitivity of the system to labor cost increases, price changes, and new equipment additions. To be sure, system models, simulating actual operations and their impact on financial factors, are primarily planning tools. But so are most control techniques. However, by making possible exceptionally quick responses to the many "what-if" questions of operating managers, system models can greatly reduce the time elapsed in correcting for deviations from plans and can materially improve control.

These and other systems which use the technology of fast computation clearly promise to hasten the day when planning all the areas of production can be more precise and controlling more effective. The drawback is not cost; rather it is the failure of managers to spend time and mental effort on conceptualizing the system and its relationships or to see that someone else in the organization does so. Nevertheless, as pointed out in Chapter 18, fast information availability can never provide true real-time controls of the time delays in any feedback system. Only a feedforward approach can overcome these delays.

OPERATIONS RESEARCH FOR PLANNING, CONTROLLING, AND IMPROVING PRODUCTIVITY

A number of techniques employed in many kinds of planning and controlling are especially useful in managing operations. This is understandable, since most of the special techniques that have been developed are based on mathematical models and the use of quantitative data. Conceptual models and fairly exact quantitative data are available in many areas for production and operations management.

It was advantageous to discuss some of these techniques in the chapters on decision making and control techniques. Of special interest here to managers of production and operations are the tools of operations research. Later in this chapter other techniques will also be discussed.

The Concept of Operations Research

Operations research is a product of World War II, although its forerunners in scientific methods, higher mathematics, and such tools as probability theory go back far beyond that period. The accelerated growth of operations research in recent years has followed the trend of applying the methods of physical scientists and engineers to economic and political problems. It has also been made possible by the development of rapid computing machines, particularly those using electronics, since much of the advantage of operations research depends upon the ability to apply, at low cost, involved mathematical formulas and to use data with complex relationships. There are almost as many definitions of operations research as there are writers on the subject. For the purposes of this discussion, the most acceptable definition is that **operations research** is *the application of scientific methods to the study of alternatives in a problem situation, with a view to obtaining a quantitative basis for arriving at a best solution.* Thus, the emphasis is on scientific method, on the use of quantitative data, on goals, and on the determination of the best means of reaching the goals. In other words, operations research might be called "quantitative common sense."

The Essentials of Operations Research

Managers have long attempted to solve management problems scientifically, but operations researchers have supplied an element of novelty in the orderliness and completeness of their approach. They have emphasized defining the problem and goals, carefully collecting and evaluating data, developing and testing hypotheses, determining relationships among data, developing and checking predictions based on hypotheses, and devising measures to evaluate the effectiveness of a course of action.

Thus, the essential characteristics of operations research as applied to decision making can be summarized as follows:

1. It emphasizes *models* — the logical physical representation of a reality or problem. Models can, of course, be simple or complex. For example, the accounting formula "Assets minus liabilities equals proprietorship" is a model, since it represents an idea and, within the limits of the terms used, symbolizes the relationship among the variables involved.

2. It emphasizes *goals* in a problem area and the development of measures of effectiveness in determining whether a given solution shows promise of achieving these goals. For example, if the goal is profit, the measure of effectiveness may be the rate of return on investment, and every proposed solution will arrange the variables so that the end result can be weighed against this measure.

3. It incorporates in a model the *variables* in a problem, or at least those that appear to be important to its solution. Managers can control some variables; others may be uncontrollable factors in the problem.

4. It puts the model, and its variables, constraints, and goals, in *mathematical terms* so that they may be clearly identified, subjected to mathematical simplification, and readily utilized for calculation by substitution of quantities for symbols.

5. It *quantifies* the variables in a problem to the extent possible, since only quantifiable data can be inserted into a model to yield a measurable result.

6. It supplements much unavailable data with such usable mathematical and statistical devices as the *probabilities* in a situation, thus often making the mathematical and computing problem workable within a small margin of error despite gaps in accurate quantifiable data.

Of all these characteristics, perhaps the basic tool — and the major contribution — of operations research is the construction and use of conceptual models. There are many types of models. Some assert logical relationships among variables. These may be referred to as "simulative" or "descriptive" if they are designed only to describe the relationship of elements in a situation. The models useful for planning are referred to as "decision" or "optimizing" models, designed to lead to the selection of a best course of action among available alternatives.

Linear Programming

A technique for determining the optimum combination of limited resources to obtain a desired goal, **linear programming** is one of the most successful applications of operations research. It is based upon the assumption that a linear, or straight-line, relationship exists between variables and that the limits of variations can be determined. For example, in a production shop, the variables may be units of output per machine in a given time, direct-labor costs or material costs per unit of output, number of operations per unit, and so forth. Most or all of these may have linear relationships, within certain limits; by solving linear equations, one can establish the optimum in terms of cost, time, machine utilization, or other objectives. Thus, this technique is especially useful in cases where input data can be quantified and objectives are subject to definite measurement.

As one might expect, the technique has had its most promising use in such problem areas as production planning, shipping rates and routes, and the utilization of production and warehouse facilities to achieve lowest overall costs, including transportation costs. Because it depends on linear relationships and many decisions do not involve these or cannot be simulated accurately enough, newer and more complex systems of nonlinear programming have come into use.

Inventory Planning and Control

Perhaps in the history of operations research more attention has been directed to inventory control than to any other practical area of operations. The essential systems relationships can be seen as a little "black box," as depicted in Figure 20-2.

In mathematical form, these conceptual relationships are expressed by the equation:

$$Q_e = \sqrt{\frac{2DS}{H}}$$

where Q_e = economic order quantity

$\quad\quad D$ = demand per year

$\quad\quad S$ = setup costs

$\quad\quad H$ = inventory holding (carrying) cost per item, per year

The model in Figure 20-2 illustrates several things. It forces consideration of the goals desired and of the need for placing values on outputs and inputs. It also furnishes a manager with the basis for plans and with standards by which to measure performance.[10] However, with all its advantages, this is a subsystem and does not incorporate other subsystems, such as production planning, distribution planning, and sales planning.

Figure 20-2

INVENTORY CONTROL MODEL.

The **economic order quantity** (EOQ) approach to determining inventory levels has been used by firms for many years. It works reasonably well for finding order quantities when demand is predictable and fairly constant throughout the year (that is, no seasonable patterns). However, for determining inventory levels of parts and materials used for some production processes, the EOQ approach does not work well. For example, poor quality of parts may increase the demand for these production inputs. Thus, demand is likely to be intermittent, resulting in inventory shortages at some times and excesses at other times. Firms determining inventory levels in these manufacturing settings have found that inventory control approaches such as material requirement planning (MRP) and Kanban (just-in-time) systems perform better than EOQ.[11]

Just-in-Time Inventory System

One reason for Japan's high manufacturing productivity is the cost reductions it achieves through its **just-in-time** (JIT) inventory method. In this system, the supplier delivers the components and parts to the production line "just in time" to be assembled. Other names for this or very similar methods are **zero inventory** and **stockless production.**[12]

The just-in-time method was successfully used after World War II by the Toyota automobile company. In the United States General Motors, Ford, Chrysler, and American Motors use more advanced versions of JIT. But other companies also have used JIT with favorable results. Consider Black & Decker, which produces, among other things, small appliances such as coffee makers and irons: When its plant in North Carolina switched to JIT, inventory was reduced by 40 percent and 30 percent fewer forklift trucks were required. Moreover, quality losses were reduced 60 percent and labor productivity increased by 15 percent.[13]

For the JIT method to work, a number of requirements must be fulfilled: (1) The quality of the parts must be very high; a defective part could hold up the assembly line. (2) There must be dependable relationships and smooth cooperation with suppliers.[14] (3) Ideally, the suppliers should be located near the company, with dependable transportation available.[15]

Distribution Logistics

An exciting and profit-promising way of using systems logistics in planning and control is the expansion of inventory control to include other factors; this system is referred to here as **distribution logistics.** In its advanced form, it treats the entire logistics of a business — from sales forecasting through purchasing and processing material and inventorying to shipping finished goods — as a single system. The goal is usually to optimize the total costs of the system in operation, while furnishing a desired level of customer service and meeting certain constraints, such as financially limited inventory levels. This gathers into one system a large mass of relationships and information in order to optimize the whole. It is entirely possible that transportation, manufacturing, or any other single area of cost will not be optimized, but the total cost of material management will be.

Schematically, a distribution logistics system might appear as shown in Figure 20-3. This model would be expressed mathematically as an operating system. The figure shows the relationships between the goal desired, the input variables and limits, and the expected outputs. By optimizing *total* costs in a broad area of operation, the system might show that it would be cheaper to use more expensive transportation on occasion rather than to carry high inventories. Or it might show that production at less-than-economic order quantities would be justified in order to get better transportation or warehousing utilization or to meet customer service standards with limited inventories.

Limitations of Operations Research

So far, operations research has been used to solve only a fairly limited number of managerial problems. Its limitations should not be overlooked.

In the first place, there is the sheer magnitude of the mathematical and computing aspects. The number of variables and interrelationships in many managerial problems, plus the complexities of human relationships and reac-

Figure 20-3

DISTRIBUTION LOGISTICS MODEL.

tions, calls for a higher order of mathematics than nuclear physics does. The late mathematical genius John von Neumann found, in his development of the theory of games, that his mathematical abilities soon reached their limit in a relatively simple strategic problem. Managers are, however, a long way from fully using the mathematics now available.

In the second place, although probabilities and approximations are being substituted for unknown quantities and although scientific method can assign values to factors that could never be measured before, a major portion of important managerial decisions still involves qualitative factors. Until these can be measured, operations research will have limited usefulness in these areas, and decisions will continue to be based on nonquantitative judgments.

Related to the fact that many management decisions involve unmeasurable factors is the lack of information needed to make operations research useful in practice. In conceptualizing a problem area and constructing a mathematical model to represent it, people discover variables about which they need information that is not now available. To improve this situation, persons interested in the practical applications of operations research should place far more emphasis on developing this required information.

Still another limitation is the gap between practicing managers and trained operations researchers. Managers in general lack a knowledge and appreciation of mathematics, just as mathematicians lack an understanding of managerial problems. This gap is being dealt with, to an increasing extent, by the business schools and, more often, by business firms that team up managers with operations researchers. But it is still the major reason why firms are slow to use operations research.

A final drawback of operations research — at least in its application to complex problems — is that analyses and programming are expensive, and many problems are not important enough to justify this cost. However, in practice this has not really been a major limitation.

OTHER TOOLS AND TECHNIQUES FOR IMPROVING PRODUCTIVITY

Besides operations research there are other techniques. Discussed below is the application of time-event networks, value engineering, work simplification, quality circles, computer-aided design, computer-aided manufacturing, and the manufacturing automation protocol.

Time-Event Networks

As discussed in Chapter 19, time-event network analysis is a logical extension of the famous Gantt chart. Often referred to as the Program Evaluation and Review Technique (PERT) and in its essentials as the Critical Path Method (CPM), this technique of planning and control has wide potential use in many applications. But PERT and its various refinements, like PERT/COST, have considerable potential for use in many aspects of planning and controlling operations.

Value Engineering

A product can be improved and its cost lowered through **value engineering,** which consists of analyzing the operation of the product or service, estimating the value of each operation, and attempting to improve that operation by trying to keep cost slow at each step or part. The following specific steps are suggested:

1. Divide the product into parts and operations.

2. Identify the costs for each part and operation.

3. Identify the relative value of the contribution of each part to the final part.

4. Find a new approach for those items which appear to have a high cost and low value.

Work Simplification

Work methods can also be improved through **work simplification,** which is the process of obtaining the participation of workers in simplifying their work. Training sessions are conducted to teach concepts and principles of techniques such as time and motion studies, work-flow analyses, and the layout of the work situation.

Quality Circles

Quality control circles, or simply **quality circles** (QC), are groups of people, from the same organizational area, who meet regularly to solve problems they experience at work.[16] Members are trained in solving problems, in applying statistical quality control, and in working in groups. Usually a facilitator works with each group, which normally consists of six to twelve members. The QCs may meet 4 hours a month. Although QC members may receive recognition, they usually do not receive monetary rewards.

Quality circles evolved from suggestion programs. In both approaches, workers participate in solving work-related problems. Although in suggestion programs the problems are usually quite specific, those dealt with by quality control circles are often more complex and require the involvement of several team members. The team consists primarily of rank-and-file workers and sometimes also includes supervisors. So-called efficiency experts are usually excluded from the team.

It is interesting to note that while the concept of quality control originated in the United States, the Japanese appear to have perfected it. More recently, American firms have "rediscovered" the importance of quality, as stressed, for example, in the advertisements for Chrysler and Ford automobiles. At any rate, there is no reason to doubt that quality circles can be used by American companies, which are now faced with a competitive situation in a world market that demands quality products.

INTERNATIONAL PERSPECTIVE:
QUALITY CIRCLES IN JAPAN

For some time now, Japanese companies have been successful in marketing products. To a great extent this has been due to the quality of their products, but this has not always been the case. In fact, in the 1950s and 1960s many products made in Japan had the image of poor quality.

In order to compete in the world market, Japanese firms had to improve the quality of their products.[17] The campaign to improve the quality of Japanese products was initiated by regulatory action taken by the Japanese government. Shortly after World War II ended, the Japanese, realizing that their economic situation depended on increasing exports, encouraged their government to set up a system of regulations mandating that all exporters submit to a government agency a sample of each product to be exported and that they meet demanding requirements for quality before receiving a permit to export.

The legislative drive for quality was supported by various management techniques encouraging or requiring product quality. One of the interesting techniques is the quality control circle, now in widespread use in Japan. At first, employees were trained in the analysis of quality problems. But now other problems are also dealt with, such as cost reduction, workshop facilities improvement, safety problems, employee morale, pollution control, and the education of employees.

PERSPECTIVE:
QUALITY CONTROL LEADERSHIP AT KODAK[18]

In Japan the concern for quality starts with the CEO, whereas in the United States quality has been the primary concern of lower-level managers and quality control engineers. But this pattern is beginning to change. Former President Reagan designated October 1988 as "National Quality Month." To reinforce the commitment to quality, some of the largest companies — such as Coca-Cola, Ford, GM, and IBM — participated in the National Quality Forum.

While there is still skepticism regarding whether most CEOs are really serious about quality, the chairman of one large, multinational corporation provides a good role model. Colby H. Chandler, Kodak's CEO, started his career as a quality control engineer. His philosophy is "Quality pays for itself many times over." Quality is closely linked to productivity and engineering, which have been greatly improved by computers and the new software programs. Kodak's strategy is driven by research and development as well as concern for productivity and quality. If top-management involvement in these issues is a trend in the United States, then companies may again achieve product leadership.

CAD/CAM and MAP

Product design and manufacturing have been changing greatly in recent years, largely because of the application of computer technology. Computer-aided design (CAD), computer-aided manufacturing (CAM), and the manufacturing automation protocol (MAP) are some of the cornerstones of the factory of the future.

CAD/CAMs help engineers design products much more quickly than they could with the traditional paper-and-pencil approach. This will become increasingly important, since product life cycles are getting shorter. Capturing the market quickly is crucial in the very competitive environment. Moreover, firms can respond more rapidly to the requests of customers with specific requirements. The ultimate aim of many companies is "computer-integrated manufacturing."[19]

Automobile companies, as well as firms such as Deere, Boeing, and Eastman Kodak, developed what is called **manufacturing automation protocol** (MAP), which is a network of machines and various office devices hooked together. MAP is a sophisticated extension of local area networks (LANs). One of the most committed supporters of MAP is Roger Smith, chairman of General Motors, who sees it as a key to the factory of the future. At General Motors, for example, MAP is used to link robots with numerically controlled machine tools. The company has achieved considerable savings by using the new method to change the production line when introducing a different kind of front axle for an automobile. What previously took 3 days now takes only 10 minutes. With the new technology, General Motors and other U.S. manufacturers hope to overtake Japanese firms, which now are quite advanced in automation.[20]

THE FUTURE OF OPERATIONS MANAGEMENT

What factors show signs of influencing future developments in this field? Several major trends can be expected in operations management:[21]

1. The increased complexity of technology will be reflected in the products themselves as well as in the processes used to produce them.[22] Fifteen years ago few people would have expected that sophisticated home computers could be produced at a price affordable by the average consumer.

2. Automation is becoming increasingly more important in the production process.[23] General Motors, which pioneered the application of robots, is importing a new generation of robots from Japan. New machine tools, microprocessors, sensory technology, and computer controls now make it possible to reduce machine setup time and costs.[24] This means a greater variety of products at lower cost. In the past, lower cost tended to be achieved through high-volume production of a particular model. Now, through high technology, setup times are reduced dramatically. This means a better use of machines with lower direct-labor costs. Moreover, work-in-process inventories can thereby be reduced. Finally, maintenance costs are reduced by simplifying processes, controls, and machines. These simplification technologies were pioneered by Toyota when it doubled its automobile model range without incurring the high costs traditionally associated with a variety of models.

3. The service industry in the United States is providing an increasingly important portion of the gross national product. This means that the concepts and principles of "production" have been advantageously adapted to such nonmanufacturing activities as banking, health care, and tourism.

4. The production function will become increasingly a global challenge.[25] Car engines produced in Japan and Germany are now installed in American cars. Moreover, major car manufacturers in the United States have made arrangements to produce cars in Japan and market them under their own names in the United States and elsewhere.

In short, then, productivity, and the concern for measuring it, will continue to be a challenge for managers operating in an increasingly competitive global market. Operations management systems are expected to become more productive through the application of operations research, a variety of other tools, and information technology

SUMMARY

Productivity is a major concern of managers. It implies measurement, an essential step in the control process. The productivity measurement of skill workers is generally easier than that of knowledge workers such as managers.

Yet managerial productivity is very important, especially for organizations operating in a competitive environment.

Production management refers to those activities necessary to manufacture products; it may also include purchasing, warehousing, transportation, and other operations. Operations management has a similar meaning, referring to activities necessary to produce and deliver a service as well as a physical product.

The operations management systems model shows inputs, the transformation process, outputs, and the feedback system. A variety of tools and techniques make operations more productive. Seven steps are often involved in planning and designing a product and its production. Companies can choose from six different kinds of production layouts. In order to operate the system, the managerial functions of organizing, staffing, and leading must be carried out effectively. Controlling requires an information system often supported by computers.

Among the various tools for planning and controlling operations is operations research, which is the application of the scientific method to the study of alternatives in a problem situation to obtain a quantitative basis for arriving at the best solution. Examples of tools are linear programming, inventory planning and control, the just-in-time inventory system, and distribution logistics. Other tools and techniques are time-event networks, value engineering, work simplification, quality circles, and a variety of computer-aided approaches.

KEY IDEAS AND CONCEPTS FOR REVIEW

Productivity	Inventory planning and control
Production management	Just-in-time (JIT) inventory system
Operations management	Distribution logistics
Operations management system	Time-event networks
Steps in product and production design	Value engineering
Production layouts	Work simplification
Operations research	Quality circles
Essential characteristics of operations research	CAD/CAM and MAP
Linear programming	Trends in operations research

FOR DISCUSSION

1. How would you measure the productivity of managers and other knowledge workers? Explain in detail.

2. Why is the field of production and operations management such a good one to use as a case example of planning and control techniques? Why do you believe that this area was favored for analysis and productivity improvement by the pioneers in the field of management?

3. Distinguish between the planning and control techniques that are usually found only in production and operations management and those that are found useful in all areas of management. Why is this so?

4. Explain the nature of and reasons for each step usually found in the development of a production and operations management program.

5. There are many typical layouts used in the design of a production program. Which one is ordinarily used for the manufacture of automobiles? Why? Which one do you believe was used for construction of the trans-Alaska pipeline. Why?

6. Real-time information can be widely used in the area of production, but this does not solve the problem of control. Why?

7. What tools generally found in operations research have been widely used in production and operations management? Do they have anything in common? If so, what is it?

8. What makes distribution logistics a more useful and complex tool of planning and control than an inventory model?

9. Why do you believe that quality control circles have been used so much in Japan?

EXERCISES/ACTION STEPS

1. After the class has been divided into groups of four or five students, consider the case below and try to answer the six questions raised by Lampert's business colleague. For the second question, each group should display a drawing of their lamp, including its main specifications (e.g., voltage) and several usages. One member of each group should try to "sell" the lamp to the class. If the class size is large enough, one group should act as an independent panel, evaluating each lamp proposal in terms of creativity, aesthetics, feasibility, and other criteria developed by the group.

2. Draw the layout of your apartment or your house, and indicate the pathways you walk while doing your typical daily chores. Show any rearrangements you could make that would increase your effectiveness and personal productivity.

CASE:
LAMPERT & SONS COMPANY

John Lampert, president of Lampert & Sons Company, a small manufacturing firm producing electrical appliances, was an entrepreneur with a technical background. He recently moved into a new house, and his wife asked him to install some spotlights to accent various areas in the house, such as bookshelves, a sculpture, and certain items in a wall unit.

At the local lighting stores, the lamps that might fit the purpose cost far more than Mr. Lampert was willing to pay. He felt that there was a real need for a low-cost, attractive spotlight or clamp-on lamp. He discussed his idea with a business colleague, who raised a number of questions such as these:

- Is there really a need for such a product?

- What should such a lamp look like?

- How or where should it be produced (e.g., in his plant in the Midwest or abroad, such as in Korea, Hong Kong, or Taiwan)?

- What arrangements would have to be made if the lamp were to be produced by Lampert & Sons?

- What kind of distribution channel (or channels) should be used to sell the product?

- How would he maintain the quality if the price of the lamp was to be kept low?

After this discussion, Mr. Lampert realized that he really had not thought through his idea and could not satisfactorily answer several of the questions.

1. If you were a small-business consultant, how would you answer the questions Mr. Lampert's colleague raised?

2. What other actions would you recommend for making the decisions to design the product, to set up a production system, and to control the operation, especially the quality?

3. What decision-making tools and techniques could assist in making these decisions?

REFERENCES

1. Certain sections of the discussion of productivity in this chapter are based on Heinz Weihrich, *Management Excellence* (New York: McGraw-Hill Book Company, 1985).

2. See, for example, Vernon M. Buehler and Y. Krishna Shetty (eds.), *Productivity Improvement* (New York: AMACOM, 1981), reporting on the experiences of companies in improving their productivity. See also Bernard J. Reilly and Joseph P. Fuhr, Jr., "Productivity: An Economic and Management Analysis with a Direction towards a New Synthesis," *Academy of Management Review* (January 1983), pp. 108–117.

3. Buehler and Shetty, *Productivity Improvement* (1981).

4. In the preparation of this chapter, the authors have received considerable assistance from Richard B. Chase and Nicholas J. Aquilano, *Production and Operations Management* (Homewood, Ill.: Richard D. Irwin, 1981).

5. The input-transformation-output model is widely used in the discussion of operations management. See, for example, Chase and Aquilano, *Production* (1981); Harold Fearon, William A. Ruch, Patrick G. Decker, Ross R. Reck, Vincent G. Reuter, and C. David Wieters, *Fundamentals of Production/Operations*

Management (St. Paul, Minn.: West Publishing Company, 1979); Elwood S. Buffa and James S. Dyer, *Management Science/Operations Research* (New York: John Wiley & Sons, 1981).

6. For a discussion of the relationship between strategy and operations management, see Wickham Skinner, *Manufacturing in the Corporate Strategy* (New York: John Wiley & Sons, 1978); Stephen C. Wheelwright, "Operations as Strategy Lessons from Japan," *Stanford GSB* (Fall 1981–1982), pp. 3–7.

7. For some interesting ideas about office layout, see Philip J. Stone and Robert Luchetti, "Your Office Is Where You Are," *Harvard Business Review* (March–April 1985), pp. 102–117.

8. See Chase and Aquilano, *Production* (1981), sec. 2; see also Arthur C. Laufer, *Operations Management* (Cincinnati: South-Western Publishing Company, 1979), chap. 16.

9. For a detailed discussion of information and control, see Edward E. Lawler III and John G. Rhode, *Information and Control in Organizations* (Santa Monica, Calif.: Goodyear Publishing Company, 1976).

10. For the application of analytical techniques and the use of graphics, see David J. Armstrong, "Sharpening Inventory Management," *Harvard*

Business Review (November–December 1985), pp. 42–58. For a variety of graphics software for the microcomputer, see David Needle, "Presentation Graphics Software," *InfoWorld* (Sept. 22, 1986).

11. Discussion with Professor Robert N. Mefford. His paper "The Productivity Nexus of New Inventory and Quality Control Techniques" has been submitted for review and publication. See also Richard B. Chase and Nicholas J. Aquilano, *Production and Operations Management*, 4th ed. (Homewood, Ill.: Richard D. Irwin, 1985), chap. 18.

12. Alan L. Saipe and Richard J. Schonberger, "Don't Ignore Just-in-Time Production," *Business Quarterly* (Spring 1984), pp. 60–66.

13. Saipe and Schonberger, "Don't Ignore Just-in-Time Production" (1984).

14. Richard C. Walleigh, "What's Your Excuse for not Using JIT?" *Harvard Business Review* (March–April 1986), pp. 38–54.

15. For an evaluation of just-in-time techniques, see Chiradet Ousawat and Kenneth D. Ramsing, "An Evaluation of the Just-in-Time Techniques in a Multi-Stage, Multi-Product Production System," in Frank Hoy (ed.), *Academy of Management Best Papers — Proceedings 1987*, Forty-Seventh Annual Meeting of the Academy of Management, New Orleans, Louisiana, August 9–12, 1987, pp. 296–300. See also Marshall Schminke and Stephen Chapman, "Organization Theory and Implementing JIT: Understanding *Why* as Well as What and How," in Frank Hoy (ed.), *Academy of Management Best Papers — Proceedings 1988*, Forty-Eighth Annual Meeting of the Academy of Management, Anaheim, California, August 7–10, 1988, pp. 303–307.

16. Edward E. Lawler III and Susan A. Mohrman, "Quality Circles after the Fad," *Harvard Business Review* (January–February 1985), pp. 65–71. See also S. G. Goldstein, "Organizational Dualism and Quality Circles," *Academy of Management Review* (July 1985), pp. 504–517.

17. For a discussion of quality circles in Japan and in the United States, see Tai K. Oh, "The Fate of QC Circles in the U.S.: A Case Study Testing the Cultural, Convergence, and Tradition-Modernity Theories," in Ryine T. Hsieh and Steven A. Scherling (eds.), *Proceedings of the Academy of International Business, Southeast Regional Conference, Taipei*, vol. 1 (June 26–28, 1986), pp. 749–759. See also Peter B. Petersen, "The Contribution of W. Edwards Deming to Japanese Management Theory and Practice," in Hoy (ed.), *Academy of Management Best Papers* (1987), pp. 133–137.

18. George Melloan, "Computers Elevate Quality Standards," *The Wall Street Journal* (Oct. 11, 1988); Eastman Kodak Company Annual Report, 1985.

19. Gene Bylinsky, "GM's Road Map to Automated Plants," *Fortune* (Oct. 28, 1985), pp. 89–102. For another discussion of computer-integrated manufacturing (CIM), see Robert S. Kaplan, "Must CIM Be Justified by Faith Alone?" *Harvard Business Review* (March–April 1986), pp. 87–95.

20. Bylinsky, "GM's Road Map" (1985). For difficulties with the new technology, especially at General Motors' Hamtramck plant in Michigan, which was supposed to be the showcase of high technology, see Amal Nag, "Auto Makers Discover 'Factory of the Future' Is Headache Just Now," *The Wall Street Journal* (May 13, 1986).

21. Fearon et al., *Fundamentals* (1979). See also Joseph Finkelstein and David Newman, "The Third Industrial Revolution: A Special Challenge to Managers," *Organizational Dynamics* (Summer 1984), pp. 53–65.

22. For a discussion of flexible automation, see Ramchandran Jaikumar, "Postindustrial Manufacturing," *Harvard Business Review* (November–December 1986), pp. 69–76. A holistic approach to developing new products has been suggested by Hirotaka Takeuchi and Ikujiro Nonaka, "The New Product Development Game," *Harvard Business Review* (January–February 1986), pp. 137–146.

23. For a discussion of how robotics are changing organizations and manufacturing tasks, see Daniel E. Whitney, "Real Robots Do Need Jigs," *Harvard Business Review* (May–June 1986), pp. 110–116.

24. "The Big Revolution on the Factory Floor," *The Wall Street Journal* (July 12, 1982).

25. For futuristic ideas about floating factories, see Alonzo L. McDonald, "Of Floating Factories and Mating Dinosaurs," *Harvard Business Review* (November–December 1986), pp. 82–86.

CHAPTER 21

Overall and Preventive Control

CHAPTER OBJECTIVES

After reading this chapter, you should understand:

1. The concept of overall control
2. The most widely used techniques of overall control of an enterprise
3. The principle of preventive control and how its nature and application differ from those of the many direct controls
4. The major challenges facing management and what needs to be done to develop excellent managers

Most controls are designed for specific things: policies, wages and salaries, employee selection and training, research and development, product quality, costs, pricing, capital expenditures, cash, and other areas where we wish performance to conform to plans. Such controls are partial in the sense that they apply to a part of an enterprise and do not measure total accomplishments against total goals. There clearly is a need for some overall measures, and, not surprisingly, many are expressed in financial terms.

Many of the controls are based on feedback by measuring deviations from plans. Also, the traditional approach is to find out who is responsible for the undesirable deviation and to get that person to correct it. This is direct control. But, as discussed later in this chapter, this kind of control is based on some questionable assumptions. Would it not be better to prevent undesirable deviations from occurring in the first place? Most people would answer, "Of course." It is therefore recommended that "preventive control" be applied; with this approach, a highly qualified manager will make fewer mistakes, thus reducing (but certainly not eliminating) the need for direct control. But let us first discuss the more traditional — and important — overall controls of budget summaries and other financial analyses.

CONTROL OF OVERALL PERFORMANCE

Planning and control are increasingly being treated as an interrelated system. Along with techniques for partial control, control devices have been developed for measuring the overall performance of an enterprise — or an integrated* division or project within it — against total goals.

There are many reasons for control of overall performance. In the first place, just as overall planning must apply to enterprise or major division goals, so must overall controls be applied. In the second place, decentralization of authority — especially in product or territorial divisions — creates semi-independent units, and these must be subjected to overall controls to avoid the chaos of complete independence. In the third place, overall controls permit measuring an integrated area manager's *total* effort, rather than parts of it.

Many overall controls in business are, as one might expect, financial. Business owes its continued existence to profit making; its capital resources are a scarce, life-giving element. Since finance is the binding force of business, financial controls are certainly an important objective gauge of the success of plans.[1]

Financial measurements also summarize, as a common denominator, the operation of a number of plans. Further, they accurately indicate total expenditures of resources in reaching goals. This is true in all forms of enterprise. Although the purpose of an educational or government enterprise is not to make monetary profits, any responsible manager must have some way of knowing what goal achievement has cost in terms of resources. Proper accounting is important not only for business but for government as well. Professor Anthony at Harvard points out that in government, accounting often hides important facts. Otherwise, how could it have happened that several cities, including New York, were nearly bankrupt before their financial conditions became clear?[2]

---

*"Integrated" is used here as meaning that an operation includes the functions necessary to gain an overall objective. Thus, a product division of a company would normally include engineering, manufacturing, and marketing, and these functions represent enough of a total operation for the division manager — even though subject to some direction and control from headquarters — to be held basically responsible for a profit. To a lesser degree, an engineering design operation might be regarded as integrated: If its head supervises all the engineering functions and specialities necessary for complete product design, he or she can then be held responsible for the efficient accomplishment of the project.

Financial controls, like any other control, have to be tailored to the specific needs of the enterprise or the position. Doctors, lawyers, and managers at different organizational levels do have different needs for controlling their area of operation.[3] Financial analyses also furnish an excellent "window" through which accomplishment in nonfinancial areas can be seen. A deviation from planned costs, for example, may lead a manager to find the causes in poor planning, inadequate training of employees, or other nonfinancial factors.

BUDGET SUMMARIES AND REPORTS

A widely used control of overall performance takes the form of a summary of budgets. A **budget summary,** being a résumé of all the individual budgets, reflects company plans so that sales volume, costs, profits, utilization of capital, and return on investment may be seen in their proper relationship. In these terms it shows top management how well the company as a whole is succeeding in meeting its objectives.

For the best control through a budget summary, a manager must first be satisfied that total budgets are an accurate and reasonably complete portrayal of the company's plans. The manager should study the budget reports and any material accompanying them to determine whether the comparison of budget and actual costs shows the real nature of any deviations. For example, a company head criticized his factory manager for being considerably over his labor budget in a month when the labor force had been materially reduced and the temporary increase in expenses was due to severance pay.

Minor discrepancies should receive appropriately little attention. The purpose of a control system is to draw attention to important variations, and both the budget reports and the attention paid to them should reflect this. Above all, a manager should never forget that a budget summary is no substitute for profitable operation. Budgeting is never more perfect than the planning behind it, and plans — especially long-range plans — are subject to the imperfections caused by change and uncertainty. There may even be times when a manager must forget the budget and take special action to meet unexpected events. Budgets are meant to be tools, and not masters, of managers.

On the other hand, managers should not underestimate the value of budget summaries in providing an effective means for overall control in situations of decentralized authority. Budget summaries furnish a means whereby enterprise objectives can be clearly and specifically defined and departmental plans can be made to contribute toward such objectives. Should the budget summary and the reports of actual events indicate that the enterprise as a whole is not tending toward its objectives, top managers have a convenient and positive means of finding out where the deviations are occurring. The summaries thus furnish a useful guide for corrective action.

PROFIT AND LOSS CONTROL

The income statement for an enterprise as a whole serves important control purposes, mainly because it is useful for determining the immediate revenue or cost factors that have accounted for success or failure. Obviously, if it is first put in the form of a forecast, the income statement is an even better control device in that it gives managers a chance, before things happen, to influence revenues, expenses, and, consequently, profits.

The Nature and Purpose of Profit and Loss Controls

Since the survival of a business usually depends on profits and since profits are a definite standard against which to measure success, many companies use the income statement for divisional or departmental control. Because it is a statement of all revenues and expenses for a given time, it is a true summary of the results of business operations. Profit and loss control, when applied to divisions or departments, is based on the premise that if it is the purpose of the entire business to make a profit, each part of the enterprise should contribute to this purpose.[4] Thus, the ability of a part to make an expected profit becomes a standard for measuring its performance.

In profit and loss control, each major department or division details its revenues and expenses — normally including a proportionate share of company overhead — and calculates periodically its profit or loss. Some units have their own accounting group; in others, the statement is prepared by the central accounting department. In either case, the organizational unit, because it is expected to turn in a separate record of profitable operation, is considered by headquarters in much the same way that subsidiary companies are considered by a holding company.

Profit and loss control usually is practicable only for major segments of a company, since the paperwork involved in building up profit and loss statements for smaller departments tends to be too heavy. Also, profit and loss control usually implies that managers of a division or department have fairly wide authority to run their part of the business as they see fit, with profit the primary standard of success. However, many companies that do not so decentralize authority have nonetheless found profit and loss control valuable. The focus on profit and the sensitivity of the organizational unit to it are worthwhile even when managers have limited independence in seeking profit as they wish.

The more integrated and complete the organization unit, the more accurate a measuring stick profit and loss control can be. For this reason, it works best in product or territorial divisions, where both sales and production functions for a product or service are under one general manager. For example, it is much easier to use the standard of profit for measuring the operations of the general manager of the Buick division of General Motors than it would be to use it for the supervisor of the motor-block-boring section of the manufacturing department of this division.

PERSPECTIVE:
KODAK'S PROFIT PICTURE IN FULL COLOR AGAIN

For a long time Eastman Kodak Company, with headquarters in Rochester, New York, was considered an excellent company. In the mid-1980s, however, the company encountered difficulties, partly because of the strong U.S. dollar and the tough competition from Japan's Fuji Films, Kodak's main rival. In 1986 the profit picture changed for the better, with an increase of about 14 percent in earnings.

What, then, accounted for the turnaround?[5] Among the various reasons for the change are the following:

1. The decline of the value of the U.S. dollar had a positive effect on profits. It also made Kodak more competitive with Fuji.

2. Cost was reduced by a reduction in the work force of almost 25,000.

3. In 1986 Kodak introduced 100 new products, including new films (for example, the VR-G films with vibrant colors) and a new 35-mm camera.

4. Kodak is also selling minilabs for developing films; these labs use great amounts of chemicals and paper made by Kodak.

5. The company diversified into areas such as optical-disk data storage, long-life batteries, and electronic publishing.

6. The reorganization resulted in seventeen fairly autonomous business units, a setup that enables the company to respond more quickly to changes in the market.

Kodak is also preparing for the more distant future, realizing that it has to expand its domain beyond photography. Thus, the company is venturing into health care, drugs (for example, to fight cancer), electronic imaging, and data storage (it acquired the floppy-disk maker Verbatim in 1985). While the future is not without problems and challenges, for now a combination of factors such as changes in the external environment, some clever strategic choices, cost cutting, and the reorganization hint at a colorful future for Kodak.

At the same time, companies organized on a functional basis do occasionally employ profit and loss control. The heat-treating department may produce and "sell" its service to the machining department, which in turn "sells" its product to the assembly department, which in turn "sells" a complete product to the sales department. This can be done, although the paperwork required is often not worth the effort, and the problem of determining the right transfer price may occasion much negotiation or many difficult executive decisions. If the transfer is made at cost, clearly only the sales department would show a profit or a loss. If it is made at a figure above cost, the question of what price to charge arises.

In most instances, profit and loss control is not applied to central staff and service departments. Although these departments could "sell" their services, the most satisfactory practice is to place them under some other form of control, such as the variable expense budget.

Limitations of Profit and Loss Control

Profit and loss control suffers its greatest limitation from the cost of the accounting and paper transactions involving intracompany transfer of costs and revenues. Duplication of accounting records, efforts involved in allocating the many overhead costs, and the time and effort required to calculate intracompany sales can make this control too costly if it is carried too far.

Profit and loss control also may be inadequate for overall performance. Top managers may not wish to give their division managers too much authority, and they may desire the additional assurances of good budgetary control. In addition, profit and loss control in and of itself does not provide a standard of desirable profits or policy controls in the area of product-line development or in other matters of long-term overall company concern.

Another limitation of profit and loss control, especially if it is carried very far in the organization, is that departments may come to compete with an aggressive detachment not helpful to enterprise coordination. On the other hand, in many companies there is not enough feeling of departmental responsibility for company profit, and departments may develop the smugness of a monopolist with an assured market. The parts fabrication department that knows its products must be "bought" by the assembly department, the manufacturing or the service department that can force its output on the sales department, and the engineering group that has a monopolistic hold on both production and sales are dangerous monopolists indeed. Profit and loss control can break down these islands of monopoly. So, in spite of limitations — and especially if accompanied by an intracompany pricing policy which requires that departments meet competitive prices of suppliers outside the enterprise, rather than a policy which is based on cost — profit and loss control can give top managers an extraordinary measure of overall control.

CONTROL THROUGH RETURN ON INVESTMENT

One of the most successfully used control techniques is that of measuring both the absolute and the relative success of a company or a company unit by the ratio of earnings to investment of capital. The return-on-investment approach, often referred to simply as ROI, has been the core of the control system of the Du Pont Company since 1919. A large number of companies have adopted it as their key measure of overall performance. This yardstick is the rate of return that a company or a division can earn on the capital allocated to it. This tool, therefore, regards profit not as an absolute but as a return on capital employed in the business. The goal of a business is seen, accordingly, not necessarily as optimizing profits but as optimizing returns from capital devoted to business purposes. This standard recognizes the fundamental fact that capital is a critical factor in almost any enterprise and, through its scarcity, limits progress. It also emphasizes the fact that the job of managers is to make the best possible use of assets entrusted to them.

The Return-on-Investment System in Action

As the system has been used by the Du Pont Company, return on investment involves consideration of several factors. Return is computed on the basis of capital turnover (that is, total sales divided by capital, or total investment) multiplied by earnings as a percentage of sales. This formula recognizes that a division with a high capital turnover and low percentage of earnings to sales may be more profitable in terms of return on investment than another with a high percentage of profits to sales but with low capital turnover. As can be seen, the system measures effectiveness in the use of capital. Investment includes not only the permanent plant facilities but also the working capital of the unit. In the Du Pont system, investment and working capital represent amounts invested without reduction for liabilities or reserves, on the ground that such a reduction would result in a fluctuation in operating investments as reserves or liabilities change, which would distort the rate of return and render it less meaningful. Earnings are, however, calculated after normal depreciation charges, on the basis that true profits are not earned until allowance is made for the write-off of depreciable assets.

Return-on-investment control is perhaps best summarized in chart form, as in Figure 21-1. Here, analysis of variations in rate of return leads into every financial aspect of the business. Rate of return is the common denominator used in comparing divisions, and differences can easily be traced to their causes.

However, other companies have taken the position that the return on investment should be calculated on fixed assets less depreciation. Such companies hold that the depreciation reserve represents a write-off of the initial investment and that funds made available through such charges are reinvested in other fixed assets or used as working capital. Such a treatment appears more realistic to operating people, partly because it places a heavier rate-of-return burden on new fixed assets than on worn or obsolete ones.

In any control through return on investment, the number of ratios and comparisons behind the yardstick figure cannot be overlooked. Although improvement in rate of return can come from a higher percentage of profit to sales, improvement may also come from increasing the rate of turnover by lowering price and reducing return on sales. Moreover, the ratio of return on investment might be improved by getting more products (and sales) out of a given plant investment or by reducing the cost of sales for a given product.

Application to Product Lines

Functional-line organizations without integrated product divisions have applied return-on-investment control to their various product lines. By grouping its many products into a number of major classifications, a typical company follows through with the allocation of sales, costs, and investment in fixed assets and working capital to arrive at the same kind of rate-of-return analysis used by multidivision companies. A simplified example of these results is shown in Table 21-1.

Figure 21-1

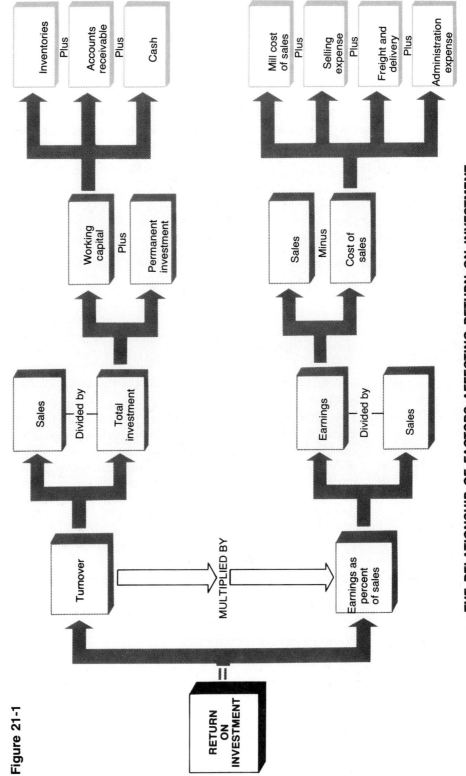

THE RELATIONSHIP OF FACTORS AFFECTING RETURN ON INVESTMENT.

Table 21-1   Comparative Rates of Return on Assets Employed: Multiproduct Company
(In thousands of dollars)

	Total sales		Assets employed		Operating income*		
	Amount	Percent of total	Amount	Per dollar of sales	Amount	Percent return on sales	Percent return on assets
Base year:							
Product A	$ 39,300	40	$ 20,700	52.9%	$ 4,800	12.2	23.1
Product B	29,500	30	16,900	57.3	2,800	9.4	16.4
Product C	19,600	20	8,900	45.1	2,100	10.8	23.9
Product D	9,800	10	2,700	27.5	500	5.1	18.5
Total	$ 98,200	100	$ 49,200	50.1%	$10,200	10.4	20.8
Current year:							
Product A	$ 48,100	25	$ 28,400	59.0%	$ 5,600	11.6	19.7
Product B	96,200	50	75,300	78.3	8,500	8.8	11.2
Product C	38,500	20	19,500	50.7	3,900	10.2	20.1
Product D	9,600	5	2,900	29.9	500	5.2	17.2
Total	$192,400	100	$126,100	65.5%	$18,500	9.6	14.6

* Before interest on borrowed money and federal income taxes.

To use the rate-of-return yardstick (as return on assets employed) for product lines, the company has allocated certain expenses and assets, but these allocations apparently have not caused much difficulty. Most production costs are maintained by product, and common costs, such as sales branch expenses, are allocated by volume of sales. More difficulty is incurred in determining asset usage by product lines, but cash, accounts receivable, and administrative and sales facilities are allocated in accordance with sales, while inventories and factory and plant equipment are prorated to the various products on the basis of special analyses.

In addition to comparing rates of return on assets of products, as indicated in Table 21-1, this company compared actual experience with trends for the various products (identified for purposes of simplicity as the "base year" in the table). An advantage of these comparisons is that the company is able to keep a sharp eye on its product lines, wih a view to determining where capital is being most efficiently employed and as a guide toward obtaining a balanced use of capital for greatest overall profit. Thus, the company has been able to identify products that are either strong and established, new and improved, or past their peak growth and profitability.

Advantages of ROI

One of the principal advantages of using return on investment to control overall performance is that it, like profit and loss control, focuses managerial attention on the central objective of the business — making the best profit possible on the capital available. It measures the efficiency of the company as a whole and of its major divisions or departments, its products, and its planning. It takes attention away from mere increase in sales volume or asset size or even from the level of costs, and it draws attention to the combination of factors that promotes successful operation.

Another advantage of control by return on investment is that it is effective where authority is decentralized. It not only is an absolute guide to capital efficiency but also offers the possibility of comparing efficiency in the use of capital within the company and with other enterprises. By holding departmental managers responsible for performance in terms of the dollars invested in their parts of the business, it forces them to look at their operations from the point of view of top management. Managers often insist on heavy capital investments for new equipment or drive for lower prices to increase sales without taking into account the possible effect of their requests on the company as a whole. They also often feel isolated, particularly in large businesses, with respect to their performance. If managers are furnished with a guide to efficiency that applies to a business as a whole, they develop a keener sense of responsibility for their department or division and top managers can more easily hold subordinate managers responsible.

A further advantage of return-on-investment control, if it is complete and shows all the factors bearing upon the return, is that it enables managers to locate weaknesses. If inventories are rising, the rate of return will be affected; or if other factors camouflage inventory variations and leave the rate looking good, tracing back influences will disclose any weakness of the inventory situation and open the way for consideration of a remedy.

Limitations of ROI

With all its advantages and its widespread use by well-managed and successful companies, this method of control is not foolproof. Difficulties involve availability of information on sales, costs, and assets and proper allocation of investment and return for commonly sold or produced items. Does the present accounting system give the needed information? If not, how much will it cost to get it, through either changes in the system or special analyses? If assets are jointly used or costs are common, what method of allocation between divisions or departments should be used? Should a manager be charged with assets at their original costs, their replacement costs, or their depreciated values? Setting up a return-on-investment control system is no simple task.

Another question is, What constitutes a reasonable return? Comparisons of rates of return are hardly enough, because they do not tell the top manager what the rate of return should be. Perhaps as good a standard as any is one that meets or surpasses the level of competing firms, since, in a practical sense, the best tends to be measured not by an absolute level but by the level of the competition for capital.

One of the dangers of overemphasis on the rate of return is that it may lead to undesirable inflexibility in investing capital for new ventures. Many companies using this important measuring tool have set minimum rates which a division, new-product program, or investment must meet before the allocation of additional capital would be approved. It is said that even Du Pont, for many years, would not approve a new product program which would not promise a minimum of 20 percent return on investment. According to one executive of the company, this rigid minimum caused Du Pont to pass up such great product opportunities as xerography and the Land (Polaroid) camera. More recently, the company has used a more flexible minimum rate of return, requiring a higher rate when risks are greater and a lower rate when results are very promising or more certain or when an investment supplements an established business.

Perhaps the greatest danger in return-on-investment control, as with any system of control based on financial data, is that it can lead to excessive preoccupation with financial factors within a firm or an industry. Undue attention to ratios and financial data can cause a firm to overlook environmental factors such as social and technical developments. It might also lead a company to overlook the fact that capital is not the only scarce resource with which a business can grow, prosper, and endure. Every bit as scarce are competent managers, good employee morale, and good customer and public relations. A well-managed company would never regard any financially based control as the sole gauge of overall performance.

DIRECT CONTROL VERSUS PREVENTIVE CONTROL

The preceding analysis of controls stresses the variety of approaches that managers follow to make results conform to plans. At the basis of control is the fact that the outcome of plans is dependent on the people who carry them out. For instance, a poor educational system cannot be controlled by criticizing its product, the unfortunate graduate; a factory turning out inferior products cannot be controlled by consigning products to the scrap heap; and a firm plagued with customer complaints cannot be controlled by ignoring the complainers. Responsibility for controllable deviations lies with whoever has made unfortunate decisions. Any hope of abolishing unsatisfactory results lies in changing the future actions of the responsible person, through additional training, modification of procedures, or new policy. This is the crux of controlling the quality of management.

There are two ways of seeing to it that the responsible people modify future action. The normal procedure is to trace the cause of an unsatisfactory result back to the persons responsible for it and get them to correct their practices. This may be called **direct control.** The alternative in the area of management is to develop better managers who will skillfully apply concepts, techniques, and principles and who will look at managing and managerial problems from a systems point of view, thus eliminating undesirable results caused by poor management. This will be referred to as **preventive control.***

---

*In previous editions of this text a different terminology was used. On the basis of colleagues' recommendations, the terms "preventive" control and "direct" control are used in this edition.

> **PERSPECTIVE:**
> **CONTROL AT APPLE COMPUTER**
>
> Apple Computer, Inc., enjoyed a phenomenal early success after it was founded in 1977 by Steve Wozniak, the technical expert, and Steve Jobs, the marketing genius.
>
> However, success did not last for very long, partly because of the introduction of the IBM Personal Computer. In the early 1980s, in the view of some observers, Apple needed tighter control and a more professional approach to managing. John Sculley was lured from the Pepsi-Cola Company to give Apple a new direction.[6]
>
> To bring the company under control, Sculley employed cost-cutting measures to improve its profitability. At the same time, however, research and development expenditures were increased so that the company could remain a technological leader in the field. The firm was also reorganized to reduce duplication of efforts, to lower the break-even point, and to reduce friction among the departments. To improve its effectiveness and efficiency, Apple introduced new reporting procedures. Furthermore, considerable efforts were made to control the inventory level, which is a serious problem in the personal-computer industry. These measures, combined with a successful strategy (Apple's Macintosh computer is making inroads into business corporations which are dominated by IBM) and helped by the popularity of desktop publishing, resulted in an increase of over 150 percent in earnings in the 1986 fiscal year.

DIRECT CONTROL

In every enterprise, hundreds, and even thousands, of standards are developed to compare the actual output of goods or services — in terms of quantity, quality, time, and cost — with plans. A negative deviation indicates — in terms of goal achievement, cost, price, personnel, labor-hours, or machine-hours — that performance is less than good or normal or standard and that results are not conforming to plans.

Causes of Negative Deviations from Standards

The causes of negative deviations will often determine whether control measures are possible. Although an incorrect standard may cause deviations, if the standard is correct, plans may fail because of (1) uncertainty and (2) lack of knowledge, experience, or judgment on the part of those who make the decisions or take actions.

Uncertainty   Elements affecting a given plan may be grouped into facts, risks, and uncertainty. Facts, such as number of employees, costs, or machine capacity, are known. Considerably less is known about the element of risk. Insurable risks are readily converted to factual status through the payment of a known premium, and costs of certain noninsurable risks may be included in a business decision on the basis of probability. But most risks arise from uncertainty. The total of facts and risks is small compared with the element of uncertainty, which includes everything about which nothing is certain. For instance, the success of a plan to manufacture aluminum pistons will depend not only on known facts and risks but also on such uncertainties as future world conditions, competition of known and yet unknown metals, and power technology that may eliminate all piston prime movers. Not even probability can be estimated for all the uncertain factors, and yet they can wreck a plan.

Managerial errors caused by unforeseeable events cannot be avoided. The fixing of personal responsibility by direct control techniques is of little avail in such situations.

Lack of knowledge, experience, or judgment Plans may misfire and negative deviations occur when people appointed to managerial posts lack the necessary background. The higher in the organizational structure managers are placed, the broader the knowledge and experience they need. Long years as an engineer, a sales manager, a production executive, or a controller may be inadequate qualifications for a top manager.

If the cause of error is poor judgment, whether due to inadequate training, to lack of experience, or to failure to use appropriate information in decision making, corrections can be made. Managers can improve their education, be transferred to acquire broader experience, or be cautioned to take better stock of the situation before making decisions.

Questionable Assumptions Underlying Direct Control

In addition to its cost, the shortcomings of direct control may also be the results of questionable assumptions which hold that (1) performance can be measured,[7] (2) personal responsibility exists, (3) the time expenditure is warranted, (4) mistakes can be discovered in time, and (5) the person responsible will take corrective steps.

Assumption that performance can be measured At first glance, almost any enterprise appears to be a maze of controls. Input, output, cost, price, time, complaints, and quality are subject to numerous standards, and the standards may be expressed in terms of goal achievement, time, weight, tolerances, averages, ratios, dollars, and indexes. In terms of usefulness, the standards may be correct, acceptable, or merely better than nothing. Close analysis will often reveal shortcomings of two types. The first type concerns measurement. The ability of a manager to develop potential managers, the effectiveness of research, and the amount of creativity, foresight, and judgment in decision making can seldom be measured accurately.

The second type of shortcoming concerns the location of the control. Managers know that critical stages exist in acquiring input factors, manipulating them to produce a finished product, and selling and delivering the product. In a factory operation, for example, critical stages would include receiving inspection, inspection for each assembly process, shipping, and billing. These are critical because effective control here will minimize costs. No amounts of control at other points can make up for lack of control at these stages.

Assumption that personal responsibility exists Sometimes no manager is responsible for poor results. An increase in interest rates or inflation may cause the costs of many activities to rise precipitously; scarcity of a particular fuel may necessitate use of less economical sources of power; and markets may shrink for reasons unconnected with the firm.

Assumption that the time expenditure is warranted Whether managers undertake the inquiry themselves or assign it to others, executive time must be spent in ferreting out causes of poor results. Large scrap losses, for example, may call for meetings attended by persons representing quality control, production planning, engineering, purchasing, and manufacturing. Because time has passed, recalling facts may be quite difficult. These drawbacks may convince managers that the cost of investigation exceeds any benefit they may derive. This often precludes investigation of clear violations of standards.

Assumption that mistakes can be discovered in time Discovery of deviations from plans often comes too late for effective action. Although true control can be applied only to future action, most controls depend on historical data — all that most managers have available. Managers should, of course, interpret such data in terms of their implications for the future.

The cost of errors in major areas — such as cash or inventories — has led to the use of feedforward techniques as the basis for control. Since these are often difficult to use, the natural tendency to rely on historical reports seriously blocks adequate controls. Feedforward control techniques offer hope, but as yet they have not been widely developed or utilized. No manager really has control unless he or she can correct mistakes. And the best way to correct mistakes is to avoid them.

Assumption that the person responsible will take corrective steps Fixing the responsibility may not lead to correction. High production costs, for example, might be traced back to a marketing manager who insists that "slight" product modification will make selling easier and that this involves "really" no change in a production run. If the marketing manager is a member of top management, a subordinate investigator may be intimidated. Although great effort may be made to correct subordinate managers, it is sometimes very difficult to correct an executive to whom one reports.

THE PRINCIPLE OF PREVENTIVE CONTROL

The principle of preventive control embraces the idea that most of the responsibility for negative deviations from standards can be fixed by applying fundamentals of management. It draws a sharp distinction between analyzing performance reports, essential in any case, and determining whether managers act in accordance with established principles in carrying out their functions. The **principle of preventive control,** then, can be stated as follows:

The higher the quality of managers and their subordinates, the less will be the need for direct controls.

The extensive adoption of preventive control must await a wider understanding of managerial principles, functions, and techniques as well as management philosophy. While such an understanding is not achieved easily, it can be gained through university training, on-the-job experience, coaching by a knowledgeable superior, and constant self-education. Moreover, as progress is made in appraising managers as managers, preventive control can be expected to have more practical meaning and effectiveness.

Assumptions of the Principle of Preventive Control

The desirability of preventive control rests upon three assumptions: These hold that (1) qualified managers make a minimum of errors, (2) managerial performance can be measured and management concepts, principles, and techniques are useful diagnostic standards in measuring managerial performance, and (3) the application of management fundamentals can be evaluated.

Assumption that qualified managers make a minimum of errors J. P. Morgan has often been quoted as saying that the decisions of good managers are right two-thirds of the time. However, an accurate analysis of the quality of decision making should not rely upon quantity of errors but should be concerned with the nature of the error. J. Paul Getty once said that his concern in his world-wide empire was not the percentage of decisions in which an executive was right or wrong — the executive could be wrong on only 2 percent of them and seriously endanger a company if the errors were critical. Managers can logically be held strictly accountable for the performance of their functions because these functions should be undertaken in conformance with the fundamentals of management.[8] However, accountability cannot be exacted for errors attributable to factors beyond managers' authority or their ability to forecast the future with a reasonable degree of accuracy.

Assumption that management fundamentals can be used to measure performance The chief purpose of this book has been to draw together concepts, principles, theory, and basic techniques or approaches of management and relate them to a system of managerial functions. As stated in previous chapters, the completeness and certitude of these vary considerably, depending largely upon the state of knowledge concerning managing. There is, for instance, greater general acceptance of some of the principles of organizing than there is of the principles relating to other functions. Nevertheless, it can be said that the fundamentals set forth here are useful in measuring managerial performance, even though this statement will undoubtedly be refined and better verified by future specialists.

Assumption that the application of management fundamentals can be evaluated Evaluation can provide for periodic measurement of the skill with which managers apply management fundamentals. This can be done not only by judging performance against these fundamentals but also by casting them into a series of fairly objective questions. An approach to the proper evaluation of managers as managers was set forth in Chapter 12. The ability to set and achieve verifiable objectives is one measure of a manager's performance, but much depends on being able to evaluate the performance of a manager as a manager. As crude as these standards of measurement may be at the present state of the art of managing, they can still highlight the extent to which an individual has the knowledge and ability required to fill the managerial role.

Advantages of Preventive Control

Controlling the quality of managers and thus minimizing errors has several advantages. First, greater accuracy is achieved in assigning personal responsibility. The ongoing evaluation of managers is practically certain to uncover deficiencies and should provide a basis for specific training to eliminate them.

Second, preventive control should hasten corrective action and make it more effective. It encourages control by self-control. Knowing that errors will be uncovered in an evaluation, managers will themselves try to determine their responsibility and make voluntary corrections. For example, a report of excessive scrap will probably cause the department supervisor to determine quickly whether the excess was due to poor direction of subordinates or to other factors. The same report will cause the chief inspector to look into whether inspections employees acted properly, the purchasing agent to check the material purchased against engineering specifications, and the engineers to determine whether appropriate material was specified. All these actions can be immediate and voluntary. Managers who conclude privately that they were in error are likely to do their best to prevent recurrence, for they realize their responsibility.

Third, preventive control may lighten the managerial burden now caused by direct controls. Preventing problems from occurring often requires less effort than correcting them after deviations have been detected.

Fourth, the psychological advantage of preventive control is impressive. Many subordinates feel that superiors do not rate fairly, that they rely on hunch and personality, and that they use improper measuring standards, but performance appraisal of the kind suggested in Chapter 12 can go far in removing this feeling. Subordinate managers know what is expected of them, understand the nature of managing, and feel a close relationship between performance and measurement.

DEVELOPING EXCELLENT MANAGERS

Although the introductory analyses of the task of the manager are presented in this book as a start toward understanding the science underlying managerial practice, more is required. There are many considerations in ensuring the development of excellent managers; some of the more important ones are discussed below. Surely, effective future managerial practice will depend, at least, on these.

Instilling a Willingness to Learn

If managers are to avoid the stultifying effect of basing too much of their learning on experience, they must be aware of the dangers of experience.[9] As indicated earlier in this book, undistilled experience can lead an individual toward assuming that events or programs of the past will or will not work in a different future. But managers need more than this. They need to be willing to learn and to take advantage of new knowledge and new techniques. This necessitates a humble approach to their successes and limitations. It demands a recognition that there is no finishing school or terminal degree for management.

Accelerating Management Development

The preceding discussion underlines the urgent importance of accelerated programs of management development. This implies not only more pertinent management seminars and conferences but also other means of transmitting to practicing managers in as simple and useful a way as possible the new knowledge and tools in the field of management.

One of the major challenges in this connection is that of compressing and transmitting the available knowledge. Every field of art based on a burgeoning science has the same problem. No field has completely solved it, although certain areas, such as specialized aspects of medicine and dentistry, have made considerable progress.

There is no adequate answer for this problem. It does appear that those on the management faculties of our universities have an obligation to practicing managers to do much of the task of compressing and transmitting this knowledge as easily and quickly as possible. There is still inadequate evidence that many university professors see the social importance of this role. Also, one might expect a greater contribution from various management associations, as well as from management consultants, who can certainly greatly improve their value to clients by doing this. Perhaps more can be done through intelligent digesting of articles and books. Also, a series of special management clinics could be established on a regular basis. By spending a day every few weeks at such a clinic, managers at all levels in alert companies could be brought up to date on a specific area of new knowledge and techniques.

Planning for Innovation

As competition becomes sharper, as problem solving grows in complexity, and as knowledge expands, one expects that the managers of the future will have to place greater importance on planning for innovation. Even now it is widely recognized that a business enterprise, at least, must "innovate or die," that new products do not just happen, and that new marketing ideas do not often occur by luck. The manager of the future must place more emphasis than ever before on developing an environment for effective planning. This will involve, even more than it does at present, planning goals which call for stretch; creating policy guidelines to channel thinking toward them without stifling imagination; designing roles in which people can be creative and yet constructive; keeping abreast of the entire external environment (discussed in greater detail in Chapters 2 and 21), which affects every kind of organization; and recognizing the urgency of channeling research toward desired ends.

Measuring and Rewarding Management

One of the significant concerns of the manager of the future will be the importance both of objectively measuring managerial performance and of rewarding good performance, imposing sanctions on a poor operation, and providing corrective action where it is indicated. Managers must be willing to work toward establishing objective measures of performance through both an analysis of verifiable results and a measurement of the abilities of individuals as managers.

Tailoring Information

Another important consideration for the manager of the future will be obtaining the right information in the right form and at the right time. Tailoring information, as outlined in this book, requires a high order of intelligence and design. Until more managers realize that very little of their operation can be planned and controlled through "handbook" approaches, and until more managers recognize that they themselves must become involved in tailoring the information they require, progress will continue to be slow in this area. As long as information design is confused with the clerical work of information gathering and summarizing, managers will understandably continue to fret about the inadequacy of the data on which they are forced to act.

Expanding Research and Development in Tools and Techniques

All the issues mentioned above should command greater managerial attention. In addition, a great need exists for more real research and development in management tools and techniques themselves. The level of research effort and support in the field of management is woefully low. It is also not particularly great in the disciplines underlying management or, for that matter, in the entire area of social science. Nevertheless, it is probable that research in the underlying disciplines far outpaces that in the central area of management.

There are many reasons for this. General management research is difficult, exceedingly complex, and dynamic. It is an area in which facts and proved relationships are hard to come by and in which the controlled experiment of the laboratory is difficult to use without dangerous oversimplification. Likewise, management research is expensive, and the funds that have gone into it are abysmally inadequate.

Still another reason for the low state of management research is that there are few clinical analyses, despite a considerable volume of clinical experience. Consulting efforts of both professional consultants and individual academics, extensive management case collections, and studies and analyses made internally in business, government, and other enterprises almost certainly encompass a huge mass of undigested, largely unsummarized, and relatively useless information. If this clinical experience could be given the analytical and summarizing work so common in the health sciences, there might now be considerable evidence of what is workable in practice and where deficiencies exist.

Undertaking this research requires patience and understanding. Perfection of analysis to include all kinds of variables is a laudable goal for a researcher. But, particularly in the field of management, a little light can be a massive beam in a hitherto dark area. We must often settle for small advances so that cumulatively, and over time, we may gain larger ones.

Developing More Managerial Inventions

Research without development is insufficient. One of the major challenges for the manager of the future is the need for developing more managerial inventions. It is interesting that so much creative talent has been channeled into the invention of physical designs and chemical compositions while so little has gone into social inventions. The Gantt chart has sometimes been regarded as the most important social invention of the first half of the twentieth century. Other management inventions include the variable budget, rate-of-return-on-investment analysis, and PERT. Mere reference to these inventions underscores the fact that they are creative tools developed from a base of principles on the one hand and needs on the other. Reference to them indicates also that they are useful devices in improving the art of managing.

Inventions tend to reflect the cultural level of an art. There are few of them in management. Surely, even the present inadequate cultural level can be coupled with urgent needs to give rise to many more management innovations, particularly if the people concerned are willing to spend some time and money to direct their energies toward these inventions. It is very easy to see that one significant management invention, such as those mentioned in the previous paragraph, can make important contributions to management effectiveness and economy of operations. Applied research and development in this field surely justify a considerable expenditure of time and money.

Creating Strong Intellectual Leadership

That intellectual leadership in management is urgently needed can hardly be denied. Managing can no longer be only a practical art requiring merely native intelligence and experience. The rapid growth of underlying knowledge and the obvious need for even more, particularly that knowledge which is organized and useful for improvement of practice, are requirements which have tremendous significance.

For people in every type of enterprise, at any part of the globe, the challenge of creating a highly productive society is great. History teaches us that when needs exist and are recognized, leadership usually rises to inspired solutions. The challenging needs are here, waiting the application of knowledge discussed in this book, which is aimed at making you more effective as a person and as a manager so that you can lead a productive organization.

SUMMARY

Many overall controls are financial. One widely used control of overall performance is the summary budget, which is a summary of all operating revenue and expense budgets. Another kind of control is profit and loss control. Still another overall control technique is the exercise of control through calculating and comparing return on investment. This approach is based on the idea that profit should not be considered as an absolute measure but as a return on the capital employed in a segment of a business. An example is the well-known Du Pont return-on-investment (ROI) model.

In carrying out the controlling function, managers have two basic approaches. The most usual one, direct control, consists of developing standards for desired performance and then comparing actual performance against these standards. The normal procedure is to trace the cause of an unsatisfactory result back to the persons responsible for it and get them to correct their practices.

The other approach is "preventive" control, in which an attempt is made to prevent negative deviations from standards by ensuring that managers at all levels apply effectively the fundamentals of management. The principle of preventive control is stated as follows: The higher the quality of managers and their subordinates, the less will be the need for direct controls. The assumptions that underlie the principle of preventive control are that (1) qualified managers make a minimum of errors, (2) management fundamentals can be used to measure performance, and (3) the application of management fundamentals can be evaluated.

Without question, the manager's role is expanding and changing. With new knowledge being developed and social forces requiring managers to take advantage of it, the danger that managers will become obsolete is growing more serious. Many factors can help avoid this possibility: managers who are willing to learn, acceleration of programs of management development, more effective planning for innovation, better methods for evaluating and rewarding managerial performance, more tailored information, and greater emphasis on managerial research, development, and inventions. The best intellectual leadership in management is urgently required to meet these challenges.

KEY IDEAS AND CONCEPTS FOR REVIEW

Budget summary	Direct control
Profit and loss control	Questionable assumptions of direct
Limitations of profit and loss control	control
Return on investment (ROI)	Principle of preventive control
Advantages and limitations of ROI	Advantages of preventive control
control	Essentials for developing effective managers

FOR DISCUSSION

1. Why do most controls of overall performance tend to be financial? Should they be? What else would you suggest?

2. "Profit and loss control is defective in that it does not emphasize return on investment; the latter is defective in that it places too great an emphasis on present results, possibly endangering future results." Discuss.

3. In applying the rate of return on investment as a control tool, would you favor using an undepreciated or a depreciated asset base?

4. If preventive control were completely effective, would a company need any direct controls?

5. Select any major area of management theory and principles, and discuss how it can be applied to reality.

6. In reference to specific management problem areas, such as new product development, organization structure, or budgets, what are the ways that managers can introduce flexibility, and what are the inflexibilities usually encountered in each?

7. How do you anticipate that the computer will affect the manager's role at the top-management level? The middle-management level? First-level supervision?

8. What can be done about the problem of top-level executive malnutrition?

EXERCISES/ACTION STEPS

1. Interview two managers in business firms and ask them about the kinds of controls used to measure overall performance. What are the similarities and differences of the responses of the two managers?

2. Choose any federal, state, or local government agency you wish, and check whether or not it has some kind of overall control. If not, could you develop a system or program for evaluating overall performance?

CASE:
BANKAMERICA CORPORATION[10]

BankAmerica, once the largest bank in the United States, ranked 299th among the 300 most admired companies identified by *Fortune* magazine.[11] In this group BankAmerica was among the least admired companies in terms of quality of management, innovativeness, and other characteristics.

In the early 1980s, the bank was one of the most profitable banks in the nation. At that time, it had over 87,000 employees and more than 2000 offices in about 100 countries. But over a period of 5 years, loans worth more than $4 billion were written off, many of them to home builders, shipping firms, farmers, and foreign customers. In 1986 Samuel Armacost stated that the situation was under control,[12] yet the stock price dropped sharply in that year. The headquarters building in San Francisco was sold, followed by the sale of Charles Schwab & Co., BankAmerica's brokerage subsidiary, in 1987.

The bank had expanded its mortgage business in 1979 and 1980 with the expectation that the interest rates would fall. Instead, they skyrocketed in the early 1980s. Being stuck with low mortgages, but paying high interest rates on deposits, put a great burden on the institution. Deregulation resulted in an easing of interest-rate ceilings and created a dynamic environment for which most financial institutions were not prepared. Savings and loan associations became more like banks in their operations. Increased competition resulted in lower margins, which, in turn, led some inefficient organizations to fail or to be acquired by others.

Competition came not only from other banks but also from many other institutions. General Motors, for example, became one of the top consumer lenders. Other firms were Sears, Ford Motor Company, National Steel, General Electric, and American Express, just to mention a few.

BankAmerica, like many other banks, also made loans to less developed countries. One of the reasons was to spread the risks for savers and investors. But some of the loans were not collectible.

In 1986 Armacost was replaced by A. W. Clausen, who was also his predecessor.

1. Did BankAmerica get out of control? If your answer is "yes," how did it happen?

2. What safeguards would you recommend so that it does not happen again? What, for example, would you recommend so that loan officers do not make risky loans?

REFERENCES

1. For a discussion of different kinds of measurement, see Joseph W. Wilkinson, "The Meanings of Measurement," in Max D. Richards (ed.), *Readings in Management*, 7th ed. (Cincinnati: South-Western Publishing Company, 1986), pp. 318–324.

2. Robert N. Anthony, "Games Government Accountants Play," *Harvard Business Review* (September–October 1985), pp. 161–170.

3. Michael J. Sandretto, "What Kind of Cost System Do You Need?" *Harvard Business Review* (January–February 1986), pp. 110–118.

4. Frances Gaither Tucker and Seymour M. Zivan, "A Xerox Cost Center Imitates a Profit Center," *Harvard Business Review* (May–June 1985), pp. 168–174.

5. Leslie Helm, "Why Kodak Is Starting to Click Again," *Business Week* (Feb. 23, 1987), pp. 134–138; Leslie Helm and Barbara Buell, "Kodak Fights Fuji with 'Me-Too' Tactics," *Business Week* (Feb. 23, 1987),

p. 138; Alex Taylor III, "Kodak Scrambles to Refocus," *Fortune* (Mar. 3, 1986), pp. 34–39.

6. Deborah C. Wise, "Can John Sculley Clean Up the Mess at Apple?" *Business Week* (July 29, 1985), pp. 70–71; Deborah C. Wise, "Apple, Part 2: The No-Nonsense Era of John Sculley," *Business Week* (Jan. 27, 1986), pp. 96–98; Katherine M. Hafner and Geoff Lewis, "Apple's Comeback," *Business Week* (Jan. 19, 1987), pp. 84–89; Brian O'Reilly, "Apple Finally Invades the Office," *Fortune* (Nov. 9, 1987), pp. 52–64; Brenton R. Schlender, "Shedding His Shyness, John Sculley Promotes Apple — and Himself," *The Wall Street Journal* (Aug. 18, 1988).

7. See also Geert Hofstede, "The Poverty of Management Control Philosophy," in Richards (ed.), *Readings in Management* (1986), pp. 302–315.

8. See also Derek F. du Toit, "Confessions of a So-So Controller," *Harvard Business Review* (July–August 1985), pp. 50–56.

9. On the other hand, the contributions of managers in their forties and fifties are often underestimated. They are often the ones who keep the organization going and should be involved in important decisions. See Jay W. Lorsch and Haruo Takagi, "Keeping Managers Off the Shelf," *Harvard Business Review* (July–August 1986), pp. 60–65.

10. The case is based on a variety of sources, including Harvey Rosenblum and Diane Siegel, *Competition in Financial Services: The Impact of Nonbank Entry*, Federal Reserve Bank of Chicago, Staff Study #83–1, p. 17; Teresa Carson, "Who Needs BankAmerica? Not Joe Pinola," *Business Week* (Feb. 23, 1987), p. 46; Jonathan B. Levine, "1985 Won't Be Any Better for BofA," *Business Week* (June 24, 1985), p. 46; "Banks Give Farmers Loans and Pray for Bailout," *The Wall Street Journal* (June 6, 1985); Harlan S. Byrne and Jonathan R. Laing, "Asset or Liability? Tom Clausen Returns to B of A," *Barrans* (October 1986); Nina Easton, "Some Branch Tightening Ahead of Bank of America," *American Banker* (Feb. 23, 1987).

11. Edward C. Baig, "America's Most Admired Corporations," *Fortune* (Jan. 19, 1987), pp. 18–31.

12. Gary Hector, "The Most Beleaguered Banker," *Fortune* (Jan. 5, 1987), p. 86.

SUMMARY OF MAJOR PRINCIPLES, OR GUIDES, OF CONTROLLING

From the discussions in the previous chapters on management control, there have emerged certain essentials, or basic truths. These, which are referred to as "principles," are designed to highlight aspects of control that are regarded as especially important. In view of the fact that control, even though representing a system itself, is a subsystem of the larger area of management, certain of these principles are understandably similar to those identified in discussions of the other managerial functions. Principles of control can be grouped into three categories, reflecting their purpose and nature, structure, and process.

The Purpose and Nature of Control

The purpose and nature of control may be summarized by the principles listed below.

Principle of the purpose of control   The task of control is to ensure that plans succeed by detecting deviations from plans and furnishing a basis for taking action to correct potential or actual undesired deviations.

Principle of future-directed controls   Because of time lags in the total system of control, the more a control system is based on feedforward rather than simple feedback of information, the more managers have the opportunity to perceive undesirable deviations from plans before they occur and to take action in time to prevent them.

These two principles emphasize that the purpose of control in any system of managerial action is ensuring that objectives are achieved through detecting deviations and taking corrective action designed to attain them. Moreover, control, like planning, should ideally be forward-looking. This principle is often disregarded in practice, largely because the present state of the art in managing has not regularly provided for systems of feedforward control. Managers have generally been dependent on historical data, which may be adequate for collecting taxes and determining stockholders' earnings but are not good enough for the most effective control. If means of looking forward are lacking, reference to history, on the questionable assumption that "what is past is prologue," is better than not looking at all. But time lags in the system of management control make it imperative that greater efforts be undertaken to make future-directed control a reality.

Principle of control responsibility   The primary responsibility for the exercise of control rests in the manager charged with the performance of the particular plans involved.

Since delegation of authority, assignment of tasks, and responsibility for certain objectives rest in individual managers, it follows that control over this work should be exercised by each of these managers. An individual manager's responsibility cannot be waived or rescinded without changes in the organization structure.

Principle of efficiency of controls   Control techniques and approaches are efficient if they detect and illuminate the nature and causes of deviations from plans with a minimum of costs or other unsought consequences.

Control techniques have a way of becoming costly, complex, and burdensome. Managers may become so engrossed in control that they spend more than it is worth to detect a deviation. Detailed budget controls that hamstring a subordinate, complex mathematical controls that thwart innovation, and purchasing controls that delay deliveries and cost more than the item purchased are instances of inefficient controls.

Principle of preventive control   The higher the quality of managers in a managerial system, the less will be the need for direct controls.

Most controls are based in large part on the fact that human beings make mistakes and often do not react to problems by undertaking their correction adequately and promptly. The more qualified managers are, the more they will perceive deviations from plans and take timely action to prevent them.

The Structure of Control

The principles that follow are aimed at pointing out how control systems and techniques can be designed to improve the quality of managerial control.

Principle of reflection of plans   The more that plans are clear, complete, and integrated, and the more that controls are designed to reflect such plans, the more effectively controls will serve the needs of managers.

It is not possible for a system of controls to be devised without plans, since the task of control is to ensure that plans work out as intended. There can be no doubt that the more clear, complete, and integrated these plans are, and the more that control techniques are designed to follow the progress of these plans, the more effective they will be.

Principle of organizational suitability   The more that an organizational structure is clear, complete, and integrated, and the more that controls are designed to reflect the place in the organization structure where responsibility for action lies, the more they will facilitate correction of deviations from plans.

Plans are implemented by people. Deviations from plans must be the responsibility primarily of managers who are entrusted with the task of executing planning programs. Since it is the function of an organization structure to define a system of roles, it follows that controls must be designed to affect the role in which responsibility for performance of a plan lies.

Principle of individuality of controls The more that control techniques and information are understandable to individual managers who must utilize them, the more they will actually be used and the more they will result in effective control.

Although some control techniques and information can be utilized in the same form by various kinds of enterprises and managers, as a general rule controls should be tailored to meet the individual needs of managers. Some of this individuality is related to position in the organization structure, as noted in the previous principle. Another aspect of individuality is the tailoring of controls to the kind and level of managers' understanding. Company presidents as well as supervisors have thrown up their hands in dismay (often for quite different reasons) at the unintelligible nature and inappropriate form of control information. Control information which a manager cannot or will not use has little practical value.

The Process of Control

Control, often being so much a matter of technique, rests heavily on the art of managing, on know-how in given instances. However, there are certain principles which experience has shown have wide applicability.

Principle of standards Effective control requires objective, accurate, and suitable standards.

There should be a simple, specific, and verifiable way to measure whether a planning program is being accomplished. Control is accomplished through people. Even the best manager cannot help being influenced by personal factors, and actual performance is sometimes camouflaged by a dull or a sparkling personality or by a subordinate's ability to "sell" a deficient performance. By the same token, good standards of performance, objectively applied, will more likely be accepted by subordinates as fair and reasonable.

Principle of critical-point control Effective control requires special attention to those factors critical to evaluating performance against plans.

It would ordinarily be wasteful and unnecessary for managers to follow every detail of plan execution. What they must know is that plans are being implemented. Therefore, they concentrate attention on salient factors of performance that will indicate, without watching everything, any important deviations from plans. Perhaps all managers can ask themselves what things in their operations will best show them whether the plans for which they are responsible are being accomplished.

The exception principle   The more that managers concentrate control efforts on significant exceptions, the more efficient will be the results of their control.

This principle holds that managers should concern themselves with significant deviations — the especially good or the especially bad situations. It is often confused with the principle of critical-point control, and the two do have some kinship. However, critical-point control has to do with recognizing the points to be watched, while the exception principle has to do with watching the size of deviations at these points.

Principle of flexibility of controls   If controls are to remain effective despite failure or unforeseen changes of plans, flexibility is required in their design.

According to this principle, controls must not be so inflexibly tied in with a plan as to be useless if the entire plan fails or is suddenly changed. Note that this principle applies to failures of plans, not failures of people operating under plans.

Principle of action   Control is justified only if indicated or experienced deviations from plans are corrected through appropriate planning, organizing, staffing, and leading.

There are instances in practice in which this simple truth is forgotten. Control is a wasteful use of managerial and staff time unless it is followed by action. If deviations are found in experienced or projected performance, action is indicated, in the form of either redrawing plans or making additional plans to get back on course. The situation may call for reorganization. It may require replacing subordinates or training them to do the task desired. Or it may indicate that the fault is a lack of direction and leadership in getting a subordinate to understand the plans or in motivating him or her to accomplish them. In any case, action is implied.

International Management and the Future

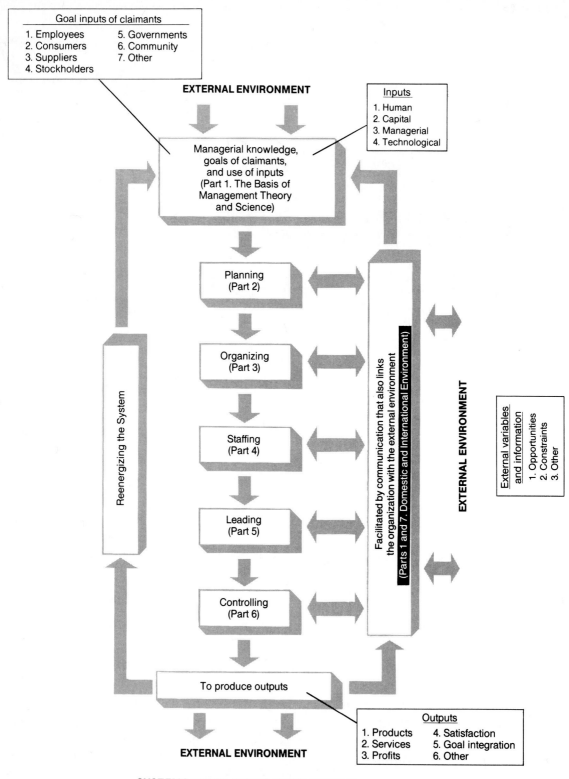

Goal inputs of claimants
1. Employees   5. Governments
2. Consumers   6. Community
3. Suppliers   7. Other
4. Stockholders

EXTERNAL ENVIRONMENT

Inputs
1. Human
2. Capital
3. Managerial
4. Technological

Managerial knowledge,
goals of claimants,
and use of inputs
(Part 1. The Basis of
Management Theory
and Science)

Planning
(Part 2)

Organizing
(Part 3)

Staffing
(Part 4)

Leading
(Part 5)

Controlling
(Part 6)

Reenergizing the System

Facilitated by communication that also links
the organization with the external environment
(Parts 1 and 7. Domestic and International Environment)

EXTERNAL ENVIRONMENT

External variables
and information
1. Opportunities
2. Constraints
3. Other

To produce outputs

Outputs
1. Products   4. Satisfaction
2. Services   5. Goal integration
3. Profits   6. Other

EXTERNAL ENVIRONMENT

SYSTEMS APPROACH TO MANAGEMENT

CHAPTER 22

International Management: Toward a Unified, Global Management Theory

CHAPTER OBJECTIVES

After reading this chapter, you should understand:

1. The differences in managing in selected countries
2. Managerial practices in Japan and the United States and the application of Theory Z
3. The nature and purpose of international business and multinational corporations (MNCs)
4. How managerial functions are carried out in the international environment
5. The trend toward a unified global theory of management

Chapter 2 focused on the external factors in the domestic environment. The constraining factors on managing are likely to be more severe for international firms. Executives operating in a foreign country need to learn a great deal about the country's educational, economic, legal, and political systems and especially its sociocultural environment.

This chapter examines more closely the environmental impact on managing in selected countries, and then it compares and contrasts more extensively Japanese and American managerial practices, including Theory Z. Then the discussion shifts to international management and the role of multinational corporations. The chapter ends with an optimistic view, pointing out the tendency toward a unified global theory of management.

INTERNATIONAL MANAGEMENT IN SELECTED COUNTRIES

It is interesting to know some of the differences in managerial practices in selected countries. This discussion, however, is illustrative rather than comprehensive, and it is based on generalizations. There are, for example, great differences among U.S. managers; the same holds true for managers in other countries. Furthermore, a society is not static, and changes do occur over time. For instance, the traditional authoritarian style of German managers is slowly giving way to a more participative approach.

France: Le Plan

In France, government planning on a national scale (legal-political environment factor) helps coordinate plans of individual industries and companies (managerial function of planning). The government's aim is to utilize most effectively the country's resources and to avoid expansion in uneconomic areas. Although governmental planning — which is also extended to regional areas — is carried out by relatively few, but competent, people, cooperation and assistance are provided by other governmental departments, employers' organizations, unions, and consumers.

The plan, which is generally revised every 5 years, attempts to obtain economic growth, price stability, a balance in foreign payments, and a favorable employment situation. Managers, then, are not only constrained by "Le Plan" but also aided by it, since it produces a great deal of information upon which they can draw for preparing plans for their own enterprises.

At times, the plan becomes a global strategy helping specific industries.[1] For example, the French government attempts to integrate the electronics industry into a whole so that it can overcome its weaknesses in information processing, consumer electronics, microelectronics, and automation. To implement the strategy, the government plans to support several national projects, such as speech synthesis, mini- and microcomputers, and large mainframe computers. Clearly, there is a close relationship between government planning and firms, especially those that are owned and directly aided by the government.

Germany: Authority and Codetermination

In the past, and to a lesser extent today, the German cultural environment favored reliance on authority in directing the work force, although it was often benevolent authoritarianism (managerial function of leading). Even today, while managers may show concern for subordinates, they also expect obedience.

It is almost a paradox that, on the one hand, the managerial style is characterized by considerable use of authority, while, on the other hand, labor, by law, is represented by and actively involved in managing large corporations (legal-political environment). In 1951 a law was passed that provided for **codetermination,** which requires labor membership in the supervisory board and the executive committee of certain large corporations. Furthermore, a labor director is elected as a member of the executive committee.[2] This position is a difficult one. Labor directors supposedly must represent the interests of the employees and, at the same time, must make managerial decisions that are in the best interest of the enterprise.

Selected Factors Influencing Managing in Other Countries[3]

Managing in *Australia* is influenced by that country's moralistic stance and its emphasis on political and social value, achievement, and risk taking.

INTERNATIONAL PERSPECTIVE:
IS MANAGEMENT CATCHING ON IN THE SOVIET UNION?

The importance of managing is even recognized by Soviet leader Mikhail Gorbachev, who is relying on the new managerial elite to modernize industry.

In the past, important decisions were largely made by central planners. However, the need for decentralization has become evident. Interviewed by *Fortune* magazine, a Soviet manager indicated that his own expectations are stated in profit and revenues but the decisions of resource allocation and salary increases for his employees are left to him.[4] The managerial power even extends to the decision of firing an employee. But this authority may be more theoretical than real, because the state guarantees employment. Thus, the dismissal may amount to a transfer of the employee to another organization. While, in the past, much of the decision authority was vested in governmental officials, the new authority relationships may cause a great deal of uncertainty among the managers themselves.

In one tractor factory, teams of about ten people worked together to earn a bonus if they exceeded the quota. Problems arose, however, when output quantities were achieved at the expense of quality. Indeed, Mikhail Gorbachev's new approach to economics and managing created a great deal of conflict. While the newly educated executives push for change and the use of economic incentives to improve productivity, old-style managers see the introduction of bonuses as an infusion of capitalistic ideas.[5]

While raising the status of the managerial elite is a new phenomenon in Russia, management education lags far behind that in most Western nations. There are only two new management schools in the Soviet Union.

Italian managers are operating in an environment of low tolerance for risks. Italians are very competitive, but at the same time they like group decision making.

Management in *Austria* (and *Germany*) is characterized by self-realization and leadership. Independence and competitiveness are valued. The tolerance for risk taking is rather low.

In *Britain*, security is important and so are resourcefulness, adaptability, and logic. Similarly, individualism is also highly valued.

Preparing Foreign Managers for Work in the United States

With the increasing investment of foreign firms in the United States, more attention must be given to the integration of managers and workers from other countries into American society.[6] This need is highlighted by the fact that the number of intercompany transferees has more than tripled from the late 1970s to the mid-1980s. The Japanese, for example, often find it difficult to be outspoken and direct in interactions with their colleagues and especially with their superiors. People from Arabian countries usually find American teaching methods too impersonal.

Various approaches have been used to reduce culture shock. These include special programs about corporate life in the United States, as well as instruction in English, books, and movies; even tax advice is given to the newcomers. Some companies have found the buddy system useful for making the foreigner feel comfortable in the new environment. In this approach an American looks after the needs of the newcomer. Other firms use role playing to demonstrate alternative ways of managerial behavior. Because of their cultural background, Japanese managers usually find it rather difficult to conduct an American-style performance review that focuses on results.

In the past, training and development focused on preparing U.S. managers and workers for overseas assignments. Increasingly, firms are realizing that they need to help foreigners reduce the culture shock they may experience upon coming to America.

JAPANESE MANAGEMENT AND THEORY Z

Japan, one of the leading industrial nations in the world, has adopted managerial practices that are quite different from those of other economically advanced countries in the Western world. The discussion below deals first with two common Japanese practices: lifetime employment and consensus decision making. Then it will compare and contrast Japanese and U.S. managerial practices, including Theory Z.

Lifetime Employment

Important features of Japanese management practice are lifelong employment (related to the staffing function), great concern for the individual employee, and emphasis on seniority. Typically, employees spend their working life with a single enterprise, which in turn provides employees with security and a feeling of belonging. This practice brings the culturally induced concept of *wa* (harmony) to the enterprise, resulting in employee loyalty and close identification with the aims of the company.

However, it also adds to business costs, because employees are kept on the payroll even though there may be insufficient work. Consequently, firms are beginning to question the practice of lifelong employment. Indeed, changes appear to be in the making,[7] but they are slow — very slow. What is often overlooked, however, is that this permanent employment practice, known as *nenko*, is used only by large firms. In fact, it is estimated that the job security system applies to only about one-third of the labor force.[8]

Closely related to lifelong employment is the seniority system, which has provided privileges for older employees who have been with the enterprise a long time. But there are indications that the seniority system may be superseded by a more open approach that provides opportunities for advancement for young people. For example, the relatively new Sony Corporation has team leaders (a point is made of not calling them supervisors) who are often young women 18 or 19 years of age. There is practically no age difference between these leaders and the operators they lead.

Decision Making

The managerial practice of decision making in Japan is also considerably different from that in the United States. It is built on the concept that change and new ideas should come primarily from below. Thus, lower-level employees prepare proposals for higher-level personnel. Supervisors, rather than simply accepting or rejecting suggestions, tactfully question proposals, make suggestions, and encourage subordinates. If necessary, proposals are sent back to the initiator for more information.

Japanese management, then, uses decision making by consensus; lower-level employees initiate the idea and submit it to the next higher level, until it reaches the desk of the top executive. If the proposal is approved, it is returned to the initiator for implementation. Although the decision-making process is time-consuming, the implementation of the decision — because of the general consensus at various levels of management — is swift and does not require additional "selling."

An important characteristic of Japanese decision making is the large amount of effort that goes into defining the question or problem; there is a great deal of communication *before* a decision is actually made. American managers are often accused of making decisions before defining the problem. In contrast, Japanese management makes a decision only after long discussions of the issue.

In summary, Japanese managerial practice still emphasizes (although changes are occurring) lifetime employment, concern for the individual, seniority, and a sense of loyalty to the firm. Furthermore, in decision making there is open communication among people at different levels of the organizational hierarchy, a great deal of collaboration, and a recognition of mutual dependence.

Japanese versus U.S. Management Practices and Theory Z

Of great concern is the declining growth rate in productivity in the United States. Thus, Americans increasingly examine Japanese management — rightly or wrongly — to find answers to this productivity crisis. The preceding discussion focused on two characteristics of Japanese management: lifetime employment and consensus decision making. But there are other characteristics that distinguish Japanese from American management practices; these are summarized in Table 22-1.[9] A word of caution must be added regarding interpretation of this table: It is obvious that not all American firms are managed the same way; this is also true of Japanese firms. In addition, few empirical studies exist on the subject, and most of the available literature is descriptive. Therefore, the contrasting managerial approaches in the table are suggestive and need to be substantiated by additional research.

In **Theory Z,** selected Japanese managerial practices are adapted to the environment of the United States. It is practiced by companies such as IBM, Hewlett Packard, and the diversified retail company Dayton-Hudson.[10] One of the characteristics of Type Z organization is an emphasis on the interpersonal skills that are needed for group interaction. Yet, despite the emphasis on group decision making, responsibility remains with the individual (which is quite different from the Japanese practice, which emphasizes collective responsibility). There is also an emphasis on informal and democratic relationships based on trust. Yet the hierarchical structure still remains intact, as illustrated by IBM, in which not only goals but also authority, rules, and discipline guide corporate behavior.[11]

Participative management facilitates the free flow of information needed to reach consensus. Formal planning and objectives are important, but numerical measures are not overly emphasized. Instead, a corporate philosophy and corporate values guide managerial actions. People are seen as whole human beings, not simply as factors in production. However, the Japanese practice of very infrequent performance evaluations and promotions is not emphasized by Theory Z–type companies. In short, these companies selectively use some Japanese managerial practices but make adjustments for the environment prevailing in the United States.

Japanese Companies Operating in the United States

In an attempt to demonstrate the effectiveness of Japanese managerial approaches, success stories of Japanese companies operating in the United States are often cited. Workers at Sony's television plant in San Diego are said to produce as well as workers in Japan. The Bridgestone Tire Company (see the Perspective) is another positive example. But other cases are not quite as convincing. YKK, Inc., a manufacturer of zippers, has experienced labor-

Table 22-1   Japanese and U.S. Management Approaches

Japanese management	U.S. management
Planning	
1. Long-term orientation	1. Primarily short-term orientation
2. Collective decision making (*ringi*) with consensus	2. Individual decision making
3. Involvement of many people in preparing and making the decision	3. Involvement of a few people in making and "selling" the decision to persons with divergent values
4. Decision flow from bottom to top and back	4. Decisions initiated at the top, flowing down
5. Slow decision making; fast implementation of the decision	5. Fast decision making; slow implementation requiring compromise, often resulting in suboptimal decisions
Organizing	
1. Collective responsibility and accountability	1. Individual responsibility and accountability
2. Ambiguity of decision responsibility	2. Clear and specific decision responsibility
3. Informal organization structure	3. Formal, bureaucratic organization structure
4. Well-known common organization culture and philosophy; competitive spirit toward other enterprises	4. Lack of common organization culture; identification with profession rather than with company
Staffing	
1. Young people hired out of school; hardly any mobility of people among companies	1. People hired out of schools and from other companies; frequent company changes
2. Slow promotion through the ranks	2. Rapid advancement desired and demanded
3. Loyalty to the company	3. Loyalty to the profession
4. Very infrequent performance evaluation for new (young) employees	4. Frequent performance evaluation for new employees
5. Appraisal of long-term performance	5. Appraisal of short-term results
6. Promotions based on multiple criteria	6. Promotions based primarily on individual performance
7. Training and development considered a long-term investment	7. Training and development undertaken with hesitation (for fear of turnover)
8. Lifetime employment common in large companies	8. Job insecurity prevailing
Leading	
1. Leader acting as a social facilitator and group member	1. Leader acting as decision maker and head of the group
2. Paternalistic style	2. Directive style (strong, firm, determined)
3. Common values facilitating cooperation	3. Often divergent values; individualism sometimes hindering cooperation
4. Avoidance of confrontation, sometimes leading to ambiguities; emphasis on harmony	4. Face-to-face confrontation common; emphasis on clarity
5. Bottom-up communication	5. Communication primarily top-down
Controlling	
1. Control by peers	1. Control by superior
2. Control focus on group performance	2. Control focus on individual performance
3. Saving face	3. Fixing blame
4. Extensive use of quality control circles	4. Limited use of quality control circles

INTERNATIONAL PERSPECTIVE:
BRIDGESTONE TIRE COMPANY

The Bridgestone Corporation, a Japanese tire firm that took over the Firestone Tire & Rubber Company plant in Tennessee, was able not only to smooth the stormy labor relations that had plagued the company for years but also to improve both productivity and quality.[12] Some of the methods used to achieve these results were indeed rather traditional. They included investing in new equipment, setting high quality standards, and using a disciplined managerial approach that required employees to work harder and to give up some seniority provisions, thus allowing the company to fill key positions with the most suitable employees. Moreover, employees were also asked to participate in decisions that affected them and their jobs. For example, workers, not just inspectors, now have responsibility for the quality of the products. And this was done with the cooperation of the union. Bridgestone also used a management-by-objectives approach which is built on the concept of self-control and self-direction.

management confrontations similar to those experienced by U.S. companies. The trend of Japanese firms investing in manufacturing facilities in the United States is probably going to continue. In 1983, 31 Japanese firms were established here, bringing the total of Japanese-owned companies to 309 in 1984; they employed 73,000 workers.[13] These firms often demand less costly labor contracts. Although Japanese firms generally resist unions, 23 percent of the 163 companies responding to a 1982 survey were unionized.

INTERNATIONAL MANAGEMENT AND MULTINATIONAL CORPORATIONS

The study of **international management** focuses on the operation of international firms in host countries. It is concerned with managerial issues related to the flow of people, goods, and money, with the ultimate aim being to manage better in situations that involve crossing national boundaries.

The environmental factors that affect domestic firms usually are more critical for international corporations operating in foreign countries. As illustrated in Table 22-2, managers involved in international business are faced with many factors that are different from those of the domestically oriented firm. Managers have to interact with employees who have different educational and cultural backgrounds and value systems; they also must cope with different legal, political, and economic factors. Thus, these environments understandably influence the way managerial and enterprise functions are carried out.

The Nature and Purpose of International Business

Although business has been conducted on an international scale for many years, international business has gained greater visibility and importance in recent years because of the growth of large multinational corporations. **Inter-**

Table 22-2 **Domestic and International Enterprises: Characteristics and Practices**

The environment	Domestic enterprise (industrialized country)	International enterprise
Educational environment:		
1. Language (spoken, written, official)	One	Multiple
2. Education system (quality, level, extent)	No or little constraint	Great constraint
Sociocultural environment:		
1. Values, attitudes (toward achievement, risk taking, scientific method, work)	Homogeneous	Heterogeneous
2. Social organization (authority, status, roles, institutions, mobility, social systems)	Similar	Different
Political-legal environment:		
1. Political orientation (power, ideologies)	Country-centered	Transnational
2. Legal environment (laws, codes, regulations)	Fairly uniform	Different
3. National sovereignties	One	Many
4. Government policies, regulations	Same	Different
Economic environment:		
1. Economic development (underdeveloped, industrialized)	At similar stages	At different stages
2. Economic system (capitalistic, mixed, Marxist)	Similar	Different

national businesses engage in transactions across national boundaries. These transactions include the transfer of goods, services, technology, managerial knowledge, and capital to other countries.

The interaction of a firm with the host country can take many forms, as illustrated in Figure 22-1. One is the *exportation* of goods and services. Another is a *licensing agreement* for producing goods in another country. The parent company may also engage in *management contracts* that provide for operating foreign companies. Still another form of interaction is the *joint venture* with a firm in the host country. Finally, multinationals may set up wholly owned *subsidiaries* or *branches* with production facilities in the host country. Thus, in developing a global strategy, an international firm has many options.[14]

The contact between the parent firm and the host country is affected by several factors; some are unifying, others can cause conflicts.

Unifying effects Unifying influences occur when the parent company provides and shares technical and managerial know-how, thus assisting the host company in the development of human and material resources. Moreover, the parent corporation and the firm in the host country may find it advantageous to be integrated into a global organization structure. Whatever the interaction, policies must provide for equity and result in benefits for both the parent firm and the host company. Only then can one expect a long-lasting relationship.

Potentials for conflict Many factors can cause conflicts between the parent firm and the host country. Nationalistic self-interest may overshadow the

Figure 22-1

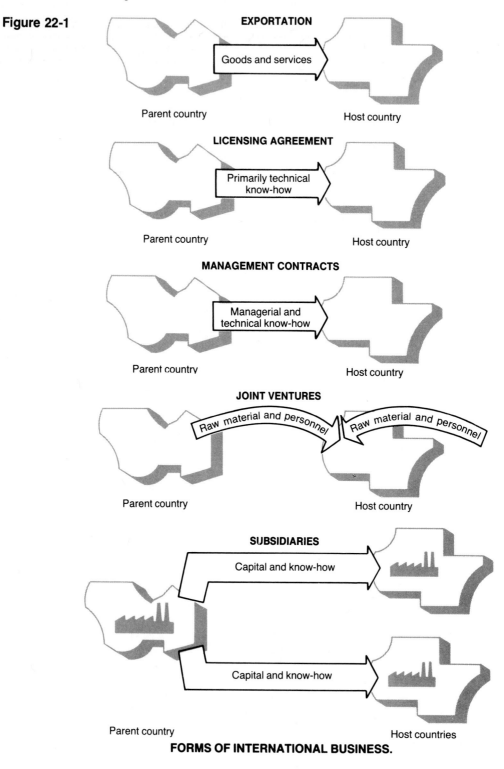

EXPORTATION

Goods and services

Parent country   Host country

LICENSING AGREEMENT

Primarily technical
know-how

Parent country   Host country

MANAGEMENT CONTRACTS

Managerial and
technical know-how

Parent country   Host country

JOINT VENTURES

Raw material and personnel   Raw material and personnel

Parent country   Host country

SUBSIDIARIES

Capital and know-how

Capital and know-how

Parent country   Host countries

FORMS OF INTERNATIONAL BUSINESS.

benefits obtained through cooperation. Similarly, sociocultural differences can lead to breakdowns in communication and subsequent misunderstandings. Also, a large multinational firm may have such overpowering economic effects on a small country that the host country feels overwhelmed. Some international corporations have been charged with making excessive profits, hiring the best local people away from local firms, and operating contrary to social customs. The international corporation must develop social and diplomatic skills in its managers in order to prevent such conflicts and to resolve those that unavoidably occur.

Multinational Corporations

Multinational corporations (MNCs) have their headquarters in one country but their operations in many countries. Of the ten largest multinational industrial corporations, ranked by 1985 sales, eight are American.[15] The ten are (1) General Motors, (2) Exxon, (3) Royal Dutch/Shell Group (Dutch-English), (4) Mobil, (5) British Petroleum (English), (6) Ford Motor Company, (7) International Business Machines, (8) Texaco, (9) Chevron, and (10) American Telephone and Telegraph.

From ethnocentric to geocentric orientation   In its early stages, international business was conducted with an **ethnocentric** outlook; that is, the orientation and type of operation was based on that of the parent company.[16] The **polycentric** attitude, on the other hand, is based on the notion that it is best to give foreign subsidiaries, staffed by local nationals, a great deal of managerial freedom. It is assumed that nationals have the best understanding of the local environment. **Regiocentric** orientation favors the staffing of foreign operations on a regional basis. Thus, a European view may be composed of British, French, German, and Italian influences. The modern multinational corporation has a **geocentric** orientation. This means that the total organization is viewed as an interdependent system operating in many countries. The relationships between headquarters and subsidiaries are collaborative, with communication flowing in both directions. Furthermore, key positions are filled by managers of different nationalities. In short, the orientation of the multi-national corporation is truly international and goes beyond a narrow nationalistic viewpoint.

Advantages of multinationals   Multinational corporations have several advantages over firms that have a domestic orientation. Obviously, the MNC can take advantage of business opportunities in many different countries. It can also raise money for its operations throughout the world. Moreover, multinational firms benefit by being able to establish production facilities in countries where their products can be produced most effectively and efficiently. Companies with worldwide operations sometimes have access to natural resources and materials that may not be available to domestic firms. Finally,

INTERNATIONAL PERSPECTIVE:
WOMAN CEO MANAGES BY THE TEXTBOOK

Illustrative of the demand for managers with an international background is the case of Marisa Bellisario, one of the most sought-after executives in Europe in 1984.[17] She was the first woman to head a major industrial firm in Italy, the state-controlled ITALTEL Societa Italiana, the biggest Italian firm making telecommunications equipment. Her background, however, is international. After receiving her degree in economics and business administration from Turin University, she worked at Olivetti in the electronics division. When Olivetti sold its data processing unit to General Electric, she spent time in Miami working on GE's worldwide marketing strategy for computers. She left GE to head corporate planning at Olivetti. Later, as the CEO at ITALTEL, she turned the company around, showing a small profit. (The firm had experienced huge losses in the past.) Her managerial approach has been characterized as "straight out of the textbook," and companies such as GTE Corporation, IBM, AT&T, and other European and Japanese firms are interested in recruiting her.

the large MNCs can recruit management and other personnel from a worldwide labor pool.

Successful U.S. multinationals   Despite the increasing competition and the cost advantages of some foreign corporations, a number of U.S. companies have done very well in the international environment.

Fortune studied a number of large companies that earn more than 20 percent of their revenues from overseas operations.[18] The reasons for the success of these firms differ greatly. IBM's size makes it possible to dominate the market. Coca-Cola is very adept at opening up new markets rather rapidly. McDonald's, on the other hand, does not rush into the market but carefully assesses the potential for success. Hewlett Packard and Boeing bring foreign managers to the United States to expose them to their organizational culture.

The MNCs that were studied structure their organization very carefully to suit the needs of each individual country. In addition, these firms are flexible in their product design and marketing. It should also be noted that the operations abroad were largely managed by foreign nationals.

Challenges for the multinationals   The advantages of the multinational operation must be weighed against the challenges and risks associated with operating in foreign environments. One problem is the increasing nationalism in many countries. Years ago, developing countries lacked managerial, marketing, and technical skills. Consequently, they welcomed the multinationals. But the situation is changing, with people in developing countries acquiring those skills. In addition, countries have not only become aware of the value of their natural resources but also become more skilled in international negotiations. Finally, multinationals must maintain good relations with the host country, a task that may prove difficult because governments frequently change and corporations must deal with, and adapt to, these changes.

THE MANAGERIAL FUNCTIONS IN INTERNATIONAL BUSINESS

Evidence shows that management fundamentals may be applicable in different countries. However, the practice of carrying out the managerial functions of planning, organizing, staffing, leading, and controlling differs considerably in domestic and international enterprises, as shown in Table 22-3.

Planning in the Multinational Corporation

Planning requires setting objectives and then selecting strategies, policies, programs, and procedures for achieving them. A critically important activity for the MNC is the assessment of opportunities and threats in the external environment. This is a complex task even for a domestic enterprise, but it becomes much more intricate when many different, ever-changing world markets must be scanned.

External threats and opportunities must be matched with the internal strengths and weaknesses of the firm. For example, a poor educational system makes it difficult to find qualified personnel. Similarly, cultural orientation toward time will affect planning. Specifically, cultural attitudes that emphasize a short time perspective will not be conducive to long-range planning. Finally, political and economic instability in a country makes it difficult to forecast and will discourage long-term commitment of resources.

Even large multinational companies may find it difficult to compete in the world market. Therefore, they form **global strategic partnerships** (GSPs).[19] General Motors formed a joint venture with Toyota to produce cars at the Fre-

Table 22-3   Managing Domestic and International Enterprises

Managerial functions	Domestic enterprise (industrialized country)	International enterprise
Planning: Scanning the environment for threats and opportunities	National market	Worldwide market
Organizing: **1.** Organization structure **2.** View of authority	Structure for domestic operations Similar	Global structure Different
Staffing: **1.** Sources of managerial talent **2.** Manager orientation	National labor pool Often ethnocentric	Worldwide labor pool Geocentric
Leading: **1.** Leadership and motivation **2.** Communication lines	Influenced by similar culture Relatively short	Influenced by many different cultures Network with long distances
Controlling: Reporting system	Similar requirements	Many different requirements

mont plant in California.[20] American Telephone and Telegraph Company shares technology with Olivetti and Philips,[21] both large multinational corporations in Europe. Kodak works with a Japanese company to produce some of its cameras. Clearly, success of the GSPs will depend on balancing cooperation with competitiveness among the firms.

Organizing the Multinational Corporation

Organization structures are established to achieve corporate objectives. The company can select from a great variety of structures.[22] An enterprise may, for example, establish a vice-presidential position at corporate headquarters with responsibility for the international division. An alternative is to organize according to geographic areas. For example, managers may be put in charge of regions such as North America, Latin America, Europe, Africa, and the Far East. Still another way of grouping organizational activities is according to product lines. For instance, at corporate headquarters, managers may be put in charge of a product line which is marketed worldwide. The truly multinational firm may integrate domestic and international business into a global structure which gives similar importance to domestic and foreign business activities.

Each structure has advantages and limitations, as discussed in Chapter 8. It is important to realize that for the large multinational corporation any one structure may be insufficient. Consequently, different organizational designs may have to be mixed, depending on the environmental and task demands.

Staffing in the Multinational Corporation[23]

The positions identified in the organization structure must be filled by qualified persons. This involves staffing.

Sources for managerial talent   Managers of the MNC can be classified in three ways. First, managers may be nationals selected from the country in which the headquarters is located. These expatriates (with *home-country nationality*) are chosen to represent and manage the enterprise abroad. These managers, because of their experience, are usually familiar with the parent company's policies and operations.

Second, a firm may select managers who are *nationals of the host country.* These managers are familiar with the country's environment, its education system, its culture, its legal and political processes, and its economic environment. They usually also know local customers, suppliers, government officials, behavioral characteristics of employees, and the public in general.

The third source for managerial personnel consists of *third-country nationals.* These are managers who have a nationality that is different from the parent company or the host country. Such managers may have gained experience by working at the company headquarters as well as in different countries. Thus, they would have developed behavioral flexibility that eases their adaptation to different cultures. These managers may be truly transcultural.

Trends in staffing multinational corporations   Each of the three sources for managers has advantages and disadvantages, and a firm may use a variety of combinations. A few factors that influence the trend in staffing MNCs are worth noting. First, the cost of sending U.S. managers abroad has increased, partly due to the declining value of the U.S. dollar in the 1970s and in 1986. Second, people in the host countries are now better prepared to assume responsible managerial positions. While conducting management development programs in Singapore, Hong Kong, and Taipei, one of the authors found that the quality of middle managers measured up to that of their counterparts in the United States. Finally, employing nationals of the host country can improve relations with that country. Therefore, as far as American firms are concerned, the trend is toward employing more host-country nationals than managers from the parent company.

Leading in the Multinational Corporation

Leading involves motivating and communicating. It requires exerting leadership by inducing employees to contribute to enterprise objectives.

Motivating and leading demand an understanding of employees and their cultural environment. For instance, participative management may work well in one country but may cause confusion among employees in another country with a tradition of autocratic rule.

Communication is often a problem in multinational firms with subsidiaries and affiliates in countries where different languages are spoken. Even a firm with operations in a country where English is the primary language may encounter communication problems because of the distance between headquarters and the subsidiary. But new communications technology has greatly improved the transmission of information. Still, a telephone call is not quite the same as a visit and a person-to-person discussion.

Controlling in the Multinational Corporation

Controlling — the measurement and correction of performance to ensure that events conform to plans — is an essential managerial function that is influenced by several environmental factors unique to international enterprises. First, revenues, costs, and profits are measured in different currencies. Second, the ratios between currencies are subject to considerable fluctuations. Third, accounting practices and financial reporting often differ from country to country. For example, accounting procedures may have to satisfy the demands of tax authorities of the host country as well as the government of the parent firm. The procedures must also satisfy stockholders in various countries, agencies in charge of regulating securities, and banks. Procedures must also be suitable to meet the internal requirements of the firm. Developing a procedure that meets all these demands at the same time is extremely difficult. Finally, and partly due to the complex nature of measurement, there is a time lag in the measurement of performance which may delay detecting deviations from standards and initiating corrective action. Computers, however, have done much to speed up the process. In all, then, these few examples indicate that controlling the international corporation is considerably more difficult than monitoring a domestic operation.

TOWARD A UNIFIED, GLOBAL THEORY OF MANAGEMENT

Today, the framework of planning, organizing, staffing, leading, and controlling (with some slight variations at times) has become the most popular way of structuring managerial knowledge.[24] Management textbooks based on this framework are widely used around the world. Still, there are challenging tasks ahead for integrating the body of managerial knowledge into a unified theory.

Chapter 1 of this book dealt with the many schools of, or approaches to, management. There is evidence that the management theory jungle not only continues to flourish but gets more dense, with nearly twice as many schools or approaches as were found more than 20 years ago.

At the same time, there are signs that the various schools of thought are converging. Realizing that these are only signs along the road to a more unified and operational theory of management, and that there is more of this road to travel, let us briefly examine some of these tendencies toward convergence.

The Empirical Approach: Distilling Basics

In reviewing the many programs that use cases as a means of educating managers, one finds that there appears to be much greater emphasis on distilling fundamentals than there was two or three decades ago. Likewise, in the field of business policy, by which term these case approaches have tended to be known, there has been increased emphasis on teaching and research that goes beyond recounting what happened in a given situation to analyzing the underlying causes.[25] One major result of all this has been a new emphasis on strategic management. Furthermore, many textbooks on policy and strategy now have many international cases and considerable text material of distilled knowledge.[26]

Systems Thinking — Not a Separate Approach

Practicing managers as well as the operational theorists increasingly use the basics of systems theory in analyzing managerial jobs. On the macro level, managers, especially those in multinational corporations, are viewing their operations as a global interdependent system. Japanese managers, for example, are in charge of their manufacturing plants in the United States, and U.S. managers direct their firms in Europe and other countries.

Situational and Contingency Approaches — Not New or Separate

It is now clear that the concepts of situational, or contingency, management are merely a way of distinguishing between science and art, knowledge and practice. As pointed out at the beginning of this book, science and art are two diffferent but complementary things. Those writers and scholars who have emphasized situational, or contingency, approaches have done the field of management theory and practice a great service by stressing that what the intelligent manager actually does depends on the realities of the situation, whether it is in the United States or abroad.

The Confluence of Motivation and Leadership Theory

Another interesting sign of the move toward a unified operational theory of management is the way that research and analysis have tended to merge motivation and leadership theory.[27] As explained in Chapters 15 and 16, leadership research and theory have found that people tend to follow those who offer them a means of satisfying their own desires. Thus, explanations of leadership have been increasingly related to motivation.

Implied by most recent research and theory is the clear message that effective leaders design a system that takes into account the expectations of subordinates, the variability of motives between individuals, the factors specific to a situation, the need for clarity of role definition, interpersonal relations, and types of rewards.

The New, Managerially Oriented "Organization Development"

Both "organization development" and the field ordinarily referred to as "organization behavior" have grown out of the interpersonal and group behavior approaches to management. Many specialists in these areas are now beginning to see that basic management theory and techniques fit well into their programs of behavioral intervention.

Fortunately, a review of the latest organization behavior books indicates that many authors in this field are beginning to understand that the study of behavioral elements in group operations must be more closely integrated with the study of organization structure design, staffing, planning, and control. This is a hopeful sign. It is a recognition that analysis of individual and group behavior, at least in managed situations, easily and logically falls into place in the scheme of operational-management theory.

The Impact of Technology: Researching an Old Problem

That technology has an important impact on organizational structure, behavior patterns, and other aspects of managing has been recognized by practitioners for many years. Fortunately, academic researchers in recent years have directed their attention to the impact of technology on managerial effectiveness.

The Merger of Theory and Practice

For some time now, scholars and practitioners looked to the total job of managing. As pointed out in Chapter 1, the 7-S framework for management analysis proposed by McKinsey & Company, a respected management consulting firm, is indeed close to the operational, or management process, model.

PERSPECTIVE:
RECENT RESEARCH SUPPORTING THE OPERATIONAL APPROACH

Some recent research studies have focused on the total managerial job. An example of this research was presented by Fred Luthans in his presidential speech at the Academy of Management in August 1986.[28] His findings are, in general, congruent with the operational approach to managing as used in this book. In his 4-year study of over 300 managers at different levels and in various kinds of organizations, he found that "real" managers carry out the following activities: (1) routine communication (see Part 5 in this book), (2) traditional managerial activities such as planning, decision making, and controlling (Parts 2 and 6 in this book), (3) human resource management activities (Parts 4 and 5), and (4) networking, by which is meant socializing, politicking, and interacting with outsiders (some of these concepts relate to the discussion of informal organization, coordination, and power presented in Part 3). Luthans found a significant relationship between networking activities and managerial success (measured by a promotion index). The next level of analysis focused on managers' effectiveness (consisting of perceived work unit performance in terms of quantity and quality, as well as subordinate commitment and satisfaction). The findings showed the strongest relationships between effectiveness with routine communication, followed by human resource management, and traditional management. Although the research does not address all the key managerial activities (such as structuring the organization or the clarifying authority-responsibility relationships), it takes a comprehensive look at what successful and effective managers really do.

Clarification of Semantics: Some Hopeful Signs

One of the greatest obstacles to disentangling the jungle has been the problem of semantics. People writing and lecturing on management and related fields have tended to use the same terms in different ways (or to use different terms for the same concept). This is exemplified by the variety of meanings given to such terms as "organization," "line and staff," "authority," "responsibility," and "policies," to mention a few. While this semantics swamp still exists and the general acceptance of standardized meanings of key terms and concepts is still a long way off, there are some hopeful signs on the horizon.

It has become rather common now for leading management texts to include a glossary of key terms and concepts, and an increasing number of textbooks are beginning to use terms in a similar way. Furthermore, the Fellows of the International Academy of Management, a select group comprising management scholars and managerial leaders from over thirty countries, have responded to the demands of members and undertaken the development of a glossary of management concepts and terms in a number of languages. It is necessary to agree not only on the translation of terms (although some terms such as "operations research" or "management" are used without translations in different languages) but on the precise meaning, understandable to all.

The Internationalization of Management

The term "global village" may appropriately describe the world we live in today. Advances in technology in aerospace, communications, fiber optics, and computers link people from around the globe.

While Japan sends its young people to the United States to study management techniques (and Japanese managers are eager readers of U.S. best-sellers on management), managers in the United States often look to Japan for implementing some of these techniques and theories more effectively. Recently, Korean managers have come with their style — which in many ways is similar to that of the Japanese — to lead their subsidiaries in the United States.[29] Samsung, Lucky Goldstar, Daewoo, and Hyundai are just a few of the Korean companies establishing themselves (quite successfully) in the United States. One Japanese manager admits that the Koreans, lacking the homogeneous culture of the Japanese, may be more flexible in adapting to the U.S. environment.

The point here is not that one approach is better than another but, rather, that many countries can contribute to managerial theory and practice. A special commission presented a sobering report on industrial competitiveness to the President of the United States.[30] In an environment of global competition, only the best companies will succeed, and management, it can be suggested, will be an important factor for this success.

A perceptive observer will note that the role of managers is expanding. New approaches are required to avoid managerial obsolescence and improve managerial productivity. There is a need for more effective planning, flexible approaches to organizing, better managing of human resources, an environment favorable for motivation, and methods for effective and efficient control that use the new information technology. Above all, the field of management urgently requires intellectual and inspirational leadership in the United States and around the world to make organizations more productive for the benefit of humanity.

SUMMARY

Managerial practices differ in various countries. In France, for example, government planning greatly influences the planning and direction of enterprises. In Germany, the use of authority and the concept of codetermination shapes managerial practices. Organizations have to be concerned not only about preparing American managers for working abroad but also about preparing foreign managers for working in the United States.

Japanese managerial practices differ greatly from those in the United States. Theory Z, which involves selected Japanese managerial practices, has been adopted by some U.S. companies. International business extends its operations across national boundaries. The educational, sociocultural, political-legal, and economic environments have a particular impact on international enterprises. Multinational corporations have developed different orientations for operating in foreign countries, ranging from ethnocentric (the foreign operation is based on the parent company's views) to geocentric (the organization is viewed as an interdependent system operating in many countries, that is, it is truly international).

While management fundamentals may be applicable in different countries, the practice of carrying out the managerial functions differs in domestic and international enterprises. For example, in an international enterprise planning is done with a worldwide market in mind. The organization is characterized by a global structure. In staffing, personnel is drawn from a worldwide labor pool. In leading, the many cultural differences are taken into account. And in controlling, the different requirements (for example, for tax purposes) of the various countries must be taken into account.

Chapter 1 highlighted the various approaches to management, which result in a kind of jungle. The operational, or management process, approach, as used in this book, is an attempt to unify these different orientations. There are indeed signs that business is moving toward a unified, global theory of management.

KEY IDEAS AND CONCEPTS FOR REVIEW

Management practices in France
Management practices in Germany
Differences in the management approaches
  in Japan and the United States
Impact of environmental factors on domestic
  and international enterprises
Ethnocentric orientation

Polycentric orientation
Regiocentric orientation
Geocentric orientation
Managerial functions in domestic
  and international enterprises
Trends toward a unified management
  theory

FOR DISCUSSION

1. Do you think the managerial concepts and practices applied in the United States can be transferred to England, France, or West Germany?

2. What are some typical management practices in Japan, and how do they compare to those in the United States?

3. What are likely to be the differences between the operation of a domestic firm and that of a multinational corporation? Select five differences and discuss their importance.

4. What advantages do multinational corporations have? What challenges must they meet? Give examples.

5. What are some of the hopeful signs that indicate business is moving toward a unified, global theory of management?

EXERCISES/ACTION STEPS

1. Contact a foreign firm operating in the United States and interview one or more managers. How do the managerial practices in the U.S. operation differ from those in the firm's home country?

2. From your knowledge of any foreign country, outline the major elements of its culture that would, in your judgment, influence managerial practices in that country.

CASE:
HONDA MOVES TO THE UNITED STATES[31]

Honda has debunked the auto industry's claim that "nobody can make an economy car in the United States at a profit." Not only is Honda's plant in Marysville, Ohio, profitable, it is said, but its cars are as well built as those made in Japan.

Since Honda holds only a relatively small share of the Japanese car market, it needed an outlet to grow. In the early 1970s, when gas became scarce and expensive, Honda introduced its fuel-efficient cars in the United States. Strong demand and growing trade friction convinced Honda that it needed to repeat the strategy that worked for its motorcycles: build a U.S. operation. The first cars rolled out in 1983 — the year quotas became effective. In 1985, Honda outsold both Nissan and Toyota and became the fourth largest car manufacturer in the United States.

The Marysville plant is not demonstrably more automated than American factories, but it works differently. All employees are treated as equals. Workers are chosen for their team skills as well as their expertise. A quarter of the first employees spent up to 3 months in Honda's plant in Japan. When they returned, they taught their coworkers how to assemble cars in teams.

New workers spend several weeks practicing on training cars before they are assigned to a team. Team members trade jobs and learn as many tasks as they can. Team leaders check the workmanship and help the team in any way they can (solving problems, replacing an absent member, and so on).

Honda attributes its success to workers who are willing to work hard for the company. The "equal partnership" gives employees a stake in the company. Mr. Honda believes that all employees are equally important. Everyone, including the plant manager, wears coveralls and shares the facilities (same lunchroom, washrooms, parking). All employees can help make decisions. Initially, workers were surprised that their supervisors asked them for advice.

The workers are very proud of their work. They like working at Honda, even though they earn roughly 20 percent less than other U.S. auto workers. Honda's labor costs are about 60 percent lower than the industry average because it has a lower overhead per worker.

Honda expects suppliers to establish the same quality standards it uses. It was willing to help U.S. parts suppliers that did not meet them. Those who insisted that Honda could simply return defective parts were replaced by Japanese suppliers. Some of them have built plants near Marysville, which, in turn, has helped Honda minimize inventory.

Although most U.S. manufacturers barely break even on compacts, Honda earns a handsome profit on each car, and it sells every car it makes. And while this is only half the profit Honda earns on the cars it imports from Japan, it expects the difference to narrow as the workers in the U.S. plant learn to be more efficient.

Now that the company is well established in the U.S. car market, Honda plans to double its U.S. capacity and build luxury cars, which should be more profitable than the less expensive cars. Honda attempts to avoid problems from its low-cost image by selling its luxury cars under another name — Acura — through different dealerships. Far from importing the large, old-fashioned Japanese luxury cars, Honda is developing "European-style" models specifically for the U.S. market. European styling has two advantages: It appeals to the growing

number of young professionals, and the cars are small enough that they can be built on Honda's existing compact-car production lines.

1. Why did Honda build a plant in the United States (what were the objectives)? How is the plant in the United States affecting the company in Japan? What problems or advantages might the U.S. operation give Honda in the future?

2. Why was Honda able to build economy cars in the United States when American car manufacturers could not? What advantages does Honda have over the American companies?

3. How much of Honda's success is due to its policies? How much is due to nonmanagerial factors?

4. Apply the steps in planning to the case.

REFERENCES

1. "France — An Electronics Plan with Global Ambitions," *Business Week* (May 31, 1982), p. 39.

2. See Simcha Ronen, *Comparative and Multinational Management* (New York: John Wiley & Sons, 1986), chap. 9; David Heenan, *The Re-United States of America* (Reading, Mass.: Addison-Wesley Publishing Company, 1983), chap. 1.

3. See Ronen, *Comparative and Multinational Management* (1986). See also the extensive studies by Geert Hofstede, such as "The Cultural Relativity of Organizational Practices and Theories," *Journal of International Business Studies,* vol. 14, no. 2 (1983), pp. 75-90; "Motivation, Leadership and Organization: Do American Theories Apply Abroad?" *Organizational Dynamics,* no. 9 (1983), pp. 42-63; *Culture's Consequences: International Differences in Work Related Values* (Beverly Hills: Sage, 1980).

4. Thomas Moore, "Managers: Russia's New Elite," *Fortune* (Nov. 25, 1985); John Pearson, "How a Soviet Manager Can Start Thinking for Himself," *Business Week* (Nov. 11, 1985), p. 93. Another indication of Soviet interest in management is the effort of translating one of the previous editions of this book into the Russian language.

5. Peter Galuszka, "A Tractor Factory Tries to Pull Its Own Weight," *Business Week* (Dec. 7, 1987), p. 79.

6. "American Culture Is Often a Puzzle for Foreign Managers in the U.S.," *The Wall Street Journal* (Feb. 12, 1986).

7. Masayoshi Kanabayashi, "In Japan, Employees Are Switching Firms for Better Work, Pay," *The Wall Street Journal* (Oct. 11, 1988).

8. Tai K. Oh, "Japanese Management — A Critical Review," *Academy of Management Review* (January 1976), pp. 14-25.

9. The information for Table 22-1 is based on a variety of sources.

Miscellaneous aspects of managing in Japan and the United States have been discussed as follows: Japanese managerial practices have been widely discussed in the literature and at professional meetings such as the Japanese–United States Business Conference held in Tokyo, Japan, April 4–8, 1983; the Pan-Pacific Conference held in Honolulu, Hawaii, March 26–28, 1984, in Seoul, Korea, May 13–15, 1985, and in Taipei, Taiwan, May 17–20, 1987. See also Fred Luthans, Harriette S. McCaul, and Nancy G. Dodd, "Organizational Commitment: A Comparison of American, Japanese, and Korean Employees," *Academy of Management Journal* (March 1985), pp. 213–219; Ikujiro Nonaka and Johny K. Johansson, "Japanese Management: What about the 'Hard' Skills?" *Academy of Management Review* (April 1985), pp. 181–191; "Remaking Japan," Special Report, *Business Week* (July 13, 1987), pp. 48–64; Oh, "Japanese Management" (1976).

Planning aspects have been discussed by Ichiro Hattori, "A Proposition on Efficient Decision-Making in the Japanese Corporation," *Columbia Journal of*

World Business (Summer 1978), pp. 7–15; Richard Tanner Johnson and William G. Ouchi, "Made in America (under Japanese Management)," *Harvard Business Review* (September–October, 1974), pp. 61–69; William G. Ouchi and Alfred M. Jaeger, "Type Z Organization: Stability in the Midst of Mobility," *Academy of Management Review* (April 1978), pp. 305–314; Steven C. Wheelwright, "Operations as Strategy Lessons from Japan," *Stanford GSB* (Fall, 1981–1982), pp. 3–7.

Aspects of **organizing** have been discussed as follows: Johnson and Ouchi, "Made in America" (1974); William G. Ouchi and Raymond L. Price, "Hierarchies, Clans, and Theory Z: A New Perspective on Organization Development," *Organizational Dynamics* (Autumn 1978), pp. 25–44; Michael Y. Yoshino, "Emerging Japanese Multinational Enterprises," in E. F. Vogel (ed.), *Modern Japanese Organization and Decision Making* (Berkeley: University of California Press, 1975), pp. 146–166.

Staffing aspects have been discussed by Terutomo Ozawa, "Japanese World of Work: An Interpretive Survey," *MSU Business Topics* (Spring 1980); Arthur M. Whitehill and Shin-ichi Takezawa, "Workplace Harmony: Another Japanese 'Miracle'?" *Columbia Journal of World Business* (Fall 1978), pp. 25–39.

Leading has been discussed by Peter F. Drucker, "Behind Japan's Success," *Harvard Business Review* (January–February 1981); Lee Smith, "Japan's Autocratic Managers," *Fortune* (Jan. 7, 1985), pp. 56–65; Hirotake Takeuchi, "Productivity: Learning from the Japanese," *California Management Review* (Summer 1981), pp. 5–20.

Controlling has been discussed as follows: Joel Dreyfuss, "Networking: Japan's Latest Computer Craze," *Fortune* (July 7, 1986), pp. 94–96; Dexter Hutchins, "Having a Hard Time with Just-in-Time," *Fortune* (June 9, 1986), pp. 64–66; Kazuo Koike, "Will America Regain Its Competitiveness?" *Economic Eye* (March 1981), pp. 26–32.

10. This discussion is based on William G. Ouchi, *Theory Z* (Reading, Mass.: Addison-Wesley Publishing Company, 1981).

11. "Life At IBM — Rules and Discipline and Praise Shape IBMer's Taut World," *The Wall Street Journal* (Apr. 8, 1982), pp. 1, 14.

12. "The Japanese Manager Meets the American Worker," *Business Week* (Aug. 20, 1984), pp. 128–129.

13. "The Japanese Manager" (1984).

14. An increasing number of overseas ventures combine direct investment, licensing, and trade. Farok J. Contractor, "A Generalized Theorem for Joint-Venture and Licensing Negotiations," *Journal of International Business Studies* (Summer 1985), pp. 23–50.

15. Alan Farnham and Carrie Gottlieb, "The World's Largest Industrial Corporations," *Fortune* (Aug. 4, 1986), p. 171.

16. David A. Heenan and Howard V. Perlmutter, *Multinational Organization Development* (Reading, Mass.: Addison-Wesley Publishing Company, 1979), chap. 2.

17. "ITALTEL's New Chief Gets What She Wants," *Business Week* (Apr. 30, 1984), p. 51; Robert Ball, "Italy's Most Talked-About Executive," *Fortune* (Apr. 2, 1984), pp. 99–102; Marisa Bellisario, "The Turnaround at ITALTEL," *Long Range Planning*, vol. 18, no. 6 (1985), pp. 21–24.

18. Kenneth Labich, "America's International Winners," *Fortune* (Apr. 14, 1986), pp. 34–46.

19. Howard V. Perlmutter and David A. Heenan, "Cooperate to Compete Globally," *Harvard Business Review* (March–April 1986), pp. 136–152; Jonathan B. Levine and John A. Byrne, "Corporate Odd Couples," *Business Week* (July 21, 1986), pp. 100–105.

20. Doron P. Levin, "GM-Toyota Venture Will Test Ability of Workers in U.S. to Match Japanese," *The Wall Street Journal* (Apr. 5, 1985); William J. Holstein, "Japan, U.S.A.," *Business Week* (July 14, 1986), pp. 45–46.

21. For additional strategies of Philips, see Jonathan Kapstein, "The Big Two of Consumer Electronics: Squeezed — but Fighting Back," *Business Week* (Dec. 30, 1985), pp. 62–64.

22. See also Ronen, *Comparative and Multinational Management* (1986), chap. 8.

23. For a human resource management model, see R. Hal Mason and Robert S. Spich, *Management — An International Perspective* (Homewood, Ill.: Richard D. Irwin, 1987), chap. 8.

24. See also Stephen J. Carroll and Dennis J. Gillen, "Are the Classical Management Functions Useful in Describing Managerial Work?" *Academy of Management Review* (January 1987), pp. 38–51.

25. See, for example, Michael E. Porter, *Competitive Advantage* (New York: The Free Press, 1985).

26. One example of a book with extensive text material, readings, and cases is George A. Steiner, John B. Miner, and Edmund R. Gray, *Management Policy and Strategy*, 3d ed. (New York: The Macmillan Company, 1986); another book with extensive text material is

Fred R. David, *Fundamentals of Strategic Management* (Columbus, Ohio: Merrill Publishing Company, 1986). An example of a book with many international cases is Thomas J. McNichols, *Policymaking and Executive Action*, 6th ed. (New York: McGraw-Hill Book Company, 1983).

27. A high degree of motivation can also be obtained through self-leadership. See, for example, Charles C. Manz, "Self-Leadership: Toward an Expanded Theory of Self-Influence Processes in Organizations," *Academy of Management Review* (July 1986), pp. 585–600.

28. See also Fred Luthans, Richard M. Hodgetts, and Stuart A. Rosenkrantz, *Real Managers* (Cambridge, Mass.: Ballinger Publishing Company, 1988). The book has also been reviewed by Craig C. Pinder in *Academy of Management Review* (October 1988), pp. 661–663.

29. Laurie Baum, "Korea's Newest Import: Management Style," *Business Week* (Jan. 19, 1987), p. 66.

30. *Global Competition — The New Reality*, The Report of the President's Commission on Industrial Competitiveness, vol. 1 (Washington: GPO, January 1985).

31. The case is based on a variety of sources, including Drexel Burnham Lambert auto analyst David B. Healy, quoted in "AMC's U.S. Car Plant May Go on the Scrap Heap," *Business Week* (June 3, 1985), p. 42; "Meanwhile Back in Marysville," *Forbes* (Mar. 12, 1984), p. 127; W. J. Hampton, "Detroit Beware: Japan Is Ready to Sell Luxury," *Business Week* (Dec. 9, 1985), p. 118; "Here Comes Honda" (interview with Tetsuo Chino), *Barron's* (Dec. 2, 1985), p. 13; Thomas Hout, Michael E. Porter, and Eileen Rudden, "How Global Companies Win Out," *Harvard Business Review* (September–October 1982), pp. 98–108; Faye Rice, "America's New No. 4 Automaker — Honda," *Fortune* (Oct. 28, 1985), p. 30.

NAME INDEX

PRODUCT AND ORGANIZATION INDEX

SUBJECT INDEX